Government and the American Economy

GOVERNMENT & THE AMERICAN ECONOMY

A New History

Foreword by
DOUGLASS C. NORTH

PRICE FISHBACK
ROBERT HIGGS
GARY D. LIBECAP
JOHN JOSEPH WALLIS
STANLEY L. ENGERMAN
JEFFREY ROGERS HUMMEL
SUMNER J. LA CROIX
ROBERT A. MARGO
ROBERT A. MCGUIRE
RICHARD SYLLA
LEE J. ALSTON
JOSEPH P. FERRIE
MARK GUGLIELMO
E. C. PASOUR JR.
RANDAL R. RUCKER
WERNER TROESKEN

The University of Chicago Press

Chicago and London

The University of Chicago Press, Chicago 60637
The University of Chicago Press, Ltd., London
© 2007 by The University of Chicago
All rights reserved. Published 2007
Printed in the United States of America

16 15 14 13 12 11 10 09 08 07   1 2 3 4 5

ISBN-13: 978-0-226-25127-1 (cloth)
ISBN-13: 978-0-226-25128-8 (paper)
ISBN-10: 0-226-25127-6 (cloth)
ISBN-10: 0-226-25128-4 (paper)

Library of Congress Cataloging-in-Publication Data

Government and the American economy : a new history /
Price Fishback . . . [et al.].
        p. cm.
    Includes bibliographical references and index.
    ISBN-13: 978-0-226-25127-1 (cloth : alk. paper)
    ISBN-10: 0-226-25127-6 (cloth : alk. paper)
    ISBN-13: 978-0-226-25128-8 (pbk. : alk. paper)
    1. United States—Economic policy. 2. United States—History.
I. Fishback, Price Van Meter.
    HC103.G676 2007
    330.973—dc22

                                        2006037643

♾ The paper used in this publication meets the minimum
requirements of the American National Standard for Information Sciences—Permanence of Paper for Printed Library
Materials, ANSI z39.48-1992.

DEDICATION PRICE FISHBACK

TO ROBERT HIGGS

This book is dedicated to Robert Higgs, one of its coauthors. Bob is many things to each of us: a close friend, a mentor, a teacher, and a student. Those of us who took courses with him consider him to be one of the best lecturers that we have ever seen at the undergraduate level. He gave such lucid and entertaining descriptions of the ins and outs of economic history and the mixed economy that his students were enthralled by what many thought would be a dry subject. Bob managed this without pyrotechnics and in a relatively quiet manner. But we could see his passion for the subject, and his dry sense of humor constantly caught us off guard. My only complaint was that he kept referring to Louisville, Kentucky, my hometown, as one of the "Seven Lost Cities of America." Bob would always tell us that the Kentucky Derby, run there every year, was actually staged on a movie back lot in California because the favorite almost never won and Hollywood loved stories in which the underdog wins.

In his graduate seminars he let his students run wild with ideas and opinions while he gently (and sometimes archly) guided us through the mixture of brilliant thought and sometimes absolute lunacy of some of the papers that we were reading. Our favorite expression of Bob's was "the look": one eyebrow arched well above the top of his glasses as he passionately tore apart an analysis that he thought was flawed. Bob allowed students to make major mistakes but never criticized them personally in class. Instead, he allowed them to figure out the errors of their ways. In one case I proudly presented a paper by a famous economic historian and thought I had ripped it to shreds. Bob allowed the discussion to reveal the true essence of the paper and the test involved. By the end of the class I knew that I had totally misunderstood the author's intentions, although Bob had never come out and told me I was wrong.

The University of Washington's written examination in economic history in the late 1970s was a weekend-long test in which three leading scholars each asked an overarching question. Bob's question was, "How had government grown in the United States in the twentieth century? Was it an evolutionary process or one marked by responses to crises?" I wrote what I thought to be a brilliant defense of the growth of government as an evolutionary process. Of course, Bob was in the early stages of writing *Crisis and Leviathan*, which took the opposite tack. Yet Bob gave me a high pass on the exam and became my dissertation chair. He was a great advisor, listening as I explored my ideas and helping me enormously in copyediting and criticizing the voluminous drafts that I kept handing him. His guidance of my thesis set the stage for a series of papers that carried me through my years as an assistant professor. In similar ways Bob helped guide all the scholars that have contributed to this book. Those who did not matriculate at the University of Washington learned from him through his writings, their conversations with him, and their correspondence.

It seems as if Bob has read everything. He devoured the literature as he did his meals at the International House of Pancakes, where he seemed to eat lunch every day of the year in the late 1970s. On any given day Bob's lunch partners could get involved in deep discourses concerning a range of subjects in economics, politics, history, and the broader social sciences. Monthly lunches with Bob, Douglass North, and Morris David Morris, in which great books in economic history were discussed, were lively affairs; each held a different point of view, and the students all chimed in with even more diverse opinions. Bob became a close friend to many of us, joining pick-up basketball games at the student recreation center and flashing his skills, hard won on the dusty courts in the San Joaquin Valley, as point guard on our championship intramural teams. He particularly liked our team name: the Poorly Defined Property Rights.

Bob has truly made his mark in his research. Doug North recognized his potential immediately. The academic labor market in economics has typically consisted of graduates-to-be in ill-fitting suits wandering the hallways at American Economic Association meetings and interviewing with faculty members in hotel sitting rooms. When Bob got to the University of Washington's room, Doug pulled him into the room and immediately offered him a job. Many departments were hiring economic historians, and Bob, one of Johns Hopkins University's best students, was already writing a dissertation about the impact of urban areas on location theory and the development of Western cities in the late nineteenth century. In the early 1970s Bob wrote *The Transformation of the American Economy, 1865–1914*. In that thin volume he deviated from the focus of most of the literature at the time. Each chapter was a gem that foreshadowed major strands of research in economic history that developed over the next several decades: the role of urban areas in stimulating inventive activity, the role of uncertainty as opposed to exploitation in the farm protest movements, the economic nature of share tenancy, the role played by discrimination and human capital in determining the wages of immigrants, blacks, and native white workers, the importance of health to the productivity of American workers, and the factors that influenced their health, to name a few.

Bob's masterpiece about the experience of black workers in the South after the Civil War, *Competition and Coercion* (1977), described the interplay of market competition, which often served to limit the discrimination faced by African Americans, and coercion by governments and others, which often effectively retarded their progress. Many models of discrimination in use at the time were based on a distaste for working with blacks. Bob suggested that the economic models applied "more to a kind of tea-party discrimination than to the blood and steel of the Southern racial scene" (9). He expanded his work on share tenancy in that book and in later articles written with Lee Alston. Bob understood share tenancy and poverty because he was born an Okie to parents who had farmed land for "thirds and fourths" and lived in a shack with no electricity in the 1930s. After moving to California in 1951, his family lived in a labor camp for a while—outdoor toilets included at no extra charge, inasmuch as there were no indoor toilets. Bob always told us that since leaving the camp in 1951 he has lived on Easy Street, that is, he has always had indoor plumbing, his one-dimensional index of economic development. After his experience in riding out the aftermath of Hurricane Katrina in southern Louisiana, he is thinking about including a second dimension: access to a hot shower.

He wrote major papers about intrafirm wage differentials for blacks and whites and about the relative changes in their wealth. His work with Robert McGuire further addressed the role played by uncertainty in determining the choice of crops planted in the South and in driving farm protest in the Midwest and the Plains states. He documented the horrendous treatment of Japanese immigrants, who were denied access to land ownership in California and other states and then shunted away to detention camps during World War II.

In the 1980s Bob became interested in the growth of government, in particular the federal government, during the twentieth century. He has noted the importance of evolutionary forces in establishing an upward trend, but in "16 Myths about the Growth of Government" he shows quite clearly why the evolutionary stories told are incomplete. In *Crisis and Leviathan* he documents a "ratchet effect" in the scope of government authority associated with the major crises of the twentieth century, the world wars and the Great Depression. Each crisis engendered an expansion in government authority that went far beyond the statistics about employment and spending and ranged into expansions in regulatory authority over decisions made by consumers and producers. As the crises receded, the government's scope receded, but it never returned to the level predicted on the basis of the evolutionary trend. Thus, the government's scope kept ratcheting up over time. People interested in using government for their own ends have increased their use of crisis language, so that smaller and smaller crises now engender government responses. Government occasionally recedes in some areas, but Bob's work predicted the expansion in government authority and agencies related to the horrible events of September 11, 2001, which he documents in *Against Government: Government Power and a Free Society.*

Among the causes of the ratchet effect were changes in the ideology of the elites and the general public that led to greater acceptance of government activity. Doug North had argued for the importance of ideology in his 1982 book *Structure and Change,* and Bob was one of the first to take these thoughts to heart as he carefully developed a framework and definition of ideology that he could use effectively in making his arguments about the growth of government.

In 1992 Bob developed a strain of research concerning the economic welfare of people during and immediately after World War II. In "Wartime Prosperity? A Reassessment of the U.S. Economy in the 1940s," published in the *Journal of Economic History,* he powerfully argued that World War II should be considered an extension of the Great Depression and not a huge Keynesian stimulus to the economy. He showed how standard government statistics misrepresented the true extent of consumption of normal goods during the war and documented the costs to the economic welfare of the American people of fighting the war. Unemployment was reduced by drafting millions of men into the armed forces, where many faced far worse conditions than they ever saw on the unemployment lines during the 1930s. We may have needed to fight the war to prevent Hitler from leaving the world in a terrible condition, but the costs were enormous and were underappreciated before Bob's article appeared

When most of us first met Bob he was a free-market economist who believed strongly that markets worked well. Over time he has become more and more closely associated with libertarian and Austrian thought. His belief in free markets and in the protection of individual freedoms from government interference increasingly marked his writing as he moved from the University of Washington to Lafayette College to Seattle University and to his current position as editor of the *Independent Review* for the Independent Institute. Bob's passion for protection of freedoms shines through strong and clear in his recent writings. He cares deeply about the state of our society; therefore, he has written lucid defenses of classical liberal thought and heartfelt and powerful criticisms of increasing limits on personal freedom. The authors of this book all are independent thinkers in their own right. We share many of Bob's views about the importance of property rights, the rule of law, and the protection of individual freedoms to the health and welfare of our society. Yet we also have our disagreements with Bob and among ourselves about how far the role of government should extend. A number of us are less skeptical than Bob is about certain roles played by the government. Yet we each can say that sharing our profession with Robert Higgs has contributed greatly to our careers. More important, sharing his friendship has enriched our lives immeasurably.

—Price Fishback

CONTENTS

TABLES AND FIGURES

LEE J. ALSTON is professor of economics at the University of Colorado at Boulder and a research associate at the National Bureau of Economic Research.

STANLEY L. ENGERMAN is the John Munro Professor of Economics and professor of history at University of Rochester and a research associate at the National Bureau of Economic Research.

JOSEPH P. FERRIE is associate professor of economics at Northwestern University and a research associate at the National Bureau of Economic Research.

PRICE FISHBACK is the Frank and Clara Kramer Professor of Economics at the University of Arizona and a research associate at the National Bureau of Economic Research.

MARK GUGLIELMO is a senior research associate at the Center for Population Economics at the University of Chicago.

ROBERT HIGGS is a senior fellow in political economy for the Independent Institute and editor of the institute's quarterly journal, *The Independent Review*.

JEFFREY ROGERS HUMMEL is assistant professor of economics at San Jose State University.

SUMNER J. LA CROIX is professor of economics and professor of population studies at the University of Hawaii.

GARY D. LIBECAP is the Donald Bren Professor of Corporate Environmental Management at the University of California, Santa Barbara, and a research associate at the National Bureau of Economic Research.

ROBERT A. MARGO is professor of economics and African-American Studies at Boston University and a research associate at the National Bureau of Economic Research.

ROBERT A. MCGUIRE is professor of economics at the University of Akron.

DOUGLASS C. NORTH is the Bartlett Burnap Senior Fellow at the Hoover Institution. He is also the Spencer T. Olin Professor in Arts and Sciences, professor of economics, and professor of history at Washington University. He received the Alfred Nobel Memorial Prize in Economic Science in 1993.

E. C. PASOUR JR. is a research fellow at the Independent Institute and professor emeritus of agricultural and resource economics at North Carolina State University.

RANDAL R. RUCKER is professor in the Department of Agricultural Economics and Economics at Montana State University.

RICHARD SYLLA is professor of economics, entrepreneurship, and innovation and the Henry Kaufman Professor of the History of Financial Institutions and Markets at the Leonard N. Stern School of Business, New York University. He is also a research associate at the National Bureau of Economic Research.

WERNER TROESKEN is professor of history at the University of Pittsburgh and a research associate at the National Bureau of Economic Research.

JOHN JOSEPH WALLIS is professor of economics at the University of Maryland and a research associate at the National Bureau of Economic Research.

THIS AMBITIOUS BOOK aims for a thorough appraisal of the role of government in the history of the American economy. Although the inspiration was Robert Higgs's pioneering exploration of this subject, the present work provides both a longitudinal view of the topic and an in-depth exploration of the role of government in the many aspects of the economy during that development. The book has three underlying themes: (1) the success story of the creation and maintenance of an open-access society throughout American history; (2) the critical role of interest groups in shaping the specific features of the polity and the economy; and (3) the role of beliefs in shaping the overall process—those of the participants and those of the authors of this book.

From earliest colonial times the American economy has provided a level of well-being that has placed it at or near the top of the economic ladder. The source of this success has been widespread participation in the political and economic processes. Persistent efforts to limit access to these processes for almost four centuries have been stopped. This is no mean achievement. The maintenance of a democratic polity and a market economy for such a long period is the hallmark of this process. In contrast to Latin America, the thirteen American colonies from the beginning of settlement created an open-access process. How did it happen? And more important, why has it been perpetuated in the succeeding centuries? Despite all the problems along the way, including the treatment of the native population, slavery, the unequal status of women, and the disadvantaged status of various groups at times, it is still an unequaled success story. The persistence of this open-access society in the course of a development that has featured an increase in population to almost three hundred million, a transformation from a rural agricultural society to an urban manufacturing giant and then to a service economy (specializing in technological development), and a devastatingly destructive civil war (to mention only a few of the fundamental changes) suggest the depth of its roots. Telling this story is a critical task of this book.

But the story of government is the story of interest groups. It could not be otherwise, as James Madison made clear in his celebrated

Federalist Paper no. 10. How have the interest groups been tamed to permit the perpetuation of the open-access economy? And how have they, at the same time, shaped the individual parts of the economy? The creation of an ongoing federalist structure and the development of well-specified property rights and effective enforcement are themes that recur throughout the book. But it is the pervasive role of interest groups that provides a rich context for the study of American economic history. The result is not simply a story of attempts to monopolize markets but, rather, a far richer story of diverse consequences, as illustrated, for example, in Sylla's account of the evolution of the financial system, Margo's story of Reconstruction and its aftermath along with the consequences for the growth and repression of African Americans, Guglielmo and Troesken's story of control and competition in the oil market, and Fishback's account of the New Deal. These are stories in which the beliefs of the players shaped the policies they pursued, and this brings me to the third issue.

How do we understand what we are doing? "Reality" is in our heads, and our understanding is a construction of the human mind. Economists are correct in their view that economics is a theory of choice, but until recently they have ignored the question of how humans make choices. Our understanding is a mixture of our culture (the beliefs and institutions inherited from the past) and new experiences that alter and modify that cultural heritage. The idea that our understanding is disembodied wisdom independent of our cultural heritage and experiences was criticized by Charles Beard in his story of the interests of the framers of the Constitution. Beard's perspective shocked (and enraged) his contemporaries but, as McGuire points out, it is surely sensible. The subjective nature of our understanding is not an argument for the prevailing folly of deconstructionism. We do test our subjective theories against evidence, as McGuire has done, and although the results are inevitably less rigorous than the results obtained in the physical sciences—because we cannot evade completely the mental processes that underlie even our empirical work—there is still a wide gap between good and bad scholarship in the social sciences. The beliefs of the actors in our history form a crucial part of the account, whether they are the racist views of post-Reconstruction southerners, the conflicting perceptions of the players in the Progressive Era, or the beliefs evident in Higgs's account of the warfare state. Understanding the beliefs of the players is essential to good economic history. But we must also understand that the beliefs of the authors of this book color their writing.

This would be devastating to good writing if the authors were not, first and foremost, good scholars. But they are, and the result is a plus rather than a minus. Whether sympathetic to the way development occurred, as Sylla is in his account of Hamilton's role, or of a libertarian persuasion, as Higgs is in his story of government's role during the world wars, they highlight aspects of the story that need telling and thereby enrich the overall work. The result is a unique account of government and the American economy.

Government and the Economy

MANY DISLIKE the impact of government on their lives. Others embrace it. Yet it is hard for societies and economies to function without it. Few enjoy the government's taking a significant part of their income via taxation, limiting their freedom of choice, or loading them down with paperwork done in compliance with arcane-seeming regulations. On the other hand, good governments provide invaluable services not easily provided by other entities, including defense against foreign predation, a stable rule of law, peaceful judgment of disputes, and protection of individual rights and property. Unfortunately, history is replete with governments that enriched a small number of powerful elites at the expense of the vast majority of the population. Such governments often hindered the economic activity of most of their people and failed to release the creativity and innovation of the human spirit in economic endeavors. Poor governments have been so common that at least one group of scholars recently referred to bad government as the "natural state." Yet a relatively small number of countries have succeeded in developing governments that allow nearly all their people enough economic freedom to promote rapid economic growth, and almost all have done so in the past 250 years.[1]

This book is about the economic history of one of those governments, that of the United States of America. The nation has been an economic success from the beginning. In the late 1700s, American colonists had per capita incomes that were among the highest in the world. Today the United States continues to be among the richest nations in history, if not *the* richest. There was no guarantee at the outset, however, that, even with favorable conditions, the nation would maintain such a high relative economic position. The people of Argentina, for example, had one of the world's highest standards of living in the early 1900s, but Argentina now ranks below the world average in per capita gross domestic product (GDP), at about one-ninth of the level of the leading countries.[2]

There are many reasons why the United States has been successful. The country has been blessed with an abundance of natural resources relative to the size of its population. The development of new technologies allowed the nation to overcome the Malthusian fear that population growth would outstrip the resource base.[3] The populace has become increasingly well-educated, and people have developed a wide range of organizations and institutions that allow them to produce more while pursuing a large variety of leisure activities. A critical element of American success and of the development of the characteristics described above has been the relatively high quality of its government. The United States has largely avoided warfare on its own soil. Government at all levels has tended to protect individual economic and political freedoms to a greater extent than have nearly all other governments, past or present. Finally, the U.S. government has experienced orderly transfers of power, has adhered strongly to the rule of law, and has an independent judiciary to adjudicate disputes. This is well illustrated by the events surrounding the presidential election of 2000. The series of legal struggles over the vote-counting rules used in Florida was ultimately settled by a Supreme Court decision that ended the recounts and installed George W. Bush as president. Although many Democrats still questioned the final vote tallies, Al Gore's gracious concession speech asked the nation to accept the decision and follow Bush's leadership. Throughout the process the American people went on about their business expecting an orderly process. The outcome was unusual in that it was met with such calm. In many other countries there likely would have been riots and a violent struggle over succession.

Assessments of the role of government in America's success must start with the foundational documents. The Constitution and the Bill of Rights codified protection of many individual freedoms. Those that were important for economic success were the freedom for individuals to make voluntary contracts with others without government interference and protection of their right to hold property of all kinds. People and goods were allowed to move freely across state boundaries even as the Constitution reserved a limited set of powers for the national government. The Constitution established a system of checks and balances within government to protect these freedoms.

But a well-written constitution was not enough by itself. More important were the subsequent decisions by U.S. governments and courts at all levels to protect most economic freedoms. With regularity, the interests of the individual were protected against the demands of the majority. The initial relatively broad distribution of property ownership and income gave the people a stake in protecting these freedoms. The result was significant economic mobility, so that newcomers to the economy had a stake in the continuation of these protections. Indices of economic freedom created by the Heritage Foundation suggest that the United States is among the world leaders today in protecting fundamental economic freedoms. Countries with similar indices also often rank very highly on measures of economic performance.[4]

The stability of government is a key feature of successful economies. Instability leads to uncertainty about the future that threatens individual decisions and retards investment. With the exception of a short invasion by the British during the War of 1812, America has managed to avoid invasions of its territory. Thus it managed to avoid the long periods of destruction of property, civilian deaths, and disruptions of the civil order that have struck many countries. The orderly and peaceful transfer of leadership has been just as important; the nation has had to deal with only one civil war.

Another key to the quality of U.S. governments has been their flexibility. Despite forces that lead to inertia, American governments have shown the capacity to correct mistakes. Governing is a messy process of trial and error. Voters often disagree about the best policy, and competing theories of government held by the experts often lead to conflicting answers. Policies that seemed useful at one time become inappropriate following technological and social change. In a setting of diverse resources and people spread across a large country, the federal structure established in the Constitution gave governments a high degree of latitude to experiment with different policies. State and local governments were left with a significant degree of autonomy. Decisions about state policies have been constrained by the mobility of people and resources, which creates a healthy competition between states. Successful policies are often imitated, whereas unsuccessful ones are not. The ability of the national government to respond to socioeconomic change is also important.

American governments have also made mistakes. Yet at all levels they constantly tinker with policies, sometimes taking backward steps, but at other times rectifying errors. The right to vote has been extended over time. Explicit segregation of government-run schools by race has been abandoned. Federal price controls and regulation of the number of firms have been tried and then abandoned. Many northern state governments chose to eliminate slavery early in their history, although slavery's ultimate demise across the country required a terrible civil war. Given the worldwide shift away from slavery, U.S. governments were flexible enough to have brokered a peaceful solution within a few decades although the practice remained economically viable to slave owners.[5]

In a complex world the government will continue to make mistakes. Part of the problem in identifying the mistakes is that people legitimately disagree about the appropriateness of various policies. Classical liberals deplore many decisions that have promoted the good of the majority, and sometimes that of a minority of well-placed groups, at the expense of limiting individual economic freedom and limiting property rights. Modern liberals argue that the policies fall well short of their desired aim of protecting people against the uncertainties of an impersonal world. These disagreements, when combined with the natural inertia of government in a democracy, imply that corrections may be slow and that some errors are never fully eliminated.

The Economics of Government

Government is unique among economic institutions because it has the coercive power to force people to take actions. This power can be used to promote the economic welfare of the many or of the few. Unfortunately, world history is filled with countless examples of governments that promoted the interests of the few: predatory states whose leaders took control of governments by force and then sought to extract wealth and power for their own ends. Recent examples include Iraq under Saddam Hussein and North Korea; historical examples include large numbers of monarchies. The lack of security for most of the populace in these countries limited people's incentives to work and save. This chilling effect on the economy was compounded by the dissipation of resources by excessive expenditures on military and self-protection costs by elites whose position required the continued use of force. At the other extreme, a few states developed institutions that limited governmental power by means of a set of internal checks and enabled the government to write and enforce a set of rules (including rules about its own behavior) that allowed the society to run more effectively. The United States is a leading example of this type of *contractual* state. In market-oriented societies such as the United States, government plays several roles in the economy.[6]

Property Rights

A key role played by governments is the definition and enforcement of property rights. The term *property rights* refers to more than simply rights to land. They include control over one's own person and decisions, control over such personal property as automobiles and clothing, control over equipment and capital, and control over such intangibles as ideas, inventions, music, and writings. Governments have adopted property rights regimes ranging from common property to communal rights to private property. The U.S. system is largely a system of private property in which people have the exclusive right to use the property, the exclusive right to derive income from use, and the exclusive right to sell the property.[7]

To appreciate the importance of these rights, consider how you would act in their absence. Begin with the property right of exclusive use. How much would you value an automobile that other people could also drive at will? Its value to you would be considerably reduced although the physical aspects of the car had not changed. Moreover, the lack of exclusive rights to use would lead you to develop costly methods, such as more complex locks, to limit access to the car. You would certainly cut back on maintenance because you would incur the costs but would be less likely to obtain the full benefits. The combination of reduced value and increased costs of ownership would lower the price you are willing to pay for the car. Lower prices ultimately would lead to the production of fewer cars.

Now consider a case where you have the exclusive right to use your car, but cars cannot be sold to someone else. This limit on your right to "alienate" the car will make you less likely to buy a car in the first place. The type of car you want to buy will change. Durable cars will become more valuable than cars that do not last because it is impossible to sell your car to someone else. Thus the physical characteristics of cars would change. Equally important, you are prevented from transferring your car to another who would get more benefits from using it. Both these limits on the property rights associated with owning a car demonstrate that economic value is a function of more than simply the physical attributes of the car. By creating better defined and tradable property rights, it is possible to create real economic value.[8]

The exclusive right to derive income from use is best illustrated by patents on new inventions. Patents give inventors a greater incentive to invent because they are the only ones who can receive income from the use of their inventions. Inventive activity generally is greater in countries with established patent laws. Patents also illustrate one of the potential trade-offs for private property rights. The patent owner obtains a monopoly that allows him or her to limit access to the invention and demand a high price for its use. The diffusion of the invention is then slowed by the patent monopoly. The U.S. government's solution to this problem has been a compromise: U.S. patent law imposes a time limit so that the invention is eventually available to everybody when the patent expires.[9]

In general, private property rights systems work best when many people own property. Broad dispersion of resource ownership generally leads to more competition in the production and sale of goods and services. In addition, more people consider the property rights system to be legitimate because they have a stake in the continuation of the system. The legitimacy of such schemes is buttressed by another empirical finding: Private property rights and protection of freedom to write contracts often have been and continue to be strongly correlated with the protection of individuals' political and social freedoms.[10]

Property rights in the United States have been curtailed in three ways. First, owners of certain types of property are required to pay the taxes levied on their property or forfeit the property to the government. The payment of taxes contributes to covering the costs of defending the individual's rights to property. It is important, however, that the checks and balances in government prevent tax rates from rising to levels at which they damage incentives to use the property productively. Second, governments at all levels have imposed regulations on land use by means of local zoning laws and state and federal regulations. Recent examples include the limits on development of property imposed by the laws protecting endangered species. Third, the Constitution gave American governments the right of eminent domain, which allows governments to take property as long as there is a public purpose, the taking meets due process, and the owner is fully compensated. *Full compensation* has typically meant "the market value of the property." In the past hundred years the protection of property against an eminent domain taking has eroded as courts have expanded the definition of "public purpose" to include urban renewal in blighted areas, the breakup of land oligopolies, and the promotion of economic development that would lead to new jobs and higher tax revenues.[11]

One key feature of private property is that it requires people who damage another's property to pay compensation for that damage. In the United States disputes about damages are handled ultimately in the civil courts, although most claims are handled by private settlements with the alternative of going to court in the background. Problems develop when the rights to resources are poorly defined. In some cases it is difficult to effectively define rights to a resource, as in the cases of air and large bodies of water. In those cases pollution often arises because polluters are not required to pay damages to an owner of the resource. Many societies have resolved this issue by treating the resource as held in common but subjecting its use to a system of rules and customs. Thus it is rare to find resources that are truly common property that everybody can use unilaterally. Usually there is some type of management process wherein groups within the society restrict resource use, while the society as a whole protects the resource from outside invaders.[12]

Systems of communal rights work best when the society has a relatively small population, all of whose members have similar interests in the resource. The first settlers in Massachusetts and Virginia started with communal systems but soon discarded them as ineffective. To some degree, communal and customary rights were the property structures chosen by various Native American tribes. As tribes grew in population, they clashed over the boundaries of their respective communal territories. The Hopi, Navajo, and Zuni tribes, for example, simultaneously laid claim to the same broad area in Arizona and New Mexico. One of the ironies of American history is that the nation values private property rights highly, yet settlers and governments were quick to show disrespect for the communal rights systems that Native Americans had established prior to the settlers' arrival. In this realm the U.S. government acted rather as a conquering nation would act. On occasion it signed treaties with the tribes for land. But constant pressure from new settlement often led to treaty violations and the replacement of existing, often implicit agreements with new property rights regimes.

Freedom to Contract and the "Regular Administration of Justice"

Another major feature of economic freedoms in the United States is the contract clause in article I, section 10 of the Constitution: "No state shall pass any . . . law impairing the obligation of contracts." This clause allows people to make binding commitments without government interference. Such commitments are particularly important for making long-term arrangements in which one side or other might seek to back out of the agreement when conditions change. In the absence of this commitment, many projects in which at least one side has to make up-front investments and stay the course to reap substantial future benefits could not be agreed on. The freedom to contract was strongly reaffirmed in *Dartmouth College v. Woodward* (1819) when the U.S. Supreme Court prevented the New Hampshire legislature from turning Dartmouth College, which was privately run, into a state university. Chief Justice

John Marshall emphasized that the college's corporate character was a contract that could not be violated by the state government. There are, however, limits on the freedom to contract. In a number of cases the courts have refused to enforce contracts that they consider unconscionable, cases in which they believe that one party was unable to contract effectively. The court doctrine that allowed workers and employers to end employment contracts "at will" prevented people from contracting to become slaves. Governments have retained the right to use their police powers to establish regulations in "the public interest" that impose limits on behavior and contracts. The Supreme Court affirmed this right to regulate in *Munn v. Illinois* (1877) by ruling that the grain warehouse company Munn and Scott had to abide by state requirements that it obtain a license and not raise rates above the maximum set by the state. The definition of *public interest* has expanded over time as first states and then the federal government increased their regulatory activity.[13]

If the system of property rights and contracts is to work well, the rule of law must be in effect. Police departments are important because they help protect property from theft and people from harm. Adam Smith argued that economies "will seldom flourish" in states that do not enjoy a "regular administration of justice" or "a certain degree of confidence in the justice of government." Given the complexities of language and negotiation and the costs of writing contracts that anticipate all eventualities, it is inevitable that parties to some contracts will disagree about how to interpret the agreement. Similarly, there will be disagreements about how to interpret the statutes written by legislatures and the clauses adopted in constitutions. In other situations, the actions of one person might damage the property of others or infringe upon their personal freedoms.[14]

A method of dispute resolution that is considered legitimate by the parties involved and the population in general is therefore central. To obtain such legitimacy, the system must establish an impartial decision maker, be it a judge or a jury of peers, to whom the parties to the dispute can turn for resolution. Since there will always be at least one side that is dissatisfied with the decision, the key to success is that people see the system as fair before the decision has been made. A history of impartial decisions over time that are also predictable on the basis of past decisions confers legitimacy on the system. Predictability matters because it gives guidance about what to expect from the arbitrators and allows better planning in the writing of contracts. This can lead to quick resolution of disputes without having to turn to the courts.

The United States adopted the British system of common law, which seeks impartiality by insulating judges and juries from political pressures. The common law develops from court decisions, although it is constrained by legislation. The goal of consistency is sought by using the principle of stare decisis such that judges are wary of reversing long-standing rulings in prior cases concerning the same topic.[15]

The Classic Public Good: National Defense

A government's use of coercive power is important in enforcing rights and laws and resolving internal disputes, but its significance is paramount in protecting against outside aggression. National defense is the classic example of a *public good*. Economists use a narrow definition of the term, such that a public good has two features: it is difficult to exclude users, and use of the good by one individual does not prevent use by another. National defense is one of the few goods that largely meet both of these conditions. All within the borders are defended. Adding a person within the borders does not reduce the defense provided to others. Such goods as sanitation and water treatment facilities, research and development, parks, and highways are considered partial public goods, and these, too, have often been provided by governments.

The difficulty of excluding people from using a public good often leads to a *free rider problem,* in which people have incentives to obtain the good without paying for it. People's voluntary contributions often are less than would be necessary for the optimal production of a public good. This would be particularly problematic in the case of national defense, in which inadequate production in the face of an external threat could lead to the demise of the society. The U.S. government resolves the problem by using its coercive power to force people to pay taxes to contribute to national defense. The U.S. Constitution gave the national government the right to collect taxes directly to alleviate fears about free riding by states. These fears arose because of problems in collecting contributions for national defense under the Articles of Confederation.[16]

Government taxing authority does not resolve all of the problems associated with provision of national defense. An equally thorny issue is the determination of the appropriate level of national defense. Ask people what they are willing to pay for a public good, and they are likely to give a low estimate, particularly if they believe that what they say will determine the tax they pay. We live in a world of uncertainty, which compounds the problem, and given the high costs of determining the precise threat to national security, there is plenty of room for disagreement about what is necessary or optimal. Spending on national defense and the military has been the central aspect of the story of government in U.S. history. Wars have led to dramatic increases in expenditures, issuance of debt, and depreciation of the dollar. Wartime borrowing influences both the tax structure and the economy in the years that follow major wars. Sacrifices made during wars extend well beyond government expenditures, the loss of lives, and the destruction of military equipment. The nation's involvement in wars has led to limits on access to normal consumer goods and restrictions on individual freedoms. Even in peacetime, Americans constantly debate the trade-off between "guns and butter." The military and the producers of military equipment consistently press for expanded production and new technologies to maintain readiness against external threats, while other segments of society raise doubts about the extent of these threats. Defense spending has therefore waxed and waned with changes in leadership, people's perceptions of potential threats, and the country's role in international politics.[17]

Choosing between Markets and Regulation

One of the leading arguments for government involvement in the economy is the market failure argument. Markets can fail to allocate goods and services efficiently in several situations. Market economies combined with common law courts that adjudicate disputes are sometimes inefficient when information is expensive, negotiation costs are high, or there are *externalities*. Externalities are created when the decisions of one person or group cause damage to (or create benefits for) other people. Moreover, critics of market economies argue that large firms tend to develop in some industries and monopolize activity.

Government has the capacity to help resolve these issues. Where information costs are high, a government may be able to force sellers to reveal information about their products or set a basic standard that all sellers must meet. Negotiations costs are particularly problematic for externalities involving large numbers of people. In developing a solution, the government can cut negotiation costs by acting as a representative of the people being harmed. In the case of roads, government funds raised by gasoline taxes might effectively cut the transaction costs involved when owners of private roads charge a toll for each use. Through antitrust activity, governments may be able to prevent anticompetitive behavior that harms consumers.

Remember, however, that government regulation might also fail to resolve these problems and in some cases could make them worse. Governments face many of the same problems in resolving issues that market actors do. Consider the case of information about product quality and characteristics. In the marketplace, producers try to reassure consumers that their goods have the appropriate quality by offering guarantees or establishing brand names and reputations for better quality. Meanwhile, some organizations specialize in providing information about quality to buyers and sellers. The government would also have to invest in obtaining and providing information about the quality of items, so the primary question is, which set of institutions, the government or the market, is best equipped to resolve the information problem?

Regulation can often be a blunt instrument when the same requirements apply to all people and places. In a highly diverse society, a specific regulation might be optimal for some groups or areas but be suboptimal for others. Thus the best choice between market and government solutions may rest on determining which solution has more flexibility in responding to diverse preferences.

A fundamental tension arises in many regulatory settings. Regulations can confer significant economic advantages to subgroups of producers. For example, licensing restrictions designed to ensure that each producer meets a certain quality standard can also serve to protect the qualifying producers against competition in their markets. Such limits on entry can lead to higher incomes for producers as they charge consumers higher prices for less output. For example, restrictions on interstate highway billboards enacted during the 1970s tended to favor big motel chains with large advertising budgets at the expense of smaller mom-and-pop operations. Safety and environmental regulations that require extensive investments in new plants and equipment may favor large producers at the expense of smaller producers. Aware of these advantages, producers have incentives to press for regulations and administrative decisions that give them favorable treatment and protection against competition. In the final analysis there is no guarantee that regulations will always be focused on resolving market failures. The optimal choice between market solutions and regulatory solutions often depends on the specifics of the situation and thus are best considered on a case-by-case basis.

The Government as a Redistributor

Nearly every move that a government makes redistributes income. The most obvious form of redistribution takes places when the government collects taxes—on income, property, sales, foreign goods, corporate profits—and then assigns the revenues to other groups in the form of subsidies and direct payments. In some situations governments seek to tie the taxation to use so that those paying taxes are funding programs from which they benefit. For example, the revenues from some gasoline taxes are used to pay for highway maintenance; some parks charge user fees. Unemployment benefits for workers come from payroll taxes paid by employers, and the system is, at least in part, "experience-rated," so that employers who consistently lay off more workers pay higher taxes. In other cases the connections are far looser. Social Security payments to the elderly are funded by payroll taxes paid by current workers and employers. The Social Security trust fund serves as an implicit guarantee that the federal government will collect enough taxes to fund the system when current workers are ready to retire and receive benefits.

All of these taxes and subsidies alter the incentive structure of the economy, and every economist will tell you that incentives matter. Increases in income tax rates and increases in welfare payments eventually lead to reductions in work and in participation in the workforce. As income tax rates increase, governments face trade-offs in terms of revenue. They collect more in revenue on each dollar of income, but the total income is likely to fall as some people reduce their economic activity. Thus the rise in total revenue from the higher tax rate tends not to reach the level predicted by applying the new tax rate to the prior income level.[18]

There is a constant tension between the collection of tax revenue and the working of a market economy. Taxation leads to distortions in the operation of a market economy. Until 1913, the federal government largely relied on sales taxes and tariffs for revenue. Imposing sales taxes in a specific competitive market typically leads to direct losses for all participants in that market. The quantity sold falls, consumers pay higher prices, and suppliers receive lower net prices after they subtract the tax paid to the government from the price paid by consumers. Whether the losses in this market are worthwhile from an economic standpoint depends on the value of government goods and services funded by the tax revenue collected. We know that there are direct losses to buyers and sellers in the market. Nearly all agree that the value of basic government services such as defense, the courts, and law and order can exceed the losses within the market taxed. As the U.S. government has expanded its role, however, there has been increasing disagreement across the population about the value of some additional programs, including the subsidies paid to farmers since 1933 and bailouts of large companies such as Chrysler, which was bailed out in 1980.

The redistributive power of government also takes more subtle forms. A tariff on foreign imports of steel favors U.S. steel producers rather than U.S. steel consumers because the tariff gives the producers latitude to charge higher prices. As the tariff rises and becomes more protective, eventually it could eliminate all foreign competition altogether. Similarly, restrictions on entry into an industry redistribute income from consumers to producers by allowing producers to charge higher prices. In 2005, for example, several states passed legislation protecting real estate agents against competition from discount competitors, forcing home buyers and sellers to pay higher commission fees. Tariffs and entry restrictions create distortions in the market that lead to decreases in the quantities being traded. The combination of higher prices and lower quantities often means that consumers likely lose more than producers gain.[19]

As discussed above, quality, safety, and environmental regulations can favor certain classes of producers. Meanwhile, regulation of electric utility prices can favor consumers rather than producers of goods. To take another example, rent controls benefit renters who have rights to remain in their apartments at the expense of landlords and other would-be renters who no longer can find apartments or face additional nonmonetary costs of searching for apartments.

The Political Economy of U.S. Governments

In his Gettysburg Address Abraham Lincoln averred that the U.S. government is "of the people, for the people, and by the people." The United States is a representative democracy in which the people elect representatives to various levels of government to make decisions about how the country, as well as state and local jurisdictions, will be governed. The American electorate has always been large and diverse. Even when suffrage was limited to white males holding property or paying taxes, there was diversity with respect to age, wealth, occupation, religious beliefs, geographical location, attitude toward the role of government, and general disposition. The electorate became more diverse as property requirements for eligibility were lifted, slaves were freed, women obtained the right to vote, the voting age was lowered to eighteen, and large numbers of foreign immigrants and their children were assimilated as citizens. Progress has moved in fits and starts with several reversals. The civil rights granted to freed slaves during Reconstruction were limited for several decades by the Jim Crow laws and segregation in the southern states. Efforts to break down segregation and return those rights met with increasing success after 1940, culminating in the achievements of the civil rights movement of the 1960s and the evolution of rights since then.[20]

The most obvious influence that each person has over the government stems from his or her right to vote. Voting gives each citizen some say in the political process, yet many do not exercise this right to its fullest extent. Each person represents such a small share of the electorate that it is extraordinarily unlikely that his or her vote will be decisive in an election. Furthermore, candidates establish their positions in such ways as to attract enough voters to win, so the difference between candidates is not often large. Thus, in many elections many people choose not to vote because their perceived benefit from casting the vote is lower than the small cost of going to the polls.[21]

Some people have more influence than others in determining policy. Some devote their time to political activism, volunteer their services during elections, or influence policy as advisors to legislators and the executive. Others devote portions of their wealth to the process and follow practices that range across a spectrum from the legal funding of political campaigns to the nefarious bribing of key decision makers. Many seek to influence the government by joining with like-minded people and forming interest groups to lobby the government for policies consistent with their position. In creating the Constitution the founding fathers fully anticipated the role to be played by these interest groups; it was eloquently outlined by James Madison in Federalist Paper no. 10.[22]

In the struggle between interest groups and the general public, *public choice* economists have identified a *special interest advantage* in lobbying for a specific policy. Although the general public has more votes, each member of the general public typically has little to lose from the special interest policy, many members have diverse interests, and it is costly to organize the general public to oppose a specific policy. Meanwhile, the special interest group is generally well organized because it is composed of a relatively small number of like-minded people, each with a relatively large amount at stake. Consider a tariff on steel that would raise $200 million for one million people in the steel industry. The average per capita gain in the steel industry would be $200 per person. Meanwhile, a loss of roughly $300 million spread among the 300 million members of the general public would cost them each only one dollar. It is easy to see that the steel interest groups would press hard for this tariff whereas members of the general public might find their personal costs of organizing to stop the policy higher than their dollar loss.

This might help explain why protectionist steel tariffs were enacted in the late nineteenth century and why George W. Bush increased steel tariffs in 2002. To some extent the U.S. system is saved from special-interest legislation run amok by countervailing special-interest groups. In many cases the benefits sought by one such group lead to harm to another that actively opposes the policy.[23]

As a result, discussions of whether the policies are in the public interest depend on whether the winners will gain more than the losers give up. One way to resolve the dissatisfaction of the losers is for the winners to make direct payments to losers to cover their losses. The transaction costs of making such direct payments are often quite large, and such obvious payments are rarely made. There are, however, more subtle ways for winners and losers to come to an agreement. Legislative acts are often compromises between the original bills and amendments proposed by advocates on both sides of the issue. Furthermore, in many situations support for one policy is traded for support of another through "logrolling," or vote trading by legislators. When the infamous Smoot-Hawley Tariff Act of 1930 was passed, for example, groups of senators representing sugar-producing states traded votes with senators from glass-producing states to raise tariffs for both products; a similar trade was made between senators representing lumber- and oil-producing states.[24] In the past few years members of Congress apparently have been making such exchanges with "earmarked" expenditures that are added as amendments to legislation.

Once policies have been legislated, they have to be administered. In the case of regulation, those being regulated and the people originally calling for regulation are in constant contact with the regulatory officials. In a number of cases those who wanted regulation have enough influence that it is binding in the way they originally sought. But the constant contact and lobbying pressure by those being regulated raises the possibility of industry *capture* of the regulatory officials. Regulating an industry requires expertise, so at least some of the regulators are often chosen from industry and are likely to be sympathetic to industry demands. At the other extreme are the more infamous and corrupt practices of bribery and intimidation. In some situations the industry itself has been the group calling for regulation, so that the capture of the regulator was established in the initial legislation. For example, there has been extensive debate about the extent to which the Interstate Commerce Commission, the first federal regulatory body, was captured by the railroads and later the trucking industry.[25]

Instituting a new government policy is often much less difficult than eliminating it. The U.S. system of checks and balances among the executive, the legislature, and the judiciary at all levels leads to inertia. This inertia is exacerbated by the development of stakeholders once a policy is in place. People who benefit from the policy actively lobby to prevent its elimination. Iron and steel tariffs, for example, lingered for a number of years after American producers were able to undercut their foreign competitors in export markets. The regulatory staffs often find ways to block the elimination of a policy or seek ways to expand their authority and remain in office. For example, the Rural Electrification Administration, established to lend funds to cooperatives in order to bring electricity for the first time to many rural areas in the 1930s, managed to find new projects and survived until 1994, long after the vast majority of rural farms had access to electric service.[26]

Although the United States has a government of the people, government officials have significant latitude in their decision making. In economists' parlance, a republican form of government is rife with the potential for *principal-agent* problems. The principal selects the agent to work to represent her interests, but the agent has enough latitude to make decisions that benefit the agent at the expense of the principal. At one level the principal is the American electorate and the agents are the president, governors, mayors, legislators, judges, and the bureaucracy. Within the government the principal might be the president and the administrators under his authority his agents. In other cases the principal is the legislature that has oversight authority over the administrators as agents. Within an agency the principal would be the head of the agency and the agents her subordinates.

Consider the voters as principals. They have some control over elected officials when the officials would like to be reelected or rise to higher office. The voters' control, however, is relatively loose because an individual vote is rarely decisive, elections come around only once every one to six years, recalls are rare, there are often multiple issues at stake in an election, and there is enough diversity among constituents within most districts that the elected official can point to some constituency that he was trying to help. Elected officials have to make enough decisions that match the dominant economic interests and ideologies of their voting constituents to stay in office or advance to higher office. Yet they have latitude to make many decisions that would not be decisive about their reelection, allowing their own economic interests and ideologies to come into play. Elected officials, like many occupational groups in society, can be arranged on a spectrum of humankind.

Table 1.1 GOVERNMENT REVENUE IN CURRENT DOLLARS PER CAPITA AND AS A PERCENTAGE OF GNP BY DECADE

	Government revenue per capita				
Year	Federal	State	Local	Total	Total as share of GNP (%)
1800	1.96	0.42			
1810	1.80	0.36			
1820	2.52	0.56			
1830	2.07	0.54			
1840	1.50	0.88	1.23	3.60	4.0
1850	1.93	0.99	1.23	4.14	4.2
1860	3.32	1.72	2.17	7.20	5.4
1870	9.82	2.34	5.48	17.64	8.4
1880	6.39	1.70	4.98	13.07	5.7
1890	5.74	1.84	5.96	13.55	6.4
1900	6.42	2.43	8.83	17.68	7.2

	Revenues as share of GNP			
Year	Federal (%)	State (%)	Local (%)	Total (%)
1902	3.0	0.8	4.0	7.8
1913	2.4	0.9	4.2	7.5
1922	5.8	1.7	5.2	12.6
1927	4.7	2.1	6.0	12.8
1934	6.0	3.8	7.6	17.4
1940	7.0	5.0	5.8	17.9
1946	22.3	3.7	3.6	29.5
1952	20.4	4.1	4.0	28.5
1957	19.3	4.6	4.7	28.6
1962	18.5	5.2	5.5	29.2
1967	19.7	5.7	5.4	30.8
1972	18.4	6.9	6.2	31.5
1977	19.2	7.6	6.0	32.8
1982	21.6	8.2	6.2	36.1
1987	21.0	9.1	6.9	37.0
1992	20.8	9.3	7.3	37.5

Source: Reprinted from Wallis 2000, p. 65.

have always played some role in daily life. During the colonial era local jurisdictions had rules to govern the market, but it is not clear how well these were enforced. The federal government had initial rules for the distribution of federal lands. The common law court decisions set guidelines and adjudicated disputes about externalities and in settings where others were hurt or defrauded.[29]

Since the late nineteenth century the government has widened its scope by setting regulatory limits and expanding the range of administrative bodies, adding work for the courts that prescribe and enforce these limits. A comparison of the situation in 1890 with today's setting illuminates this expansion in scope. In most states, a manufacturing firm that hired a worker in 1890 generally filed no record of the hiring with any governmental authority. The firm had the obligation to exercise due care to prevent the worker from being injured and to not defraud the worker of his wages. If something bad happened, the worker would have the ultimate option of taking the firm to court. In some states there were guidelines for reporting some basic information about the firm and its workers. Today such a firm is required to meet guidelines in hiring and the running of the workplace that are established by the Equal Employment Opportunity Commission, the Fair Labor Standards Act, the National Labor Relations Board, the Internal Revenue Service, workers' compensation and unemployment insurance administrators, the Immigration and Naturalization Service, the Occupational Safety and Health Administration (OSHA), and other agencies. Similarly, the same firm seeking to build a new plant in 1890 would establish the deed and would have to meet local building code and state boiler inspection rules. If the plant damaged another's property there might be a lawsuit. Today, in addition to those costs, the firm would have to meet guidelines set by the Environmental Protection Agency, OSHA, and other state, local, and federal government agencies.

Economists and social scientists who are interested in the topic have offered an array of explanations for the expansion of government. Population growth, modernization, technological change, and industrialization have led to much greater interaction between people, and this has raised transactions costs and problems with externalities. Americans have higher incomes and thus can afford to prevent environmental damage and provide minimum incomes for the poor in ways that were not available when the income remaining after meeting subsistence needs was much smaller. Bureaucracies tend to expand as administrators seek to maximize their budgets. The early expansion of government led to feedback effects, and rent seekers learned new and better ways to demand more from government. The passage of the income tax amendment in 1913 removed a key constraint on revenue that held spending in check. All these factors contribute to the growth of government, although various scholars give them different weights.

Three major themes deserve to be highlighted in discussing the growth of American government. First, there has been a large-scale increase in the costs of providing security against external aggression and in expanding the nation's role in world affairs. Second, many people have sought greater protection against bad outcomes even at the risk of restrictions on personal freedom. Third, ideological changes concerning the role of government have played an important role, and these have been fueled in part by major crises.[30]

Since the founding of the country, national security has been a touchstone of American government. The rise in national defense costs has been dramatic. During the eighteenth and nineteenth centuries the natural protection of the oceans kept the costs of maintaining national security relatively low. The primary defense costs were associated with the internal strife of the Civil War. Americans were often content to ignore events outside the Western Hemisphere, and a relatively small share of the population had invested in resources in other countries because the balance of investments flowed into the United States from other countries. Pressure to remain isolationist persisted during World War I and through the beginning of World War II. From the 1940s to the present, the United States has played a larger and more important rule on the world stage. The development of new military technologies at home and abroad has meant that the natural defense offered by oceans has become less effective. Advances in military technology have become more and more expensive. Increased globalization means that American businesses now have extensive interests and employment abroad. Therefore, the pressure for the United States to defend its own lands and the lands of allies have risen. This expansion in activity has caused peacetime national defense expenditures to rise dramatically from 1 percent of GDP in peacetime before 1940 to between 4 and 8 percent of GDP in peacetime since 1950.

Possibly more important to the expansion of government has been the increasing demand for security against adverse economic events. From the country's founding, many local governments accepted limited responsibility for people in trouble, providing temporary housing and some cash payments to them. Charitable societies and churches provided additional help. The proportions of aid from public and private sources waxed and waned throughout the nineteenth century, but the temporary payments to the poor typically made up about 40 percent of the average wage. Because people might rely too much on such payments, societal norms often attached shame to dependence on government handouts. Land and opportunity were so abundant that people found it easy to blame the recipients of poor relief for their plight. The limits on provision of funds and the ostracism associated with accepting support led many to rely on their families and friends for aid in times of need. Meanwhile, the populace was less averse to providing aid to the less able. Local and state governments therefore provided for asylums for the insane, schools for the deaf and blind, and help for the disabled.[31]

Beginning in the late nineteenth century there was a trend among the developed countries toward expanding the degree of economic security and social insurance available and to formalize and depersonalize the arrangements for aiding low-income people. The United States joined this trend relatively late. At the turn of the century, the federal government expanded eligibility for Civil War disability pensions to such a degree that many of the elderly in the North were receiving disability pensions. During the early 1900s states began establishing pensions for widows with children and expanded the number of workplace accident victims receiving compensation by replacing the old common-law fault system with a specific set of workers' compensation requirements. Some explored separate programs for payments to the blind and the elderly poor. During the Great Depression, the federal government temporarily took over the lion's share of the relief obligations. With the Social Security Act of 1935, a national old-age pension system was established, and a series of joint state-national programs was created to provide unemployment insurance and to provide public assistance to dependent children, the blind, and the aged. Meanwhile, new programs allowed farmers to obtain a floor price for many crops. A number of businesses were propped up in hopes of preventing bankruptcy. The federal government began to insure deposits in banks and in savings and loans and mortgage loans for housing. Since the 1930s, economic security has expanded to include federal disability payments and federally funded medical care for the aged and the poor. Despite controversy about the farm programs, they remain in place, and even programs that seem to have been eliminated are rejuvenated in new forms. Governments still occasionally bail out companies considered too big to fail.[32]

In the past century, the process of obtaining relief has become more professional and impersonal. Rather than controlling overuse of relief largely by ostracism, the programs rely on professional administrators who apply rules designed to limit use. Bad times, however, lead to weakening of the rules. For example, a rise in the length of time people were receiving unemployment insurance during the 1990s led to temporary increases in the maximum period for which they could do so. The degree to which people rely on families and friends for aid has declined. It is clear that there has been a sea change in attitudes toward social insurance and public assistance and that these trends have been driven by the demands of large segments of the population. Many people seeking aid prefer the more impersonal process of applying for aid. As the economy becomes more specialized, at home and abroad, more people fear that they can lose their jobs or their incomes owing to decisions and events far beyond their control. People feel more entitled to benefits because they have paid for them with their income taxes. The link between payments and benefits is tighter still for social insurance programs designed so that the worker or the employer pays into funds from which the benefits are distributed.

The search for protection has moved beyond direct transfers of income and social insurance to regulations that protect against dangerous products and working conditions, the malfunctioning of products, incompetent service, changes in price, and monopoly. Businesses have increasingly sought protection against what they consider to be unrestrained and unhealthy competition.

As the country became increasingly industrialized during the nineteenth century, the ethos of caveat emptor—let the buyer beware—developed. The courts established a framework for compensating people after the fact when products or employment led to injury. The common-law decisions implied that sellers or employers shown to be at fault could be found liable to compensate the injured. If the buyer or worker had adequate information about the danger in advance or had contributed to the danger, however, the liability was reduced or eliminated. In the late 1800s state governments began to establish regulations that prescribed rules for production and work and created administrative bodies to enforce the regulations. The federal government also began to regulate a variety of activities involved in interstate commerce. Opportunities to regulate at the federal level continued to expand as the economy became more fully integrated. The courts have continued to play an important role in these areas, serving as arbiters when regulations are violated. Court decisions made since World War II, particularly in product safety cases, have increasingly disallowed the use of contractual language in purchase agreements as a bar against compensation of the injured.[33]

The focus of many of these regulations is to find ways to prevent bad outcomes in advance of events by regulating the process or the exchange, while continuing to compensate people after a bad event occurs. There have been numerous pressures for these changes. As discussed above, supporters of regulation argue that it benefits workers and consumers by helping solve several forms of market failure: high information and transaction costs, externalities, and monopoly.

All of these factors contribute to the demand for greater regulation. Yet it often confers benefits on sellers and employers as well by indirectly limiting entry. Many regulations were adopted or put in place as the result of political processes wherein building a winning coalition required reformers to join forces with at least a subset of the affected sellers or employers. These coalitions were common when workplace safety regulations, child-labor laws, and limits on women's' working hours were adopted during the Progressive Era. Thus, regulation was a compromise with which those to be regulated could live. This does not imply that the general population has been hoodwinked by the rise of regulation. Instead, the political realities have meant that the search for security regulation has dovetailed with the interests of subsets of firms and employers. The result has been a series of complicated tradeoffs among safety, higher prices, limited entry, and expanded opportunities.[34]

During the past century the United States has seen an ideological shift concerning the role of government, and particularly the federal government. Prior to 1900 there was a bias against an expanded role of government in the economy. In the course of World War I, the Great Depression, and World War II, attitudes toward government shifted such that by 1950 the majority of elites and the general public easily turned to government when they saw a problem they thought should be solved. Robert Higgs suggests that after each major crisis, the scale and scope of government ratcheted upward. During World War I, in the face of a major military crisis, the federal government experimented with a wide variety of controls of economic activity and off-budget government corporations to execute the war. Fears that these moves would severely hinder the economy were rampant. But those who administered the programs found many ways to resolve the information and allocation problems that arose. The new system worked less well than did regular markets at reflecting the true opportunity costs of many decisions, but it worked well enough to achieve the U.S. goal of winning the war. Many of the programs were dismantled in peacetime, but a cadre of administrators publicized their wartime successes. After the Great Depression began in 1929, four years of horrendous unemployment and declines in output led to great uncertainty. The cadre of WWI administrators was ready and willing to describe their prior success and press for the reinstitution of their methods. Hoover's Reconstruction Finance Corporation (RFC) and many of Roosevelt's New Deal programs had antecedents in the wartime programs. During World War II, New Deal philosophies and the World War I programs were put to use. The ability to win the war and reach an economic recovery in the postwar era led people to see the government's efforts as success stories.[35]

The counterfactual question of how well the nation would have done in the absence of many of the government programs often is difficult to answer because numerous alternative scenarios can be constructed. Opinions vary widely in American society. The program participants saw their efforts to overcome tremendous adversity as successes and thus defend the programs. Many stand ready to supply their services and ideas in the next crisis. Since World War II, as society has faced each new crisis, large or small, there has been a greater tendency to seek a governmental solution than in the late nineteenth century. A recent crisis, the terrorist strike on the World Trade Center and the Pentagon on September 11, 2001, led to the government's taking over responsibility for airport security under the Transportation Security Administration and an expansion in the Justice Department's powers to detain and monitor individual activities under the Patriot Act.

Shifts in Responsibilities within the Federal System

A prominent feature of government in the United States has always been the federal structure: the division of powers and responsibilities among many levels and types of government. In the colonial period it had some federal features because the Crown to whose authority it was subject was a long distance away. Under the Continental Congress during the Revolution and the Articles of Confederation afterward, the national government had substantially less power than it would have under the Constitution. The Constitution gave more powers to the national government but reserved most to state governments. By 1997 the U.S. structure had evolved to encompass one national government, fifty state governments, several territorial governments, more than three thousand county governments, and more than eighty-seven thousand other local governments including municipalities, townships, special purpose governments, and school districts. Most of these forms have their own separation of powers between an executive, a representative legislative body, and a court system.

The different levels of government typically specialize in different functions. The national government originally focused on the distribution of lands that it held, national defense and foreign policy, the post office, and the establishment of a basic monetary standard. The state and local levels maintained control over most other governmental functions, with the state distributing authority to local governments. The latter often focused on provision of local public goods such as police and fire protection, sanitation, public health, some poor relief, and eventually education. The degree of specialization of governments has increased over time as the federal government has become more involved in welfare and educational policies.

The expansion of government in American history has taken place at all levels, particularly in the past century, when such simple measures as government revenue as a share of GDP rose sharply (see table 1.1). The relative share of government activity at different levels has shifted over time. Warfare has always led to expansions of the national government relative to other governments. After wars the collections of tax revenues continued at high levels to help pay down the wartime debt.

Dramatic shifts in activity between the different levels of government occur in peacetime as well. From the adoption of the Constitution through the Civil War there was constant tension regarding the roles played by the national and state governments. In Congress and on the campaign trail the issue of states' rights was a constant theme, as the debates about slavery, the tariff, the Bank of the United States, and a variety of economic issues centered on the limitations of the national government's authority. Most authority over economic activity, however, was still centered in the states. The Civil War ultimately settled the issue in favor of a strong union with the national government operating the governments of the southern states through the end of Reconstruction.

Between 1790 and 1840, the state governments were the primary governments investing heavily in internal projects including banks, canals, and other transportation improvements. They experimented actively with the corporation as a way to accomplish public policy goals and to promote individual initiative. In the worlds of James Hurst, states "worked to release the latent energy" of the American economy by means of a thorough overhaul of the legal system. State government served as the primary conduit through which a large amount of capital, both foreign and domestic, could be funneled into investment projects. The national government played only a limited role in these areas, overseeing the two incarnations of the Bank of the United States and the building of a national road. Local governments were small because the large majority of the people lived in rural places. One sign of this difference in activity is the level of debt issued by each of the governments, shown in table 1.2. State debt in 1841 was $193 million, local debt was approximately $25 million, and national debt was $5 million.[36]

The heyday of state internal improvements ended in the early 1840s, when eight states and the Territory of Florida defaulted on debts they

Table 1.2 GOVERNMENT DEBT BY LEVEL OF GOVERNMENT, SELECTED YEARS

Year	Government debt, in millions of current dollars			Share at each level		
	State	**Local**	**National**	**State (%)**	**Local (%)**	**National (%)**
1838	172	25	3	86.0	12.5	1.5
1841	190	25	5	86.4	11.4	2.3
1870	352	516	2,436	10.7	15.6	73.7
1880	297	826	2,090	9.2	25.7	65.0
1890	228	905	1,122	10.1	40.1	49.8
1902	230	1,877	1,178	7.0	57.1	35.9
1913	379	4,035	1,193	6.8	72.0	21.3
1922	1,131	8,978	22,963	3.4	27.1	69.4
1932	2,832	16,373	19,487	7.3	42.3	50.4
1942	3,257	16,080	67,753	3.7	18.5	77.8
1952	6,874	23,226	214,758	2.8	9.5	87.7
1962	22,023	58,779	248,010	6.7	17.9	75.4
1972	59,375	129,110	322,377	11.6	25.3	63.1
1982	147,470	257,109	919,238	11.1	19.4	69.4
1992			2,998,639			

Source: Reprinted from Wallis 2000, p. 66.

had incurred in order to build or buy the banks, canals, and railroads. As a result, states began scaling back their development activities after 1842. New state constitutions and amendments to existing ones limited state borrowing, limited state assistance to private corporations, and in some cases prohibited investments altogether. After 1842 much of the activity in internal improvements shifted to local governments, although the national government was heavily involved in subsidizing transcontinental railroads. By the late nineteenth century the growing local governments were investing heavily in schools, roads, municipal buildings, and public health improvements. Local governments were also pressing for more freedom from interference by state legislatures. By 1902, local debt was eight times total state debt, and most of the local debt was for public infrastructure investments (see table 1.2). At the same time, local government revenues exceeded national and state government revenues combined.[37]

During the late nineteenth century and during the Progressive Era, the states became increasingly active in using their police powers to regulate actors in their respective economies. In the nineteenth century they had always regulated banks and had begun to regulate railroads. By the early 1900s states had established an extensive set of regulations of labor markets and some product markets. In addition, they had become more intimately involved in public assistance, education, and some forms of social insurance. Although many forms of regulation were considered the purview of the states, the federal government began regulating activities involving interstate commerce, including national banks and railroads, and foodstuffs.

The demarcations between federal, state, and local government were revolutionized during the New Deal. Many economic concerns, such as unemployment, had long been considered local problems. But the nationwide depression led many to consider the economy a national problem. The result was a dramatic shift in the role of the national government as it became heavily involved in public assistance, social insurance, agricultural programs, and a broad array of regulations. This dramatic peacetime shift in responsibility was further consolidated during World War II. According to various measures, the national government has remained the largest level of government to this day.

Outline of the Book

The goal of this book is to discuss the role of government in the American economy from colonial times to the present. The co-authors describe the impact of government policies on the economy and the political economy of the policy making process. The book highlights the insights of economic theories of government and the results of an extensive amount of research conducted in the past thirty years by economic historians and social scientists. It offers the advantages of a chronological discussion of the development of government in the economy and special chapters interwoven throughout that focus on long-term changes in specific areas. The chronological story allows us to weave together the changes in government during specific periods, and the case studies highlight important features of the government's role in more depth and allow for greater appreciation of the ways it has changed over time.

Many features of American governments did not simply spring from the minds of the founding fathers in 1787. Instead, they developed from our colonial heritage. Chapter 2, by Stanley L. Engerman, shows how the various colonial governments developed in response to their environments and documents the different features of government that were retained and discarded as British rule gave way to the United States of America. In chapter 3 Robert A. McGuire discusses the economic problems that the Constitutional Convention was meant to resolve and how the ideologies and economic interests of the founding fathers and the society at large influenced the document. The Constitution provided only a basic framework for government; the true nature of its operation

was established during the federal period. John Joseph Wallis documents in chapter 6 the ways in which the national and state governments
interacted in the new federal system and illuminates the constant tensions that developed regarding which level of government would have
responsibility for which facets of policy. Disagreements about the rights
of states, the enslavement of African Americans, and various economic
issues eventually culminated in the Civil War. In chapter 7 Jeffrey Rogers
Hummel traces these developments as well as the impact of the war on
the American economy, and the way the outcome of the war and Reconstruction established the strength of the federal government. Mark
Guglielmo and Werner Troesken document the changes at all levels of
government during the Gilded Age in chapter 9. The growth of cities
and changes in technology and industry led to an expansion in local
government spending on education as well as professional police and
fire departments while leading to diverse arrangements for the provision of sewers, water, electricity, and natural gas. Many states began
to explore the use of regulation while the federal government became
increasingly involved in regulating interstate commerce in the railroad
and food industries and established the first major antitrust law.

The twentieth century witnessed a dramatic expansion in activity by
all levels of government. In chapter 10 Price Fishback documents the
changes that took place during the Progressive Era as a kaleidoscope of
interest groups pushed to establish new forms of government activity.
Most of the changes were small steps that set the stage for larger expansions of government in response to three major crises. Robert Higgs
portrays the experiments with the command economy that were conducted during the two world wars and the legacies that they established
in chapter 14, and in chapter 13 Price Fishback discusses the widespread
changes made during the New Deal that contributed to a permanent
expansion of all governments and in the federal government's role in
the economy. In chapter 17 Fishback discusses the search for security in
a complex world that has led to continued expansion of national defense
and the regulations and social insurance programs designed to protect
the populace against adverse outcomes.

Several facets of the government and economy receive special attention. Discussions of economic development center on the key inputs: capital, land, and labor. In chapter 5 Richard Sylla traces the government's
role in establishing a financial system that was the envy of the developed world in the nineteenth and twentieth centuries. Gary D. Libecap
describes the long-term development of our system of private property

rights and the policies adopted by the federal government to distribute the public lands in chapter 4. In chapter 11 Sumner J. La Croix examines the government's role in labor markets from the development of government sponsorship of schools to the changes in the rules associated with collective action. Not all groups have shared equally in the American success story. Robert A. Margo traces the governments' role in policy toward African Americans in chapter 8, encompassing the promotion and protection of slavery, the development of Jim Crow laws and segregated schools in the southern states, and the modern era, when government policies have been more favorable in protecting blacks' rights.

Three aspect of government in the twentieth century receive particular attention: the rise of the federal bureaucracy, the expansions in federal farm programs, and the dramatic changes in welfare and public assistance. In chapter 12 Gary D. Libecap describes the development of the federal bureaucracy from a system run primarily via patronage to the modern civil service system. Randal R. Rucker and E. C. Pasour Jr. lay out the development of the leading farm programs and examine their impact on the farm sector and the rest of the economy in chapter 15. Lee J. Alston and Joseph P. Ferrie, the authors of chapter 16, describe the development of federal welfare policy and show how various interest groups, particularly changing economic interests in the South, have influenced the forms of public assistance seen in modern programs.

Knowledge of the history of government in the U.S. economy is central to anyone's understanding of the roles that government plays today. As it has for the past two centuries, the relation between the government and the economy is likely to continue to change. The relative inertia of government institutions and policies, however, means that our future choices will be strongly influenced by the historical path we have followed.

Notes

1. See North, Wallis, and Weingast 2005 for discussion of the "natural state." See O'Driscoll, Feulner, and O'Grady 2003 and Gwartney and Lawson 2004a for current ratings of governments around the world with respect to economic freedom. Gwartney and Lawson's data can be downloaded from Gwartney and Lawson 2004b. There is a huge literature about the role of government policy in economic growth across countries by economic historians and economists. See, e.g., North 1981, 1991, 2005; Landis 1998; Rostow 1960; Barro and Martin 2004, chap. 12; Acemoglu, Johnson, and Robinson 2002; Knack and Kiefer 1995; and Scully and Landis 1988. Barro and Martin (2004) developed empirical estimates for modern economies that show that countries

tend to have faster economic growth in areas where the rule of law is strong. The impact of enhanced electoral rights is positive as countries move away from totalitarian regimes, but once the value reaches the midpoint of their measure, expanding democracy tends to have a negative effect, possibly because electoral majorities use the political process to redistribute income away from minorities in ways that retard growth. The higher the ratio of government spending on factors other than national defense and education to real GDP, the lower the growth rate.

2. On Argentina, see Taylor 1992. Maddison (1991, 2001) documents the changes in relative status of countries over the course of the past few centuries.

3. Thomas Malthus was a famous economic philosopher in the early nineteenth century who argued that population often grew more rapidly than available resources. When this happened, wars, diseases, and other disasters would lead to sharp reductions in population.

4. Gwartney and Lawson (2004a, 5) state that "the key ingredients of economic freedom are personal choice, voluntary exchange, freedom to compete, and protection of person and property. Institutions and policies are consistent with economic freedom when they provide an infrastructure for voluntary exchange and protect individuals and their property from aggressors seeking to use violence, coercion and fraud to seize things that do not belong to them."

5. Had the governments considered the direct and indirect costs of the war and brokered a peaceful compensation of slave owners, the slave owners would have received the market values of their slaves at 1860 prices and each of the slaves would have received a significant grant of land and tools and a significant amount of back wages (Goldin and Lewis 1975).

6. For discussions of the economic role of government, see North 1981, 1991.

7. For longer discussions of this issue, see Libecap 1989; Hughes 1977, chap. 2; Eggertsson 1990; and chapter 4 of this book.

8. In this case cars, like prescription drugs, would be items that you can buy but cannot sell.

9. See Khan and Sokoloff 2001 for the development of patent rights in American history.

10. See Pipes 1999, Scully 1988, Knack and Kiefer 1995, Barro and Martin 2004, and Feng 2003.

11. See Kelo et al. v. City of New London et al., no. 04-108 (June 25, 2005). http://supremecourtus.gov/opinions/04slipopinion.html (accessed September 1, 2005).

12. For examples of communal and customary rights, see Ostrom 1990 and Simmons and Anderson 1992.

13. Trustees of Dartmouth College v. Woodward, 17 U.S. 518 (1819); Munn v. Illinois, 94 U.S. 113 (1877). For a broad overview of the development of the legal system see Hughes 1977 and Hughes and Cain 2003.

14. The quotations are from Smith (1937, 862).

15. Friedman (1985) and Hurst (1956) have written extended histories of American law. A good introduction to the economic history of the legal system is provided in Hughes and Cain 2003.

16. Experimental studies of free riding in public-good settings suggest that at least initially some of the public good will be produced. In the experiments,

economic logic suggested that everybody would free ride and thus the public good would not be produced. In early rounds participants contributed enough to produce roughly 40 to 50 percent of the optimal amount of the public good. This is a partial triumph for the socialization process or our natural instinct for cooperation. In later rounds, however, the participants tended to reduce their cooperation, and less than 20 percent of the public good was provided (Isaac and Walker 1988).

17. See Higgs 1987, 1990.

18. Tax rates can reach a level high enough that further increases in rates cause tax revenues to actually fall. There were heated debates during the Reagan era about supply-side economics that centered on determining the point at which higher rates would lead to reductions in revenue. Much of this debate was centered on the very top part of the income distribution and on discussions of legal and illegal forms of tax avoidance for investment income.

19. Irwin (1996) discusses the history of economic thought on tariffs. The laws passed to protect realtors from discount competitors are described in "Review and Outlook: The Realtor Racket," *Wall Street Journal,* August 12, 2005, A8.

20. Keyssar (2000) provides a history of voting.

21. See Mueller (1989, chap. 18), Downs (1957), and Tullock (1967).

22. Hamilton, Madison, and Jay 1961, 77–84. For a sampling of economists' discussions of interest groups, see Mueller 1989, Stigler 1971, Peltzman 1980, Buchanan, Tollison, and Tullock 1980, and Becker 1983.

23. Public choice economics is the study of the way self-interested individuals make decisions to influence government policy inside and outside government. For broad surveys of public choice, see Mueller 1989, Buchanan and Tullock 1962, Buchanan, Tollison, and Tullock 1980, and the journal *Public Choice.* A partial equilibrium analysis of the tariff suggests that consumers would lose more than producers would gain from the creation of a tariff. On past steel tariffs, see Taussig 1964. On the Bush tariff see Samuelson 2003.

24. For the Smoot-Hawley logroll see Irwin and Kroszner 1996. For other examples see Stratman 1995 and Mayhew 1966.

25. For discussions of capture, see Kolko 1965, Stigler 1971, Glaeser and Shleifer 2003, and Buchanan, Tollison and Tullock 1980. For discussions of corruption, see Shleifer and Vishny 1998.

26. On the long life of steel tariffs, see Taussig (1964, 346–47). On the REA, see *Columbia Electronic Encyclopedia* 2005.

27. The Lincoln quotation is taken from Carman and Luthin (1943, 6). For more on the transition from patronage to civil service see chapter 12 of this book.

28. Higgs (1987, 1991), North and Wallis (1982), Wallis and North (1986), and Wallis (2000) provide perspectives on long-term government growth in the United States.

29. Hughes (1977) describes the various local market rules in the colonial period.

30. Higgs (1987, 1991) and Borcherding (1977) offer discussion of various economic theories about the growth of the U.S. government in the twentieth century.

31. Ziliak (1996, 2002) describes the shifts between private and public aid for the poor and the 40 percent figure for aid as a share of the average wage.

32. Lindert (2004) describes the development of social welfare policies for many nations.

33. Huber (1988) describes the changes in court rulings concerning product safety.

34. See chapter 10 for more details concerning the reformer-business coalitions that passed legislation.

35. For more detail see Higgs 1987.

36. See Hurst 1956. Callendar (1902) provides the classic statement of the state's role as a financial intermediary in promoting investments in canals, railroads, and banks.

37. Goodrich (1960) describes the states' roles in developing transportation networks in the nineteenth century.

References

Acemoglu, Daron, Simon Johnson, and James A. Robinson. 2002. "Reversal of Fortune: Geography and Institutions in the Making of the Modern World Income Distribution." *Quarterly Journal of Economics* 117 (November): 1231–94.

Barro, Robert, and Xavier Sala-i-Martin. 2004. *Economic Growth*. 2d ed. Cambridge: MIT Press.

Becker, Gary. 1983. "A Theory of Competition Among Pressure Groups for Political Influence." *Quarterly Journal of Economics* 98 (August): 371–400.

Borcherding, Thomas. 1977. "The Sources of Growth of Public Expenditures in the United States." In *Budgets and Bureaucrats: The Sources of Government Growth*, ed. Thomas E. Borcherding, 45–70. Durham, NC: Duke University Press

Buchanan, James, Robert Tollison, and Gordon Tullock. 1980. *Toward a Theory of the Rent Seeking Society*. College Station: Texas A&M University Press.

Buchanan, James, and Gordon Tullock. 1962. *Calculus and Consent*. Ann Arbor: University of Michigan Press.

Callender, Guy. 1902. "The Early Transportation and Banking Enterprises of the States in Relation to the Growth of the Corporation." *Quarterly Journal of Economics* 17 (November): 111–62.

Carman, Harry J., and Reinhard H. Luthin. 1943. *Lincoln and the Patronage*. New York: Columbia University Press.

Coase, Ronald. 1937. "The Nature of the Firm." *Economica* 4 (November): 386–405.

———. 1960. "The Problem of Social Cost." *Journal of Law and Economics* 3 (October): 1–44.

The Columbia Electronic Encyclopedia. 2005. 6th ed. "The Rural Electrification Administration." 6th ed. http://www.infoplease.com/ce6/history/A0842689.html (accessed August 23, 2005).

Downs, Anthony. 1957. *An Economic Theory of Democracy*. New York: Harper & Row.

Eggertsson, Thrainn. 1990. *Economic Behavior and Institutions*. New York: Cambridge University Press.

Feng, Yi. 2003. *Democracy, Governance, and Economic Performance.* Cambridge: MIT Press.

Friedman, Lawrence. 1985. *A History of American Law.* 2d ed. New York: Simon & Schuster.

Glaeser, Edward L., and Andrei Shleifer. 2003. "The Rise of the Regulatory State." *Journal of Economic Literature* 41 (June): 401–25.

Goldin, Claudia, and Frank Lewis. 1975. "The Economic Cost of the American Civil War: Estimates and Implications." *Journal of Economic History* 35 (June): 304–9.

Goodrich, Carter. 1960. *Government Promotion of American Canals and Railroads.* New York: Columbia University Press.

Gwartney, James, and Robert Lawson. 2004a. *Economic Freedom of the World: 2004 Annual Report.* Washington, DC: Cato Institute.

———. 2004b. *Economic Freedom of the World: 2004 Annual Report, Data Downloads.* Vancouver: Fraser Institute. www.freetheworld.com (accessed September 5, 2005).

Hamilton, Alexander, James Madison, and John Jay. 1961. *The Federalist Papers.* New York: New American Library Times Mirror.

Higgs, Robert. 1987. *Crisis and Leviathan: Critical Episodes in the Growth of American Government.* New York: Oxford University Press.

———, ed. 1990. *Arms, Politics, and the Economy: Historical and Contemporary Perspectives.* New York: Holmes & Meier.

———. 1991. "Eighteen Problematic Propositions in the Analysis of the Growth of Government." *Review of Austrian Economics* 5:3–40.

Huber, Peter. 1988. *Liability: The Legal Revolution and Its Consequences.* New York: Basic Books.

Hughes, Jonathan. 1977. *The Governmental Habit: Economic Controls from Colonial Times to the Present.* New York: Basic Books.

Hughes, Jonathan, and Louis Cain. 2003. *American Economic History.* 6th ed. New York: Addison-Wesley.

Hurst, James Willard. 1956. *Law and the Conditions of Freedom in the 19th Century United States.* Madison: University of Wisconsin Press.

Irwin, Douglas. 1996. *Against the Tide: An Intellectual History of Free Trade.* Princeton, NJ: Princeton University Press.

Irwin, Douglas, and Randall Kroszner. 1996. "Log-Rolling and Economic Interests in the Passage of the Smoot-Hawley Tariff." *Carnegie-Rochester Conference Series on Public Policy* 45 (December): 173–200.

Isaac, R. Mark, and Walker, James M. 1988. "Group Size Effects in Public Goods Provision: The Voluntary Contributions Mechanism." *Quarterly Journal of Economics* 103 (February): 179–99.

Keyssar, Alexander. 2000. *The Right to Vote : The Contested History of Democracy in the United States.* New York: Basic Books.

Khan, B. Zorina, and Kenneth L. Sokoloff. 2001. "Intellectual Property Institutions in the United States: Early Development." *Journal of Economic Perspectives* 15 (Summer): 233–46.

Knack, Stephen, and Philip Keefer. 1995. "Institutions and Economic Performance: Cross-Country Tests Using Alternative Institutional Measures." *Economics and Politics* 7 (November): 207–77.

Kolko, Gabriel. 1965. *Railroads and Regulation, 1877–1916*. New York: Norton.

Landis, David. 1998. *The Wealth and Poverty of Nations: Why Some Are So Rich and Some So Poor*. New York: Norton.

Libecap, Gary D. 1989. *Contracting for Property Rights*. New York: Cambridge University Press.

Lindert, Peter H. 2004. *Growing Public: Social Spending and Economic Growth since the Eighteenth Century*. New York: Cambridge University Press.

Maddison, Angus. 1991. *Dynamic Forces in Capitalist Development: A Long-Run Comparative View*. New York: Oxford University Press.

———. 2001. *The World Economy: A Millennial Perspective*. Paris: Development Centre of the Organisation for Economic Co-operation and Development.

Mayhew, D. R. 1966. *Party Loyalty among Congressmen*. Cambridge: Harvard University Press.

Mueller, Dennis. 1989. *Public Choice II*. New York: Cambridge University Press.

North, Douglass C. 1981. *Structure and Change in Economic History*. New York: Norton.

———. 1991. *Institutions, Institutional Changes, and Economic Performance*. New York: Cambridge University Press.

———. 2005. *Understanding the Process of Economic Change*. Princeton, NJ: Princeton University Press.

North, Douglass C., and John Joseph Wallis. 1982. "American Government Expenditures: A Historical Perspective." *American Economic Review* 72 (May): 336–40.

North, Douglass C., John Joseph Wallis, and Barry Weingast. 2005. "A Framework for Understanding Recorded Human History." Paper presented at the National Bureau of Economic Research Summer Institute on the Development of the American Economy, Cambridge, MA, July.

O'Driscoll, Gerald, Edwin J. Feulner, and Mary Anastasia O'Grady. 2003. *2003 Index of Economic Freedom*. Washington, DC: Heritage Foundation and the Wall Street Journal.

Ostrom, Elinor. 1990. *Governing the Commons: The Evolution of Institutions for Collective Action*. Cambridge: Cambridge University Press.

Peltzman, Samuel. 1980. "The Growth of Government." *Journal of Law and Economics* 23 (October): 209–87.

Pipes, Richard. 1999. *Property and Freedom*. New York: Vintage.

Rostow, Walter. 1960. *The Stages of Economic Growth*. New York: Cambridge University Press.

Samuelson, Robert. 2003. "A Trade War We Don't Need," *Newsweek*, November 17, 53.

Scully, Gerald W. 1988. "The Institutional Framework and Economic Development." *Journal of Political Economy* 96 (April): 652–62.

Shleifer, Andrei, and Robert W. Vishny. 1998. *The Grabbing Hand: Government Pathologies and Their Cures*. Cambridge: Harvard University Press.

Simmons, Randy, and Terry Anderson, eds. 1992. *The Political Economy of Customs and Culture: Informal Solutions to the Commons Problem*. Savage, MD: Rowan & Littlefield.

Smith, Adam. 1937. *An Inquiry into the Nature and Causes of the Wealth of Nations*. 1776; New York: Modern Library.

Stigler, George. 1971. "The Theory of Economic Regulation." *Bell Journal of Economics and Management Science* 2 (Spring): 3–21.

Stratman, Thomas. 1995. "Logrolling in the U.S. Congress." *Economic Inquiry* 33 (July): 441–56.

Taussig, F. W. 1964. *The Tariff History of the United States.* 8th ed. New York: Capricorn.

Taylor, Alan. 1992. "External Dependence, Demographic Burdens, and Argentine Economic Decline after the Belle Epoque." *Journal of Economic History* 52 (December): 907–36.

Tullock, Gordon. 1967. *Toward a Mathematics of Politics.* Ann Arbor: University of Michigan Press.

Wallis, John Joseph. 2000. "American Government Finance in the Long Run." *Journal of Economic Perspectives* 14 (Winter): 61–82.

Wallis, John Joseph, and Douglass C. North. 1986. "Measuring the Transaction Sector in the American Economy, 1870–1970." In *Long-Term Factors in American Economic Growth,* ed. Stanley L. Engerman and Robert E. Gallman, 95–148. Chicago: University of Chicago Press.

Ziliak, Stephen. 1996. "The End of Welfare and the Contradiction of Compassion." *Independent Review* 1 (Spring): 55–73.

———. 2002. "Some Tendencies of Social Welfare and the Problem of Interpretation." *Cato Journal* 21 (Winter): 499–513.

STANLEY L. ENGERMAN

2

Government in Colonial America

THE SETTLEMENT of colonial America entailed the movement of people from elsewhere into areas previously resided in by Indians. It required the attraction of free immigrants, mainly from the British Isles, and the acquisition of slaves from Africa, as well as the need to control those already there, or, at least, to work out mutually satisfactory arrangements for coexistence. For free immigrants it meant a relocation into an area quite different from that which they had left, and for African slaves it also meant a loss of freedom and control.

The role of colonial governments was to provide the following within the colonies: defense and protection, including the raising of militias when needed, laws in regard to property rights for individuals, and certain public goods such as poor relief, the establishment of religions, and the regulation of activities of private individuals and businesses. In dealings outside the colonies the governments provided for regulations regarding trade (although these were often imposed by England) and defense against foreign attack (again, generally provided by England). Governmental rules could be the basis of a laissez-faire economy or a centrally controlled one. In either case government played a major role. Although the thirteen colonies were subject to control by the English until they achieved independence, they did have some flexibility in determining who had the right to vote and to hold office, what laws could be passed, and who had control over financial issues. Those not able to vote could be the beneficiaries of government policy nonetheless and also were able to bring pressure on the governments to offset losses in the economic and political spheres.[1]

Early European Settlement of the New World

The nations of western Europe began their moving into and across the Atlantic in the late fourteenth and fifteenth centuries. The pioneering nations in settling the Americas were Spain and Portugal. Portugal had first moved onto the offshore African islands, including the Azores, Madeira, the Cape Verde Islands, Fernando Po, Principe, and São Tomé, and Spain settled the Canary Islands, before both crossed the Atlantic to settle in the Americas. The Portuguese settled in Brazil while the Spanish explored several parts of mainland North America, the Caribbean, and Central and South America, primarily settling in what would be called Latin America, several of the islands in the Caribbean (Cuba, Puerto Rico, and Hispaniola), and a few scattered parts of mainland North America, mainly in the Southwest and Florida. British expansion overseas, initiated for the purpose of trade, began with the granting of charters to several trading companies, beginning with the Muscovy Company (1553), and by the end of the sixteenth century British companies were trading with the Levant, North Africa, and India, and, after the mid-seventeenth century, West Africa.[2]

Spain had a one-century lead on the northern nations of western Europe—France, Britain, and the Netherlands—and settled in the areas of the Americas that had the greatest wealth and had by far the greatest numbers of American Indians. Spain's possessions provided great wealth from the use of Indian labor in mining gold and silver for shipment to Spain, whence it was exported to other parts of Europe and to Asia to finance Spanish purchases of consumer and military goods.[3]

The British and other Europeans were not, of course, the first to settle in the Americas; they had been preceded by the Native Americans. The locations of Indians at the time of European contact pointed to significant differences in settlement patterns. The areas of Spanish conquest had about three-quarters of the Indian population, mainly in the wealthy and politically sophisticated Inca and Aztec empires, with populations resident in urban areas, military organizations, high agricultural productivity, and large-scale slavery and imperialism. Even with the exceptional mortality that took place after contact with the Spanish, primarily due to diseases, these areas continued to have large Indian populations and still do today. In mainland North America the Native Americans were many fewer, and they lived in much smaller political units than did those in Latin America.

The pattern of Indian-European contact was rather mixed. It involved conflict and warfare, as well as some early enslavement and sale of Native Americans by Europeans. Some Europeans formed coalitions with Indian groups, often in opposition to other Europeans, but peaceful arrangements between Europeans and natives in the absence of

European rivalry also persisted. The French in Canada were heavily involved in the fur trade with Indians, and the British, in their colonies, were also able to establish trade with the Indians. Furs were traded for foodstuffs, alcohol, tobacco, and other goods. Whether trade was peaceful or antagonistic, Europeans generally pushed inland, with the Indians often being forced to relocate further inland. Thus, the land base of the British colonists on mainland North America expanded greatly after initial settlement, as did that of the French in Canada before they lost it to the British in 1763.[4]

Colonial Organization in the Settlement of North America

As noted above, when the three major northern European nations came to explore and settle in the New World they were left with what were regarded as limited opportunities relative to Spain's and Portugal's. The areas that were still available had small Indian societies of relatively limited wealth. Before settling on the mainland, Europeans had settled in the generally unoccupied islands of the Caribbean. After an early period of using white indentured labor to produce tobacco, they transformed these islands into major sugar-producing areas, using mainly slave labor brought from Africa. Sugar was produced for export to European markets on large plantations, often using one hundred to two hundred or more slaves. The rivalry between the British and the Dutch, in Europe and in the New World, led the British to introduce the Navigation Acts after 1651 to control export and import markets and shipping patterns. The acts regulated the trade of their colonies, requiring that exports were to go to Britain, imports were to come from Britain, and goods were to be carried in British or colonial vessels. All Europeans pursued similar policies of mercantilism, intended to increase the production and trade of the home country at the expense of other nations.

It was only at the end of the seventeenth century that the migration from Britain shifted from the Caribbean to go primarily to the colonies of mainland North America. Settlement on the mainland had begun earlier in the century, but it was not yet considered as attractive a location for settlement as was the Caribbean, and the demand for slave labor was much smaller. At that time several other groups had settled on the mainland: the French, mainly in Canada; the Swedes, in Delaware; and the Dutch, in what was called New Netherland.

The means of establishing colonies varied among European nations. The Spanish and the Portuguese colonies were often state enterprises, with state decision making and with a strong role played by the Catholic

Church. British colonies were established according to charters issued by the Crown. Yet they were settled by individuals or groups, not by the government, and they made decisions in their own or the colony's interests. There were two basic British patterns of colonial establishment and operation. The first was the proprietorship, established by a grant made to specific individuals and groups. Sometimes such colonies were established for particular religious or philanthropic purposes. The second was the use of a joint stock company to finance settlement and to establish the group controlling the political life of the colony.

The earliest attempts by the British to establish settlements in North America, both unsuccessful, were proprietorships for Newfoundland (1583) and Roanoke Island, North Carolina (1585). Both involved small numbers of settlers and lasted for a very short period, as did the joint stock company established for the settlement of Kennebec River, Maine (1607). The first successful settlement was that of Virginia, based on a charter granted in 1606, a settlement founded in 1607, and a new charter that created a joint stock company in 1609, with land grants used to encourage colonization. The settlement was to be successful, but the company was not. It failed financially and, in 1624, Virginia became the first royal colony. Joint stock companies were used to settle Plymouth, Massachusetts in 1620 and Massachusetts in 1629 (via the Massachusetts Bay Company). The former was an attempt at a communal economic system, but it was seen as a financial failure in 1627, and there was a shift to private ownership at that time. The communal system did not work well because individuals and families were not willing to work as long and hard as they would if they had privately owned property on which they need not share their gains with others. In the case of the Massachusetts Bay Company there was a subsequent shift of political power by the Puritans to a representative system of local residents in 1634.

In the 1620s the British formed several colonies in the Caribbean. The first, St. Kitts, was initially settled in 1623, colonized by the French and the British, and came under a grant in 1627. Barbados was first settled after 1624 and was given a grant in 1627—the same grant that covered St. Kitts and most of the British Leeward Islands in the Caribbean. Barbados was a proprietorship, and this status led to a series of political disputes in subsequent years. It became a royal colony in 1650, although some provisions concerning the sharing of profits with creditors and leaseholders remained in effect for the length of the lease. A Puritan joint stock company, following the same laws as the Massachusetts Bay Company, had been established on Providence Island off the coast of

Belize in 1630, but this was neither an economic nor a social success, and it was captured by the Spanish in 1641. The largest of the British colonies in the Caribbean, Jamaica, was settled after being taken from Spain in 1655. As such, it was initially treated by the British government as a dependency. The varying patterns of organization in the Caribbean and the mainland indicate the flexibility of British political controls and settlement arrangements.

The first settlements on the mainland after 1629 were undertaken by the granting of proprietorships, several of which became Crown colonies within several decades of their establishment. Maryland, settled in 1634, was formed as a proprietorship granted to the Catholic Lord Baltimore, became a Crown colony in 1691, and reverted to a proprietorship in 1715. New York, which in 1664 had been captured from the Dutch (who had tried to establish a joint stock company in 1613), became a Crown colony in 1683; New Jersey, initially settled by Swedes and Finns, was captured by the Dutch in 1655, then by the British in 1664, and it became a Crown colony in 1702. The Carolinas (1670) became Crown colonies in 1729. The other two colonies were a colony including numerous Quakers with the name Pennsylvania and Delaware (1681), which was to become socially and economically successful, and Georgia (1732), initially a philanthropic venture. Georgia was not successful, and in 1751 it was returned to the Crown, at which time it reversed its earlier policy of excluding slave labor. All thirteen colonies became economically successful over time, and whatever the original provisions of their foundation, became equivalent states after the Revolution.[5]

Attracting Labor to the Colonies

All colonies had to solve the same set of problems: attracting labor and capital in order to survive economically. Although these factors of production were in short supply, a third factor, land, was quite abundant and quite fertile. It could be used, after clearing, in efficient agricultural production. The lower cost of producing food and other agricultural goods in the colonies was offset by the higher cost of producing manufactured commodities due to the scarcity of labor and capital. The Navigation Acts were meant to encourage British manufacturers and limit colonial manufacturers. But, as can be seen by the patterns of production in the early nineteenth century in the United States, these acts were, at least as far as manufacturing was concerned, unnecessary or redundant. The controls on shipping of colonial commodities were, however, more important, and they did restrict shipping by the Dutch, raising the cost of the commodities in British and other European markets and reducing the colonies' incomes.

The colonial governments adopted several different methods in their attempts to acquire labor. Land, whether granted directly to immigrants or to those who brought them over, was used to encourage immigration. It was sometimes granted immediately and sometimes after the period of time needed to establish permanent residence had passed. A system of indentured labor, along the lines of British apprenticeship, was rapidly introduced. Most immigrants lacked the funds to cover the costs of passage to the New World and of establishing themselves, so they traded a number of years of coerced labor for their transportation from the British Isles to the colonies. It is estimated that this system accounted for about three-fifths of all white migration to the mainland colonies, and it was particularly important for the southern colonies. At the end of the period of indenture, money or land might be given to the laborer as an additional subsidy to encourage migration. The colonies regulated the terms of transportation across the Atlantic and were responsible for the enforcement of the terms of the contracts and disputes between owners and servants. The mixture of land grants and indenture contracts attracted settlers from many areas of Europe, including all parts of the British Isles, Germany, the Netherlands, Sweden, and Finland, and groups such as English Pilgrims and the French Huguenots came seeking religious freedom. Nevertheless, Britain was the dominant presence on the mainland.

Another source of labor that was important in the southern states and in the Caribbean was that of slaves, initially purchased from Africa. The first slaves were introduced to the North American mainland about 1620. Patterning their laws after the major slave laws in Barbados in 1661, most colonies introduced slave codes to define slaveowners' rights, including the provision for the inheritance of the slave status by children born to slave mothers. The relative importance of these forms of labor—free versus slave—varied by region, based on the profitability of different crops. All colonies, despite their religious or political background, had legalized slavery, and no colony was to end slavery until the Revolutionary War.[6]

Attitudes and Political Economic Institutions

Some of the basic economic characteristics of the different colonies seemed similar at the start, but over time there developed significant differences in the nature of agriculture production and in the importance of agriculture relative to other economic sectors. The proprietors and investors in the colonies were generally from among the wealthiest and most politically important families in the British Isles. They had generally participated in the political life of England and were often the recipients of charters and grants from the king that provided monopoly privileges. They had been involved with commercial transactions and trade, both internally and externally, and had contacts with nations on the European continent as well as with Africa and Asia. They had seen the advantages, at least to themselves, of private property and had developed a concern with incentives for individuals and groups for private operations, with only limited reliance on government controls and operations or communal activities. They had achieved a comparatively high standard of living, the outcome of a willingness to labor or to organize labor to achieve that goal. They lived in a British economy that included banks and money exchanges, taxation of property, and a productive agricultural sector based on of hired labor and tenants. Therefore, it is not surprising that many of the North American proprietors and settlers with large landholdings sought to transfer these institutions to the New World.

Key questions for understanding successful long-term growth are, how pervasive were these commercial attitudes among the remainder of the free population, and how consistent were these commercial, if not fully capitalist, attitudes with their religious and cultural attitudes? In general, the desire to seek commercial gains and the willingness to respond to various price and income incentives permitted the attraction of migrants from Europe as well as increased economic productivity and geographic expansion in the colonies. There was not, of course, a narrow focus on pure profit maximization, as seen in choices regarding leisure, family and children, and religion, but obviously a concern to achieve high living standards.

The earlier settlers also carried over an attitude toward political and legal life that built on, and, indeed, expanded beyond that in the metropolis. English common law was firmly established in the colonies by the time of the Revolutionary War. Although the rules concerning eligibility to vote, which were based on property holding, were initially similar to those in Britain, the substantial difference in the proportion of colonists that was able to meet the requirements did lead to important political differences. The basic requirements for eligibility to vote and to hold office generally included minimum amounts of freehold, personal property, tax payments, income, or wealth, and these varied by colony and over time. Several colonies initially restricted voting by

certain religious groups, primarily Catholics and Jews. Blacks and Indians were not legally citizens and thus could not vote. Suffrage was also
restricted with regard to age, gender, race, and ethnicity. Nevertheless,
whereas about 15 percent of adult males could vote in early eighteenth-
century Britain, it is estimated that in the colonies 50 to 80 percent of
white males were qualified to vote. The distribution of land ownership
and wealthholdings was broader in the colonies than in the metropolis, and this had a significant influence on the economic and political
behavior of the colonies. This difference in voting patterns helps explain many of the observed policy differences. Unlike Europe, there
were relatively few religious limitations on voting in the colonies, and
the British ones, unlike the Spanish, had no religious restrictions on immigration. This meant that religious freedom was more fully developed
in the British colonies than in other nations' colonies or in Europe.

The expanded landholding, with its important impact on the economy
and the size of the electorate, was not the outcome of the basic policy of
landholding introduced in the colonies at the onset of settlement. Many
of the original settlers had been landholders in Britain, and they wished
to adopt the manorial, or feudal, system with which they were familiar.
This meant, at first, the allocation of land in large units, with the minimum
acreages sold being greater than the size of farms needed for individual
or family production of most food crops. Over time, however, the average size of farms and of landholdings was reduced as a result of the realities of production methods and political influence. Average farm size in
the New England and middle colonies was smaller than that in the southern states, although the large holdings of Dutch patroons in the Hudson
River valley of New York were maintained by the British after 1664. This
decrease in the size of landholdings in the North reflected not only the
pattern of land sales adopted by the colonies but also the frequency of
adoption of more egalitarian laws and practices, including inheritance
practices and the granting of headrights by colonial governments to encourage immigration from abroad and the settlement of frontier areas
within the colonies. Whereas, in regard to land, England maintained the
practice of primogeniture (inheritance by the oldest son), many of the colonies provided for an equal division of land among heirs and otherwise
limited the share going to the eldest son. In the southern colonies there
were also many small landholdings, but the emergence of plantations to
produce rice and tobacco using slave labor resulted in more large units
than in the North, although these plantations were smaller than were the
sugar plantations of the Caribbean. The rise of slave-based plantations

reflected more the nature of the crops grown than it did any fundamental initial differences in land law or in settlers' beliefs concerning slavery.[7]

The Structure of Colonial Government

Each of the thirteen colonies had its own legal and political systems, based initially on its governmental charter, although, in retrospect, many of these differences were relatively minor and inconsequential. This system, resembling what would later be regarded as federalism, did allow for mobility and competition among colonies. Each colony had elective assemblies and a governor, often appointed by the Crown. It set its own suffrage requirements, made its own budgetary decisions, and was responsible for its own fiscal arrangements. The outcomes, however, were often somewhat similar across colonies, as were the legal codes.

Yet these thirteen colonies were not able to behave as fully independent powers because they, and their Caribbean counterparts, were still part of the developing British Empire and subject to metropolitan controls. All were bound by the terms of the metropolitan Navigation Acts, influencing exports, imports, and shipping, and no colony could opt out of their provisions. The Navigation Acts were part of the system of mercantilism, aimed at increasing shipping, shipbuilding, production, and incomes of merchants, all to benefit residents of England. Although some of the English were to be gainers, the losers were the British colonies, foreign countries, and British consumers of colonial products. Depending on the importance and magnitude of exports and imports, the acts could, however, have had dramatically different impacts across colonies and generated differing amounts of controversy and debate. Similarly, when most of the settlements became Crown colonies, colonial legislatures had to obtain final approval of their decisions from the British Parliament, which could overrule them. In time of warfare the colonies fought on the side of the British, and colonial militias, generally formed as needed in the absence of a standing army, were often called to fight in wars against the French and the Indians. The basic costs of the army and the navy were, however, paid for by the British, saving the colonies much of the expense of defense and reducing the need for manpower. Colonies were thus a mixture of colonized nation and independent region, with their own leaders and legislatures.[8]

Geography's Impact on Demographic and Economic Structures

Despite some basic similarity in patterns of belief and behavior among British settlers and an early similarity of institutions, major differences soon emerged in economic and demographic structures. This led to sharp differences in institutions and in the nature of labor regimes. Fundamental to these changes were differences in climate, resources, and crops that were growable in the various regions.

The Caribbean islands were first settled by indentured servants producing mainly tobacco, but generally they soon became sugar-producing islands using mainly slave labor. Slaves made up 80 to 90 percent of their populations, and the high mortality and low fertility of the slave population meant a continued need to import large numbers of slaves from Africa. Sugar was grown on large plantations, and most of it was exported. First it went to Britain, and then some was reexported to other parts of Europe. The total of nonhuman wealth (land, buildings, and equipment) per free capita in the Caribbean was considerably above that in the mainland colonies, and the politically influential planter class was able to get favorable legislation from the British government, including legislation, such as the Molasses Act of 1733, that benefited them at the expense of mainland colonies. This act placed a high tariff on sugar, molasses, rum, and spirits that the colonies had imported from the French and other foreign sugar colonies.

The mainland is conventionally divided into three areas: New England, the Middle Atlantic, and the South. Each had quite different economic and demographic patterns. The New England colonies were characterized by very high rates of population growth, due to high fertility and low mortality. There were few indentured laborers and few slaves, the labor force consisting mainly of free members of the population. New England experienced a high rate of natural increase, with only a rather limited immigration from Britain and elsewhere after the initial period of settlement. Agricultural production took place on small farms growing mostly grains, often owner-operated; the region's relatively limited exports went mainly to the British West Indies.

The Middle Atlantic region had somewhat more slaves and indentured laborers than did New England, but it was also characterized by agricultural production of foodstuffs on relatively small units with a level of exports per capita similar to that of New England. These two regions (known collectively as the North) were not considered by the British to provide the principal benefits of colonization. They produced crops similar to those of Britain and thus provided a limited basis for becoming major trading partners.

The southern colonies fit much better Britain's mercantilist ideal, specializing in crops that it was not able to produce and exporting them to there for both British consumption and reexport to the Continent.

The major crops were tobacco from the Chesapeake and later rice and indigo from South Carolina and Georgia. The importance of tobacco as an export led to the imposition of various regulations by Virginia and Maryland over the course of the seventeenth and eighteenth centuries, including inspection requirements, regulation of quality, and export restrictions. Exports from the southern colonies per free capita were about seven times those of the northern regions at the start of the eighteenth century and roughly three times greater prior to the Revolution. White indentured laborers and free workers were the earliest settlers of the southern colonies, but in the eighteenth century there was a sharp growth in the size of the slave population from about 6 percent of total population in 1680 to 41 percent in 1770. Slaves were of particular importance mainly in export production of rice and tobacco on units larger than the family farm. The natural rate of population growth in the region, free and slave, was unusually rapid, but the growth rate also benefited from large migrations from Britain and from Africa.

The mainland colonies had roughly similar nonhuman wealth per capita (free and slave), which is a crude index of overall productivity. More useful as measures of differential political influence were the total (nonhuman and human, the latter only valued for slaves) wealth per free capita, the South's being more than twice that of the North, and the nonhuman wealth per free capita, the South's being about 1.5 times that of the North. The mainland's wealth per free capita was considerably below that of Jamaica and the Caribbean. The distribution of this wealth among wealthholders was similar for residents of New England and the South, but that for the Middle Atlantic was somewhat more equal than the other regions, a point that, possibly, favorably influenced its subsequent economic and political development. The relative equality of incomes and wealth led to a larger number of voters, and this, in turn, influenced the decisions made as to education, land distribution, and chartering of banks and businesses.

Although most mainland colonies became Crown colonies, British officials were permitted to limit the rights of colonial governments. Each colony remained responsible for certain key political decisions. Colonies had legislative bodies and governors appointed by the Crown to rule internally and generally also had elective offices. Usually voting was reserved for property holders, as was the case in England and elsewhere, but, as noted above, the broad distribution of landholdings meant that a higher share of the population was eligible to vote than in Britain and on the European continent at the start of the eighteenth century.[9]

Important Colonial Government Policies

Each colony made key decisions pertaining to property rights; the allocation of land, including the size and price of holdings made available for grants or for purchases; control of labor, free, slave, and indentured; regulations regarding shipping and trade, including tariffs, taxes, quality controls, and the use of product trademarks; the issuance of paper money; the provision of state militias; and the general policies concerning taxation and expenditures. The functions performed by the colonial governments did not differ dramatically from those later undertaken by state and local governments, and some, such as poor relief, control of market prices and regulations about the quality of goods, resembled those still existing in Britain. As always, the degree of enforcement of any law may have been limited.

Unlike the Caribbean, with its large percentage of African slaves, and Mexico and South and Central America, with large numbers of Native Americans, mainland North America was predominantly populated by the British. European settlers made up about 60 percent of the population of the southern colonies, and this proportion was higher in other regions. Because of the nature of the settlement process set out by the Crown, thirteen colonies were making decisions about laws, taxes, and finances, though they were subject to the overriding power of the British government. Certain aspects of economic and political structure, such as the rules controlling the trade in exports and imports and shipping arrangements, were binding on all colonies, but the specifics of tax and expenditure policies remained within colonial discretion. As part of the empire's currency union, the mainland faced constraints on financial and monetary policies such as those that would affect the rest of the world in the nineteenth and twentieth centuries, involving gold standards and currency unions. The role of gold and silver specie and basically fixed definitions of colonial and British rates of exchange did not allow for substantial and persistent, as contrasted with temporary, variations in colonial monetary laws and money issues. The British Currency Acts of 1751 and 1764 restricted issues of paper money by colonies because it was not considered legal tender, although a 1773 act allowed the use of paper money to pay provincial taxes. Nevertheless, a land bank was established in Massachusetts, and more than one-half of the colonies issued paper money, which was particularly important as a means of temporary wartime financing to be retired at a war's end.

The range of legislation enacted in the colonies was rather broad; as J. R. T. Hughes pointed out, during that era virtually every aspect of economic life was subject to nonmarket control, "and there is very little in the way of nonmarket control of the economy that does not have a colonial or English forerunner." [10] That being said, the colonies were able to experience relatively rapid economic growth by the standards of the time and to achieve levels of per capita income similar to that of Britain while receiving large number of immigrants and sustaining an exceptionally high rate of natural population increase.

This reflected, in part, the relatively stable monetary situation; there were no prolonged periods of price inflation (or deflation), so loans of foreign capital, mainly from Britain, continued throughout the period. Furthermore, rates of taxation in the colonies, even with some allowance for the burden of the Navigation Acts, were relatively low compared to rates in Britain and much of Europe. The British government imposed tariffs on the external trade of the colonies, but not until the Stamp Act of 1765 (later repealed in part) was a major internal tax introduced.

Different colonies imposed rather mixed sets of taxes, including property taxes, faculty (per person) or income taxes on individuals, poll taxes, import and export duties, excise or internal taxes, and land taxes based on improved acreage, total acreage, or assessed value. Tax rates did vary with circumstances, such as wars, but in the absence of a standing army or navy, and with the primary defense shield provided by the British, overall military expenditures were generally small. And although the local governments in the colonies were responsible for bridges, fences, roads, and schooling, these were often financed by tolls and fees, by the granting of land or of monopoly franchises, or by taxes paid in the form of labor. Political conflicts—between proprietors and settlers, between large and small landholders, between landholders and the landless, between merchants and farmers, between tidewater and frontier populations—occurred at periodic intervals but did not lead to dramatic overhauls of the political system, although these pressures led to measures that indicated the flexibility of the colonial political system.

These basic legal provisions and regulations seemingly did not interfere with economic growth or, at the least, were consistent with what developed: economic growth at a relatively high rate for the time. The granting of relatively unconstrained rights to private property, generally without government confiscation or the other forms of failure to maintain these property rights, was very important. The Quebec Act of 1774 limited the ability of the colonists to expand westward as the British government took control of the western lands from the colonies that had rights to them, but in the same year regulations provided for land rights in several areas to be sold or given as grants to proprietors. Some colonies required that the land be either used or improved within a limited number of years before title was final, foreshadowing the Homestead Act of 1862. In some colonies Indians were not permitted to own land. The purchasers or grantees had rights to own, use, bequeath (although primogeniture was not abolished until the Revolutionary War), or sell the land, as long as the taxes (quitrents) were paid. Given the great amounts of land available and the great importance of agriculture to national output, this security of land title played a key role in economic growth. Although early in the settlement process the intent was to have land be made available in large units, over time the minimum size of units was reduced, and more parcels of fifty to one hundred acres were granted to encourage population growth and relocation. Most free males were able to acquire land.

The colonies adopted the English system of common law, which paid great attention to lawyers and legal matters, as seen in the numerous volumes of state law codes and published legal decisions. Important sets of laws controlled black slavery, indentured labor, and apprenticeship, but there was no serfdom or, for whites, slavery. At times colonies imposed regulations on wages and working hours, as well as regulations regarding occupations. The English poor laws, which provided for local controls on vagabonds and vagrancy, with workhouses and poor relief as well as various terms regarding settlement, were carried over. Controls on exports were introduced to provide for better marketing, including inspection systems and quality controls, and colonies could introduce their own tariffs. Opening and closing hours for stores and inns were set as part of various types of business regulations. Thus within the basic framework of property rights and free markets, the economies of the colonies were regulated, in terms of law if not by actual enforcement. The colonists may have benefited from the seeming certainty of transactions and behavior, but complications due to having thirteen colonies and legal systems may have introduced some costs to society. The establishment of thirteen colonies did lead to some competition and choice in settlement decisions, which may have had some influence on policies.[11]

The Colonial Legacy

A guide to the attitudes of the times regarding mercantilist regulations may be seen in the aftermath of the Revolutionary War. Alexander Hamilton introduced a set of basic policies concerning shipping, imports, and so on, suggesting that there was no conceptual opposition by colonists to mercantilist policy. Rather, the issues of concern were whose mercantilistic policies to choose and whether it would be possible to force the British to behave appropriately. Hamilton's various proposals regarding manufacturing, a national bank, the distribution of public lands, and the assumption of the colonial, state, and national government debts formed a basis for postrevolutionary economic policy and were carried forward for many years. With regard to other matters, the Revolution led to an increase in taxation due to the states' absorbing the military expenditures previously paid for by the British, but the basic commitment to property rights and free markets, along with the practices of slavery and indentured labor, were carried forward into the new nation. Nevertheless, the war did not lead immediately to economic success. It took about two decades for the new system to become economically successful and for its per capita income to rise above the prerevolutionary level.[12]

The colonial legacy for the new nation was one that permitted an early establishment of some characteristics that were necessary for economic and political success. The mix of centralized power and decentralization established with the Constitution provided for flexibility in decision making. Federalism entailed the ability to have policy differences among the states that were useful for the most part but permitted the continuation of slavery in parts of the nation. Many important legal and political features were carried forward from earlier times. Some, such as the common law and the belief in protection of property rights, were vestiges of the British background; others, such as a broad franchise, a state-determined banking system, and some relatively generous policies of land dispersal, reflected adaptations made by the colonists.

Notes

1. Of the numerous histories of colonial America and of its changing governmental structure, this is a very limited listing of interesting and useful works: Nettels 1938, Middleton 1996, Gallman 1964, Egnal 1998, and Engerman and Gallman 1996. An important work about the general role of institutions in economic development is North 1990.

2. The New World was not the earliest arena for England's westward expansion, politically or demographically. In 1541 the Irish Kingship Act established the English king as king of Ireland and attempted to set Protestantism rather than Catholicism as the state religion. In the seventeenth century alone, about 180,000 people from England and Wales migrated to Ireland, most after 1649, subsequent to Cromwell's triumphs.

3. For descriptions of European expansion overseas, see, e.g., Canny 1994 (especially the essays by Canny and by Cullen), Eltis 2000, Davies 1974, Lockhart and Schwartz 1983, and Fieldhouse 1966.

4. For the Native American population of North America, see Denevan 1976 and Verano and Ubelaker 1992. For broader issues regarding Native Americans, see Washburn 1975. For a description of Indian and European enslavement of Indians in the earlier years of settlement, see Gallay 2002.

5. For the most complete examination of the process of colonial settlement in America, see Andrews 1934–38. The settlement of the West Indies is described in Pitman 1917 and in Watts 1987. The key role of sugar in the settlement of the Americas is described in Deerr 1949–50. For a discussion of the Navigation Acts, see Harper 1939. See Craven 1953 for a brief discussion of the settlement process.

6. For different aspects of colonial labor supply, see Galenson 1981, Smith 1947, Dunn 1972, Curtin 1969, Morgan 1998, and Bailyn 1986.

7. For political aspects of colonial development, see Rusk 2001; Dinkin 1977, 1982; Greene 1986; and McKinley 1905. In regard to inheritance, see Shammas et al. 1987.

8. For the role of government control in the colonial economy see Hughes 1976, 1991; Farnam 1938.

9. For the development of agriculture and some of its implication, see Engerman and Sokoloff 2002, Gray 1933, Carr et al. 1991, Kulikoff 1986, Bidwell and Falconer 1925, Rothenberg 1992, McCusker and Menard 1991, Perkins 1988, J. T. Main 1985, and G. Main 2001. For tobacco regulation, in addition to Gray, see Wyckoff 1936.

10. See Hughes 1991, 53.

11. For colonial taxation, see Becker 1980, and for discussion of colonial finance, see Studenski and Kroos 1963. For land policy, see Gates 1968. For the economy of the colonial era as well as the broad rules of regulation, see Hughes 1976.

12. For descriptions of the impact of the Revolution on colonial incomes, see Jones 1980 and Walton and Shepherd 1979.

References

Andrews, Charles M. 1934–38. *The Colonial Period of American History.* 4 vols. New Haven: Yale University Press

Bailyn, Bernard. 1986. *Voyage to the West: A Passage to the Peoples of America on the Eve of the Revolution.* New York: Knopf.

Becker, Robert A. 1980. *Revolution, Reform, and the Politics of American Taxation, 1763–1783.* Baton Rouge: Louisiana State University Press.

Bidwell, Percy Wells, and John I. Falconer. 1925. *History of Agriculture in the Northern United States, 1620–1860.* Washington, DC: Carnegie Institution.

Butler, Jon. 2000. *Becoming America: The Revolution before 1776.* Cambridge: Harvard University Press.

Canny, Nicholas, ed. 1994. *Europeans on the Move: Studies on European Migration, 1500–1800.* New York: Oxford University Press.

Carr, Lois Green, Russell R. Menard, and Lorena S. Walsh. 1991. *Robert Cole's World: Agriculture and Society in Early Maryland.* Chapel Hill: University of North Carolina Press.

Craven, W Frank. 1953. "The Early Settlements: A European Investment of Capital and Labor." In *The Growth of American Economy.* 2d ed., ed. Harold F. Williamson, 19–43. New York: Prentice-Hall.

Curtin, Philip D. 1969. *The Atlantic Slave Trade: A Census.* Madison: University of Wisconsin Press.

Davies, K. G. 1974. *The North Atlantic World in the Seventeenth Century.* Minneapolis: University of Minnesota Press.

Deerr, Noel. 1949–50. *The History of Sugar.* 2 vols. London: Chapman and Hall.

Denevan, William, M., ed. 1976. *The Native Population of the Americas in 1492.* Madison: University of Wisconsin Press.

Dinkin, Robert J. 1977. *Voting in Provincial America. A Study of Elections in the Thirteen Colonies, 1689–1776.* Westport: Greenwood.

———. 1982. *Voting in Revolutionary America: A Study of Elections in the Original Thirteen States, 1776–1789.* Westport: Greenwood.

Dunn, Richard S. 1972. *Sugar and Slaves: The Rise of the Planter Class in the English West Indies, 1624–1713.* Chapel Hill: University of North Carolina Press.

Egnal, Marc. 1998. *New World Economies: The Growth of the Thirteen Colonies and Early Canada.* New York: Oxford University Press.

Eltis, Davis. 2000. *The Rise of African Slavery in the Americas.* Cambridge: Cambridge University Press.

Engerman, Stanley L., and Robert E. Gallman, eds. 1996. *The Cambridge Economic History of the United States.* vol. 1, *The Colonial Era.* Cambridge: Cambridge University Press.

Engerman, Stanley L., and Kenneth L. Sokoloff. 2002. "Factor Endowments, Inequality, and Paths of Development among New World Economies." *Economía* 3 (Fall): 41–88.

Farnam, Henry W. 1938. *Chapters in the History of Social Legislation in the United States to 1860.* Washington, DC: Carnegie Institution.

Fieldhouse, D. K. 1966. *The Colonial Empires from the Eighteenth Century.* New York: Delta.

Galenson, David. 1981. *White Servitude in Colonial America: An Economic Analysis.* Cambridge: Cambridge University Press.

Gallay, Alan. 2002. *The Indian Slave Trade: The Rise of the English Empire in the American South, 1670–1717.* New Haven: Yale University Press.

Gallman, Robert E. 1964. *Developing the American Colonies, 1607–1783.* Chicago: Scott Foresman.

Gates, Paul W. 1968. *History of Public Land Law Development.* Washington, DC: Government Printing Office.

Gray, Lewis Cecil. 1933. *History of Agriculture in the Southern United States to 1860.* 2 vols. Washington, DC: Carnegie Institution.

Greene, Jack P. 1986. *Peripheries and Center: Constitutional Development in the Extended Politics of the British Empire and the United States, 1607–1788.* Athens: University of Georgia Press.

Harper, Lawrence A. 1939. *The English Navigation Laws: A Seventeenth-Century Experiment in Social Engineering.* New York: Columbia University Press.

Hughes, Jonathan R. T. 1976. *Social Control in the Colonial Economy*. Charlottesville: University Press of Virginia.

———. 1991. *The Governmental Habit Redux: Economic Controls from the Colonial Times to the Present*. Princeton: Princeton University Press.

Jones, Alice Hanson. 1980. *The Wealth of a Nation to Be: The American Colonies on the Eve of the Revolution*. New York: Columbia University Press.

Kulikoff, Allan. 1986. *Tobacco and Slaves: The Development of Southern Cultures in the Chesapeake, 1680–1800*. Chapel Hill: University of North Carolina Press.

Lockhart, James, and Stuart B. Schwartz. 1983. *Early Latin America: A History of Colonial Spanish America and Brazil*. Cambridge: Cambridge University Press.

Main, Gloria L. 2001. *Peoples of a Spacious Land: Families and Cultures in Colonial New England*. Cambridge: Harvard University Press.

Main, Jackson Turner. 1985. *Society and Economy in Colonial Connecticut*. Princeton: Princeton University Press.

McCusker, John J., and Russell R. Menard. 1991. *The Economy of British America, 1607–1789*. 2d ed. Chapel Hill: University of North Carolina Press.

McKinley, Albert Edward. 1905. *The Suffrage Franchise in the Thirteen English Colonies in America*. Philadelphia: University of Pennsylvania Press.

Middleton, Richard. 1996. *Colonial America: A History, 1585–1776*. Oxford: Blackwell.

Morgan, Philip D. 1998. *Slave Counterpoint: Black Culture in the Eighteenth-Century Chesapeake and Lowcountry*. Chapel Hill: University of North Carolina Press.

Nettels, Curtis P. 1938. *The Roots of American Civilization: A History of American Colonial Life*. New York: Appleton-Century-Crofts.

North, Douglass C. 1990. *Institutions, Institutional Change and Economic Performance*. Cambridge: Cambridge University Press.

Perkins, Edwin J. 1988. *The Economy of Colonial America*. 2d ed. New York: Columbia University Press.

Pitman, Frank Wesley. 1917. *The Development of the British West Indies, 1700–1763*. New Haven: Yale University Press.

Rothenberg, Winifred Barr. 1992. *From Market-Places to a Market Economy: The Transformation of Rural Massachusetts, 1750–1850*. Chicago: University of Chicago Press.

Rusk, Jerrold G. 2001. *A Statistical History of the American Electorate*. Washington, DC: CQ Press.

Shammas, Carole, Marylynn Salmon, and Michel Dahlin. 1987. *Inheritance in America from Colonial Time to the Present*. New Brunswick: Rutgers University Press.

Smith, Abbot Emerson. 1947. *Colonists in Bondage: White Servitude and Convict Labor in America, 1607–1776*. Chapel Hill: University of North Carolina Press.

Studenski, Paul, and Herman E. Krooss. 1963. *Financial History of the United States*. 2d ed. New York: McGraw-Hill.

Verano, John W., and Douglas H. Ubelaker, eds. 1992. *Disease and Demography in the Americas*. Washington, DC: Smithsonian Institution Press, 1992.

Walton, Gary M., and James F. Shepherd. 1979. *The Economic Rise of Early America*. Cambridge: Cambridge University Press.

Washburn, Wilcomb E. 1975. *The Indian in America*. New York: Harper & Row.

Watts, David. 1987. *The West Indies: Patterns of Development, Culture, and Environmental Change since 1492*. Cambridge: Cambridge University Press.

Wyckoff, Vertrees J. 1936. *Tobacco Regulation in Colonial Maryland*. Baltimore: Johns Hopkins University Press.

ROBERT A. MCGUIRE

3

The Founding Era, 1774–1791

CENTRAL TO THE PROCESS
of creating a nation is the
creation of the fundamen-
tal rules for the legal-
political order, the rules
for governance of the
nation. When a government is formed, rules are chosen that specify
the way collective, or governmental, decisions within the nation will
be made. What rules will be used for making future collective decisions?
How will collective decision making be allocated within the nation?
Who will have the authority to make collective decisions? What rights
will citizens have? What types of behavior will the fundamental rules
allow? What constraints will be placed on government and on individual citizens?

Because the fundamental rules (what defines a nation's government)
determine the incentive structure within a nation, these rules are crucial
to a nation's economic and political development. This is well understood, but the way these rules are chosen is not. That is, how is a nation's
constitution created? A constitution is the key legal-political institution
that contains the collective decision-making rules, specifying the allocation of political power within the nation. These rules delineate the
constraints placed on government and citizens. As such, a constitution,
which is designed to be appreciably more difficult to change than ordinary laws, is intended to be long-lasting. This leads to two important
questions: Who creates a nation's constitution? And how is it adopted?

The fundamental rules for the legal-political order of the United
States, which are contained in the U.S. Constitution, were designed and
adopted more than two hundred years ago by representatives of the
American people when a few dozen of America's political leaders drafted
and ratified the Constitution. Political representatives, not individual
citizens, made the constitutional choices because the decision-making
costs of governing a nation with a direct democracy in which every citizen
has an input or a vote on every issue increase as the number of citizens

increases. As a result, it is in a citizen's interest to choose other citizens to represent him in the governing process. In a representative form of government the decision-making costs of governance are lower than in a direct democracy. In the former, individual citizens with a comparative cost advantage in leadership skills and representing other citizens choose to specialize in leading and representing citizens. These specialists then become the representatives, politicians, or political elites who offer their expertise to citizens and compete among themselves for the citizens' approval to act on their behalf.

This representative form of government had emerged in what became the United States before the Constitution was drafted in the summer of 1787. In fact, as discussed in chapter 2, the roots of American representative government go back to the nation's colonial beginnings and to parliamentary government in Britain. Consequently, America's political leaders, the Founding Fathers, designed the Constitution, and they and other political representatives voted on ratifying it in conventions of the thirteen states; the citizens did not directly design or vote on ratifying the Constitution.

This leads to other important questions: What factors explain the choices of George Washington, James Madison, Benjamin Franklin, and the other Founding Fathers who drafted the U.S. Constitution? What factors explain the manner in which they apportioned representation and allocated political power within the nation? Why did they design the Constitution with a vastly strengthened central government? Why did they include a prohibition on state paper-money issues? Why did they fail to adopt a clause requiring a two-thirds majority in the national legislature to establish laws concerning commerce or a clause giving the national government an absolute veto over state laws? This chapter attempts to provide answers to these and many other questions concerning the design and adoption of the U.S. Constitution.

The Continental Congress, the Revolutionary War, and the Articles of Confederation

From America's colonial beginnings at Jamestown, Virginia, in 1607 through the declaration of independence from Britain in 1776, in addition to local governments and colonial assemblies in each colony, there was a "central" government to which the colonial governments were accountable. That central government consisted of the British Crown and Parliament in London. Although it is accurate to describe the general form of government in the American colonies as a representative form

rather than a direct democracy, the colonists had no political representatives of their own in the central government in Britain. Consequently,
during the 170 years of American colonial history, the colonies became
increasingly disenchanted with and distant from their central government, which, many colonists believed, was becoming increasingly tyrannical and unrepresentative of their interests. As a result, in the year
just prior to the beginning of the Revolutionary War and the colonies'
decision to break from Britain, they formed their own central government made up of representatives from the thirteen American colonies;
they formed the First Continental Congress.

The Continental Congress

The colonies appointed delegates to a continental congress because,
in the words of the Massachusetts House of Representatives, "This
house having duly considered, and being deeply affected with the unhappy differences which have long subsisted and are encreasing between Great Britain and the American Colonies, [we] do resolve, that
a meeting of Committees from the several Colonies on this Continent
is highly expedient and necessary, to consult upon the present state of
the Colonies, and the miseries to which they are and must be reduced
by the operation of certain acts of Parliament respecting America, and
to deliberate and determine upon wise and proper measures, to be by
them recommended to all the Colonies, for the recovery and establishment of their just rights & liberties, civil & religious, and the restora-
tion of union & harmony between Great Britain and the Colonies, most
ardently desired by all good men." Moreover, according to the governor
of Rhode Island, delegates were appointed to join others "in consult-
ing upon the proper measures to obtain a repeal of the several acts of
the British parliament, for levying taxes upon his Majesty's subjects in
America, without their consent, and particularly an act lately passed for
blocking up the port of Boston." By the time of the First Continental
Congress, not only did America's political leaders share a deeply held
ideology or belief in liberty and in a republican—a popularly elected,
representative—government, but many colonists did as well. This ideology, which had evolved from the shared experiences of Americans with
British rule over the years, played a major role in the colonies' decisions
to form their own central government.[1]

The First Continental Congress met from September 5, 1774, to
October 26, 1774. The Second Continental Congress met each year from
May 10, 1775, to March 2, 1789, until the new national government under

the U.S. Constitution, which created the U.S. House of Representatives and U.S. Senate, went into effect on March 4, 1789. Apparently, America's colonial leaders did not so much dispute the importance of a central government as they disputed who should be represented in it. The colonies' call for a continental, or general, congress in 1774 was the culmination of earlier steps toward common measures of response taken in the early 1770s by various colonial committees of correspondence and colonial assemblies to British policy toward the colonies. The First Continental Congress limited itself to declarations of colonial grievances and petitions for relief. When the Continental Congress assembled again in May 1775, it was too late for more petitions for relief from Britain because fighting between colonial militiamen and British troops had taken place at Lexington and Concord on April 19, 1775.

Although the fighting had begun in 1775, it was not until July 2, 1776, that a formal and unanimous declaration of the independence of the thirteen "united" states was approved in the Continental Congress and announced on July 4. Congressional actions thereafter were decisions of the "United States, in Congress assembled." Although the general form of the new central government of the thirteen united states, a confederation of mainly independent states, was decided early on during the deliberations of the Continental Congress, the Articles of Confederation and Perpetual Union were not agreed to until November 15, 1777, and more than three years passed before the Articles of Confederation were formally approved. The Articles became the law of the land when they were finally ratified by all thirteen states, Maryland being the last to ratify after New York finally decided to cede its western land claims to the Continental government, and the Articles were declared in force on March 1, 1781. The Articles were the nation's first formal document to specify the legal-political rules for the central governance of the newly independent but united states.

At the same time that the form of the new central government was being considered in Congress, the former colonies were creating new state governments as well. Consequently, among the first actions of state political leaders after the declaration of independence from Britain was the design of constitutions for the governance of their states beginning in 1776. their states. These new state constitutions generally expressed the beliefs and ideals of the revolutionary era; in fact, the very idea of a written state constitution expressed the new American ideal of "constitutionalism," a system of government founded on a written set of fundamental rules for the legal-political order. The state constitutions incorporated the ideal of republican government by the people, in which authority was embodied in popularly elected representative assemblies to prevent tyrannical rulers or governors from impinging on liberty.[2]

The Revolutionary War

From the early beginnings of the confederation among the thirteen states, the new central government, the Continental Congress, had to prepare to fight the Revolutionary War with Britain and coordinate the war efforts of thirteen mainly independent states. When the Second Continental Congress convened on May 10, 1775, less than a month after the fighting had begun at Lexington and Concord, it authorized the formation of a continental army and began purchasing arms and ammunitions. The Continental government not only had to mobilize for war, but it also had to make decisions about funding it. Throughout history, providing a military and financing wars have been among the most fundamental of government activities. This was no easy task, however, for a central government overseeing a confederation of mainly independent states, each with its own constitution, militia, and source of revenue.

The new central government had no existing sources of revenue or authority to impose coercive taxation. The states never authorized the Continental Congress to enact any national-level taxes. Consequently, to finance the war effort Congress first authorized the establishment of a continental currency (bills of credit backed only by the credit of the Continental government) that circulated as money domestically, and later it authorized borrowing funds from both domestic and foreign sources. Following suit, individual states also emitted their own bills of credit (state currency backed by the credit of the state government) ands borrowed funds to finance the war effort. Thus the time-honored government methods of financing wars with paper money emissions (the continental dollar and state currencies) and borrowed funds, rather than instituting taxes to raise sufficient revenues, were employed by the new central government and the states. Nevertheless, during the war years, the Continental Congress unsuccessfully made several attempts to enact national-level taxes to help finance the war and made various attempts to convince the states to provide more of the funding to the Congress than had been requested of them. In each case, Congress never received the support of enough states to enact tax legislation or to increase the amount of state funding of the central government.

The emissions of the continental dollar and most emissions of state currencies were carried out well before the Articles of Confederation were formally adopted in 1781. The Continental government alone issued a total of more than $241 million continental dollars from 1775 to 1779, when the gross domestic product of the thirteen united states was probably less than $200 million annually. To say the least, emissions of this magnitude led to significant inflation and a fall in the value of the currency. This led to the derisive phrase "not worth a continental" because the overissue of currency caused prices to rise; in this case, it led to the worst inflation in U.S. history. The state governments contributed to inflation as well, for during the 1775–81 period they issued another $216 million in state currency, which likewise lost much of its value. In response to this wartime inflation, some state governments organized conventions within their states to enact governmental wage and price controls to legally cap prices, another time-honored government action. At last, the Continental Congress eventually authorized the military to simply seize private property for the war effort, another traditional government act, because its ability to finance the war with currency emissions and borrowing declined precipitously as the continental dollar became nearly worthless by 1780. This created serious doubts that the Continental government could honor its bills of credit or ever repay its loans.[3]

Fighting the Revolutionary War was no easy task for the newly created Continental Army, which was often short of arms, munitions, and provisions. The war was especially difficult given the Continental government's limited resources, chronic shortfall of revenues, and lack of popular support—no more than about a third of the population actively backed the revolutionary cause. (Another third is said to have supported the British, and the other third was probably indifferent toward the war.) In total, an estimated two hundred thousand Americans participated in military efforts during the entire 1775–83 period. The direct costs of the war have been estimated at $100 million in current expenditures, which translates to around $2.2 billion in 2004 dollars but which was probably more than half of one year's gross domestic product at the time. This cost estimate represents only the direct expenditures on the war; it does not include any future payments to officers who served in the war, damage to the country's infrastructure, the implicit cost of wartime inflation, or the cost of American military casualties, which included 4,435 dead and 6,188 wounded.[4]

After the military defeat of the British at Yorktown, Virginia, on October 19, 1781, the fighting was all but over; all that remained was a determination of the terms of the peace. While the peace negotiations between the British and the Americans were proceeding in 1782, the

Congress continued to work on ways to finance the war obligations of the United States. The Congress had determined that by the war's end the outstanding foreign debt of the United States stood at $8 million and the outstanding domestic debt stood at $42 million, for a total national debt of $50 million, with annual interest payments alone of $2.5 million per year. This was at a time when the Confederation government had no sources of revenue independent of the states and when the state governments continued to supply insufficient revenues to the central government for it to meet its outstanding debt obligations.[5]

The Articles of Confederation

Under the Articles of Confederation, the American political system consisted of a confederation, or loose union, of independent states and a weak central government. The central government (now referred to as the Confederation government) had no legal power independent of the individual states to raise revenues or taxes and consequently had difficulty repaying its debts. It also experienced other fiscal problems, which were threefold. First, the thirteen states did not fully contribute to the public finances of the central government because the system of state requisitions was uninformed. Each state sent between two and seven delegates to the Confederation Congress (Articles of Confederation, Article V, Section 2), which determined the government's fiscal and military requirements and then requested each state to contribute its share of money or troops to the central government (Article VIII; Article IX, Section 5). Each state's share was initially based on the value of its land (Article VIII) but ultimately was based on the number of white inhabitants. A state was to assess its citizens an amount necessary to meet the requisition, collect the taxes at the state level, and forward the requisition to Congress. But without an enforcement mechanism, state payments to the central government ultimately were voluntary. Confederation revenues thus fell short of requests. This made prosecution of the Revolutionary War during the early years of the confederation quite difficult.[6]

This raises an interesting economic question: Why did the state governments supply any requisitions at all to the confederation government when there was no enforcement mechanism? The state governments actually supplied nontrivial amounts of their requisitions to the central government and provided many men for the war effort. Why did not a particular state government merely attempt to free ride on the contributions of other states? That is, why not let some other state provide funds to the central government and then receive the benefits for free? Why didn't all states simply free ride? In short, the answer is that the Confederation government provided services (military action against the British) that also benefited the states; thus, when a state government expected to directly benefit from the military campaign of the Continental Army it was willing to voluntarily provide revenues (at least part of its requisitions) and to supply men to produce the shared "public good." But that wasn't always enough.[7]

The second fiscal problem under the Articles was that each state had a single vote in the Confederation Congress (Article V, Section 4), and the unanimous consent of the thirteen states was required in order for the Congress to amend the Articles of Confederation (Article XIII) and enact any Confederation taxes. A single state thus could block national-level tax legislation. This de facto veto power on the part of each state created prohibitively high decision-making costs for Congress and prevented proposed confederation imposts (import duties) from ever being enacted under the Articles of Confederation, which left the central government without an independent source of taxation and chronically short of revenues. The third fiscal problem was that the approval of nine of the thirteen states (70 percent) was required for most other confederation fiscal policies, such as the coining of money, ascertaining the expenses and sums necessary for the defense and welfare of the United States or of any state, emitting bills of credit, borrowing money on the credit of the United States, or even appropriating money (Article IX, Section 6). This requirement created high decision-making costs, thus making it difficult for Congress to enact most ordinary fiscal policies and, in the early years of the Confederation government, to prosecute the Revolutionary War.

There were other problems under the Articles of Confederation as well. The central government lacked the legal power to enforce uniform commercial regulations—either at home or abroad—that might have been conducive to the development of a common economic trading area. But state and local interference in interstate or international trade was not a major problem at the time. There was a reasonably large common trading area at the time because few of the states imposed duties on goods imported from other American states, and the tariff duties they imposed on foreign trade were quite low overall and no protectionist in nature. Many commercial interests, nonetheless, still feared that local and state barriers to trade could develop in the future under the Articles of Confederation. The Confederation government also possessed uncertain authority to negotiate with foreign powers on behalf of the states, making peace negotiations after the defeat of the British at Yorktown in 1781 more difficult. Part of the difficulty in negotiating with foreign powers was that under the Articles there was no executive branch of the central government, nor was there a judicial branch to settle national-level issues or to settle disputes among the states. The central government's problems in raising revenues and repaying existing debts created additional uncertainty about its financial viability. And western landowners were often impatient with the Confederation government because of its inability to establish order on the frontiers.[8]

The story of growing dissatisfaction with the Articles of Confederation among America's political leaders and the movement toward constitutional reform during the early 1780s is well known. At the conclusion of the Revolutionary War and the Treaty of Paris in 1783, some of the nation's leaders had already been calling for a strengthened central government. Dissatisfaction with the way the Congress and the Confederation government operated in terms of financing and manning the war was a major source of discontent among many leaders. Not only did the Confederation government have a difficult time waging the war, but the war's aftermath was not considered much better. Although by the mid-1780s the economy was improving, approaching pre-war levels of economic activity in most New England and Middle Atlantic states, the level of overall economic activity and trade, especially in the first years after the war and in the southern states, was still below pre-war levels. It took time to recover from the disruption of commerce and trade during the war and its immediate aftermath.

In response to ongoing commercial concerns involving the two states, commissioners from Maryland and Virginia met in 1785 to consider issues concerning free navigation on the Potomac Pocomoke Rivers, signing a "compact" that resolved far broader issues between the two. Yet the meeting, known as the Mount Vernon Conference, had not received prior congressional approval. Given that the Articles of Confederation did not allow any state to enter into a treaty with another state without the approval of Congress (Article VI), and given the increasing dissatisfaction with economic conditions and the Confederation government, the Maryland and Virginia legislatures, at the suggestion of James Madison, invited all states to a meeting in Annapolis the following year "to consider how far a uniform system in their commercial regulations may be necessary to their common interest."[9] This meeting became known as the 1786 Annapolis Convention. Although all were invited, only five states sent delegations, and nothing of substance was accomplished. But those in attendance did urge Congress to call another meeting of the states for the following spring to discuss revising the Articles of Confederation and consider constitutional reform more generally.

At the same time, other events combined to make another meeting of the states inevitable. Shays's Rebellion, an armed uprising in western Massachusetts against the state government, took place from the summer of 1786 through the winter of 1787; it was quite possibly the crystallizing event that occasioned the constitutional change that occurred during the summer of 1787. The rebellion involved the forced closings of several state courts, an attempted takeover of the federal arsenal at Springfield, and various battles and skirmishes between insurgents and state and local forces.

The conventional wisdom is that the rebels were poor, debt-ridden farmers from the backcountry of Massachusetts who were trying to avoid payment of their debts. Recent research, though, indicates that participants were neither deeply in debt nor mainly debtors, suggesting instead that government tax policies were paramount in fomenting the rebellion. In the mid-1780s, state legislators had decided to pay the entire debt that Massachusetts had accumulated during the war with specie (silver or gold). To raise the necessary revenues, the legislators enacted direct taxes on land and men (poll taxes). The taxes, due in specie and enforced by the courts, were especially burdensome for western Massachusetts' farmers, who lacked specie but not land and sons. After several unsuccessful petitions for tax relief, the backcountry farmers took up arms against the state. In their view, they were opposing a tyrannical state government in Boston and a repressive court system.[10]

The rebellion's aftermath was much bigger than the rebellion itself, since the Boston elite portrayed the rebellion as a threat to the entire nation. As a consequence, the nationalists and the involved in the movement for a stronger national government resorted to the rallying cries of anarchy, mob rule, and democratic excesses. As a result, the call for another meeting of the states to consider constitutional reform was successful. Twelve states eventually attended the Philadelphia convention that drafted the Constitution in 1787. Although debate still exists concerning actual economic and political conditions, the historical evidence suggests that neither the economy nor the Confederation government was performing admirably during the 1780s. The evidence also indicates that the Confederation Congress believed it was politically necessary to call a convention of the states to consider revising the Articles of Confederation.[11]

One of the major contributions of Robert Higgs (1987) to our understanding of the historical evolution of government, and a theme repeated in much of this book, is his thesis that crisis is a primary factor behind appeals for government action, which sets in motion societal changes leading to bigger and more intrusive government. Interestingly, Higgs's thesis appears to fit well the case of the movement toward constitutional reform of the Confederation government during the 1780s. The primary contemporaneous argument for why revision of the Articles of Confederation was necessary was that economic and political crises existed in the nation; it was said at the time that the central government and the economy were in a shambles. As proof, the nationalists only needed to call attention to Shays's Rebellion. Whether there was a real crisis in the Confederation government or in the economy at the time is not transparent from the historical record. What it does reveal is that, whether real, imagined, or manufactured, the existence of economic and political crises was used to justify calling the Philadelphia convention to revise the Articles of Confederation and create a national government. Even the so-called Father of the Constitution, James Madison, argued powerfully that the Constitution was necessary because there was a crisis in government and in the economy at the time of its drafting.[12]

The Drafting and Adoption of the United States Constitution

The Philadelphia Constitutional Convention

The Constitutional Convention was originally to begin May 14, 1787, in Philadelphia, but less than a majority of the states were represented that day, so the delegates adjourned from day to day until delegates from a sufficient number of states arrived. As a result, the convention did not begin until May 25, when twenty-nine delegates from nine of the thirteen states were finally in attendance; they promptly elected George Washington the president of the convention. The Congress of the Confederation authorized the convention to consider amendment and revision of the Articles of Confederation. The convention was to consider revising the Articles to strengthen the central government's power over taxation, its authority to regulate interstate and international commerce, its authority to negotiate with foreign nations, its ability to provide national defense, and its authority over a national judiciary. America's political leaders disagreed not so much about their desire for constitutional reform as about the magnitude of that reform.[13]

But they disagreed enough about the importance and urgency of reform that nineteen of the seventy-four delegates appointed by their states to attend the Philadelphia meeting chose not to attend. Patrick Henry, for example, did not attend, purportedly saying, "I smelt a Rat."

Apparently not all of America's political leaders were convinced there was a genuine crisis in the nation.[14]

The delegates decided that the convention's decisions would be made by majority voting by state delegations, with the votes of each state decided by majority voting among that state's delegates, a rule that was contrary to the requirement of unanimous consent of the states to amend the Articles of Confederation. This majority rule was crucial to replacing the Articles with the Constitution; evidence from the convention's debates indicates that the convention would have gone nowhere had there been a unanimity rule. The convention generally operated as a committee of the whole although it did organize itself into various committees throughout the summer of 1787. Its mode of operation essentially allowed individuals who were present the freedom to propose and discuss almost any issue. Scrutiny of the debates, which took nearly four months, suggests that many of the important votes taken were votes either in favor of a strong national form of government or in favor of a confederation form of government. Indeed, the major question at Philadelphia was whether there would be a strengthened, more powerful central government with essentially independent sovereign states or a strong, nationally oriented central government with much less, if any, state sovereignty. Would there be a national system or a continued confederation? The answer came on September 17, 1787, with the scrapping of the Articles of Confederation and the presentation of the United States Constitution, which established a strong national government but one that would not be supreme for many decades.[15]

During the summer of 1787, a total of fifty-five men attended the convention in Philadelphia that drafted the Constitution, but no more than about forty were ever present at the same time. Less than a year after the convention was over, New Hampshire became the ninth state to ratify the Constitution, as drafted, on June 21, 1788.[16] As a result, the Confederation Congress declared the Constitution to be in force beginning March 4, 1789, because ratification by only nine of the thirteen states was required for it to be considered adopted by the ratifying states (U.S. Constitution, Article VII). The Constitution replaced the Articles of Confederation and its political system of a loose confederation of independent states, which had been in effect only since March 1, 1781, with a political system that greatly strengthened the central (national) government at the expense of the states and their former sovereignty. This change in the nation's fundamental legal-political institution was to have a profound influence on the economic history of the nation.[17]

How the Constitution Strengthened the Power
of the Central Government

The Constitution included powers assigned specifically to the national government as well as prohibitions on the actions of the state governments. The power to tax (the "power of the purse") was firmly delegated to the national government (Article I, Section 8), providing it with an independent source of revenue, which improved the prospects for the central government's financial future. The power to borrow on the nation's credit and to pay its debts, along with the authority to settle past Confederation debts, was also firmly delegated to the national government (Article I, Section 8 and Article VI, respectively), which, along with the power to tax, reduced uncertainty about repayment of government debt, improving the nation's overall financial conditions and capital markets (markets for loans).

The Constitution, unlike the Articles of Confederation, required only a simple majority vote of the individual representatives in both chambers of Congress to enact tax legislation with the approval of the president. There were, and are, checks on simple majority voting, however. The president can veto congressional legislation, and it takes a two-thirds vote in Congress to override a presidential veto (Article I, Section 7). These constraints on simple majority voting do not create anything near the magnitude of the decision-making costs that were created by the requirement of a unanimous vote to amend the Articles so that tax legislation could be enacted, or with the nine-state rule under the Articles for other fiscal acts of the central government.

The power to regulate both interstate and international commerce, including the power to lay duties on trade, was delegated solely to the national government by the Constitution (Article I, Section 8). Moreover, Congress was prohibited from enacting any duties on exports from states (Article I, Section 9). These provisions were expected to prevent state and local interference with interstate and foreign trade as well as prevent national government interference with the export trade. Meanwhile, to allow a united front in trade negotiations, the power to make treaties with foreign nations was firmly delegated to the central government as well (Article II, Section 2) and prohibited to the state governments (Article I, Section 10).

The assignment of the sole right to coin money to the national government (Article I, Section 8) and the prohibition against the coining of money and emitting "bills of credit" by the states (Article I, Section 10) also were expected to improve overall financial conditions in the country and capital markets in particular. The Constitution also authorized the national government and Congress to provide defense, declare war, and create an army and a navy (Article I, Section 8). A national executive was created to run the government (Article II, Section 1), and a national judiciary was created to adjudicate disputes related to national and interstate matters (Article III, Section 1).

The Constitution, compared to the Articles of Confederation, greatly strengthened the central government at the expense of the state governments. The basic framework for a national government—with its own legislative, executive, and judicial branches, with powers of taxation and regulation of commerce, authority to borrow, provide a military, and settle disputes among the states, and with power to negotiate with foreign nations—was designed into the Constitution. Although three-quarters of a century would pass before the supremacy of the national government over the states ultimately would be settled with a civil war, the framework was in place in the Constitution drafted in Philadelphia in 1787.

How a Stronger Central Government Affected the Economy

Many economic historians conclude that the most important changes for the economy associated with the Constitution "were those changes that strengthened the framework for protection of private property and enforcement of contracts." This is so because these changes increased the benefits of exchange (the cornerstone of a market economy) and created incentives for individuals to specialize in economic activities in which they had a particular advantage and then engage in mutually advantageous exchange (trade) with individuals specializing in other economic activities. Specific provisions in the Constitution that helped increase the benefits of exchange were those that prohibited the national government from enacting ex post facto (retroactive) laws (Article I, Section 9) and that prohibited states from passing any ex post facto law or law impairing contractual obligations (Article I, Section 10).[18]

These prohibitions were important to the development of a market economy because they constrained governments (especially state governments) from interfering with existing economic agreements, making the returns to economic activity more secure. The astute reader will note, however, that only state governments are prohibited by Article I, Section 10 from passing laws "impairing the Obligation of Contracts." During the Confederation period, many of America's national leaders became increasingly dissatisfied with the behavior of state legislatures and their willingness to pass debt moratorium legislation, which suspended payment of existing debts and as a consequence impaired "the Obligation of Contracts."

Because the economies of the thirteen states were not as dependent on each other in the 1780s as they are today, the *immediate* economic consequences for the nation of adopting the Constitution might not have been at all that large. But this change in the nation's fundamental legal-political institution was ultimately to have a profound influence on the economy, because over time the Constitution became the foundation of the supremacy of the national government over the state governments in the United States. In this regard, that the Constitution granted to the national government the sole right to regulate interstate (as well as international) commerce (Article 1, Section 8) was critically important for the economy. The principal gain from this provision was the development of a common trading union across the nation with no state barriers to internal trade. But this gain to the nation did not fully materialize until near the end of the nineteenth century. There were, in fact, state-level occupational licensing and inspection laws during the nation's first hundred years, which the Constitution allowed in Article 1, Section 10. These state laws served as disguised taxes on out-of-state products and thus acted as barriers to internal trade and prevented the completely free flow of goods and people across state borders. The laws placed some constraints on internal trade until they were eventually declared unconstitutional in several U.S. Supreme Court commerce clause cases between 1875 and 1890, indicating the important role of the Supreme Court (created by Article 3, Section 1) in the history of the American economy.[19]

How did this fundamental change come about? Why did our nation's founders replace the Articles of Confederation with the Constitution? In defending the newly drafted Constitution, Alexander Hamilton observed in late 1787: "It has been frequently remarked that it seems to have been reserved to the people of this country . . . to decide the important question, whether societies of men are really capable or not of establishing good government from reflection and choice, or whether they are forever destined to depend for their political constitutions on accident and force." How did this country "decide the important question"? Since the middle of the nineteenth century, hundreds of scholars have studied and debated the possible explanations for such an important change in the fundamental legal-political institution of the nation. Many historians have concluded that the Constitution was drafted and adopted as a result of a consensus that the Articles of Confederation were fatally flawed. Other scholars have argued that the limitations of the Articles could have been eliminated without fundamentally altering the balance of power between the states and the central government. Others have suggested that the adoption of the Constitution was the product of conflict between various economic and financial interests within the nation, between those who, because of their interests, wanted a stronger national government and those who, because of their interests, did not.[20]

Charles A. Beard's Economic Interpretation

In 1913, Charles A. Beard consolidated various scholarly views of the Constitution and, in the process, offered what became identified as *the* economic interpretation of it. Beard argued that at the heart of the Constitution was a conflict based on competing economic interests— interests of the proponents and the opponents. In his view, the Federalists, the founders who supported a strong, centralized government and favored the Constitution during its drafting and ratification, were individuals whose primary economic interests were tied to personal property. They were mainly merchants, shippers, bankers, speculators, and holders of private and public (government) securities. The AntiFederalists, the opponents of the Constitution and supporters of a more decentralized government, were individuals whose primary economic interests were tied to real property. These opponents consisted primarily of less-commercial backcountry farmers, who often were also debtors, and large manorial planters along the Hudson River in New York. Beard maintained, however, that many southern slaveowning planters, who held much of their wealth in personal property, had much in common with the northern merchants and financiers and should be included as supporters of the Constitution.

Beard claimed that support for his argument could be found in the economic conditions prevailing in the 1780s: during the Confederation period, the American economy faced severe problems. The independence of the former colonies from the British Empire seriously disrupted shipping and foreign trade. As noted above, although trade had been improving after the Revolutionary War, it had not fully recovered. Individuals who held Confederation government securities did not always receive interest when due, and many feared a loss of principal. After the war, depreciation of the currency caused by the overissue of confederation and state bills of credit during the war and state debt moratorium (debt suspension) measures enacted after the war made hard-money advocates and creditors fearful. The central government and state governments were experiencing problems raising revenues and repaying their debts, harming individuals who held public securities. Because prices had fallen rapidly from their wartime levels by the mid-1780s, state legislatures were under political pressure to emit paper money, increase land taxes, and declare debt moratoria.

As a result of these economic conditions, Beard suggested, the primary beneficiaries of the Constitution would have been individuals with commercial and financial interests—in particular, those with public securities holdings who, according to Beard, had a clause included in the Constitution requiring the assumption of existing Confederation government debt by the new national government. Commercial and financial interests also would benefit because of increased certainty in the rules of commerce, trade, and credit markets under the Constitution. Less-commercial backcountry farmers, debtors, paper money advocates, and the northern planters along the Hudson River would have been the primary beneficiaries under the status quo. With a decentralized government, they would have had greater ability at the state level to avoid heavy land taxation—levied to pay off the public debt incurred during the Revolutionary War—and to promote paper money and debt moratorium measures that advanced their economic interests. Consequently, they opposed the Constitution.[21]

Critics of an Economic Interpretation: Robert E. Brown and Forrest McDonald

Beard's thesis soon emerged as the standard historical interpretation and remained so until the 1950s, when it began to face serious scholarly challenges. The most influential and lasting of the challenges were those by Robert E. Brown (1956) and Forrest McDonald (1958). Brown maintained that Beard's arguments that (1) eighteenth-century America was not very democratic, (2) the wealthy were strong supporters of the Constitution, and (3) those without personal property generally opposed the Constitution are factually incorrect. A couple of years later, McDonald examined evidence concerning the wealth, economic interests, and votes of the delegates to the Constitutional Convention and of the delegates to the thirteen state ratifying conventions that considered the Constitution's adoption afterward. He divided the delegates into the broad groups that Beard had suggested and found that in many cases the members of the groups did not all vote in the same way. As a result, McDonald concluded that "anyone wishing to rewrite the history of those proceedings [the Philadelphia convention] largely or exclusively in terms of the economic interests represented there would find the facts to be insurmountable obstacles." He reached a similar conclusion about the thirteen ratifying conventions.

Brown and McDonald are still credited today by many scholars with having delivered the fatal blows to Charles Beard's economic interpretation of the Constitution. Yet examples abound of scholars who take Brown and McDonald at face value, crediting one or both of them with having proved Beard wrong without having conducted their own analysis of the issues.[22]

The New Quantitative Approach

In the early 1980s, economic historians began a reexamination of the behavior of the founders concerning the creation and adoption of the Con-stitution. These scholars collected large amounts of data about the economic, financial, and other characteristics of the men who drafted and ratified the Constitution, and they applied formal economic models and modern statistical techniques to examine how these characteristics influenced the founders' voting behavior. The reexamination recognizes that each individual was not a member of a single group or social class but often had multiple economic interests. Nearly every delegate represented more than one economic activity and owned more than one economic asset, in addition to holding more than one fundamental belief or ideology. A delegate, for example, might have been a slaveowner, a financier, and an owner of western lands and might have represented a state, county, or township with economic and other interests and beliefs similar to or in conflict with his own.[23]

The delegates who drafted the Constitution at Philadelphia and the delegates who attended the thirteen ratifying conventions, though often wealthier than the average freeman, represented widely diverse economic and other interests as well as varying beliefs and ideologies and owned economic assets of widely diverse amounts. Slaveowners, non-slaveowners, planters, merchants, financiers, less-commercial farmers, debtors, and backcountry folk were among those present at the Constitutional Convention and the state ratifying conventions. Because of these widely diverse and potentially conflicting interests and beliefs, the delegates could not all be satisfied, and many had to make compromises and tradeoffs. Nor was any framer or ratifier in a position to have satisfied all his interests and beliefs with a single decision. Each had to make choices regarding which interests and beliefs he would satisfy and which ones he would compromise or trade off as he decided to support a particular issue. In trying to do what was right, the delegates had to weigh the likely ramifications of choosing a particular action. Taking a certain position might have directly benefited or harmed them or others. At other times, taking another position might have put them at odds with long-held beliefs and ideologies. As a result, the Constitution that was adopted contained various compromises with which some individuals and interests were satisfied while other individuals and interests were not.

To examine the impact of these diverse interests, the scholars matched the founders' observed votes on a particular issue at Philadelphia or on ratification with measures of the economic interests and ideologies of the founders and their constituents. The relationship between votes on a particular issue and each measure of the economic interests and ideologies was then statistically estimated. The statistical estimation produces for each explanatory variable an estimate that captures the direction and magnitude of the variable's influence on the probability of the founders' having voted in favor of an issue, holding the influence of all other variables constant. The benefit of this statistical approach is that each explanatory variable is examined separately from the influence of the other factors while controlling for the influence of these other potentially confounding factors. For example, if the relationship between the vote on a particular issue and the founders' slaveholdings is examined in isolation, a positive relationship may be indicated. But if other interests are taken into account (for example, the founders' public securities holdings), the relationship with slaveholdings could change and, in fact, be negative.

The modern evidence indicates that the founders' specific economic and financial interests can be principally identified with one side or the other of an issue, contrary to earlier scholarly views that they cannot. When specific issues arose at the Philadelphia convention that had a direct impact on important economic interests of the founders, these interests, even narrowly defined, in several cases significantly influenced the specific design of the Constitution, and the magnitudes of the influences were often quite large. The types of economic interests that mattered for the choice of specific issues were those that were likely to have accounted for a substantial portion of the overall wealth of the founders or represent their primary livelihood. Even when the founders were deciding on the general issue of the basic design of the Constitution to strengthen the national government, economic and other interests significantly influenced them. That is, when they were making fundamental constitutional choices rather than more specific-interest ones, their choices were still consistent with self-interested and partisan behavior. The modern evidence, however, does indicate that fewer economic and financial interests mattered for the basic design of the Constitution than for specific-interest aspects of it.

The finding that self-interest influenced the design and adoption of the Constitution does not mean that either the framers or the ratifiers of the Constitution were motivated by a greedy desire to "line their own pockets" or by some dialectic concept of class interests. Nor does it mean that some conspiracy among the founders or some fatalistic concept of "economic determinism" explains the Constitution. Nor does it mean that the founders were completely selfish in a purely financial sense. It does mean that the pursuit of one's interests both in a narrow pecuniary sense and a broader nonpecuniary sense can explain the drafting and ratification of the Constitution.

Specific Findings for the Constitutional Convention and State Ratifying Conventions

Financial Securities. The founders' ownership of financial securities often had a significantly large influence on their behavior. Whether a founder had private securities (owned bank stock or held private loans) or had public securities (owned Revolutionary War debt issued by the Confederation Congress or by the state governments) indicates whether he was a private or a public creditor. For a small number of the important issues considered at the Philadelphia convention, the founders' financial securities significantly affected the vote. This does not mean that all securities-owning delegates voted together at Philadelphia. What it does mean is that the ownership of financial securities, controlling for other influences, significantly increased the chance of supporting some of the important issues at the Philadelphia convention, particularly those that strengthened the central government (or weakened the state governments).[24]

One issue that the financial securities owners were more likely to have supported at Philadelphia, for example, was a proposal to absolutely prohibit state governments from emitting bills of credit (issuing paper money). Not surprisingly, the twelve framers who owned private financial securities voted unanimously in favor of the prohibition. Likewise, those who owned public securities were significantly more likely to have favored it. The evidence also indicates that a delegate with any amount of public securities who at the same time possessed the average (the mean) values of all other interests represented at the convention had nearly a 30 percent greater chance of voting in favor of the prohibition than an otherwise average delegate who owned no public securities. These findings suggest that creditors at the convention might have desired to constrain the states' ability to inflate away the value of their securities by expanding the supply of state paper money, rather than acting merely on a desire to improve overall financial conditions and capital markets in the country. Another recent study, moreover, contends that the framers of the Constitution included the prohibition on state paper money not because they wanted to improve capital markets but because the merchant-bankers at the convention wanted to increase their personal power and wealth by prohibiting states from issuing paper money that would compete with the issuance of private banknotes.[25]

During the ratification process, the ownership of financial securities had an even greater influence. A delegate's financial securities, controlling for other influences, significantly increased his chance of voting in favor of ratification at his state convention. Specifically, private or public creditors, especially those who owned large amounts of public securities, had a significantly greater chance of voting in favor of ratification. The overall evidence for private and public creditors implies that to the extent that some delegates who owned financial securities voted against strengthening the central government at Philadelphia or voted against ratification, it was the effects of their other interests that influenced them to vote in those ways.

Slaveowners. The view of many historical scholars is that delegates who were slaveowners and those who represented slaveholding areas generally supported strengthening the central government and ratifying the Constitution. This may be correct as far as it goes, but the issue of the influence of slaveholdings on the behavior of the Founding Fathers, as is the influence of any factor, is more complex. The modern evidence indicates that, although a majority of slaveowners and a majority of delegates from slaveholding areas generally voted for issues strengthening the central government or for ratification, the actual influence of slave interests was to significantly *decrease* a delegate's chance of voting for strengthening the central government or voting for ratification. For example, a major issue that slaveholders at Philadelphia were less likely to have voted for was a proposal that would have given the national legislature an absolute veto over state laws. If the national veto had been put into the Constitution, Congress, especially if it had a majority of

non-slaveholding representatives, could have vetoed state laws concerning slavery. This would have given Congress the power to limit the economic viability of slavery as early as 1789, if it so chose. Not surprisingly,
the modern evidence indicates that a delegate who owned the most
slaves at the convention, for example, and had the average values of all
other interests, was virtually certain to vote *against* the national veto
of state laws while an otherwise average delegate with no slaveholdings
had a roughly fifty-fifty chance of voting *for* the national veto. Likewise,
during the ratification process, slaveholding, controlling for other influences, significantly decreased the chance of voting in favor of ratification. This evidence implies that in the case of the slaveholding delegates
and delegates from slaveholding areas who voted to strengthen the central government or voted for ratification, it was the effects of their other
interests that influenced them to do so.

Commercial Interests. When the Constitution was drafted, the more
commercial areas of the states, in which merchandizing, production, and
other economic activities were generally oriented to the marketplace,
were highly correlated with residing in or near coastal areas or near
navigable water where colonial cities and urban areas were located. The
less commercial areas of the states, in which production and life in general were primarily oriented to the home or at most the local area, were
highly correlated with residing in more isolated, backcountry areas far
from coastal areas or from navigable water. The modern evidence con-
firms that the framers and ratifiers who were from areas near navigable
water generally voted differently than those from areas far from navigable water. The former had a significantly greater chance of voting for
clauses in the Constitution that strengthened the central government
and a significantly greater chance of voting for ratification. The latter
were less likely to support strengthening the central government and
less likely to vote for ratification.

The Specific Founding Fathers Mattered:
How the Constitution Might Have Been Different

The modern evidence attests to the paramount importance of the
specific political actors involved in the founding of America's system of
government. The estimated magnitude of the influence of many of the
economic and financial interests and beliefs and ideologies on the design of the Constitution are large enough that the product of the Constitutional Convention most likely would have been dramatically different
had men with dramatically different interests been involved.

For instance, had all the delegates at Philadelphia represented a state with a population the size of the most populous state and possessed the average values of all other interests represented at Philadelphia, the Constitution almost certainly would have contained a clause giving the national government an absolute veto over all state laws. If the national veto had been put into the Constitution, given that representation in the House of Representatives was based on a state's population (rather than each state possessing an equal vote as under the Articles of Confederation), representatives from the most populous states could have controlled legislative outcomes. This would have given more populous states potential control over less populous ones.

Or, had all the delegates at Philadelphia represented a state with the greatest concentration of slaves and possessed the average values of all other interests, the Constitution likely would have contained a clause requiring a two-thirds majority of the national legislature to enact commercial laws. If the two-thirds majority requirement had been put into the Constitution, it would have been *more* difficult to enact commercial laws, laws that could have regulated the slave-based export economies of the southern states. The two-thirds requirement would have made it more difficult for a future northern majority to affect the southern economy by means of commercial regulation.

The Specific Ratifiers Mattered More: How the Constitution Might Not Have Been Ratified

Once drafted, the Constitution had to be ratified by nine state conventions. The results of the statistical tests of the influence of interest groups on ratification indicate that economic interests and ideologies and beliefs might have had even more influence on the votes to ratify the Constitution than they did at the Philadelphia convention. The outcome of ratification appears to have depended even more on the specific individuals involved. The estimated influences were considerable enough that the outcome of ratification almost certainly would have been different had men with different interests and beliefs attended the ratifying conventions.

For example, at the Massachusetts ratifying convention, an otherwise average delegate who was a debtor was highly unlikely to vote for ratification, but if the delegate was not a debtor, there was more than a 60 percent chance that he would vote to ratify. In North Carolina, an otherwise average delegate who was not a merchant had little chance of voting for ratification (much less than 20 percent), but if a merchant, he was nearly certain to vote to ratify the Constitution. In Virginia, an otherwise average slaveowner had slightly less than a fifty-fifty chance of voting to ratify; if not a slaveowner, he had nearly an 85 percent chance of voting to ratify.

Differences of these magnitudes suggest that ratification of the Constitution strongly depended on the specific economic interests and ideologies of the specific individuals who attended the state ratifying conventions. Had there been more Baptists, debtors, less-commercial farmers, and delegates from the backcountry in attendance at the ratifying conventions, the outcome likely would have been different; the Constitution likely would *not* have been ratified. These types of economic interests and beliefs were more prevalent among the opponents of a national government and the Constitution. These opponents, most of whom were for a "federal" form of government (they generally supported a confederation among the states) though they were labeled Anti-Federalists, contended that the Constitution was an unknown system that set up a consolidated national government that would destroy state sovereignty. In their view, the proposed national government under the Constitution was a movement toward a monarchy. As a result, the people, they believed, required a bill of rights in the Constitution to protect their rights from the tyrannical use of power, and since the Constitution did not include one, it should not be ratified.

The importance of the specific delegates involved in the ratification process cannot be overstressed. Had only a few more Anti-Federalists been involved, the Constitution would not have been ratified. Indeed, the vote in four of the state conventions was so close that small changes in their votes would have defeated the Constitution. In Massachusetts, the ratification vote was 187–168; in New Hampshire, it was 57–47; in New York, it was 30–27; and in Virginia, it was 89–79. (A fifth state, Rhode Island, actually had the closest vote, 34–32, but that vote took place well after the issue was moot because the Constitution had already been ratified.) If ten yes votes in Massachusetts had been switched to no votes, the new Massachusetts vote would have been 177–178; if six yes votes in New Hampshire had been switched, the new vote would have been 51–53; if two yes votes in New York had been switched, the new vote would have been 28–29; and if six yes votes in Virginia had been switched, the new vote would have been 83–85. Thus a change of twenty-four yes votes of a total of 684 votes cast in these four ratifying conventions—less than four percent of the votes cast—would have changed the outcome. Without Massachusetts, New Hampshire, New

York, and Virginia, or two or three of them, there would have been no union, at least not under the terms of the Constitution as drafted.

Ratification of the Constitution and the Bill of Rights

Although it did not defeat the Constitution during ratification, the opposition did help cause the inclusion of a bill of rights in an amended Constitution *after* ratification. Given that not all delegates at the thirteen ratifying conventions could be completely satisfied with the Constitution, a number of compromises were struck during the ratification process. The most important was that Federalists from many states allowed recommended amendments to the Constitution concerning a bill of rights to be open for debate and subject to vote in their ratifying conventions. Consequently, instead of rejection of the Constitution, ratification with recommended amendments took place in more than half of the state conventions. This compromise was essential to the Federalist success, because many Anti-Federalists were willing to vote to ratify only because they believed that their recommended amendments would be taken seriously by Congress when the new government convened.

Although conditional ratification, strictly speaking, may not have been permitted, many borderline Anti-Federalists were persuaded to vote for ratification when the recommended amendments were offered. It is quite likely that there were enough of these votes to have affected the final outcome. Sam Adams (a Massachusetts delegate) was one of those with doubts and reservations about the Constitution. At the Massachusetts ratifying convention, after John Hancock—president of the convention—proposed recommended bill of rights amendments, Adams admitted that "the proposition submitted [would] have a tendency to remove such doubts" for him. Several states also declared their own interpretations of the meaning of the Constitution in their letters of ratification. Ratification with recommended amendments took place in seven states—Massachusetts, New Hampshire, New York, North Carolina, Rhode Island, South Carolina, and Virginia—the last five of which also included the declarations of constitutional interpretation. The importance of these "conditional" ratifications cannot be minimized; they placed the new Congress under great pressure to consider bill of rights amendments as soon as possible. And Congress did![26]

Within three months after the new government went into effect on March 4, 1789, James Madison presented a draft of a bill of rights to Congress on June 8, 1789. After considerable debate in Congress from June to September on Madison's draft as well as on other proposals, the

U.S. House and the U.S. Senate agreed on twelve articles of amend-ment and sent them to the states for approval. Two years later, in 1791, ten of the original twelve were ratified by the states and became part of the Constitution as amendments. All ten became collectively known as the "Bill of Rights," though only the first nine apply explicitly to the people (the Tenth Amendment applies to the states).[27]

As incongruous as it may seem today, the Bill of Rights at the time of its adoption, consistent with the Constitution as the framework for the national government, was commonly understood to prohibit only the ac-tions of the national government, not the actions of states. For instance, whereas the national government was prohibited from violating the free-dom of the press, states were free to regulate the press because the First Amendment to the Constitution declares: "*Congress* shall make no law respecting an establishment of religion, or prohibiting the free exercise thereof; or abridging the freedom of speech, or of the press; or the right of the people peaceably to assemble, and to petition the government for a redress of grievances" (emphasis added). This was not a major issue at the time because all state constitutions had bills of rights, many of which paralleled the U.S. Constitution's Bill of Rights. That only the actions of the national government were prohibited is consistent with the beliefs of the Anti-Federalists who pushed for a bill of rights during the ratifica-tion campaign and who, as advocates of states' rights, strongly opposed government prohibitions on the actions and sovereignty of the states.

It would be a century and a half before most of the U.S. Constitution's Bill of Rights applied to the actions of state governments. This result fol-lowed from numerous U.S. Supreme Court decisions, indicating again the important role of the Supreme Court in the history of the American economy. The privileges and immunities, due process, and equal treat-ment clauses in the Fourteenth Amendment, one of the Reconstruc-tion amendments adopted in 1868 following the Civil War, are generally thought to intend to extend from the national to the state governments nearly all protections contained in the Bill of Rights. Nonetheless, the actual process of "incorporating" the Bill of Rights' protections so that they are enforceable with respect to actions of state governments began in earnest more than a half-century later. Two cases that reached the Su-preme Court, *Twining v. New Jersey,* decided in 1925, and a *Adamson v. California,* in 1947, were among the pivotal cases in this process. The "modern view," which is reflected in *Duncan v. Louisiana,* decided in 1968, is that the protections in the Bill of Rights that are "fundamental to the American scheme of justice" (a jury trial in serious criminal cases) are "incorporated" but other protections (a jury trial in civil cases involving more than $20) are not. These cases all revolved around whether the Fourteenth Amendment incorporated the protections of the Bill of Rights.[28]

Implications of the Constitution for the Nation's Future

The Constitution may not have been drafted nor ratified by a group of disinterested and nonpartisan demigods motivated only, or even primarily, by high-minded political principles to promote the nation's interest. It was drafted and eventually ratified by a group of men whose decisions were influenced by their own economic interests, the interests of the states they represented, and their own religious and political beliefs. No single interest group got precisely what it wanted. In fact, many of the individuals who drafted the Constitution had conflicting interests regarding a single issue. The result was a document shaped by interests and beliefs through various agreements and compromises.

The Constitution and the Bill of Rights that arose from this process have played a major role in the long-term success of the American economy. The protections of individual freedoms and property rights gave economic actors tremendous flexibility in pursuing economic development and their own interests in the context of an ever-changing world that could not have been anticipated in 1787. Although some states restricted the completely free movement of goods and people across state lines with state-level inspection and occupational licensing laws, these restrictions were limited and were ultimately prohibited by several U.S. Supreme Court decisions in the late nineteenth century. As a result, resources and opportunities eventually were easily spread throughout the country. The assignment of responsibility for national defense and foreign affairs to the national government allowed the nation to present a unified front in foreign negotiations.

Because the Constitution included many agreements, compromises, and potential ambiguities owing, in large part, to the diversity of economic interests and ideologies in the nation, its adoption in 1789 could not possibly have settled all the potential disputes and issues that might arise. For example, the Constitution did not completely settle the issue of the allocation of power between the states and the central government. Consequently, conflicts between the states and central government and among various economic interests and ideologies would continue for many decades. Some of the greatest conflict arose concerning the issue of slavery and differences between the northern and southern economies.

For instance, the framers compromised on how slaves would be counted for purposes of political representation and direct taxation, counting them as three-fifths of other persons. This never satisfied every southerner or northerner, and it became a basis of future conflict. Another particularly telling example concerns one of the most important economic agreements made during the Constitution's drafting. Southern exporting interests (in particular, slaveholders in the lower South) are said to have agreed to settle for a simple majority (rather than a two-thirds majority) congressional vote to enact commercial regulations, including those concerning taxation, in exchange for northern commercial interests' agreeing to a prohibition on export tariffs and a twenty-year prohibition on congressional interference in the slave trade.

This North-South agreement ultimately led to economic and political conflict for the nation that lasted many decades. Because a tax on income or on expenditures, including a tax on international transactions, has similar economic consequences, the ability to tax imports (international expenditures), which Article 1, Section 8 of the Constitution permits, has consequences similar to those of a tax on exports (international income). As a result, the effect of the export tariff prohibition in this agreement was largely procedural, not economic. At the same time, adoption of the simple majority vote made it easier for the national government to enact import tariffs. That the bulk of U.S. exports originated in the South meant that easier-to-enact import tariffs, which act as de facto export tariffs, would fall heavily on southern economic interests. The part of the agreement related to the slave trade meant only a twenty-year prohibition on *national* interference in the international slave trade. This constitutional agreement fostered much sectional conflict once the nation began to enact import tariffs. Indeed, one of the nation's early constitutional crises, South Carolina's 1831 Nullification Crisis, was caused by the 1828 Tariff of Abominations, which South Carolina tried to nullify because the extremely high tariff rates contained in it were particularly harmful to the export-based southern economy. The Tariff of Abominations certainly would not have been enacted had a two-thirds majority been required to enact commercial regulations.[29]

That the Constitution did not settle North-South differences regarding slavery and commercial and tariff policies can be seen as a result of the inability to design a set of fundamental rules that completely satisfied the wide diversity of economic interests and beliefs in the nation. Ultimately, it would take the four-year Civil War beginning in 1861, which caused the death of 625,000 Americans and the destruction of property worth at least $1.5 billion, and many U.S. Supreme Court cases to settle the issues of slavery, commercial and tariff policies, and state versus national authority.

Notes

1. For a general treatment of the influence of the ideals of liberty and republicanism on the American Revolution, see Wood 2002. The quotation from the Massachusetts assembly is from *Journals of the Continental Congress* (September 5, 1774, 15–16). The quotation from the Rhode Island assembly is from *Journals of the Continental Congress* (September 5, 1774, 16–17).

2. Wood (2002) is of the view that the original state constitutions incorporated the principle of republican government to safeguard liberty (see esp. 67).

3. More on the history of government currency emissions in the United States and inflation is presented in chapter 5. Rockoff (1984) discusses governmental wage and price controls during the Revolutionary War.

4. The casualty and cost estimates are from U.S. Civil War Center [2004].

5. The discussion in this section on financing the Revolutionary War is based on Baack 2001a, 2001b.

6. A copy of the Articles of Confederation is contained in Appendix B.

7. This paragraph is based on the material presented in Dougherty 2001.

8. Evidence of the low prevalence of interstate duties and low level of international tariffs during the Confederation period is offered in Shepherd 1993.

9. The quotation is from the Virginia General Assembly, January 21, 1786, as quoted in Kurland and Lerner 1987, 1:185.

10. The analysis of Shays's Rebellion in this paragraph is based on Richards 2002.

11. For studies of economic conditions during the 1780s, see Ferguson 1961, Nettles 1962, Bjork 1963, 1964, Shepherd and Walton 1976, Walton and Shepherd 1979, McCusker and Menard 1985, and Shepherd 1993. Jensen (1964), Rossiter (1966), and Kelly and Harbison (1970) discuss the movement for constitutional reform during the 1780s.

12. See Paper no. 10, by James Madison, in *The Federalist* (1788 [1937]).

13. The entire section on the drafting and adoption of the Constitution borrows freely from McGuire 2003.

14. The quotation is from H. B. Grigsby, *History of the Virginia Federal Constitution of 1788* (1:32), as cited in Farrand 1911, 3:558, n. 2.

15. For a record of the debates, see Farrand 1911, which is reputed to be the best single source of information concerning what took place in Philadelphia. Farrand's three volumes contain, among other things, a copy of the official journal of the convention, James Madison's highly respected notes of the entire proceedings, the diaries, notes, and memoranda of seven other framers (Alexander Hamilton, Rufus King, George Mason, James McHenry, William Pierce, William Paterson, and Robert Yates), the plans of government presented to the convention by Virginia and New Jersey, several documents

recording the work of the Committee of Detail, which presented the first draft of the Constitution to the convention on August 6, 1787, and numerous pieces of correspondence of many of the founders and their contemporaries.

16. Elliot (1836 [1888]) presents a record of the debates at many of the state ratifying conventions. For a record of the views of the opponents of ratification, see Storing 1981, which contains memoranda, letters, and various writings of the Anti-Federalists, the opponents of the Constitution.

17. Many issues concerning national as opposed to state sovereignty were not settled with the drafting of the Constitution in the summer of 1787. These issues are discussed below. The reader should compare the Articles of Confederation to the United States Constitution, which are reprinted in Appendices B and C, respectively.

18. The quotation is from Walton and Shepherd 1979, 187–88.

19. The contention that occupational licensing and inspection laws acted as state barriers to internal trade until the late nineteenth century is derived from McCurdy 1978.

20. The quotation is from *The Federalist* 1788 [1937], Paper no. 1, 3.

21. The descriptions of Beard's views in this section come from Beard 1913 [1935], 16–51.

22. For examples of studies that cite Brown, McDonald, or both as discrediting Beard without conducting their own analysis, see Buchanan and Tullock 1962, Wood 1969, 2002, Riker 1987, and Ackerman 1991. The quotation comes from McDonald 1958, 110.

23. The first reexamination of the behavior of our Founding Fathers during the drafting and ratification of the Constitution appeared in McGuire and Ohsfeldt 1984, which was followed by a series of studies on the Constitution (see McGuire and Ohsfeldt 1986, 1989a, 1989b, 1997; McGuire 1988, 2001), culminating in McGuire 2003.

24. Unless otherwise noted, the specific findings discussed here are taken from McGuire 2003.

25. Grubb (2003) espouses this view. Grubb's study has been recently challenged by Michener and Wright 2005. But see Grubb's (2005) response.

26. Riker (1987) makes a strong case that ratification with recommended amendments was essential to the ratification process. The quotation comes from Elliot 1836 [1888], 2:123.

27. The Bill of Rights is reprinted in Appendix D.

28. The issue of whether the Bill of Rights is enforceable with respect to actions of state governments because of the Fourteenth Amendment is considered "one of the most important and long-lasting debates" in constitutional interpretation. For more on the "incorporation debate," see Linder 2005. Also, see *The U.S. Constitution Online* and *U.S. Courts: The Federal Judiciary*. The Supreme Court cases cited in the paragraph are Twining v. New Jersey, 268 U.S. 652 (1925), Adamson v. California, 332 U.S. 46 (1947), and Duncan v. Louisiana, 391 U.S. 145 (1968).

29. For an examination of the South's views of tariffs vis-à-vis how the South handled them when it drafted its own constitution in 1861 for the Confederate States of America, see McGuire and Van Cott 2002. McGuire and

Van Cott (2003) present an easily accessible demand-and-supply explanation of the symmetry between import and export tariffs. Baack, McGuire, and Van Cott (2005) outline the political economy of the North-South agreement concerning exports, the slave trade, and congressional voting on commercial regulations during the drafting of the U.S. Constitution, describing the way the agreement played a critical role in the North-South conflict leading up to southern secession in 1861 and the Civil War.

References

Ackerman, Bruce. 1991. *We the People*. 2 vols. Cambridge: Harvard University Press, Belknap Press.

Baack, Ben. 2001a. "Forging a Nation State: The Continental Congress and the Financing of the War of American Independence." *Economic History Review* 54:639–56.

———. 2001b. "The Economics of the American Revolutionary War." In *The EH.Net Encyclopedia of Economic and Business History*, ed. Robert Whaples. EH.Net (November). http://www.eh.net/encyclopedia/baack.war.revolutionary.us.php.

Baack, Ben, Robert A. McGuire, and T. Norman Van Cott. 2005. "The Political Economy of Constitutional Design: Did the Southern Framers Get It Right in 1787?" Mimeograph, the University of Akron.

Beard, Charles A. 1913 [1935]. *An Economic Interpretation of the Constitution of the United States*. New York: Macmillan.

Bjork, Gordon Carl. 1963. "Stagnation and Growth in the American Economy, 1784–1792." PhD diss., University of Washington.

———. 1964. "The Weaning of the American Economy: Independence, Market Changes, and Economic Development." *Journal of Economic History* 24:541–60.

Brown, Robert E. 1956. *Charles Beard and the Constitution: A Critical Analysis of an Economic Interpretation of the Constitution*. Princeton: Princeton University Press.

Buchanan, James M., and Gordon Tullock. 1962. *The Calculus of Consent: Logical Foundations of Constitutional Democracy*. Ann Arbor: University of Michigan Press.

Dougherty, Keith L. 2001. *Collective Action under the Articles of Confederation*. New York: Cambridge University Press.

Elliot, Jonathan, ed. 1836 [1888]. *The Debates in the Several State Conventions on the Adoption of the Federal Constitution as Recommended by the General Convention at Philadelphia, in 1787*. 5 vols. Philadelphia: Lippincott.

Farrand, Max, ed. 1911. *The Records of the Federal Convention of 1787*. 3 vols. New Haven: Yale University Press.

The Federalist: A Commentary on the Constitution of the United States, Being a Collection of Essays written in Support of the Constitution agreed upon September 17, 1787, by the Federal Convention. 1788 [1937]. New York: Modern Library.

Ferguson, E. James. 1961. *The Power of the Purse: A History of American Public Finance, 1776–1790*. Chapel Hill: University of North Carolina Press.

Grubb, Farley W. 2003. "Creating the U.S. Dollar Currency Union, 1748–1811: A Quest for Monetary Stability or a Usurpation of State Sovereignty for Personal Gain?" *American Economic Review* 93 (December): 1778–98.

———. 2005. "State 'Currencies' and the Transition to the U.S. Dollar: Reply—Including a New View from Canada." *American Economic Review* 95 (September): 341–48.

Higgs, Robert. 1987. *Crisis and Leviathan: Critical Episodes in the Growth of American Government.* New York: Oxford University Press.

Jensen, Merrill. 1964. *The Making of the Constitution.* New York: Van Nostrand.

Journals of the Continental Congress, 1774–1789. 1904–37. 34 vols. Washington, DC: Library of Congress. http://memory.loc.gov/ammem/amlaw/lwjc.html.

Kelly, Alfred H., and Winfred A. Harbison. 1970. *The American Constitution: Its Origins and Development.* 4th ed. New York: Norton.

Kurland, Philip B., and Ralph Lerner. 1987. *The Founders' Constitution.* 5 vols. Chicago: University of Chicago Press.

Linder, Doug. 2005. *Exploring Constitutional Law.* http://www.law.umkc.edu/faculty/projects/ftrials/conlaw/incorp.htm.

McCurdy, Charles. 1978. "American Law and the Marketing Structure of the Large Corporation." *Journal of Economic History* 38:631–49.

McCusker, John J., and Russell R. Menard. 1985. *The Economy of British America.* Chapel Hill: University of North Carolina Press.

McDonald, Forrest. 1958. *We the People: The Economic Origins of the Constitution.* Chicago: University of Chicago Press.

McGuire, Robert A. 1988. "Constitution Making: A Rational Choice Model of the Federal Convention of 1787." *American Journal of Political Science* 32 (May): 483–522.

———. 2001. "Economic Interests and the Adoption of the United States Constitution." In *The EH.Net Encyclopedia of Economic and Business History,* ed. Robert Whaples. EH.Net. (August). http://www.eh.net/encyclopedia/mcguire.constitution.us.economic.interests.php.

———. 2003. *To Form a More Perfect Union: A New Economic Interpretation of the United States Constitution.* New York: Oxford University Press.

McGuire, Robert A., and Robert L. Ohsfeldt. 1984. "Economic Interests and the American Constitution: A Quantitative Rehabilitation of Charles A. Beard." *Journal of Economic History* 44 (June): 509–19.

———. 1986. "An Economic Model of Voting Behavior over Specific Issues at the Constitutional Convention of 1787." *Journal of Economic History* 46 (March): 79–111.

———. 1989a. "Self-Interest, Agency Theory, and Political Voting Behavior: The Ratification of the United States Constitution." *American Economic Review* 79 (March): 219–34.

———. 1989b. "Public Choice Analysis and the Ratification of the Constitution." In *The Federalist Papers and the New Institutionalism,* ed. Bernard Grofman and Donald Wittman, 175–204. New York: Agathon.

———. 1997. "Constitutional Economics and the American Founding." *Research in Law and Economics* 18:143–71.

McGuire, Robert A., and T. Norman Van Cott. 2002. "The Confederate Constitution, Tariffs, and the Laffer Relationship." *Economic Inquiry* 40:428–38.

———. 2003. "A Supply and Demand Exposition of a Constitutional Tax Loophole: The Case of Tariff Symmetry." *Constitutional Political Economy* 14:39–45.

Michener, Ronald W., and Robert E. Wright. 2005. "State 'Currencies' and the Transition to the U.S. Dollar: Clarifying Some Confusions." *American Economic Review* 95 (June): 682–703.

Nettles, Curtis P. 1962. *The Emergence of a National Economy, 1775–1815.* New York: Holt, Rinehart, and Winston.

Richards, Leonard L. 2002. *Shays's Rebellion: The American Revolution's Final Battle.* Philadelphia: University of Pennsylvania Press.

Riker, William H. 1987. "The Lessons of 1787." *Public Choice* 55:5–34.

Rockoff, Hugh. 1984. *Drastic Measures: A History of Wage and Price Controls in the United States.* Cambridge: Cambridge University Press.

Rossiter, Clinton. 1966. *1787: The Grand Convention.* New York: Macmillan.

Shepherd, James F. 1993. "State Tariff Policies in the Era of Confederation." Paper presented at the 68th annual meeting of the Western Economic Association International, Lake Tahoe, Nevada, June 21.

Shepherd, James F., and Gary M. Walton. 1976. "Economic Change After the American Revolution: Pre- and Post-War Comparisons of Maritime Shipping and Trade." *Explorations in Economic History* 13:397–422.

Storing, Herbert J. 1981. *The Complete Anti-Federalist.* 7 vols. Chicago: University of Chicago Press.

U.S. Civil War Center. [2004]. "Statistical Summary, America's Major Wars." Based on table 2-23, "Principal Wars in which the US Participated: US Military Personnel Serving and Casualties." Washington Headquarters Services, Directorate for Information Operations and Reports, U.S. Department of Defense Records. www.cwc.lsu.edu/cwc/other/stats/warcost.htm (accessed May 24, 2005).

The U.S. Constitution Online. http://www.usconstitution.net/consttop_bor .html.

U.S. Courts: The Federal Judiciary. http://www.uscourts.gov/outreach/fedstate _amendment14.htm.

Walton, Gary M., and James F. Shepherd. 1979. *The Economic Rise of Early America.* New York: Cambridge University Press.

Whaples, Robert. 1995. "Where Is There Consensus among American Economic Historians? The Results of a Survey on Forty Propositions." *Journal of Economic History* 55:139–54.

Wood, Gordon S. 1969. *The Creation of the American Republic, 1776–1787.* Chapel Hill: University of North Carolina Press.

———. 2002. *The American Revolution: A History.* New York: Modern Library.

GARY D. LIBECAP

4

Property Rights and
Federal Land Policy

THE AMERICAN ECONOMY, generally speaking, is a market-oriented one with a smaller role for government than is found, for example, in western European economies. Throughout American economic history, most decisions regarding resource use and answers to questions regarding what, how, and for whom to produce have been based on private property rights and market incentives. Although the institution of private property was well established in Europe and followed European immigrants as they migrated to North America, its strong position throughout the American economy was promoted by the establishment of secure private property rights to land.

In the rural agricultural economy of the colonial and early republic periods, ownership of land and other natural resources was of overriding importance. These ownership institutions set precedents for private ownership of other, less-tangible assets such as financial instruments and allowed for the development of private financial institutions and markets such as banks and stock exchanges. Had American land and other natural resource property rights remained uncertain and confused, it is doubtful that financial markets would have developed as they did or, more broadly, that the overall economy would have emerged and grown as successfully as it did. The property rights assignment scheme molded the way expectations were formed regarding appropriation of the returns to investment and entrepreneurial activities as well as mobility and economic advancement. Correspondingly, the property rights structure determined how adaptable the economy would be in responding to changes in factor and product prices. In contrast, in most parts of Latin America, Africa, and Asia the process of land titling has not been so smooth and, accordingly, the development of a market economy has been more problematic.

The way property rights to land were allocated in the United States also was important because it largely determined the distribution of

income, wealth, and political power. On the northern agricultural frontier, land policy supported the formation of small farms. In the absence
of important economies of scale in grain farming, these small units were
economically viable, and they led to the establishment of political jurisdictions dominated by smallholders with a stake in the economic and
political growth of their communities. Conservative, prosperous agricultural regions consisting of small farms developed, with the population
providing for public goods such as education and transportation that
were essential for longer-term economic growth. Moreover, this piece-
meal allocation of land brought the promise of ownership. Any ambitious individual could claim and establish a farm of his or her own, if not
in the immediate area, then to the west. This broad distribution of land
allowed for a sense of optimism in widely shared opportunities for owning land, prospering, and being a valuable and viable part of the community. This expectation certainly was a major factor behind the draw
of America for immigrants and the creation of the American Dream.

In Latin America land distribution generally favored elites and often
led to the establishment of very large farms, or *latifundia*. A wage agricultural labor force developed instead of a system of smallholders, and
serious tensions over the distribution of wealth and opportunity have
characterized those societies in a way that has never occurred in the
United States.

For all of these reasons, it is important to understand how American
land policy worked, where it was successful, and where it was not. But
before turning directly to land policy, it is worthwhile to briefly review
the role of private property rights in an economy and why they are the
fundamental institution for markets.

Property Rights

Property rights institutions underlie the performance and income
distribution of an economy. By defining the parameters for the use of
scarce resources and assigning the associated rewards and costs, the prevailing system of property rights establishes incentives and time horizons for investment, production, and exchange. They delineate decision-
making authority over economic resources, determine the relevant time
periods for those decisions, specify permitted asset uses, define transferability, and direct the assignment of net benefits. By outlining the
costs and rewards of decision making, property rights establish the factors that are privately considered in determining resource use.

In the limit, if property rights are so completely defined and enforced that private and social net benefits are equalized, there will be

no externalities. Economic decisions made in circumstances where all social costs and benefits are considered will maximize total wealth, given the existing income distribution and market demand composition. Production will be at the right level with no uncompensated third-party effects such as those we observe with air pollution or excessive harvesting of open-access fisheries. In these latter two cases, transaction costs, including those of measurement and enforcement, prevent the complete definition and assignment of property rights to the air and to the stock of fish.

An alternative though complete property rights assignment will have a correspondingly different income distribution, demand structure, and production mix. Nevertheless, the output chosen will maximize aggregate wealth under the new rights distribution. In general, for efficiency's sake, the key consideration is the completeness of the definition of property rights and not the specific allocation (Libecap 1986). But distribution matters. If the assignment of property rights to valuable resources in an economy is so skewed that most of the society is left out, and if there are few obvious means for obtaining property rights and participating as owners, then the number of people with a political stake in the ownership structure will be small. Under these circumstances, property rights institutions will be unstable. We observe this situation in parts of the world where land ownership and wealth are very unevenly distributed and landless squatters invade and occupy large farms. Such invasions increase ownership uncertainty and reduce economic returns and incentives for investment, production, and trade. And if ownership uncertainty is widespread, the economy will not perform to its potential and the society will be poorer overall.

Communal ownership of assets may be an attractive alternative to private property rights from an equity point of view because it can avoid the distributional conflicts associated with private ownership. Even so, collective property rights can have problems of their own. Although nongroup members are excluded from using the resource, constraints on members' behavior must be implemented; otherwise, open-access conditions can emerge within the group, leading to excessive and wasteful use and depletion of the value of the resource. Hence, there must be some form of property rights within the group to govern behavior. These critical intragroup controls are not free of distributional pressures. Although formal titles are not assigned, the intragroup regulations still must determine access and individual ability to collect income from the resource. This means that distributional conflicts can continue to mold collective action within communal systems, much as they do with more formal private property rights. Further, common ownership and decision making work best when the group is small and relatively homogeneous so that the members share similar objectives and have similar costs. Under these circumstances, it is possible for group decision making to take place effectively. But as group size increases, perhaps as the value of the asset rises and attracts more entry, such cohesion breaks down and decision making and monitoring of behavior become more costly, controversial, and ineffective. Private decision making, because it involves the objectives of only one party, can work much more smoothly in the face of exogenous shifts in resource values.

Private property rights may involve a variety of rights or opportunities including the right to exclude nonowners from access, the right to capture the stream of income and costs from the use of and investments in the resource, the right to modify the resource, and the right to sell or otherwise transfer the resource to others (including heirs). Property rights institutions range from formal arrangements, including constitutional provisions, statutes, and judicial rulings, to informal conventions and customs regarding the allocation and use of property (Libecap 1989, 1–19). Property rights also are found along a continuum from completely open access, in which no ownership exists and the resource is wide open to all, to increasing levels of specificity and exclusion. Property rights also can be private and individually held, private but held by a group (as with common property), state-owned (as with socialism), or a combination of these.

The nature of a rights system depends on a number of factors: the value of the asset and the corresponding costs and benefits of well-defined and enforced ownership, the social structure and acceptability of private ownership and individualism, legal precedent as codified in constitutional provisions, legislation, and court opinions, prevailing regulatory and tax policies, and the physical nature of the asset.

Highly valued assets are more likely to have secure property rights, all else being equal, because they are potentially most subject to costly competition for ownership and hence theft. They therefore bring the greatest returns from defining property rights. If the ownership of a valuable asset is unclear, then competing claimants will waste at least part of its value in their efforts to seize it. There may be costly violence in the struggle for control, and there will be short time horizons because no party will be confident in the security of their holdings. Long-term and otherwise valuable investment will be impractical under these circumstances. Trade will be inhibited because traders will have little security in the ownership of what they are exchanging, and resource prices will be reduced. These are some of the losses associated with the "tragedy of the commons" described by Garrett Hardin in his famous 1968 *Science* article and extended for the case of open-access and often depleted fisheries by H. Scott Gordon (1954) and Stephen N. S. Cheung (1970). To avoid the wastes of open-access systems, property rights tend to be made more complete through collective action with more effective enforcement as resource values rise. Not only are these resources more subject to costly competition for control, but their added value compensates for the increased costs of greater rights definition and enforcement (Libecap 1978; Demsetz 1967).

As argued by Harold Demsetz, social, political, and religious conventions influence the nature of property rights adopted by a society at any point in time. If individual ownership and decision making are discouraged within the society, then private property rights arrangements will be more costly to implement and protect (Demsetz 1967). Because property rights ultimately are political institutions, defined and sanctioned by law and custom, they also will be subject to broader regulations that govern asset use and exchange or that tax part of the asset's value. The more onerous the regulatory and tax structure, the weaker will be the property rights regime. Although regulation and tax policies may have important bases in the desire to provide public goods, they nevertheless compromise the private property rights structure and its corresponding benefits.

Ownership also is more difficult to assign and defend if the asset is very large, mobile, unboundable, or otherwise unobservable, conditions that characterize many fisheries, the atmosphere, some deep mineral deposits, aquifers, and oil and natural gas reservoirs. Private property rights may also be limited by the state if there are important public goods aspects of resource use, as with navigable water ways, where ownership is restrained under the "public trust" doctrine. Low-cost navigation on inland rivers, important for extending markets and facilitating economic growth, for example, could be seriously jeopardized if many individual riparian property owners held up shipping. The public trust doctrine requires that such waterways be left unrestricted for navigation.

This short overview illustrates the importance of a secure property rights structure for the growth of a market economy. I now turn to an examination of U.S. land policy to show where it facilitated the assignment of clear property rights to the huge federal estate that covered much of North America and where it did not. American land policy developed gradually in the late eighteenth and nineteenth centuries by means of a complex political process. Early on, Congress faced the conflicting political objectives of maximizing revenue from the sale of federal lands, of meeting growing constituent demands for low-cost access to natural resources, of reacting to the high costs of enforcing federal government holdings against private claimants, and the desire to extend settlement in order to strengthen American claims to frontier regions. These factors molded the timing and nature of the land laws that emerged.

Federal Land Policy

After the Revolutionary War, some of the newly independent states claimed large tracts of land to the west of the Appalachian Mountains as part of their future proposed boundaries. Conflicts developed about conflicting claims, and had this pattern continued, there might have been no federal land policy but rather, thirteen contentious ones. Fortunately, the states gradually ceded their land claims to the federal government. In addition, between 1781 and 1853 the federal government acquired more than 1,327,000,000 acres of new land via the Louisiana Purchase (1803) and the additions of Texas (1845), Oregon (1846), and the Mexican Cession (1848). The Gadsden Purchase (1853), Alaska (1867), and Hawaii (1898) rounded out the major acquisitions. But it was the first group that formed the vast amount of land that was part of the U.S. domain and on which federal land policy was focused.

Had the federal government maintained ownership of this huge estate and tightly regulated its access and use, the nature of American society and its economy would have been very different. As it was, most of the land was opened for private patenting. The way title was assigned critically affected the formation of the American agricultural economy and the distribution of income and wealth in the country.

Alternatively, large estates might have emerged from huge land grants to political and economic elites, but that did not happen generally in the United States, at least along the northern agricultural frontier. Instead, smaller distributions were made. In the early nineteenth century, revenues from land sales formed a major source of income for the federal government, and large political constituencies sought to own federal land. Accordingly, politicians were anxious to promote the rapid transfer of natural resources, and federal land policies reflected these objectives. Further, some lands were distributed from the federal government to veterans in the form of land warrants in payment for their military service. Other tracts were granted to the states to help finance public schools, land grant colleges, and other public goods. The railroads also received grants of land in the West as stimuli for extending transportation systems to sparsely populated regions. Lands also were auctioned to private claimants or transferred to settlers at minimum prices under the Pre-Emption Acts. Finally, the largest distributions came via the Homestead Act of 1862 and similar land laws, whereby 160-acre allocations were provided to actual farmers after residency and improvement of the land.

As a result of these policies, until about 1880 secure property rights to land were assigned to viable farming units to lands in the United States east of the ninety-eighth meridian. A largely rural agricultural economy developed and flourished. Investments in land improvements, new processes, new equipment, and new seed types occurred in an environment of predictable, enforced private ownership. Land and capital markets emerged. In addition, capital gains from land sales on the frontier became the major way by which individuals could amass wealth.[1]

The outcome of federal land policy was similar for mineral lands, although there was no explicit federal policy for transferring private mineral rights until the passage of the Mining Law of 1872. The federal government's early response to mineral claims was quite similar to that for agricultural land, at least until 1920 and enactment of the Mineral Leasing Act. The Forty-Niners and others who braved the perils of migrating across North America or of traveling around the Horn to the Pacific Coast and the gold and silver deposits of the Sierras and the Rockies could obtain locally devised property rights to mineral land. In 1872 these mining camp rules were explicitly recognized by the federal government. The rules and the security they provided promoted exploration and production. The American mining industry developed, and the United States became a world leader in the production of hard-rock minerals and in mining engineering.

As we will see, however, federal land policy was less effective for agricultural and timber lands west of the ninety-eighth meridian. In that region the small-farm model that dominated northern frontier agriculture was maintained, largely owing to political pressure on Congress to facilitate as many land claims as possible and to a lack of understanding of the implications of the region's semiarid climate. This land policy contributed to the allocation of property rights to farm land in plots that were too small to be economically viable over the long run. Hundreds of thousands of individuals migrated to the Great Plains, and once they had borne those costs and were established on the frontier they were reluctant to leave even as their farms struggled during droughts.

There were few options other than outmigration, which subsequently took place, often after one generation had tried to make a go of it on the plains. Given the many "homestead busts" in the region, there were fewer of the rags-to-riches stories of frontier settlers on the Great Plains than along the earlier frontiers of the Midwest and the East.

Similarly, land policy was not well adapted for granting rights to timberland in the West. In the East and the Midwest, individuals acquired rights to timberland by means of farm land purchases and consolidation. Large holdings, such as those of Ezra Cornell in Wisconsin, were assembled via the purchase of military script given by the federal government to soldiers and sailors as payment for their service. Although the focus of land policy was on agriculture, it was possible for individuals to garner enough timberland through federal land purchases to support a lumber industry; this occurred in the upper Great Lakes states of Michigan, Wisconsin, and Minnesota (Johnson and Libecap 1980). But in the West, where settlement generally did not occur until after the Civil War and took place under the Homestead Act and similar land laws, farm plots of 160 acres were far too limited to form effective holdings of timberland. Hence, much illegal lumbering occurred on federal land without secure property rights. This resulted in waste, timber theft, and depredation.

The strict focus of land policy on small farm allocations based on climatic and soil conditions in the eastern United States meant that private claimants for viable dryland farms and ranches on the Great Plains and in the Great Basin could not legally obtain title to the property they used. The same was true for those who sought sufficient tracts of timberland in the Pacific Northwest, where there were economies of scale in timber cruising and in the production of lumber, to support lumber mills. As a result, these land claimants occupied or used federal natural resources without obtaining formal title. The practice of informally using federal property on the frontier was viable for much for much of the nineteenth century, but after the turn of the twentieth century the federal government began to gradually withdraw the lands from private entry. Today, large tracts of the western continental United States and much of Alaska remain federally owned largely because of the inflexibility of federal land policy in these regions.

Where U.S. Land Policy Worked: The Northern Agricultural Frontier

The Treaty of Paris of 1783 ceded to the United States all lands south of Canada, east of the Mississippi, and north of Florida, an area that became known as the Northwest Territories and the area around which U.S. land policy developed.[2] Although there was never any sense that the federal government would retain ownership, there were nevertheless competing pressures for the disposal of federal estate. Some wished to raise revenue by selling the land at full value. Others wanted the land given away in a manner that achieved the democratic objectives of small farm ownership and met constituent demands for low-cost access to federal land. There was also a desire to maximize the number of American settlers in the frontier to support U.S. claims to the region. And finally, it was very difficult for the federal government with its limited resources to effectively enforce its land claims against private entry. Until the Civil War, revenue generation remained an important but declining factor, and the government auctioned land or made it available for purchase at minimum prices ranging from $1 to $2 per acre. In 1862 small farmers' objectives prevailed with passage of the Homestead Act; most federal land was offered for free in 160-acre plots, subject to occupation and improvement, or at $1.25 or $2.50 per acre, depending on the land law.

The framework for distributing federal lands was created by the Land Ordinances of 1785 and 1787, which called for the orderly, systematic distribution of federal property to private claimants. Surveying was to proceed with the delineation of plots within a rectangular grid relative to east-west longitudinal and north-south latitude base lines, with further division into townships six miles square with thirty-six sections of 640 acres each.[3] Surveyed lands then could be offered for sale at public auction to raise revenue. Initial minimum prices were high and minimum acreages large. But gradually both of these minima were reduced. Administration of land sales was difficult, sales and revenues were below expectations, squatters moved ahead of the survey and staked claims, and the whole process of land disposal was politically controversial.

Constituencies that favored rapid settlement of the frontier via the low-cost transfer of federal lands to private claimants gained political ascendancy, so that the terms of land sales were liberalized repeatedly in legislation passed after 1800. In addition, squatters disliked the system of land auctions because the minimum plots were often larger than they wanted, and they lacked the capital to compete with more affluent land developers. By occupying lands ahead of surveys and auctions and organizing claims clubs to intimidate those who would compete with them for their lands, squatters could disrupt planned land auctions or at least limit participation in them to members of their clubs. As these distributional conflicts intensified, Congress responded with laws enacted in 1830 and 1841 that gave preference, or "pre-emption," to squatters, allowing them to buy 160 acres at $1.25 per acre. The 1854 Graduation Act further reduced the price for unsold federal lands to 12½ cents per acre. And there was political pressure to do even more. The combined political muscle of frontier land developers, or speculators (and most frontier migrants engaged in land speculation), settlers and prospective settlers, transportation companies (canals and later, famously, the railroads), and territorial boosters seeking statehood created a formidable constituency that few politicians could ignore.

There also was an important distributional objective in U.S. land policy, at least for the northern agricultural frontier, that increased the political attractiveness of a liberal property rights allocation. The dominant focus came to be one of small-farm distribution, as called for by Thomas Jefferson: "The earth is given as a common stock for man to labor and live on. . . . The small landholders are the most precious part of the state."[4]

A political coalition formed to reserve federal lands for small farmers and "working men" and to oppose the perceived development of monopoly baronial estates and landlordism. Advocates maintained that every man had a right to a share of frontier land and that this property rights allocation would not only serve as a remedy for poverty, unemployment, and the privation of the working class but would ensure the extension of democracy throughout a nation of prosperous small landholders who had a stake in the society. Such a nation would have the distributive balance to be politically conservative and free of the damaging social and political conflicts that characterized Europe. Federal land, allocated freely in small plots, could help mitigate any of the social pressures that might build up in eastern cities. Immigrants could be channeled to the frontier to reduce the supply of urban workers, maintaining acceptable manufacturing wages.

Although the practical effect of this "safety-valve" process has been questioned, it appears to have contributed to the political foundation for the more liberal federal land policies adopted in the mid-nineteenth century.[5] Federal lands also were used in other ways to promote rapid settlement of the frontier. Land was granted to developers in exchange for private internal investments in roads, turnpikes, canals, and railroads. Land grants were made to the states to help underwrite primary and secondary education and to establish land grant colleges (pursuant to the Morrill Act of 1862), and federal lands were used to compensate veterans of the Revolutionary War, the War of 1812, the Mexican War, and the Civil War.

In 1844 the National Land Reform Association, led by Horace Greeley and others, was organized to secure enactment of a homestead act. They petitioned Congress for "free homes for a homeless people."[6] After 1854, the new Republican Party put free land into its platforms Hibbard 1965, 358; Gates 1979, 390–99. An act that authorized the free transfer of up to 160 acres of federal land to pioneers once they paid a registration and filing fee and occupied and improved the land for a set period of time would have been the most liberal option. But it ran into sectional opposition, especially from southern Democrats who could not reconcile its objectives with those of expanding slave-based agriculture on the frontier. Southern Democrats also were concerned about maintaining the balance in the Senate between free and slave states.

The free-land movement was thwarted by southern Democrats until the secession of the South and the election of Lincoln as president. In 1862 the first Homestead Act was passed, and it became the most important policy vehicle for allocating federal land through the end of federal land transfer in 1935. Under the 1862 law, any family head who was at least twenty-one years old could claim between 40 and 160 acres, and on paying fees and commissions and satisfying the five years' continuous residence and improvement (cultivation) requirement, receive title.[7] The act was modified slightly in 1909 to allow 320-acre claims and in 1912 to reduce the residency requirement to three years.[8]

Although most people by far used the Homestead Act to secure government land after 1862, other mechanisms by which federal land was transferred included the Desert Land Act of 1877, which authorized the purchase of 640 acres for $1.25 per acre if the land would be irrigated, the 1878 Timber and Stone Act, which granted parcels of 40–160 acres for accessing timber or stone for agricultural purposes, the 1904 Kinkaid Act, which authorized 640-acre claims in western Nebraska, and the 1916 Stock Raising Homestead Act, which allowed for 640-acre parcels for grazing in other selected states.[9] Figure 4.1 illustrates the pattern of land property rights transfer from the federal government to private individuals between 1800 and 1935.

Homestead allocations worked well in northern agriculture east of the ninety-eighth meridian, which runs through the Dakotas and Texas. There were no important economies of scale in grain production, and sufficient rainfall (usually more than thirty inches per year), high soil quality, and familiar conditions allowed farmers to use agricultural

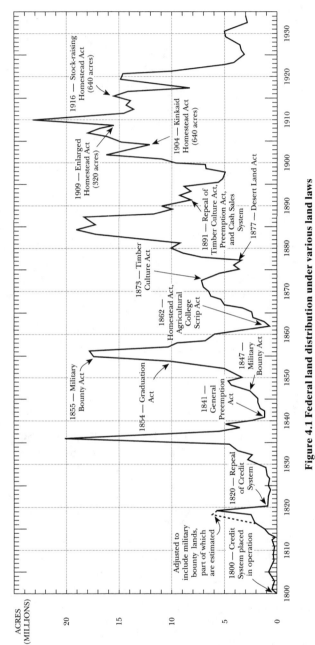

Figure 4.1 Federal land distribution under various land laws
Source: Robbins 1942, 344, as printed in Atack and Passell 1994, 257.

knowledge gained in the East or in Europe. As migrants moved across the frontier, they brought farming practices and crops that had been appropriate in their places of origin. Under these circumstances, property rights were assigned quickly and agriculture developed rapidly. The Midwest was settled successfully with prosperous small farms so that the political objectives of the Homestead Act were met.

Where Land Policy Worked: By Default in the Western Mineral Lands

The discovery of valuable gold and silver ore deposits in the Far West beginning in 1848 and continuing through the rest of the nineteenth century brought dramatic increases in land values in an area where private property rights to land were not yet defined and where no legal procedures existed for assigning mineral rights. Generally, the ore was found in remote, mountainous areas where there were no existing land claims, at least none that were recognized in Washington, D.C.

The miners who rushed to the far West were aware of the general transfer of federal lands to private claimants. As with agricultural lands, the mining frontier was seen as a source of great opportunity for individual advancement and for the overall development of American society and the economy. The practices used in allocating agricultural land helped form individual expectations for claiming federal mineral land: there was no question, in the minds of prospectors, at least, that the government would retain ownership, the land was open for private entry and eventual patenting, and the distribution would be in the form of small plots.

Ostensibly, the policy of the federal government regarding mineral lands was to retain title in order to extract rents for the federal treasury. But because there had been few important ore discoveries prior to 1848, the retention policy was not put to a serious test. Congress required that new states created in the West accept its ownership of mineral lands, and these lands were not included in the Preemption Act or other land laws designed to transfer agricultural lands to private claimants. Congress experimented with leasing of lead and copper deposits in Michigan, but this effort proved difficult to enforce (Libecap 1989, 36). When gold was discovered in the foothills of the Sierra Nevadas in 1848, enforcement of federal ownership became even more costly. Troops who would have been used by the U.S. military governor in Monterrey deserted for the new mines, and given the remoteness of the ore strikes relative to the rest of the country, there was little the federal government could do to assert its claims.

Under these conditions miners were left to assign private rights locally as part of mining camp rules. Mining camps emerged throughout
the central Sierras with rules drafted by miners to outline procedures for
staking, marking, recording, and maintaining private mineral claims.
The rules detailed allowable claim sizes and numbers of claims that
individuals could hold, along with arbitration procedures and the establishment of local miners' courts. The California camp rules were repli-
cated in Nevada with the discovery of the Comstock Lode in 1858 and in
Montana, Colorado, and elsewhere in the West. Given the remote possibility that any single claim would prove to be a bonanza, prospectors
did just as their name suggests: they migrated from gulch to gulch and
region to region prospecting for ore. In doing so, they could carry with
them knowledge of which of the miners' property rules worked which
did not.

Most studies of western mineral rights indicate that ownership arrangements were adopted quickly and without significant and costly
violence (Hallagan 1978; Libecap 1978, 1979; McCurdy 1976; Umbeck
1977a, 1977b; Zerbe and Anderson 2001). Another study, however, suggests that there may have been more uncertainty in the rights structure,
especially in the very early gold rush period, when the location of ore was
not known and searching was important (Clay and Wright 2005). Over
the longer term, though, dependable mineral rights institutions emerged.

A reasonably secure property rights arrangement was necessary if
miners were to be able to focus on mining and not on defense or predation. There appears to be no evidence of widespread conflict or long-
lasting uncertainty about ownership of mining claims that dampened
incentives for subsequent investment in mining and smelting. Although
the ore initially found in California was largely in placer or surface
deposits where significant investment in tunneling was not required,
the deeper ore mined later in California and elsewhere in the West required such investments. They would not have taken place had there
been important concerns regarding the stability of ownership. A stock
exchange was organized in San Francisco to facilitate the trade of mining properties and the raising of capital for deep-vein mining, railroad
spurs to mining camps, mills and smelters, and elaborate aqueducts.
The San Francisco exchange was especially important for mining investment on the Comstock Lode, which became the country's premier
silver-producing region (Libecap 1978).

Although the mining industry developed around locally devised property rights, these rules were not recognized by the federal government

until 1866, when the first federal mineral rights law authorized the transfer of title to private claimants. The 1866 law ratified the distribution of ownership outlined by local mining camp rules. And these same provisions were kept intact in the Mining Law of 1872, which remains in effect today, for patenting private hard-rock mineral claims on federal lands.

Under this institutional arrangement, the mining industry flourished, often becoming the first industrial sector in most western states. To support it, territories and states enacted legislation to provide a court system for arbitrating disputes and enforcing mining claims. Other supportive legislation was enacted (Libecap 1979). In addition, schools such as the Montana School of Mines, the Colorado School of Mines, and the Arizona College of Minerals and Mines were opened to provide the local technology and knowledge necessary for extracting ore.

Where U.S. Land Policy Failed: The Semiarid Great Plains

Land policy did not always establish clear property rights to natural resources, however. Between 1863 and 1880 the northern agricultural frontier moved across the Midwest from Ohio, Indiana, and Illinois through Iowa, Wisconsin, and Minnesota to the eastern parts of Kansas, Nebraska, and the Dakotas. Between 1863, the year after the Homestead Act was passed, and 1880, claimants filed 469,882 original homestead entries covering 55,667,035 acres of federal land. The average claim size was 118 acres. Fifty-nine percent of the claimed acreage was in these states (excluding the Dakotas).[10] The one-size-fits-all homestead model seemed to work well.

By 1880, however, the frontier reached the Great Plains (figure 4.2), where conditions were quite different. The region was much drier than the areas to the east. Either the ninety-eighth or the hundredth meridian usually defines the start of the semiarid Great Plains (Webb 1931; Stegner 1953; Rabin 1997).

The distinguishing characteristics of the Great Plains were their relative aridity and fluctuating rainfall. The region received one-third to one-half the annual precipitation of the Midwest and was subject to periodic droughts. In a report made to Congress in 1878, John Wesley Powell warned that past methods of agricultural settlement could no longer be relied on and called for homesteads of a minimum of 2,560 acres for "pastoral regions." Two bills to change federal land policy were included in his report, but they were not considered.[11] Allocations of this size were *sixteen times* the size of existing homestead allocations and were considered extreme and unnecessary. They would have drastically

The Great Plains

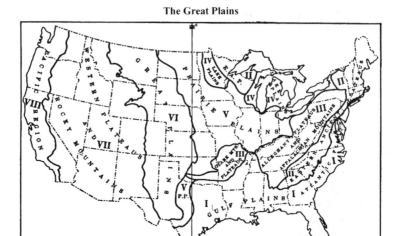

Figure 4.2 The Great Plains
Source: Hansen and Libecap 2004.

reduced the number of farmers who could settle in the region, reducing the options for economic development and the likelihood that the region would emerge culturally and politically in a manner comparable to the Midwest.[12] They were rejected, and no significant modifications in the land laws were made.

Despite Powell's report, most members of Congress did not believe that the remaining federal lands were sufficiently arid to require major revision of the land laws. There was insufficient scientific evidence to support Powell's claim about the region's weather and the implications for farm size and appropriate agricultural products and practices. The strong political sentiment for maintaining the Homestead Act and its emphasis on the formation of small farms was illustrated by the statement of Representative George W. Julian of Indiana: "If our institutions are to be preserved, we must insist upon the policy of small farms, thrifty villages, compact settlements, free schools, and equality of political rights, instead of large estates, slovenly agriculture, wide-scattered settlements, popular ignorance and a pampered aristocracy lording it over the people. This is the overshadowing question of American politics."[13]

In the congressional debates of 1879, representative Martin Maginnis of Montana asserted that under current settlement policies the West would be "one of the richest and greatest parts of the vast domain of the United States."[14] Representative Thomas Patterson of Colorado emphasized the desire of western representatives to have as much land as possible made available to as many claimants as possible: "[O]ur agricultural lands . . . are limited, and the number of our population following agricultural pursuits must also be limited. But to have that number as great as possible, to swell it to its maximum, the 160-acre homestead must not be exceeded." [15]

Prior to the arrival of homesteaders, many parts of the Great Plains had been occupied by individuals who assembled ranches of a thousand acres or more. Under the federal land laws, however, ranchers could not obtain title to units of that size. They were restricted to plots of 160 acres, which, given the semiarid nature of the region, was too little for livestock raising when twenty-five acres or more were needed to sustain one cow or five sheep for a year. Ranchers who settled the area ahead of homesteaders claimed as much as they legally could given the land laws, and then informally claimed larger tracts to support viable herd sizes. Their informal prior appropriation claims were recognized by local livestock associations, which also organized joint herd management and recorded livestock brands (Dennen 1976).

The livestock associations were similar to the local mining camps, and their rules played a similar role in defining and enforcing property rights. But unlike miners and their mining camps, ranchers and livestock associations soon were to face competition from homesteaders. Because they appeared to lock up large amounts of land at a time when a clear understanding of the agricultural potential of the Great Plains was limited, livestock associations lacked consistent and broad-based political support in the territories and states in which they were located and in Congress.

Accordingly, after 1880, when conflicts between ranchers and homesteaders increased, homesteaders had the law on their side. One homesteader complained: "I took up 160 acres of government land. . . . It happened to be in a Big Cattle outfit's meadow, and when I went to do my Improvements as required by the laws of the United States of America, this same Cattle outfit shut and locked the gates and forbid me to come on my Homestead" (Libecap 1981b, 32). In response to complaints by homesteaders, the federal government removed many of the fences placed by ranchers to control access to pastures. As a result, overgrazing may have increased on the opened range. In any event, many of the large ranches were broken up as homesteaders arrived. [16]

Had the land laws been different, large farming units closer to the sizes already in existence and to the size of those advocated by Powell, with mixed ranching and grain crops, might have characterized the region.

But as it was, homesteading brought a decline in average farm size when new settlers claimed and subdivided occupied federal land. For example, in 1904 Fergus County, Montana, prior to major homestead migration to the northern plains, had 472 farms or ranches with an average size of 1,300 acres. By 1916, during the last major homestead migration in the country, the number of farms had grown more than eightfold to 3,843, and average farm size had fallen to 322 acres, a decline of 75 percent.[17]

Indeed, homestead settlement led to the proliferation of small farms throughout the Great Plains. Between 1880 and 1925 in western Kansas, Nebraska, the Dakotas, and eastern Colorado and Montana, 1,078,123 original homestead entries were filed, laying claim to 202,298,425 acres.[18] Unfortunately, this small-farm settlement occurred when there was little understanding of the region's weather or requirements for agriculture. An analysis of the problem caused by lack of weather information for the Great Plains in the late nineteenth and early twentieth centuries reveals the rise of folk theories to explain the weather, such as the saying "rain follows the plow," and to pseudoscientific prescriptions for farming practices such as "dryfarming doctrine."[19] The former held that precipitation would increase with settlement and cultivation. The latter held that even if drought occurred, its effects could be overcome by the use of specified tillage methods. Hence, in either case, there was no cause for alarm.

The notions that rainfall would increase with settlement and that drought could be defeated with diligent and proper cultivation of the soil fit nicely with the optimism and sense of manifest destiny that were associated with the western frontier. The taming of the wild prairies would lead not only to the establishment of small farms for the "home seeker" but also to the benevolent transformation of the climate or to its mastery. Ultimately, land that previously had been "the natural habitat of cactus" would be transformed into a breadbasket (Libecap and Hansen 2002). These beliefs in the evolutionary march of progress across a resisting landscape were part of the Progressive Era. They also were politically popular because they supported the formation of large numbers of homesteads at the expense of a few large ranches.

By the time severe drought made the vulnerability of small homesteads painfully clear (in 1893–94 in Kansas and the central plains and in 1917–21 in eastern Montana and the northern plains), the Great Plains were populated by hundreds of thousands of small farmers, who were persuaded to migrate by a generous federal land policy and unusually wet conditions. When rainfall was at or above the mean, yields

were plentiful and the predictions of the region's most optimistic proponents seemed to be verified, while those of naysayers such as Powell
were shown to be unduly pessimistic. Unfortunately, the farming units
prescribed by land policy were subsequently revealed to be unsustain-
able when drought returned. Limited and variable rainfall was to be
the critical factor in agricultural success, and drought was to take a toll.
The droughts in Kansas and Montana caused farm yields and incomes
to collapse. Small wheat-growing homesteads were deserted and the
population moved away, leaving the skeletons of abandoned dreams of
agricultural prosperity.

Between 1890 and 1900 the number of farms fell by 37 percent and the
population by 27 percent in the twenty-four counties of western Kansas,
and average farm size doubled from 221 acres to 468 acres, rising to
504 acres by 1920. In eastern Montana, perhaps 60,000 of the 191,965
original homestead claims filed between 1900 and 1920 were abandoned
(Libecap and Hansen 2002). "Homestead busts" on this scale were unusual in the American frontier experience, and they have dominated the
historiography of the Great Plains. Had there been greater understanding of the region's climate, Congress might have been more cautious
about the kinds of farmers and farms that the land laws encouraged.
Initial farm sizes might have been closer to those advocated by Powell.

Because federal land policy encouraged the formation of homesteads
that subsequently were to fail, the population of *two-thirds* of the counties in the Great Plains peaked in 1930 or earlier.[20] And in the Dakotas,
Nebraska, and Oklahoma the figures are more dramatic, with approximately *80 percent* of the counties peaking in population in 1930 or
before. But these populations could not be sustained. The decline in
population that occurred throughout the region, with its legacy of deserted homesteads and empty town sites, is testimony to land policies
that brought far too many farmers and small farms to the Great Plains.

Where Land Policy Failed: Western Timberlands

Efforts to secure property rights to federal lands in plots larger than
160 acres in the Great Plains were not successful. Further, although nonagricultural claims for mineral lands ultimately were ratified by the federal government, this was not the case for western timberlands. By the
time settlement reached the Pacific Northwest and the northern Rockies in the late 1870s, the federal government was in a better position to
enforce its holdings than had been the case in the mining camps of California in 1848. Moreover, by that time the dispute between ranchers

and homesteaders about large land claims had solidified political positions against major liberalization of the land laws.

Accordingly, except for lands that were part of railroad grants, there were no provisions in the land laws for commercial timber claims in the Pacific Northwest. Ownership of 160-acre plots of timberland could be obtained only by bona fide settlers for domestic use under the Preemption Act, the Homestead Act, and the Timber and Stone Act.

These restrictions, however, posed important problems for the development of commercial lumbering in the rich virgin forests of the West. The lands generally were n ot suited for agriculture, but the timber stands could provide lumber for the booming cities of San Francisco and Denver, as well as for the Great Plains, where trees of any kind were scarce.

At the same time, many logging operations were becoming highly capital-intensive, requiring spur railroad lines and other equipment for the transport of logs. There were economies of scale in cruising timber for the best stands and in harvesting. Efficient lumber operations, therefore, required both secure property rights to support investment and large amounts of timberland for production. But neither was easily possible under the land laws.

Timber claimants responded by illegally and rapidly harvesting federal timberlands. Given the remoteness of the region, federal timberlands were vulnerable to speedy, clandestine cutting. The overall magnitude likely was small because of the lack of incentive for lumber companies to invest sufficiently in access. Nevertheless, the Commissioner of the General Land Office annually charged that trespassers were denuding the federal timberlands of the West. The commissioner labeled the areas as "a common property which is preyed upon."[21] Although the 1879 report of the Public Lands Commission called for the classification and sale of western lands according to their best use, nothing was done to act on this recommendation.

Claimants also resorted to fraud to circumvent the restrictions of the land laws. The principal way for lumber companies to obtain title to federal timberland was by hiring entrymen to stake fake claims for farmland under the Pre-emption, Homestead, and Timber and Stone Acts. Entrymen were recruited by agents for the timber companies to travel to the Pacific Northwest. Some were sailors enticed from their ships.

Each entryman could obtain provisional title from the federal government to 160 acres of land after agricultural use and improvement (not required for Timber and Stone Act claims) for six months if using the commutation provision of the Homestead Act or for one month if using the Pre-emption Act. Claimants had to pay $1.25 per acre for lands claimed under the commutation provision of the Homestead Act and the Pre-emption Law and $2.50 per acre for Timber and Stone Act claims. The three laws required each entryman to swear that he "did not apply to purchase the same on speculation, but in good faith to appropriate it to his own exclusive use and benefit; and that he has not directly or indirectly, made any agreement or contract, with any person or persons whomsoever, by which title he might acquire from the Government . . . should inure" to others. Once the provisional title was received from the local federal land office, however, it was handed over to the timber company, and the entryman went on his way.[22] Later, full title would be sent from Washington, DC, and transferred to the company.

The historical literature has made much of the use of fraud to acquire federal lands, arguing that speculators, timber companies, and mining companies illegally claimed land that should have gone to actual settlers. The negative conclusion emphasizes the distributional implications: farmers were denied their rightful chance to secure a piece of the federal domain. This may have been the case in some areas, but many of the timberlands of concern in the Far West were not suitable for farming and would have been unlikely locations for founding successful new farms. The impact of federal land law, instead, was to raise the costs of obtaining secure property rights to land, thereby dissipating some of the value of the land in the use of costly fraud, delaying the process of assigning ownership, and limiting the overall extent of private ownership.

Fraud was costly because the hired entrymen had to act as if they were farmers, constructing makeshift cabins and in some cases actually occupying the land. Further, because the General Land Office, the federal agency charged with administering land policy, investigated fraud, title might not be obtained. All of this raised the transactions costs of titling. One calculation of the added costs involved between 1875 and 1903 in California, Oregon, and Washington indicates that that they were $670 per 160-acre Timber and Stone Act claim and $870 per Homestead Act or Pre-emption Act claim (Libecap and Johnson 1979). These costs represented about 78 percent of the value of the land. Overall, in the Pacific Northwest, the dissipation of rent due to the forced use of federal land laws designed for the ownership of farmland rather than timberland may have been as high as $17,000,000, or 60 percent of the value of the land involved.[23]

These wastes suggest the potential social gains from a revision of the land laws to allow for large nonagricultural claims, just as there would have been for larger agricultural claims in the semiarid Great Plains. But the political economy of land distribution was such that few advocated major change, and the land laws remained intact.

Conclusion

Property rights play a critical role in the formation and operation of a market economy. The successful development of private property rights to land in America provided the basis for the subsequent establishment of private ownership to other assets. Had land rights been retained by the federal government, America would have been fundamentally different.

Federal land law was the mechanism by which federal land was transferred to private owners. It worked well for agricultural land in the eastern United States but less well for agricultural land in the semiarid West and for nonagricultural timberlands. Private mineral rights developed effectively, primarily because the initial private mineral claims were made when the federal government had little ability to enforce its own claims. The mineral rights system that emerged followed the general patterns of small farm settlement—federal mineral lands were open for private claiming in relatively small plots.

The rigid adherence to a property rights allocation process that was designed to grant ownership to farmland in small plots raised the costs of obtaining private property rights to federal land that did not fit well with the one-size-fits-all policy. Accordingly, much federal land in the West was never claimed. In 1891 the General Revision Act began a gradual retention of ownership of land by the federal government. It repealed the two most liberal laws used to obtain private title to federal land, the Timber Culture Act and the Pre-emption Act, and authorized the establishment of the forest reserves that became the national forests. In 1934 the Taylor Grazing Act withdrew semiarid rangeland from private patenting, and in 1935 the Homestead Act was repealed.

In the end, one-third of the continental United States remained under the federal government's ownership. Sixty percent of the area of the thirteen far western states was never transferred to private owners (Libecap 1994, 266). This remaining federal estate exists despite the objectives of early U.S. land policy. It certainly would shock Thomas Jefferson and other supporters of a liberal land policy.

The mixed record of federal land policy regarding property rights reflects the political process of institutional change. Property rights are ultimately political institutions, and their nature depends on the influence of competing constituencies, information, legal and social precedents, the value of the assets involved, marking and enforcement costs, and the physical nature of the asset. As a result, property rights institutions vary in their effectiveness in promoting investment, production, and exchange, even in the American economy, which otherwise is noted for its support of private ownership.

Notes

1. For discussion of successful frontier experiences see Danhof 1969, Ferrie 1994, and Herscovici 1998.

2. Atack and Passell 1994, 249. The subsequent discussion draws from ibid. 249–70 and Gates 1979.

3. For discussion of U.S. land policies and the origins and administration of the Homestead Acts, see Gates 1979, 387–461, Hibbard 1965, and Robbins 1942.

4. Quoted in Hibbard 1965, 143.

5. For discussion of the safety-valve thesis, see Danhof 1969 and Shannon 1945.

6. *Congressional Globe,* 37th Cong., 2nd sess., May 7, 1862, p. 1915.

7. Act of May 20, 1862, ch. 75, 12 Stat. 392.

8. Act of February 19, 1909, 35 Stat. 693. The law was passed on February 19, 1909 in the 60th Congress, 2d session. In 1912 the residency requirement for the 1909 law was reduced to three years and the cultivation requirement was reduced to 160 acres. Analysis of the recorded vote suggests that representatives of northeastern states tended to vote against the change, perhaps fearing greater labor migration, whereas western representatives supported the small adjustment. For discussion, see Gates 1979, 504–7.

9. Another law, the Timber Culture Act, which granted 160 acres if settlers planted 40 acres with trees, was repealed in 1891. For discussion of the land laws, see Gates 1979, 399, 512–17.

10. These figures were compiled from the annual reports of the Commissioner of the General Land Office for the fiscal years 1863–80 (*Annual Report* 1863–1925). During this period homestead entries include those made under the Timber and Stone Act.

11. Powell's report, *Report on the Lands of the Arid Region,* 45th Cong., 2d sess., 1878, H. Rep. 73, was transmitted to the Commissioner of the General Land Office on April 1.

12. For discussion of the reaction to Powell's report, see Stegner 1953, 219–42. See Peffer (1951, 8–62, 135–68) regarding the political controversy over homestead farm size, the claims of ranchers, and efforts to adjust the federal land laws.

13. Quoted in Worster 2001, 375. See also statements by Julian in *Our Land Policy—Its Evils and Their Remedy,* House of Representatives, March 6, 1868, Washington D.C.: Office of the Great Republic.

14. *Congressional Record,* 45th Cong., 3d sess., 1879, pp. 1202–3.

15. Thomas Patterson, *Appendix to the Congressional Record,* 1879, 45th Cong., 3d sess., p. 221. See Maginnis's warning concerning monopoly and large estates like those of the Spanish land grants, ibid., p. 1201.

16. For discussion, see Libecap 1981a, 1981b; Dennon 1976.

17. Hansen and Libecap 2004b. See Peffer (1951, 8–62, 135–68) regarding the political controversy over homestead farm size, the claims of ranchers, and efforts to adjust the federal land laws.

18. *Annual Report* 1863–1925. The calculations, from the reports for 1880–1925, are for state totals.

19. Libecap and Hansen 2002. Worster (2001, 358–63) claims that congressional inaction resulted from a lack of desire on the part of the politicians to consider the scientific evidence concerning the region. Libecap and Hansen (2002) argue that the science was too inconclusive to support politically controversial changes in federal land distribution.

20. Hansen and Libecap 2004b. Some of the environmental costs are described in Hansen and Libecap 2004a.

21. Quoted in Libecap 1989, 54. This discussion is drawn from Libecap and Johnson 1979.

22. Copp 1883, quoted in Libecap 1989, 55.

23. See Libecap 1989, 57–59.

References

Annual Report of the Commissioner of the General Land Office to the Secretary of the Interior. 1863–1925. Washington, DC: Government Printing Office.

Atack, Jeremy, and Peter Passell. 1994. *A New Economic View of American History.* 2d ed. New York: Norton.

Cheung, Stephen N. S. 1970. "The Structure of a Contract and the Theory of a Non-Exclusive Resource." *Journal of Law and Economics* 13.1 (April): 49–70.

Clay, Karen, and Gavin Wright. 2005. "Order without Law? Property Rights during the California Gold Rush." *Explorations in Economic History* 42.2 (April): 155–83.

Copp, H. N. 1883. *Public Land Laws.* Washington, DC: Government Printing Office.

Danhof, Clarence. 1969. *Change in Agriculture: The Northern United States, 1820–1870.* Cambridge: Harvard University Press.

Demsetz, Harold. 1967. "Towards a Theory of Property Rights." *American Economic Review* 57.2 (May): 347–59.

Dennon, R. Taylor. 1976. "Cattlemen's Associations and Property Rights in Land in the American West." *Explorations in Economic History* 13.4 (November): 423–36.

Ferrie, Joseph P. 1994. "The Wealth Accumulation of Antebellum European Immigrants to the U.S., 1840–60." *Journal of Economic History* 54.1 (March): 1–33.

Gates, Paul W. 1979. *History of Public Land Law Development.* New York: Arno.

Gordon, H. Scott. 1954. "The Economic Theory of a Common Property Resource: The Fishery." *Journal of Political Economy* 62.2 (April): 124–42.

Hallagan, William S. 1978. "Share Contracting for California Gold." *Explorations in Economic History* 15.2 (April): 196–210.

Hansen, Zeynep K., and Gary D. Libecap. 2004a. "The Allocation of Property Rights to Land: U.S. Land Policy and Farm Failure in the Northern Great Plains." *Explorations in Economic History* 41.2 (April): 103–29.

———. 2004b. "Small Farms, Externalities, and the Dust Bowl of the 1930s." *Journal of Political Economy* 112.3 (June): 665–94.

Hardin, Garrett. 1968. "The Tragedy of the Commons." *Science* 162:1243–48.

Herscovici, Steven. 1998. "Migration and Economic Mobility: Wealth Accumulation and Occupational Change Among Antebellum Migrants and Persisters." *Journal of Economic History* 58.4 (December): 927–56.

Hibbard, Benjamin H. 1965. *History of Public Land Policies.* 1924; repr., New York: Macmillan.

Johnson, Ronald N., and Gary D. Libecap. 1980. "Efficient Markets and Great Lakes Timber: A Conservation Issue Reexamined." *Explorations in Economic History* 17.4 (October): 372–85.

Libecap, Gary D. 1978. "Economic Variables and the Development of the Law: The Case of Western Mineral Rights." *Journal of Economic History* 38.2 (June): 338–62.

———. 1979. "Government Support of Private Claims to Public Minerals: Western Mineral Rights." *Business History Review* 53.3 (Autumn): 364–85.

———. 1981a. "Bureaucratic Opposition to the Assignment of Property Rights: Overgrazing on the Western Range." *Journal of Economic History* 41.1 (March): 151–58.

———. 1981b. *Locking up the Range: Federal Land Use Controls and Grazing.* Cambridge, U.K.: Ballinger.

———. 1986. "Property Rights in Economic History: Implications for Research." *Explorations in Economic History* 23.3 (July): 227–52.

———. 1989. *Contracting for Property Rights.* New York: Cambridge University Press.

———. 1994. "The Political Economy of Institutional Change: Property Rights and the General Revision Act of 1891." In *Capitalism in Context,* ed. John James and Mark Thomas, 265–78. Chicago: University of Chicago Press.

Libecap, Gary D., and Zeynep K. Hansen. 2002. " 'Rain Follows the Plow' and Dryfarming Doctrine: The Climate Information Problem and Homestead Failure in the Upper Great Plains, 1890–1925." *Journal of Economic History* 62.1 (March): 86–120.

Libecap, Gary D., and Ronald N. Johnson. 1979. "Property Rights, Nineteenth-Century Federal Timber Policy, and the Conservation Movement." *Journal of Economic History* 39.1 (March): 129–42.

McCurdy, C. W. 1976. "Stephen J. Field and Public Land Law Development in California, 1850–1866: A Case Study of Judicial Resource Allocation in Nineteenth Century America." *Law and Society Review* 10.2 (Winter): 235–66.

Peffer, E. Louise. 1951. *The Closing of the Public Domain: Disposal and Reservation Policies.* Stanford: Stanford University Press.

Powell, John Wesley. 1878. *Report on the Lands of the Arid Region of the United States,* 45th Cong., 2nd sess., Executive Document no. 73. Washington D.C.: Government Printing Office.

Rabin, Jonathan. 1997. *Bad Land: An American Romance.* New York: Vintage.

Robbins, Roy M. 1942. *Our Landed Heritage: The Public Domain, 1776–1936.* Princeton: Princeton University Press.

Shannon, Fred A. 1945. "A Post Mortem on the Labor-Safety-Valve Theory." *Agricultural History* 19 (January): 31–38.

Stegner, Wallace. 1953. *Beyond the 100th Meridian: John Wesley Powell and the Second Opening of the West.* Boston: Houghton Mifflin.

Umbeck, John. 1977a. "The California Gold Rush: A Study of Emerging Property Rights." *Explorations in Economic History* 14.3 (July): 197–226.

———. 1977b. "A Theory of Contract Choice and the California Gold Rush." *Journal of Law and Economics* 20.2 (October): 421–37.

Webb, Walter Prescott. 1931. *The Great Plains.* Boston: Ginn.

Worster, Donald. 2001. *A River Running West: The Life of John Wesley Powell.* New York: Oxford University Press.

Zerbe, Richard O., and C. Leigh Anderson. 2001. "Culture and Fairness in the Development of Institutions in the California Gold Fields." *Journal of Economic History* 61.1 (March): 114–43.

5

Reversing Financial Reversals: *Government and the Financial System since 1789*

MOST INFORMED observers today would agree that the United States has just about the best financial system in the world. Its problems are newsworthy mostly because they arise in a context of a well-functioning financial order, not one that is disorderly. The federal government easily collects tax revenues to cover most of its expenditures, and it manages a huge national debt of $8 trillion. Agencies of the government hold about half of that debt. Of the remainder that is in the hands of the public, foreign investors own about half. On smaller scales, state and local governments do the same. The U.S. dollar remains the world's preeminent currency. Some countries tie their currencies to it. Others adopt the dollar as their own currency.

The U.S. banking system is dynamic and efficient. The central bank, with branches around the country and international ties, is virtually the world's central bank. The United States has the world's largest and arguably most innovative securities markets. Its corporations are world leaders in many industries. All of these institutions, instruments, and markets are networked in a financial system that is the envy of the world.

Remarkably, informed observers two centuries ago could well have had similar sentiments. Only the United Provinces of the Netherlands (the Dutch Republic) and Great Britain had developed comparable articulated financial systems by the beginning of the nineteenth century. The Dutch were the leaders. At the beginning of the seventeenth century, they used financial and commercial innovations to propel their little republic toward independence from Spain, great-power status in the world, and the "embarrassment of riches" that characterized the seventeenth-century Dutch golden age. After the Glorious Revolution of 1688 Great Britain adopted and extended Dutch financial innovations, which played a large role in Britain's rise to political and economic eminence in the eighteenth century. A century later, the United States, after gaining independence, began quickly to follow the Dutch-British pattern leading from financial development to economic and political power.[1]

The United States circa 1800 was a small player on a world economic and political scene dominated by large European powers. The nation's public finances and debt management were orderly. The dollar was linked to gold and silver, which made it stable in terms of other currencies similarly linked. The U.S. banking system was rapidly developing in innovative corporate ways with limited liability that would later be copied by the banking systems of the world. Securities markets actively functioned in several U.S. cities. They were linked with one another and with those in Europe by the communications technologies of that era. In the first years of the nineteenth century, European investors owned more than half of the securities issued by the U.S. government and about half of all American securities, public and private. States were busily chartering nonbank financial corporations such as insurance companies, as well as nonfinancial corporations in far greater numbers than in other countries. As they did in banking, these countries would later emulate U.S. practices by creating numerous limited-liability business corporations. The Bank of the United States (BUS), a central bank with branches around the country, connected the elements of a rapidly developing financial system—the public finances, the dollar, the banks, the securities markets, the corporations, and other enterprises—into one all-encompassing financial network, which it, along with the U.S. Treasury, oversaw.[2]

Because all this financial development was happening in a nation where most people were farmers of one sort or another, and because few Americans realized how advanced their modern financial system was in comparison with those in most other countries, it was easy to miss the significance of it. But the modern sector of the U.S. economy—we can lump into it finance, foreign and domestic commerce, manufacturing, transportation, and professional services—small as it was in the vast farmer's field that was the early United States, began to grow very rapidly from the 1790s onward. By 1840, the U.S. economy in the aggregate already had reached the level of modern economic growth (sustained increases in per capita income averaging about 1.6 percent per year) that has persisted ever since.[3]

We can think of this process of becoming modern as one in which an initially small modern sector began to grow quite rapidly compared to growth in the farmer's field. From the 1790s to the 1840s the modern sector became a much larger part of the economy, and growth proceeded from then on at modern rates. If we had annual GDP data for the early decades as reliable as what we have for later periods, GDP per capita would likely show a gradual acceleration in those decades. Less-than-comprehensive estimates for these early decades already point in that direction. But the real story of modernization is what made the modern sector start and continue to grow rapidly. In the U.S. case, arguably it was the modern financial system. It was the main new economic institution of the 1790s, and that is when the modern sector began to grow at high rates.[4] That system, moreover, was to a great extent created and sustained by government actions.

In this chapter I trace the development of the U.S. financial system over the course of two centuries in terms of the political economy of its interactions with government. I emphasize the early period because it is less thoroughly studied than later periods. Understanding the early period is important for showing that progress in finance, even in the United States, should not be taken for granted. The U.S. story is not one of uniform progress. Between the state-of-the-art financial system of two centuries ago and the state-of-the-art system of today there were reversals, as the recent work of Rajan and Zingales shows with regard to national financial systems of the twentieth century. In reversals, which often result from responses to economic and financial crises, such a system gets worse than it was in key ways. But according to Rajan and Zingales, such reversals can work to the advantage of "incumbents," that is, established firms in finance, as competition is stifled. Politicians and governments, sometimes but not always well intentioned, often contributed to these reversals.[5]

Historical experience and economic analyses of the effects of asymmetric information on market outcomes would appear to argue that government has a duty to oversee and regulate a financial system. Financial regulation is essentially due diligence toward institutions that government did much to create and on which governments as well as businesses and individuals depend. But the exercise of due diligence can be overdone, just as it can be underdone. In either case, financial reversals can occur. Due diligence could be well intentioned, but it can backfire, creating new problems or making old ones worse rather than better. For example, governments may sponsor deposit insurance programs to make bank depositors more secure. But the existence of such insurance could prompt bankers to take greater risks in pursuing profits, while making it less likely that depositors will care much about the risks bankers are taking. If the bankers' risky bets pay off, they and bank owners benefit. If the bets go bad, government insurance funds and taxpayers may have to absorb losses.

When governments engineer financial reversals to benefit particular constituencies, such as the incumbents of Rajan and Zingales, they are responding to rent seeking. *Rent seeking* refers to attempts by some economic interests to use the power of government to gain economic advantages not available to others. Unfortunately, due diligence and rent seeking in financial regulation are not always easy to disentangle. The latter will invariably be described as the former, especially by those seeking rents.

Fortunately, most financial reversals in U.S. history later were reversed. At the start of the twenty-first century, the U.S. financial system is in the best shape it has been in for about two centuries. So for now the story related here has a happy ending. Whether future financial crises will lead to constructive reforms or to reversals is, however, not easy to predict from experience.

Creating a Modern Financial System, 1789–1833

Because government essentially created the financial sector as we know it in U.S. history, we should not be surprised that from first to last government continued to use and sometimes abuse its creation through its demands on it and its regulation of it. By way of contrast, no one would seriously contend that government created the agricultural, commercial, manufacturing, transportation, and service sectors of the economy. Other agents did that. Government became involved in various ways with all of these sectors, but it did not create them.

Why did government create the financial system? Governments are instituted to serve purposes, and most of those purposes cost money. There is a never-ending debate about what the range of the purposes is and what it should be. But even a limited-government thinker such as Adam Smith argued that the purposes of government included defense, justice, certain public works, and maybe education. Smith, moreover, devoted more than a quarter of book 5 of his influential 1776 work *The Wealth of Nations* to the items that warranted governmental expenditures and to the ways in which they might be financed.

As is often remarked, in the year Smith's work appeared, the American colonists declared their independence from his government in Great Britain. Because the British government deemed this a treasonous act, it sent large naval and land forces to put down the rebellion of the self-styled United States of America. For the American rebels of the thirteen former colonies and their Continental Congress, that created a need for defense, Smith's first purpose of government. Defense, like other governmental activities, had to be financed.

History seems to have come up with only three or four ways of financing government. The three major ways are taxing, borrowing, and printing money. The fourth might be asset sales or income from assets. But that merely raises the question of how a government came to own the assets. The answer likely would involve one of the three major methods of finance. If the assets are confiscated, we might regard that as a form of taxation. One could well regard the lands that various Euro-American governments came to own, for example, as obtained by means of taxing them away from Native Americans. And the first three methods might be reduced to one: taxing. For borrowing incurs an obligation to repay, and if a governmental debt is to be reduced or eliminated, it can only be done by taxation in the future. And paper money printed by governments is not much more than a type of government debt, so if it also has to be redeemed, as some say it should be, that would involve taxation. One form of such taxation might be the "inflation tax" that makes prices higher than they would be had no money been printed.

The rebellious Americans of 1776 were to try all three of the major ways of financing their defense. Mostly they did it by borrowing and by printing money. They did not like taxation without representation—one of their gripes against the mother country—or even taxation with representation in their own state and local governments. Moreover, their tax systems were not up to financing much of their revolutionary venture. So they borrowed by means of voluntary and forced loans. And they printed paper money to such excess that there was a large inflation tax that made the paper worthless.[6]

Luckily, with no small help from the French, who wanted to reduce the power and colonial territory of their British rival, it worked. The American rebels prevailed. The British state, divided at home about the war, isolated internationally, embarrassed by battles lost in America, and financially overburdened, decided to negotiate a treaty of peace recognizing U.S. independence in 1783.

It was a very dicey outcome for Americans, but some of them had learned a lot about finance, politics, war, and government during the war. The one who seemed to have learned the most, at least about finance, was a young Continental Army officer, Alexander Hamilton. While in the army from 1776 to 1781 Hamilton absorbed key lessons of financial history, called on national leaders to apply them, and in his mind began to shape plans for a new and modern financial system. There is ample evidence of all three of these points in a long letter Hamilton wrote to Robert Morris, Congress's newly appointed Superintendent of Finance, in April 1781, in which he said, " 'Tis by introducing order into our finances—by restoreing [sic] public credit—not by gaining battles, that we are finally to gain our object." A decade later Hamilton would have his financial plans refined, and as the nation's first Secretary of the Treasury, he would be given the authority to implement them.[7]

In 1783 the national government of the newly independent Americans had large domestic and foreign debts. Without taxing powers granted under the Articles of Confederation, the charter of government adopted by Congress in 1777 and ratified by the states in 1781, the national government had no revenue of its own, and hence no means of paying its debts or the interest on them. All it could do was ask the states for contributions. But the states had debts of their own incurred in the war, so they did not contribute much to the national treasury. For some, state debts were so large that they also were not serviced. The unserviced debts were essentially junk bonds in default, valued in scattered exchanges at small percentages of face value in the hope that they might one day be paid.

States at least could levy taxes to service their debts. But it was a risky business if taxes became onerous, as Massachusetts found out when some of its taxpayers, led by Daniel Shays, launched an armed rebellion in 1786. At the other extreme, Rhode Island discharged its debts by printing paper money (which rapidly depreciated) and forcing it on state creditors. Money consisted of state paper issues and specie (gold and silver, plate, and foreign coins), with the former depreciating in value relative to the latter. Apart from specie, there was no national money or monetary base. There was one small bank, the Bank of North America, which had opened in Philadelphia in 1782. There were few corporations of any kind. Financially, it was a pretty grim situation.[8]

In the most dramatic response to these problems, the Americans of the 1780s reinvented their government by writing and adopting a new plan of national government. Hamilton and other nationalists, who soon would call themselves Federalists, were at the forefront of the movement for the Constitution drafted at Philadelphia in 1787 and adopted by the requisite number of states the following year. Hamilton became the finance minister of the new federal government in 1789, when President Washington appointed him to lead the Treasury Department. The new government had taxing and monetary powers. The latter included the power to define what U.S. money would be and regulate its value.

Hamilton and his supporters in Congress used these powers right away to launch a modern financial system.[9]

The first pillar of the new system, enacted in 1789, consisted of a national tariff on imports and duties on ship tonnage to provide revenue for the new government. Because the purpose was revenue, not protection, tariff and duty rates were modest. Soon these taxes on international trade were supplemented by domestic excise taxes. Nonetheless, the federal revenue system had to be built from scratch, forcing Hamilton to rely extensively on loans from domestic banks and foreign lenders to fund the government and his reform program while federal revenues gradually grew during his term, from 1789 to 1795.

The second pillar, put in place in 1790, was a restructured and funded national debt. Domestic national and state debts incurred during the War of Independence and represented mostly by a variety of securities in default and some near-worthless paper currency were exchanged for three new issues that would pay interest in hard money or its equivalent (that is, convertible banknotes). Par value of the new domestic debt amounted to about $64 million. The debt was termed "funded" because the government's tax revenues were pledged first to pay interest on the debt. Hamilton and his allies also established a sinking fund, ostensibly to retire the debt down the road but in reality to allow him to practice what today would be called open market operations to promote financial stability. Other provisions were made for servicing the country's foreign debt, which Hamilton managed in Europe through contacts with Dutch bankers.[10]

The third pillar of Hamilton's system was the Bank of the United States, approved by Congress and launched in 1791. It was a national bank with branches in leading U.S. cities and something of a central bank, although the concept was new then. As the government's fiscal agent, the BUS received federal revenues as deposits and made government payments, sometimes with the assistance of other banks in a formative U.S. banking system. The government owned 20 percent of BUS stock, financing it with a loan from the bank, the first of many loans the bank would make to the government. The other 80 percent of the stock was subscribed for by private investors, who could pay for three-fourths of it by tendering the new national debt securities, the main issue of which quickly rose to par value in newly active securities markets. The bank was capitalized at $10 million (25,000 shares of $400 par value each), an amount several times the combined capitals of the three or four other banks in existence in 1791.[11]

The fourth pillar was the new U.S. dollar, defined in terms of weights of gold and silver in Hamilton's 1791 report on the establishment of a mint the recommendations of which Congress adopted. Essentially, this pillar defined the monetary unit of account and established the monetary base of the country. It would give the United States a monetary system like those of other leading trading nations, replacing the fiat paper systems that had been used and sometimes abused by the colonies, by Congress and states during the Revolution, and by states during the 1780s. Hamilton envisioned that most Americans would use as money not gold and silver coins but rather notes and deposits of the BUS and other banks. They would do this because the bank obligations were to be convertible into the gold and silver base at the defined dollar rates and were more convenient to use than coins in making many payments. He also envisioned that securities such as the national debt issues and BUS stock would serve as near moneys since they could be used as collateral for bank loans or easily liquidated in securities markets.[12]

The markets? The other banks? Where did they come from? Hardly any existed before 1789. As Treasury Secretary, Hamilton could exert direct influence on issues such as public finance (including national debt restructuring and management), the BUS, and the choice of a monetary base. Part of Hamilton's financial genius was to formulate and execute key elements of a plan that would induce others to complete it. Consider first the securities markets. When the huge volume of new federal debt securities and equity shares of the Bank of the United States were issued in 1790 and 1791, people began immediately to trade them in the streets. The frenzied birth of the U.S. securities culture created a host of problems best solved by organizational change. So traders and brokers in New York and Philadelphia began to form securities-trading clubs that evolved into stock exchanges. Boston also had a thriving securities market in the early 1790s. Other cities, starting with Baltimore around 1800, eventually would follow these leads. The New York Stock Exchange, today far and away the world's largest as measured by the market capitalization of its listed securities, began, according to legend, under a buttonwood (sycamore) tree in Wall Street, as just such a broker's club with a few rules in May 1792.[13]

Consider next the banks. There were but two banking corporations, one in Philadelphia and one in Boston, and one joint-stock bank, the Bank of New York, in the United States when Hamilton introduced his proposal for the BUS in December 1790. When it was enacted in February 1791, the New York state legislature almost immediately granted a charter to the Bank of New York, something it had refused to do several times since its founding (by Hamilton and others) in 1784. Why the change of heart? The charter of the Bank of the United States allowed it to establish branches where it pleased, and one likely site would be New York City. If the state did not have a bank there that it had chartered itself, it would be ceding the business of banking to the controversial new national government or perhaps to other states. The New York legislator James Kent said as much at the time: "It is as requisite to have a state bank to control the influence of a national bank as for a state government to control the influence of a general government. . . . Besides, our money will be carried to a great degree to Philadelphia, a rival city, unless we incorporate our bank." So the legislature acted to ensure that the New York state government would have a bank that was beholden to it.[14]

With variations, the same bank-chartering story played out in other states. Rhode Island, for example, chartered a bank in Providence because merchants there hoped (vainly, it turned out) that having a bank would induce the BUS to open a branch there and extend the available banking facilities. But Hamilton encouraged formation of the Providence Bank and others by directing collectors of customs to deposit moneys collected in such state banks. By 1795 the United States had twenty state-chartered banks and five branches of the BUS where there had been no banks before 1782 and only three in 1790. The half-decade 1791–95 marks the emergence of a U.S. banking system as well as a central bank. From that start the network of banks grew and grew. Today there are about seventy thousand banks and branches.[15]

The financial revolution of Hamilton and his Federalist allies was complete by the time he left office in 1795. It resulted in strong federal finances and debt management, a stable dollar currency convertible into a hard-money base, a banking system, a central bank, securities markets, and proliferating corporations, financial and nonfinancial, chartered by U.S. states. This was a giant leap toward economic modernity for the United States. Nothing quite as well planned and well executed had taken place elsewhere. The Netherlands, Great Britain, and the United States were perhaps the only three countries with modern financial systems as they entered the nineteenth century. It is likely not a coincidence that the three successively have been the world economic leaders of the past four centuries.

One particularly dramatic consequence of the financial revolution came in 1803. In perhaps the single largest international financial transaction in world history up to that year, the United States doubled its size with the Louisiana Purchase. It paid the $15 million price to Bonaparte's France by issuing $11.25 million worth of new dollar-denominated 6 percent bonds redeemable after fifteen years and by assuming $3.75 million worth of French obligations to U.S. citizens resulting from French depredations on American shipping during the Quasi War of 1798–1800. The Louisiana Purchase bonds were shipped to Europe, where Dutch and English bankers placed the bonds with European investors, paying the proceeds (after deducting their charges) to Bonaparte's government. Such was the international credit and credibility of the United States in 1803. Fifteen years earlier the transaction would have been unthinkable. There is some irony, given the political rivalry between Thomas Jefferson and Alexander Hamilton, that the greatest achievement of Jefferson's presidency relied on the financial system constructed in great part by Hamilton.

The effects of the U.S. financial revolution in accelerating the growth of modern sectors of the economy were immediate. From 1790 to a peak in 1802, industrial production (the new Davis index, with 1790 as the initial year) grew at 5.4 percent per year, well in excess of the rate of population growth. The rate is slightly higher than the 5.3 percent rate of growth from the peak of 1815 to that of 1833, when the country was industrializing rapidly. From 1790 to 1913, the rate of growth was 5.0 percent per year. From 1860 to 1913, when the United States became the industrial leader, the rate was 4.8 percent. The new evidence indicates that high growth in *the modern sector* of the U.S. economy—the sector most actively served by the new financial system—was there from the start. In the Davis index, industrial production expands at 7.4 percent per year from 1790 to a peak in 1796. A comparable annual GDP series for the period 1790–1840 that showed a gradual acceleration of the growth rate (as likely it would) would result not from all sectors' gradually accelerating their growth but from high-growth modern sectors such as manufacturing and commerce's becoming an ever-larger proportion of the U.S. economy.[16]

An Early Reversal and Correction, 1801–1832

Clever politicians styling themselves Republicans outmaneuvered the Federalists in the elections of 1800, making one of them, Thomas Jefferson, president in 1801. Jefferson, owner of many slaves, in part owed his election to the Electoral College, which provided electoral weight for the southern states' large slave population even though slaves could note vote. He and his followers let it appear to contemporaries and later historians as a victory for democracy and the common man, an effective political strategy. James Madison, who also owned slaves, became Secretary of State. He would succeed Jefferson as president in 1809. Together, Madison and Jefferson had attacked the new financial system from its inception in 1790, perhaps, as some have argued, because it built up the federal government's powers more than those of the states, or perhaps, as others have argued, because a strong federal government might circumscribe or end slavery. The two arguments are related, and Jefferson and Madison were right about them. A strong federal government did end slavery decades later. Another interpretation is that the Jeffersonian Republicans detested British institutions, which they deemed corrupt, and therefore to them Hamilton's financial system seemed too British. If so, it seems they did not appreciate that the new U.S. Constitution had created safeguards against corruption and restraints on governmental action that were not present in Great Britain at that time.[17]

In control of the U.S. government after 1801, the Jeffersonian Republicans could do mischief to the financial system. They did. First they slashed domestic federal taxes, which brought in more than a million dollars in 1801 and next to nothing by 1811. Second, provoked by European powers' predations and their loathing of Great Britain, the main trading partner of the United States, they enacted a trade embargo in 1808. That action cut customs revenues by more than half. Third, they allowed the twenty-year charter of the Bank of the United States to expire without renewal in 1811. Fourth, having enfeebled the country's finances, they declared war on Great Britain in 1812.

The war did not go well. The United States was embarrassed militarily and financially. The British shelled Baltimore and burned government buildings in Washington, including the White House, after President Madison had fled. Inflation rose, and convertibility of bank money to the monetary base was suspended everywhere outside New England, where political leaders reacted to Republican economic policies by broaching the idea of secession from the United States. The war officially though inconclusively ended with a negotiated treaty of peace late in 1814. But the news of its end did not reach the United States soon enough to prevent the Battle of New Orleans in January 1815. There the American general Andrew Jackson and his army routed combined British land and naval forces. Jackson became a national hero. In less than fifteen years, his heroism would make him president. That would put Jackson in a position to do more damage to the financial system, which he did.

But that is getting ahead of the story. As might be guessed, the economy did not do as well under Republican financial and trade policies as it had done earlier and would do later. True, the trade boom that resulted from U.S. neutrality while Europe warred and that ended with the U.S. embargo of 1808 expanded customs revenues. That allowed the Jefferson administration to pay down the national debt. This policy was questioned at the time, for it returned capital to Europe, saving an interest cost of about 6 percent at a time when capital could earn substantially more than 6 percent in the United States. The Davis industrial production index shows growth at a rate of only 3.9 percent per year between the peaks of 1802 and 1815, substantially lower than the 5.4 percent annual rate of 1790–1802 and the 5.3 percent rate of 1815–33. The embargo and the less drastic "nonintercourse" policy that replaced it supposedly stimulated manufacturing in the United States by cutting off competing imports. Yet the growth rate from the peak of 1807 to that of 1815 is only 4.2 percent, not much more than a rate of 3.4 percent between the 1802 and the 1807 peaks. The new industrial production index thus casts doubt on long-held opinions that Jefferson's embargo and Madison's nonintercourse and war policies provided hothouse conditions for U.S. industrialization. Industrial output grew faster before and after those policies were in effect.

Chastened by what had happened to the country during the war, the Republicans made it an early order of business to undo the damage to the financial system. They raised tariffs in 1816, some to protective levels. In the same year, they reinstituted the Bank of the United States on an enlarged scale (capital of $35 million, or 350,000 shares of $100 par value each) and asked it to guide the country back to convertible money. Madison, a nationalist and co-author with Hamilton of *The Federalist* in the 1780s before becoming a Republican to build his political base in Virginia, signed the bill. Hamilton had gone to his grave in 1804 alarmed about the direction of national policy. Now the first financial reversal had been reversed. Although restoring the specie standard in the parts of the country where it had been suspended led to a financial panic in 1819, that was followed by renewed economic growth in what has been termed "the era of good feeling."

The states continued to charter banks and other corporations. In 1810 there were more than a hundred banks. By 1820 more than three hundred had been chartered, and by 1833, more than five hundred. To that number we can add the home office of the Bank of the United

States in Philadelphia and its twenty-five branches (the first BUS had a maximum of eight) in Baltimore; Boston; Buffalo; Burlington, Vermont; Charleston; Cincinnati; Fayetteville, North Carolina; Hartford; Lexington, Kentucky; Louisville; Mobile; Nashville; Natchez; New Orleans; New York; Norfolk; Pittsburgh; Portland, Maine; Portsmouth, New Hampshire; Providence; Richmond; St. Louis; Savannah; Utica, New York; and Washington, DC. Thus from the 1790s to the 1830s, when Andrew Jackson vetoed Congress's rechartering of the BUS, the United States effectively had nationwide branch banking, something it would not have again until the 1990s. By the early 1830s, this was the best and the fastest-growing banking system in the world, furnishing extensive credit and an efficient payments system to the world's fastest-growing economy.[18]

But it was far from a perfect system. At the state and the national levels, banking had become highly politicized. Bank charters conferred on their possessors virtually a right to print money and lend it out at interest, a profitable activity. And the politicians in the state legislatures conferred bank charters. We might expect, therefore, that they would demand something in return. They did. Sometimes it was a bonus payment into the state coffers. Sometimes it was a portion of shares of stock in a bank, so that bank dividends would accrue to a state. Or the legislature might order a bank, as a condition of receiving a charter, to spend money on public projects and purposes that otherwise the state might have to finance. The obligations imposed on banks seem in principle to be legitimate, if perhaps not always wise, forms of compensation for granting charters. The rents were there, and someone would get them. But charter granting also could become corrupt if the rent money went directly to the politicians or to their favored political supporters, as it often did, rather than to state coffers. Starting in the 1830s governments would seek to solve this problem by removing bank chartering from state legislatures and making it a routine administrative function by means of so-called free banking laws, discussed in more detail below.[19]

Banks and banking systems can be prone to instability, and when they are, they can destabilize an economy. On one hand, banks provide convenient forms of money—banknotes and checkable deposits—and they operate a payment system for the economy by creating and redeeming bank money. To redeem notes, banks must hold reserves of the base money, which consisted of gold and silver in this period. On the other hand, banks are profit-seeking enterprises, and profits go up as reserves go down by being lent out at interest. The tension of modern banking is in this potential conflict of two good things: stability and profit. A balance needs to be struck, and government regulation can sometimes help by reminding bankers of their double duty.

The United States had the best banking system in the world from the 1790s to the 1830s in large measure because the two Banks of the United States played a major role in the payments system and provided discipline for state banks. By receiving banknote and check payments to the government, the two federal banks became creditors of state banks. By redeeming state banknotes and checks for base-money reserves, the federal banks could discourage the state banks from running down reserves in favor of pursuing profits. They did this. As a consequence, by the early 1830s the U.S. public had so much confidence in banking stability that a tremendous volume of bank credit was maintained by a relatively low quantity of banking reserves. In what might seem a paradox—finance has many of these—banking discipline actually led to a greater scope for banking expansion. When holders of banknotes knew that they could promptly convert them to the specie base money, they were willing to hold them instead of redeeming them. Thus more banknotes could be issued, and money was also held in the form of bank checking deposits. Nonetheless, many state banks resented the discipline and thought they would be better off if there were no Bank of the United States. There would be less regulatory discipline, and the state banks might also obtain the federal government's deposits.[20]

Banking discipline by no means required a federal bank. The Suffolk Bank of Boston, a Massachusetts state bank, provided it by demanding that other New England banks keep reserves with it if they wanted their notes to be redeemed in Boston, the region's trade center, toward which banknotes flowed. If they did not, the Suffolk Bank would quickly present the notes it received at the other banks and drain them of their reserves. Most of them joined the Suffolk system, which operated from 1818 to the Civil War, and many resented having to do so. The Suffolk system thus disciplined New England's banks. As a result, from the 1830s to the 1860s New England had the best banking of any U.S. region, whereas the rest of the country retreated from disciplined banking.[21]

New York came up with another way of regulating and inspiring confidence in banks. Its Safety Fund Law of 1829 provided insurance for holders of banknotes and deposits. The Safety Fund charged banks to fund the insurance. But the law was poorly designed, and when too many Safety Fund banks failed in the early 1840s, the fund was bankrupted and collapsed. By that time, New York was already implementing another solution, free banking (discussed further below). The Safety Fund's failure foreshadowed the problems federal deposit insurance would have in the savings and loan crisis a century and a half later.[22]

The United States also continued to develop fine securities markets. Government seemingly kept securities-market regulation to a minimum. States would pass an occasional law, usually during a period of financial crisis, of which there were not many. If such laws went against market interests and customs, they were typically ignored. The securities markets practiced self-regulation. The formal stock exchanges, in particular, made and enforced their own rules and regulations to protect the interests of participants and the integrity of the markets. The conflicts that sometimes arose tended to be settled in the courts, indicating the importance of legal and judicial systems for modern financial systems. The courts, of course, were creations of government, so it can hardly be said that U.S. securities markets thrived because government took no interest in them.[23]

The early United States was far in advance of other countries in chartering business corporations. Proliferating numbers of corporations raised problems of corporate governance. Principal-agent problems—conflicts of interest between managers of companies and their stockholder-owners—tended to be handled by elaborate charter provisions, by the continuing monitoring of corporate affairs by stockholders, and by the discipline provided by securities markets. All in all, the banking, securities-market, and corporate sectors of the early U.S. financial system worked remarkably well, with much less formal regulation than later would be deemed necessary.[24]

The Great Reversal, 1832–1863

In 1816 the second Bank of the United States received a twenty-year charter from Congress. In 1832, an election year, politicians friendly to the BUS introduced a bill to renew the charter before they needed to. They were hoping to gain some political advantages over the president, Andrew Jackson, who was known to be unfriendly to the bank, before the elections. After Jackson's supporters in Congress investigated the bank and made a variety of charges (most having little validity) against it, both the House and the Senate passed the bill to renew the charter. Jackson vetoed it, and his veto could not be overridden. This was perhaps *the* great reversal of U.S. financial history.

Unlike the reversal of the early 1800s, the Jacksonian reversal was not corrected in five years. Instead, it unleashed a decade's worth of financial excess and revulsion, featuring panics, suspensions of bank money convertibility to base money, the debt defaults of eight U.S. states and the Territory of Florida, a deep depression, and the embarrassment of the United States and its governments in Europe. Also unlike the Jeffersonian reversal, which was exposed by the War of 1812 and then quickly corrected, all this occurred in a time of peace. After the 1830s reversal, financial course corrections, unfolding in steps, took the better part of a century.[25]

Why did the great reversal happen? The volumes written about it suggest two broad answers: political due diligence and rent seeking. Some contend that Jackson sincerely believed that the Bank of the United States was unconstitutional. Or that, as a large financial institution with a special relation to the federal government and owned by wealthy private investors, it was a threat to democracy and the common people of the country. Or that because some banks had failed, bank money of any kind was suspect. Or that banking was better left to the states to handle in whatever ways they would choose to handle it. Or that ownership of BUS stock by foreign investors posed a loyalty problem for the BUS, although its charter precluded foreign stockholders from voting their shares or having a voice in BUS management. Those provisions were unmentioned in Jackson's veto message, which contained far scarier words: "Should the stock of the bank principally pass into the hands of subjects of a foreign country, and we should unfortunately become involved in a war with that country, what would be our condition? Of the course which would be pursued by a bank almost wholly owned by the subjects of a foreign power, and managed by those whose interests, if not affections, would run in the same direction there can be no doubt. All its operations within would be in the aid of the hostile fleets and armies without. Controlling our currency, receiving our public moneys, and holding thousands of our citizens in dependence, it would be more formidable and dangerous than the naval and military power of the enemy." This was little more than demagoguery.[26]

Nonetheless, Jackson, the chief magistrate, claimed to be exercising due diligence with his veto. The arguments he used were strained. The BUS had existed for the better part of four decades, its constitutionality had been affirmed several times, the paper currency was in fine shape, the country had become more democratic, and the common man had done quite well. Regarding the constitutional issue, the venerable James Madison, who had been opposed to the first BUS in 1791 and as president had approved the second in 1816, justified his actions and implicitly

undercut Jackson's arguments when he said in 1831, "[L]egislative precedents, expounding the Constitution, ought to guide succeeding legislatures, and to overrule individual opinions."[27]

Rent seeking provides a better explanation of the motives behind
Jackson's veto. Jackson's advisors and supporters thought they would
gain personally by doing in the BUS, and they played on what may have
been his cherished beliefs to encourage his opposition to it. Many of
them had connections to state banks. If the BUS were no longer regulating them, they might be able to run down the reserves and make
more of those profitable loans. Because the federal bank not only regulated state banks but also competed with them in markets served by
both, the state banks would get rid of a competitor. Then they would be
the logical places for the federal government to hold its funds, further
expanding their business. In fact the so-called pet banks of the Jacksonians did for a time take over the government's deposits from the BUS,
until the financial chaos unleashed by the veto forced the government
to forswear bank connections altogether and retreat for a time into a
shell that was called the Independent Treasury. Moreover, Jacksonians
in Boston and New York, who resented the headquartering of the BUS
in Philadelphia, floated plans for a new central bank in their cities, with
branches in other states if—this was the states' rights angle—the states
authorized such branches. The Jacksonians were not against a central
bank at all; they merely wanted it to be *their* central bank.

Whatever the reasons for Jackson's veto, its financial and economic
effects were ominous. The chaos of the following decade included tight
money and recession in 1833–34 as the administration began to move
government deposits from the BUS and the BUS reacted by contracting its loans and discounts. Inflation and speculation (mostly in land)
marked the recovery up to 1837. Although the inflation and the monetary expansion that caused it seem less deeply rooted in the veto and
the removal of BUS restraint than once was thought, the absence of the
BUS as a regulator probably made the inflation and the subsequent depression worse than they might have been. Financial panics broke out
in 1837, 1839, and 1842. Bank money convertibility was suspended in
1837 and 1839. Widespread business failures, bank failures, and stock
market declines as well as the debt defaults of nine states marked the
depression of 1839–43. The United States had 901 state banks in 1840
and only 691 three years later. To the extent that Jacksonian policies
were intended to "liberate" U.S. banking from the discipline of a central bank, they had backfired.[28]

This sounds grim, but it was far from a disaster. The nation had a lot going for it. From its peak in 1833 to its peak in 1839, the industrial production index grew at a rate of 4.5 percent per year. This was less than the rate of 5.3 percent between the peaks of 1815 and 1833 and far less than the 9.9 percent annual rate achieved from 1828 to 1833, but still not bad. Moreover, after contracting in 1840, industrial production began a sustained advance during the next two decades. Its rate of growth from the peak of 1839 to that of 1860 was 5.9 percent per year. Most manufacturing took place in the northeastern states with long-established financial arrangements—tax systems, banks, stock markets, corporations—that were least damaged by the financial chaos of the 1830s and early 1840s.

The newer states of the trans-Appalachian South and West suffered most from the absence of the BUS. They had few banks and still fewer well-run, well-capitalized ones. The branches of the BUS had furnished them with loans and discounts, a stable paper currency, and an interregional payments system that integrated their developing frontier economies with the those of older states and the international economy. After the Jacksonian financial reversal, all of that had to be rebuilt with state and private initiatives, less efficiently and at higher costs. The eminent banking historian Bray Hammond summed up this reversal as follows:

> Having ended federal restraint on bank lending and federal responsibility for the monetary system, the Jacksonians gloried in what was a triumph of *laissez faire* in a field in which *laissez faire* had no place. Sovereign and unified control of the monetary system is needed in any economy, whatever freedoms may be proper otherwise. Consequently, from possession of what was generally considered the best monetary system in the world, the country fell back into one of the most disordered. But the period was one of such prodigious growth in population, territory, natural wealth, and accumulated wealth that the cost could be borne. The Americans . . . are the only people who with a light heart have trusted to the energy of growth to insure them against the effects of their mistakes.[29]

New England's Suffolk Bank system continued to give that region perhaps the best banking and payments system in the country. New York made an improvement that was later to have national implications when it enacted a landmark free banking law in 1838. The law more or less ended the corruption involved in legislative chartering by making the granting of charters an administrative rather than a legislative function of state government. The law allowed any group of would-be bankers that met its specifications to obtain a bank charter. This was termed *free entry.* Free banks could issue banknotes only by depositing collateral, in the form of state and federal bonds and mortgages on lands in the state, to back the notes. If a free bank failed, the collateral would be liquidated and the note holders compensated with the proceeds. Free banking was emulated elsewhere, especially during the 1850s. It worked so well that the federal government essentially adopted the system in its National Currency Act of 1863 and the National Banking Act of 1864 (see below).

Free banking is sometimes considered an alternative to central banking, possibly because the United States adopted its version of free banking—free entry and collateralized note issues—right after the Bank of the United States departed from the scene in the mid-1830s. But that was an accident of history. There is no reason to think that free banking and central banking are incompatible, unless, that is, one defines free banking, as some libertarians tautologically do, as meaning the absence of a central bank, and central banking as a monopoly of note issue. Had Jackson not vetoed the rechartering of the BUS, New York and other states could still have introduced free banking. Its main ideas were hardly new in the 1830s. Eighteenth-century British economists such as Sir James Steuart and Adam Smith had advocated free entry, and the early nineteenth-century British economist David Ricardo had advocated bond-secured note issues. Free banking American-style was more significant in promoting the idea that free incorporation of businesses was a right worth having than it was in creating an alternative to central banking. In establishing rights of business to freely adopt the corporate form of organization, the United States again was in advance of other countries.[30]

The main costs to the U.S. economy of not having a central bank were a less efficient, more costly payments system and a greater potential for financial instability, which raised the cost of financial capital. Between 1790, when the financial system began to be put in place, and 1836, when the charter of the second BUS expired, the United States had only two financial panics. One was in 1792, within months of the opening of the first BUS. The other was in 1819, when the brand-new second BUS, working with the U.S. Treasury, had to carry out orders to get the country back to a convertible currency in the only way it could, namely, by contracting the paper currency. After 1836 there were three panics in short order, those of 1837, 1839, and 1842. Things settled down a bit after that, but major panics appeared again in 1857, 1873, 1884, 1893, and 1907. No matter how one cuts and averages these data, panics

were more frequent when a central bank was absent. A less stable financial world is one with a higher cost of capital because people have to be
paid for bearing risk. It would be decades before Americans and American governments could borrow again on terms as generous as those of
the 1820s and early 1830s. What that cost the United States in terms of
economic growth is a matter of counterfactual speculation, but there
can be little doubt that it cost something.

A Small Step Forward: National Banking
with a Uniform Currency, 1863–1913

When the Civil War broke out in 1861, the United States had about
sixteen hundred state-chartered banks. Most of these banks issued notes
in several denominations, so the country had approximately ten thousand different-looking pieces of paper money in circulation, each of
which had words and numerals on it saying that it was some number of
U.S. dollars. Counterfeiting flourished in these circumstances, as did
publications called banknote reporters and counterfeit detectors. These
publications cost something to produce and to purchase. But they were
necessary for anyone handling much paper money. Sellers of goods and
services had to spend time using them to determine whether the issuing banks were sound and whether the notes were real or counterfeit.
It was a system of states' rights and laissez-faire with a vengeance. Had
the BUS lasted, it might by then have become the sole issuer of paper
currency, as the U.S. central bank is now, and the nation's other banks
would have become deposit banks, as they are now.

Congress and the Lincoln administration, responding to widespread
concerns about the currency chaos, seized the opportunity to solve some
of their war financing problems while improving the nation's currency.
They introduced the National Currency Act of 1863, its amendment in the
National Banking Act of 1864, and a prohibitive tax on state banknotes
in 1865. The first two made the New York free banking act of 1838 national in scope. That law required banks to back their notes by purchasing government bonds and pledging them as collateral for banknotes.
The U.S. government needed to sell bonds to obtain resources to face the
armed rebellion of the Confederacy. So it adopted a version of the New
York law, printing uniform national banknotes and distributing them to
new federally chartered banks after they had purchased U.S. bonds and
deposited them with a federal official, the Comptroller of the Currency.
The comptroller's office, located in the Treasury Department, would also
inspect the national banks frequently and would otherwise oversee and
regulate the system. The name of the bank was stamped on the otherwise

uniform national notes. When not all banks responded to this patriotic wartime appeal, Congress passed the prohibitive tax on state banknotes.

Not all state banks joined national banking system, however. Larger city banks had already gotten out of the note-issuing business, so the tax on state banknote issues provided no incentive for them to join, and state charters were sometimes more liberal than federal charters. Any bank could continue deposit banking under its state charter and merely cease to issue notes. But most state banks in the 1860s did join the national system, especially after a revision of the original act relaxed some objectionable provisions, such as the requirement that a bank joining the national system give up entirely any evidence of its old name.

That is how the United States at long last obtained a uniform paper currency that consisted of obligations of the federal government. It was a step forward. No longer did money handlers have to consult banknote reporters and counterfeit detectors.[31]

The national banking system, however, did not correct the stability problem that surfaced after the BUS disappeared. Financial panics continued with greater frequency than they had in the early decades of U.S. history. Across the Atlantic, just the opposite was happening. Great Britain, which had more financial panics than did the United States from the 1790s to the 1830s, had fewer of them thereafter. Britain had improved its financial system, in part by adopting U.S.-style corporate banking, and the Bank of England always had its charter renewed. By the second half of the nineteenth century, it had adopted the theory (which was new) and the practice (which was not) of central banking. Britain thus had a more stable economy and lower interest rates than the United States, although the latter was surpassing it in income and wealth. This, it appears, is the origin of historians' widely held opinion that Britain had the most effective financial system of the nineteenth century, although that was not the case before the 1830s, when by law banks in England and Wales had to be small partnerships of no more than six persons, in contrast with America's larger banking corporations. Such laws were rent seeking, British style; they were designed to protect the monopoly privileges of the Bank of England in ways American law never protected the privileges of the Banks of the United States. When the United States began its great reversal, Britain was in the early stages of improving its system by reducing the privileges of the Bank of England rather than eliminating it.[32]

The U.S. national banking system, moreover, had flaws in addition to the absence of a central bank. Far from establishing a free banking system with free entry, the law was loaded with restrictions on entry and other operations. There were, for example, minimum capital

requirements, legal reserve requirements, limits on note issue, and restrictions on types of loans allowed. The system, although adequate for
conditions in the Northeast, was not attuned to conditions in the South
and the West. The restrictive provisions of national banking constituted
entry barriers for would-be banks in those regions. That is why, after
almost being eliminated, state banking revived, and indeed, by the late
nineteenth century state banks surpassed the national banks in number. Since then the United States has had a dual system of federally and
state-chartered banks and bank regulatory authorities.[33]

The early Comptrollers of the Currency also decided to interpret the
National Banking Act in such a way that a federally chartered national
bank could have only one office (unit banking) and was otherwise subject to the banking regulations of the state in which it was located. Hence,
a national bank could not open branches within a state or bank across
state borders. Far from being national, as the Bank of the United States
had been, the national banking system was in effect state banking with
a federal charter and without a central bank.[34]

During this era substitutes for the central bank included the U.S.
Treasury, which could and did move money out of government coffers
to increase banking-system liquidity in times of stress, and bank clearinghouses, institutions that in ordinary times settled on a daily basis
the balances due to and from member banks that received checks from
one another. Clearinghouses invented the loan certificate as a method
of stretching bank reserves in periods of financial stringency and crisis,
thus increasing liquidity as a central bank might. Another substitute
consisted of the large national banks of New York City, the nation's
financial center. Because they held balances of other banks scattered
throughout the United States, these banks knew they would need to be
liquid in periods of stringency and crisis when other bankers' balances
would be withdrawn. In the event, these substitutes for a central bank,
neither individually nor in tandem, could prevent financial stringencies,
panics, and crises from upsetting the U.S. economy in 1873, 1884, 1890,
1893, and 1907. Gradually it dawned on Americans that they needed
something other than substitutes.

Monetary policies and politics further complicated financial problems before 1900. A return to specie convertibility at pre–Civil War
parity required a deflation of prices to undo the war era's inflation. Exi-
gencies of war had forced a suspension of convertibility in 1862, and
the federal government had quickly issued the greenback, a fiat paper
currency, that caused the price level to more than double. After the war,

money creation was held in check while the U.S. economy grew. The combination produced deflation until 1879, when the prewar price level returned and the government and the banks resumed converting their paper liabilities into gold. But the deflation had uneven impacts across economic sectors, and political movements rose up to demand policy changes that would end the deflation.

One such movement was the Greenback Party, which called for expansion, not contraction, of federally issued fiat paper. Another was the "free silver" movement, which called for free coinage of silver into dollar coins to increase the monetary base and alleviate problems caused by deflation. Neither movement was successful in achieving its goals, but the supporters of free silver did achieve partial victories in 1878 and 1890, when Congress enacted laws calling for monetization of some silver, which U.S. mines produced in large quantities.

In another financial paradox, the attempt to expand the money supply had the opposite effect. Foreign investors—then as now the United States was a magnet for foreign capital—sensed that silver legislation posed a threat to the gold standard, the monetary standard of most leading nations. The investors began to liquidate their U.S. investments, converting the proceeds to gold and withdrawing the gold from the United States. As they did so, Treasury and bank gold reserves declined, causing the money stock to contract rather than expand. Silver monetization thus backfired. The problem became acute in the 1890s. Money was the hot-button issue of national politics in that decade. Gold's backers defeated the proponents of silver, and Congress committed the country to gold in 1900.[35]

Correcting the Great Reversal: The Federal Reserve, 1914–2004

The third Bank of the United States, the Federal Reserve System (more popularly, the Fed), received a charter from Congress in 1913 and opened its doors in 1914. The great financial panic of 1907 revealed that the largest and richest economy had a financial system that was in many ways outmoded, although it held 30 percent of total world deposits and 36 percent of commercial bank deposits. So to remedy deficiencies in its financial arrangements, after a hiatus of seven decades the United States once again reinstituted a central bank with branches around the country. Like its two predecessors the Fed was designed to give the United States a bank for the federal government, a more uniform currency, a more efficient national payments system, a manager of U.S. international financial relations, an overseer and supervisor of the banking system, and methods for nipping incipient and actual financial crises in the bud through injections of liquidity. The Jacksonian financial reversal of the 1830s was finally and fully reversed.[36]

There were some differences between the two Banks of the United States and the Fed. The Fed was controlled much more by the government than by its nominal owner-shareholders, namely, its member banks. In contrast, the BUS had been controlled by private shareholders and management, with the government having only a minority interest. The Fed did not compete in banking markets with the banks it regulated and supervised, whereas the BUS had. And the Fed's control over the money stock derived from being a debtor to, rather than a creditor of, its member national and state banks. Instead of receiving the notes and checks of state banks and returning them to the state banks for conversion to the monetary base, the Fed achieved control by requiring member banks to hold base-money reserves with it and by controlling the quantity of base-money reserves available to the U.S. banking system.

The advantages of one approach to central banking were the disadvantages of the other. The Fed, which did not compete with other banks, had a political advantage; BUS, which competed with other banks had a political disadvantage because the other banks would just as soon not have that competition. On the other hand, a greater insulation from political interference in routine central banking was an advantage of the BUS that the Fed lacked; operating on a specie-based monetary standard, the old Banks would not have caused or acquiesced to, as the Fed did, the Great Inflation of 1966–81 (discussed further below). In short, the Banks of the United States were designed to be, and were, more independent of governmental pressures than has been the case with the Fed.

In the nine-decade history of the Fed, the United States has had only one financial crisis comparable to the many crises it had from 1837 to 1907. It lasted from 1930 to 1933. And the Fed was culpable, having failed to do one of things it had been designed to do: prevent or alleviate the several waves of bank failures that shook the country by adding to the liquid reserves of the financial system and acting as a lender of last resort to illiquid but solvent banks. In perspective, this was the abuse of an institution that is essentially, or at least potentially, useful.[37]

Another abuse, not nearly as bad as that of 1930–33, occurred during the above-mentioned Great Inflation of 1966–81. The Fed sponsored a too-rapid expansion of the money stock, with the result that U.S. inflation averaged 6 percent per year and price indexes tripled in a decade and a half. Like the 1930–33 episode, this one derived from a combination at the Fed (and elsewhere) of flawed economic analysis and weak leadership. Now, after a quarter-century of relatively stable economic growth and a better macroeconomic performance than that achieved in most countries, there are grounds for contending that the central bankers at the Fed learned something from the big mistakes of the 1930s and the 1970s. If that learning persists, history may record that in the quarter-century from 1980 to 2005, U.S. central banking at last achieved in practice the economic-stabilization abilities it was thought to have in theory.

A Mixed Record, 1933–1990

Like the crisis of the 1780s that led to the Federalist financial revolution, the crisis of the early 1930s unleashed a great wave of financial reforms. Most of the reforms helped restore confidence in the financial system and bring the economy up from the depths to which it sunk in the Great Depression. In the long term, some of the reforms have been more successful than others.

Consider first the monetary reform. In the 1790s the dollar had been defined as fixed weights of gold and silver. From then to the 1930s, the price level, though fluctuating over shorter periods, exhibited long-term stability. Money therefore tended to retain its value. During most of the fourteen decades from 1790 to 1930, the holder of a paper dollar could exchange it for roughly the amounts of gold or silver specified in the 1790s. That right was taken away in 1933. The federal government nationalized the gold holdings of Americans and then devalued the dollar. It agreed to exchange gold for dollars held by foreign countries and central banks; a gold exchange standard replaced the gold standard, in which anyone could convert paper money to gold at fixed rates.

The gold exchange standard continued in the Bretton Woods System, established at the end of World War II, in which other countries defined their currencies in terms of dollars and the United States held most of the world's reserves of monetary gold. During the following two decades, the United States, for a variety of reasons, flooded the world with dollars but did not increase its gold reserves. When some countries began to convert their excess dollar holdings to gold, the United States saw the handwriting on the wall and detached the dollar entirely from gold in the early 1970s. The action was followed by rising rates of inflation in that decade. Because the dollar price of gold in free markets in 2006 was about fifteen times what it was before the dollar's detachment from gold and more than twenty-five times what it was from 1791 to 1933, one might say that the few remaining advocates of a return to the gold standard have some historical basis for their position that the gold standard encouraged monetary discipline.[38]

After banks failed in large numbers in the early 1930s, a major goal of U.S. financial policy in President Franklin Roosevelt's New Deal was to make banking safe. Essentially this was done by turning the banking system into a cartel, reversing good reforms of earlier U.S. history (such as free entry into banking), adding ones that had proved problematical (such as deposit insurance, which had failed in a number of states starting with the New York Safety Fund a century earlier), and adding more regulations (such as government-controlled interest rates) and layers of regulation (such as the Federal Deposit Insurance Corporation) to banking. These reforms supported unit banking, because the thousands of unit banks felt threatened when a branch of a larger bank, or indeed another unit bank, moved into their market. Another measure, the Glass-Steagall Act of 1933, forced a split of commercial and investment banking that was intended to end perceived conflicts of interest when a bank engaged in both. Existing banks that combined both types of banking had to choose one or the other or break the two activities into separate entities.[39]

As a result of the New Deal financial reforms, U.S. banking by the middle decades of the twentieth century became incredibly safe—a bank seldom failed from the 1930s through the 1960s—and it also became rather stodgy. Starting in the 1950s, larger money center banks, sensing that new business opportunities would arise if they could gather more resources and enter new markets, began to find ways around the stodginess of New Deal banking regulations and cartelization by means of mergers, one-bank holding companies, and other financial innovations. Among the innovations were negotiable certificates of deposit and commercial paper issued by bank holding companies to finance greater lending by banks. These allowed a bank to make any loan it wanted to make by going out to the markets and buying the money to make it: true financial intermediation. The greatest boon of all was in international banking, where U.S. money-center banks discovered all the large foreign holdings of dollars that were undermining Bretton Woods (so-called Eurodollars), looser regulations than in the United States, and markets that craved American capital and financial expertise. As these banks, like U.S.-based multinational corporations in other industries, did more and more of their business outside of the United States, pressure rose for U.S. financial regulators to ease up, end the cartels, and allow greater freedom to U.S. banks.[40]

The more enlightened reforms of the 1930s related to securities markets, which American governments had largely allowed to regulate themselves from the 1790s until early in the twentieth century. Self-regulation continued from the 1930s, but it was buttressed by government oversight. The breakthrough came with disclosure laws. Until the twentieth century securities markets were mostly the concern of wealthy individuals and institutions, their bankers and brokers, and the governments and corporations that issued securities. They were large markets by most countries' standards, but they were not mass markets.

That began to change early in the century as rising incomes and wealth for the masses drew more and more of them into securities investments. The masses, however, did not have access to the information, or the power to act on it, that great bankers such as J. Pierpont Morgan and his rich clients did. As a result, many of them got burned in the boom and bust of the 1920s. In the aftermath, the federal government decided to level the playing field by requiring issuers of securities as well as the bankers and brokers who sold them to make standardized disclosures of financial information to one and all, in the form of quarterly income statements and annual balance sheets, among other things. A new Securities and Exchange Commission became the overseer of the securities industry and markets, or Wall Street. The reforms were designed to alleviate the asymmetry of financial information that existed when corporate managers and Wall Street bankers knew a lot more about companies' affairs and conditions than did the masses of investors who owned corporate securities.

Wall Street at first hated this allegedly unwarranted government interference in free markets. But the Street, in another of the paradoxes that arise in financial history, soon came to like government intervention. Securities regulation, especially disclosure, renewed the shaken confidence of the investing public. That investing public grew year by year as the country became ever richer, and they flocked back to Wall Street, sending its profits to previously undreamed-of heights. Today it is estimated that roughly half of the adult population of the United States participates directly or indirectly (through mutual and pension funds) in corporate securities investments.[41]

Full Circle

Since the 1970s a lot has transpired to make the U.S. financial system a state-of-the-art one. Historically strong federal finances and debt management have become even stronger. Concerns about the absolute levels of federal budget deficits and a rising national debt appear less serious than implied when they are related to a rising GDP and declining levels of market interest rates. The dollar is more stable at home and abroad than it was in prior decades. One who does not trust the government or the central bank to keep inflation under control has, since the late 1990s, been able to purchase from the Treasury or the markets some TIPS, that is, Treasury Inflation Protected Securities.

The banking system is solid, and—miracle of miracles—since 1994 U.S. banks have been able to open branches throughout the country, just as the first and second Banks of the United States did from the 1790s to the 1830s. Belatedly, the United States caught up in branch banking with most of the developed world. Congress repealed the Glass-Steagall separation of commercial and investment banking in the 1990s, so banks can again participate in both of these businesses. Although it is not clear that doing so will achieve greater efficiencies and profits or avoid the potential for conflicts of interest that motivated Glass-Steagall, at least U.S. banks are free to try. Credit is more widely available, and at lower rates, than it has been in a couple of generations.

The third Bank of the United States, the Fed, has never had more prestige at home and abroad than it does now, and that status appears to be deserved. Securities markets and corporations, with nudges from elected officials, regulators, and the courts, are cleaning up some recent messes that exposed conflicts of interest and manipulations of corporate information. The recent messes do not appear to have shaken the public's confidence much. And confidence is the sine qua non of modern financial systems.

This is a return to a set of conditions happily created for the United States by enlightened financial statesmen more than two hundred years ago. At that time, the installation of a modern financial system did much to get the country rolling economically, rolling so well in fact that even less enlightened financial leadership in later periods could not long delay the rise of the United States in the world. The nation's financial history is a story of political economy that Americans and others in less affluent settings would do well to study. Its lessons of substantial achievements often prompted by government policies, and of financial reversals often prompted by government policies, are of relevance for improving financial policies, regulations, and institutions.

Notes

1. Good accounts of early Dutch and British financial developments are provided by Hart et al. 1997, de Vries and van der Woude 1997, Dickson 1967, and Neal 1990. The phrase "embarrassment of riches" is the title of a book by Schama 1987.

2. For an account of early U.S. banking and securities market developments, see Sylla 1998. Wilkins (1989) documents the increasing flows of foreign investment capital to the United States that began at the time of the U.S. financial revolution in the 1790s. Sylla (1985) and Wright (2002) study innovative U.S. developments in the area of business corporations.

3. Gallman (1965) establishes that the U.S. economy was growing by the 1830s and 1840s at modern rates that have persisted since that era. J. H. Davis (2004) demonstrates that industrial production, an important component of the initially small modern sector, grew at high rates of 4–6 percent per year from peak to peak from the inception of his annual series with an essay on the year 1790. More details about Davis's evidence are presented below.

4. Rousseau and Sylla (2005) explore the relationship of financial development to economic growth in the early United States.

5. See Rajan and Zingales 2003, 2004.

6. For an excellent account of the American revolutionary and postrevolution financial experience, see Ferguson 1961.

7. See Hamilton 1961–1987; the quotation from the letter to Morris is at 2:606.

8. See Ferguson 1961 and Perkins 1994 for extended discussions of the financial and other problems of the 1780s.

9. Two fine biographies of Hamilton provide extensive treatments of the political economy of financial reforms during the 1780s and 1790s: McDonald 1979 and Chernow 2004.

10. See Hamilton 1961–87, particularly the Report [to Congress] Relative to a Provision for the Support of Public Credit, January 9, 1790, 6:51–137.

11. See Final Version of the Second Report [to Congress] on the Further Provision Necessary for Establishing Public Credit (Report on a National Bank) in Hamilton 1961–87, 7:305–42.

12. See Final Version of the Report [to Congress] on the Establishment of a Mint, January 28, 1791, in Hamilton (1961–87), 7:570–607 for the document that defined the new U.S. dollar.

13. See Wright 2002, 2005 and Sylla 2005 for accounts of the origins and functions of the first U.S. securities markets.

14. The quotation from Kent is cited in Wright 1995, 144. Kent later became Chancellor Kent, one of New York State's top judicial officers.

15. On the proliferation of banks in the early 1790s and the encouragements given to them by the Secretary of the Treasury, see J. S. Davis 1917, vol. 2, chap. 2.

16. See J. H. Davis 2004 for the details and annual data of the new U.S. industrial production index starting with 1790.

17. For arguments that Jefferson and Madison wanted a weak federal government in order to protect American slavery, see Wills 2003 and Ellis 2000, chap. 3. For arguments that they were worried about British-style corruption, see Banning 1978.

18. For good accounts of early U.S. banking developments and their relation to economic expansion, see Hammond 1957; Bodenhorn 2000, 2003; and Wright 2002.

19. See Sylla, Legler, and Wallis 1987 and Wallis, Sylla, and Legler 1994 for accounts of the fiscal interests of state governments in U.S. banking.

20. For a positive view of the effects of BUS regulation on monetary growth, see Engerman 1970.

21. Bodenhorn (2003) compares banking regulation across states and regions during the antebellum era.

22. For an account of how the New York Safety Fund worked, and failed, see ibid., chap. 7.

23. Banner (1998) and Wright (2002) provide valuable perspectives on the workings of early U.S. securities markets.

24. Wright (2002) has much to say about early corporate governance in the United States.

25. Temin (1969) provides a thorough account of the ups and downs of the U.S. economy in the 1830s, although he rather minimizes the role played by Jackson's destruction of the central bank. Rousseau (2002) provides counterpoint that stresses the perverse effects of Jacksonian policies.

26. Hammond (1957) provides a thorough discussion of Jackson's possible motives in vetoing the BUS recharter in 1832. The veto message, quoted here, can be found in Chandler and Tedlow 1985, 133–35, as the end of an excellent case study of the BUS.

27. Madison's letter is quoted in Gordon 1968, 106.

28. See Hammond 1957 and Temin 1969 for thorough accounts of economic and financial issues during the 1830s.

29. Hammond 1957, 741–42.

30. On free banking and free incorporation, see Bodenhorn 2003 and Sylla 1985.

31. For a detailed account of financial changes that took place during the Civil War, see Hammond 1970. Less detailed accounts are given by Studenski and Krooss 1963, among others.

32. Wood (2005) discusses the entire history of central banking in Great Britain and the United States, with interesting comparisons of the two cases.

33. Sylla (1975) discusses the entry barriers created by the national banking system.

34. Two excellent financial histories of the national banking era from 1863 to 1913 (and its aftermath) are James 1978 and White 1983.

35. The early chapters of Friedman and Schwartz 1963 cover the monetary history of the period from 1867 to 1913 in considerable detail.

36. For international comparisons of national banking systems and securities markets in the 1870–1914 period, see Michie 2003.

37. On the history of the Fed from 1914 to 1960, see Friedman and Schwartz 1963. An even meatier account is that of Meltzer (2003), who stops at 1951 but promises a second volume with the later history.

38. For a thorough account of the Bretton Woods era, see Bordo and Eichengreen 1993.

39. For a thorough survey of trends in U.S. financial regulation, see Calomiris 2000.

40. Sylla (2002) discusses these banking trends, pointing out that what Europeans considered to be an invasion of large U.S. banks in the 1960s and 1970s might as well be regarded as an escape from rigidities in financial regulation within the United States.

41. Smith and Sylla (1993, 1996) discuss two centuries of U.S. capital market regulation and the role of capital markets in U.S. economic development.

References

Banner, Stuart. 1998. *Anglo-American Securities Regulation: Cultural and Political Roots, 1690–1860*. Cambridge: Cambridge University Press.

Banning, Lance. 1978. *The Jeffersonian Persuasion*. Ithaca: Cornell University Press.

Blodget, Samuel. 1806. *Economica: A Statistical Manual for the United States of America*. Washington, DC: Samuel Blodget.

Bodenhorn, Howard. 2000. *A History of Banking in Antebellum America: Financial Markets and Economic Development in an Era of Nation-Building*. Cambridge: Cambridge University Press.

———. 2003. *State Banking in Early America: A New Economic History*. New York: Oxford University Press.

Bordo, Michael D., and Barry Eichengreen, eds. 1993. *A Retrospective on the Bretton Woods System: Lessons for International Monetary Reform*. Chicago: University of Chicago Press.

Calomiris, Charles W. 2000. *U.S. Bank Deregulation in Historical Perspective*. Cambridge: Cambridge University Press.

Chandler, Alfred D., Jr., and Richard S. Tedlow. 1985. *The Coming of Managerial Capitalism: A Casebook on the History of American Economic Institutions*. Homewood, IL: Irwin.

Chernow, Ron. 2004. *Alexander Hamilton*. New York: Penguin.

Davis, Joseph H. 2004. "An Annual Index of U.S. Industrial Production, 1790–1915." *Quarterly Journal of Economics* 119 (November): 1177–1215.

Davis, Joseph Stancliffe. 1917. *Essays in the Earlier History of American Corporations*. 2 vols. Cambridge: Harvard University Press.

De Vries, Jan, and An van der Woude. 1997. *The First Modern Economy: Success, Failure and Perseverance of the Dutch Economy, 1500–1815*. Cambridge: Cambridge University Press.

Dickson, P. G. M. 1967. *The Financial Revolution in England: A Study in the Development of Public Credit, 1688–1756*. London: Macmillan.

Ellis, Joseph J. 2000. *Founding Brothers: The Revolutionary Generation*. New York: Knopf.

Engerman, Stanley L. 1970. "A Note on the Economic Consequences of the Bank of the United States." *Journal of Political Economy* 78 (July–August): 725–28.

Ferguson, E. James. 1961. *The Power of the Purse: A History of American Public Finance, 1776–1790*. Chapel Hill: University of North Carolina Press.

Friedman, Milton, and Anna Jacobson Schwartz. 1963. *A Monetary History of the United States, 1867–1960*. Princeton: Princeton University Press.

Gallman, Robert E. 1965. "Gross National Product in the United States, 1834–1909." In *Output, Employment, and Productivity in the United States after 1800*, ed. Dorothy S. Brady, 3–76. New York: Columbia University Press.

Gordon, T. F. 1968. *The War on the Bank of the United States*. 1834; repr., New York: Augustus M. Kelley.

Hamilton, Alexander. 1961–1987. *The Papers of Alexander Hamilton*. 27 vols. Ed. Harold C. Syrett. New York: Columbia University Press.

Hammond, Bray. 1957. *Banks and Politics in America, from the Revolution to the Civil War*. Princeton: Princeton University Press.

———. 1970. *Sovereignty and an Empty Purse: Banks and Politics in the Civil War*. Princeton: Princeton University Press.

Hart, Marjolein't, Joost Jonker, and Jan Luiten van Zanden. 1997. *A Financial History of the Netherlands*. Cambridge: Cambridge University Press.

James, John A. 1978. *Money and Capital Markets in Postbellum America*. Princeton: Princeton University Press.

McDonald, Forrest. 1979. *Alexander Hamilton: A Biography*. New York: Norton.

Meltzer, Allan H. 2003. *A History of the Federal Reserve*. Vol. 1: *1913–1951*. Chicago: University of Chicago Press.

Michie, Ranald. 2003. "Banks and Securities Markets, 1870–1914." In *The Origins of National Financial Systems: Alexander Gerschenkron Reconsidered*, ed. Douglas J. Forsyth and Daniel Verdier, 43–63. London: Routledge.

Neal, Larry. 1990. *The Rise of Financial Capitalism: International Capital Markets in the Age of Reason*. Cambridge: Cambridge University Press.

Perkins, Edwin J. 1994. *American Public Finance and Financial Services, 1700–1815*. Columbus: Ohio State University Press.

Rajan, Raghuram G., and Luigi Zingales. 2003. "The Great Reversals: The Politics of Financial Development in the 20th Century." *Journal of Financial Economics* 69:5–50.

———. 2004. *Saving Capitalism from the Capitalists: Unleashing the Power of Financial Markets to Create Wealth and Spread Opportunity*. Princeton: Princeton University Press.

Rousseau, Peter L. 2002. "Jacksonian Monetary Policy, Specie Flows, and the Panic of 1837." *Journal of Economic History* 62 (June): 457–88.

Rousseau, Peter L., and Richard Sylla. 2005. "Emerging Financial Markets and Early U.S. Growth." *Explorations in Economic History* 42 (January): 1–26.

Schama, Simon. 1987. *The Embarrassment of Riches: An Interpretation of Dutch Culture in the Golden Age*. New York: Knopf.

Smith, George David, and Richard Sylla. 1993. "The Transformation of Financial Capitalism: An Essay on the History of American Capital Markets." *Financial Markets, Institutions, and Instruments* 2.2:1–62.

———. 1996. "Capital Markets." In *Encyclopedia of the United States in the Twentieth Century*, ed. Stanley I. Kutler, 3:1209–42. New York: Charles Scribner's Sons/Simon & Schuster.

Studenski, Paul, and Herman E. Krooss. 1963. *Financial History of the United States: Fiscal, Monetary, Banking, and Tariff, Including Financial Administration and State and Local Finance*. 2d ed. New York: McGraw-Hill.

Sylla, Richard. 1975. *The American Capital Market, 1846–1914: A Study of the Effects of Public Policy on Economic Development*. New York: Arno.

———. 1985. "Early American Banking: The Significance of the Corporate Form." *Business and Economic History*, 2d ser., 14:105–23.

———. 1987. "Banks and State Public Finance in the New Republic, 1790–1860." *Journal of Economic History* 47 (June): 391–403.

———. 1998. "U.S. Securities Markets and the Banking System, 1790–1840." *Federal Reserve Bank of St. Louis Review* 80 (May–June): 83–104.

———. 2002. "U.S. Banks and Europe: Strategy and Attitudes." In *European Banks and the American Challenge: Competition and Cooperation in International Banking under Bretton Woods,* ed. Stefano Battilossi and Youssef Cassis, 53–73. Oxford: Oxford University Press.

———. 2005. "Origins of the New York Stock Exchange." In *The Origins of Value: The Financial Innovations That Created Modern Capital Markets,* ed. William M. Goetzmann and K. Geert Rouwenhorst, 299–312. Oxford and New York: Oxford University Press.

Sylla, Richard, John B. Legler, and John Joseph Wallis. 1987. "Banks and State Public Finance in the New Republic." *Journal of Economic History* 47 (June): 391–403.

Temin, Peter. 1969. *The Jacksonian Economy.* New York: Norton.

Wallis, John Joseph, Richard Sylla, and John B. Legler. 1994. "The Interaction of Taxation and Regulation in Nineteenth-Century U.S. Banking." In *The Regulated Economy: An Historical Approach to Political Economy,* ed. Claudia Goldin and Gary Libecap, 121–44. Chicago: University of Chicago Press.

White, Eugene Nelson. 1983. *The Regulation and Reform of the American Banking System, 1900–1929.* Princeton: Princeton University Press.

Wilkins, Mira. 1989. *The History of Foreign Investment in the United States to 1914.* Cambridge: Harvard University Press.

Wills, Garry. 2003. *Negro President: Jefferson and the Slave Power.* Boston: Houghton Mifflin.

Wood, John H. 2005. *A History of Central Banking in Great Britain and the United States.* Cambridge: Cambridge University Press.

Wright, Robert E. 1996. "Banking and Politics in New York, 1784–1829." PhD diss., State University of New York at Buffalo. Ann Arbor: UMI Dissertation Services, no. 9719191.

———. 2002. *The Wealth of Nations Rediscovered: Integration and Expansion in American Financial Markets, 1780–1850.* Cambridge: Cambridge University Press.

———. 2005. *The First Wall Street: Chestnut Street, Philadelphia, and the Birth of American Finance.* Chicago: University of Chicago Press.

6

The National Era

WHEN AMERICANS decided in favor of independence in the spring of 1776 they faced many difficult decisions. They declared themselves to be independent states. John Adams, leader of the Continental Congress and later president of the United States, believed that the real declaration of independence was made on May 6, 1776, when Congress asked the individual states to write their own constitutions. But they also declared their independence together, as a nation. After that, political genius was required to create a national government strong enough to defend the country from external threats and weak enough internally that it did not threaten the independence of the states. It took a long time to get the balance right. The first national constitution, the Articles of Confederation, created a national government strong enough to secure independence, but not strong enough to pay off its debts, deal adequately with international affairs, or referee disputes between the states. The second constitution, adopted in 1787, created a stronger national government but left unsettled so many of the details about sharing power between national and state governments that internal debate about the proper constitutional powers of the national government brought the nation to the brink of disunity several times and finally to civil war in 1861. The biggest issue facing American government between 1790 and 1860 was internal, not external. How were Americans to govern themselves? How were power and policies to be shared between the national and state governments?[1]

The division of responsibility between national and state governments was a source of constant debate. Some functions of government were divided and some were shared between the two levels, and any history of government between 1790 and 1860 must take both levels into account. In order to understand the government's role in economic development, we must understand its structure. I begin by tracing in rough outlines the size and structure of government before the Civil War, then

148

briefly sketch the sources of growth in the American economy. Then I discuss the main policies of the national and state governments, identifying what each level did to promote economic development.[2]

Constitutions, the Division of Powers, and the Sharing of Powers

By 1780 every state but two had written a new constitution. Connecticut and Rhode Island adopted their colonial charters as constitutions. Almost every new constitution incorporated the idea of British-style mixed government with a bicameral legislature and an independent executive. Although all were democratic republics, the extent of democracy varied (all states had some restrictions on voting and office holding based on wealth, property, or taxpaying), as did the internal relationships between the legislative bodies and between them and the executive. Over the course of the next fifty years most states adopted universal white male suffrage, streamlined their legislative machinery, and clarified the role and structure of the judiciary.[3]

The Articles of Confederation were proposed in 1777 but not ratified until 1781. Maryland ratified them last, and only after New York agreed to cede its western land claims to the national government and other states agreed, in principle, to cede their claims as well. The Articles gave Congress control over international relations and the military but otherwise did not create a strong national government. States retained the sole power to levy taxes, and the national government could only request funds from the states. The inability of the national government to raise revenues hampered its ability to provide national defense, the reason for its existence. By 1785 it was bankrupt.[4]

Writing a new constitution that would give the national government power to raise revenue to provide for external defense threatened internal liberties. How could a national government with the power to tax be controlled? The new Constitution used three devices. First, it equated taxation with representation. Second, it divided authority and decision making among the legislative, executive, and judicial branches at the national level. Third, it delegated only specific powers to the national government, placed prohibitions on specific state government powers, and gave the states the power to act as external checks on the national government via the direct appointment of senators by states. As seen in chapter 3, the Constitution gave the national government the sole power to regulate international relations and trade, provide for the national defense, regulate and mint coins and control the currency, and regulate the movement of goods across state borders. Both levels of government shared the power to tax, the police power to promote the general welfare, and all the powers of sovereignty associated with the common-law powers of government in Britain. Given these constitutional mandates and restrictions, what did American governments actually do?

The Size and Functions of American Government

The true size of government cannot be simply measured by the size of revenues, expenditures, or debt. Nonetheless, a look at basic fiscal measures is a good place to begin describing what government did between 1790 and 1860. The figures show the small size of the national government in the pre–Civil War era relative to later eras. Several important functions of government not reflected in the budget data are discussed below. The tables A.1 and A.2 (see appendix A) present information about the size of revenues by level of government for the nineteenth and twentieth centuries.

National government finances followed a distinct pattern driven by war finance. Figures 6.1 and 6.2 show national government's expenditures and revenues annually in nominal dollars per capita from 1791 to 1936. Figure 6.3 shows debt per capita and the deficit or surplus in the national budget. The plot line for debt measures the total amount of debt outstanding, and the plot line for deficit or surplus measures the change in debt from year to year. The War of 1812, the Civil War, and World War I stand out in all three figures. The national government paid for wars in part by raising taxes and in part by borrowing money.[5]

Where did the revenues come from? Figure 6.4 shows the share of total revenues from customs, land sales, and internal revenue. In the

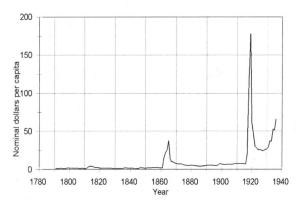

Figure 6.1. Federal expenditures per capita (nominal dollars)

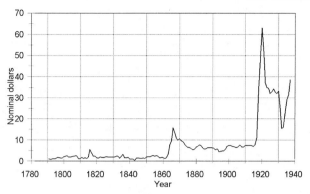

Figure 6.2. Federal revenues per capita (nominal values)

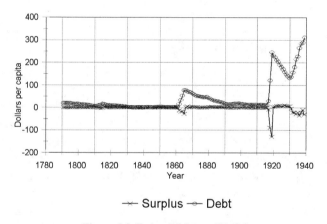

—×— Surplus —◦— Debt

Figure 6.3. Federal debts and deficits

nineteenth century the latter consisted primarily of excise taxes on alcohol and other products, and after 1917 it included the income tax. There have been three distinct federal revenue structures. The first, which lasted from 1790 to 1860, was dominated by customs revenues; the second, from 1860 to 1912, was a combination of customs revenues and internal revenues; and the third, in effect after 1919, was dominated by internal revenues, specifically the income tax. Wars also exert their effect on revenues. In the War of 1812, excise taxes were increased sharply and then eliminated after the war. In the Civil War new excise and income taxes were imposed. The income taxes were removed after the war, but the excise taxes were not. Just before World War I the income tax was made constitutional, and during that war sharply higher income taxes were collected.

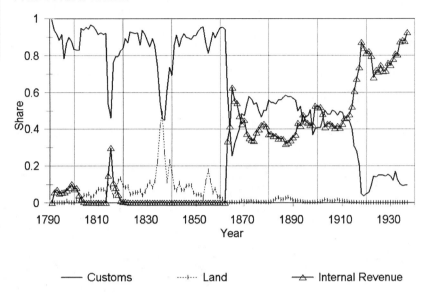

Figure 6.4. Custom, land, and internal revenues (share of total revenues)

Figure 6.5 shows the share of national expenditures going to the military and to interest payments on the national debt. Interest payments on the national debt acquired during the Revolution dominated expenditures in the early years of the republic. Until the 1820s outlays for the army, the navy, and interest usually totaled 80 percent of national expenditures. During the War of 1812, the debt increased, but it was quickly paid off. By 1835 the debt was zero, and interest payments fell accordingly. Until the Civil War, defense expenditures averaged about one-half of federal expenditures. During the Civil War military expenditures peaked, and interest payments remained high for several decades after the war as debt was gradually paid off. The defense share fell to roughly 20 percent of national expenditures after the Civil War but rose again to about 40 percent during the Spanish-American War and World War I.[6]

Looking closely at the period between 1790 and 1860, we see the same pattern. After 1790 the national government paid off the revolutionary war debt by running persistent budget surpluses and using the surpluses to retire debt. During this period customs revenue accounted for 85 percent of federal revenues. Excise taxes were unpopular. In 1794 President Washington had to call out troops to suppress a protest in western Pennsylvania of the excise tax on whiskey. Land sales rarely contributed significantly to federal revenues, except in years such as 1835 and 1836, when land sales boomed. Tariffs ultimately became a divisive political issue in Congress, but at no time was the national government in a position to remove tariffs entirely or to raise them to prohibitive levels on most imports. There was no feasible or popular alternative to import duties in the early nineteenth century.[7]

On the expenditure side, between 1790 and 1860, 52 percent of federal expenditures were for military defense and another 12 percent were for interest payments. Of the remainder, the largest portion went to general administration: the costs of running the administration, Congress, and the federal courts. There were no large or significant expenditures for any other functions except the post office. Expenditures on transportation, including roads, rivers and harbors, and other improvements, made up only 3 percent of the total during this time.

The numbers in table A.1 (see appendix A) give a rough measure of the relative size of state and national governments in the early nineteenth century. We can ask which was bigger in fiscal terms, but it turns out that it depends on which states we look at. Aggregate averages conceal the wide variety in state taxes and spending. Figure 6.6 presents average annual per capita revenue from all (nonloan) sources for the federal government and for Indiana, New Hampshire, Maryland, and South Carolina. Collectively, as seen in table 6.1 (below), state revenues averaged about 20 to 25 percent of national revenues from 1800 to 1830. For comparison, national revenues per capita were around $2.00 and income

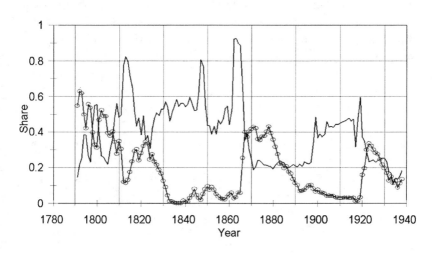

Figure 6.5. Interest and military expenditures (share of total federal expenditures)

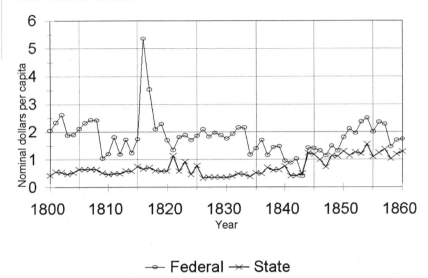

Figure 6.6. Federal and state per capita revenues (federal land sales excluded)

per capita was in the neighborhood of $100. In the decade between 1835 and 1844, state revenues rose in absolute terms and as a percentage of national revenues from less than $.50 to $.88 per person and from 20 to 25 percent to slightly more than 50 percent of national revenues. One reason is that by 1835 the national debt had been fully paid, and there was no need to levy taxes to pay interest on the debt. State revenues continued at this higher level throughout the 1850s. The rise in state government activity, caused by a boom in state investments in canals, banks, and railroads in the 1830s, is discussed in more detail below.[8]

There was, however, considerable variation from year to year and from state to state. In Maryland, for example, per capita revenues were between $.30 and $.50 until the 1830s. In the late 1820s Maryland began borrowing money to invest in the Chesapeake and Ohio canal. Because the canal never made any money, the state eventually raised taxes to service its debts. In 1842 it was forced to temporarily default on its state bonds, not resuming interest payments until 1848. By the mid-1840s, per capita tax revenues in Maryland were $2.00 per person, four to six times higher than they had been in the 1820s and early 1830s, and equal to national taxes in those years.

Indiana and New Hampshire were both small rural states with very small state governments. Per capita revenues in both states ran about $.10 to $.20, respectively, in the 1820s. In the mid-1830s, Indiana began construction on its ambitious canal and railroad network. At a time when the state population was about five hundred thousand and the annual budget about $50,000, the state legislature authorized a bond issue of $10,000,000 in 5 percent bonds. Annual interest payments on the bonds came to $1.00 per person, a tenfold increase in size of the state government. Its leaders thought that the canals and railroads would return a profit to the state. When they did not, Indiana, like Maryland, was forced to default on its bonds for a time and to raise taxes to service it debts. In the 1840s and 1850s, per capita revenues in Indiana ranged between $1.50 and $2.00, again comparable to federal revenues. In contrast, New Hampshire, which did not borrow money to invest in canals, railroads, or banks, maintained low and steady revenues for the entire period up to 1860.

South Carolina was an early and active supporter of canals and banks. Before 1830, it borrowed to finance investments, and state revenues were always relatively high, between $.40 and $1.00 per person. South Carolina, however, did not participate in the investment boom of the 1830s. Like New Hampshire, per capita revenues stayed stable for the entire period up to the beginning of the Civil War.

What did states spend money on, and where did they get their revenues from? The year 1831 was typical of Maryland before the canal boom, and Maryland expenditures are representative of the general pattern of expenditures in many states. In that year, 40 percent of expenditures went for government administration, 10 percent for education, and 10 percent for charities (including asylums), in total a bit more than half of all state expenditures. Miscellaneous expenditures made up roughly a quarter of the total, the content of which, of course, varied from year to year.[9]

The main element with respect to which states differed was the amount spent on "internal improvements," which in the early nineteenth century meant investments in banks or in the construction and operation of roads, turnpikes, and canals. South Carolina made early investments in transportation and banking. Virginia had a Board of Public Works in 1816. Pennsylvania invested in turnpikes in the 1790s. The sharp increase in Maryland's revenues in the 1840s resulted from the need to finance large canal investments made in the mid-1830s. By 1841 the state's expenditures had more than tripled and work on the canal had almost ceased, but interest payments alone accounted for two-thirds of the budget. All of the increase in expenditures in that decade was for the canal. The internal improvement boom of the 1830s, which was critically important for states, is discussed in more detail below.[10]

States differed more widely with regard to revenue. Revenues came from four general sources: property taxes, poll taxes, business taxes, and income from assets. Property taxes were levied on land and other wealth, sometimes on a per-acre basis but more commonly *ad valorem,* that is, on the assessed value of the land and other wealth subject to taxation. Poll taxes were head taxes imposed on voters. Business taxes encompassed a wide variety of fees, licenses, permits, bonuses for corporate charters, and taxes on capital. Asset income was income earned directly in the form of dividends on state investments in corporations or in the form of tolls on state transportation projects.

States always had the option of taxing land but preferred to eliminate the property tax if possible. Many states with other sources of revenue eliminated the state property tax (not the local property tax) completely before 1830. These were well-established eastern states with substantial income from business taxes and assets. On average, property taxes made up only 2 percent of state revenues in the eastern states in the late 1830s. A few New England states continued to rely on the property tax. In Connecticut, New Hampshire, and Vermont the average property tax share was 58 percent of total revenue. States in the West relied heavily on the property tax, an average of 43 percent of total revenue.[11]

The internal improvement boom of the 1830s eventually collapsed into the debt crisis of the 1840s, and states defaulted, had to raise property tax rates and other taxes, or both to service the debts incurred in the 1830s. Maryland, Pennsylvania, Illinois, Michigan, Indiana, Florida, Mississippi, Louisiana, and Arkansas all defaulted on their debts in 1841 and 1842. Property taxes rose dramatically from $.03 to $.87 per capita in Maryland, from $.02 to $.53 in Pennsylvania, from $.01 to $.14 in New York, from $.14 to $.22 in Indiana, from $.21 to $.52 in Ohio, and from $.23 to $.34 in Indiana.[12]

The distinct regional differences in the share of state revenues made up by property taxes reflects the ability of eastern states (with exceptions in New England) to tax businesses and to acquire ownership interests in private enterprises. Massachusetts, New York, Pennsylvania, Maryland, Virginia, South Carolina, Georgia, and Alabama all held significant amounts of bank stock at some time before 1830. Massachusetts, Connecticut, and Rhode Island taxed bank capital. In fact, the bank capital tax made up more than 50 percent of Massachusetts revenues in the 1830. In the 1820s and 1830s taxes on bank capital or charter fees made up more than 25 percent of revenues in Connecticut, Delaware, Pennsylvania, and North Carolina. Dividends from their bank investments allowed Georgia and Alabama to eliminate their state property taxes in the 1830s.[13] Eastern states also levied an array of taxes on corporate capital, business licenses, and fees of all types.

Western states simply didn't have the businesses to tax; they had land and people, and that is what they taxed. Half of Indiana's 1835 revenues of $50,000 came from poll taxes and half came from property taxes.

Economic Growth and Government Promotion of Economic Development

The United States was an agrarian society in 1783. Three-quarters of the labor force was directly engaged in farming, and a large share of the other quarter worked in processing, packing, shipping, or selling farm products. Perhaps 10 percent of the labor force was employed in manufacturing. Agriculture and manufacturing were the two primary sources of economic growth in the early nineteenth century. Growth in both sectors was related to the growth of the domestic economy, but what each required from governments in terms of legal and financial support was very different.[14]

The single most important resource Americans possessed until the Civil War was land: more wealth was held in the form of land than in any other form. The peace settlement with Britain gave the new country extensive holdings from the Appalachians to the Mississippi, millions of acres of land the federal government wanted to sell to private individuals. Opening the West to settlement and cultivation was the biggest potential source of economic growth and the nation's number one economic priority. But the process wasn't cheap. There were two elements to the cost. One was borne directly by the farmers, and the other fell on the larger society.[15]

Land is usually not treated as part of the capital stock because land possesses certain features such as location that are not the result of investment and savings, but improvements to land are definitely capital investments. Raw land, covered with trees or prairie grasses, could not be brought into production without a substantial investment in clearing, fence building, and farm building. The land itself was cheap, but making a farm was expensive. In 1860 the state of Minnesota estimated that a 160-acre farm cost $775 to establish and that only $200 of that cost was for the land itself. The cost of building farms fell on individuals. Robert Gallman's estimates of the capital stock in the early nineteenth century show that improvements to land made up the single largest element in investment before 1840.[16]

Fertility and distance from transportation routes determined the value of land. Land situated along the Atlantic and Gulf seaboards and along navigable inland waterways that ran to the ocean was much more valuable than land in the interior. Western lands were inherently productive but were in the wrong place. The cost of transporting bulk agricultural products over the Appalachian Mountains in 1800 exceeded the value of the products. The economic viability of farming in the Northwest depended on the building of a national transportation system linking the Ohio and Mississippi River valleys with the Eastern Seaboard. The costs of building such a system far exceeded the financial capacity of individual farmers. Many private firms such as the Schuylkill and Susquehanna Navigation Company in Pennsylvania, the Western and Northern Inland Lock Navigation Company in New York, and the Potomac Company in Virginia asked states for charters to build canals to the West in the 1780s and 1790s. These companies all tried and failed to breach the Appalachian Mountains. In the end, state governments took the lead in successfully building a national transportation network.

Farm building and investment in transportation were two of the three elements necessary to bring all the nation's farmers into a national market. The third element was a financial system capable of providing short-term credits to the farmers, shippers, and wholesalers who moved the crops from farms to urban and international markets. A farmer in Ohio faced the problem of selling his crop in the East. One possibility was to sell his wheat in Cincinnati to someone who would arrange to transport it to New York and sell it there. Another possibility was to arrange shipment with a freight line, ship his crop to an agent in New York, and have the agent sell it and send the profits back to him (net of the agent's costs). The difference in these two methods was the ownership of the wheat. If the farmer sells in Cincinnati, the shipper owns the wheat and bears the risk of any rise or fall in the price. If the farmer consigns his crop to an agent, the farmer bears the risk of any change in the price. Most commonly the farmer consigned his crop and bore the risk of price fluctuations.[17]

The farmer, as a result, was not paid in cash for his crop in Cincinnati. Instead, the agent to whom he consigned his crop typically authorized the farmer to draw a "bill of exchange" on the agent's representative in New York. This bill was like a check that the farmer wrote in Ohio, to be honored by the agent's representative in New York in the future.[18] Since no one in Ohio wanted to be paid with a check drawn on the account of an individual in New York, the farmer usually took the bill to the local bank (if there was one) and sold it to the bank for cash. The bank paid the farmer less than the face value of the bill and then arranged to collect the amount due in New York in the future. The bank's profits came from the difference between what it paid to the farmer and the face value it received when the bill matured. The "discount" between the two prices represented the interest on the loan made to the farmer. Since the farmer wrote the bill in the first place, the farmer was ultimately responsible for honoring it if the New York agent did not pay it. Sound complicated? It was, but it was the cheapest way of doing business over a long distance when communication and transportation were expensive and took a long time.

To get an idea of the relative importance of transportation and finance costs and their decline over time, consider the difference in the price of a barrel of flour in Cincinnati and New York between 1820 and 1860. In 1820 a barrel of flour (weighing 196 pounds) cost about $8 in New York and $5.52 in Cincinnati; in 1860 the price was about $5 in New York and $4.72 in Cincinnati. Over time, the difference in price between the two markets fell from $2.48 per barrel to $.28 per barrel, a decline of almost 90 percent. The bulk of the decline was caused by falling transportation costs. In the early 1830s, Ohio completed two canals that linked southern Ohio with Lake Erie and, via the lake, with the Erie Canal and New York city. Transportation costs fell to $1.05 per barrel in 1836–40, the first full five-year period after the canals were in operation. The next major drop occurred at the very end of the period, when the difference dropped to $.28 per barrel in 1855–60, after the railroads reached across the Appalachians (the Baltimore and Ohio was the first) in the early 1850s.[19]

One can approximate the cost of financial services by examining the interest costs on a ninety-day loan to finance the shipment of flour eastward. Interest rates on such transactions fell from roughly 24 percent in 1820 to 8 percent in 1860 as the riskiness of loans was reduced by improved communications. Interest costs of $.33 per barrel made up 6 percent of the Cincinnati price in 1820, and costs of $.09 percent made up only 2 percent of the Cincinnati price in 1860. On the other hand, interest costs made up only 13 percent of the price differential in 1820, whereas they accounted for 33 percent of the price differential in 1860. As the physical cost of transporting goods dropped, financial costs became increasingly important as a wedge between producer and consumer prices.[20]

Interest costs were only some of the transaction costs of getting goods to market. Freight handling, insurance, and warehousing all added to transaction costs. Once the Ohio canals were open, tolls steadily declined as both New York and Ohio tried to keep as much freight as possible moving over their canals. Despite lower canal tolls, the price difference between Cincinnati and New York widened in the 1840s and fluctuated over time. The price differential widened from $1.02 in the 1836–40 period to $1.68 in the 1846–50 period. The widening gap must have been the result of the higher cost of transaction services because transport costs were falling. Financial services formed a substantial part of the cost of getting goods to market, and banks played a central role in reducing that cost. The disruptions caused by the failure of the federal government to recharter the Bank of the United States, financial market instability from 1837 to 1843, and the collapse of state government borrowing all probably contributed to a reduction in the efficiency of the financial system that contributed to the widening price differential.[21]

There were several important advantages to establishing local banks in western and southern states. First, banks printed their own money in the form of bank notes, redeemable in gold, that circulated in the local economy. Keeping with the numbers in the previous example, suppose that money could be borrowed in the form of gold coins (specie) in Indiana at an interest rate of 24 percent. A bank that printed $3 in bank notes for every $1 in gold coins it held in its vaults could discount three times as many bills of exchange in bank notes as it could in gold. The bank could break even if it discounted the bills of exchange for 8 percent, that is, its return on the gold it held would be 24 percent. By creating banks, western states could provide liquidity to their local markets, in the form of bank notes, at much lower cost than the same amount of money in gold coins. Second, the establishment of local banks created local information about the creditworthiness of local borrowers. A banker in Indianapolis could better judge the credit risk of his neighbors than could a banker in New York. Once the Indianapolis banker established his creditworthiness in New York, he could borrow money in New York to lend in Indianapolis to his profit and to the benefit of his neighbors. Finally, the establishment of local banks and currency provided local markets with some independence from fluctuations in the bank notes of other cities. It is not surprising, then, that every state wanted to encourage the establishment of banks within its boundaries. Southwestern states with access to ocean transport invested heavily in banks but invested almost nothing in transportation.

Bringing the West into the national market required improvements in transportation and in financial services. The major beneficiaries of the improvements were farmers in the West who shipped bulky, low-value agricultural products to the East and on to international markets. But the investment in the transportation and financial system directly stimulated the growth of manufacturing in the Northeast. During colonial times Americans imported many of their manufactured goods from Britain, a pattern that withstood the stress of the Revolution. American markets for higher quality manufactured goods—hats, clothes, textiles, cutlery, crockery, books, and so on—were dominated by British firms. American producers could compete with Britain in two ways. The first was the establishment of protective tariffs, raising American prices high enough to allow high-cost production by Americans. The second was the production of cheap, lower-quality goods naturally protected by the high transportation costs of shipping goods across the Atlantic.

Because of their higher value and lower weight, manufactured goods always can be profitably shipped farther than most agricultural products. Opening up the internal domestic market in the United States by reducing transportation and financing costs offered northeastern manufacturers a growing market in cheap, durable, easily repaired or replaced manufactured goods. Whereas agriculture was geographically extensive, expanding output in manufacturing was geographically intensive. Producers bunched together in small geographic areas where costs were lower because of a price advantage (cheap labor or water power) or because knowledge was more readily available (a key in the new manufacturing technologies) and then distributed their products over a wider area. This geographically intense pattern was made possible by a more efficient distribution system. American manufacturers in the early nineteenth century were producing not for international export (this would change in the later part of the century) but for domestic consumption.

Manufacturing was concentrated in the Northeast. Agriculture spread throughout the rest of the country, with grain and meat production in the North and cotton production in the South. Economic growth built on advances in transportation and finance. Promotion of economic growth required investments in banks, canals, and later railroads. Whether governments promoted economic development or not depended on their ability to stimulate development of transportation and financial systems.

The National Government and Promotion of Economic Development

Not everything a government does is reflected in large revenues or expenditures. Indeed, one of the most important government contributions to economic growth is to provide a stable and unbiased legal environment. The costs of running the judicial system may be unrelated to whether the government provides effective justice, since corrupt courts might require more expenditures than do fair courts. Therefore it is important to examine the activities of the national government in this era to see which may have had an impact on economic growth regardless of amount budgeted for them.

The national government provided military defense, conducted international relations, ran the postal and patent systems, and administered the federal courts. All are important functions. Occasionally major debates arose concerning the conduct of federal policy, but there was never any serious question that the government would cease providing these services. On the other hand, Congress regularly debated import tariffs, support for internal improvements (transportation), public land policy, the existence of a nationally chartered bank, and the continued existence of and regulation of slavery. The previous section identified the reasons why tariffs, transportation, use of western land, and banking were important determinants of economic growth in the early nineteenth century. Slavery was very much an economic matter. The major issue facing Congress, the president, and the national courts in the early nineteenth century was how much, if anything, the national government should do to promote economic development through active policy making in these areas.

The Constitution of 1787 explicitly assigned responsibility for tariffs, public lands, and elements of the financial system to the national government. Despite an ongoing debate about whether the national government should carry out transportation projects and regulate slavery (at least in the territories), the fact is that it did do these things. There was never any doubt that the national government *could* do these things. This doesn't mean that people didn't argue about whether it *should* do such things. Some people, including several presidents, claimed that a federal bank was unconstitutional or that the national government couldn't build a road or a canal without a constitutional amendment or that it had no power over slavery. The national government was never prohibited from establishing a bank, controlling the emission of money, building a road or a canal, regulating slavery, levying a tariff, fighting a war, or controlling the settlement of western lands because those actions were somehow declared unconstitutional. People, politicians, and presidents sometimes argued that one of these policies was unconstitutional, but that was a political argument, not a constitutional one.[22]

Yet if the national government had the constitutional power to promote economic development in these ways, did it use those powers? The question is a subtle one. The national government did not have the option of not having a policy. For example, giving the federal lands away for free is just as much a policy as not selling them. The questions, rather, are (1) whether the policy it did have was intended to promote growth, (2) how the policy changed during this seventy-year period, and (3) whether the changes were intended to increase or decrease promotion of economic development. It appears that the federal policies put in place by 1791 were intended to promote economic development, but after 1791 the national government found it extremely difficult to expand promotion of economic development farther than the status quo.

The easiest policy to quantify and understand is transportation policy, or internal improvements. There had always been a strong argument for national support of transportation projects. George Washington had been an early organizer and supporter of the Potomac Company, which aimed to build a canal from the Chesapeake Bay into the Ohio River valley. Even Thomas Jefferson, later an opponent of national support for internal improvements, said in his second inaugural speech in 1805 that "the revenue thereby liberated [from paying off the national debt] may, by a just repartition among the states, and corresponding amendment of the constitution, be applied, *in time of peace,* to rivers, canals, roads, arts, manufactures, education, and other great objects within each state." Jefferson mentions a constitutional amendment, one allowing the national government to spend money on transportation. This implies that he believed that such a policy would be unconstitutional without an amendment—an interesting position, because Jefferson himself had signed into law the 1803 enabling act that required the national government to spend 2 percent of the revenues from the sale of public land in Ohio on transportation improvements leading to or within Ohio. Congress and Jefferson had already decided it was constitutional for the national government to spend money to build roads.[23]

Between 1790 and 1860 the national government spent a total of $54 million on transportation improvements. By far the largest share of national expenditures went to rivers, harbors, and aids to navigation, all explicitly allowed in the Constitution. The single largest project was the National Road, which grew out of the promise made to Ohio to spend a portion of the revenues derived from land sales on roads. But of $9 million spent on roads, a large share went to short roads built within one state. When Andrew Jackson vetoed the appropriation for the Maysville Road in 1830 on the "constitutional" grounds that it lay entirely within Kentucky (it happened to be the route home for his political archrival Henry Clay), he conveniently ignored the precedents of many similar grants that had already been made.[24]

How important were national expenditures on transportation? State and local governments spent more than $450 million on transportation projects, nine times the amount spent by the national government. Most of the federal spending went to small river and harbor improvements and to lighthouses; only a few were projects on the scale of the National Road. Why did the federal government accomplish so little? The main reason can be found in the kind of projects it did fund. "Rivers and Harbors" bills contained lots of small projects for congressional districts scattered around the country. No section, East, West, North, or South, was willing to support a large appropriation that would go exclusively to one region.

The public lands were always closely related to internal improvements. Land values rose when transportation improvements were made. The national government adopted a system of public land sales in 1785 and 1787, before the Constitutional Convention, that was designed to maximize revenues from land sales. Land sales, however, rarely constituted an important source of federal revenue. Only in land booms such as those of 1818, 1836, and 1854 did land sales approach 20 percent of federal revenues, and in most years they were well below 10 percent. The original system offered land for sale in open auctions, in minimum parcels of 640 acres at a minimum price of $2.00 an acre, with the option of buying land on credit. There were no upper limits on the size of a purchase. Between 1785 and 1841, a series of acts gradually lowered the minimum purchase to 80 acres. The minimum price was lowered to $1.25 per acre. Credit sales were abolished in 1820 when it became clear that most of the people who bought on credit did not pay. Preemption—occupying land without title—was illegal, but widespread, throughout the West. Dislodging farmers who had built farms on preempted land was politically unpopular. As a result, the national government periodically passed preemption acts that recognized the rights of preempters to buy land at the minimum price *ex post*. In 1841, the national government finally gave up and made preemption a permanent way to acquire land. At that point the national government accepted that revenues from land sales would never amount to much since preempters only paid the minimum price.[25]

What did these changes mean for economic development? They meant almost nothing. Land policy itself was very important, but the shape of land policy was in place by 1787, and the changes made after that date were minor. Smaller minimum purchase sizes had some effect, but individuals could still purchase larger parcels. Legitimizing preemption was not a significant change because the government had rarely been willing to evict occupants without clear title and had set a definite precedent of allowing squatters to eventually purchase the land they had claimed. Feller thus concluded his history of federal land policy between 1790 and 1841: "Considering its central place in the Jacksonian debate over political economy, federal land policy did not change much during those years."[26]

The fact that little was done in the area of land policy and internal improvements does not mean that nothing was proposed or discussed. Congress considered 117 pieces of internal improvement legislation between 1815 and 1829. Almost every session of Congress saw bills to give the public lands to the western states, bills to give land sales revenues to states for education, and bills to distribute land revenues to support internal improvements. As with internal improvements, there was a continual conflict between western states with public lands within their borders and wealthy eastern states with no public land but a desire to see federal land revenues shared.[27]

Slavery was another area of federal responsibility (shared with the states) regarding which much was debated and little was changed. The focal debate about slavery in Congress involved the process of creating territorial governments in the West from which new states would be formed. If slavery were allowed during the territorial phase, then the citizens would be likely to allow slavery in their constitutions when the territory became a state. If slavery were prohibited in a territory, the territory would be likely to prohibit slavery when it became a state. Debates about slavery were inextricably linked to land policy established in the land ordinances of 1785 and 1787. The Land Ordinance of 1787 governed settlement in what would become the states of Ohio, Indiana, Illinois, Michigan, and Wisconsin. Article VI of the ordinance stated, "There shall be neither slavery nor involuntary servitude in the said territory, otherwise than in the punishment of crimes. . . *Provided always,* That any person escaping into the same, from whom labor or service is lawfully claimed in any one of the original States, . . . may be lawfully reclaimed, and conveyed to the person claiming his or her service as aforesaid." Because the ordinance preceded the national constitution, there was no room for debate about slavery in the Northwest, nor was there any doubt that the national government was committed to enforcing fugitive slave laws.[28]

Kentucky was created in 1791 from the state of Virginia, so federal public land law never applied there. North Carolina ceded Tennessee to the national government in 1790. The terms of the cession allowed all existing private claims to be honored, and most of Tennessee had been sold or granted to private individuals. The terms required that Congress "assume the government of the said ceded territory, which they shall execute in a manner similar to that which they support in the territory west [sic] of the Ohio; . . . *Provided always,* That no regulation made or to be made by Congress shall tend to emancipate slaves." In 1798 Congress created the Mississippi Territory, encompassing the land that would become Alabama and Mississippi, stating that "the President of the United States is hereby authorized to establish therein a government in all respects similar to that now exercised in the territory northwest of the Ohio, excepting and excluding the last article of the ordinance made for the governance thereof by the late Congress, on the thirteenth day of July, one thousand seven hundred and eighty-seven."[29] The last article of the Northwest Ordinance was Article VI, prohibiting slavery. Land and slavery in Kentucky and Tennessee were excluded from federal control by the Virginia and North Carolina grants. In the northern arm of western settlement slavery was prohibited; in the southern arm of western settlement slavery was allowed.

Slavery was the most controversial national policy in the early nineteenth century, and the history of slavery continues to be contentious today. But no matter where one stands regarding the constitutionality of national government regulation in the territories, one cannot escape the fact that by 1800 the national government had already, by simple legislation and not by constitutional amendment, prohibited slavery in the Northwest Territory, permitted slavery in the Mississippi Territory, and allowed residents of Kentucky and Tennessee to continue their practice of slaveholding without interference from the national government. The policy precedent was clear: the national government could do whatever it wanted with respect to slavery in the territories because it had already pursued widely divergent policies in different territorial areas.

The first big crisis came when Missouri petitioned for admission as a state in 1820. Missouri was the second state created from the Louisiana purchase, Louisiana was the first in 1811. The terms of the Louisiana and Orleans Territorial Act of 1804 prohibited importation of slaves into the territory from outside the United States and prohibited the importation of slaves into the territory from the United States if they had been imported into the United States after 1798 but allowed the importation of slaves into the territory from other states in the Union as long as it was done "by a citizen of the United States removing into said Territory for actual settlement, and being at the time of such removal *bona-fide* owner of such slave or slaves." It was legal to bring slaves into Missouri, and people did. The question raised in 1820 was whether slavery would be allowed in the remainder of the Louisiana Purchase. The Missouri Compromise, engineered by Henry Clay, brought Missouri into the Union as a slave state, brought Maine into the Union as a free state (Maine was originally part of Massachusetts), and prohibited slavery "in all that territory ceded by France to the United States, under the name of Louisiana, which lies north of thirty-six degrees and thirty minutes north latitude, not included within the limits of the state contemplated by this act."[30]

The Missouri Compromise acknowledged the "balance rule," which stated that slave and free states should have equal total numbers of senators in the U.S. Senate. The compromise governed settlement in Minnesota and Iowa (free) and Arkansas (slave) and put off until the 1840s the question of what would be done with land further to the west. The recognition, annexation, and admission of Texas as a slave state in 1845 created another intense debate between the South and North, a debate that escalated with the Mexican War. Ultimately another round of compromises took place in 1850, the last of the famous compromises arranged by Henry Clay. After 1850, the status of the Kansas-Nebraska territory sparked a crisis that could not be resolved by compromise and led the nation into civil war.

Did federal policy regarding slavery change substantially because of these crises? The answer, as with public lands and internal improvements, has to be no. The national government decided to draw the line regarding slave and free territories in 1820 and moved the line around in the 1850s. After that it debated, argued, and finally broke up, with exactly the same policy put into place in 1787. Federal policy in all three areas—land, internal improvements, and slavery—was regularly debated. The debates were so intense that small changes in policy seemed to be major accomplishments, but in retrospect the lack of substantive policy change reflects the strong disagreements about what should be done and an inability to reach a consensus on a new federal policy.[31]

In three other major areas of national responsibility—import tariffs, finance, and defense and international affairs—the national government did take action as allowed by the Constitution. Federal tariff and financial policies were intertwined from the beginning by Alexander Hamilton's proposal for funding the revolutionary war debt, putting the government on a sound financial footing, and promoting the development of American trade and manufacturing. Hamilton's plan established new funding for most of the existing national and state debt from the Revolution by creating new bonds that were traded for existing bonds.

A national bank, which issued its own currency, was created to act as the national government's financial agent, the place where national tax receipts would be deposited and where checks were drawn for expenditures (including payments on the national debt). Finally, import tariffs were imposed, both to generate revenue and to protect manufacturing.[32]

All three elements of the plan were passed by Congress and signed by President George Washington, despite intense debate and opposition. Attorney General Edmund Randolph and Secretary of State Thomas Jefferson thought the bank was unconstitutional. Their arguments turned on the power of the government to create a corporation, a power the Constitution had not explicitly enumerated and therefore, under the reserved powers clause, a power possessed by states but not the national government. Hamilton argued, successfully, that the power to create a corporation was inherent in the powers of a sovereign government:

> The latter [Randolph], expressly admits, that if there is anything in the bill which is not warranted by the Constitution, it is the clause of incorporation. Now it appears to the Secretary of the Treasury [Hamilton] that this *general principle* is *inherent* in the very *definition* of government, and *essential* to every step of the progress to be made by that of the United States, namely: That every power vested in a government is in its nature *sovereign,* and includes by *force* of the *term,* a right to employ all the *means* requisite and fairly applicable to the attainment of the *ends* of such power, and which are not precluded by restrictions and exceptions specified in the Constitution, or not immoral, or not contrary to the *essential ends* of political society.[33]

In Hamilton's view, the Constitution contained an implicit and inherent grant of power to the national government sufficient to perform the functions it was assigned in the Constitution. But you can see how Hamilton's reading of the Constitution differed from Jefferson's. Hamilton saw limits on the national government in the Constitution only where there were explicit restrictions; Jefferson saw powers given to the national government only where there were explicit grants. The two positions remain poles of argument today.

The national government granted a charter to the Bank of the United States (BUS) in 1791. The bank had branches throughout the country, issued its own bank notes, served as a depository for federal tax receipts (mostly customs, as we have seen), and moved federal funds around the country through its branch system as needed to meet the federal government's needs. Revenues were collected primarily in seaports in the Northeast and in New Orleans, and the bulk of expenditures went to military defense, much of it on the frontiers. The BUS enabled the government to perform these functions efficiently and at low cost. The BUS was a private corporation whose stock was owned, in part, by the national government.

Congress failed to renew the charter of the BUS when it expired in 1811, and the national government's financing of the War of 1812 suffered as a result. In 1816 Congress passed a bill chartering a new Bank of the United States (known as the Second BUS). President Madison signed the bill despite his opposition to the first bank in 1791. He acknowledged that experience had proved the bank useful and constitutional. Both banks provided an important link in the development of a nationally integrated financial system. The bank notes of the branches of the BUS were accepted at par (face value) at all branches of the system, providing the country with a uniform paper currency. The notes of state-chartered banks tended to trade at a discount that increased with the distance of the note from its issuing bank. As important, the BUS facilitated the movement of payments between the regions of the country in the process of carrying out its role as the agent of the national government. It bought bills of exchange in different regions and delivered them for payment at their maturity. Because the BUS was involved in every region of the country, it could turn a tidy profit on the business at the same time that it provided a more orderly market for these critically important financial instruments.

The charter of the Second BUS was due to expire in 1836. When Congress renewed the charter in 1832, the renewal was vetoed by President Jackson. Although Jackson attacked the bank on constitutional grounds, the force of his argument was directed toward the privileges granted to the bank. These extensive privileges and the profits they created, some of which went to foreign stockholders, made the bank a "monster of corruption." There would not be a national bank again until 1914, although the national government would resume chartering banks in 1863 under the National Banking Act. The national government did try to promote economic development by chartering a national bank; Hamilton laid out the rationale and drew up the blueprints in 1790. But a national bank always generated vigorous political opposition, and the national government was unable to sustain the national banks in 1811 and in 1832.[34]

Tariffs were different, if only because the government relied on them for 85 percent of its revenues before 1860. Hamilton proposed moderate tariffs. He wanted an import tariff both to raise revenue and to promote manufacturing development. Tariffs that were too high provided protection but no revenue. Tariffs that were too low provided neither revenue nor protection. Hamilton's proposed tariffs were generally implemented by Congress in the 1790s. Measuring tariff rates is complicated by several factors. Tariffs can be imposed on units, weight, or value, and tariffs vary from product to product. So the overall burden of tariffs depends on how they are imposed and on the types of goods on which they are imposed.[35]

Figure 6.7 shows tariffs as a share of dutiable value of imports (that is, the official value on which the tariffs were levied) from 1821 to 1955. Tariffs rates rose from the 1790s to the 1820s. There was pressure to increase tariffs from manufacturing interests in the Northeast and pressure to reduce tariffs from the cotton exporters in the South. Pressure for higher tariffs peaked with the enactment of the "Tariff of Abominations" in 1828, and tariff rates as a share of dutiable value peaked at 61 percent in 1831. Exporting interests always opposed high tariffs, but the Tariff of Abominations brought extraordinary opposition from the South. In 1832, South Carolina "nullified" the tariff, refusing to allow it to be collected within its borders. Jackson threatened South Carolina with military occupation if it did not back down, vehemently denying any state's ability to nullify a federal act. In 1832 a compromise, again arranged by Henry Clay, allowed South Carolina to rescind its nullification without an invasion by federal troops but in the "Force Act" gave the president the authority to use force should it be necessary and promised to reduce tariff rates by 10 percent per year for the succeeding ten years. Clay's compromise ended the nullification crisis, but it also signaled the end of the protective tariff as an active policy tool to promote development. Tariff rates declined steadily from 1832 to 1860.[36]

The national government started the 1790s with the power and the tools to promote economic development through banks and tariffs. Wielding those powers, however, was politically controversial. By 1832, with the ascendance of the Jacksonian Democrats, the national government backed away from both a national bank and a protective tariff. Only in the area of defense and international relations did the national government continue to forge an active policy.

We have already seen the importance of land to the American economy in the early nineteenth century. Between 1790 and 1867, the land area of the United States more than quadrupled. The nation occupied 525 million acres after the Revolution. The Louisiana Purchase in 1803 added 523 million acres, the annexation of Texas in 1845 added 247 million acres, the Oregon Compromise with Britain in 1846 added

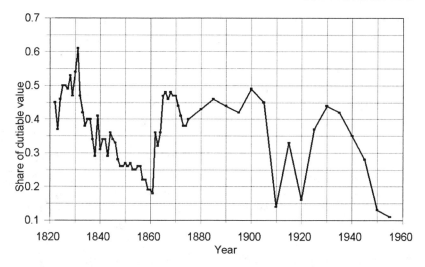

Figure 6.7. Tariff rates as a share of dutiable value

180 million acres, the Treaty of Guadalupe Hidalgo that ended the Mexican War added 334 million acres, and the purchase of Alaska in 1867 added 365 million acres. This dramatic expansion into the West was the fruit of diplomatic negotiation and of war. Not all attempts to increase the size of the United States were successful; the War of 1812 began with a failed invasion of Canada. As we saw above in the case of slavery, the movement into western lands always involved internal debate about how land should be acquired and who should settle it. But from its inception, the national government carried out an active program of expanding the country, and, via army expenditures on the frontier (the single largest item in the federal budget), provided security and government along the western expanse.[37]

In 1790 the national government possessed the constitutional powers to promote economic development via public land policy, internal improvements, banking and financial investment, tariffs, and international expansion. National land and slavery policies hardly changed at all from 1790 to 1860, and the national government's efforts in the field of transportation were less than one-ninth of state and local investment. Hamilton's blueprint for economic development included national action in banking and a protective tariff, both of which were enacted, but by 1832 those policies had been eclipsed by political opposition. Only the drive to add more land continued unabated from 1790 to 1860, but the development of the new lands in the West, and their connection with established areas in the East by building transportation and financial systems, would depend on actions taken by state governments.

State Governments and the Promotion of Economic Development

It is easy to see why historians focus on the national government. States did nothing so exciting as making war on the British, the Mexicans, or the Indians; did not decide the fate of any manufacturing interests by setting tariffs; did not distribute hundreds of millions of acres of public land; and did not decide whether there would be a national bank. Successful state politicians aspired to be senators; senator rarely aspired to be governors. The national constitution prohibited states from declaring war, conducting international relations, emitting bills of credit, levying a tariff, or otherwise effecting international trade or even domestic trade across state lines. The national government was the only government involved in the expanding the nation's boundaries in the West. How could states possibly influence the pace and pattern of economic growth in the early nineteenth century?

The process of opening the West required enormous resources and turned the economic focus and energies of the country inward. In comparison to the colonial economy, which revolved around international exports and imports, the nineteenth-century economy became increasingly independent of foreign markets. The major economic opportunities, except for an export product such as cotton, were within the United States, and the most important and potentially profitable investments were in transportation and finance. The role of states in these areas far outstrips that of the national government in importance. The financial system that arose between 1790 and 1860 was based on banks not only chartered by but in some cases owned by state governments. Nine of every ten dollars spent on public transportation investment came from state and local governments. By 1860, portions of the transportation system, particularly in the East, were passing out of the hands of states and coming under private control, but that should not blind us to the origins of the nation's transportation system in actions by the states. Banking was always under the control of state governments, with the exception of the two Banks of the United States, and the national government did not take an active role in chartering and regulating banks until 1863. State governments were at the center of the development process.

There were no banks in America before the Revolution. States began chartering banks in the 1780s and 1790s. At first the numbers were small, but they increased steadily with time. By the 1830s there were more than six hundred state-chartered banks with capital of more than $400 million. A corporate charter usually endowed the bank with limited liability, which was important to bankers whose profits came mainly from borrowing money in the form of bank notes. The legal ability to issue bank notes soon became a privilege that required a bank charter. Bank charters were valuable licenses to engage in a profitable activity. It is not surprising that the first banks often gave the state ownership shares in the bank as part of the cost of obtaining the charter. Massachusetts, New York, Pennsylvania, Maryland, Virginia, and South Carolina all came to hold a financial interest in banks in this way. As I pointed out above, dividends on bank stock were important to the revenues of state governments in the East.[38]

Once a state acquired an ownership interest in a bank, it faced conflicting incentives when asked to charter a second bank. The profitability of a bank depended, in part, on competition. As more banks were chartered, rates of return on the capital invested in individual banks declined. Existing banks opposed the formation of new banks, but states were constantly asked to open new banks, particularly in developing areas where financial systems were primitive (for example, the western parts of New York and Pennsylvania between 1810 and 1820). States that held large amounts of stock in existing banks were less likely to charter new banks; this was the case in Pennsylvania. Other states, such as Massachusetts, decided to sell their bank stock and tax bank capital. These states tended to have many more banks and smaller banks. By the second decade of the century all of the states on the Eastern Seaboard were promoting or involved in banking in some way.[39]

In places such as New York, Philadelphia, Baltimore, and Boston there were many groups of businessmen who aspired to have a bank. In these places states could sell bank charters and receive substantial revenues from doing so. In per capita terms, there were more banking services in the Northeast than in the rest of the country. West and south of that region, however, the size and sophistication of commercial centers decreased (with the exception of New Orleans), the number of banks decreased, and the number of farmers increased, but the need for banking services did not decline. States in the South and the West wanted banks just as much as New Englanders did, but the low population density, the high share of farmers, and the geographic concentration of crops meant that banking was riskier. Banks in Mississippi, for example, made loans directly to cotton farmers so that they could plant crops and, by discounting bills of exchange, facilitate getting the crops to market.

If the crop failed or cotton prices collapsed, banks in Mississippi were in trouble. The Mississippi banks had limited ability to diversify their risk, unlike banks in major eastern commercial centers with many opportunities to diversify their risk. The same was true in the Northwest, except there it was markets for wheat, corn, and other grains that mattered.[40]

States in the South and the West responded in two ways. First, they invested their own funds in banks, providing bankers with larger amounts of public capital (as opposed to Eastern states, which usually received bank stock as part of the charter process and did not put state funds *into* the bank). Second, there were fewer banks, and they tended to be larger (see table 6.1). Ohio and Louisiana were the only states west of the Appalachians with more than ten banks, and they were the two oldest and most highly developed western states by the 1830s. Most frontier states had fewer than five banks. Southern states in general had larger banks than did northern states, but in both regions banks were much larger in the West than in the East. Banks in the Southwest had ten times the average capital of banks in New England.[41]

The last three columns of table 6.1 provide some insight into state investment in banks in the West. Column 4 shows the amount of state debt incurred to invest in banks up to 1837. Only states in the frontier South and West invested in banks. Column 5 shows state investment as a share of total bank capital. With the exception of Kentucky, Ohio, and Michigan, state governments provided more than half of bank capital in each of these states. State involvement was critically important to the development of banks in these two regions. Column 6 shows the share of all state borrowing that went to investments in banks.

Table 6.1 BANKS, BANK CAPITAL, AND STATE INVESTMENTS IN BANKS, 1837

	(1) Banks and branches	(2) Capital	(3) Capital per bank	(4) Bank debt	(5) State debt as share of bank capital	(6) Share of state debt for banks
New England	304	$64,232,766	$211,292	0	0	0
Mid-Atlantic	204	$78,454,919	$384,583	0	0	0
South Atlantic	38	$31,377,856	$825,733	0	0	0
Southwest	31	$62,307,111	$2,009,907	$42,250,000	68%	87%
Northwest	49	$23,892,863	$487,609	$8,890,000	37%	29%

Note: All figures are calculated from H. Doc. #111, 26th Cong., 2nd sess. 1841. New England includes ME, NH, VT, MA, RI, and CT. Mid-Atlantic includes NY, NJ, PA, DE, MD, and DC. South Atlantic includes VA, NC, SC, and GA. Southwest includes FL, AL, LA, MS, and TN. Northwest includes KY, MO, IL, IN, OH, and MI.

Both Banks of the United States were extremely important to the development of American financial systems. They spanned the country, provided a uniform paper currency, and stabilized the conduct of national financial activities. But they were not the most important elements of the banking system that developed in the early nineteenth century. By 1836, state-chartered banks had ten times the capital of the Second BUS. When it lost its charter, it was quickly rechartered as the Bank of the United States of Pennsylvania. The banking system continued to develop without a national bank, and there is no reason to believe that the system would not have developed before 1836 if there had not been a national bank, although the system would have looked somewhat different.

State involvement in transportation investment has as a long history as well. By the 1780s states were chartering private companies, providing subsidies, and purchasing stock in canal, bridge, road, and turnpike companies. Virginia chartered the Potomac Company and the James River Company in 1785 and the Dismal Swamp Company in 1790. In 1792 New York chartered two companies, the Western Inland Lock Navigation Company and the Northern Inland Lock Navigation Company, to open canals to Lake Ontario in the West at the St. Lawrence River and in the North via Lake Champlain. Maryland chartered the Chesapeake and Delaware Canal in 1799. By 1811 Pennsylvania had spent $825,000 to build turnpikes. Massachusetts also invested in turnpikes. Unlike their investments in banks, however, transportation projects were rarely profitable for state governments. For a few brief years around 1805, it appeared the national government might get involved in transportation. Jefferson's second inaugural message, cited above, led Congress to ask the Secretary of the Treasury, Albert Gallatin, to prepare a report laying out a possible system of internal improvements. Gallatin's famous report proposed a network of canals that would have connected the disparate parts of the country at a cost of more than $20,000,000. Most of the projects envisioned in the report were eventually carried out in one form or another by state or private interests, but the national government spent very little on transportation before the 1820s.[42]

Despite inaction at the national level, there was widespread support for internal improvements. In 1811 the New York legislature authorized the issue of $5,000,000 in state bonds to build a canal, a plan sidetracked by the outbreak of the War of 1812. Virginia created a Board of Public works in 1816. In 1817, after failing to receive the support of the national government, New York embarked on the largest infrastructure project of its time, the Erie Canal. The canal turned out to be a phenomenally successful investment. Completed in 1825, it soon returned funds to the state over and above maintenance costs and interest payments. It now appeared that canals could prove as profitable as banks.

The pattern of state transportation investment after the Erie Canal's success was influenced by two factors. The first was geography. States with access to ocean transportation did not need to build canals, although they often improved their rivers and built short canals to bring their interior regions into contact with ports. The real payoff was the construction of interregional canals, like the Erie, that reached into the northwestern interior. In the late 1820s Ohio, Pennsylvania, and Maryland started canals, all with hopes that they would pay for themselves and return a handsome dividend to the state treasury. Virginia, South Carolina, and Georgia contemplated projects that would open up routes into Tennessee and Kentucky.

The second factor was the youth of western states. Indiana became a state in 1816, Mississippi in 1817, Illinois in 1818, Alabama in 1819, and Missouri in 1820. Indiana, the largest of those states in 1820, had a population of only 147,000. Not until the early 1830s did western economies expand in response to rapid population inflows. The expansion swelled the budgets of western states, enabling them to contemplate transportation investments of their own. In 1836 and 1837, Indiana, Illinois, and Michigan started new canal and railroad systems. In the same years, New York, Ohio, and Pennsylvania committed to expanding their existing systems. Rising western populations raised land prices; rising land prices stimulated public land sales; increased sale of public land raised the property tax base; and states began to think they could afford to build better transportation systems, which would further raise land prices, increase land sales, and expand the property tax base. The direction of causation in this story is difficult to disentangle, but all the factors came together to produce a major economic boom in the 1830s.

The boom affected southwestern states just as it affected northwestern states. Southern states, however, were not in need of major transportation investments. Their already navigable rivers ran to the sea. In the South, states invested predominantly in banks. Louisiana invested $23 million in banks beginning in 1824. Alabama, Georgia, and Florida made substantial investments in the early 1830s, and Mississippi and Arkansas committed millions of dollars to banks in 1837 and 1838. More than half of the banking capital in each of these states by 1837 came from state investment, and almost all of the debt in these states was issued for the purpose of investing in banks. Northwestern states needed banks, too; Illinois and Indiana made significant investments in their state banks.[43]

States had always borrowed money to finance long-term capital projects. But the pace of state borrowing increased dramatically in the 1830s. State debt expanded from a few million dollars in 1820 to $80 million in 1830 and to $200 million in 1841. Figure 6.8 shows the amount of state debt issued each year in the 1830s. The relative size of some of the state debts is truly amazing. In 1836, Indiana, with a population of roughly 500,000 and a state budget of $50,000 a year, authorized a bond issue of $10,000,000 in 5 percent bonds. Michigan, with a population of no more than 200,000 and state revenues of $17,000 in 1836, authorized a bond issue of $5,000,000 in 5 percent bonds in 1837. Above we saw the implications for tax revenues in Indiana. Per capita tax revenues in the 1840s were ten times higher than they had been in the 1830s. Total and per capita state debts outstanding in 1841 are given for each state in table 6.2.[44]

In 1837 the American economy was hit by a financial panic, and in 1839 a depression began that lasted until 1843. Many of the transportation and banking projects of the western states were abandoned. Indiana, Illinois, Michigan, Arkansas, Louisiana, Mississippi, Florida (still a territory), Maryland, and Pennsylvania stopped making interest payments on their state bonds in 1841 and 1842. Mississippi and Florida formally

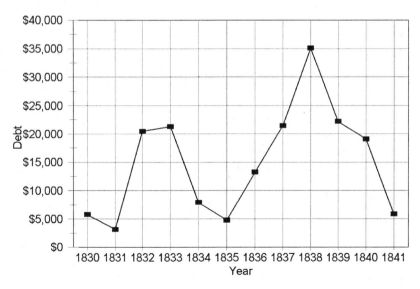

Figure 6.8. Debt authorized by year (thousands of dollars)

Table 6.2 TOTAL STATE DEBT, DEBT PER CAPITA, AND DEFAULTS, 1841

State	Total debt	Debt per capita	Default?
FL	$4,000,000	$74.07	Y
LA	$23,985,000	$68.14	Y
MD	$15,214,761	$32.37	Y
IL	$13,527,292	$28.42	Y
AK	$2,676,000	$27.31	Y
MI	$5,611,000	$26.47	Y
AL	$15,400,000	$26.06	N
PA	$33,301,013	$19.32	Y
MS	$7,000,000	$18.62	Y
IN	$12,751,000	$18.59	Y
NY	$21,797,267	$8.97	N
MA	$5,424,137	$7.35	N
OH	$10,924,123	$7.19	N
WI	$200,000	$6.45	N
SC	$3,691,234	$6.21	N
TN	$3,398,000	$4.10	N
KY	$3,085,500	$3.96	N
ME	$1,734,861	$3.46	N
VA	$4,037,200	$3.23	N
MO	$842,261	$2.19	N
GA	$1,309,750	$1.90	N
NH	$0	$0.00	N
CT	$0	$0.00	N
VT	$0	$0.00	N
RI	$0	$0.00	N
NC	$0	$0.00	N
NJ	$0	$0.00	N
DE	$0	$0.00	N

Source: Wallis, Sylla, and Grinath 2004.

repudiated their bonds, and Louisiana, Arkansas, and Michigan ultimately failed to repay part of the money they had borrowed. The other
states eventually resumed payments on their bonds and in the end repaid all of the principal and most of the back interest.[45] New York, Ohio,
and Alabama narrowly avoided default.

It is tempting to think that the canal boom of the 1830s took place
because naive western states optimistically thought they could borrow
to build canals, railroads, and banks and live on the dividends and tolls.
Such a view is inconsistent with the history recounted in this section.
States had been deeply involved in the creation of banks and transportation companies since the 1780s. In the case of banks, state involvement
had proved profitable in the sense that states that owned stock in banks
received substantial and steady dividends, and those that taxed banks
earned a hefty share of their revenues from bank taxes. In the case of

transportation, until the building of the Erie Canal, state investments had rarely been directly profitable, but there is little reason to doubt that the overall returns to the state treasury in terms of higher property tax revenues on increased land values made them good investments. What happened after 1839 was an unexpected economic depression that was caused, in part, by the terrible fix in which the states found themselves.[46]

States reacted predictably to the immediate crisis. New York passed a "Stop and Tax" law in 1842 requiring it to stop construction on the canals and reinstate the property tax. Indiana's new constitution, passed in 1851, left it up to the voters to ban banking entirely (they chose not to) and made it unconstitutional for the state to borrow to finance internal improvements. But by and large this revulsion against internal improvements was temporary. What changed permanently was the way states approached the process of promoting economic development. As early as 1837 Michigan and New York had adopted "free banking." In a state with a free banking act, anyone who met minimum requirements for capital investment could obtain a bank charter. Free banks were regulated; the "free" referred to entry, not to regulation. Twenty states had free banking systems by 1860. The corollaries to free banking in manufacturing and other sectors of the economy were general incorporation acts. In every state in 1790, a corporate charter could only be obtained by an act of the state legislature. This made charters valuable, as we have seen, but it also raised the possibility that business interests and politicians would conspire to limit competition. This was always a problem if the state relied on corporate charters or investment dividends for revenues. Eleven states adopted general incorporation clauses in their constitutions in the 1840s, and most states had general incorporation acts in place by 1900. When states began moving toward free banking and general incorporation, the importance of asset income necessarily declined, and state property taxes rose in importance as a share of state revenue.[47]

The depression of 1839 ended state investment in transportation in some states. Indiana, Illinois, Michigan, and Maryland wouldn't spend a penny on transportation until well after the Civil War. But voters in New York approved a bond issue to complete the canal system in the 1850s. Ohio struggled through the 1839 depression to finish its canal network. Louisiana, despite being in default on bank bonds issued in the 1820s, borrowed in national and international capital markets to build railroads in the 1850s. Nobody would lend money to Mississippi or Florida, but Missouri borrowed millions of dollars to build railroads in the 1850s.

Active promotion of economic development shifted in the later nineteenth century from state to local governments. In 1841 state government debt was eight times local government debt. Almost all of the debt was incurred to invest in banks, canals, and railroads. In 1902, when the first complete census of American governments was taken, local government debt was eight times state debt. Local debt was, as before, primarily incurred for economic development: railroads, water and sewage, public power, and education. American governments kept promoting economic development, but the level of government changed.

Conclusions

The history of American government cannot be written without including governments at all levels. Policies designed to promote economic development have moved from one level of government to another constantly throughout the nation's history. In 1776 there were fourteen individual government policies, not one. By the 1830s there were twenty-six states, each pursuing its own development agenda. By the end of the nineteenth century local governments had taken the lead in infrastructure investment. In 1940, when a complete count was taken, there were 140,000 governments in the United States (today there are about 80,000). Keeping track of how the American government interacts with the economy first requires that we keep track of what all American governments are doing.

From the nation's very beginnings in 1776, state governments, not the national government, took the lead in economic policy. The Articles of Confederation gave the federal government a monopoly of defense and international relations but gave it power over very little else. Such a weak central government could not provide even the basic service required of it: national defense. The Constitution, written in 1787, created a stronger national government, one possessing its own independent source of tax revenues. The Constitution gave the national government the sole power to conduct international affairs and military defense, to regulate the currency, to regulate international trade, and to disperse the western lands. At the same time, it hemmed in the national government by granting unenumerated powers to state governments.

In the 1790s, the federal government set up an active policy of financial promotion and protective revenue tariffs. Tariffs accounted for 85 percent of federal revenues, and military defense took up more than 52 percent of federal expenditures between 1790 and 1860. But using the tariff to actively promote American manufacturing raised substantial political opposition, and after the Tariff of Abominations was passed in 1828, tariff rates gradually declined and talk of using the tariff as a means of economic development diminished. The two federally chartered banks did exert a regulating influence on the money supply between 1791 and 1836, but they also generated intense political opposition. Congress failed to renew the first bank's charter in 1811 and could not override President Jackson's veto of the charter's renewal in 1832. The main functions of the federal government continued to be military defense (and at times military offense) and international relations.

The states developed active policies to promote economic development by encouraging public and private investment in banking and transportation. State development policy began to take shape in the 1780s and continued to grow in size and importance. States were often investors in early banks, and banking became an important source of revenue in several eastern states. As western states entered the Union, they too sought to develop banks and canals. Frontier states invested heavily in banks in the 1820s and 1830s. Following the success of the Erie Canal, eastern states such as Pennsylvania, Maryland, and Massachusetts began canal and railroad projects, followed in the 1830s by a wave of transportation investments in the Northwest. In the economic depression that began in 1839, many of the latter came to a bad end. States in some parts of the country began retreating from active investment, although others continued to actively invest right up to the Civil War.

In the 1840s, following the default crisis, states began putting in place arrangements that made it easier for corporations to form and guaranteed equal access to corporate charters for all members of the economy. Free banking laws and general incorporation acts implemented these policies. Many states wrote explicit provisions into their constitutions requiring legislators to write general incorporation acts. The result was a growing number of corporations and banks throughout the country.

Throughout the early nineteenth century, the national government wanted to promote economic development but found the political complexity of reaching a consensus about what should be done too daunting. National policy changed very little, except to back away from development-promoting policies, between 1790 and 1860. State governments, on the other hand, actively experimented with new ways to promote development, to help farmers get their goods to market with better transportation and finance, and to raise land values, which helped the farmers and the state treasuries that depended on the property tax. Not everything they tried worked, and some of their projects failed spectacularly.

But the idea that government should play a positive role in the economy was never seriously challenged, although it was often intensely debated.

Notes

1. For Adams's view see J. Adams 1961, 335–37.

2. This chapter omits two important areas of government action: education and the law. State governments provided a minimum amount of support for public education before 1860, but local governments, with wide variety across the country, began moving toward funding public schools. State and federal courts made large contributions to the promotion of economic development. Two features stand out. First, by the lights of the early nineteenth century, the courts were independent and unbiased. The "rule of law," the idea that governments should be of laws, not men, and in particular that governments and politicians should abide by the same laws they made for everyone else, was an important ideological element in the American legal system. Second, judges and lawyers thought systematically about how law affected the economy and effectively began changing the structure of American common law to "release energy," in the words of James Willard Hurst (1964).

3. Pennsylvania, Vermont, and Georgia all started out with a unicameral legislature, a governor, and an executive council. The council was elected by the voters in Pennsylvania and Vermont and chosen from within the legislature in Georgia. All three states intended to create a government constituted of balanced and separated powers. For a discussion of the first state constitutions see W. Adams 2001; Lutz 1980, 1988; Tarr 2001; Green 1966; and Kruman 1997. For the ever-changing state of suffrage see Keyssar 2000. Judicial independence was a principle of American constitutional theory, but as in the national constitution, the actual form that judicial institutions took was initially a legislative matter. Over time states adopted much more specific constitutional forms of judicial systems, and the national government has left the federal judiciary to the Congress.

4. The story of national finances during and after the war is told in Ferguson 1961 and in chapter 5 of this book.

5. Adjustments for inflation and deflation would not change the basic features of government discussed here.

6. Military expenditures would be substantially higher if benefits for Civil War veterans were included in the defense category.

7. Slaughter (1986) discusses the 1794 protests in Pennsylvania. In discussions of debt it is important to note that repaying the principal on government debts is clearly an expense for the government, but it is not treated as an "expenditure" in the government accounts. To do so would be to double-count the borrowed money. If the government borrows $100 to build a bridge, the construction costs are counted as an expenditure. If the repayment of the $100 principal were also counted as an expenditure, then total expenditures would be $200, when the government really spent $100. Interest payments on debts are expenditures. In a similar way, borrowed funds are not counted as revenues.

8. The four states are regionally representative and are ones for which we have relatively complete data. Individual state revenues are weighted by population to construct the average in the figure.

9. The figures for Maryland can be found in Hanna 1907.

10. See Goodrich 1960 for a history of transportation investment in the states.

11. The eastern state average is calculated for New York, Pennsylvania, Maryland, Massachusetts, Delaware, Rhode Island, North Carolina, and South Carolina. The western state average includes Ohio, Indiana, Illinois, Michigan, Arkansas, Kentucky, and Mississippi.

12. These figures are taken from the state financial documents that underlay the figures and the appendix tables on the nineteenth century. See Wallis 2000.

13. Wallis, Sylla, and Legler 1994, 126.

14. Figures for the labor force are available in Weiss 1992.

15. My assertion that land was the most important form of wealth holding before the Civil War is based on the figures presented in Gallman 1992.

16. For the cost of farm building see Atack and Passell 1994, 75–79. For the share of capital held in the form of land improvements see Gallman 1992.

17. Eventually, the development of futures markets for agricultural products enabled farmers to purchase contracts to sell wheat, for example, at a fixed price in the future.

18. This type of bill of exchange was often a "sight" bill, meaning that the agent's representative in New York had sixty days from the presentation of the bill, the sight, to pay cash.

19. The price differentials between Cincinnati and New York are taken from Berry 1943, 106, the prices in New York and Philadelphia from U.S. Department of Commerce 1975, 209.

20. The $.33 figure for 1820 is 24 percent of the $5.52 price of a barrel of flour in Cincinnati, divided by four, since the interest rate is annual and we want the cost of a ninety-day loan.

21. Scheiber (1969) discusses how Ohio and New York worked together to get freight on their systems. See chapter 5 of this book for more discussion of the financial turmoil that took place between 1837 and 1843.

22. With respect to slavery, in the Dred Scott decision of 1857, the Supreme Court declared the Missouri Compromise unconstitutional and ruled that Congress had no authority to exclude slavery from the territories. Neither Supreme Court decisions nor the endless debates and compromises in Congress settled the issue of slavery in the territories. Ultimately, the Civil War settled the debate.

The distinction between political and constitutional argument may be a bit difficult for modern ears to follow. In the twenty-first century it is clear that the Supreme Court is the final arbiter of what is "constitutional." The Constitution declares itself the law of the land but is vague about the mechanism. In the early nineteenth century it wasn't clear what was and was not constitutional; more important, it was not at all clear who should decide. Presidents Madison and Jackson both vetoed important legislation on the grounds that it was unconstitutional (the Bonus Bill of 1817 and the Maysville Road bill of 1830, respectively), but their stands (particularly Jackson's) appear to have been motivated more by political objections than constitutional ones. Earlier and later Congresses and presidents passed and signed legislation that did exactly what Madison and Jackson had vetoed without changing the Constitution. Madison's and Jackson's assertion that something was unconstitutional nonetheless carried considerable weight at the time because no one had yet figured out how a congressional act or state law was to be declared unconstitutional.

23. Jefferson is quoted in Richardson 1897, 367.

24. Federal expenditures for transportation are analyzed in detail in Malone 1998.

25. For more on land sales, see chap. 4.

26. Feller 1984, 194.

27. Nettels (1924, 353) analyzes these 117 pieces of legislation.

28. *An Ordinance for the government of the territory of the United States northwest of the river Ohio.* Confederate Congress, July 13, 1787, reported in Poore 2003, 432.

29. The quotations are found in Poore 2003, 1664 (for First Cong., 2d sess., 1790), 1050 (for Fifth Cong., 2d sess., 1798).

30. The quotations are found in Poore 2003, 694 (Eighth Cong., 1st sess., 1804), 1104 (*Enabling Act for Missouri,* Sixteenth Cong., 1st sess., 1820).

31. Keep in mind the distinction between economic and political importance. Did the Kansas-Nebraska Act, which allowed those territories to decide for themselves whether to allow slavery, mean much to the economic development of the United States? The answer has to be no. Did the passage of the act mean much to the political development of the United States? Of course it did, because the act was a critical event leading up to the Civil War.

32. Hamilton's plans were laid out in a series of reports to Congress: First Report on the Public Credit, January 14, 1790; Report on a National Bank, December 14, 1790; Report on Manufacturers, December 5, 1791; and Second Report on the Public Credit, January 16 and 21, 1795. These are reprinted in McKee 1934.

33. Hamilton's letter to Washington about the constitutionality of a national bank is found in McKee 1934, 101, emphasis in original.

34. For more on the Second Bank of the United States, see chapter 5.

35. See Irwin 2003 for the success of Hamilton's tariff plan in Congress.

36. Ellis (1987) tells the history of the nullification crisis.

37. The numbers are taken from Gates 1968, 86. Other additions to the public domain included the cession of Florida and the Gadsden purchase.

38. Fenstermaker (1965) provides detailed information about the chartering of state banks before 1837.

39. The relation between ownership and taxation of banks to the number of banks charted in Pennsylvania, Massachusetts, and other states is examined in Wallis, Sylla, and Legler 1994.

40. See Bodenhorn 2000, 63; 2003.

41. The numbers for Mississippi and Michigan are larger because of the creation of banks in 1835 and 1836.

42. The classic history of government involvement in transportation remains Goodrich 1960, which has been supplemented by Larson 2001.

43. Arkansas became a state in 1837, and the first act of the state legislature was to create a bank capitalized by state bonds.

44. I nformation about state finances in the 1830s and 1840s is available in Sylla, Legler, and Wallis 1993.

45. The amount and speed of repayment varied from state to state. Pennsylvania and Maryland resumed payments by 1848 and paid the back interest in full. Indiana and Illinois were still struggling in the 1850s.

46. For a paper that estimates the effect of railroad construction on land values and property tax revenues in the late nineteenth century see Heckelman and Wallis 1997; for a direct measure of canal construction on land values in Indiana in the mid-1830s, see Wallis 2003.

47. For evidence concerning incorporation acts, see Evans 1948.

References

Adams, John. 1961. *Diary and Autobiography of John Adams.* Ed. L. H. Butterworth. Cambridge: Harvard University Press, Belknap Press.

Adams, Willi Paul. 2001. *The First American Constitutions.* Expanded ed. Lanham, MD: Rowman & Littlefield.

Atack, Jeremy, and Peter Passell. 1994. *A New Economic View of American History.* New York: Norton.

Berry, Thomas, Sr. 1943. *Western Prices before 1861.* Cambridge: Harvard University Press.

Bodenhorn, Howard. 2000. *A History of Banking in Antebellum America.* Cambridge: Cambridge University Press.

———. 2003. *State Banking in Early America: A New Economic History.* Oxford: Oxford University Press.

Callender, Guy Stevens. 1902. "The Early Transportation and Banking Enterprises of the States." *Quarterly Journal of Economics* 17.1 (November): 111–62.

Ellis, Richard E. 1987. *The Union at Risk: Jacksonian Democracy, States' Rights, and the Nullification Crisis.* Oxford: Oxford University Press.

Evans, George Heberton. 1948. *Business Incorporations in the United States, 1800–1943.* New York: National Bureau of Economic Research; Baltimore: Waverly Press.

Feller, Daniel. 1984. *The Public Lands in Jacksonian Politics.* Madison: University of Wisconsin Press.

Fenstermaker, J. Van. 1965. *The Development of American Commercial Banking, 1782–1837.* Kent, OH: Kent State University, Bureau of Economic and Business Research.

Ferguson, E. James. 1961. *The Power of the Purse: A History of American Public Finance, 1776–1790.* Chapel Hill: University of North Carolina Press.

Gallman, Robert. 1992. "Capital Stock." In *American Economic Growth and Standards of Living before the Civil War,* ed. Robert Gallman and John Joseph Wallis, 79–120. Chicago: University of Chicago Press.

Gates, Paul Wallace. 1968. *History of Public Land Law Development.* Washington, DC: Government Printing Office.

Goodrich, Carter. 1960. *Government Promotion of American Canals and Railroads*. New York: Columbia University Press.

Green, Fletcher M. 1966. *Constitutional Development in the South Atlantic States, 1776–1860*. New York: Norton.

Hammond, Bray. 1957. *Banks and Politics in America: From the Revolution to the Civil War*. Princeton: Princeton University Press.

Handlin, Oscar, and Mart Flug Handlin. 1969. *Commonwealth: A Study of the Role of Government in the American Economy; Massachusetts, 1774–1861*. Cambridge: Harvard University Press, Belknap Press.

Hanna, Hugh Sisson. 1907. *A Financial History of Maryland (1789–1848)*. Johns Hopkins University Studies in Historical and Political Science, ser. 25, nos. 8–10. Baltimore: Johns Hopkins University Press.

Heckelman, Jac, and John Joseph Wallis. 1997. "Railroads and Property Taxes." *Explorations in Economic History* 34 (January): 77–99.

Hurst, James Willard. 1964. *Law and the Conditions of Freedom*. Madison: University of Wisconsin Press.

Irwin, Douglas A. 2003. "The Aftermath of Hamilton's 'Report on Manufacturers.'" Working Paper no. W9943, National Bureau of Economic Research, Cambridge, MA (September).

Keyssar, Alexander. 2000. *The Right to Vote: The Contested History of Democracy in the United States*. New York: Basic Books.

Kruman, Marc W. 1997. *Between Authority and Liberty: State Constitution Making in Revolutionary America*. Chapel Hill: University of North Carolina Press.

Larson, John Lauritz. 2001. *Internal Improvement: National Public Works and the Promise of Popular Government in the Early United States*. Chapel Hill: University of North Carolina Press.

Legler, John B., Richard E. Sylla, and John Joseph Wallis. 1988. "U.S. City Finances and the Growth of Government, 1850–1902." *Journal of Economic History* 48 (June): 347–56.

Lutz, Donald S. 1980. *Popular Consent and Popular Control: Whig Political Theory and the Early State Constitutions*. Baton Rouge: Louisiana State University Press.

———. 1988. *The Origins of American Constitutionalism*. Baton Rouge: Louisiana State University Press.

Malone, Laurence J. 1998. *Opening the West: Federal Internal Improvements before 1860*. Westport, CT: Greenwood.

McKee, Samuel Jr., ed. 1934. *Alexander Hamilton's Papers on Public Credit, Commerce and Finance*. New York: Columbia University Press.

Nettels, Curtis. 1924. "The Mississippi Valley and the Constitution, 1815–1829." *The Mississippi Valley Historical Review* 11 (December): 332–57.

Poore, Benjamin Perley. 2003. *The Federal and State Constitutions, Colonial Charters, and Other Organic Laws of the United States*. 2d ed. 1878; repr., Clark, NJ: Lawbook Exchange.

Richardson, James D. 1897. *Messages and Papers of the Presidents*. Washington, DC: Bureau of National Literature.

Scheiber, Harry N. 1969. *Ohio Canal Era: A Case Study of Government and the Economy, 1820–1861*. Athens: Ohio State University Press.

Schwartz, Anna 1987. "The Beginning of Competitive Banking in Philadelphia." In *Money in Historical Perspective*. Cambridge, MA: National Bureau of Economic Research; Chicago: University of Chicago Press.

Slaughter, Thomas P. 1986. *The Whiskey Rebellion: Frontier Epilogue to the American Revolution*. New York: Oxford University Press.

Sylla, Richard, John B. Legler, and John Joseph Wallis. 1987. "Banks and State Public Finance in the New Republic." *Journal of Economic History* 47 (June): 391–403.

———. 1993. "Sources and Uses of Funds in State and Local Governments, 1790–1915: [United States]." Inter-University Consortium for Political and Social Research (ICPSR) Data set 1993-05-13. University of Michigan at Ann Arbor.

Tarr, Alan. 2000. *Understanding State Constitutions*. Princeton: Princeton University Press.

United States Department of Commerce. 1975. *Historical Statistics of the United States: Colonial Times to 1970*. Washington, DC: Government Printing Office.

Wallis, John Joseph. 2000. "American Government Finance in the Long Run: 1790 to 1990." *Journal of Economic Perspectives* 14.1 (January 2000): 61–82.

———. 2001. "History of the Property Tax." In *Property Tax*, ed. Wallace E. Oates, 123–47. Cambridge, MA: Lincoln Institute.

———. 2003. "The Property Tax as a Coordination Device: Financing Indiana's Mammoth System of Internal Improvements." *Explorations in Economic History* 40.3 (July 2003): 223–50.

Wallis, John Joseph, Richard Sylla, and Arthur Grinath. 2004. "Sovereign Default and Repudiation: The Emerging-Market Debt Crisis in American States, 1839–1843." Working Paper no. W10753, National Bureau of Economic Research, Cambridge, MA.

Wallis, John Joseph, Richard Sylla, and John Legler. 1994. "The Interaction of Taxation and Regulation in Nineteenth Century Banking." In *The Regulated Economy: A Historical Approach to Political Economy,* ed. Claudia Goldin and Gary Libecap, 121–44. Chicago: University of Chicago Press.

Weiss, Thomas. 1992. "Labor Force." In *American Economic Growth and Standards of Living Before the Civil War*, ed. Robert Gallman and John Joseph Wallis, 19–78. Chicago: University of Chicago Press.

JEFFREY ROGERS
HUMMEL

7

The Civil War and Reconstruction

THE CIVIL WAR is a defining event in American history. Far more than the American Revolution, it forged a consolidated nation-state, politically, economically, and ideologically. With the triumph of American nationalism, never again would any section of the United States even threaten, much less attempt, independence. The war also brought about the final eradication of black chattel slavery within the country's borders, an accomplishment whose significance cannot be overestimated. The United States had previously stood out as one of the few remaining world powers striving to uphold this ancient but waning institution. Now it had dramatically and decisively joined the cause of abolition.[1]

But these watershed changes came at an enormous cost. Contrary to the expectations of leaders on both sides, the Civil War raged for four soul-wrenching years. The total number killed on both sides—620,000, with an additional 400,000 wounded—ranks the conflict as the bloodiest in all of United States history. That figure is half again the number of American deaths that resulted from World War II and represents six times as many on a per capita basis. Several of the Civil War's major battles, including that at Gettysburg, Pennsylvania, individually yielded more American casualties than the fighting in all previous U.S. wars combined. On top of the human devastation was the insurgency's economic cost, reaching a total of $6.6 billion (in 1860 prices), about evenly divided between the two sides. The North's portion alone was by some estimates enough to buy all slaves and set up every freed family with forty acres and a mule.[2]

It is unsurprising that the American Civil War had a decisive impact on government and the economy. Part of that impact is aptly captured in the maxim "War is the health of the State." Enunciated by Randolph Bourne, the young progressive radical, as he gazed in dismay at the Wilson administration's excesses during World War I, this maxim holds in two respects. During wartime, government swells in size, scope, power, and intrusiveness, as it taxes, conscripts, and regulates the people, generates inflation, and suppresses civil liberties in its single-minded pursuit of military victory. Then, after the war is over, there is what Robert Higgs and others have identified as a ratchet effect. Postwar retrenchment almost never returns government to its prewar levels. The State has assumed new functions, taken on new responsibilities, and exercised new prerogatives that continue long beyond the fighting's end.[3]

These two phenomena are starkly evident in nearly every American war. Yet the Civil War witnessed them both plus something more—and something unique. Despite wars and their ratchets, governments must *sometimes* recede in reach, else all peoples would have been groaning under totalitarian regimes long ago. It is commonly agreed that Americans once enjoyed a degree of liberty from government that was extraordinary in the annals of civilization. Whether one thinks that was desirable or not, all acknowledge that the government within the United States is more active today than in the past. Total government spending (national, state, and local) now exceeds one-third of the U.S. economy's output, and government regulation is so pervasive that many economics texts properly classify the U.S. not as a market economy but as a mixed one, combining elements of command and markets.

A major question for economic history is, how did this come about? How did the United States become so free from government in the first place, and what caused the reversal? Many conservatives and liberals date the turning point to the Great Depression of 1929. Americans are alleged to have self-reliantly resisted the temptations of tax-financed largess and confined federal power within strict constitutional limits, until Roosevelt's New Deal ushered in an age of government extravagance and paternalism. Others push the critical reversal back to the Progressive Era. I contend that America's decisive transition with respect to State power, as with respect to so much else, must be dated even earlier, during the conflict of 1861–65.

Prior to the Civil War, American politics had been dominated by four successive ideological surges: the radical republican movement that spearheaded the American Revolution, the Jeffersonian movement, which had arisen in reaction to the Federalist State, the Jacksonian movement, which followed the War of 1812, and the roughly contemporaneous abolitionist movement. Although each was unique, all were American manifestations of the worldwide thrust toward classical liberalism. Each had contributed to the secular erosion of government power at all levels, despite intermittent wars with their ratchet effects. The great irony of the Civil War is that at the very moment of the abolitionist triumph, with the final elimination of the last major coercive blight on the landscape, the American polity started marching in the opposite direction. Thereafter, the long-term tendency would be for local, state, and central governments to expand their functions and reach, particularly as a result of wars, and at a rate faster than the economy's growth. The Civil War thus represents a simultaneous culmination and repudiation of the radical principles of the American Revolution.

To support this contention, as well as to trace the Civil War surge in government control and the postwar ratchet effect, I must begin with a brief survey of how the relation between the U.S. economy and government was evolving in the antebellum years. I also examine slavery both as labor system and as cause of sectional strife. Then I look at the war's impact on government in four overlapping realms: military mobilization, public finance, civil liberties, and economic mobilization. Bear in mind that the Civil War involved two central States: the Union and the Confederacy. We will discover that in most respects, they were mirror images, with a few intriguing variations on a theme. Finally, I take up the war's legacy as it played out in the South under Reconstruction and in the nation overall.

The Antebellum United States

The United States prior to Lincoln's election in 1860 had a central government that was minuscule by modern standards. The highest annual outlays reached was $74.2 million in 1858, which translates into a little more than $1.5 billion in 2005 prices. On a per capita basis, the government in Washington was spending approximately $2.50 in 1858, or the equivalent today of about $50, for every man, woman, and child. That was less than 2 percent of the economy's total output. We have poor records of how much state and local governments spent at the time, but all estimates put the level at less than twice as much as the national government spent, which was the approximate ratio after 1902, the first year for which we have complete information. Total spending then for all levels of government was around 5 percent of national income.[4]

The national debt, for all intents and purposes, had been completely paid off in 1835. By 1860, mainly as a consequence of the Mexican War, it stood at a modest $65 million—*less* than annual outlays in 1858. What makes this doubly amazing is that there were only two sources of federal

THE CIVIL WAR AND RECONSTRUCTION

revenue at the time: a tariff, with relatively low duties because this was an era of expanding free trade; and the sale of public lands, on which Congress had been steadily reducing the price because of the growing appeal of homesteading. In short, most Americans paid no taxes whatsoever directly to the central government. Their only regular contact with representatives of national authority would have been through the United States Post Office—if they had any contact at all. Indeed, in New York City, the government delivered only one million letters in 1856, as compared with ten million carried by private companies (Nevins 1959, 240).

The indebtedness of state governments during the 1830s and 40s had greatly exceeded that of the national government. This was mainly the consequence of a craze for canal building and other internal improvements that engulfed the states after the War of 1812. These projects generally turned out to be lavish and wasteful malinvestments that by the 1840s had forced many states into some kind of financial stringency and eight of them, plus the Florida Territory, into default. But this fiscal crisis had the salutary effect of encouraging constitutional limits on state indebtedness along with the adoption of general incorporation laws, eliminating the monopoly privileges previously associated with individual corporate charters granted by the state legislatures. The states would now be far more restrained and circumspect in their promotion of railroads, which unlike canals tended to remain privately owned. In short, state governments were receding during the antebellum years as well.[5]

Even the monetary system was significantly deregulated as a result of the Jacksonian "divorce" of banking and government at the national level. There was no federally chartered central bank, and the Treasury, as much as feasible, avoided dealing with the many state-chartered banks. The only legally recognized money was specie, that is, gold and silver coins. Although banks were still regulated by the state governments, many states had instituted a de facto regime of quasi-free banking. The economy's currency consisted solely of state bank notes redeemable for specie on demand. Private competition thus regulated the circulation of paper money. Despite trumped-up charges of wildcat banking, it was by comparison a relatively stable and crisis-free monetary system, as attested to by the painless financing of the Mexican War from 1846 to 1848 and the unprecedented quiescence of monetary issues in national politics in the decade prior to the Civil War.[6]

The major exception to this widespread decline of coercive authority was, of course, chattel slavery, or what southerners referred to as their "peculiar institution." Of a U.S. population of 31.5 million in 1860, nearly four million were African American slaves, concentrated within the southern states. Three quarters of these bondsmen and -women toiled on plantations and farms, producing tobacco, sugar, rice, or cotton for world markets. This deeply imbedded institution, moreover, spun out political ramifications that impinged on the liberty of free white Americans in the South and the North.

Slavery had not always divided the two sections. But the American Revolution's liberating spirit had induced the northern states, where the institution was less economically entrenched, to become the first jurisdictions in the Western Hemisphere to enact either outright abolition or gradual emancipation. During the same period, in contrast, slavery underwent an economic resurgence in the American South as a cotton boom enticed settlers into the rich lands of the Gulf of Mexico, converting the formerly slave-free southern frontier to plantation agriculture. Not until the decade following the War of 1812 did slavery fully divide the South from the North. Yet the United States slave population was three times what it had been at the outset of the Revolution.

Thus, while bondage was disappearing elsewhere, it was expanding in the southern states. Simultaneously, the free states were beginning to overwhelm the slave states in total population and outvote them in the House of Representatives. Only the Senate tended to maintain a balance between the country's two sections, and that ended in 1850. With black slavery now surviving only in Puerto Rico, Cuba, Brazil, the Dutch West Indies, and the United States, southern slaveholders felt increasingly encircled. Slaveholders were a minority within their own states. By 1860, only one-fourth of white southern households owned slaves, and about half of those owned fewer than five. Still, the total value of all slaves was between $2.7 and $3.7 billion, making it an asset that exceeded the value of all U.S. manufacturing and railroad capital combined. Political power was therefore concentrated in the hands of large planters, who constituted a special interest that dominated not only southern state and local governments but the national government as well.[7]

Slaveholders consequently secured government subsidies at all levels. State and local ordinances that regulated the activities of the small numbers of free blacks, that restricted masters from manumitting their own slaves, that outlawed teaching slaves to read or write, and that imposed harsh penalties on anyone advocating abolition were nearly universal throughout the South. The chief mechanism by which states and localities socialized slavery's enforcement costs, however, was a system of slave patrols, established in every slave state save Delaware. Although sometimes tax-financed in the upper South, patrol duty was usually compulsory for most able-bodied white males. The national government likewise bolstered the South's peculiar institution, most conspicuously as a result of the Constitution's fugitive slave clause. The clause required the return of escaped slaves even from free states and was the reason the celebrated Underground Railroad, which assisted runaways, terminated in Canada rather than Pennsylvania.[8]

Although increasing northern reluctance to return runaway slaves generated tension between northerners and southerners, the most acrimonious source of sectional strife was slavery's status in the territories. As the borders expanded from the Atlantic to the Pacific, the Union successfully withstood three severe territorial impasses: the Missouri crisis of 1819–20, the crisis ended by the Compromise of 1850, and the crisis over Kansas, which erupted in 1854. Each crisis was patched over with a congressional compromise, but each compromise made it evident that the North and the South were drifting apart in a reinforcing cycle of southern isolation and escalation. Because the political power of the slave states eroded steadily with their declining relative population, they escalated demands for national guarantees to their peculiar institution. But each successive guarantee alienated greater numbers of northerners.

The cumulative impact was to foster antislavery sentiment. The newly formed Republican Party mobilized this sentiment, reducing it to its lowest common denominator by only opposing slavery's extension into the territories. In 1860, the Republicans elected as president Abraham Lincoln, a northerner who did not carry a single slave state and, within ten of them, did not get a single recorded vote. Nothing could make the looming political impotence of the slave states starker. Almost overnight a special interest that had dictated policy to Congress, to the Executive, on the Supreme Court, and usually to both major parties was politically dispossessed. Although leaving the Union was a risky gamble, many slaveholders felt they had nothing to lose.

Slavery was the underlying motive for the secession of the southern states, but it initially had little to do with the northern refusal to let the South go in peace. The Republican Party had politically triumphed where more radical opponents of slavery had failed because it had promised free-state voters that they could have *both* antislavery and Union. Now that the Union was imperiled, the Republicans had to take decisive action or face political oblivion. Lincoln insisted, both before and after the firing on Fort Sumter, that he wanted only to preserve the Union, and Congress confirmed this war aim. Nevertheless, the emancipation of black slaves ultimately became the paramount and most propitious unintended consequence of suppressing southern independence.[9]

Military Mobilization: From Voluntarism to Conscription

One of the reasons why government was so unobtrusive before the Civil War is that, unlike most European and Latin American powers, the United States maintained a Lilliputian standing army during peacetime. Few realize that, at the outset of the Mexican War in 1846, despite having twice the population and a much more prosperous economy, the United States had a regular army that was less than one-fourth the size of Mexico's: 7,300 to 32,000. To fight that war, the U.S. government had expanded its military to a conquering force of nearly 50,000, but by the time South Carolina seceded in 1860 only 16,000 regulars remained scattered across outposts mainly in the far West and along the coast.

Thus, both the Union and the Confederacy had to create gargantuan military establishments essentially from scratch. In both cases, the foundation for this unprecedented mobilization was the volunteer militia. And the operative word is *volunteer,* for the militia system of 1860 was quite different from the militias of the early Republic. Originally the colonial and state militias had comprised a decentralized system of universal military training and conscription. Every able-bodied male, with some occupational exemptions, had been enrolled and required to muster for regular training days. In "calling out the militia," a seemingly innocuous phrase, each militia district received a quota. If volunteers were sufficient to fill the quota, fine, but if not, names would be chosen from the militia rolls for compulsory service. As a result, there had been widespread conscription during both the American Revolution and the War of 1812. One of the unsung Jacksonian achievements at the state level had been a militia reform that had not only successfully assailed the system's compulsory features but in many respects had privatized it. Volunteer units—sometimes organized, recruited, and equipped by wealthy or prominent individuals—sprung up throughout the country in the years following the War of 1812 and almost completely supplanted the old common militia. The Mexican War, therefore, became the first U.S. war to be fought entirely with volunteers.[10]

At the Civil War's outset, this decentralized system brought in more enthusiastic volunteers than either side could process. Military historians have endlessly denounced the seeming unpreparedness and disorganization. Yet if we make an honest assessment, it was one of the most rapid and effective mobilizations in world history. The Union army multiplied by a factor of fifteen within four months of the firing on Fort Sumter, despite the defection of nearly half the country and many professional officers. Compare that with U.S. Army's mere threefold growth, under rigid conscription, in the first four months after the U.S. entered World War I.[11]

By the end of the Civil War, the Union army was a million strong, making it the largest military machine on the planet. That, in and of itself, was a dramatic transformation, but there had also been a profound alteration in the organizing principle. For as the war dragged on and the initial enthusiasm faded, both the Union and the Confederacy resorted to conscription. The South, which unlike the North had never completely dismantled its compulsory militia, did so first in April 1862. Although not, as often stated, the first conscription in American history, it was the first centrally administered conscription in American history, and for that reason it represents a momentous step.

The Confederacy's draft initially applied to all men between eighteen and thirty-five years of age. Yet exemptions were numerous, and men could also avoid service by paying a substitute to serve for them, a feature carried over from the militia laws. The primary function of the early Confederate legislation was to prolong the terms of all draft-age veterans to three years. Later acts, however, made avoiding conscription steadily tougher. Eventually the eligible ages were extended to cover all males between seventeen and fifty years of age. The rebel legislature repealed substitution in December 1863. Conscientious objectors still could pay a $500 exemption fee, but only if they were Quakers, Dunkers, or Mennonites as of October 1862.

Conscription furnished somewhere between one-fifth and one-third of southern military manpower. Nearly every soldier, whether volunteer or conscript, was held in the army until the war ended—or he was wounded or killed. No Confederate war measure aroused more popular resentment. Nonslaveholders were particularly galled by an exemption for one white man on each plantation of twenty or more slaves. This precaution against servile insurrection and declining labor discipline was derisively denounced as the "twenty-nigger law." It led to the widespread quip, "rich man's war, poor man's fight."[12]

The Union imposed a national militia law in July 1862, shortly after passage of the Confederacy's first conscription act. But the measure with real teeth was the Enrollment Act of March 1863. Men between the ages of twenty and forty-five were made liable for three years of military service, and this eventually would apply to noncitizens residing in the country, too. Although there were no occupational exemptions, anyone could hire a substitute or pay the government a flat $300 commutation fee. Much maligned by historians, these practices made conscription more efficient, equitable, and palatable, not less. Many military-age men put money into draft insurance clubs that would hire substitutes for any member called up. And in contrast to the Confederacy, the Union honored a soldier's original enlistment and exempted him from all future draft calls.

The resulting turnover, however, required the Union to find a greater number of fresh recruits. Congress mainly designed the Enrollment Act, like the militia law passed a year earlier, to stimulate volunteering. Each congressional district received a troop quota. Along with the stick of conscription, national, state, and local authorities tried to raise the troops with the carrot of monetary bounties. Ranging from $300 all the way up to $1,500, these incentives gave rise to professional bounty brokers as well as the charming vice of bounty jumping, whereby a man would enlist in one community, get his bounty, desert, and enlist in another area. The bounty-jumping record of the North went to John O'Connor, who succeeded in thirty-two desertions before being apprehended and jailed in 1865. Less fortunate bounty jumpers caught earlier were summarily shot or hung. During the course of the war, Union and Confederate authorities executed a combined total of five hundred of their own troops, more than in all other American wars combined, and two-thirds of those were executed for desertion (Robertson 1988, 135).

Only if a northern district failed to meet its quota with volunteers would federal enrollment officers take over. Rather than obligating citizens to come forward and register, as in the military drafts of more recent times, the Enrollment Act sent these officers on a house-to-house canvass. As the reader can imagine, this became an extremely hazardous occupation. Enrollment officers were gunned down in Illinois and Indiana. At one point in 1863, Secretary of War Edwin M. Stanton faced simultaneous calls from about two hundred cities, towns, and counties throughout the loyal states for troops to suppress draft disturbances.

But nothing matched the fury of the outbreak in New York City during July 1863. The drawing of the first draftees' names touched off four days of uncontrolled rioting, mostly among the city's teeming population of Irish workingmen and women. With well over one hundred dead and as many wounded, many of them hapless free blacks whom the rioters blamed for the war, it was the worst urban riot in American history. After inspiring all this commotion, conscription directly provided only about 6 percent of the men who served in the Union armies. Monetary payments in the form of generous bounties or, secondarily, substitution remained the main inducements for enlistment. And perhaps as many as 160,000 northerners illegally evaded the draft altogether.[13]

Wartime Public Finance, North and South

Wars are very expensive. Nearly all governments throughout history have spent more on waging and preparing for war than on anything else. Yet Abraham Lincoln's Secretary of the Treasury, Salmon Portland Chase, in addition to being a radical opponent of slavery, despised government debt, paper money, and internal taxes. Good government, in Chase's eyes, was frugal government. Imagine, then, his mortification when he learned that the Union's wartime deficit for only the first three months after Fort Sumter would exceed $17 million. By 1865, central government spending had soared from less than 2 percent of the economy's total output to well over 20 percent, approximately what the central government spends today during peacetime. It is hard to decide from which angle this statistic is more remarkable: that spending rose from such infinitesimal lows to today's heights in only four years, or that today federal authorities regularly spend as much as they did during the most expensive year of the country's bloodiest war. These unprecedented expenditures struck at the very moment that anticipated revenues were falling. Although the outgoing Congress had raised the tariff before President James Buchanan left office, the Treasury Department was not going to be able to collect any duties from the South in the foreseeable future. Meanwhile the prices charged for public lands had been declining, and in 1862 the Homestead Act finally passed Congress, implementing the demand that settlers get free title to 160 acres of government land after five years of settlement.[14]

Chase therefore found himself resorting to a mixture of all the financial expedients he hated. Congress started off in 1861 with a direct tax of $20 million on real estate. This was the first internal tax Americans had paid to Washington City in nearly forty years, but at least it was administered by the state governments. Such was not the case with the Internal Revenue Act passed by Congress one year later. Rather than recite all the myriad details of this all-encompassing measure, I quote James G. Blaine, an up-and-coming Maine Republican, who reported how the act tried to tax nearly everything.

"One of the most searching, thorough, comprehensive systems of taxation ever devised by any Government," he called it. "Spirituous and malt liquors and tobacco were relied upon for a very large share of revenue. . . . Manufactures of cotton, wool, flax, hemp, iron, steel, wood, stone, earth, and every other material were taxed three percent. Banks, insurance and railroad companies, telegraph companies, and all other corporations were made to pay tribute. The butcher paid thirty cents for every beef slaughtered, ten cents for every hog, five cents for every sheep. Carriages, billiard-tables, yachts, gold and silver plate, and all other articles of luxury were levied upon heavily. Every profession and every calling, except the ministry of religion, was included within the far-reaching provisions of the law and subjected to tax for license. Bankers and pawnbrokers, lawyers and horse-dealers, physicians and confectioners, commercial brokers and peddlers, proprietors of theaters and jugglers on the street, were indiscriminately summoned to aid the National Treasury."[15]

With all these excise, sales, and license taxes, Blaine neglected to mention that the Internal Revenue Act of 1862 also introduced stamp taxes on most legal documents and an inheritance tax. Collection required the creation of an extensive internal revenue bureaucracy with 185 districts reaching into every hamlet and town. Evasion became a major problem, especially for the whiskey excise, as bootleg liquor displaced taxed liquor on the market. Congress's most portentous revenue measure, however, was a national income tax. Authorized in August 1861, this was the first such tax in United States history. It ultimately covered all incomes higher than $600 per year ($12,700 in 2005 prices) at graduated rates from 5 to 10 percent. To ensure compliance, the government adopted a British practice and withheld money from people's income when it could. The sources most vulnerable to withholding were government salaries, as well as dividends and interest from the stocks and bonds of banks, railroads, and other corporations. At the war's close the United States could boast higher taxation per capita than any other nation. But all the new and old taxes combined were just sufficient to cover about one-fifth of the Civil War's monetary cost.[16]

Borrowing covered another two-thirds of the war's cost. Chase floated some loans directly to the general public, with the aid of an extravagant publicity campaign handled by private financier, Jay Cooke. For most of its borrowing, however, the Union had to rely on banks, and this required that Congress undermine the restraints built into the antebellum financial system. The Treasury's initial war loan of $150 million had put a heavy strain on the northern banks that had subscribed. Once the financial community realized that the war would not be quick or easy, Treasury securities dropped in value. As gold reserves drained from the bank vaults, governments authorized suspension of specie payments in December 1861, a resort banks had always depended on during panics. These twelve hundred institutions were soon issuing more than $100 million worth of irredeemable notes, depreciating at different rates.

So in order to harness banking more tightly to the war effort and create a market for the Treasury's debt, the Republicans drafted the National Currency Acts of 1863 and 1864. These acts fashioned a network of nationally chartered banks, regulated by a new federal Comptroller of the Currency. National banks could issue bank notes supplied to them by the Comptroller, but only if they purchased a roughly equivalent value of war bonds. Congress attempted to bestow a currency monopoly on the national banks with a 2 percent tax on state bank notes, and when that failed to drive state bank notes out of circulation, it raised the tax to a prohibitive 10 percent in 1865. The state-chartered banks were thereafter confined to providing other financial services.

The last 15 percent of the war's financial outlay was covered by the first fiat money issued since the Constitution's ratification. In early 1862, Congress passed the Legal Tender Act, empowering Secretary Chase to issue a form of paper bills that became popularly known as greenbacks. The greenbacks were different from national bank notes in several respects. Greenbacks were unbacked, directly issued by the government, and made legal tender for all payments, public and private, except tariff duties and interest on the Treasury's debt. The national bank notes, although guaranteed by the government, were nominally the liability of private institutions and contractually exchangeable for bank reserves (which meant they were exchangeable exclusively for greenbacks until resumption of specie payments).[17]

The final total of greenbacks put into circulation reached $431 million, supplemented by a small quantity of interest-bearing notes and other currency. All this government paper, coupled with the private bank notes, doubled the Union's money stock by 1863. The consequent inflation put specie at a premium. Greenback dollars had fallen in July 1864 to a low of 35 cents' worth of gold. Banks in the Northeast offered deposits denominated either in gold dollars or greenback dollars. On the west coast, gold was still the circulating money and greenbacks were only accepted at a discount.[18]

Union finance occasioned some instructive sidelights. The flood of paper money caused a rise in counterfeiting, justifying the creation of a new federal agency to hunt down the culprits, the Secret Service, set up just as the conflict ended. This illustrates that more often than not, if one traces the origin of some government agency seemingly unrelated to national defense, one discovers that it arose in the fertile soil of war. Another way the government tightened its control over money during the war was by banning private coinage for the first time. Although the official United States mint had issued gold, silver, and copper coins since George Washington's presidency, up until the Civil War these had competed alongside coins issued by foreign governments and by privately owned domestic mints. Congress even tried to interfere with holding specie as protection from inflation by shutting down the exchange for contracts promising future delivery of gold in the summer of 1864. But this threatened further to disrupt foreign commerce, which depended on the metal. Congress had to back off hastily, and thereafter the Treasury confined any efforts at manipulating the gold exchange to the issue of gold certificates, authorized the year before and convertible on demand, but not actually put in circulation until 1865.

THE CONFEDERATE STATES of America faced serious disadvantages in military resources. Not counting the divided 3.2 million inhabitants of four border slave states that had not seceded, the Confederate population was 9.1 million, compared with the Union's 19.1 million. More than one-third of this population consisted of slaves, who were presumably unavailable for military service. The South's economic disabilities were even greater. Per capita income was higher among northerners, who owned three-quarters of the nation's material wealth. The output of northern industry was ten times that of the South. Indeed, the products manufactured in all eleven Confederate states combined amounted to less than one-fourth the total value manufactured in New York State alone. The North had twice the railroad mileage and built fourteen of every fifteen locomotives.[19]

The Confederacy's conventional military strategy, however, ensured that it, like the Union, would bear staggering wartime expenditures. So it likewise turned to a mixture of heavy taxation, government borrowing, and fiat money. With less abundant wealth to call on, taxation covered less than 7 percent of the South's total war costs. That was not for any lack of trying, although the Confederacy, like the Union, delayed truly confiscatory measures because it expected a short war. The rebel government, as soon as it was established, imposed duties on imports and also on exports, something the United States Constitution prohibited.

Yet a self-inflicted cotton embargo early in the conflict, along with the subsequent federal blockade, severely circumscribed any revenue from those sources. The Confederate Congress's first stab at internal taxation, like the Union's, was a direct tax on the state governments. Yet most southern states converted this tax into a war loan by issuing state bonds to finance their shares. Eventually, in April 1863, the Confederate government adopted a comprehensive revenue measure that included a graduated income tax, an excess profits tax, license taxes, excise taxes, and a 10 percent tax in kind. Farmers paid the tax in kind by directly surrendering their agricultural products. The southern economy's lack of monetary development necessitated this expedient, but the high-handed behavior of the TIK men who enforced it engendered widespread resistance.

One-fourth of the Confederate government's income came from borrowing. Most southern banks ceased paying specie immediately after secession and therefore had enough gold and silver left in their vaults to subscribe to much of the first Confederate loan, which was for $15 million. The South later floated an $8.5 million loan abroad through the French financier Emile Erlanger. Greater amounts came from produce loans, which were fiscally analogous to the tax in kind. At first planters and farmers would subscribe a share of their crop, sell it themselves for hard money, and loan the proceeds to the government. But later they exchanged cotton and other commodities directly for Confederate bonds. Churches, ladies' societies, and patriotic citizens also donated more than $2 million during the course of the war. Finally, a sequestration law, passed in response to the Union confiscation acts, expropriated all private property owned by northerners within Confederate jurisdiction and provided the government with some additional resources.[20]

But overall the Confederacy relied on paper money for more than half of the war's cost. Starting in March 1861 with $1 million of one-year Treasury notes bearing 3.65 percent, the Confederate Congress by August of the same year had authorized more than $100 million of non-interest-bearing notes. Although this paper money was acceptable for most tax payments to the central government, what really helped it circulate was the willingness of the state governments and state banks to receive it. Indeed, the Confederate Secretary of the Treasury compelled the conservative New Orleans banks, which had continued to pay out gold and silver after the Sumter crisis, to stop doing so in order to prevent specie from competing with Confederate currency.

The Confederate Treasury ultimately issued more than $1 billion worth of currency, more than twice the amount of greenbacks. This monetary expansion spurred ruinous price increases that made the Union's wartime inflation seem trivial. The blockade and an additional $45 million in paper currency issued by individual southern states contributed to the monetary depreciation. A Confederate dollar was worth 82.7 cents in specie in 1862, 29.0 cents in 1863, and 1.7 cents in 1865. Between 1860 and 1864 prices did not quite double in the North but multiplied by a factor of twenty-seven in the South. Only southern banks exercised any restraint, having no central bank or national banking system to encourage their monetary expansion. As the war dragged on, bank notes circulated at a premium, despite being immediately redeemable only in Confederate paper. The rebel Congress attempted a currency "reform" in February 1864, but this amounted to nothing more than a phased devaluation and repudiation. After January of the following year, the government would not accept its old currency at all, although it continued to issue new currency. The skyrocketing inflation worked a great hardship on the southern people. As this hidden tax diverted resources to the Confederate war effort, prices climbed faster than incomes. Real wages fell by almost two-thirds. Food riots swept through Richmond and other southern cities in the war's third year, with wives and mothers at the forefront of the rioters.[21]

The state governments attempted to step in and aid suffering families. They blocked debt collection with stay laws and tried to prevent speculative hoarding. Previously relief had been handled at the local level, but now the state legislatures appropriated millions of dollars for this purpose. Georgia spent more in 1863 than during the entire decade of the 1850s. Inflation accounted for some of this increase, and nearly half of this spending was for the military, but the other half was for welfare. By 1864, more than thirty-seven thousand families were receiving some form of relief from the state of Alabama—37 percent of all families in the state. Unfortunately, government welfare was powerless to create more real resources and so was doomed to futility as long as the military's appetite remained unabated.[22]

The rebel government, unlike the Union, never made its paper money legal tender. It did, however, force much of this money into circulation through the impressment of supplies. Commanders in the field initiated the practice, and the Confederate Congress formally systematized impressments in 1863. The Commissary and Quartermaster Bureaus would seize food and other items as needed in exchange for Confederate currency at officially fixed prices, a step beyond anything the Union did. Because the fixed prices were invariably lower than the inflationary market prices, shortages became rampant. Impressments made southerners suffer almost as much from the proximity of their own armies as from the invasions of Union armies.

Suppression of Civil Liberties

It has become a commonplace historical observation that Lincoln delayed calling Congress into session for nearly three months after the firing on Fort Sumter so that he could exercise arbitrary power. He thus mobilized seventy-five thousand militia, enlarged the regular army, ordered the blockade, dispersed government funds, authorized government borrowing, suspended habeas corpus, and instituted postal censorship, all before the legislature convened. Congress, however, retroactively approved almost all of these actions, and I am less concerned with the wartime relations among the various branches of government than with the government's treatment of its citizens.

The demeanor of the Lincoln administration first became evident in the border slave states. Four states—Delaware, Maryland, Kentucky, and Missouri—did not secede. Of these, only Delaware was unquestionably loyal. Maryland, in particular, was vital to the Union, and a glance at a map reveals why. The state isolated the nation's capital from the free states further north and also contained Baltimore, the country's third-largest city. Popular sentiment within the state was bitterly divided. The Maryland governor was timidly pro-Union, whereas the majority of the legislature leaned toward secession. The first regiment to answer Lincoln's call, the Sixth Massachusetts, had to march between train stations in Baltimore, where they were set upon by a pro-southern mob. In the ensuing melee four soldiers and at least nine civilians died, with many more injured. As the Sixth Massachusetts limped into Washington, Baltimore officials burned the railroad bridges and cut the telegraph wires.

After more regiments began pouring into the beleaguered capital, Lincoln suspended the writ of habeas corpus along "the military line" between Philadelphia and the District of Columbia and imposed a military occupation on Maryland. This permitted military authorities to imprison prominent secessionists without trial. One of the incarcerated Marylanders, John Merryman, appealed to the courts. The Chief Justice of the Supreme Court, Roger B. Taney, sitting as a circuit judge, ordered Merryman released, but federal officials, acting under Lincoln's instructions, refused. Whereas Lincoln simply ignored Taney's opinion, he did not overlook the increasingly outspoken Maryland legislature when it lodged a sharp protest with Congress. Instead, Secretary of State William Seward ordered a lightning raid that jailed thirty-one legislators, the mayor of Baltimore, one of the state's Congressmen, and key antiadministration publishers and editors. At the state's next election in the fall of 1861, federal provost marshals stood guard at the polls and arrested any disunionists who attempted to vote. Thus the new legislature was solidly behind the war.[23]

Similar measures not only held the other border states in the Union but also soon spread throughout the North. Opposition to emancipation and other policies of the Lincoln administration led increasing numbers of Democrats to question the war altogether. Northern sympathy for the Confederacy was particularly strong among Catholic immigrants in the cities and rural residents of the lower Midwest. Some Copperheads, as northern peace advocates were derisively labeled, formed secret societies such as the Knights of the Golden Circle and the Order of American Knights.

To intimidate and control these groups, the president extended the suspension of habeas corpus, previously limited to certain areas, to all the states in September 1862. This was a response to the first draft disturbances, but even before this blanket suspension, Union authorities were routinely arresting without trial or charges any northerners they suspected of disloyalty. First the State Department and later the War Department loosely coordinated surveillance through a network of special agents, U.S. marshals, Pinkerton detectives, local police, private informers, and above all, military officials. One widely circulated story claimed that Seward bragged about his power to the British Ambassador: "I can touch a bell on my right hand and order the arrest of a citizen of Ohio; I can touch a bell again, and order the imprisonment of a citizen of New York, and no power on earth, except that of the President of the United States, can release them. Can the Queen of England do as much?"[24]

To be sure, many of those arrested secured release within a month or two, usually after swearing a loyalty oath. The greater number were residents of either the border states or the Confederacy itself. Nevertheless, the Lincoln administration imprisoned at least fourteen thousand civilians throughout the course of the war, and state and local authorities probably seized many more. The federal government simultaneously monitored and censored the mails and telegraphs and for the first time demanded passports of those entering and leaving the country. No one who was eligible for the draft could depart. It also suppressed newspapers. More than three hundred, including the *Chicago Times*, the

New York World, and the *Philadelphia Evening Journal,* had to cease publication for varying periods. If the Postmaster General banned an antiwar paper from the mail, it had received the kiss of death.[25]

Confederate president Jefferson Davis, unlike Lincoln, rarely acted without congressional authorization. But this merely made the Confederacy's suppression more decentralized than the Union's. As early as 1862 the Confederate Congress empowered the president to suspend habeas corpus and declare martial law in threatened areas. Richmond was one of the first sectors where Davis exercised this option. General John H. Winder, assuming command of the capital, prohibited the sale of liquor and seized all privately owned firearms. Within the first two weeks of Winder's rule, he had arbitrarily arrested thirty persons, including a former two-term Congressman. A passport system regulated movement in and out of the city. Hotels and railroads were required to provide lists of all guests and passengers. Winder shortly afterward threatened to stop the *Richmond Whig* from publishing for undermining confidence in the government. He also tried price-fixing for a few weeks until he discovered that farmers would no longer bring products into the city.

Davis put other areas under martial law at one time or another, and Confederate commanders occasionally instituted martial law at their own discretion. Only military force, mass arrests, and several executions for sabotage kept the strongly Unionist eastern part of Tennessee in the Confederacy. In other sections bordering on the North, the authorities imposed loyalty oaths and arrested those who refused to comply. Indeed, in August 1861, the Confederate Congress had given all individuals born in the North forty days to swear loyalty or go into exile, with their property forfeit. The courts viewed anyone not supporting the Confederacy as an enemy alien, denied any legal protections accorded to citizens. Disloyal families in Virginia were deported beyond rebel lines and had their homes destroyed, and the military in Florida burned down one community that harbored deserters and confined its women and children to refugee camps.

The South had always relied on local and private vigilance committees to monitor community norms, and such groups now imposed, to the point of lynching, their own versions of loyalty. During the early secession crisis, an Arkansas mob had dragged a St. Louis newspaper distributor off a steamboat and hanged him for selling Horace Greeley's *New York Tribune.* By October 1862, an outbreak of war hysteria in eastern Texas culminated in rump trials and the execution of at least fifty victims. The Confederate Congress at intervals renewed and revised the suspension of habeas corpus, making it general throughout the Confederacy for certain disloyal acts in February 1864. Although the government left southern newspapers generally unmolested, Tennessee officials did banish the Unionist editor of the *Knoxville Whig*. The military's provost marshals required passports of travelers in nearly all Confederate-held territory. These travel restrictions, analogous to the pass system already employed to control the slaves, were far more stringent than those in the North.[26]

Republican Neomercantilism versus Confederate War Socialism

The Republican Party started out as an antislavery coalition of former Whigs and former Democrats. Lincoln himself had been a Whig, as had Secretary of State Seward. But prior to the attack on Fort Sumter, no fewer than eight ex-Democrats had served as Republican governors, seven as Republican senators, and many more as Republican congressmen. Even Lincoln's Secretary of the Treasury, Chase, belongs in this list. The prewar Republican platform, therefore, had to gloss over the economic differences between Whigs, who wanted the central government to promote economic growth, and Democrats, who tended to support the prevailing regime of free trade and laissez-faire economics. Once the fighting got under way, however, the natural dynamics of wartime intervention brought to fruition the traditional Whig program of government subsidies and economic regulation.[27]

The Whigs, for instance, had been the guardians of the defunct Bank of the United States. Although the Jacksonian legacy was virile enough to block reestablishment of a single central bank, the new national banking system nevertheless undid the divorce between the banks and the central government. Similarly, the Whigs had long believed in protective tariffs. After raising duties in 1861 for revenue purposes, Republican legislators took advantage of the southern departure from Congress to raise the rates higher and higher. The war's internal taxes helped justify steep tariffs, because domestic industry would otherwise face unfair foreign competition. Protectionists also exploited the clandestine activities of Confederate agents who operated out of Canada as an excuse to repeal the reciprocity treaty that had permitted free trade with that nation since 1854. By war's end, average duties had risen to 47 percent and the free list had been cut in half.

Even before the southern states seceded, Republicans had officially embraced the Whig policy of federally funded internal improvements (as had northern Democrats). Sectional rivalry had prevented government sponsorship of a transcontinental railroad before the war, but in 1862 the Republicans were able to pass the Pacific Railway Act. It chartered two private corporations, the Union Pacific and Central Pacific. They received ten square miles of public land for every mile of track constructed along a central route, supplemented by generous loans from the public treasury. The Union's relationship with existing railroads was also intimate. Congress authorized the president to seize any rail and telegraph line at his discretion, and all the railways in occupied portions of the South were under full military management. Inside the North, however, the War Department directly controlled only a few tracks close to the front; the government's influence derived primarily from being the rail companies' largest customer.

The Lincoln administration enlisted other interests with a shower of legislative and administrative favors. Farmers were courted with a new Department of Agriculture in 1862. The Contract Labor Law of 1864 attempted to help employers offset the wartime decline in immigration. It established the post of Commissioner of Immigration and gave government sanction—until its repeal four years later—to twelve-month labor contracts for immigrants, resurrecting a practice that had died with indentured servitude. The Morrill Act of 1862 bestowed huge tracts of the public domain on the loyal state governments for the purpose of endowing colleges that would offer agricultural, mechanical, and military instruction. This not only involved national support for higher education; it also promoted military training in an arena where such training had been rare. Almost unnoticed, Congress also took the first small step toward pulling unsettled wilderness off the market entirely to create expansive reaches for government-managed conservation and parks; in 1864 it granted the Yosemite lands to California as a nature preserve.

There were a few government-run enterprises that operated in the North during the war. Of the two federal armories that existed beforehand, only the one at Springfield, Massachusetts, continued to fashion rifles, the Confederates having put the one at Harper's Ferry, Virginia, out of operation. The Ordnance Department controlled four other manufacturing arsenals that produced accoutrements and ammunition, including the new arsenal at Rock Island, Illinois. The government set up clothing factories in Cincinnati and Philadelphia, meat-packing houses in Tennessee and Kentucky, and several drug and medicine laboratories. Establishing the Government Printing Office and the Bureau of Engraving and Printing allowed the national government to conduct its own printing and publishing. And in 1863, Congress created the National Academy of Sciences to seek out technological innovations that would be useful for the war effort.

The Union mobilization of the economy, however, relied generally on profitable war contracts. These forged new and close partnerships between private businesses and governments at every level. Charges of graft and profiteering became widespread, especially with respect to the strictly licensed trade in occupied territory. No matter what the extent of corruption, the war created an intimacy between the military and industry that brought back the abandoned policies of seventeenth-century mercantilism. An economic boom in the northern war industries fostered an illusion of general prosperity. But the wartime prosperity, in reality, did not extend to all sectors of the northern economy. Adjusting for inflation, workers' wages actually fell by one-third. Laborers sometimes organized unions to keep abreast of living costs, but the Lincoln administration broke new ground in the employment of federal troops against strikers. For instance, in July 1864 the War Department operated the Philadelphia and Reading Railroad because striking engineers had interrupted the delivery of coal to Philadelphia, marking the first presidential seizure of private property during a labor dispute.

Modern historians have discovered that the Civil War in fact retarded economic growth. The 1860s saw the American economy's worst performance of any decade between 1840 and 1930, with real income per capita falling by 3 percent. Some of this loss stemmed from wartime destruction in the South. But if the North is considered in isolation, the Civil War still hampered prosperity. Most of the war industries, except woolens, experienced a slump, despite increased participation of women in the workforce. Iron production for arms rose, but that increase was more than offset by declining production for railways. Output in the Massachusetts boot and shoe industry fell by 30 percent because military contracts did not counteract the loss of southern markets. Overall the war erased five years' wealth accumulation.[28]

Whereas the Civil War saw the triumph in the North of Republican neomercantilism, it saw the emergence in the South of full-blown State socialism. Nowhere did the Confederacy have greater disadvantages than in industrial output. Except for the Tredegar Iron Works in Richmond, the South did not have a cannon foundry at the war's outset. With little native industry to call on, the rebel government moved immediately and directly into its own war production. General Josiah Gorgas, the Pennsylvania-born Chief of Confederate Ordnance, took the lead in establishing government-owned facilities. By 1863 the Confederacy was dotted with small-arms factories, foundries, a powder mill, and a chemical plant, all belonging to and operated by Gorgas's Ordnance Bureau. The Confederate Navy also set up its own cannon foundry and powder mill, as well as numerous shipyards. The Nitre and Mining Bureau extracted and refined coal, iron, copper, nitre, and lead. The Confederate Quartermaster Bureau ran its own clothing, shoe, and wagon factories. The southern state governments also operated arsenals, powder mills, textile mills, flour mills, saltworks, and a variety of other enterprises.[29]

When the authorities did purchase supplies from private firms, they dictated prices and profits. The rebel government sometimes loaned one-half the start-up capital to businesses, which in turn had to sell two-thirds of their production to the government. Because rigid regulations and soaring inflation made genuine profits impossible, private owners, one after another, turned their factories over to the public officials. Right from the conflict's beginning, the Confederacy had violated its constitution by loaning money for the completion of strategic railway links. Seven-eighths of the freight and two-thirds of the passengers transported on the Virginia Central Railroad during one year, to cite only one example, were for the government's account. Toward the end, President Davis took possession of all uncaptured southern railroads, steamboats, and telegraph lines outright, incorporating their employees and officers into the military (Cappon 1941).

Managing the ubiquitous system of war socialism was a central government bureaucracy that had grown from nothing to seventy thousand civilians in 1863. The Confederate Constitution, moreover, in an effort to limit political patronage, had inadvertently laid the basis for an entrenched civil service by denying the president authority to fire most of these government employees. A quick glance at Augusta, Georgia, one of the new urban centers in the Confederate South, shows the results of this expansion. The Ordnance Bureau's powder works there was the second largest in the world, after the famed Waltham Abbey Works in England. An army clothing factory employed 1,500 female workers. The government ran flour mills, meatpacking and vegetable canning factories, distilleries, a military bakery with twelve ovens, an ordnance manufacture, two cotton presses, and a manufacture of clothing, uniforms, and shoes for the navy. The city's major private firm, the Augusta Textile Factory, did 92 percent of its work for the government.[30]

Confederate war socialism was not merely confined to manufacturing and transportation. The states, in their efforts to stimulate food production and help enforce the cotton embargo, imposed limits on the acreage of cotton and tobacco that planters could grow and prohibited the distillation of liquor. The central government, meanwhile, acquired such large stockpiles of cotton from its produce loans and the tax in kind that it quickly became the market's largest cotton merchant. Although this staple could not directly feed or equip southern soldiers, it provided collateral for the Erlanger loan. It also brought in vast quantities of war supplies through an illicit but flourishing trade with the enemy. Both sides formally banned the trade. But whereas the Lincoln administration gave exemptions to private businesses, the Davis government allowed military commanders to monopolize the exchange of cotton across the lines. When the embargo proved a diplomatic failure, the government dominated the reopened export trade in this commodity as well (Hill 1936).

The rebel government shifted from its command over cotton to shipping. The Navy Department and North Carolina already were competing against private blockade-runners with one vessel each. The Confederate War Department in 1863 bought its own ships, acquired majority interest in others, and commandeered one-third to one-half the outbound cargo space on the remainder. The following year, the Confederate Congress granted President Davis total regulatory control over foreign exports and banned the importation of any goods it considered "non-essential." The South had now completely nationalized its foreign commerce.

Conscription was a crucial cog in the wheel of Confederate war socialism. Draft exemption was the mechanism for manipulating the labor market. Any southern business that did not conform to military priorities found itself without workers. War Department control over labor became still more overt in February 1864. The rebel Congress abolished many occupational exemptions and replaced them with the discretionary assignment of soldiers to industrial jobs. Insofar as these detailed soldiers were conscripts, the Confederacy was running its factories with coerced labor. The internal logic of military conscription had led the nation of black agricultural slavery to the ironic but appropriate adoption of white industrial slavery.

Forced industrialization guaranteed that the agrarian South never lacked for arms and ammunition, even as it verged on starvation. Accompanying all these policies were public exhortations for sacrifice to the common cause. *De Bow's Review,* a southern journal that had been in the forefront of the secessionist movement, printed one such call in 1862: "Every man should feel that he has an interest in the State, and that the State in a measure leans upon him; and he should rouse himself to efforts as bold and heroic as if all depended upon his single right arm. . . . It is implied in the spirit which times demand that all private interests are sacrificed to the public good. The State becomes everything, and the individual nothing" (De Bow 1862).

One of the Civil War's enduring myths is that the South's unbending commitment to states' rights paralyzed its war effort. In actuality, Confederate war socialism was more economically centralized than the Union's neomercantilism, which relied more on private initiative. Furthermore, rebel central planning, while adequately serving the goal of supplying conventional armies, otherwise misallocated resources, fostered inefficiencies, and sapped morale. What may have paralyzed the Confederacy was not a central government with too little power but one with too much.[31]

The Postwar Legacy

How much of this surge in government power persisted after the conflict ceased? Obviously, Confederate war socialism was swept away with military defeat. But as the South underwent Reconstruction for another decade, the ongoing military occupation required a postwar U.S. Army of about sixty thousand men—four times its immediate prewar size. The most prominent presence of the War Department in the South was the Bureau of Refugees, Freedmen, and Abandoned Lands, established before the fighting had ceased. The Freedmen's Bureau, as it was commonly known, was soon dispensing free food and clothing from surplus army stocks and free medical care to southern refugees, white and black. It also found employment and supervised labor contracts for the freed slaves and provided them with schools. As the first federal relief agency in U.S. history, it was run by the military until phased out in 1872.[32]

The Republican state governments that military force propped up in the South during Reconstruction remain a complex topic. These governments were responsible for many genuine accomplishments, especially with respect to racial equality. They also introduced the same kind of general incorporation laws that had already spread throughout the northern states in the antebellum years and opened up market competition. But for some of their alleged accomplishments, the Reconstruction regimes actually deserve censure. Postwar state governments, in the South as elsewhere in the Union, promoted private railroads with reckless abandon. These pro-business subsidies usually diverted resources away from more urgent needs, and the costs fell particularly heavily on southern farmers, already destitute from wartime losses. Railroad appropriations, furthermore, were the occasions for most of the political fraud perpetrated below the Mason-Dixon line.[33]

The southern states also imported the Yankee system of tax-supported, compulsory schools. Even without much government support, literacy among white southerners before the firing on Fort Sumter had exceeded 80 percent, slightly below that of northerners and better than the rate in Britain or any other European country outside Sweden and Denmark. Admittedly this figure omits the slaves, whom it was illegal to educate. But only during the Civil War had compulsory school attendance become standard across the North. To permanently fasten government schools on the defeated South, Congress created a federal Department of Education in 1867, downgraded the next year to a bureau within the Interior Department. National aid to education eventually became a platform plank of the Republican Party, although the proposal never could make it through the Senate. By 1872 every southern state had established a school system, and generally these were more centrally administered and funded than in the North, where local districts played a larger role. Moreover, the public schools created during congressional Reconstruction were all racially segregated, except, briefly, those in New Orleans. Once captured by the forces of white rule, they could be turned into engines of racial exploitation.[34]

Other new expenditures instituted by southern states during Reconstruction included orphanages, insane asylums, and homes for the poor. Alabama charged its new commissioner of industries with the task of encouraging commercial activity. Some states set up bureaus of immigration to foster settlement. South Carolina's first land commissioner financially aided those purchasing real estate. All these functions were costly, with the result that the war-ravaged South suffered under some of the heaviest state and local taxation in proportion to wealth in U.S. history. Tax rates in 1870 were three or four times what they had been in 1860, though property values had declined significantly. Many who had not lost their land already were forced into bankruptcy. At one point 15 percent of all taxable land in Mississippi was up for sale because of tax defaults. Coming on the heels of war-engendered confiscations, Radical Reconstruction foisted on the biracial South the worst of two worlds: significant turbulence in white land titles with hardly any compensating distribution to the freedmen.[35]

Many of the poor southern whites and former Unionists who initially had been receptive to the Republican coalition became disenchanted with the extravagance of the Reconstruction governments, which had racked up $130 million worth of indebtedness. This was one major factor, along with northern weariness of the expense and frustration of maintaining what some self-styled Liberal Republicans were openly denouncing as "bayonet rule," that permitted white southerners to engage during the 1870s in a process euphemistically labeled Redemption. Continuing violence, coupled with social ostracism and economic pressures, kept blacks away from the polls and forced whites out of Republican ranks. The Redeemers overturned Republican rule in state after state and instituted a regimen of retrenchment, economy, and partial debt repudiation, along with (of course) white supremacy.

Fortunately, the Thirteenth Amendment to the Constitution, ratified in 1865, had put the total elimination of chattel slavery where no state government, no future Democratic administration, no Supreme Court ruling could reverse it. A second Reconstruction amendment, the Fourteenth, was dubiously ratified in 1868. Few constitutional modifications have proved as far-reaching. Intended to extend from the national to the state governments nearly all the restrictions contained in the Bill of Rights, in a single stroke it subjected much state legislation to federal review. Congress, reacting to Lincoln's myriad habeas corpus cases, had already expanded the size and scope of the federal judiciary in 1863, bringing many matters that were previously confined to state courts within federal jurisdiction. Then, in 1870, the Fifteenth Amendment made voting rights for African Americans, at least on paper, permanent and nationwide. It stands as the pinnacle of Reconstruction; none of the other nations that had abolished slavery in the nineteenth century had even formally granted their former slaves citizenship rights equal to those of whites.[36]

The political turmoil of Reconstruction was only the Civil War's most visible legacy. The war had dramatically altered American society and institutions. The South, of course, would never be the same, but the transformation of the North was also profound. The national government that emerged victorious from the conflict dwarfed in power and size the minimal Jacksonian State that had commenced the war. The number of civilians in federal employ swelled almost fivefold. A distant administration that had little contact with its citizens had been transformed into an overbearing bureaucracy that intruded into daily life with taxes, drafts, surveillance, subsidies, and regulations.[37]

An ideological surge in nationalism complemented the surge in actual government power. Northerners now viewed the United States as a single nation, rather than a confederation or union of states. A seemingly

minor shift in word usage highlights this change. "Before the Civil War,"
emphasizes David H. Donald, "many politicians and writers referred to
the United States in the plural, but after 1865 only a pedant or the most
unreconstructed Southerner would dream of saying the 'the United
States *are*.'" Abandoning the word *Union,* Lincoln instead called the
United States a nation a total of five times during his short Gettysburg
Address, in contrast to his predecessors, who tended to avoid the term
(Donald 1978, 215).

Although the final end of Reconstruction in 1877 allowed further
military cutbacks, the total number of armed forces would never fall
below a level half again as high as that before the war. Nor did this end
political employment of the U.S. Army, which had been fashioned into
a reliable enforcer of domestic laws to an extent previously undreamed
of. In addition to finishing off the Indians and herding them on to reservations, the post-Reconstruction army was used most often to break
strikes. It militarily intervened in scores of labor disputes, most notably
the General Railroad Strike of 1877 and the Pullman Strike of 1894.
The state militias went on strike duty even more frequently as they were
transformed, beginning with New York's, from mass-based citizen soldiers into tax-financed elite professionals. The term *National Guard*
was borrowed from the French in an effort to identify these state military formations more closely with national authority.[38]

The war taxes lingered well after the fighting had ended. Congress
did not let the inheritance tax lapse until 1870, the income tax until
1872. The latter was reinstituted, declared unconstitutional, and finally
made permanent with ratification of the Sixteenth Amendment in 1913.
The other internal levies were gradually pared down but never completely abolished, especially the sin taxes on alcohol and tobacco. None
of the post-Appomattox campaigns for tariff reform achieved much,
either. Republican protectionism continued to dominate trade policy
mercilessly for the next three-quarters of a century.[39]

Because the South remained an exporting region, it—especially the
deep South—bore a disproportionate burden from the nation's new high
tariffs. To further ensure that the rebellious states would help cover the
Union's war costs, the direct tax of 1861 had been levied against them,
with a 50 percent penalty for their failure to collect it themselves. A
particularly onerous increase in the federal excise on cotton extracted
another $68 million from the South before being repealed in 1868. Note
that the Republican Party's economic exploitation of the defeated South
harmed blacks as well as whites.

THE CIVIL WAR AND RECONSTRUCTION 215

Postwar taxation, furthermore, undid an unwritten constitutional bargain of the antebellum years in which the central government had been confined to external taxes, while internal taxes remained the province of the state governments. A separation of taxing powers had been one of the most insistent modifications proposed by the states that demanded a bill of rights when they first ratified the U.S. Constitution. The first ten amendments had failed to include any curbs on internal taxes collected by the national government. But the system operated this way in practice once Thomas Jefferson was elected president in 1800, except during the War of 1812. Such structural independence, probably as much as any other factor, had made secession a realistic option.[40]

The greenbacks bequeathed a continuing source of economic conundrums and political discord. A resumption of the gold standard at the prewar parity required significant price deflation, so both the timing and the eventuality itself were contested. Chief Justice Salmon P. Chase, in one of the most astonishing cases of intellectual honesty on the part of a public official, implicitly branded his prior actions as Secretary of the Treasury unconstitutional when the Court struck down the greenbacks' retroactive legal-tender provision in the *Hepburn* decision of 1870. President Ulysses Grant, however, soon packed the Court so that it effectively reversed itself the following year. Only in 1879, more than a decade after Lee's surrender at Appomattox, did this paper money circulate at par with specie and did the banks resume payments in gold.[41]

The national banking system, despite creating a national currency, was riddled with features that ended up interdicting the flow of savings to northern and southern farmers alike. Nationally chartered banks could not legally make real-estate loans at all until 1913. The general prohibition on branch banking made it more difficult to shift credit out of areas where interest rates were low to where the demand was greatest. High capital requirements for bank charters, the Comptroller of the Currency's restriction of entry, and initial ceilings on bank notes also discriminated against rural regions. After the ceilings were removed, the requirement that national bank notes be matched by investments in an ever-shrinking supply of Treasury securities made it less profitable to issue these notes where interest rates were highest.[42]

State-chartered banks, which might have filled the gap, could no longer issue notes. They could offer deposits and, for that reason, experienced a resurgence by the turn of the century, but modern readers often fail to appreciate how the widespread use of the checking account—a liability of private institutions that forms the bulk of today's money supply—depends on advanced technologies of credit verification. During the nineteenth century, the privilege of writing an open-ended draft against a bank was confined to individuals of recognized wealth or unquestioned probity. The poor or undistinguished had to borrow currency, commodities, or nothing at all.

The national banking system contributed to starving the agricultural South not only for credit but also for money in small denominations. So long as the price level can freely adjust up and down, there can never be a shortage of money per se, but a denominational shortage can seem like one. Wartime inflation had caused much of the Treasury's subsidiary silver coinage to be melted down for its metallic value. By 1869 circulation had dwindled to nearly one-fourth the prewar level of $21 million. Despite the new ban on private mints, many businesses and municipalities began issuing notes, tickets, and due bills of their own that circulated as small change, whereas the government facilitated such use for postage stamps. Yet the privately and locally issued "shinplasters," as they were called, could not completely ease the shortage so long as they remained technically illegal, and the notes of nationally chartered banks were artificially scarce, as already observed. Although the government's paper money was printed in fractional denominations lower than the $1 limit (close to $20 in today's prices) set for national bank notes, the Treasury initially contracted its total circulation during Reconstruction.[43]

This government-induced derangement inhibited the South's monetary system just at the moment when its needs had leapt upward. The slave plantation had been a mini-planned economy within which food, clothing, and other resources were allocated under the planter's central direction. On emancipation, most blacks entered the market for the first time. Now they had to purchase their own necessities. But the denominational shortage often reduced freed slaves to an inefficient reliance on barter. Sharecropping, after all, was a barter transaction—cotton exchanged for the use of land—and many of the farmers who rented land at fixed rates paid not "cash rent" in the form of money but "standing rent" in the form of crops. Even agricultural laborers often received nonmonetary "share wages."[44]

In short, the national banking system throttled both financial intermediation and monetary exchange in the agricultural sector. This fueled political crusades for inflationary policies of either printing greenbacks or coining silver. The wartime banking legislation had also tied note issue to the national debt, so that any debt retirement automatically contracted part of the money stock. After creating an inelastic currency, the banks faced a new source of runs that left the financial system more vulnerable than ever to panics.

The postwar national debt had climbed to $2.8 billion. The interest alone on this debt commanded about 40 percent of the central government's outlays into the mid-1870s. An unbroken string of twenty-eight annual budget surpluses from the war's end to the depression of 1893 could have eliminated this liability. But national expenditures as a percentage of the total economy, despite collapsing from their wartime high, were still often more than twice their prewar level and never dipped much below 3 percent of output. Because the Confederate debt had been repudiated, the recipients of this interest, paid in gold under the Public Credit Act of 1869, were initially northerners and tended to remain so. Although the debt did fall below $1 billion in 1892, the Republicans were more interested in spending the surpluses on internal improvements and other pork-barrel legislation. Already by 1873 Congress had allotted 155 million acres of land and $64 million in credit to four chartered transcontinental railroads. These subsidies and the Crédit Mobilier scandal that surrounded them epitomized the national government's neomercantilist coalition with business.[45]

The most extravagant appropriations, however, were for soldiers' benefits. The Grand Army of the Republic, a pressure group comprised of Union veterans, became a powerful bulwark of the Republican Party. Every Republican who was elected president from Ulysses Grant through William McKinley had served as a Civil War officer. Veterans' pensions grew from 2 percent of all federal expenditures in 1866 to 29 percent in 1884, replacing interest payments on the war debt as the largest single item. The pension system constituted in essence the national government's first system of old-age and disability insurance and qualifies as a precursor to Social Security. And none of this money was paid to Confederate veterans. In other words, the primary fiscal activities of the postwar central government—debt service and veterans' benefits—extracted wealth from the impoverished and war-ravaged southern economy and transferred it northward.[46]

The war also brought a proliferation in government activism at the state and local levels. War expenditures had added more than $100 million to the indebtedness of northern states, and some means had to be found to finance this obligation. In addition, people had become accustomed to government attempts at solving social problems. Reformers consequently turned more than ever before to local and state authorities, who undertook a myriad of new tasks. These included everything from public health measures to business regulations, from professional licensing restrictions to anti-liquor and anti-vice measures. "The war . . . has tended, more than any other event in the history of the country," declaimed Republican governor Richard Yates of Illinois in 1865, "to militate against the Jeffersonian idea, that 'the best government is that which governs least.' The war has not only, of necessity, given more power to, but has led to a more intimate prevision of the government over every material interest of society."[47]

New York City, for instance, established a professional fire department in 1865 to replace volunteer companies that Republican lawmakers found too closely tied to the city's Democratic machine. The New York legislature within the next two years enacted the country's first housing regulations, set up a Board of Charities, and established a string of eight teacher-training colleges. Massachusetts created a statewide constabulary in 1865. This formative state police unit enforced ordinances against prostitution, gambling, and liquor. In 1869 the state erected a Board of Health and a Bureau of Labor Statistics. Chicago's city government was so decentralized prior to the firing on Fort Sumter that it was run virtually on user fees and only adopted general taxes to fund wartime expenditures, particularly bounties paid to fill troop quotas. Overall, Massachusetts, New Hampshire, and New York had each nearly doubled tax collections per person between 1860 and 1870, even after making allowances for price changes. In New Jersey per capita real taxes increased by a factor of 2.5, and in Connecticut they increased by a factor of 3.5. During the six years prior to the Panic of 1873, city debt in Boston, New York, and Chicago expanded threefold.[48]

Not all government interventions had their primary effects in the fiscal arena. In Republican-controlled Illinois, postwar controls over freight rates and grain warehouses reached an apex in 1871 with the creation of a railroad commission. Starting in 1865, state after state chartered bar associations, which became exclusive licensing agencies for lawyers. Ohio became the first state to restrict effective competition in the practice of medicine in 1868, and from there stronger medical licensing requirements spread north and south. The legacy of the Civil War was even felt in the seemingly unrelated area of obscenity. The first act to regulate mail content was passed in March 1865, just prior to the cessation of fighting. Responding to complaints that troops were ordering obscene material, Congress made mailing such material a crime. The Republicans demonstrated their ongoing commitment to being the "Party of Piety" by adding a postal ban on lotteries and other schemes deemed fraudulent in

1868. A series of new enactments beginning in 1872 steadily strengthened both bans, which were further reinforced by various state laws combating obscenity and vice. These laws empowered the infamous Anthony Comstock, as special postal agent, to conduct a veritable witch hunt.[49]

The Yankee Leviathan, in short, had acquired for central authority such functions as subsidizing privileged businesses, managing the currency, providing welfare to veterans, and protecting the nation's morals — at the very moment that local and state governments were also expanding. And it had set precedents with respect to taxes, fiat money, conscription, and the suppression of dissent. It had permanently reversed the implicit constitutional settlement that had made the central and the state governments revenue-independent. All these countless changes mark the Civil War as America's real turning point. In the years ahead, coercive authority would wax and wane with year-to-year circumstances, but the long-term trend would be unmistakable. In contrast to the whittling away of government that had preceded the Civil War, the United States had commenced its halting but inexorable march toward the welfare-warfare State of today.

Notes

1. I capitalize the word *State* when using it in its broader sense, meaning government in general, to distinguish that meaning from the constituent states within a federal system of government such as the United States. The scholarly literature about the Civil War is overwhelming, and these endnotes are nowhere near exhaustive. When not documenting specific factual details, they merely direct readers to the more important or influential works concerning various topics.

2. Goldin and Lewis 1975. Temin (1976) contends that Goldin and Lewis overstated the South's portion of the war's cost. See also their exchange: Goldin and Lewis 1978; Temin 1978.

3. Bourne 1977, 360. No work deserves greater credit for popularizing knowledge of war's ratchet effect than Higgs 1987, although its naming dates back at least to Porter 1980.

4. U.S. Department of Commerce 1975, pt. 2, ser. Y335-8, Y457-65, Y493-504, Y671-81. I have used the Composite Consumer Price Index calculated by McCusker 1992, supplemented by more recent numbers from the Consumer Price Index, to deflate amounts to 2005 prices. Berry (1988) estimates nominal output at $3.7 billion in 1858 and $3.9 billion in 1859; Weiss (1992) revises the latter figure to $4.2 billion. Ransom and Sutch have their own similar conjecture, appearing in Ransom (1989, 256), of $4.1 billion for 1859. Gallman's widely used but never published annual series, as provided to me by Weiss, estimates U.S. GNP in 1858 at $3.982 billion. For a comparison of these various

estimates, see Myers 1992, 1994. My results conform with the earlier work of Kendrick (1955), who put national expenditures at 1.5 percent of GNP in 1859. The research of Wallis (2000), Legler, Sylla, and Wallis (1988), and Sylla, Legler, and Wallis (1987) finds total state and local revenue as averaging 1.41 times national revenue in the decade 1836–45 and 1.15 times in the decade 1846–55. Any conceivable differences between government *revenue* and *expenditures* could not possibly push those ratios above 2.00. According to these estimates, total government revenue averaged 4.0 percent and 4.2 percent of GNP, respectively, in the two antebellum intervals. Detailed data about expenditures of only state governments are presented in Holt 1977. See also the 1860 Census, U.S. Census Bureau 1866, 4:511; *American Almanac* 1861, 240–41, 248–376; and Davis and Legler 1966.

5. For further details about canals and their impact on state finances, see chapter 6 of this volume and Goodrich 1960.

6. On various aspects of the free banking era, see Bodenhorn 2000, 2003; Hummel 1999; and Rockoff 1971.

7. Stampp 1956, 29–30. The fraction of southern households that owned slaves had been declining since 1830, and it varied from state to state, approaching one-third in 1860 for the states that would comprise the Confederacy. Goldin (1973) provides the more often cited lower figure for the total value of all slaves. The higher comes from Rose 1964. Ransom and Sutch (1988) put the number at $3.1 billion, midway between the two. The 1860 U.S. Census, as summarized by Kennedy 1862, 190, 231, estimates the total value of railroad capital at $1.2 billion and of manufacturing capital at $1.1 billion. See also Gallman 1986.

8. Hadden 2001 is an in-depth study of slave patrols.

9. Space does not permit citing the overwhelming literature about either American slavery or the causes of the Civil War, but for surveys see Hummel 1996 and 2001a. Some recent contributions that are of economic interest include Grant 2000, Huston 1999, Majewski 2000, and Ransom and Sutch 2001.

10. Three good overviews of the antebellum militia are in Cunliffe 1968, Weigley 1984, and Hummel 2001b.

11. The first military historian to make this observation was Williams 1949–50, 1:60–66, 114–48, 2: 796–98.

12. Although General Jonathan S. Preston, Superintendent of the Confederate Conscription Bureau, in U.S. War Department 1880–1901, ser. 4, v. 3, 1101, reported that 81,993 of less than one million total southern soldiers entered as draftees, and another 76,206 were induced by conscription to volunteer, this low-end estimate of less than 20 percent is incomplete, covers only the area east of the Mississippi, and does not take into account those who had their terms of service coercively extended. Moore (1924, 356–57) credits the Confederate draft with assigning 300,000 men east of the Mississippi—one-third the total number of those who served.

13. Geary 1991, 78–84. If hired substitutes are included, then the conscription acts furnished 13 percent of Union soldiers during the last two years of the war. State militia drafts garnered another 87,500 nine-month men, 11 percent of the total during the war's first two years. Other studies of Union military mobilization include Leach 1952, Murdock 1967 and 1971, and Shannon 1928. Bernstein (1990) treats the New York City draft riots.

14. Hammond (1970), Newcomb (1865), Sharkey (1959), and Rein (1962) provide overviews of Union finances.

15. Blaine 1884, 1:433. Details about Union taxation are available in Smith 1914.

16. Although Congress first authorized the income tax on August 5, 1861, at the same time as it passed the direct tax on the states, Congress failed to provide for enforcement, and Chase declined to implement the income tax. Whereas the direct tax took effect eight months after passage, the income tax was not collected until Congress included a more stringent measure as part of the comprehensive Internal Revenue Act of July 1, 1862.

17. The status of the greenbacks is much misunderstood by noneconomists. Some attribute the Confederacy's monetary problems to a failure to make its currency legal tender in private transactions. In fact, as the monetary history of the American colonies makes clear, all that is necessary to get government paper money to circulate is making it usable for payment of taxes, along with some restraint on the amount issued and good prospects that the government will survive. As Calomiris (1991) has pointed out, the Union made greenbacks legal tender not to support the currency but to assist the banks. This facilitated bank suspension by making greenbacks legal substitutes for specie. As a result, bank liabilities would fall in value at the same rate as their primary assets, Treasury bonds and notes.

18. McCandless (1996) attempts to pinpoint how war news affected the value of Union and Confederate currency.

19. For surveys of Confederate finances, see Ball 1991, Schwab 1901, and Todd 1954.

20. The standard estimates, given in Lerner 1954, are 5 percent from taxation, 5 percent from seizures and donations, 30 percent from borrowing, and 60 percent from the seigniorage of fiat money. Hirshleifer (1963, 41–43), however, points out that these percentages ignore the resources gained from uncompensated impressments. Adding them into seizures changes the percentages to 7 percent from taxes, 17 percent from seizures and donations, 24 percent from loans, and 52 percent from seigniorage. See also Burdekin and Langdana 1993.

21. Among the many studies specifically treating Confederate monetary policy are Burdekin and Weidenmier 2001, Godrey 1978, and Lerner 1955, 1956. For an economic analysis of the contributing role of the Union blockade, see Surdam 2001.

22. Martin 1932, 128. Also see Escott 1977.

23. Lincoln's holding Maryland is covered in Duncan 1974 and Sprague 1965.

24. As reported in Sanborn 1907, 229.

25. Neely 1991 has become the standard apology for the Lincoln Administration's violations of civil liberties. Neely not only contends that these measure were either necessary or desirable but also contrasts them favorably with all the conceivable repression that that did *not* occur. Older studies are Randall 1951 and Hyman 1973.

26. Neely (1999) also provides the most comprehensive study of civil liberties in the Confederacy. Other treatments are Tatum 1934 and Freehling 2001.

27. General works about northern politics and economic legislation include Curry 1968, Fite 1910, Rawley 1974, and Richardson 1997.

28. Beard (1927) and Hacker (1940) were the most prominent proponents of the notion that the Civil War contributed to U.S. economic growth. Engerman 1966, oft-cited and often reprinted, remains the definitive refutation of the Beard-Hacker thesis, but see also other contributions in Andreano 1967 and Gilchrist and Lewis 1965. There is some debate among economists about what caused the decline in northern real wages; DeCanio and Mokyr (1977) provide a good introduction to the debate.

29. For assorted discussions of the southern home front, consult Ramsdell 1944 and Vandiver 1952.

30. The growth of the Confederate civil service is covered in Van Riper and Scheiber 1959; this description of Augusta comes from Corley 1960.

31. The most succinct statement of the pervasive belief that the South lost the war because its government was less centralized and more feeble than the North's is Donald 1960. The "Died of Democracy" thesis is dispatched in the two best overviews of Confederate war socialism—Thomas 1971 and Luraghi 1978—as well as in Bensel 1990. M. Thornton and Ekelund 2004 is a brief survey that cites the more technical articles of the two economists who have done the most to show how such socialism actually harmed the Confederate cause. See also Escott 1978.

32. Bentley (1955) covers the Freedmen's Bureau.

33. Summers 1984 is a study of railroad politics in the Reconstruction-era South.

34. See Fishlow 1977, Foner 1988, and Warren 1974.

35. J. M. Thornton 1982, 371. The year was 1871 and the amount 3,330,000 acres. Wallenstein (1987) provides a corroborating study of public policy in postwar Georgia.

36. The original intent of the Fourteenth Amendment is contested, but the account I find most convincing is Curtis 1986.

37. Van Riper and Sutherland (1965) provide the numbers for government employment. More wide-ranging explorations of expanding federal functions include Elazar 1971, Keller 1977, and White 1958.

38. See Higham 1989 on domestic employment of the military.

39. For the post–Civil War evolution of the federal income tax, see chapter 10 of this volume.

40. Storing (1981) calls attention to the Anti-Federalist desire for revenue independence during the ratification debates, whereas Slaughter (1986) is the best at revealing the importance of repealing internal taxes to the Jeffersonian Revolution of 1800.

41. Mitchell 1903 and 1908 are classic economic studies of the greenbacks.

42. Sylla, in chapter 5 of this volume, presents a more positive view of the national banking system, although in one of his earlier writings (1969), he was among the system's detractors. Other critical assessments include James 1978, 1981; Hetherton 1990; Selgin 2000; Selgin and White 1994; Laird and Rinehart 1968; and Friedman and Schwartz 1963, 168–73.

43. One monetary economist who treats this denominational shortage seriously is Timberlake 1993, 118–28. For historical details, consult Carothers 1930, whereas a highly technical analysis of the problem applied to another place and time is Sargent and Velde 2002.

44. The scholarly literature about the economics of sharecropping is vast, and, like that about chattel slavery, beyond the scope of this chapter. But a work that clearly perceives the barter nature of so many of the postbellum arrangements in southern agriculture is Jaynes 1986. Higgs (1977) compares the impact of competition versus coercion on the welfare of the freed slaves. A brief historiographical review of the Civil War's economic consequences with particular emphasis on emancipation's ramifications is O'Brien 1988.

45. Patterson (1954) and Williamson (1974) delve into the post–Civil War debt, whereas Fogel (1969) questions the economic desirability of subsidized transcontinental railroads.

46. Skocpol 1992 is the definitive work about veterans' benefits as the precursor of modern social insurance.

47. Final Message to the Illinois General Assembly, 2 January 1865, *Chicago Tribune*, 5 January 1865, 2. Mohr (1976) looks generally at northern state governments during Reconstruction, and Bremner (1980) chronicles the increasing government role in social welfare.

48. See Einhorn 1990 on Chicago city government. The figures for state taxation are from 1870 Census, U.S. Census Bureau 1872, 3:10–11, whereas the figures for city debt are from the 1880 Census, U.S. Census Bureau 1884, 7:722–31. All northern states had real per capita tax increases over the course of the decade.

49. Miller (1971) and Brock (1984) investigate post–Civil War economic regulation at the state level. Hyman and Wiecek (1982, 299, 346) cover licensing of lawyers. Although the American Medical Association had been founded in 1847 and twenty states plus the District of Columbia had experimented with some form of medical licensing prior to 1860, Hamowy (1979) finds that none of these effectively limited entry until Ohio enacted its restrictions in 1868. On postal censorship and the crusade against obscenity, see Fowler 1977 and Sears 1977.

References

The American Almanac and Repository of Useful Knowledge for the Year 1861. 1861. Boston: Crosby, Nichols, Lee.

Andreano, Ralph L., ed. 1967. *The Economic Impact of the American Civil War*. 2nd ed. Cambridge, MA: Schenkman.

Ball, Douglas B. 1991. *Financial Failure and Confederate Defeat*. Urbana: University of Illinois Press.

Beard, Charles A., and Mary R. Beard. 1927. *The Rise of American Civilization*. 2 vols. New York: Macmillan.

Bensel, Richard Franklin. 1990. *Yankee Leviathan: The Origins of Central State Authority in America, 1859–1877*. Cambridge: Cambridge University Press.

Bentley, George R. 1955. *A History of the Freedmen's Bureau*. Philadelphia: University of Pennsylvania Press.

Bernstein, Iver. 1990. *The New York City Draft Riots: Their Significance for American Society and Politics in the Age of the Civil War*. New York: Oxford University Press.

Berry, Thomas Senior. 1988. *Production and Population since 1789: Revised GNP Series in Constant Dollars.* Richmond: Bostwick.

Blaine, James G. 1884. *Twenty Years of Congress: From Lincoln to Garfield, with a Review of the Events Which Led to the Political Revolution of 1860.* 2 vols. Norwich, CT: Henry Bill.

Bodenhorn, Howard. 2000. *A History of Banking in Antebellum America.* Cambridge: Cambridge University Press.

———. 2003. *State Banking in Early America: A New Economic History.* Oxford: Oxford University Press.

Bourne, Randolph. 1977. "The State." In *The Radical Will: Selected Writings, 1911–1918,* ed. Olaf Hansen, 355–95. New York: Urizen.

Bremner, Robert H. 1980. *The Public Good: Philanthropy and Welfare in the Civil War Era.* New York: Knopf.

Brock, William R. 1984. *Investigation and Responsibility: Public Responsibility in the United States, 1865–1900.* Cambridge: Cambridge University Press.

Burdekin, Richard C. K., and Farrokh K. Langdana. 1993. "War Finance in the Southern Confederacy, 1861–1865." *Explorations in Economic History* 30 (July): 352–76.

Burdekin, Richard C. K., and Marc D. Weidenmier. 2001. "Inflation Is Always and Everywhere a Monetary Phenomenon: Richmond vs. Houston in 1864." *American Economic Review* 91 (December): 1621–30.

Calomiris, Charles W. 1991. "The Motives of U.S. Debt-Management Policy, 1790–1880: Efficient Discrimination and Time Consistency." In *Research in Economic History: A Research Annual,* vol. 13, ed. Roger L. Ransom and Richard Sutch, 67–105. Greenwich, CT: JAI.

Cappon, Lester J. 1941. "Government and Private Industry in the Southern Confederacy." In *Humanistic Studies in Honor of John Calvin Metcalf,* 151–89. Charlottesville: University of Virginia Press.

Carothers, Neil. 1930. *Fractional Money: A History of the Small Coins and Fractional Paper Currency of the United States.* New York: John Wiley & Sons.

Corley, Florence Fleming. 1960. *Confederate City: Augusta, Georgia, 1860–1865.* Columbia: University of South Carolina Press.

Cunliffe, Marcus. 1968. *Soldiers and Civilians: The Martial Spirit in America, 1775–1865.* Boston: Little, Brown.

Curry, Leonard P. 1968. *Blueprint for Modern America: Nonmilitary Legislation of the First Civil War Congress.* Nashville: Vanderbilt University Press.

Curtis, Michael Kent. 1986. *No State Shall Abridge: The Fourteenth Amendment and the Bill of Rights.* Durham, NC: Duke University Press.

Davis, Lance, and John Legler. 1966. "The Government in the American Economy, 1815–1902: A Quantitative Study." *Journal of Economic History* 26 (December): 514–55.

De Bow, James D. B. 1962. "Our Danger and Our Duty." *De Bow's Review,* old ser., 33 (May–August): 46.

DeCanio, Stephen, and Joel Mokyr. 1977. "Inflation and the Wage Lag during the American Civil War." *Explorations in Economic History* 14 (October): 311–36.

Donald, David Herbert. 1960. "Died of Democracy." In *Why the North Won the Civil War,* ed. David Donald, 79–90. Baton Rouge: Louisiana State University Press.

———. 1978. *Liberty and Union.* Boston: Little, Brown.

Duncan, Richard R. 1974. "The Era of the Civil War." In *Maryland: A History, 1632–1974,* ed. Richard Walsh and William Lloyd Fox. Baltimore: Maryland Historical Society.

Einhorn, Robin L. 1990. "The Civil War and Municipal Government in Chicago." In *Toward a Social History of the American Civil War: Exploratory Essays,* ed. Maris A. Vinovskis, 117–38 Cambridge: Cambridge University Press.

Elazar, Daniel J. 1971. "Civil War and the Preservation of American Federalism." *Publius* 1 (1971): 39–58.

Engerman, Stanley L. 1966. "The Economic Impact of the Civil War." *Explorations in Entrepreneurial History.* 2nd ser., 3 (Spring–Summer): 176–99.

Escott, Paul. 1977. "'The Cry of the Sufferers': The Problem of Welfare in the Confederacy." *Civil War History* 23 (September): 228–40.

———. 1978. *After Secession: Jefferson Davis and the Failure of Confederate Nationalism.* Baton Rouge: Louisiana State University Press.

Fishlow, Albert. 1977. "Levels of Nineteenth-Century American Investment in Education." *Journal of Economic History* 26 (December): 418–36.

Fite, Emerson David. 1910. *Social and Industrial Conditions in the North During the Civil War.* New York: Macmillan.

Fogel, Robert William. 1969. *The Union Pacific Railroad: A Case of Premature Enterprise.* Baltimore: Johns Hopkins University Press.

Foner, Eric. 1988. *Reconstruction: America's Unfinished Revolution, 1863–1877.* New York: Harper & Row.

Fowler, Dorothy Ganfield. 1977. *Unmailable: Congress and the Post Office.* Athens: University of Georgia Press.

Freehling, William W. 2001. *The South vs. the South: How Anti-Confederate Southerners Shaped the Course of the Civil War.* New York: Oxford University Press.

Friedman, Milton, and Anna Jacobson Schwartz. 1963. *A Monetary History of the United States, 1867–1960.* Princeton: Princeton University Press.

Gallman, Robert E. 1986. "The United States Capital Stock in the Nineteenth Century." In *Long-Term Factors in American Economic Growth,* ed. Stanley L. Engerman and Robert E. Gallman, 165–213. National Bureau of Economic Research, Studies in Income and Wealth, vol. 51. Chicago: University of Chicago Press.

Geary, James W. 1991. *We Need Men: The Union Draft in the Civil War.* DeKalb: Northern Illinois University Press.

Gilchrist, David T., and W. David Lewis, eds. 1965. *Economic Change in the Civil War Era: Proceedings of a Conference on American Economic Institutional Change, 1850–1873, and the Impact of the Civil War Held March 12–14, 1964.* Greenville, DE: Eleutherian Mills–Hagley Foundation.

Godrey, John Munro. 1978. *Monetary Expansion in the Confederacy.* New York: Arno.

Goldin, Claudia. 1973. "The Economics of Emancipation." *Journal of Economic History* 33 (March): 66–85.

Goldin, Claudia, and Frank D. Lewis. 1975. "The Economic Cost of the American Civil War: Estimates and Implications." *Journal of Economic History* 35 (June): 299–322.

———. 1978. "The Post-Bellum Recovery of the South and the Cost of the Civil War: Comment." *Journal of Economic History* 38 (June): 487–92.

Goodrich, Carter. 1960. *Government Promotion of American Canals and Railroads, 1800–1890.* New York: Columbia University Press.

Grant, Susan-Mary. 2000. *North over South: Northern Nationalism and American Identity in the Antebellum Era.* Lawrence: University Press of Kansas.

Hacker, Louis M. 1940. *The Triumph of American Capitalism: The Development of Forces in American History to the End of the Nineteenth Century.* New York: Columbia University Press.

Hadden, Sally E. 2001. *Slave Patrols: Law and Violence in Virginia and the Carolinas.* Cambridge: Harvard University Press.

Hammond, Bray. 1970. *Sovereignty and an Empty Purse: Banks and Politics in the Civil War.* Princeton: Princeton University Press.

Hamowy, Ronald. 1979. "The Early Development of Medical Licensing Laws in the United States, 1875–1900." *Journal of Libertarian Studies* 3 [Spring]: 73–119.

Hetherington, Bruce W. 1990. "Bank Entry and the Low Issue of National Bank Notes: A Re-examination." *Journal of Economic History* 50 (September): 669–75.

Higgs, Robert. 1977. *Competition and Coercion: Blacks in the American Economy.* Cambridge: Cambridge University Press.

———. 1987. *Crisis and Leviathan: Critical Episodes in the Growth of American Government.* New York: Oxford University Press.

Higham, Robin, ed. 1989. *Bayonets in the Streets: The Use of Troops in Civil Disturbances.* 2nd ed. Manhattan, KS: Sunflower University Press.

Hill, Louise B. 1936. *State Socialism in the Confederate States of America.* Charlottesville, VA: Historical.

Hirshleifer, Jack. 1963. *Disaster and Recovery: A Historical Survey.* Santa Monica, CA: Rand Corporation.

Holt, Charles Frank. 1977. *The Role of State Government in the Nineteenth-Century American Economy, 1820–1902: A Quantitative Study.* New York: Arno.

Hummel, Jeffrey Rogers. 1996. *Emancipating Slaves, Enslaving Free Men: A History of the American Civil War.* Chicago: Open Court.

———. 1999. "Martin Van Buren: America's Greatest President." *Independent Review 4* (Fall): 255–81.

———. 2001a. "Deadweight Loss and the American Civil War: The Political Economy of Slavery, Secession, and Emancipation." PhD diss., University of Texas at Austin.

———. 2001b. "The American Militia and the Origin of Conscription: A Reassessment." *Journal of Libertarian Studies* 15 (Fall): 29–77.

Huston, James L. 1999. "Property Rights in Slavery and the Coming of the Civil War." *Journal of Southern History* 65 (May): 249–86.

Hyman, Harold M. 1973. *A More Perfect Union: The Impact of the Civil War and Reconstruction on the Constitution.* New York: Knopf.

Hyman, Harold M., and William M. Wiecek. 1982. *Equal Justice Under Law: Constitutional Development, 1835–1875.* New York: Harper & Row.

James, John A. 1978. *Money and Capital Markets in Postbellum America.* Princeton: Princeton University Press.

———. 1981. "Financial Underdevelopment in the Postbellum South." *Journal of Interdisciplinary History* 11 (Winter): 443–54.

Jaynes, Gerald David. 1986. *Branches without Roots: Genesis of the Black Working Class in the American South, 1862–1882.* New York: Oxford University Press.

Keller, Morton. 1977. *Affairs of State: Public Life in Late Nineteenth Century America.* Cambridge: Harvard University Press.

Kendrick, M. Slade. 1955. *A Century and a Half of Federal Expenditures.* New York: National Bureau of Economic Research.

Kennedy, Joseph C. G. 1862. *Preliminary Report on the Eighth Census, 1860.* Washington, DC: Government Printing Office.

Laird, William J., and James R. Rinehart. 1968. "Deflation, Agriculture, and Southern Development." *Agriculture History* 42 (April): 115–245.

Leach, John Franklin. 1952. *Conscription in the United States: Historical Background.* Rutland, VT: Tuttle.

Legler, John B., Richard Sylla, and John J. Wallis. 1988. "U.S. City Finances and the Growth of Government, 1850-1902." *Journal of Economic History* 48 (June): 347–56.

Lerner, Eugene M. 1954. "Monetary and Fiscal Programs of the Confederate Government, 1861–65." *Journal of Political Economy* 62 (December): 506–22.

———. 1955. "Money, Prices, and Wages in the Confederacy." *Journal of Political Economy* 63 (February): 20–40.

———. 1956. "Inflation in the Confederacy, 1861–65." In *Studies in the Quantity Theory of Money,* ed. Milton Friedman, 161–75. Chicago: University of Chicago Press.

Luraghi, Raimondo. 1978. *The Rise and Fall of the Plantation South.* New York: Watts.

Majewski, John. 2000. *House Dividing: Economic Development in Pennsylvania and Virginia before the Civil War.* Cambridge: Cambridge University Press.

Martin, Bessie. 1932. *Desertion of Alabama Troops from the Confederate Army: A Study in Sectionalism.* New York: Columbia University Press.

McCandless, George T., Jr. 1996. "Money, Expectations, and the U.S. Civil War." *American Economic Review* 86 (June): 661–71.

McCusker, John J. 1992. *How Much Is That in Real Money? A Historical Price Index for Use as a Deflator of Money Values in the Economy of the United States.* Worcester, MA: American Antiquarian Society.

Miller, George H. 1971. *Railroads and the Granger Laws.* Madison: University of Wisconsin.

Mitchell, Wesley Clair. 1903. *A History of the Greenbacks: With Special Reference to the Economic Consequences of Their Issue, 1862–65.* Chicago: University of Chicago Press.

———. 1908. *Gold, Prices and Wages Under the Greenback Standard.* Berkeley: University of California Press.

Mohr, James C., ed. 1976. *Radical Republicans in the North: State Politics During Reconstruction.* Baltimore: Johns Hopkins University Press.

Moore, Albert Burton. 1924. *Conscription and Conflict in the Confederacy.* New York: Macmillan.

Murdock, Eugene. 1967. *Patriotism Limited, 1862–1865: The Civil War Draft and the Bounty System.* Kent, OH: Kent State University Press.

———. 1971. *One Million Men: The Civil War Draft in the North.* Madison: State Historical Society of Wisconsin.

Myers, Charles J. 1992. "A Compilation of Estimates of U.S. GNP, 1790–1840." Golden Gate University.

———. 1994. "Retirement of the First Federal Debt: A Test of Vincent Ostrom's Theory of Democratic Administration." PhD diss., Golden Gate University.

Neely, Mark E., Jr. 1991. *The Fate of Liberty: Abraham Lincoln and Civil Liberties.* New York: Oxford University Press.

———. 1999. *Southern Rights: Political Prisoners and the Myth of Confederate Constitutionalism.* Charlottesville: University Press of Virginia.

Nevins, Allan. 1959. "A Major Result of the Civil War." *Civil War History* 5 (September): 237–50.

Newcomb, Simon. 1865. *A Critical Examination of Our Financial Policy during the Southern Rebellion.* New York: D. Appleton.

O'Brien, Patrick K. 1988. *The Economic Effects of the American Civil War.* Basingstoke, U.K.: Macmillan Education.

Patterson, Robert T. 1954. *Federal Debt-Management Policies, 1865–1879.* Durham: Duke University Press.

Porter, Bruce D. 1980. "Parkinson's Law Revisited: War and the Growth of Government." *Public Interest* no. 60 (Summer): 50–68.

Ramsdell, Charles W. 1944. *Behind the Lines in the Southern Confederacy.* Baton Rouge: Louisiana State University Press.

Randall, James G. 1951. *Constitutional Problems Under Lincoln,* rev. ed. Urbana: University of Illinois Press.

Ransom, Roger L. 1989. *Conflict and Compromise: The Political Economy of Slavery, Emancipation, and the American Civil War.* Cambridge: Cambridge University Press.

Ransom, Roger L., and Richard Sutch. 1988. "Capitalists without Capital: The Burden of Slavery and the Impact of Emancipation." *Agricultural History* 62 (Summer): 133–60.

———. 2001. "Conflicting Visions: The American Civil War as a Revolutionary Event." In *Research in Economic History,* ed. Alexander J. Field, Gregory Clark, and William A. Sundstrom, 20:249–301. Amsterdam: JAI.

Rawley, James A. 1974. *The Politics of Union: Northern Politics during the Civil War.* Lincoln: University of Nebraska Press.

Rein, Bert W. 1962. *An Analysis and Critique of the Union Financing of the Civil War.* Amherst, MA: Amherst College Press.

Richardson, Heather Cox. 1997. *The Greatest Nation of the Earth: Republican Economic Policies during the Civil War*. Cambridge: Harvard University Press.

Robertson, James I., Jr. 1988. *Soldiers Blue and Gray*. Columbia: University of South Carolina Press.

Rockoff, Hugh. 1971. "Money, Prices, and Banks in the Jacksonian Era." In *The Reinterpretation of American Economic History,* ed. Robert W. Fogel and Stanley L. Engerman, 448–58. New York: Harper & Row.

Rose, Louis. 1964. "Capital Losses of Southern Slaveholders Due to Emancipation." *Western Economic Journal* 3 (Fall): 39–51.

Sanborn, Alvan F., ed. 1907. *Reminiscences of Richard Lathers: Sixty Years of a Busy Life in South Carolina, Massachusetts and New York*. New York: Grafton, 1907.

Sargent, Thomas J., and François R. Velde. 2002. *The Big Problem of Small Change*. Princeton: Princeton University Press.

Schwab, Christopher. 1901. *The Confederate States of America, 1861–1865: A Financial and Industrial History of the South during the Civil War*. New York: C. Scribner's Sons.

Sears, Hal D. 1977. *The Sex Radicals: Free Love in High Victorian America*. Lawrence: Regents Press of Kansas.

Selgin, George. 2000. "The Suppression of State Banknotes: A Reconsideration." *Economic Inquiry* 38 (October): 600–615.

Selgin, George, and Lawrence H. White. 1994. "Monetary Reform and the Redemption of National Bank Notes." *Business History Review* (Summer): 205–43.

Shannon, Fred Albert. 1928. *The Organization and Administration of the Union Army*. 2 vols. Cleveland: Clark.

Sharkey, Robert P. 1959. *Money, Class and Party: An Economic Study of Civil War and Reconstruction*. Baltimore: Johns Hopkins University Press.

Skocpol, Theda. 1992. *Protecting Soldiers and Mothers: The Political Origins of Social Policy in the United States*. Cambridge: Harvard University Press.

Slaughter, Thomas P. 1986. *The Whiskey Rebellion: Frontier Epilogue to the American Revolution*. New York: Oxford University Press.

Smith, Harry Edwin. 1914. *The United States Federal Internal Tax History from 1861 to 1871*. Boston: Houghton Mifflin.

Sprague, Dean. 1965. *Freedom under Lincoln*. Boston: Houghton Mifflin.

Stampp, Kenneth M. 1956. *The Peculiar Institution: Slavery in the Ante-Bellum South*. New York: Knopf.

Storing, Herbert J. 1981. *What the Anti-Federalists Were FOR*. Chicago: University of Chicago Press.

Summers, Mark Wahlgren. 1984. *Railroads, Reconstruction, and the Gospel of Prosperity: Aid under the Radical Republicans, 1865–1877*. Princeton: Princeton University Press.

Surdam, David. 2001. *Northern Naval Superiority and the Economics of the American Civil War*. Columbia: University of South Carolina Press.

Sylla, Richard. 1969. "Federal Policy, Banking Market Structure and Capital Mobilization in the United States, 1863–1913." *Journal of Economic History* 29 (December): 657–86.

Sylla, Richard, John B. Legler, and John J. Wallis. 1987. "Banks and State Public Finance in the New Republic: The United States, 1790–1860." *Journal of Economic History* 47 (June): 391–403.

Tatum, Georgia Lee. 1934. *Disloyalty in the Confederacy.* Chapel Hill: University of North Carolina Press.

Temin, Peter. 1976. "The Post-Bellum Recovery of the South and the Cost of the Civil War." *Journal of Economic History* 36 (December): 898–906.

———. 1978. "Reply to Goldin and Lewis." *Journal of Economic History* 38 (June): 493.

Thomas, Emory M. 1971. *The Confederacy as a Revolutionary Experience.* Englewood Cliffs: Prentice-Hall.

Thornton, J. Mills, III. 1982. "Fiscal Policy and the Failure of Radical Reconstruction in the Lower South." In *Region, Race, and Reconstruction: Essays in Honor of C. Vann Woodward,* ed. J. Morgan Kousser and James M. McPherson, 349–94. New York: Oxford University Press.

Thornton, Mark, and Robert B. Ekelund, Jr. 2004. *Tariffs, Blockades, and Inflation: The Economics of the Civil War.* Wilmington, DE: SR Books.

Timberlake, Richard H., Jr. 1993. *Monetary Policy in the United States: An Intellectual and Institutional History.* Chicago: University of Chicago Press.

Todd, Richard Cecil. 1954. *Confederate Finance.* Athens: University of Georgia Press, 1954.

U.S. Census Bureau. 1866. *Eighth (1860) Census.* Washington, DC: Government Printing Office. Vol. 4.

———. 1872. *Ninth (1870) Census.* Washington, DC: Government Printing Office. Vol. 3.

———. 1884. *Tenth (1880) Census.* Washington, DC: Government Printing Office. Vol. 7.

U.S. Department of Commerce. 1975. *Historical Statistics of the United States: Colonial Times to 1970.* 2 vols. Washington, DC: U.S. Government Printing Office.

U.S. War Department. 1880–1901. *The War of the Rebellion: A Compilation of the Official Records of the Union and Confederate Armies.* Washington, DC: Government Printing Office. ser. 4, vol. 3.

Vandiver, Frank E. 1952. *Ploughshares into Swords: Josiah Gorgas and Confederate Ordnance.* Austin: University of Texas Press.

Van Riper, Paul P., and Harry N. Scheiber. 1959. "The Confederate Civil Service." *Journal of Southern History* 25 (November): 450–70.

Van Riper, Paul P., and Keith A. Sutherland. 1965. "The Northern Civil Service, 1861–1865." *Civil War History* 11 (December): 351–69.

Wallenstein, Peter. 1987. *From Slave South to New South: Public Policy in Nineteenth-Century Georgia.* Chapel Hill: University of North Carolina Press.

Wallis, John Joseph. 2000. "American Government Finance in the Long Run, 1790 to 1990." *Journal of Economic Perspectives* 14 (January): 61–82.

Warren, Donald R. 1974. *To Enforce Education: The History of the Founding of the Office of Education.* Detroit: Wayne State University Press.

Weigley, Russell F. 1984. *History of the United States Army,* enl. ed. Bloomington: Indiana University Press.

Weiss, Thomas J. 1992. "Estimates of Gross Domestic Output for the United States." Working paper, University of Kansas.
White, Leonard D. 1958. *The Republican Era, 1869–1901: A Study in Administrative History.* New York: Macmillan.
Williams, Kenneth P. 1949–1950. *Lincoln Finds a General: A Military Study of the Civil War.* 4 vols. New York: Macmillan.
Williamson, Jeffrey. 1974. "Watersheds and Turning Points: Conjectures on the Long Term Impact of Civil War Financing." *Journal of Economic History* 34 (September): 631–61.

ROBERT A. MARGO

8

Government and the American Dilemma

AMERICANS ENJOY one of the highest per capita standards of living in the history of world, and there is little doubt that good institutions have played a key role in producing this outcome. Private property rights are secured by a Constitution and a tradition of common law and are enforced by an independent judiciary. Elections are held at periodic and predictable intervals, and transitions of government officials are routine and generally without incident. Within the boundaries of the United States there are common markets in goods, currency, and factors of production. Subject to certain limitations, individuals have freedom of speech, freedom of movement, and other human rights. Government activities are divided among the local, state, and federal levels, ensuring a degree of competition and experimentation. Although the overall structure of these institutions is largely fixed, the implementation of policy has been and continues to be extraordinarily flexible.

The history of the United States is not, however, without its stains, of which race is one of the most scarring and certainly one of the most enduring. Prior to 1865, the securing of private property rights included securing the right to own another human being in certain parts of the country. Although in principle slavery could have been divorced from skin color, black Africans and their descendants were overwhelmingly the enslaved and white Americans (with very few exceptions) were overwhelmingly the slaveowners. Most whites, whether they were or were not slaveowners, accepted, or at least did not challenge in public, a belief system that held blacks to be inferior. In the 1850s an epic struggle ensued over slavery, one that culminated in a terrible civil war. Although the war ended slavery, the belief system prevailed for much longer before it came under scrutiny and, ultimately, changed for the better.

This chapter has two goals. The first is to describe changes over time in the absolute and relative living standards of African Americans,

232

from the era of slavery to the present. I survey the work of economic historians who have studied intensively the economic history of African Americans in the past several decades. The second goal is to ask how government affected this history, for better or for worse. My economic narrative has several key elements.

The first is that slavery, as it was practiced in the southern United States before the Civil War, was economically profitable and viable. Because slaves were valuable as productive assets, treating slaves poorly in material terms potentially carried economic costs to the slaveowner. The economic costs faced by slaveowners for failing to provide opportunities for slaves to acquire human capital and accumulate wealth, however, appear to have been quite minimal. Slaves could not participate directly in the polity, and they had no legal freedom of movement or other constitutional rights enjoyed by free persons. The "rules of the game" permitted the vast majority of the economic rents produced by the slave economy to accrue, by design, to slaveowners and to consumers of the products of the slave economy, but not to the slaves. There is every reason to believe that on the eve of the Civil War slavery was economically viable and therefore no reason to believe that the institution was on the verge of collapsing of its own accord.

The second element is that the dominant long-term characteristic of the economic history of African Americans since 1865 is racial convergence—that is, a narrowing of racial differences. In the immediate aftermath of the Civil War former slaves were, on average, in a state of relative economic backwardness—they generally lacked artisanal or managerial skills, seldom owned physical capital, and almost wholly lacked exposure to formal schooling. Since the end of the Civil War, the black-to-white ratio of per capita income in the United States has increased by a factor of three and that of wealth by a factor of seven; racial difference in average years of schooling is much smaller than it was shortly after the end of the war; and a black "middle class" comprised of workers in professional and other skilled occupations has emerged. At the same time, saying that racial convergence was a dominant feature does *not* mean that racial equality has been or soon will be achieved.

Third, the economic actions that individual blacks took in response to economic incentives embedded in the free market played an important role in producing convergence. As slaves, blacks could do relatively little to improve their lot, and, in the final analysis, were always at the mercy of their owners. As free workers, they could and did make decisions to invest in human capital, accumulate wealth, and, perhaps most important, move from one place to another. In doing so, they experienced gains in economic status that, in the long run, outpaced those experienced by whites.[1]

It is possible that racial convergence after emancipation could have occurred continuously as each successive generation of African Americans acquired more wealth and human capital, migrated in search of better economic opportunities, and so on. This leaves out two crucial features, however: the persistence of the prevailing ideology and government. These two features make up the fourth element of the narrative.

The belief system that accommodated slavery and survived its downfall slowed the process of racial convergence after the Civil War. The belief system supported discrimination by whites against blacks in various ways in the private economy—for example, refusal to sell property to black farmers or to hire black workers—and in the public sector as well. In the South this took the form of a complex array of laws that enforced racial segregation in all aspects of public life—for example, in the public schools—and a general failure to adequately protect the private property rights of African Americans. Public-sector discrimination was facilitated, particularly in the South, by disenfranchisement. The abrogation of black voting rights in the South took hold in the late nineteenth century and remained entrenched until the passage of federal voting rights legislation in the 1960s.

In the South the ideology of racial inferiority became a way of life, deeply rooted and resistant to change. In the North the same ideology was active, but it was directed more towards residential segregation than toward disenfranchisement and economic subjugation. When the South emerged from the Civil War its economy was in shambles, and it remained a poor, backward region relative to the North for a long time afterward. In the immediate aftermath of the war and, indeed, for many years, most ex-slaves and their descendants lived in the South, in spite of the ideology and the grinding poverty. Their economic fortunes were inextricably tied to those of the region, always subject to the constraints imposed by the belief system and the policies implemented in response to those beliefs.

This historical reality created the preconditions for racial convergence to be discontinuous rather than continuous. Discontinuities could occur when blacks decided to move in large numbers from the South, where incomes were low, to the North, where incomes were high, as happened during the world wars. Discontinuities could also occur if events caused the belief system to be revised.

There is strong evidence that racial convergence was concentrated in particular episodes of time. These episodes were four in number. The first coincided with the period that historians refer to as Reconstruction, from the end of the Civil War to the late 1870s. During this episode many of the worst aspects of the ideology were temporarily held in check by the federal government's efforts to reconstruct the former Confederacy. The second and third episodes coincided with the two world wars. World War I is an example of a shock-induced discontinuity. The war temporarily arrested the flow of European immigrants to northern cities, creating a labor shortage that was exacerbated by legislative restrictions on immigration that were enacted shortly after the war. This labor shortage was eased by migration of persons from the South, including blacks. The extent of black migration from the South between 1910 and 1920 (and into the 1920s) was in excess of what would have been expected in the absence of World War I or the cutoff in immigration.

World War II was a similar if larger shock, but it also involved the first serious attempts on the part of government to revise the belief system. The war and various interventions in the economy by the federal government altered national labor supplies and demands such that wage differentials between skilled and unskilled, or more or less well-educated, labor declined substantially. African Americans benefited from the wage compression, because they were less skilled and less well-educated on average, than white workers.

At the federal level, the ideology began to come under attack in the 1940s. The first attack came in the form of an executive order issued by President Franklin Roosevelt that was aimed at mitigating discrimination in defense employment. It came under additional scrutiny later in the decade by President Harry Truman, progressed further in the 1950s, and then culminated in the fourth episode of discontinuous change, from the early 1960s to the mid-1970s.

This episode coincides with the civil rights movement and with the passage of federal legislation that banned racial discrimination in public accommodations, in voting, in various labor market contexts, and in housing. The passage of this legislation, particularly the central Civil Rights and Voting Rights Acts, dramatically altered the institutional structure, making it far more difficult for any politician to claim allegiance to the belief system in public and be elected to national office. As blacks began to vote, the number of black elected officials at the state and local levels, particularly in the South, rose sharply.

The racial convergence that occurred during this fourth episode eventually petered out. Some scholars blame the slowdown on fundamental changes in the American economy that have reduced the demand for less-skilled and less well-educated labor. Others attribute the slowdown to unintended consequences of the implementation of antidiscrimination legislation and to the expansion of certain types of government programs, such as welfare, that (allegedly) stifle incentives to work and to invest in human capital. Still others emphasize the changing political fortunes of the Democratic Party, which originally championed the cause of civil rights but which has seen its national political support subsequently erode. Finally, others claim that, although the institutional reforms banished overt racial discrimination in its grossest forms, discrimination remains pervasive in subtle ways in the American economy.

The Economic Impact of Slavery

At the turn of the twentieth century roughly 90 percent of African Americans lived in the South. Per capita income in the South at the time was 51 percent of the national average. Although location was far from the only reason why black incomes at the turn of the century were less than white incomes, it was a key reason.

Why was the South so poor at that time? One possibility is that it was always thus, and "always thus" was a consequence of the "peculiar institution"—slavery. The South was poor because slavery made it so. The argument has a long tradition in historical circles and reputable economics to back it up. According to this view, slave labor cannot survive for very long in competition with free labor. Free labor is modern, slave labor, archaic. The forces of modernization will eventually win the day, and slavery will out on its own.

For nearly five decades, economic historians have been intensively studying the workings of the slave economy of the antebellum South. Some of their results seem unsurprising, but others are quite surprising indeed. Slavery was highly profitable, meaning simply that the rate of return on owning a slave exceeded the next best alternative investment. Given the growth and obvious prosperity of the slave economy, profitability is not very surprising. Slavery was also economically viable. Viability means more than profitability; it means that it was economically rational for the system to reproduce itself. Slavery was profitable and viable because the slaveowner, by definition, could exploit the slave economically. *Exploit* as used here is a technical economic term: it means that the value of the slave's economic contribution—the value of his "marginal product"—exceeded the value of his maintenance costs (food, clothing, shelter, and so on).[2]

There is no question that exploitation in this sense occurred, but the amount of exploitation does not seem sufficient to account for the level of profitability. Most economic historians believe that something deeper and much more insidious made slavery profitable. According to this view, slave agriculture was technically more efficient that free agriculture: using the same nonlabor inputs (capital, land, and so on), slaves could produce more output per worker than could free laborers. Many scholars object to this finding on moral grounds, because it seems to suggest that there was something good about slavery. But there was nothing good about slavery, and the finding that slave labor was technically efficient is not a statement in favor of the system.[3]

The evidence concerning profitability makes it clear that slaveowners benefited from slavery. What technical efficiency implies is that consumers of the products of the slave economy also benefited from the system, because these products would have been more expensive had they been produced using free labor. These consumers were scattered throughout the country, and indeed all over Europe.

Technical efficiency was not a foregone conclusion. It was achieved primarily by the use of the gang system. The gang system was to agriculture what the factory system was to manufacturing. In gang system agriculture, tasks were highly specialized, there was much division of labor, and laborers of all ages and both sexes were utilized with ruthless effectiveness. Free labor shunned the gang system; slavery was the only way to reap its rents. The slaveowner who wished to extract the full benefits of the gang system had, first, to assemble a gang—a group of at least fifteen productive slaves. The labor had to be extracted from the slaves with a delicate balance of sticks and carrots. Too much of the stick—the whip and other punishments—and the extra profits could vanish owing to sabotage or merely a slowdown in work effort undetected by the slave driver or the owner. Too little of the carrot—inadequate food—and the same could occur.

None of this is meant to imply that slaves were well-treated in an absolute sense, because they were not. At best, the typical slave received an allotment of basic necessities that, on average, was roughly comparable to that received by poor, unskilled free labor. But slave labor was seriously disadvantaged in other ways.

Slave labor was almost wholly illiterate labor. This was, of course, true of some free labor at the time, but rates of illiteracy among slaves were vastly higher than corresponding rates among free labor. Merely teaching a slave to read or write was a crime. The literate slave was feared for one simple reason—he could revolt.

Slave labor was generally unskilled labor. Scholars have long disputed the precise level of skills embodied in the slave population. The debate persists because it is clear that black labor was grossly underrepresented in skilled and professional occupations at the end of the nineteenth century. The issue is whether the underrepresentation was a product of slavery or of a later era. But even the most optimistic estimates clearly imply that most adult male slaves, in particular, held unskilled occupations, chiefly in agriculture.

Slaves were dirt poor. Most slaves, except in a very limited sense, possessed no private property and had little or no means to accumulate any and pass it on to their descendants, who were slaves at birth.

Although slavery generated benefits for slaveowners and consumers of the products of the slave economy, it did little economically for the slaves. It was extremely difficult for a slave to accumulate human capital or physical wealth. The hallmark of the antebellum economy was a high rate of geographic and occupational mobility among free laborers. Free laborers could and did migrate where the returns to labor were highest. Slaveowners moved or sold their chattel to capture higher returns, but these returns did not accrue to the slaves.[4]

Finally, although the evidence shows that slavery was both economically profitable and viable on the eve of the Civil War—and therefore in no apparent danger of disappearing on economic grounds—it does not follow that slavery would have continued indefinitely. The technical advantage that slavery conferred was concentrated in a small number of crops (for example, cotton) rather than being general in application. In the absence of the Civil War it is highly likely that at some point the southern economy would have modernized to a sufficient extent that the demand for slave labor relative to free labor would have declined such that it would no longer have been in the interest of slaveowners to maintain the institution. Yet even a relatively small delay in emancipation, say, two decades, would have been extraordinarily costly to enslaved African Americans. The tenacity of white southerners in resisting the abolitionist movement and the fierceness of their resistance to the Union Army attest to the strength of the belief system underlying slavery. As the war approached, most southerners were not slaveowners, but many who were not were evidently willing to die to preserve the southern way of life, which, at the time, included the peculiar institution.

Racial Convergence after the Civil War

In 1865 the Civil War ended, and with it the enforced enslavement of millions of African Americans. Measuring the extent and timing of racial convergence since emancipation is difficult. Not until 1940 did the federal census include a question about income. The censuses of 1850, 1860, and 1870 did include questions about wealth, but there were no similar questions in subsequent censuses. Enough evidence survives, however, to piece together to a reasonably reliable and complete picture of change over time.

Estimates of per capita black incomes in the immediate aftermath of the Civil War have been made by Robert Higgs. Higgs's estimates are based primarily on contemporaneous reports of agricultural incomes. According to Higgs, the ratio of black income to white income in 1865 was approximately 0.25.[5] This is not very surprising. As noted in the previous section, the typical ex-slave was illiterate and had very few occupational skills. The American economy in 1870 was not yet one in which educated labor played a large role, but it was an economy that nevertheless paid a wage premium for educated labor, and it also paid a wage premium for skilled labor. But these are not the only factors that affected the wage ratio just after the Civil War.

The South experienced a sharp decline in per capita income after the war, one of the few instances of such declines in American history apart from the Great Depression. This decline was manifested in a steep reduction in nominal and real wages in South, both in absolute terms and relative to nominal and real wages outside the region. This decline was a consequence of a number of factors, chief among them reduced demand for labor. The gang system, which had elevated labor productivity in southern agriculture before the war (on the backs of slave workers), disappeared. Output per worker fell sharply in agriculture; one manifestation of this was a decline in wages. The vast majority of blacks in 1870 were ex-slaves living in rural areas of the South, engaged in agricultural activity. The majority of whites, however, were not rural southerners. Consequently, another reason why the black-white income ratio was so low in 1870 was that so many blacks lived in the South.[6]

Convergence in incomes of blacks and whites has occurred since the end of the Civil War. The most recently available estimate of the black-white per capita income ratio by the United States Census Bureau, the one for 2001, is 0.62.[7] Differences in wealth have also converged for blacks and whites over the long haul. As noted above, the 1870 census recorded major elements of personal and real wealth. These data refer to gross, not net, wealth (that is, they are not adjusted for debt holdings), and the 1870 census is widely believed to have been one of the poorest in quality of the nineteenth century. According to these data, the black-white wealth ratio in 1870 was a scant 0.025—that is, for every dollar of wealth held by whites, blacks held 2.5 cents. The vast majority of adult black men listed in the census reported that they owned no wealth at all.

Today, the Federal Reserve periodically conducts household-level surveys of wealth. In these the data pertain to net worth (assets minus liabilities), which can, of course, be negative (unlike gross wealth). The Federal Reserve data are far more comprehensive than those collected in the nineteenth century, and the scientific sampling methods ensure that the sample statistics, for example, medians or averages, are the best available estimates of population parameters. According to the most recent analysis of such data, the black-white wealth ratio in the mid-1990s was 0.16, approximately a sevenfold increase since 1870.[8]

Racial convergence in schooling has also occurred in the long run. Data about years of schooling or highest grade completed were first collected in 1940; data about literacy were collected before then, however. The 1870 census was the first of the pre-1940 censuses to provide nationally representative evidence of literacy by race.[9] These, like nearly all census data, were self-reported. Survey evidence suggests that, on average, exposure to a limited amount of formal schooling—as little as one to two years—was sufficient for a person to declare himself or herself literate to the census taker. The opposite, therefore—illiteracy—can be taken as an indicator of very little or no formal schooling.

In 1870, 13 percent of whites aged ten and over nationwide reported themselves as illiterate. This figure was higher in the South, but even there, the overwhelming majority of whites were literate. This was not so, however, among African Americans: nationwide, the black illiteracy rate was 81 percent. The rate for the South was virtually the same (83 percent), because the overwhelming majority of blacks in 1870 lived in the South.

The census no longer collects data about literacy, having substituted a question about educational attainment in 1940. These data have been periodically modified since 1940 and are not really comparable to the literacy data. Blacks still lag behind whites in educational attainment, but there is no question that the gap is vastly smaller than it was in the previous century.[10] To be sure, the census data for educational attainment do not adjust for school quality, and there is widespread belief that the quality of schooling received by African Americans falls short, on average, of the quality received by whites. The same was true in the past, however, and thus adjusting for school quality would not alter the conclusion that racial differences in educational attainment have narrowed substantially since 1870.

In sum, a variety of evidence, including much that I have not surveyed here, points to long-term convergence in economic outcomes between blacks and whites. Nonetheless, we live in a county in which racial gaps in income, wealth, and other measures of economic "success" are still very large in absolute terms. Measured in terms of equality, rather than convergence, the most has been achieved in schooling, and the least in wealth, with income in between.

Indeed, although proportionately more convergence took place in wealth than in income, the fact remains that the racial wealth gap today is extremely large. Why this is so is currently a topic of considerable interest among economists and other social scientists. Racial differences in income, rates of return, and demographic factors play a role, but much of the difference appears to be due to a lesser rate of intergenerational transfers among blacks as well as racial differences in portfolio structure.[11]

Government Policies and Convergence

In the preceding section I showed that long-term racial convergence in income, education, and wealth has occurred since the end of the Civil War. In theory convergence might have taken place continuously. The theory is quite simple. Under slavery, blacks faced extraordinary difficulty in accumulating human capital and physical wealth. This left them underendowed with both types of capital at the end of the Civil War. With slavery ended, the economic fortunes of blacks were tied to the market economy, and the market paid positive returns to human capital and physical wealth. Ex-slaves, therefore, had especially strong incentives to acquire wealth—incentives that, at the margin, almost certainly exceeded those of whites. Moreover, blacks no longer faced the virtually binding constraints on upward mobility that slavery imposed on them. Provided that rates of return to these activities did not differ fundamentally by race, convergence would take place—indeed, until equality was achieved.

Even in this ideal scenario, convergence would not have taken place overnight, because the required investment was huge. Absent the ability to borrow, the opportunity cost of investing in physical capital is today's consumption. Investment in human capital takes time, and the opportunity cost of time spent investing in human capital is time spent working, which also translates directly into today's consumption. But convergence would nevertheless have been steady.

There are reasons to question the "steady as it goes" story on a priori grounds. For example, the American economy has always been beset by ups and downs in the business cycle. Typically, the poor bear the brunt of these fluctuations when the economy turns sour. Periodic recessions, in other words, must have slowed the convergence process—and, indeed, there is good evidence that this was so for the post–World War II period as well as the biggest downturn of them all, the Great Depression. But the upside of a recession is a boom, and during a boom, the economic prospects of lower-income workers would get a boost. But these are movements around a trend, not the trend itself. And the trend—convergence—is positive. Shifts due to the business cycle in the relative economic fortunes of blacks cannot be the full story of long-term convergence.

A stronger reason is that the "free market" does not exist independent of the institutions that support it, notably, those associated with the definition and protection of private property. Accumulation of wealth means little if wealth can be easily stolen or destroyed and victims are unable to procure justice or recover damages. Accumulation of human capital means little if individuals are at daily risk of bodily harm. The responsibility for defining and ensuring the protection of private property rests primarily, if not exclusively, with the public sector. A governmental failure to adequately protect life, limb, and physical property of individuals dampens their incentives to invest, and in the limit, might thwart economic growth altogether.

An equally strong reason is that the ideology of black inferiority impinged on the process of convergence. In one of the standard economic models of discrimination, that of Gary Becker (1957), one group, the majority, is said to have "tastes for discrimination," or prejudice against another group, the minority. These tastes generally will differ across members of the majority; some may be without prejudice, others may be rabidly biased. If members of the majority group act on their prejudices, certain gains from trade between the two groups will not be realized. The amount of the foregone gains depends on, among other factors, the precise distribution of prejudice across the majority. If the discrimination is severe enough, convergence will be slowed considerably and perhaps stopped altogether.

The gains from trade result from private market transactions. But government can be harnessed in support of the majority's prejudices. If, motivated by prejudice, a member of the majority commits a criminal act against a member of the minority—a whipping, for example—and no action is taken against the perpetrator, the government has failed to protect private property rights. Government might outlaw certain types of exchanges between the two groups—for example, marriage or residential integration—that again can result in so-called deadweight losses. One can also imagine a model of discrimination in which the government imposes taxes on the minority and redistributes the proceeds to majority.[12]

Then, as now, the United States was made up of governments at several levels, and the ability of any one of them to discriminate was partly dependent on the actions of other governments at the same level (if any), and whether higher levels of government (if any) constrained the behavior of the lower levels. The actions of other governments at the same level matter if members of the minority group are mobile across jurisdictional boundaries and if "voting with one's feet" imposes costs on the majority. Today, a local government could never impose a law that discriminated against blacks for purely racial purposes (that is, motivated by racial animus) simply because such a law would be deemed unconstitutional on its face by either a state or a federal court, and the court order would be enforced. But this was not the case historically (see below).

The ability to harness the government to discriminate is most directly contingent on the majority's political clout relative to the minority. If members of the minority can vote, and their votes in the aggregate matter enough to the political support of the government, the majority may fail in its quest. Disenfranchisement of the minority is neither a necessary nor a sufficient condition for government discrimination to exist. It is not a necessary condition because the votes may not matter to the government, and there may be insufficient safeguards elsewhere to prevent the discrimination from taking place. It is not a sufficient condition because certain types of discrimination might impose economic harm on the majority in excess of whatever the majority gains in satisfaction from seeing its prejudices exercised or, if the discrimination is imposed at lower level and there are members of the majority who are less prejudiced (or without prejudice) elsewhere, and these engage a higher level of government to stop the discrimination by the lower government. These caveats are important in theory as well as in fact; however, there is no question that disenfranchisement can facilitate government discrimination if the other fundamentals are in place.

Slavery did not survive the Civil War, but the ideology of black inferiority that justified slavery in the eyes of slaveholders (and others) did. Indeed, it would have suited former slaveholders just fine if the peculiar institution could somehow have been reconstituted after the war in its essential elements and blacks "kept in their place." But it was in the interest of the Union to see the former Confederacy reconstructed.

Although Reconstruction was not an unmitigated blessing, on the whole African Americans benefited from its most important aspects, which were the ratification of the Fourteenth and Fifteenth Amendments to the Constitution (in 1868) and the establishment of public schools for black children in the South.[13]

Reconstruction formally ended in 1877, but the processes it put in place continued for some time thereafter and, in the case of schools, were permanent. There is clear evidence of racial convergence in wealth from 1870 to shortly after the turn of the century. This evidence comes from reports conducted by state authorities in various southern states that divided taxable wealth by race. These reports show that taxable wealth per adult black male increased more rapidly than among whites, with one exception. For example, in Georgia in 1880, the black-white ratio of per capita (taxable) wealth stood at 0.028—2.8 cents of taxable wealth per black person for every dollar held by whites. By 1910 the ratio was 0.063. This evidence is complemented by other data from census reports documenting substantial growth in the proportion of black farmers who were owner-operators by the turn of the century.[14]

More impressive is the substantial reduction in black illiteracy rates that occurred after 1870. This reduction shows up most dramatically among post–Civil War birth cohorts, the first to have widespread access to formal schooling. Hence the point made above:: if public schools for blacks had not been a key component of the effort to reconstruct the South, black illiteracy rates would have continued to be very high into the late nineteenth century.[15]

In the aftermath of Reconstruction the South underwent a major detour in its racial politics. In particular, beginning in the 1880s in some states and largely complete by the early twentieth century, a number of southern states effectively disenfranchised the black population along with many poor whites. The disenfranchisement era was also associated with the rise of "Jim Crow," the legislative embodiment of segregation. Taken to absurd lengths, segregation infected every nook and cranny of southern life.[16]

This period also witnessed a substantial deterioration in the relative amount of resources provided to black schools in the South. Earlier there had been a rough sort of racial equality in the schools, but once disenfranchisement took hold, resources per black pupil relative to resources per white pupil fell steeply.[17]

The rise of Jim Crow also coincided with a general deterioration in the security of blacks' property rights. Nothing illustrates this better than the extraordinary cruelty of southern lynch mobs, who imposed their own form of punishment on black men rather then let the justice system run its course. Newspaper and other accounts record the deaths of thousands of black men who met their maker at the hands of such mobs. The exact number will never be known.

To avoid summary justice, a beating, or a burning cross, blacks in the South had to follow a code of behavior that forced them to acquiesce to the ideology of inferiority. Even this might not be enough, so it paid to have a powerful white as a patron. We are now so far from this era and this type of society that it is difficult—impossible, really, for a white person—to comprehend the kind of day-to-day accommodations in behavior that blacks had to make merely to survive.

The combination of disfranchisement, Jim Crow, and increased educational discrimination appears to have slowed the pace of racial convergence in incomes to a crawl prior to World War I. As noted, the South was very poor at the turn of the century. Blacks who desired a better life and who remained in the South faced a difficult battle.

One of the more puzzling features of African American history is the continued presence of large numbers of blacks in the South after the Civil War, especially after their political fortunes took a turn for the worse. Why didn't more blacks leave the South, especially since there appear to have been substantially higher real incomes outside the region? Economic historians have written about this question for years, and there are many answers on the table. One answer claims that a "North Atlantic labor market" developed during the nineteenth century and that the northern United States and western Europe participated but the South did not. As the North continued to industrialize after the war, it drew its manufacturing workers from the pool of available talent in this labor market. The South could have joined, too, but, according to the story, southerners were busy with Reconstruction. Another hypothesis suggests that migrants from the South, black or white, tended to be much better educated than those who stayed behind. The South lagged substantially behind the rest of the nation in education. This story suggests that, over time, more blacks should have left the South as convergence in schooling took place. There is clear evidence of this in the census data, but there is also clear evidence of the importance of shock-induced migration.[18]

The first shock was World War I. During the war the demand for manufacturing labor in the North increased, but the usual supply of European immigrants was interrupted. The interruption subsided at war's end, but Congress followed with the implementation of quotas in 1924. Blacks migrated to take advantage of job openings during the interruption. Once the flow started, it appears to have sustained itself. Most of the migration was to select cities, and in these cities black ghettos emerged. Some cities such as St. Louis erupted in race riots initiated by whites angry about the black influx.

It is difficult to prove directly that the shock-induced migration of World War I led to discontinuous change in black-white income ratios because the requisite data are lacking. But the circumstantial evidence is strong, because wages in the South were far lower than wages in the North, and the evidence of a discontinuous jump in black migration from the South is compelling.

World War II was another shock, far bigger in size and in its long-term implications than was the Great War. Large numbers of blacks left the rural South (as did whites), settling in southern cities or, more often than not, cities outside the region, including the far West. In this case the evidence for discontinuous change in migration is very strong, as is the evidence of discontinuous convergence in incomes. Indeed, virtually all of the convergence in black-white income differences that occurred after 1940 took place in two periods, one of which was the 1940s.[19]

The 1940s witnessed the "Great Compression," a substantial reduction in the degree of wage inequality manifested by a decline in the returns to schooling and a narrowing of wage differentials between skilled and unskilled occupations. Blacks benefited disproportionately from the Great Compression because at its start (1940) they were mainly low-wage workers. Among the compression's many causes was direct intervention by the federal government in the form of wage controls. Shifts in wartime demand also favored low-wage labor, as did shifts in labor supply (including the draft). Unlike a similar compression during World War I, that of the 1940s remained largely intact well after the war ended, and thus the gains experienced by blacks owing to the compression were sustained as well.[20]

The decade also witnessed an important attack by the federal government on the ideology of racial inferiority. It is true that the ideology had already been under attack from many quarters prior to the 1940s, but only the federal government possessed the ability, in principle, to enforce implementation of antidiscrimination regulations on a nationwide basis. In 1943 Franklin Roosevelt issued an executive order barring discrimination in defense hiring. At the same time the Fair Employment Practices Committee (FEPC) was set up. It did not have the ability to punish violators by, say, putting them in jail or fining them, but it could conduct hearings, which could bring adverse publicity. Recent work by has shown that, contrary to received wisdom, the FEPC was effective in getting blacks hired in defense industries. These employment gains were sustained after the war and, because these industries paid above-average wages, were important in generating the disproportionate wage gains experienced by blacks in the 1940s.[21]

As more blacks moved to the North, they were able to exert more political pressure on government to intervene on their behalf. State governments began to pass fair employment laws. These laws do not seem to have had much effect, but they nevertheless created important precedents for national legislation. Blacks in northern cities became important "swing voters" in national elections. It is no accident that Harry Truman, who benefited from such swing votes in the 1948 election, was a proponent of antidiscrimination legislation. But significant change at the national level was held up for many years in the Senate by senators from the South, who opposed changes in racial policies, particularly in matters of integration.[22]

The attack on the ideology of racial inferiority continued in the 1950s. In 1954 the Supreme Court ruled that "separate-but-equal" public schools were unconstitutional in a case that was the culmination of a long series of court battles and social activism. The order of the Court was to be implemented with "all deliberate speed" because the white South was very far from ready to accept integration from above.

The emergence of a civil rights movement in the 1950s, which reached its zenith with the March on Washington in 1963, and Martin Luther King Jr.'s "I Have a Dream" speech coincided with the national ascendancy of the political career of Lyndon Johnson. Johnson wanted the presidency but knew by the late 1940s that he could never be elected if he toed the strict segregationist party line—by that time, he would never win enough votes outside the South. He first achieved passage of federal civil rights legislation in 1957 while in the Senate, but his crowning achievements were as president with the passage of the Civil Rights Act in 1964 and the Voting Rights Act in 1965. In an executive order issued in 1965, Johnson also establishment the principle of "affirmative action," whose implementation has been a subject of controversy ever since.

Did the sea change in the federal government's role make a difference? Recent work by the labor economists John Donohue and James Heckman strongly suggest that it did. Donohue and Heckman show that, at the national level, the period from 1963 to 1975 coincided with a

substantial convergence in black-white income ratios. On further scrutiny, however, it is clear that most of the convergence occurred in the
South. The authors point out that much of the initial enforcement of
federal antidiscrimination legislation was targeted at the South; but
even so, the extent of the enforcement seems relatively puny compared
with the apparent gains experienced by blacks.

Donohue and Heckman resolve the puzzle in two ways. First, at least
some elements in southern white society wanted to change, including
many in business. Racism gave the South a bad image in the rest of the
country and in the rest of the world, and a bad image was bad for business. In public, the external impetus to change was deeply resented by
many in the region, but cooler heads realized that the change served a
good purpose.

Second, Johnson's executive order was perfectly timed. After World
War II the South received a disproportionate share of defense spending. Defense spending, by its very nature, is federal contracting. The
South Carolina textile industry is a case in point. The industry's labor
force was almost entirely white, and had been for decades, but this was
hardly true of the state. Yet the industry suddenly began to hire black
workers after 1965. Nothing had changed except that the executive order had bee issued and many firms in the industry were federal contractors during the Vietnam War. In the late 1960s racism no longer paid,
and black-white income differences narrowed accordingly.[23]

The changes that took place in the 1960s were, in hindsight, unprecedented, but they did not come fast enough, nor were they complete
enough, to satisfy many African Americans. An incredible number of
American cities erupted in race riots in the 1960s, many after the as-
sassination of Martin Luther King in April 1968. A recent econometric analysis suggests that the riots had negative effects on outcomes for
black in the labor market.[24]

The dramatic convergence associated with the civil rights era slowed
in the mid-1970s. Beginning in the late 1970s and picking up steam during the Reagan administration, the ensuing debate in the courts about
affirmative action and other federal antidiscrimination efforts did not
lead to the reversal of the policies, but there is no question that their
reach has been circumscribed. The opportunities that emerged in the
wake of the civil rights movement have been seized on by many blacks
eager for economic advancement, and the results can be seen in all walks
of American life. But some have been left behind, and the results are
also visible, in the form of high crime rates in inner cities, drug-related

violence, and low levels of employment. These problems are exacerbated further by the continued high levels of residential segregation in many American cities. Black incomes have also been adversely affected by increasing wage inequality in the labor market, whose origins rest with skill-biased technical change and declines in the demand for manufacturing labor.[25]

Conclusion

Near the end of World War II the Swedish economist Gunnar Myrdal (1944) published his monumental two-volume study *The American Dilemma: The Negro Problem and American Democracy*. Page after page of Myrdal's work recounted the consequences of racism and the profound paradoxes that racism raised in light of the Constitution. How could a country committed to the ideals expressed in the Constitution tolerate the abuses of human rights that black Americans faced day in and day out?

Racism still exists, but its grossest, its vilest forms, so evident to Myrdal, have been banished from American public life. African Americans today still have lower incomes and far less wealth and are more often unemployed than their white counterparts; their life expectancies are lower; they have more health problems and more stress. These differences are a still a challenge for the United States. The American dilemma is not over.

Yet there has unquestionably been change for the better over the long sweep of American history since emancipation. We have had convergence, first and foremost, because slavery was abolished and because during the immediate aftermath of slavery, a variety of safeguards put in place and enforced by the federal government took hold. But government has been a fickle partner in the process of racial convergence. It was the institutions of American government that maintained slavery in the first place. It is, of course, possible that a peaceful solution—peaceful emancipation, perhaps with compensation to slaveowners—might have been worked out, but there is no reason to believe on economic grounds that slavery would have died out peacefully on the eve of the Civil War.

In the aftermath of slavery the federal government maintained its presence in the South for a while, but eventually it left, and African Americans soon faced the brunt of the region's racism. Geographic mobility in the form of the market offered some protection against discrimination and exploitation, but there is no question that, in the South, the government was an ally to whites who wished to keep blacks in their place.

Around the turn of the century the disenfranchisement movement in the South effectively banished blacks from the electorate. Segregation became a way of life hat many in the region were extremely reluctant to give up, to the point of violence.

Although blacks began to leave the South as soon as they were able, the flow was never very large until the two world wars greatly speeded up the process of out-migration. Black migrants faced a great many challenges in the urban North, but at least they had the benefit of higher incomes. As black communities were established in northern cities, the political landscape began to change, and blacks' votes became valuable as swing votes. Blacks' political clout increased over time, receiving another boost with the passage of federal voting rights laws passed as part of a wave of federal antidiscrimination legislation in the 1960s. This legislation unquestionably improved the lives of many African Americans, and the timing of the legislation coincides with an episode of convergence in incomes. But although some racial gaps now seem quite small, others, notably the gap in wealth, still are very large.

The fickleness of the government was not random. Government was, and is, a conduit for the public expression of the prevailing ideology of race in American society. When the prevailing ideology favored racial discrimination, it was in the interest of many politicians to accommodate it. When the prevailing ideology changed, so did the incentives of politicians. Nevertheless, although public expressions of racism by politicians, once very common, are no longer permissible in public life, America is still a country with a large racial divide in private. There are signs of a thaw (for example, in rates of intermarriage), but true racial integration in the United States is far off.

I began this chapter by noting that, in comparison with most countries in the history of the world, the United States has been marked by "good government. But by its very nature, government is coercion. Americans have not been immune to the temptations of using the coercive powers of the state for immoral ends. Change was often very slow in coming, and there were many reversals but, in the final analysis, the racist ideology that accommodated slavery and that festered in its aftermath gave way.

Notes

1. References in these notes are deliberately sparse and are meant to guide further reading rather than provide definitive documentation. See Higgs 1977

for an analysis of the role of market competition in the economic progress of African Americans after the Civil War.

2. Conrad and Meyer 1958 is the classic analysis of profitability, and Yasuba 1971 is the classic analysis of viability. For additional evidence, see Fogel and Engerman 1974; Fogel 1989.

3. Evidence about the relative efficiency of slave agriculture is presented in Fogel and Engerman 1974, 1992.

4. See Margo 2000 for evidence of the relation between migration and geographic differentials in real wages during the antebellum period.

5. See Higgs 1977.

6. On the decline in per capita income in the South see Engerman 1971 and Goldin 1979; on the decline in wages in the South, see Margo 2004.

7. See table P.3 in www.census.gov/hhes/income/histinc.

8. See Pope 2000 for estimates of the black-white wealth ratio in 1870; see Blau and Graham 1990 and Wolff 1998 for estimates for the late twentieth century.

9. The 1850 and 1860 censuses also report data about literacy, but these pertain solely to free persons.

10. For additional evidence about racial differences in schooling, including evidence about long-term convergence, see Collins and Margo 2003.

11. See Blau and Graham 1990.

12. See Margo 1991 for an example of such a model.

13. For a general discussion of Reconstruction, see Foner 1988; on the postemancipation experience in other countries, see Engerman, Haber, and Sokoloff 2000.

14. Higgs (1977, 1982) and Margo (1984) provide evidence for black wealth accumulation in the South in the late nineteenth century based on state auditors' reports.

15. Data and analysis of racial differences in literacy after the Civil War are presented in Collins and Margo 2003.

16. The classic reference for the rise of Jim Crow is Woodward 1955. Kousser (1974) discusses the various disenfranchisement mechanisms adopted in the South in the late nineteenth century and their effects on the race of voters in the South.

17. For evidence on the evolution of racial differences in school expenditures in the South in the late nineteenth and early twentieth centuries, see Margo 1990.

18. The argument that a separate southern market emerged after the Civil War is developed at length in Wright 1986. For evidence of the role of schooling and shocks, see Margo 1990 and Collins 1997.

19. On the discontinuous nature of black-white wage convergence see Donohue and Heckman 1991.

20. See Goldin and Margo 1992 on the Great Compression and Margo 1995 on the implications of wage compression on black-white wage convergence in the 1940s.

21. See Collins 2001.

22. On the impact of fair employment legislation, see Collins 2003.

23. See Donohue and Heckman 1991. The case of South Carolina textiles is analyzed in Heckman and Payner 1987.
24. See Collins and Margo 2004.
25. On the emergence of so-called bad ghettos, see Wilson 1987 and Cutler and Glaeser 1997; on declining employment opportunities, see Bound and Freeman 1992.

References

Becker, Gary. 1957. *The Economics of Discrimination.* Chicago: University of Chicago Press.
Blau, Francine D., and Graham, J. W. 1990. "Black-White Differences in Wealth and Asset Composition." *Quarterly Journal of Economics* 105 (May): 321–39.
Bound, John, and Richard B. Freeman. 1992. "What Went Wrong? The Erosion of Relative Earnings and Employment among Young Black Men in the 1980s." *Journal of Political Economy* 107 (February): 201–32.
Collins, William J. 1997. "When the Tide Turned: Immigration and the Delay of the Great Black Migration." *Journal of Economic History* 57 (September): 607–32.
———. 2001. "Race, Roosevelt, and Wartime Production: Fair Employment in World War Two Labor Markets." *American Economic Review* 91 (March): 272–86.
———. 2003. "The Labor Market Impact of State Anti-Discrimination Laws, 1940–1960." *Industrial and Labor Relations Review* 56 (January): 244–72.
Collins, William J., and Robert A. Margo. 2003. "Historical Perspectives on Racial Differences in Schooling." National Bureau of Economic Research Working Paper no. 9770. Cambridge, MA: National Bureau of Economic Research.
———. 2004. "The Labor Market Effects of the 1960s Riots." In *Brookings-Wharton Papers on Urban Affairs 2004,* ed. W. Gale and J. Pack, 1–34. Washington, DC: Brookings Institution Press.
Conrad, Alfred, and John Meyer. 1958. "The Economics of Slavery in the Antebellum South." *Journal of Political Economy* 56 (February): 95–130.
Cutler, David, and Edward L. Glaeser. 1997. "Are Ghettos Good or Bad?" *Quarterly Journal of Economics* 112 (August): 827–72.
Donohue, John, and James J. Heckman. 1991. "Continuous versus Episodic Change: The Impact of Civil Rights Policy on the Economic Status of Blacks." *Journal of Economic Literature* 29 (December): 1603–43.
Engerman, Stanley L. 1971. "Some Economic Factors in Southern Backwardness in the Nineteenth Century." In *Essays in Regional Economics,* ed. J. Kain and J. Meyer, 279–306. Cambridge: Harvard University Press.
Engerman, Stanley L., Stephen H. Haber, and Kenneth L. Sokoloff. 2000. "Inequality, Institutions, and Differential Paths of Growth among New World Economies." In *Institutions, Contracts, and Organizations: Perspectives from New Institutional Economics,* ed. C. Menard, 108–134. Cheltenham, U.K.: Edward Elgar.

Fogel, Robert W. 1989. *Without Consent or Contract: The Rise and Fall of American Slavery*. New York: Norton.

Fogel, Robert W., and Stanley L. Engerman. 1974. *Time on the Cross: The Economics of American Negro Slavery*. Boston: Little, Brown.

———. 1992. "Explaining the Relative Efficiency of Slave Agriculture in the Antebellum South" and "Reply." In *Without Consent or Contract: The Rise and Fall of American Slavery* (technical papers), ed. Robert W. Fogel and Stanley L. Engerman, vol. 1, *Markets and Production*, 241–303. New York: Norton.

Foner, Eric. 1988. *Reconstruction: America's Unfinished Revolution, 1863–1877*. New York: Harper & Row.

Goldin, Claudia. 1979. "'N' Kinds of Freedom." *Explorations in Economic History* 16 (January): 8–30.

Goldin, Claudia, and Robert A. Margo. 1992. "The Great Compression: The Wage Structure in the United States at Mid-Century." *Quarterly Journal of Economics* 107 (February): 1–34.

Heckman, James J., and Brooks Payner. 1989. "Determining the Impact of Federal Anti-Discrimination Policy on the Economic Status of Blacks: A Study of South Carolina." *American Economic Review* 79 (March): 138–77.

Higgs, Robert. 1977. *Competition and Coercion: Blacks in the American Economy, 1865–1914*. New York: Cambridge University Press.

———. 1982. "Accumulation of Property by Southern Blacks before World War One." *American Economic Review* 72 (September): 725–37.

Kousser, J. Morgan. 1974. *The Shaping of Southern Politics: Suffrage Restriction and the Establishment of the One-Party South*. New Haven: Yale University Press.

Margo, Robert A. 1984. "Accumulation of Property by Southern Blacks before World War One: Comment and Further Evidence." *American Economic Review* 74 (September): 768–76.

———. 1990. *Race and Schooling in the South, 1880–1950: An Economic History*. Chicago: University of Chicago Press.

———. 1991. "Segregated Schools and the Mobility Hypothesis: A Model of Local Government Discrimination." *Quarterly Review of Economics* 106 (February): 61–73.

———. 1995. "Explaining Black-White Wage Convergence, 1940–1950." *Industrial and Labor Relations Review* 48 (April): 470–81.

———. 2000. *Wages and Labor Markets in the United States, 1820–1860*. Chicago: University of Chicago Press.

———. 2004. "The North-South Wage Gap, before and after the Civil War." In *Slavery in the Development of the Americas*, ed. D. Eltis, F. Lewis, and K. Sokoloff, 324–51. New York: Cambridge University Press, 2004.

Myrdal, Gunnar. 1944. *An American Dilemma: The Negro Problem and Modern Democracy*. New York: Harper & Row.

Pope, Clayne. 2000. "Inequality in the Nineteenth Century." In *The Cambridge Economic History of the United States*, vol. 2, *The Long Nineteenth Century*, Stanley L. Engerman and Robert E. Gallman, 109–42. New York: Cambridge University Press.

Wilson, William J. 1987. *The Truly Disadvantaged: The Inner City, the Underclass, and Public Policy.* Chicago: University of Chicago Press.

Wolff, Edward. 1998. "Recent Trends in the Distribution of Household Wealth." *Journal of Economic Perspectives* 12 (Winter): 131–50.

Woodward, C. Vann. 1955. *The Strange Career of Jim Crow.* New York: Oxford University Press.

Wright, Gavin. 1986. *Old South, New South.* New York: Basic.

Yasuba, Yasukichi. 1971. "The Profitability and Viability of Plantation Slavery in the United States." In *The Reinterpretation of American Economic History,* Robert W. Fogel and Stanley Engerman, 362–68. New York: Harper & Row.

MARK GUGLIELMO AND
WERNER TROESKEN

9

The Gilded Age

Introduction
The Gilded Age was
fraught with paradox. On
one hand, it was a period of
economic centralization
and integration; on the other, it was a period of social fragmentation and
isolation. The forces driving centralization and integration were powerful and manifold, including the rise of national stock and financial markets, a modern rail system, and the emergence of nationwide industrial
enterprises known as trusts. The forces driving fragmentation and isolation were the same as those that drove centralization and integration.
In particular, as new modes of transportation and economic organization linked producers and consumers as far away as Maine and southern
California, many farmers, artisans, and small-time manufacturers were
displaced by anonymous producers in some faraway place. The people
that felt squeezed by industrialization and market integration did not go
down without a fight. On the contrary, their anger and frustration with
processes beyond their immediate control spilled over into the political
arena and in the short run reshaped electoral politics and in the longer
run altered the country's ideological and regulatory framework.

This paradox—this inevitable conflict between economic integration
and social anomie, between the rise of big business and the ruination
of smaller enterprises—runs through most of the major regulatory and
legislative changes of the late nineteenth century. For example, the
Sherman Antitrust Act of 1890, the country's first federal antitrust statute, grew out of a battle between Standard Oil and small oil refiners that
were unable to adopt the nationwide distribution techniques employed
by Standard and other large oil companies. Similarly, the move to subject all meat shipped across state lines to federal inspection stemmed
from a conflict between the meat-packing trust and small-town butchers who could not compete with the low-cost production techniques of
the large meat packers. More broadly, one can observe the workings
of the paradox in various social protest movements including agrarian

agitation and the Social Gospel movement. As explained in greater detail below, in each of these movements one finds groups that were disaffected by economic change seeking institutional remedies.

Agrarian Unrest

The period between the end of the Civil War and 1900 was a time of unprecedented and nearly continuous turmoil in the agricultural sector of the economy. This discontent spawned four political movements that succeeded in getting many local candidates elected to office. The Grangers, concentrated in the Midwest in the 1870s, successfully secured the passage of state laws setting maximum railroad rates (upheld by the U.S. Supreme Court in *Munn v. Illinois* in 1876) and also established a number of farmer-owned cooperatives including stores, grain elevators, and mills. The Greenbacks focused on increased circulation of government-issued paper money to inflate prices and reached their height in the midterm elections of 1878, when the Greenbacks elected fourteen candidates to Congress, mostly from Midwestern states. The Farmer's Alliance, which came to popularity in the South and the Midwest in the 1880s, pressed for debt relief, greater government control of railroad rates, and the formation of cooperatively run grain elevators, farm equipment factories, and banks. The Populist Party, at its zenith in the South, the Midwest, and the West in the 1890s, advocated a government-sponsored increase in the money supply, an income tax, government ownership of the railroads, and strict controls on immigration. The Populist Party's presidential candidate received more than one million votes in 1892, and the party combined with the Democrats to support William Jennings Bryan in 1896.[1]

It is difficult to rationalize agrarian protest by appealing to the economic hardships of farmers alone, in part because at least some of the complaints levied by farmers were unjustified. Farmers complained about falling agricultural prices and rising prices for manufactured goods. They attributed these trends, in part, to the creation of industrial trusts that monopolized particular markets. Yet when one examines such data, there is strong evidence that the prices of agricultural goods were generally rising relative to the prices of industrial goods during the nineteenth century. There were, however, a few important exceptions to this general pattern. Consider, for example, the experience of cotton farmers and the jute-bagging trust. Jute bags (burlap sacks) were used to transport cotton, and during the late 1880s there was a 50 percent increase in the price of jute bags. When compared to previous price increases in the industry, this change is unusually large. The increase in price followed, in very short order, the creation of a trust in the jute-bagging industry. There is also anecdotal evidence that farmers were not unreasonable in attributing price increases in other industrial sectors to the creation of trusts.[2]

The idea that farm incomes were falling over the course of the nineteenth century has a long and mistaken history dating back to agrarian protest movements. Real per capita income of farmers rose during every decade of the second half of the nineteenth century at a respectable average annual rate of 1.3 percent. Although this is less than the 1.6 percent average annual rate of increase in per capita income for the nation as a whole for the same period, this difference is due entirely to the poor agricultural performance of the South in the decades following the Civil War. The average annual rate of growth in agricultural real per capita income actually rose at a robust 1.8 percent in the areas of greatest agricultural unrest.[3]

Farmers also had more specific complaints regarding mortgage rates, futures markets, federal land policy, and railroad rates. Although there is evidence that railroad rates did not fall over the course of the nineteenth century (see the discussion below regarding railroad regulation), the evidence for farmers' other complaints is mixed. As for interest rates on farm mortgages, the vast majority of farmers did not have mortgages at all; only about 29 percent of U.S. farms were mortgaged. Most of these mortgages were relatively short-term, with an average life of three to four years. These periods are so short that it is unlikely that unanticipated price changes could have imposed great hardship on the farmer before a new rate could be negotiated. One authority concludes that "capital losses on mortgages due to unanticipated changes in the price level had only a slight effect on the average profit of farmers," reducing it by only about one-half of a percentage point per year. Moreover, these capital losses on mortgages from interest rate risk must be adjusted for capital gains that farmers earned from a rise in the value of their land, which averaged about one to two percent per year for most of the United States from 1859 to 1899. Having said this, mortgage rates were higher for five states with active agrarian protest movements—North Dakota, South Dakota, Kansas, Nebraska, and Minnesota—and though farmers were mistaken as to the causes of such interest rate differentials, their beliefs as to the existence of higher interest rates in the West were not unreasonable.[4]

As for federal land policy, farmers complained that speculators hoarded prime farmlands for themselves, thereby getting rich without ever doing any farming. The Homestead Act passed by Congress in

1862 allowed settlers to purchase federal lands at discounted prices provided that they lived on the land and cultivated it for five consecutive years. The federal government continued to sell public lands at auction and to donate land to railroad companies and the states. There is, however, a conceptual problem with objecting to speculators' making undue profits. As Robert Higgs has rightly pointed out, "in a private property system every owner of an asset is necessarily a speculator in the sense that he bears the risk of reductions in the value of the asset but hopes that the value will rise." Almost all settlers to the west purchased land, sold it, and moved on to new land several times. In this sense, everyone who purchased western land was a speculator.[5]

In addition to equity concerns, some have argued that federal land policy was inefficient because it allowed public lands to be sold at auction to large-scale investors who kept out of production lands that would otherwise have been used in agriculture. Economic research has shown, however, that investors would have had an incentive to dispose of land quickly. This research suggests that the economic costs of such speculation, if there were any, could not have been very large. Another charge was that federal land use policy released land from the public domain too quickly and, by requiring settlers to cultivate the land for five years to purchase land for the favorable price, it may have induced too much capital and labor to go into agriculture to the detriment of manufacturing. As a result, national income was lower than it would otherwise have been. Yet any losses that might have resulted from this system were purely transitory; once all federal requirements had been met, the value of the land would have been determined by its income-earning capacity, and whoever owned it would have applied the efficient amounts of capital and labor to it.[6]

Finally, many nineteenth-century farmers objected to the presence of futures markets because they believed that such markets lowered agricultural prices. Yet modern research has shown that the futures market was invaluable to the international grain trade because it reduced risk to millers, dealers, and exporters, which in turn helped narrow the difference between the average price paid to farmers and the average price charged to final consumers. Futures markets also combined with the vast U.S. storage system to allow American shippers to withhold grain when Liverpool prices were low and to reduce their stocks when prices were high. As a result, the volume of American trade was far more sensitive to prices abroad than that of any other exporting nation, and the prices that farmers received for their product were far more stable. Far from gaining vast profits at the expense of farmers, as some have charged, futures traders provided farmers with a valuable service. Moreover, on the whole, traders suffered heavy losses prior to 1896 and made only modest gains after prices started rising beginning in 1897.[7]

The previous discussion suggests that the usual economic explanations for agrarian unrest are not especially compelling. With perhaps the exception of railroad rates, farmers' complaints have received little empirical support, and there is strong evidence that in absolute terms the economic lot of farmers improved over the course of the late nineteenth century. Given the futility of traditional economic approaches to explain the origins of agrarian unrest, it seems wise to broaden the analytical perspective and ask a more general set of questions. In particular, if one wants to understand the origins of groups such as the Grange and the Alliance one needs to answer the following questions. Why did farmers join these groups? What did these groups offer to attract farmers? By the same token, one might ask why a group such as the Grange persisted for more than a century whereas groups such as the Alliance imploded after a few years.[8]

The Grange was founded in 1867 by Oliver Hudson Kelley, an employee of the U.S. postal service. Kelley had traveled the country and observed at first hand the hardships of a rural farm life. Kelley believed that farmers' difficulties stemmed from their social isolation and that their lot could be improved by breaking down the barriers to social interaction. Despite the common impression that the Grange was mainly a political organization—an impression that has only been reinforced by the unfortunate term *Granger laws*—Kelley wanted the Grange to promote the social and economic integration of farmers. Accordingly, he saw the organization primarily as a vehicle to improve the literacy of farmers and their children and to disseminate information about new farming techniques. Toward these ends, the Grange established libraries and created venues where farmers could exchange ideas about farming and form friendships.

Although these ideas resonated with many farmers, the vehicle that attracted most farmers to the Grange was the promise of gaining economic power through cooperative buying and selling. Farmers hoped that by using the Grange to pool their market power, they would be able to buy inputs at lower prices and simultaneously drive up the price of their crops. The Grange claimed that these cooperatives saved farmers up to 50 percent on such diverse goods as sewing machines, lumber, farm implements, and groceries. In Iowa alone, Grange agents had bought and sold more than $5 million in goods during the 1870s. At its peak in 1875, the Grange had attracted around 450,000 members through its promotion of economic cooperatives.

Unfortunately, the cooperatives did not work nearly as well as farmers had initially hoped. In some areas, farmers complained that Grange coops would sell to nonmembers; others complained that the discounts they offered were not significantly larger than those they secured from normal merchants; and still others complained that the coops sold low-quality goods. Dissatisfaction with the coops caused membership in the Grange to fall to sixty-five thousand by 1880, and although the organization persisted well into the twentieth century, the Grange never regained the popularity it enjoyed during the 1870s.

Of all the agrarian protest groups, the Grange was the least political and the most successful. Others such as the Wheel and the Southern Farmer's Alliance were overtly political from their inception. Furthermore, politics and economic issues do not appear to have attracted farmers to the Grange. Instead, the Grange's economic and social programs, which offered farmers direct and immediate benefits, caused them to join. That they were attracted by these features should not be a surprise. During the late nineteenth century, farmers were becoming more isolated and more alone as agriculture's position in American society was steadily eroded. The percentage of the labor force employed in agricultural pursuits fell from 48 percent in 1870 to 36 percent in 1900. Furthermore, population growth was concentrated in urban areas while the population of agricultural regions stagnated or declined. Through cooperative buying and selling, and the related educational programs, the Grange and to a lesser degree the Alliance offered farmers the promise that they, too, might benefit from the economic centralization and integration that were taking place.

Moreover, historians, economic and otherwise, have tended to assume that questions about high interest rates, unfair railroad rates, futures markets, and the like were issues that united farmers. Most farmers, it would seem, agreed about the economic sources of their discontent and the political changes necessary to alleviate their suffering: rein in the railroads and the trusts; abandon the gold standard and increase the money supply. Yet this interpretation is far from adequate. If anything, it appears that these issues divided farmers and undermined the viability of farm groups. For example, heated debates about politics and monetary policy led many members and leaders to drop out of the Southern Farmer's Alliance and eventually resulted in the organization's demise. The only factor that seemed to compensate for the group's political struggles was that the cooperatives promised farmers benefits in the form of increased buying power for inputs and market power in output markets.

The Social Gospel Movement

During the Gilded Age, most Americans—including, apparently, most farmers and laborers—opposed the radical extension of governmental powers to redistribute wealth "because they believed that such a government would be not only counterproductive but immoral." This was true even during the depression of 1893–98, the largest economic contraction in U.S. history prior to the Great Depression. In spite of this, neither the federal nor any state government adopted public works programs to relieve unemployment in the 1890s. All aid for the unemployed continued to come from the traditional sources: private charities and local governments. The Secretary of Agriculture for President Grover Cleveland, a Democrat, also resoundingly rejected a proposal from the Russian minister in Washington that the major wheat-exporting nations form a cartel to control prices, arguing that "it is not the business of government to attempt . . . to override the fixed laws of economics." One authority concludes that "in the late nineteenth century most activities, including virtually all purely economic decision-making, were considered 'not the proper business of government'—especially the federal government."[9]

One reason for this widespread aversion to helping the unemployed and disadvantaged, even during a time of crisis, was the dominance of social Darwinism. This was an attempt to apply to humans the theory of natural selection, which Darwin had originally developed to explain the evolution of plant and animal species in nature. Led by Herbert Spencer in England, who coined the phrase "survival of the fittest," and William Graham Sumner in the United States, social Darwinists argued that economic and cultural struggle among individuals would result in the survival of the best human traits and the continuing improvement of the population in general. In such a model, wealth is a sign of positive attributes such as industriousness, temperance, and frugality, whereas poverty is a sign of negative attributes such as idleness, drunkenness, and prodigality. Attempts by the state or other organizations to aid the poor, especially via income redistribution, would therefore be counterproductive because they would interfere with natural processes, ensuring that those with undesirable characteristics would survive and reproduce to the general detriment of the human population.[10]

This ideology was also shaped by the pseudo-scientific theory of eugenics—the idea that by engineering human reproduction, and in particular by limiting the growth of "undesirable" populations, the condition of the human race could be improved. Eugenicists argued that the underlying cause of social problems such as pauperism, alcoholism, crime, and prostitution was not the structure of society but the inheritance of defective germ plasm. In consequence, they advocated mandatory sterilization of individuals deemed to be defective as a means of preventing the birth of other defectives that would have to be cared for by the state. In 1907, Indiana enacted the first law allowing for involuntary sterilization on eugenic grounds. By 1914, eleven additional states had enacted such laws. At one time or another, thirty-three states had such statutes, under which more than sixty thousand Americans underwent forced sterilizations, which continued into the 1970s. Such laws were upheld by the U.S. Supreme Court in 1926 in *Buck v. Bell,* a case that has never been formally overturned. Many states passed laws prohibiting anyone who was epileptic, imbecilic, or feeble-minded from marrying.[11]

Eugenics was also used to justify state laws prohibiting interracial marriage. According to eugenicists such as Madison Grant, the biological dangers of mixing the races would inevitably result in the decline of higher racial types (for example, Nordic whites) without elevating lower racial types. By 1915, twenty-eight states had prohibited marriages between whites and blacks, including six states that included this prohibition in their constitutions. A third area of public policy in which eugenics was applied was in immigration restriction. Labor activists had urged immigration restrictions for decades as a way of propping up wages by restricting the labor force but had made little headway. But by the early twentieth century eugenicists began to provide biological arguments to support such limits. For example, in 1920 the eugenicist Harry Laughlin argued that the American gene pool was being polluted by an onrush of intellectually and morally defective immigrants from eastern and southern Europe. The Immigration Restriction Act, passed in 1924, restricted immigration from these undesirable areas.[12]

Over time, this dominant ideology was challenged by statistical and theoretical advances in the social sciences. Darwinism implied that over time, natural selection would ensure that the quantity of the members of a species displaying a desirable trait would rise relative to the quantity of the members lacking that trait. Yet from the late nineteenth century onward, the birth rates of the upper classes were falling while those of the lower classes were rising. Social scientists also discovered that traits that had been linked with genetics were actually more closely related to environment. Robert Fogel, D. J. P. Barker, and others have shown that conditions in early life are linked to later-life health outcomes. This is because many conditions and diseases are closely linked to nutrition, which is closely linked to poverty. If a parent is in poor health, undereducated, or unproductive because of malnutrition brought on by poverty, his or her children are also at high risk of suffering from these conditions. If this is true, improving the conditions of the poor will lead to better health and to a better-educated and more productive labor force, improving the overall quality of the species.

Eugenics was also challenged by the work of Franz Boas of Columbia University, the founder of modern anthropology. In a study of the head sizes and shapes of eighteen thousand people, he found that the variance of subjects within a particular race exceeded the variance between races. These and other studies convinced Boas that the inherent differences between races were minor when compared to their similarities and that all races were capable of forming sophisticated cultures. Weakened by the advances in social science in the early twentieth century that challenged its major tenets, eugenics was thoroughly discredited by the Nazis, who carried these tenets to their logical extremes.[13]

Confronted with this new evidence, the dominant American ideology toward government intervention in the economy changed over the course of the late nineteenth and early twentieth centuries. Much of this was due to changing economic conditions. In early nineteenth-century America, land was cheap and widely available. In such a world, there was little unemployment or distressing poverty among able-bodied males. The poor mainly included the elderly, widows, orphans, and the sick and disabled, whose needs could be met by private institutions. In New York State in 1820, this group included only one percent of the population. In such an environment it was easy to believe that, at least for the able-bodied, poverty was a sign of some moral or genetic defect. There were few impediments to work, and there was a lot of virgin land available for those who were dissatisfied with their current condition. Since most enterprises were small, employing fewer than one hundred people, it was possible for the humblest worker to imagine that with hard work, some day he to might become a master.[14]

But after the Civil War these conditions changed. The new situation included the rise of big businesses that often had monopsony power, a wave of immigration, rapid technological change that made some skilled workers obsolete, a series of short but sharp economic contractions, and the problems associated with rapid urbanization. The average industrial unemployment rate from 1893 to 1898 was 20 percent. Events such as the depression of the 1890s left little room for the belief that there was still excess demand for labor and that every adult male who wished to could become a prosperous yeoman. Having said this, the late nineteenth and early twentieth centuries generally saw rising real wages and declining numbers of hours worked per week.[15]

These changing economic and social conditions combined with changes in theology to produce the Social Gospel movement. In the early nineteenth century, religious theology was based on the biblical concepts of original sin and the innate depravity of man. In such a view, aid to the poor, particularly able-bodied males, would be counterproductive, reinforcing the natural tendencies of the lower classes towards sloth, lust, and drunkenness. But over the course of the century, science challenged biblical suppositions that had previously been unquestioned. The geologist Charles Lyell argued that the earth was much older than the Bible implied, and the naturalist Charles Darwin developed the theory of evolution that challenged creationism. In response, a new theology emerged that advocated a less literal interpretation of the Bible and stressed the natural goodness of man. Social Gospelists, who saw the Bible as a social document and based their theology on the Sermon on the Mount, held that social reform was a precondition for the personal salvation of those in the grip of poverty. According to this view, if people were corrupt, it was the result of a sinful social order that denied them the education and opportunities needed to choose virtuous behavior. Social Gospelists therefore believed that a minimum standard of living was necessary to give people the strength to fight sin. They even used the tenets of social Darwinism to support their own agenda. Charles Loring Brace, for example, the founder of the Children's Aid Society in New York and an early convert to evolution, argued that "history provided abundant evidence for the survival, by natural selection, of superior moral qualities, and that continuation of this process would lead to 'a new principle in the distribution of wealth' according to which surplus riches would be 'continually distributed by means of education, of wise charity and of public improvement.'" It was only after this change in the prevailing ideology that government could respond to economic hardship with redistributive programs, as it did during the Great Depression.[16]

The shift in economic philosophy can be seen in the views of Francis Wayland and Richard T. Ely. The former was a leading economist during the mid-nineteenth century; the latter was a leading economist during the late-nineteenth and early twentieth centuries. Wayland was the president of Brown University and the author of a popular economics textbook published before the Civil War. He held that unions were worthless because they thwarted the laws of competition and deprived workers of the right to dispose of their labor as they saw fit. He also opposed charity to able-bodied workers because it caused idleness. Ely was a member of the faculty of the University of Wisconsin and the first president of the American Economic Association. He argued that capital had become too powerful and that the state should therefore intervene on the side of labor by recognizing and promoting labor unions, taxing monopoly profits to finance antipoverty programs, setting minimum wages, limiting labor supply via immigration controls, restricting female and child labor, and limiting on the length of the workday and the workweek.[17]

Railroad Regulation

The railroad industry grew rapidly during the 1800s: in 1830 there were 23 miles of (operative) track in the United States; by 1850 there were 9,021 miles; by 1870 there were 52,992 miles; and by 1890 there were 166,703 miles. Most of this new railroad construction was heavily subsidized by the federal government. The development of the railroad had far-reaching effects. In terms of industrial and manufacturing activity, as the previous discussion showed, the railroads promoted centralization in the oil-refining and meat-packing industries. In terms of agriculture, the railroads reduced the burden on American farmers of transporting their crops to urban areas and to coastal ports for international export. Nonetheless, one should not overstate the significance of the railroad. It was important but not essential for American economic development. For example, in response to those who argue that the railroad hastened the development of the American iron and steel industries, it should be pointed out that more iron was used to make nails and wood-burning stoves than was used in the building of the rail system. (The railroads used even less steel during the late 1800s.) Similarly, independent estimates suggest that the savings in transport costs to farmers and other shippers that resulted from the railroads amounted to between 5 and 10 percent of GNP circa 1890.[18]

The sector of the economy that appeared the most politically sensitive to developments in the railroad industry was agriculture. This sensitivity was logical. In some areas of the country, the railroad freight charges incurred by farmers ate up as much as half of the market value of the crops shipped. Moreover, there is evidence that on short hauls railroads had market power and increased their rates to near monopoly levels. Because they faced much more competition on long-haul routes—from each other as well as from canals and shipment by river and ocean—the railroads were forced to charge lower rates on these routes. As a result, farmers often had to pay more to ship their crops one hundred miles than they would have had to pay to ship those same crops one thousand miles. This anomalous result infuriated farmers and helped fuel agrarian agitation. Finally, before 1896, railroad rates were stagnant over the long run (after adjusting for the general deflation of the late 1900s), and with the exception of a few short-term dips in price, farmers faced constant railroad rates over time.[19]

Given the disparities in long- and short-haul freight rates and persistently high rates generally, farmers grew increasingly dissatisfied with the monopolistic practices of the railroads and began lobbying for regulatory changes. Between 1860 and 1880 farmers successfully lobbied several state legislatures to pass laws regulating railroad rates. Although there was some concern that these laws might discourage future investment in the railroad industry, most farmers appear to have supported them and enjoyed lower freight rates as a consequence of state regulation. The railroad industry, however, challenged the constitutional basis of regulation, claiming that it violated their substantive due process rights and the Constitution's commerce clause. The courts ruled against the railroads' claim that regulation, in and of itself, violated substantive due process, but in the now-famous *Wabash* decision, the Supreme Court held that state railroad regulation did violate the constitutional provision against state regulation of interstate trade. The ruling that the states could only regulate the rates on routes within the state in question meant that all interstate rail traffic was not subject to regulation. This, in turn, helped fuel the demand for federal regulation of the railroads.[20]

Passed in 1887, the Interstate Commerce Act created the Interstate Commerce Commission (ICC) and was the first law empowering the federal government to regulate the rates and behavior of the nation's railroad companies. Traditionally the Interstate Commerce Act has been seen as a law designed to rein in the power of the railroads and bring farmers reduced freight rates. There is some truth to this interpretation because the lobbying efforts of farmers and shippers helped shape the ultimate structure of the law. There is also evidence, however, that the railroads probably had the greatest impact on the law. In particular, the stock market enthusiastically endorsed the legislation, with railroad stocks rising significantly with passage of the act. The patterns in the stock prices of railroads suggests that financial markets believed that federal regulation would be much less onerous than state regulation and that federal regulation might help the railroads collude in setting long-haul rates. Unfortunately for the railroads, the subsequent history of the ICC would prove these early predictions and hopes entirely incorrect. By the early 1900s, the ICC was captured by farmers and other shippers, and the commission drove railroad rates so low that many railroads became insolvent.[21]

State and Federal Regulation: Antitrust Legislation and Meat Inspection

The Origins of Antitrust Laws

Passed in 1890, the Sherman Antitrust Act was the nation's first federal antitrust law. In its essential features, the act declared combinations in restraint of trade to be illegal, authorized individuals damaged by monopolistic combinations to sue for treble damages, and allowed violators to incur a fine up to $5,000 and a prison term of up to one year. Historians have traditionally interpreted the Sherman Act as a genuine effort to rein in the power large industrial combinations and to bring consumers lower prices. This interpretation is only half right. The act was indeed designed to undermine the economic position of large businesses, but it was not intended to bring consumers lower prices. On the contrary, the act was designed to protect small, inefficient (high-price) producers from their larger, lower-price competitors.[22]

Evidence of small businesses' support for antitrust laws is especially clear in the oil-refining industry. Over the course of the late nineteenth century, John D. Rockefeller's notorious Standard Oil Company came to dominate the country's oil-refining industry. Between 1870 and 1880, Standard's share of industry capacity rose from around 10 percent to more than 90 percent. Between 1880 and 1900 Standard controlled between 70 percent and 95 percent of the industry's refining capacity, though its share of capacity fell steadily after 1890. In terms of market share, around 1900, Standard sold 40 percent of the country's lubricating oil, 50 percent of petroleum-based waxes, and 85 percent of fuel oil and gasoline.[23]

The rise of Standard Oil was associated with sharp reductions in the price of refined oil, the real price of which fell by nearly 80 percent between 1860 and 1893. The sources of this decline were threefold. First, production of crude oil, the primary input in oil refining, rose dramatically during this period, driving down the price of crude oil. Second, increases in consumer demand for refined oil, particularly lighting oil, enabled refiners to expand output and exploit economies of scale. Third, innovations in transportation during the 1870s and early 1880s reduced the cost of shipping oil. In particular, pipelines that ran from oil wells to railheads reduced the cost of shipping crude oil, and tank cars reduced the cost of shipping refined oil via the railroads.[24]

Given their connection to the Sherman Act and the origins of antitrust laws, it is useful to specify why tank cars and pipelines represented such an improvement over barrels and other modes of shipment. Before the introduction of pipelines, crude oil had to be transported from the wells to the railroad in barrels carried by teams of horses. As the oil industry developed, pipelines were built linking oil drilling centers in rural Pennsylvania and Ohio to refining centers in such urban areas as Cleveland and Pittsburgh. This allowed refiners to bypass the railroads entirely in the movement of crude.[25]

As for the introduction of tank cars, prior to their introduction, refined oil to had to be shipped to retail centers in barrels. Barrels were inferior to tank cars in many ways. Barrels leaked and allowed much of the oil to evaporate; tank cars allowed roughly 50 percent less oil to evaporate. Barrels had to be repaired and replaced constantly, which meant refiners typically had to hire a team of coopers to maintain an adequate stock of barrels; tank cars required much less maintenance. Barrels were costly to load and unload; tank cars were not. When shipping oil in barrels, there was a significant risk of accidental explosion; tank cars reduced that risk. In addition, because tank cars required much less handling by railroad workers—the responsibility for unloading barrels typically fell on the railroad, not the refiner—railroads offered refiners who shipped their oil in refiner-owned tank cars significant rate reductions relative to those who continued to use barrels.[26]

Standard Oil aggressively pursued low-cost production and transportation techniques, including tank cars. By 1889, Standard owned more than 50 percent of all tank cars then in use, owned and operated large pipelines to transport crude, and possessed relatively large and efficient refineries. Its efforts in these areas played a central role in Standard's rise to market dominance. Innovation alone, however, might not account for all of that success. Rivals claimed that Standard dominated the late nineteenth-century refining industry because it pursued anticompetitive strategies, including the use of predatory pricing and vertical restraints to forestall entry. Many historians and economists have raised serious questions about the reliability of these charges. There is, in particular, documentary evidence that claims about predatory pricing are incorrect, and there is economic logic to suggest that if it had, it probably would have been ineffective.[27]

As Standard and other efficient refiners adopted new distribution techniques, small refiners that were not so savvy in terms of adopting new technologies found themselves at a competitive disadvantage and were gradually forced out of business. Consider the margin between the price of refined oil and the price of crude oil, which fell sharply between 1870 and 1900. Because crude oil is the primary input used in producing refined oil, the margin provides a rough indicator of the efficiency of the least productive refineries. When the margin was large, relatively inefficient refineries were able to stay in business because they could waste large amounts of crude and charge enough for refined oil to cover such waste. But as the margin fell and the price of refined oil and crude converged, the ability to make such mistakes shrank and there was less room to pass along mistakes to consumers in the form of higher prices for refined oil. Before Standard ascended to market dominance, the margin between refined oil and crude was very large at about sixty dollars per barrel. This left plenty of room for small, inefficient refineries to allow crude and refined oil to evaporate away in barrels. But as Standard Oil grew and imposed more advanced technologies on the industry, the margin fell sharply, and by the late 1890s it hovered around six dollars per barrel, one-tenth the level observed thirty years earlier. This new and improved oil industry left little room for inefficient firms unable to the adopt low-cost production and distribution techniques.[28]

Unable to compete head-on with Standard and other large refiners, the small firms turned to the market for political favors and enlisted the support of a powerful ally: Senator John Sherman of Ohio. Sherman, the brother of William Tecumsah Sherman, was the longest-serving member of the U.S. Senate. During the late 1880s, Sherman received numerous letters from small oil companies requesting that he take action against Standard Oil. These companies lamented the fact that Standard Oil, as well as other large refiners, often received rebates from the railroads, ostensibly because they shipped their oil via tank cars instead of barrels. Small oil companies that continued to ship their oil in barrels objected to these reduced rates, claiming that they gave large refineries an unfair advantage. Although small oil companies eventually lobbied John Sherman to prohibit rebates for tank cars, these companies first used state legislatures and state courts. In 1878 and 1879, small oil companies in western Pennsylvania brought suits against Standard Oil and the Pennsylvania Railroad, claiming that they conspired against them. These suits failed to bring an end to the rebates, as did later efforts to get the Interstate Commerce Commission to order the railroads to cease granting rebates.[29]

The small oil companies asked Sherman to introduce legislation prohibiting rebates for use of tank cars. One letter, from the Great Western Oil Works, provided Sherman with the precise language it wanted the proposed law to use. Sherman responded by introducing the law and by repeating verbatim the words used by the Great Western Oil Works. As requested, the bill was in the form of an amendment to the Interstate Commerce Act of 1887, and it stated that it "shall be unlawful for any" railroad to grant special reduced rates for shippers using tank or cylinder cars to transport their wares.

Not all independent oil companies, however, supported the anti–tank car bill. In particular, W. C. Warner, the secretary of the National Oil Company of Titusville, Pennsylvania, opposed the bill. According to Warner, Standard was not the only oil refiner that used tank cars to receive favorable railroad rates. Warner claimed that of the 8,000 tank cars in use in 1889, 1,700 were owned by the railroads; 4,200 were owned by Standard; and 2,100 were owned by independents with no affiliation to Standard. Consequently, by outlawing rebates to all users of tank cars, Sherman's proposed measure would undermine the competitive position of the independent oil companies that used tank cars. Moreover, because Sherman's bill outlawed rebates for tank cars in all industries (not only oil), the bill promised to increase the price of other commodities as well. Warner explained: "Very many other fluid commodities are now also carried in tank cars. We used to get all of our sulphuric acid in glass carboys. If a law were passed saying we must pay the same rate in tank cars as in carboys, it would increase the cost nearly 50 percent." For these reasons, Warner argued, Sherman's bill was "a boomerang club thrown at the Standard Oil Trust by a reckless and thoughtless hand," a club that would "knock out innocent independent refiners and lose its force before reaching the object at hand."

In congressional debates about the bill, several senators argued that tank car rebates were based on economic efficiency and ultimately brought consumers lower prices. Senator Gray, a Democrat and an outspoken advocate of free trade, argued that tank cars offered "great economy in the distribution" of oil. Similarly, Senator Cullom, while he denied wanting to defend Standard Oil, argued that if the antitank car bill were passed "the result would be inevitably that the price of oil to the people of this country, the consumers, would be increased instead of re-duced. More willing to publicly defend Standard Oil, Senator Call main-tained: "The Standard Oil Company has certainly reduced the price of oil to the people of this country, and in consideration of this subject spe-cially directed towards oil and its transportation this fact should have weight and influence." At one point during the debate, Senator Reagan of Texas argued, "I do not think there is any human being on earth who will contradict or take issue with" the claim that tank cars reduced the costs of transporting oil.

Sherman countered these arguments, stating that the legislation would preserve competition by keeping Standard's smaller competitors alive: "All this [legislation] is designed to do is to guard against the mo-nopoly which, under the ordinary course of business, the oil-transporting companies with their tank cars will have over the others." He pleaded: "All that is asked by these people, most of whom are struggling now for their existence, is that their oil . . . shall be carried at the same rate per gallon in the barrels . . . as the Standard Oil and other companies." But despite this plea the bill was defeated. Afterward, three small oil companies wrote Sherman thanking him for introducing the bill and en-couraging him to continue his efforts against Standard Oil. When Sher-man discovered that he would probably never secure passage of his tank car bill, he turned his efforts to antitrust legislation. The ultimate result of these efforts was the Sherman Antitrust Act of 1890. As described by one small producer who had been driven out of business by Standard Oil, the Sherman Act was "one of the best laws ever written."

State and Federal Antitrust Enforcement

It is easy to be pessimistic about the fate of small oil refiners in par-ticular and small businesses in general. Their efforts to secure a federal anti–tank car law were unsuccessful, and though they did manage to se-cure passage of the Sherman Antitrust Act, all of the available evidence suggests that its subsequent enforcement failed to slow the growth of the trusts. Comparing market concentration in Britain (which had no anti-trust laws) and the United States, one authority argues that the Sherman Act has had no discernible impact on market structure. Another study has shown that the dissolution of Standard Oil and American Tobacco in 1911 failed to reduce firm profitability. There is also evidence that the breakup of railroad cartels in 1897 failed to reduce firm profitability or consumer prices. One renegade scholar argues that the Sherman Act might have hastened the rise of large business enterprises by discouraging less formal modes of combination such as cartels. About the only area where the Sherman Act appears to have had any noticeable effect was labor law: early enforcement of the act resulted in the dissolution of some labor unions.[30]

Initially, state antitrust enforcement appears to have been much more effective than federal enforcement, or at least that is how it was perceived by the large industrial combinations that were subject to state and federal laws. For example, early state-level decisions against the whiskey trust, the Chicago gas trust, and the sugar trust during the 1880s and early 1890s all induced large reductions in the stock market value of these combinations. Sometimes these reductions were as large as 50 percent, suggesting that investors believed that state antitrust enforcement would dramatically reduce the profitability of these enterprises. This stands in stark contrast to passage of the Sherman Antitrust Act, which had little impact on the stock market's valuation of trust-related enterprises. Moreover, if one compares the text of state and federal antitrust statutes, it is clear that state laws were much harsher and more aggressive in defining illegal actions than was the Sherman Act. These comparisons have prompted some observers to suggest that large enterprises might have welcomed the Sherman Act because they saw federal legislation as a means of undercutting state antitrust enforcement.[31]

Interpretation

While Standard Oil and other large refining businesses grew rich by adopting new distribution technologies and fully exploiting the development of the railroads, smaller oil companies found themselves at a competitive disadvantage and saw their fortunes dwindle. The oil companies that were displaced by tank cars and pipelines lobbied Sherman to pass legislation that would have thwarted the use of these new technologies and generally slowed the position of Standard Oil and other large industrial trusts. In this way the evolution of the oil industry illustrates how technological change and innovation made some rich and others poor, and it shows how those harmed by change turned to politics in an effort to minimize their losses.

Who won the political battles in the oil industry? Was it Rockefeller or the small refiners? If one looks solely at federal regulation, it appears that Rockefeller won. The anti–tank car law, which was clearly aimed at Standard Oil, was defeated and the Sherman Antitrust Act was at best a pyrrhic victory for small oil companies. In the long run the act had little effect, if any, on the operation of the oil industry. If one looks state regulation, small enterprises appear to have had more success. As stated above, at least initially market observers and the popular press believed that state antitrust laws and regulations posed a much more serious threat to Standard Oil and other large industrial combinations than did the Sherman Act. Having said this, it is also clear that over the long haul state regulations were as ineffective as the Sherman Act in reining in the power of trusts such as Standard Oil.

The impotence of federal and state antitrust regulation seems to support the idea that during the Gilded Age the interests of a narrow set of wealthy individuals (for example, John D. Rockefeller) trumped the interests of broader social groups (for example, small oil refiners). To the extent that one equates the interests of small businesses with broader societal interests, this is true. But it is not at all clear that one should define "broader societal interests" so narrowly. The rise of Standard Oil, for example, might have harmed small refiners, but it was boon to consumers, who saw the price of refined oil and kerosene plummet. Before 1890, more than 90 percent of the American populace used oil for lighting.[32]

Meat Inspection

The general patterns observed in the history of state and federal antitrust regulation hold true for other areas of industrial regulation as well. Consider, for example, the case of state and federal meat inspection. During 1880s and 1890s, many states began passing meat-inspection laws. These laws were passed at the behest of local butchers who were being undercut by the large Chicago meatpackers. More precisely, the development of refrigerated railroad cars allowed for the centralized, large-scale slaughtering of livestock in Chicago and for shipments to local markets in the United States and for international export. This gave the large meatpackers economies of scale that local butchers could not match. Further, since unsalable parts of the animal need not be shipped, shipping dressed beef in refrigerated cars saved processors 35 percent on freight costs compared with the shipment of live cattle. Shipping dressed beef also allowed the large meatpackers to avoid weight losses of ten to fifteen percent and injuries from crowding that resulted from the shipment of live cattle.[33]

Faced with this severe competition, a national organization of small, local meatpackers, the Butcher's Protective Association, had been created to seek relief in state legislatures. They proposed a statute prohibiting the sale of dressed beef, mutton, or pork unless the animals had been inspected by state officials twenty-four hours prior to slaughter. Such a law would have effectively shut out the large Chicago meatpackers from all but the Chicago market. In 1889, the state legislatures of Minnesota, Indiana, and Colorado adopted this law, and about twenty other states were considering its adoption. Faced with an immediate, sharp erosion in the size of their market, the large shippers of dressed beef promptly challenged the law in the Supreme Court in *Minnesota v. Barber.*[34]

The facts of this case appeared to strongly favor the state legislatures. All previous case law had supported the rights of states to inspect goods, even if doing so put out-of-state producers at a disadvantage. In conceding these facts, the defendant, an agent for Armour and Company, argued that the law should be overturned nonetheless because if a state could prohibit interstate commerce in beef unless the livestock were first inspected, it could prohibit interstate commerce in fish unless they were first inspected when caught. The end result would be that "there is no product of the agriculture or manufacture of other States that this State may not thus exclude; [and] none of this state that every other may not exclude." The defendant also argued that fresh meats had never been inspected before slaughter in Minnesota prior to April 1889, that death or injury from exposure to diseased meat had always been rare, and that the purpose of the law must have been therefore "to protect the competitive position of local butchers rather than to promote public health." The Supreme Court agreed.[35]

Thus, if the legitimate concerns of public health were to be met, an alternative to state inspection had to be found, for example, federal inspection. Just two weeks prior to the Supreme Court's decision in *Barber,* a bill had been reported to the U.S. Senate calling for federal inspection of meat products destined for export but looking to the states for inspection to protect American consumers. In response to the *Barber* decision, Congress amended this bill to provide for the inspection of all U.S. meat products intended for either international or interstate trade. The Meat Inspection Act of 1891, which created the Federal Meat Inspection Service, was the first time federal government was "called upon to certify food quality."[36]

According to one authority, however, concerns about the safety of meat, and dressed meat in particular, were largely spurious. Large meatpackers, who had made substantial investments in stockyards, centralized slaughterhouses, refrigeration cars, and wholesale distributors of refrigerated meat, had every incentive to maintain high quality to ensure consumer acceptance of their products. Because the typical consumer purchase of meat products was small but frequent, the large meatpackers had little to gain but much to lose from cheating their customers by providing substandard products. Local producers, however, squeezed by their more efficient if distant competitors, had every incentive to attempt to cast doubt in the public mind on the quality of refrigerated meats by taking advantage of the potential information problem that arose against any new, poorly understood product. Foreign producers engaged in similar tactics against all American meat products. Congress therefore passed the Meat Inspection Act more to remove the pretense that diseased U.S. livestock was being exported by the large meatpackers than in response to any actual threat from the U.S. food supply. At the time, the most serious threat to American beef consumers was bovine tuberculosis, which could spread from cattle to humans when infected cattle were consumed. Bovine TB, however, was a more serious problem in Europe than in the United States, where it was, moreover, effectively addressed by state-level inspection and compensated-slaughter programs.[37]

Meat inspection was closely tied to the passage of the Sherman Act. Meatpacking was one of the most heavily concentrated industries in the United States during the Gilded Age, and Midwestern cattle raisers tended to blame the large Chicago meatpackers for using their monopsony power to drive down cattle prices after 1885. They recognized that even if federal meat inspection laws increased the demand for their products, they would not increase the prices that they received for their livestock so long as the large meatpackers were allowed to continue to exploit their power to keep prices down. Therefore, Midwestern cattle raisers pressed for passage of strict antitrust legislation in addition to federal meat inspection.[38]

Urbanization and State and Local Political Economy

The industrialization that characterized the Gilded Age went hand-in-hand with urbanization. Between 1880 and 1910, the proportion of the American population living in urban areas (places with more than twenty-five hundred persons) almost doubled, growing from 26 to 46 percent. During the same period, the proportion of the population living in large cities (places with more than one hundred thousand persons) almost quadrupled, growing from 2.4 percent to 9.2 percent. Initially, migration to cities overwhelmed existing infrastructure and housing stock and was associated with declining health. By 1900, life expectancy at birth in New York, the largest city in the United States, was about thirteen years lower than that observed in rural areas. Although the development of urban infrastructure often failed to keep pace with population growth, this does not imply that this period did not experience expansion in urban infrastructure. On the contrary, during the Gilded Age and later during the Progressive Era, politicians in American cities saw to it that gas, electricity, trolley, road, water, and sewer systems were rapidly expanded.[39]

Consider, for example, the development of urban water and sewer systems. Around 1870, access to public water and sewer mains was limited to the very wealthiest segments of society and a few businesses. By 1890, between 25 and 34 percent of the local population of a typical city was connected to public sewers, and by 1909, more than 70 percent of the population in cities with populations greater than thirty thousand was connected to public sewers. In the case of water, the results are even more impressive. By 1915, officials estimated that in most American cities, more than 95 percent of the local population had access to the public water supply. The gas and electric industries developed at a less rapid pace. By 1900, about 12 percent of the U.S. population used either coal gas or electricity to light their homes, and by 1920 roughly 70 percent of the population was using one of these for lighting.[40]

The changes wrought by the introduction of gas, electric, and water service in urban areas were, on the whole, positive. The development of gas and electricity saved families countless hours of labor transporting coal and oil into their homes for cooking, heating, and light. These new technologies were also much safer and cleaner than their predecessors. Similarly, the introduction of public water supplies economized on the labor previously expended transporting water from wells and other sources.

Public water supplies also played a major role in eliminating waterborne diseases and improving health in urban areas. In 1900, for example, about one-half of the American population had experienced a waterborne disease such as typhoid fever at least once. Although typhoid fever usually killed no more than 5 to 10 percent of its victims, its sequelae were severe and left its survivors vulnerable to tuberculosis, heart failure, and influenza. By 1940, diseases such as typhoid fever had largely been eliminated from American cities. Roughly 25 percent of the improvement in human mortality observed in the United States between 1900 and 1940 can be attributed to the introduction of pure water supplies and the associated eradication of typhoid fever. For the poor, the benefits of pure water were especially large. In particular, whereas public water filtration reduced the death rate from typhoid fever among whites by 15 to

20 percent, it reduced the death rate from the disease among blacks by 50 to 60 percent. As this brief discussion suggests, the social returns to investments in public water systems were on the order of 150 percent.[41]

Despite the improvements in well-being that came with these new urban technologies, there was often widespread dissatisfaction with their distribution and pricing. In particular, consumers lamented the high prices and poor service associated with private monopolies in gas, electric, and water supply. This gave rise to new forms of regulation akin to those described for the railroads, oil refiners, and meatpackers. It also generated protest movements similar to those seen in the history of populism.[42]

Regulating Public Utilities

Initially, private utility companies were regulated by means of municipal franchises. Such a franchise was in effect, a contract between the utility and the municipality in question. The franchise imposed obligations on both parties, offering the private company the right to operate in the city in return for specific promises regarding rates and quality of service. The granting of these franchises was tainted by corruption and often provided consumers little protection against exorbitant rates and poor service. For example, in the early 1900s, in Grand Rapids, Michigan, the mayor and multiple members of the city council were implicated in a scheme to sell a lucrative franchise to a private water company. The promoters of this company paid politicians bribes of around $3,000 (about $42,000 in current dollars) each. The politicians and the promoters were eventually caught, tried, and convicted. But even when there was no corruption involved, franchises typically failed to specify rate regulations that were binding. It was simply too difficult for local politicians to predict all of the technological changes that would ultimately drive down the costs of producing and distributing gas, electricity, and water.[43]

If this sounds as though utilities were getting the better end of the bargain, it is important to recognize that monopolistic rates did not last for long. City governments gradually acquired more and more regulatory power and soon began using that power to aggressively reduce rates and win votes from local consumers. In a speech before the Pacific Gas Association delivered during the early 1900s, an officer of a San Francisco gas company explained: "When the time for the regulation of rates arises, a [city] councilman or supervisor, elected on a platform that calls for a reduction in the gas and electric rates, is hardly in a proper frame of mind to listen to evidence and impartially vote thereon. No matter what the evidence is, if he does not vote for a reduction a large number of citizens, and all of the daily papers, will accuse him of being biased in favor of the corporation."[44]

To understand the often politicized nature of municipal regulation consider the experience of Chicago. In 1905, Illinois granted the Chicago City Council the authority to regulate gas rates. A few years later, Carter Harrison ran as a mayoral candidate. Harrison and several candidates for the city council promised that, if elected, they would reduce gas rates in the city from 85 cents to 70 cents per thousand cubic feet. After Harrison and his friends won, they launched an investigation into the costs of manufacturing and distributing gas. The expert they hired, W. J. Hagenah of the Wisconsin Public Utilities Commission, recommended a 77-cent rate, 10 percent higher than Harrison had promised the voters. According to Hagenah, a rate lower than 77 cents would not allow producers a reasonable rate of return. Chicago authorities promptly fired Hagenah and hired Edward Bemis. After paying Bemis five times the salary they paid Hagenah, the authorities got the result they wanted. Bemis recommended, and the city eventually passed, an ordinance setting the rate at 70 cents. Ironically, earlier in his political career, Carter Harrison had opposed attempts by the city to regulate gas rates. As Chicago's mayor in 1900, he claimed that the city would use the power to regulate rates only as a way of "blackmailing" Chicago gas companies—if the gas companies did not pay off the city council, the city would order them to reduce rates.[45]

This sort of political gamesmanship undermined the long-term development of utility industries and had serious consequences for city residents. By 1910 private utility companies were refusing to extend service and improve infrastructure without a new round of legally binding promises from local governments that they would refrain from enacting overzealous and politicized regulations. For example, in Akron, Ohio, the local water company refused to build a new filtration system until the city promised that it would renew its franchise, which was set to expire. Similarly, in New Orleans and in Billings, Montana, local water companies refused to install new water lines without additional promises from local authorities regarding future regulatory behavior. More general evidence comes from statistical studies linking investment patterns in the gas and water industries to municipal regulatory regimes: these studies show that in cities where private gas and water companies faced a relatively high risk of future political expropriation, private investments in gas and water mains and other forms of capital were sharply reduced.[46]

THE GILDED AGE 279

Dissatisfaction with the various forms of municipal regulation grew, and during the early 1900s eventually gave way to state regulation, which was much less politicized. Between 1907 and 1922, nearly thirty states created commissions to regulate the behavior of public utilities and restrain the capricious ways of municipal governments. In the short run, these commissions worked reasonably well. They kept the rates charged by utilities companies in check and promoted investment and service quality. Over time, however, their efficacy declined as the commissions were captured by industry insiders and their policies took on a decidedly pro-producer bias. In the long run, the failure of state utility regulation gave rise to the deregulation and privatization movements of the 1980s.[47]

State regulation was the mode of governance used to control mainly gas and electric companies. Water supplies were usually subjected to another form of governance, notably municipal ownership. Between 1880 and 1932, the number of municipally owned water companies in the United States grew by a factor of 26, from 293 to 7,832. Similarly, the proportion of municipally owned companies increased by 59 percent, from 43 percent in 1890 to 68 percent in 1920. The rise of public water companies was associated with large and rapid extensions in local water systems. Although public water companies were no more likely to invest in water filtration systems than were private companies, they were much more likely to extend mains to outlying and less densely populated areas. Private companies were reluctant to provide service to these low-density areas because higher capital costs per customer implied reduced profitability. As a result, consumers in these low-density areas benefited from the public acquisition of private waterworks. Furthermore, because African Americans tended to congregate in these areas, they benefited disproportionately from public ownership. Recent econometric evidence shows, for example, that the move to publicly owned water supplies reduced typhoid fever rates among blacks but had little effect on rates among whites.[48]

Patronage at the Local Level

The rapid expansion of municipal services that occurred during the late nineteenth century was associated with a sharp increase in patronage employment. This was a system whereby local politicians exchanged lucrative public-sector jobs for electoral support. At the state and local levels, patronage flourished throughout the late nineteenth and early twentieth centuries. A few statistics highlight the costs of patronage. Public-sector employees in cities where patronage was rife enjoyed wages that were 40 percent higher and worked 16 percent fewer hours per week than their private-sector counterparts. But the former had to return some of these "excess earnings" to their political superiors. A survey conducted by the National Civic Federation in 1907 found that state and municipal employees often had to pay sizeable annual assessments to incumbent politicians. Such assessments were intended to defray the costs of local elections. Workers that failed to pay their assessments were fired. Data reported by the National Civic Federation suggest that the size of assessments ranged between 2 and 4 percent of a worker's annual salary, depending on the worker's occupation.[49]

In addition, the federation found that state and local employees were often required to work in local elections. Politicians also hired more workers than needed merely so that they would have more supporters come election time. Describing conditions at the Wheeling Gas Company, a municipally owned and operated firm, the civic federation stated that the superintendent of the gas works "requires his employees to assist in the primaries and the elections." Moreover, because of their usefulness as political operatives, the superintendent "employed about 20 per cent more men than" was "needed to do the work." The superintendent also made his appointments "as much as possible to conciliate the Councilmen." Similarly, in New York City, there were at least twelve thousand municipal employees who, while on the city's payroll, performed no work for the city. Rather, these employees were expected only to work for the political machine. Their duties included attending and serving as delegates to local primary elections, keeping track of voters, promising favors or threatening retribution, and identifying and bringing into the machine other supporters (Troesken 1999, 426–27).

The experience of Boston suggests that political patrons were rewarded handsomely for their support. According to Progressive-Era reformers, clerical work was the primary source of "waste and inefficiency" in Boston government. Between 1895 and 1907, the number of clerks working for the city grew by 75 percent, while the population of the city grew by only 23 percent. During the same period, salaries rose rapidly, and by 1907 city clerks were paid three times more than clerks in the private sector. The increase in wages and the clerical workforce stemmed from "continual pressure from political sources" and persisted "regardless of the amount of work to be done" or "the appropriations for the year." Reformers argued that "discipline had been abandoned" in the management of labor. "Incompetence and insubordination were seldom visited by suspension" and "still less frequently by discharge" (Troesken 1999, 427–28).

Although workers were not fired for these causes, they were fired for their politics. When politicians lost elections, all of their patrons lost their jobs. Because of the politicized nature of employment, public-sector employees did not enjoy long and stable careers, as they often do today. This was true even in police departments, an area where one would like to believe that sound public policy rose above local politics. As one prominent historian has written: "It was still the case—especially in big cities—that American police departments were more overtly political than, say, in England. In this country, police officers were primarily tools of local politicians; when the winds of politics changed, during or between elections, jobs and policy changed with [them]. In Cincinnati, for example, 219 of 295 patrolmen were dismissed after the election of 1880; six years later, after another election, 238 of 289 patrolmen and 8 of 16 lieutenants lost their jobs."[50]

In an effort to eliminate patronage during the nineteenth century, a few states such as Massachusetts and New York passed civil service laws. These laws, however, were notoriously ineffective and did very little to curtail patronage. This was so for two reasons. First, they affected only a tiny fraction of all state and municipal workers. Second, they were easily circumvented. For example, under the New York law, potential employees ostensibly had to pass a civil service exam before the city could hire them. Local bosses circumvented the law by informing only their favorite candidates of the dates and locations of the exams. They then saw to it that the exams were graded with appropriate leniency—an illiterate candidate once scored nearly 100 percent on a written exam. Another common strategy was to employ "temporary workers," who were not typically classified as civil servants. Because of such abuses, patronage workers dominated the payrolls of state and local governments throughout the nineteenth century.

Between 1900 and 1920, reform groups tried to extend the coverage and effectiveness of civil service laws. Reformers successfully pushed through legislation in Illinois (1905), Wisconsin (1905), Colorado (1907), New Jersey (1908), California (1913), Ohio (1913), and Maryland (1921). Among large cities, reformers also realized success. By 1923, of the twenty-five cities with populations of 250,000 or more, only one (Indianapolis) did not have some type of civil service commission. Of the sixty-eight cities with populations of 100,000 or more, only fourteen did not have civil service commissions. Most historians portray these laws as more effective than the state-level laws passed during the nineteenth century. After 1920, efforts to extend civil service reforms continued, but at a slower pace. By 1959, of all the cities with populations greater than 100,000, about 5 percent were without civil service commissions.

Concluding Remarks

There is a tendency to view the Gilded Age with pessimism. According to this view, the history of the era is mainly a story about how big business and social elites ran roughshod over the interests of smaller business enterprises and marginalized social groups. It is, in other words, a story about how the political and economic battles of the era were resolved in favor of the rich and powerful at the expense of the poor and disaffected, a story about how the advance of new technologies destroyed older and simpler ways of life. Certainly there is something to this view. For example, the populist movement ultimately did little to slow the exodus of the population from small farming communities, and the Sherman Antitrust Act failed to slow the growth of big business and might have hastened it.

Yet observers should also make room for optimism in their interpretations of the Gilded Age. To see this, it is useful to look at the period through a different set of lenses. If, for example, one looks at legislative change at the state level, as opposed to the federal, there is strong evidence that farmers and small businesses secured laws and regulations that improved their lot, at least temporarily; as a case in point, state-level antitrust laws were far more effective and caused the trusts much more consternation than did the Sherman Act. That state and local regulations were much harder on big business than federal regulation is one of the key themes to emerge from the historical narratives given above. More generally, if one considers indicators of overall material well-being—wages, hours worked, per capita income, and so on—it is clear that material improvements were not limited to the wealthiest segments of American society and that broad cross-sections of the populace benefited from the economic changes of the Gilded Age. This is not said to minimize the hardships experienced by those displaced by economic change, but instead to help explain why disaffected groups were not more successful in thwarting economic and technological change by political means.

Notes

1. See Buck 1913; Goodwyn 1976; McMath 1977. The case is Munn v. Illinois, 94 U.S. 113 (1877).

2. Bowman and Keehn 1974; Troesken 1994.

3. Fogel and Rutner 1972, 9–11; Fogel 1989; and Tostelby 1957.

4. The quotation is from Fogel and Rutner 1972, 17. On the reasonableness of farmers' complaints regarding interest rates, see Eichengreen 1984.

5. Higgs 1971, 91.

6. See Higgs 1971; Fogel and Rutner 1972.

7. Pashigian 1986; Rothstein 1960.

8. The discussion in this section draws from Barns 1967; Buck 1913; Ferguson 1942; McMath 1977; Nordin 1974; and Parsons et al. 1983.

9. Higgs 1987, 83, 87.

10. Spencer 1967; Sumner 1963.

11. Allen 1986; Lombardo 1985, 1988; Buck v. Bell, zz U.S. zzz (1926).

12. Lombardo 1985, 1988.

13. Davidson 2000; Fogel 2000.

14. Fogel 2000.

15. Ibid.

16. Quoted in Brock 1984, 33. See Higgs 1987.

17. Fogel 2000.

18. Fogel 1964; Fishlow 1965.

19. Gilligan, Marshall, and Weingast 1989; Higgs 1970; and Kanazawa and Noll 1994.

20. Kanazawa and Noll 1994; Hughes 1991, 106–9; Wabash, St. Louis, & Pacific Railway v. Illinois, 118 U.S. 557 (1886).

21. This paragraph draws on Kolko 1965, Prager 1989, and Martin 1971.

22. See Grandy 1993; Thorelli 1955, 194–203; Bork 1966; Letwin 1965; DiLorenzo 1985; and DiLorenzo and High 1988.

23. Williamson and Andreano 1962.

24. Williamson and Daum 1959; Chandler 1977, 323–29.

25. Williamson and Daum 1959; Troesken 2002.

26. Williamson and Daum 1959; Troesken 2002.

27. Troesken 2002; Granitz and Klein 1996; Tarbell 1904; McGee 1958; and Telser 1978, 1987.

28. Troesken 2002.

29. This paragraph and the ensuing discussion are drawn from ibid.

30. See Stigler 1985, Burns 1977, Binder 1988, and Bittlingmayer 1985.

31. Troesken 1995, 2000.

32. Lebergott 1993.

33. This paragraph and much of the discussion that follows are based on McCurdy 1978 and Libecap 1992.

34. Minnesota v. Barber, 136 U.S. 313 (1890).

35. McCurdy 1978, 642–43.

36. Libecap 1992, 250.

37. Olmstead and Rhode 2004.

38. Libecap 1992.

39. U.S. Bureau of the Census 1976; Haines 2001.

40. Troesken 2004, 39, 74; Troesken 1996, 25.

41. Troesken 2004, 34–38, 124–26; Meeker 1974.

42. Jacobson 2000; Troesken 1996.
43. *New York Times,* November 22, 1903, 1, and December 1, 1903, 1. See also Folk 1903; Troesken 1996, 5–27.
44. *American Gas Light Journal,* September 28, 1908, 527.
45. Troesken 1996, pp. 67–73.
46. Troesken 1997; Troesken and Geddes 2003.
47. Troesken 1996, 76–92; Twentieth Century Fund 1948; Stigler and Friedland 1962.
48. Troesken and Geddes 2003; Troesken 2001.
49. The section that follows is drawn almost entirely from Troesken 1999.
50. Friedman 1993, 149–50.

References

Allen, Garland E. 1986. "The Eugenics Record Office at Cold Spring Harbor, 1910–1940: An Essay on Institutional History." *Osiris* 2:225–64.
Barns, William D. 1967. "Oliver Hudson Kelley and the Genesis of the Grange: A Reappraisal," *Agricultural History* 41:229–42.
Binder, John J. 1988. "The Sherman Antitrust Act and the Railroad Cartels." *Journal of Law and Economics* 31:443–67.
Bittlingmayer, George. 1985. "Did Antitrust Policy Cause the Great Merger Wave?" *Journal of Law and Economics* 29:7–118.
Bork, Robert H. 1966. "Legislative Intent and the Policy of the Sherman Act." *Journal of Law and Economics* 6:7–48.
Bowman, John D., and Richard H. Keehn. 1974. "Agricultural Terms of Trade in Four Midwestern States, 1870–1900." *Journal of Economic History* 34:592–609.
Brock, William R. 1984. *Investigation and Responsibility: Public Responsibility in the United States, 1865–1900.* New York: Cambridge University Press.
Buck, Solon Justus. 1913. *The Granger Movement.* Cambridge: Harvard University Press.
Burns, Malcolm R. 1977. "The Competitive Effects of Trust-Busting: A Portfolio Analysis." *Journal of Political Economy* 85:717–39.
Chandler, Alfred D. 1977. *The Visible Hand: The Managerial Revolution in American Business.* Cambridge: Harvard University Press, Belknap Press.
Davidson, Keay. 2000. "Boas, Franz." *American National Biography Online.* http://www.anb.org/articles/14/14-00059.html.
DiLorenzo, Thomas J. 1985. "The Origins of Antitrust: An Interest-Group Perspective." *International Review of Law and Economics* 5.2:73–90.
DiLorenzo, Thomas J., and Jack C. High. 1988. "Antitrust and Competition, Historically Considered." *Economic Inquiry* 26.3:423–35.
Eichengreen, Barry. 1984. "Mortgage Interest Rates in the Populist Era." *American Economic Review* 74:995–1015.
Ferguson, James S. 1942. "The Grange and Farmer Education in Mississippi." *Journal of Southern History* 8:497–512.
Fishlow, Albert. 1965. *American Railroads and the Transformation of the Antebellum Economy.* Cambridge: Harvard University Press.

Fogel, Robert W. 1964. *Railroads and American Economic Growth: Essays in Econometric History.* Baltimore: Johns Hopkins University Press.

———. 1989. *Without Consent or Contract: The Rise and Fall of American Slavery.* New York: Norton.

———. 2000. *The Fourth Great Awakening and the Future of Egalitarianism.* Chicago: University of Chicago Press.

Fogel, Robert W., and Jack L. Rutner. 1972. "The Efficiency Effects of Federal Land Policy, 1850–1900: A Report on Some Provisional Findings." In *The Dimensions of Qualitative Research in History,* ed. W. O. Aydelotte, A. G. Bogue, and R. W. Fogel, 47–85. Princeton: Princeton University Press.

Folk, Joseph W. 1903. "Municipal Corruption." *Independent* 55:2804–6.

Friedman, Lawrence M. 1993. *Crime and Punishment in American History.* New York: Basic.

Gilligan, Thomas W., William J. Marshall, and Barry R. Weingast. 1989. "Regulation and the Theory of Legislative Choice: The Interstate Commerce Act of 1887." *Journal of Law and Economics* 32:35–61.

Goodwyn, Lawrence. 1976. *Democratic Promise: The Populist Moment in America.* New York: Oxford University Press.

Grandy, Christopher. 1993. "Original Intent and the Sherman Antitrust Act: A Re-examination of the Consumer-Welfare Hypothesis." *Journal of Economic History* 53:359–76.

Granitz, Elizabeth, and Benjamin Klein. 1996. "Monopolization by Raising Rivals Costs: The Standard Oil Case." *Journal of Law and Economics* 39:1–48.

Haines, Michael R. 2001. "The Urban Mortality Transition in the United States, 1800–1940." National Bureau of Economic Research Historical Paper 134. Cambridge, MA: National Bureau of Economic Research.

Hicks, John D. 1961. *The Populist Revolt.* Lincoln: University of Nebraska Press.

Higgs, Robert. 1970. "Railroad Rates and the Populist Uprising." *Agricultural History* 4:291–97.

———. 1971. *The Transformation of the American Economy, 1865–1914: An Essay in Interpretation.* New York: Wiley.

———. 1987. *Crisis and Leviathan: Critical Episodes in the Growth of American Government.* New York: Oxford University Press.

Hughes, Jonathan R. T. 1991. *The Governmental Habit Redux: Economic Controls from Colonial Times to the Present.* Princeton: Princeton University Press.

Jacobson, Charles. 2000. *Ties That Bind: Economic and Political Dilemmas of Urban Utility Networks, 1800–1990.* Pittsburgh: University of Pittsburgh Press.

Kanazawa, Mark, and Roger Noll. 1994. "The Origins of State Railroad Regulation: The Illinois State Constitution of 1870." In *The Regulated Economy: An Historical Approach to Political Economy,* ed. Claudia Goldin and Gary Libecap, 13–54. Chicago: University of Chicago Press.

Kolko, Gabriel. 1965. *Railroads and Regulation, 1877–1916.* Westport, CT: Greenwood.

Lebergott, Stanley. 1993. *Pursuing Happiness: American Consumers in the Twentieth Century.* Princeton: Princeton University Press.

Letwin, William. 1965. *Law and Economic Policy in America: The Evolution of the Sherman Antitrust Law.* Chicago: University of Chicago Press.

Libecap, Gary D. 1992. "The Rise of the Chicago Packers and the Origins of Meat Inspection and Antitrust." *Economic Inquiry* 30.2:242–62.

Lombardo, P. A. 1985. "Three Generations, No Imbeciles: New Light on *Buck v. Bell.*" *New York University Law Review* 60:30–62.

———. 1988. "Miscegenation, Eugenics, and Racism: Historical Footnotes to *Loving v. Virginia.*" *University of California Davis Law Review* 21:421–52.

Martin, Albro. 1971. *Enterprise Denied: The Origins of the Decline of American Railroads, 1897–1917.* New York: Columbia University Press.

McCurdy, Charles. 1978. "American Law and the Marketing Structure of the Large Corporation, 1875-1890." *Journal of Economic History* 38:631–49.

McGee, John S. 1958. "Predatory Price Cutting: The Standard Oil (N.J.) Case." *Journal of Law and Economics* 1.1:137–69.

McMath, Robert C, Jr. 1977. *Populist Vanguard: A History of the Southern Farmers' Alliance.* New York: Norton.

Meeker, Edward. 1974. "The Social Rate of Return on Investment in Public Health, 1880–1910." *Journal of Economic History* 34:392–421.

Nixon, Herman Clarence. 1928. "The Cleavage within the Farmers' Alliance Movement." *Mississippi Valley Historical Review* 15:22–33.

Nordin, Dennis S. 1974. *Rich Harvest: A History of the Grange, 1867–1900.* Jackson: University of Mississippi Press.

Olmstead, Alan, and Paul Rhode. 2004. "An Impossible Undertaking: The Eradication of Bovine Tuberculosis in the United States." *Journal of Economic History* 64 (September): 734–72

Parsons, Stanley B., Karen Toombs Parsons, Walter Killilae, and Beverly Borgers. 1983. "The Role of Cooperatives in the Development of the Movement Culture of Populism." *Journal of American History* 69:866–85.

Pashigian, B. Peter. 1986. "The Political Economy of Futures Markets." *Journal of Business* 59:S55–S84.

Prager, Robin A. 1989. "Using Stock Price Data to Measure the Effects of Regulation: The Interstate Commerce Act and the Railroad Industry." *Rand Journal of Economics* 20.2 (Summer): 280–90.

Rothstein, Martin. 1960. "America in the International Rivalry for the British Wheat Market, 1880–1914." *The Mississippi Valley Historical Review* 47: 401–18.

Spencer, Herbert. 1967. *Principles of Sociology.* Chicago: University of Chicago Press.

Stigler, George J. 1985. "The Origin of the Sherman Act." *Journal of Legal Studies* 14:1–12.

Stigler, George J., and Claire Freidland. 1962. "What Can Regulators Regulate? The Case of Electricity." *Journal of Law and Economics* 5:1–16.

Sumner, William Graham. 1963. *Social Darwinism: Selected Essays.* Introd. by Stow Persons. Englewood Cliffs, NJ: Prentice-Hall.

Tarbell, Ida M. 1904. *History of the Standard Oil Company.* New York: Macmillan.

Telser, Lester G. 1978. *Economic Theory and the Core*. Chicago: University of Chicago Press, 1978.

———. 1987. *A Theory of Efficient Competition and Cooperation*. Cambridge: Cambridge University Press.

Thorelli, Hans B. 1955. *The Federal Antitrust Policy: Origination of an American Tradition*. Baltimore: Johns Hopkins University Press.

Tontz, Robert L. 1964. "Memberships of General Farmers' Organizations, United States, 1874–1960." *Agricultural History* 38:143–56.

Tostelby, Alvin S. 1957. *Capital in Agriculture: Its Formation and Financing*. Princeton: Princeton University Press.

Troesken, Werner. 1994. "Agrarian Agitation and the Jute-Bagging Trust." Department of History, University of Pittsburgh.

———. 1995. "Antitrust Enforcement before the Sherman Act: The Break-up of the Chicago Gas Trust Company." *Explorations in Economic History* 32:109–36.

———. 1996. *Why Regulate Utilities? The New Institutional Economics and the Chicago Gas Industry, 1849–1924*. Ann Arbor: University of Michigan Press.

———. 1997. "The Sources of Public Ownership: Historical Evidence from the Gas Industry." *Journal of Law, Economics, and Organization* 13:1–27.

———. 1999. "Patronage and Public-Sector Wages in 1896." *Journal of Economic History* 59: 424–46.

———. 2000. "Did the Trusts Want a Federal Antitrust Law? An Event Study of State Antitrust Enforcement and Passage of the Sherman Act." In *Public Choice Interpretations of American Economic History*, ed. Jac C. Heckleman, John C. Moorehouse, and Robert M. Whaples, 99–124. Boston: Kluwer Academic.

———. 2001. "Race, Disease, and the Provision of Water in American Cities, 1889–1921." *Journal of Economic History* 61:750–76.

———. 2002. "The Letters of John Sherman and the Origins of Antitrust." *Review of Austrian Economics* 15:275–96.

———. 2004. *Water, Race, and Disease*. Cambridge: MIT Press.

Troesken, Werner, and Rick Geddes. 2003. "Municipalizing American Waterworks, 1897–1914." *Journal of Law, Economics, and Organization* 18:24–47.

Twentieth Century Fund Power Committee. 1948. *Electric Power and Government Policy*. New York: Twentieth Century Fund.

U.S. Bureau of the Census. 1976. *Historical Statistics of the United States, Colonial Times to 1970, Parts 1 and 2*. Washington, DC: Government Printing Office.

Williamson, Harold F., and Ralph L. Andreano. 1962. "Competitive Structure of the American Petroleum Industry, 1880–1911: A Reappraisal." In *Oil's First Century*, ed. staff of the *Business History Review*, 86–92. Cambridge: Harvard Business School.

Williamson, Harold F., and Arnold R. Daum. 1959. *The American Petroleum Industry: The Age of Illumination, 1859–1899*. Evanston: Northwestern University Press.

PRICE FISHBACK

10

The Progressive Era

THE PERIOD between the mid-1890s and the early 1920s has been enshrined as the Progressive Era. It was truly a "bridge to modern times," as attitudes toward the proper role of government shifted from the limited role preferred in the nineteenth century to the increasingly expanded role chosen in the twentieth. Many general studies of the period and biographies of leading reformers emphasize the economic and political reform movements. The economic reforms included expanded regulation, increased antitrust activity, establishment of an income tax, and the development of social insurance programs. The shift toward "direct democracy" during the era gave women the vote, professionalized government, gave the voters more say in electing and recalling political officials, and allowed for referenda on specific issues. America loves the underdog, and these studies tell stirring tales of how muckraking journalists, reformers, and the leading progressive politicians overcame a corrupt system to reform the government and use the government to curb the worst excesses of the rise of industry.[1]

On closer inspection the changes adopted during this era were far more evolutionary than revolutionary. There was no unified program to which all Progressives subscribed. The people who called themselves progressives with regard to at least one issue included the social reformers, workers, the middle class, farmers, big businessmen, and union leaders. In fact, the Progressive Era might better be described as interest group politics writ large. The old political regime and the large corporations did not simply wither away. Successful adoption of new policies often required compromises and adjustments that attracted enough supporters to form a winning coalition. Thus, there were few major victories in which social reformers routed big business. The actual impact of the grand-sounding reforms shouted out in the policy debates were muted by compromise, and the ultimate policies adopted sounded more like whispers. Eventually, many of these policies evolved into stronger policies and set precedents for more dramatic changes later in the century.[2]

The Dynamic Economic Background

When America came out of the depths of the depression of the 1890s, the economy entered a period of relatively rapid growth. The growth, though marred by occasional downturns, was striking. The long-term expansion in industry continued to reduce the farms' share of employment while attracting hundreds of thousands of new immigrants into the mines, factories, and shops of America. The rise in industry also was associated with a rapid expansion in the size of industrial enterprises. Economic growth and changes in the structure of the economy always create new problems. Each downturn engendered fears of the return to the harshness of the Depression of the 1890s and led to calls for methods to limit the downturns and help those harmed by the consequences.[3]

Employment relationships changed as the spread of large-scale enterprises meant that employers and workers no longer worked together in close quarters. The explosion of immigration from southern and eastern Europe created new frictions. Both forces served to loosen personal ties between employer and worker, which in turn made it less likely that employers would accept informal responsibility for their injured or unemployed workers. The rise of large businesses was accompanied by an expansion in union membership. The leading unions in mining, railroading, and construction were often relatively conservative, focusing on shortening workdays and improving wages and working conditions. The relatively small numbers in the more radical organizations such as the International Workers of the World, however, drew an outsized share of the attention with more extreme tactics and cries for more radical changes.[4]

New technologies, better health, and better education, among many factors, contributed to a higher standard of living and demands to expand the franchise. During the early days of the Republic, the founding fathers thought it important to limit the franchise to property holders and taxpayers on the grounds that they were responsible citizens with a stake in the system. The expansion of the nonagricultural sector throughout the nineteenth century had altered economic relationships so that a large share of the populace was now working for wages. The foundations for wealth and income shifted so that the education and skills that make up human capital became more central. These economic changes contributed to expansions of the view of who should be considered responsible enough to vote. Further, voters were demanding a greater say in the political process as governments at all levels were rocked by scandals during the late nineteenth century.

Major Policy Changes of the Progressive Era

During the Progressive Era governments introduced an impressive array of new policies at all levels. The federal government expanded its regulation of interstate commerce, established a central bank, and began to apply its antitrust policies to large-scale businesses. State governments expanded regulations of labor and product markets and established new forms of social insurance. Local governments expanded ownership and regulation of utilities and built a broad range of public health facilities. Table 10.1 lists the major policy initiatives, while this section lays out a broad outline of the era using the reform rhetoric of the period. A complete picture of the reforms can only be drawn by a closer examination of the interest groups pressing for the policies and the benefits they ultimately received from the changes in policy. The rest of the chapter examines several key reforms in this light.

The progressive reforms swelled upward from cities to state governments to the federal government. During the late nineteenth century many cities were infamous for haphazard, amateurish, and at times corrupt operations. The Tweed Ring in New York in the 1860s became synonymous with dishonesty but was thought to be only one of many examples of petty corruption. The reform movements of the Gilded Age had focused on putting the right people in office to clean up the problems. By the time the depression of the 1890s hit, these reforms were recognized as inadequate. Taxes continued to rise, and the reformers were discovering how difficult it was to clean up the administrative problems. The Progressive solutions focused not only on moral inadequacies of city politicians and administrators but also on restructuring city governments. Cities were chartered by state governments, which continued to exercise oversight over city affairs. Reformers therefore had to push for change not only locally but also in state legislatures. Supposed victories over local bosses were dashed in the state legislature at the hands of the local bosses' cronies in the state machine. Progressives therefore pressed for home rule to give cities more independence in their administration and fiscal affairs.[5]

Convinced of the weaknesses of the ward system of geographic representation, those who sought "good government" wanted to reduce the number of elected officials and pressed for citywide elections of

Table 10.1 MAJOR PROGRESSIVE-ERA POLICY CHANGES

	Law or policy	Year	Effects
National economic changes	Adamson Act	1916	Eight-hour day legislated for railroad workers
	Civil Service Retirement Act	1920	Established a generous pension program for federal workers
	Clayton Antitrust Act	1914	New antitrust restrictions
	Federal Conciliation Service	1918	Federal mediation and conciliation of labor disputes
	Federal Employer Liability Act	1908	Expanded railroad employers' liability for workplace accidents
	Federal Reserve System	1913	Established a central bank
	Federal Trade Commission	1913	Agency established to administer antitrust laws
	Immigration restrictions	1916, 1921, 1923	Limits on entry of immigrants into the U.S., particularly later immigrants
	Income tax amendment	1913	First household income tax
	Mann-Elkins Act	1910	ICC given oversight over telephone, telegraph, radio, and cable
	Federal meat inspection	1892, 1906	Federal inspection of meat
	Mine safety	1911	Established agency to collect and disseminate information on mine safety
	Newlands Conservation Act	1903	Conservation
	Prohibition: Volstead Act and 18th Amendment	1920	Prohibited "intoxicating liquors"
	Pure Food and Drug Act	1906	Regulation of food and drug quality
	Railroad regulations amended	1890s→	Expansions in railroad regulation include safety regulations, mediation services, and regulation of hours and rates
	Shepherd-Towner Maternity and Infancy Act	1920	Distribution of national funds to states to promote maternal and infant care
	Underwood tariff reduction	1913,	Reduction in tariffs
	Workers' compensation for federal employees	1908, 1916	Compensation for federal workers for all injuries arising from or in the course of employment
State-level economic changes	Aid to the blind	1920s–1930s	Monetary support for blind persons living on their own
	Child labor laws	1890s→	Limitations on child labor
	Cigarette bans	1895–1921	Bans on sale of cigarettes
	Compulsory schooling laws	1880s→	Required school attendance
	Employer liability laws	1890–1911	Expanded employers' liability for workplace accidents
	Factory inspectors	1879→	Factory inspectors designated
	Expansion of insurance regulations	1890–1930	Oversight of insurance policies

(continued)

Table 10.1 (CONTINUED)

	Law or policy	Year	Effects
	Labor arbitration and mediation services	1880s→	State agencies to help arbitrate and mediate labor disputes
	Establishment of labor departments	1869→	Labor departments to collect data, inspect workplaces, and administer rules
	Liquor bans	1890s–1921	Various laws limiting sale and manufacture of liquor
	Minimum wages for women	1910–1920	Floor for women's wages in some states
	Mining regulations	1869→	Regulation of accident reporting and labor
	Mothers' pensions	1910–1930	Support payments to widows with children
	Old-age pensions	Late 1920s	Support payments to elderly persons living on their own
	Professional licensing laws	1880s→	Minimum standards for various occupations
	Food purity regulations	1880s	Regulation of food quality
	Regulation of women's hours	1910–1920	Limitations on working time for women
	Workers' compensation laws	1911–1948	Compensation for all injuries arising from or in the course of employment
	Industrial commissions	1911–1930	Commissions established to administer labor policies
Local-level economic changes	High school expansion	1890s→	Expansion of high schools and teachers' colleges
	Regulation and ownership of city utilities	1890s→	Municipal control of electricity, water, sewer, and other utilities
	Sewage and water treatment facilities	1880s→	Building of treatment facilities to enhance public health
National political changes	Women's suffrage	1919	Women given right to vote in national elections
State-and-National-level change	Direct election of senators	1900–1914	Election of senators by popular vote, first in state laws and then in 17th Amendment to the Constitution
State-level changes	Initiatives and referenda	1898→	Voters given the right to vote directly on issues
	Recall elections	1890s→	Provision for votes to recall officials
	Women's suffrage	1869→	Women given the right to vote in state elections
	City commissions	1901→	Creation of city commissioners
	City managers	1908→	Professionalized administration of cities
	Home rule	1875→	Cities given more freedom from state restrictions on their activities

council members. Many of the reforms were designed to separate politics from administration. More offices became appointive and subject to civil service rules. Reformers, who were often backed by business leaders, adopted the language and practices of business. "Economical and efficient" government administered by "professionals" became the watchword. Municipal research bureaus imported and disseminated municipal versions of scientific management methods such as "Taylorism," which included new accounting and budgeting techniques, time and motion studies, and inventory controls. Between 1901 and 1911 more than 150 cities had adopted a commission plan of government that instituted nonpartisan elections, abandoned the separation of powers, and gave full authority to a small body of commissioners to make policy and administer the city. Critics of commission government argued that spreading administrative authority across several commissioners gave too many cooks opportunities to spoil the broth. Their solution was to hire a professional city manager. After achieving success in Dayton, Ohio, ca. 1915, the movement expanded among small- and medium-sized cities. By 1970 roughly half of American cities with populations between ten thousand and five hundred thousand had hired city managers.[6]

An alternative group of social reformers focused less on applying business practices to city governments than on improving the quality of life in cities and lowering the costs of such public utilities as gas, light, and transportation. The Progressive Era saw a rapid expansion in the development of parks, high schools, and new ways to aid the unfortunate. The building of sewers and water treatment facilities and the introduction of public health departments (along with higher incomes) contributed to reductions in death and disease rates. This class of urban reformers considered that the businesses and utilities that dealt with the city through franchises and contracts and benefited from tax breaks and city services were major sources of corruption. The ownership and regulation of local utilities—water, sewer, electricity, and gas—became hot-button issues in many cities. Many utilities provided services where there were economies of scale, that is, where the long-term average costs of providing the service fell as the size of the operation increased. Often the provision of service required the building of facilities and of pipelines that snaked through the cities. A desire to save money by not building multiple pipelines to the same houses meant that it was economically optimal from a cost standpoint to have a single provider. But a single firm has every incentive to charge monopoly prices. Cities experimented with various ways of dealing with this problem. Some regulated the utilities, others sought public ownership of them, and some bounced back and forth between regimes. Eventually, regulation of utilities in many cases was taken over by the states.[7]

By the early 1900s the Progressive movement had expanded into state governments and the federal government. A major theme of reform rhetoric was the fear of trusts. Large corporate enterprises were said to be not only dominating the economy but having undue influence on the political process as they developed cozy relationships with political bosses via political contributions and corrupt practices. In its first decade of operation, the Sherman Antitrust Act of 1890 did little more than had been done by the state antitrust acts and prior court decisions to control the anticompetitive actions of these large organizations. In fact, the Sherman Act had been applied more consistently against labor unions for combination in restraint of trade than it had been against large enterprises until the early 1900s. Theodore Roosevelt developed a reputation as a trust buster when his Justice Department began challenging mergers and pressing for the disintegration of large firms. The Justice Department successfully challenged the use of a holding company designed to merge control of the Great Northern and Northern Pacific Railroads in the *Northern Securities* Supreme Court decision of 1904. In 1903 Congress established the Bureau of Corporations to investigate major industries, giving Roosevelt the authority to publicize the bureau's findings concerning "bad" trusts and quash reports about the "good" trusts. Roosevelt used his discretion to publicize reports about the meatpacking and oil industries while avoiding publicizing potential Sherman Act violations by International Harvester. By the end of his administration, the Justice Department had filed antitrust suits that led to the break-ups of Standard Oil and the American Tobacco Company in 1911 after forceful prosecution by both the Roosevelt and the Taft administrations. Woodrow Wilson campaigned on the promise to expand antitrust enforcement to new areas and to add a powerful body to join the Justice Department in overseeing antitrust actions. He kept this promise with the passage of the Clayton Act and the establishment of the Federal Trade Commission in 1914.[8]

In the 1912 presidential campaign Wilson railed against the tariff, in particular the Payne-Aldrich tariff adjustment of 1909, as another symbol of corporate greed aided and abetted by political bosses. Economists are in nearly uniform agreement that taxes on imports harm consumers by leading to higher prices on both imports and domestic products. These losses tend to exceed the gains in profits and wages going to owners and

workers within the industry. Wilson was able to deliver on his promise to reduce tariffs with the passage of the Underwood Act of 1913.[9]
The Progressives who distrusted the correctives imposed by product market discipline argued that consumers needed protection with
respect to product quality and safety. They argued that companies too
easily succumbed to the temptation to cut corners on quality, sometimes
with disastrous health consequences. Upton Sinclair's *The Jungle* buttressed these claims with grisly descriptions of the meatpacking industry. Such muckraking novels added to the pressure for laws to give the
federal government the power to monitor and promote the quality of
food and contributed to the passage of the Pure Food and Drug Act and
the Meat Inspection Act of 1906. Temperance groups sought to protect
people from their own folly. Fifteen states passed laws banning the sale
of cigarettes. After thirty-five states passed some form of prohibition
of alcohol, the Eighteenth Amendment to the Constitution banned the
manufacture, sale, or transportation of intoxicating liquors nationwide,
effective in 1920. Prohibition did not appear to keep the Twenties from
Roarin'; it was repealed in 1933.[10]

As one means of shifting some of the burdens of industrialization
onto large corporations and the wealthy, Progressives pushed for the
federal government to introduce the first peacetime income taxes. Congress had passed legislation establishing a federal income tax in 1894,
but it was struck down as an unconstitutional direct tax by the Supreme
Court in 1895. In 1909 a tax of one percent on corporate profits greater
than $5,000 and a progressive tax on household incomes were passed.
The adoption of the household income tax required the states to ratify
a constitutional amendment, a process that culminated in the Sixteenth
Amendment in 1913. Until the 1940s the income tax was paid by only
a small share of the public. The original tax passed in 1913 was paid by
less than 2 percent of households, and the maximum rate of 7 percent
was imposed on households earning more than five hundred times the
average annual income of workers in 1913. This compares with a top
rate in 2002 of 35 percent on incomes that are roughly eight times the
average household income.[11]

Fears of the trusts extended to the intermittent downturns, which
were associated with bank panics that many thought were spurred by
unseemly speculations by large corporations. Contemporaries and modern economists suggest that presidential attacks on the trusts in speeches
and tighter antitrust enforcement may have contributed to the panic atmosphere. After the harsh but short downturn associated with the panic

in 1907–8, the National Monetary Commission was formed to find new ways to solve the problems. In 1913 the Federal Reserve System (known as the Fed) was established as the nation's first full-scale central bank. Fears of dominance by large corporate interests led to an unusual structure with twelve regional banks and a relatively weak governing board. The Fed was given the hazy charge of working to provide an "elastic currency" that could fluctuate substantially in the short term to adjust to cyclical or seasonal changes in business activity or accommodate international gold flows tied to the U.S. commitment to the gold standard. What was meant by *elastic currency* was heavily debated during the passage of the enabling act. In practice, problems arose because conflicting policies might have been required to counteract bank panics and to accommodate the gold standard at the same time. The tensions between these two demands came to a head in the late 1920s and early 1930s and contributed to monetary policy responses to the bank panics of the Great Depression that many characterize as "too little, too late."[12]

Labor reformers were convinced that the increasingly industrialized economy left workers more vulnerable to unemployment and injury. Throughout the nineteenth century the candidates for poor relief and almshouses were often seen as personally responsible for their plight. The rising scale of enterprise, the expansion of workplace machinery, and the increasing impersonality of employment relations helped shift attitudes toward the belief that unemployment and injuries were not always under the workers' control. Increases in their standard of living led workers to demand better working conditions, and the exercise of voice by increasing numbers of workers via strikes and union representatives put additional pressure on employers to take steps to improve conditions.

Progressive-Era changes in the legal relationships between employers and workers were largely dealt with at the state level. To help workers harmed in industrial accidents, many states passed employer liability laws, soon to be followed by workers' compensation. Circa 1900 workers in dangerous jobs typically were paid higher wages but usually could purchase only limited amounts of accident and life insurance. Once injured, a worker could obtain compensation for the injury if he or she could show that the accident was caused by the employer's negligence. The employer could avoid liability if the worker knew of the risk in advance and had accepted it (the defense of assumption of risk), if the worker's negligence had contributed to the accident (contributory negligence), or a fellow worker's negligence had caused the accident (fellow servant). The initial employer liability laws eliminated all or a subset of these additional defenses. Yet the continued emphasis on fault under the common law meant that many injured workers and their families would receive nothing. The shift to workers' compensation provided that all workers injured on the job would receive compensation of up to two-thirds of their lost wages plus medical expenses. This legislation was supplemented by expansions in workplace safety regulations in mines and factories. The legislation passed during the Gilded Age was often designed to collect information and suggest basic practices for mines and some factories. As the Gilded Age blended into the Progressive Era, states passed more specific legislation, introduced inspectors to enforce the laws, and increased the administrative loads.[13]

The federal government enacted safety legislation for its own employees and those of the railroads. Federal employees were among the first in the nation to receive workers' compensation protection in 1908, and the benefits enacted in the revision of 1916 gave them among the most generous benefit packages available. Federal employees began receiving generous retirement benefits under the Civil Service Act of 1920. Despite the presence of many state laws concerning railroads, the establishment of the Interstate Commerce Commission in 1887 had opened the door for federal involvement in all aspects of railroading, particularly because so many workers and passengers were constantly crossing state lines. A series of federal regulations required the railroads to adopt safety technologies. With the Federal Employers Liability Act of 1908, the federal government had removed the fellow-servant defense and weakened the contributory negligence defenses that employers could invoke in workplace accident suits.[14]

As workers and labor leaders negotiated for higher wages and reduced hours, they joined forces with reformers to press for legislation to impose maximum hours and minimum wages. One of the central tenets of labor contract law was the individual's freedom to contract with any employer under the Fourteenth Amendment to the Constitution. State and federal courts used the freedom-of-contract argument to strike down attempts to regulate wages and hours for male workers. On the other hand, the governments could regulate the wages and hours of government employees and those in the public transportation sector. Eventually, the Wilson administration successfully imposed the eight-hour day on the railroad industry with the Adamson Act of 1916. A number of states passed laws preventing workers from signing away their rights to sue for negligence for accidents prior to the time when an accident occurred. This latter limitation on contractual rights played an important role in the adoption of workers' compensation.[15]

Women and children were treated differently on the ground that they needed more protection. A significant number of states passed legislation setting maximum working hours for women. The Supreme Court upheld the legislation in the 1908 *Muller v. State of Oregon* decision, declaring: "As healthy mothers are essential to vigorous offspring, the physical wellbeing of woman is an object of public interest. The regulation of her hour[s] of labor falls within the police power of the State." A few states passed women's minimum wage laws, but some were not mandatory, others set very low minimums, and enforcement efforts were often limited by fears of court challenges to the minimum. Nearly all states passed some form of legislation that limited child labor, and the laws were regularly expanded and updated to reduce the number of children in the workforce. Complementary legislation that compelled children to attend school was a response to the demands for more and better education for children as standards of living rose. The children were not simply required to go to school but were given opportunities for more advanced schooling as the high school movement swept the country.[16]

State governments began passing legislation to provide payments to people struck by misfortune or temporarily down on their luck. By 1900 many state governments had long been providing institutions for orphans, the deaf, the blind, and the insane. An indeterminate number of local governments had been providing shelters (indoor relief) and temporary payments (outdoor relief) as outgrowths of the old British poor law system. The Progressive-Era innovation was the beginning of *state*-level legislation to make direct payments to disadvantaged people that would allow them to live on their own. Nearly every state passed mothers' pension laws that provided for payments to widows with children between 1910 and 1920. In the latter part of that decade a few states gave counties the option to provide payments to the low-income elderly to allow them to live outside old-age homes. By the early 1930s about half of the states were making direct payments to aid blind people who were living outside of institutions. In the late 1920s and early 1930s the states began making county-level cash payment programs for the elderly mandatory, so that by 1932 eighteen states were making relief payments to allow the elderly poor to live on their own. The federal government had already been providing disability benefits for veterans of the Civil War who fought for the North. Eligibility rules had become lax enough that infirmity due to age qualified the veterans for aid. The state programs and the veterans' benefits were the forerunners of joint federal-state welfare and old-age pension programs legislated by the Social Security Act of 1935.[17]

The economic changes in society, the rise in the breadth and level of education, the dissatisfaction with the operations of government, and the stench of corruption all contributed to political movements aimed at expanding the accountability of governments to voters. In a short span of time many states passed legislation or amended their constitutions to establish direct popular elections of U.S. senators, opportunities for recall elections for state officials, initiatives and referenda that allowed direct popular votes on issues, and women's enfranchisement. The federal government followed by establishing women's suffrage in 1919.

Who Were the Progressives

The range of Progressive-Era policies is so broad and the supporters of different policies so varied that there is no single group that backed them all. Generally, the policies were forged in clashes and compromises that arose from the interest group struggles envisioned by James Madison in his Federalist Paper no. 10 (Hamilton, Madison, and Jay 1961). The term *Progressive* referred to a kaleidoscope of interests, ranging from muckraking journalists to social reformers to crusading politicians to leading businessmen.

Most attention is paid to the muckraking journalists and the social reformers of the early 1900s. Among many other, Upton Sinclair vividly portrayed the horrors of meatpacking plants in *The Jungle,* Ida Tarbell wrote exposés of Standard Oil's business practices in *McClure's,* and Lincoln Steffens uncovered the shame of the cities. Social reformers such as Jane Addams pressed for new ways of dealing with the unfortunate. Many future New Dealers played significant roles in administering government positions or in nongovernmental agencies helping the poor, including Harold Ickes (future head of the Public Works Administration and Secretary of the Interior), Frances Perkins (future Secretary of Labor), and Harry Hopkins (future head of the Federal Emergency Relief Administration, Civil Works Administration, and Works Progress Administration). Leading academic economists also pressed for reforms both in their writings and by taking active roles in commissions, including John L. Commons, Edwin Witte, Richard Ely, Isador Lubin, and John C. Andrews. The social reformers and muckrakers had outsized clout relative to their numbers. They often helped frame the debate by highlighting new problems, keeping issues alive before the press and the government, proposing new policies, and pressing strongly for their passage. Often specific groups of reformers focused on one or two issues, and at times the reformers themselves clashed over such matters as the appropriate role for unions. The success of their efforts was often determined by the alignments of interest groups in the lobbying process.[18]

At the state and local levels there were thousands of reform-minded progressive politicians, and there were no clear divisions along party lines. Among the most famous was Robert LaFollette, who pushed through a broad set of progressive changes as the reform Republican governor of Wisconsin from 1900 to 1906. He was a leading force for Progressivism at the national level in the Senate and continued to press the Progressive platform long after the 1912 Roosevelt candidacy, as he ran for president on the Progressive ticket in 1924. His son Robert Jr. replaced him in the Senate in 1925 and carried on the cause through the New Deal and beyond.

Progressivism was such a big tent that all three presidential candidates in the 1912 election were supporters of its causes. Theodore Roosevelt, dissatisfied with the policies of his successor William Howard Taft, broke away from the Republican Party and ran as a Progressive in 1912. His platform was seen as the ultimate expression of the movement's values. Democratic candidate Woodrow Wilson also ran on such a platform, many of which were established during his presidency. Roosevelt and Wilson were Progressives of different stripes. Roosevelt believed that the rise of big business was natural and that larger businesses were often the "most efficient units of industrial organization." Regulation was needed to limit the excesses and control the influence of businesses. Wilson, on the other hand, believed that "[m]onopoly developed amid conditions of unregulated competition. 'We can prevent these processes through remedial legislation, and so restrict the wrong use of competition that the right use of competition will destroy monopoly.'" Even the Republican candidate, Taft, supported a number of progressive policies. Although Roosevelt was considered the trust buster, Taft's Justice Department brought the breakups of Standard Oil and American Tobacco Company to their successful conclusion and prosecuted substantially more antitrust cases than did the Roosevelt administration. The Taft administration also supported the income tax amendment, which passed Congress in 1909.[19]

The trusts were often targets of attacks because they wielded so much power. Yet many owners and executives of large-scale business enterprises actively supported subsets of Progressive policies. Large enterprises were often in the forefront in reducing their dependence on child labor and supporting educational reforms. Many employers supported the introduction of workers' compensation. A number of large firms and some small ones practiced "welfare capitalism." They provided funds for workers who were injured or fell sick and built model towns, recreational facilities, and training facilities. Larger firms tended to pay higher wages and offer better working conditions. The very wealthy practiced philanthropy: building libraries, supporting research into new social methods for reducing poverty, and funding a variety of parks, museums, and foundations. Many of these practices were merely good business. Welfare capitalism was designed to reduce turnover in the workforce, which allowed companies to raise productivity by devoting fewer resources to training new workers. It was also a method to stave off the expansion of unions into their workforces and to eliminate criticisms that might lead to more regulation of their activities. Most leading businessmen had a strong antipathy toward unions. To combat the spread of unionization, they improved wages and working conditions. Some pressed state governments for injunctions and other legal methods to slow unionization, whereas others resorted to violence and illegal means. The extremes are best illustrated with an example. The housing and working conditions at the Colorado Fuel and Iron Mines, owned by John D. Rockefeller, were among the best in the coal industry in the period from 1910 to 1920. Yet the company is most infamous in labor history for its role in the long and violent strike of 1913–1914, which culminated in the horrible Ludlow tragedy when a number of women and children lost their lives during a pitched battle between state militia, company police, and striking miners.[20]

The unions held complex and changing views about the reform movements. In the early 1900s they distrusted many attempts to regulate workplaces on the grounds that employers held sway in most state legislatures and thus would have too much influence on the laws to be passed. Their experiences with legislation that treated unions as unlawful combinations and the continued application of the Sherman Act and injunctions that limited union activity contributed to this view. The unions argued instead that more success would come from the expansion of union recognition, which would allow workers to negotiate improvements themselves. On the other hand, unions pressed strongly for limitations on hours worked as they continued their campaign for shorter work days. As their political clout grew with expanded membership, the American Federation of Labor and other conservative unions began to press for more regulatory activity.

Given the wide range of Progressive policies and the idea of the big tent, it is hard to find anybody who was not considered a Progressive with regard to at least a subset of issues. That bigger government had come to be seen as irresistible—only its precise form remained to be worked out—signaled a profound transformation of the ideological environment. Businessmen had always sought to use the government to protect their own interests, but the scope of governmental authority that they found acceptable expanded dramatically. Robert Higgs suggests that the development of universities and the expanding numbers of economists and sociologists played important roles in shaping the new ideology. Many had studied the social insurance and regulatory policies adopted by European countries in the 1880s and 1890s. Ready and anxious to apply their knowledge, many social scientists and their students became reformers who wrote for leading publications, formed associations to lobby for their prescriptions, worked on government commissions, and sometimes became government administrators.[21]

The Importance of the Federal Structure

The interplay of interest groups and government took place within the nation's federal structure of governments, which influenced the locus of regulation. The Constitution gave authority over many issues to the states. Social insurance, public assistance, sanitation, streetcars, education, and regulation of workplaces were largely considered the purview of state and local governments, which led to several patterns in the adoption of legislation. Opponents of new regulations often argued that new regulations would put their states at a competitive disadvantage. Supporters often feared that states would "race to the bottom" in their competition to attract firms.

To counteract this problem, supporters developed national organizations, which then proposed "uniform" bills simultaneously in multiple legislatures. Thus, successful legislation such as workers' compensation and mothers' pensions, tended to be adopted in nearly all states within a decade. The geography of the adoption of legislation showed that neighboring states were likely to adopt legislation with similar features within the same time frame. Proposals that received less support from business groups often foundered. Reformers sometimes were able to establish a beachhead in one or more states, as was the case for the minimum wage for women, but their efforts would then founder in the face of business opposition in the remaining states.[22]

The diversity of state policies was advantageous in some respects. Populations and economic structures varied significantly across states; therefore, no single policy necessarily fit all the states equally well. People and businesses therefore had the option move to the states with policies that best matched their situations. In addition, the states' experimentation with diverse policies later informed the choice of federal policies that took over similar functions during or after the New Deal. The Constitution limited the states' powers to regulate by preventing states from erecting barriers to interstate commerce. After the 1886 *Wabash* decision limited the states' ability to regulate interstate commerce, leading to the creation of the federal Interstate Commerce Commission to regulate railroads, the federal government became the locus for regulation of industries that were clearly involved in exchanges across state lines.[23] By 1920 the country had developed an odd admixture of federal and state regulation of railroads. When it could be clearly shown that railroad workers, for example, were moving across state lines, an injured worker might be covered by the federal liability rules for railroads. On the other hand, a railroad worker who rarely left the state might be covered by the state's workers' compensation program.

The introduction of regulation of food processing during the late nineteenth and early twentieth centuries offers an example of the transition from state regulation to combinations of state and federal regulations. The central issues were safety, product quality, and competitive advantage. All three factors motivated industry, consumer, and reform groups to lobby for regulatory changes. Although for most foodstuffs there were few documented cases of actual poisonings or damaging health effects, there nevertheless was broad concern about product content and quality and whether consumers were getting what they paid for. In addition, industry groups took advantage of this uncertainty and anxiety to push for legislation that weakened their competitors.[24]

Technological advances in canning and refrigeration, and the creation of new foods allowed large firms to distribute foods nationwide in the late nineteenth century. The new products led to competition that led local butchers, dairy producers, cattlemen, and other traditional producers to fear that their livelihoods were jeopardized. Meanwhile, concerns about food quality increased because local retailers and consumers knew less about the original source of the food. There was particular concern about ingredients as the new technological advances gave firms the opportunity to adulterate their products in ways not easily detectable by consumers.

Between 1880 and 1900 states introduced a variety of food purity regulations in response to demands from producers and consumers. The stories behind specific regulations illustrate the most common competing views of regulation: *rent seeking* and *capture* versus resolution of information problems. Dairy producers were infamous for their rent-seeking pressure on state legislators to adopt regulations that limited competition from oleomargarine. The regulations generally succeeded at slowing the decline in butter prices and expanding butter consumption. Meanwhile, local butchers combined forces with cattlemen to lobby for meat inspection laws and antitrust legislation at the state and federal levels in order to limit competition from the large Chicago meatpackers.

Capture and rent seeking do not tell the whole story, however. Firms used a variety of methods to reassure customers that their products met a specific standard of quality: money-back guarantees, replacements of defective products, and independent testing and certification of the product. Local sellers often relied on establishing a long-term relationship with their customers, while national firms established brand names and marketed extensively. Producers of brand-name goods worked to ensure quality because consumers who like a good tell their friends and expand demand. Bad experiences lead to bad word of mouth, reducing sales and likely leading to losses that speed the demise of the firm. Despite their efforts, firms still faced problems in convincing consumers that there was no significant adulteration of the items. State regulations that included laboratory testing of products appear to have reassured consumers about the quality of certain foods, leading them to increase consumption. In most cases producers did not benefit from obtaining higher prices. Producers who had not been adulterating their goods benefited from the expansion in consumption, however, because their reputations were no longer tarred by the actions of the producers who had been adulterating products.

Dissatisfaction with food and drug regulation at the state level in the 1890s led to pressures for national legislation. National producers were frustrated because they found it costly to adapt products to match a wide variety of requirements across states. Each state had its own set of regulations, some well enforced and others treated as "dead letters." The serious state regulatory bodies were frustrated by their inability to control the production procedures of out-of-state firms that sold food in original and unbroken packages. Attempts to pass national pure food regulation foundered between 1890 and 1903 as state regulators found it difficult to yield authority to the federal government and each industry pressed for a version of the bill that favored its interests. Producers of baking powder containing cream of tartar sought bans on alum-based baking powders, distillers of straight and blended whiskeys sought rules that disadvantaged each other, and there was tremendous conflict over whether patent medicines and drugs would be covered by the regulations. Meanwhile, the vast majority of consumers remained unorganized and largely ignored the issue. Ultimately, the legislative stalemate was broken when the muckraking press awakened consumer interest in pure food legislation. The coalition of consumer and producer groups that developed raised the political rewards to senators and House members to establish regulation with the Pure Food and Drug Act of 1906.

As at the state level, the early years of regulation of food and drug production revealed signs of both capture and improved information flows. There is evidence that the Bureau of Chemistry's early enforcement of the law favored straight whiskey makers and manufacturers that did not use preservatives. Such favoritism apparently ended when Dr. Harvey Wiley resigned his post as head of the bureau in 1911. The Bureau of Chemistry had very limited enforcement powers but served to aid producers in verifying their claims of quality by providing quality certification or direct technical advice in improving their products.[25]

Were the Policies Revolutionary or Evolutionary?

Richard Hofstadter, one of the leading historians of the era, suggested that the Progressive movement "may be looked upon as an attempt to develop the moral will, the intellectual insight, and the political and administrative agencies to remedy the accumulated evils and negligences of a period of industrial growth." So how successful were the policies at achieving these aims? We should not expect dramatic, revolutionary changes. Hofstadter argues that the Progressives were not "revolutionists" but rather "were attempting to work out a strategy for orderly social change." Thus, they were working within the existing political system, a structure that, the reform rhetoric charged, was dominated by "the interests" including big business. If the rhetoric was correct, why would we expect that the interests would roll over in the face of the proposed reforms? The reformers might have expected success if they could persuade a large enough share of the voting public, but they would be even more successful to the extent that they could persuade the powers that be of the worthiness of their proposals. To some extent they succeeded, as we can see by the wide range of people who supported at least some progressive causes. But a closer inspection of the policies that specific groups supported suggests that those groups agreed to them because they expected to benefit from the new policies.[26]

Because the Progressives were working within the system, we should expect that few if any of the policies they backed were major victories of the "people" over the "interests." Most of the economic policies that were adopted fell into one of several categories. First was the "win-

win" category, in which the majority of members of the affected interest groups expected to gain. Workers' compensation legislation appears to have fit this category because the concept of providing some benefits for all injured workers received support from workers, employers, and insurance companies. Second was a category in which reform legislation was proposed but had differential impacts on powerful interest groups, say, a child labor law that largely dovetailed with the practices of a number of leading businessmen. Thus, a coalition formed among reformers, workers, and this subset of businessmen to pass the legislation. The impact of the law on the number of child workers was therefore likely to be smaller than many might have expected because only a subset of businesses was affected. Third, when two parties hotly disagreed about an issue, legislative changes were impermanent and often were undone when control of the legislature switched hands. Fourth, reform legislation was proposed but others offered counterproposals, and the compromise legislation with the grand title provided little in the way of reform. The laws might merely have codified standard practices for an activity, or they might have provided for no inspection or for so few resources for inspection and such small penalties that they were largely ignored. Some forms of workplace safety legislation passed during the period might have fit the latter category. Fifth, new legislation might have benefited one special interest at the expense of another. The immigration restriction acts of 1916 and the early 1920s were the classic examples of government discrimination against specific ethnic groups that redounded to the benefit of native-born workers by reducing the competition from foreign workers for jobs. In other cases the benefits of policies that appeared to be targeted toward one group were likely not as large as they were for other groups. For example, laws limiting women's hours appear to have benefited men more than women.

Workers' Compensation as a Win-Win Policy

Workers' compensation laws were probably the leading example of win-win legislation. Their intent was supported by workers, employers, and insurers. Employers became interested owing to increasing dissatisfaction with the existing system of negligence liability, which generated friction between them and their workers and which seemed to be increasing the costs of workplace accidents. Further, the costs of increasing the expected level of post-accident compensation for workers were not large because employers were able to pass a portion of the costs back to nonunion workers in the form of lower wages. Workers gained even if they "bought" workers' compensation with wage reductions, because they ended up better insured against workplace accident risk. Insurers were happy as long as there was no state insurance; they could sell more insurance because workers' compensation overcame information problems that had sharply limited the amount of accident insurance they could offer workers.[27]

Workers' compensation laws were complex. Although the fundamental policy was popular, bitter struggles developed over specific aspects, such as benefit levels and state insurance of the compensation, that determined who received the lion's share of the gains from enacting the laws. In the vast majority of states employers and insurers were effective at limiting the demands of organized labor. For example, organized labor actively lobbied for the elimination of private insurance of workers' compensation risk. They succeeded in only seven states, where organized labor was a very strong force or could combine forces with a strong progressive movement that gained hegemony in both houses of the legislature. In ten other states, they reached compromises in which private and state insurance both were allowed, and in the majority of states no state insurance scheme was established. Employers also influenced the setting of benefit levels. Employers in more dangerous industries and in high-wage states succeeded in pressing legislatures for lower benefits, although workers succeeded in obtaining higher benefits in states where unions were strong, party control of the legislature had shifted (often in favor of reform groups), and an agency was established to administer workers' compensation.

The success of workers' compensation as opposed to other forms of social insurance is instructive vis-à-vis the importance of employer support for the issue. Employers supported this but not other forms of social insurance in part because the common law already forced them to compensate some workers for accidents. Reformers' attempts to enact unemployment insurance and establish state-mandated health insurance benefits, policies that had been enacted in some European countries, foundered. Employers had had no legal responsibility for these issues under the common law, and few supported such changes. With employers indifferent or actively opposed, no winning coalition could be developed.

Protective Legislation Codifying Preexisting Trends

Child labor laws appear to exemplify existing social trends' coinciding with or preceding legislation. Between 1880 and 1920, the labor market participation rates of children fell nearly sixfold, while a well-organized social movement pressured state legislatures to enact limits on child employment. Studies of this period suggest that relatively little of the decline in child participation rates can be attributed to the introduction of child labor legislation. The employers' demand for child labor was reduced substantially by changes in technology, increases in the supply of unskilled workers due to massive immigration, and rising real wages. As their demand for child labor fell, the employers who had already eliminated it reduced their opposition to child labor laws. In fact, they may have actively supported the legislation to force recalcitrant employers to follow in their footsteps.[28]

State laws limiting the number of working hours for women may also have passed after many employers had substantially reduced hours for women. Recent studies have found that the laws had relatively little effect. Many employers and women were already negotiating for reduced hours in response to changes in technology, the workers' standard of living, firm size, and the ethnic composition of the workforce. The legislation acted mainly to limit hours for a small number of women who had not yet succeeded in negotiating reductions in hours. The group that benefited most from these appear to have been male workers. Labor unions in male-dominated industries had actively lobbied for such laws because they expected—rightly, it turns out—that restrictions on work by women would shift the demand for labor more in favor of men.[29]

The Impermanence of Tariff Reform

Two of Woodrow Wilson's key platform planks in the 1912 presidential campaign were the reduction of the tariff and the expansion of trust-busting. Both were designed to limit the power of big business and monopolies, Wilson's main bogeymen. The reduction of the tariff in 1913 illustrates the impermanence of policy regimes when the parties have established positions that are polar opposites. Meanwhile, the expansion of antitrust legislation with the Clayton Act and Federal Trade Commission Act of 1914 shows how regulation can involve substantial compromise that fell well short of reformers' expectations.

Between the Civil War and the 1930s, Democrats and Republicans struggled mightily over tariffs. Tariff increases during the protectionist Republican administrations were typically counteracted by tariff reductions when Democrats returned to power. Republican Congresses raised tariffs in 1872 and 1875. After lowering them slightly in 1883, they passed the McKinley Act of 1890, which raised tariffs significantly for manufactured goods but left sugar and many raw products duty-free. A

Democratic Congress temporarily cut tariffs with the Wilson-Gorman Act of 1894, but the Republicans countered with the Dingley Act of 1897, which raised legislative rates more than did the acts of 1875 and the McKinley Act of 1890 combined. In 1912 Wilson campaigned heavily for tariff reductions as a means of reducing the monopoly power afforded to big business by the tariffs. Oddly enough, he condemned the Payne-Aldrich tariff of 1909, which actually served to lower overall tariff rates somewhat. His charge that the act served special interests made sense, however, because tariff rates for goods produced in some industries were raised. Economists generally agree that Wilson's instincts were right and that lower tariffs would benefit consumers. On average, the Underwood Tariff Act, signed by Wilson in 1916, lowered rates enough to offset the rate increases enacted in 1897. The Wilson administration deserves still more credit for not allowing tariff rate increases when import prices skyrocketed during World War I and lowered the tariff as a percentage of prices. Wilson's success at cutting tariffs was short-lived, though. Once the Republicans returned to power in the 1920s, they sharply increased tariffs in the Fordney-McCumber Tariff Act of 1922 and in the highly protectionist Smoot-Hawley Tariff of 1930.[30]

Compromise on Antitrust Legislation

Reformers and unions had long sought strong restrictions on the actions of the trusts and immunity against the use of antitrust laws to break up unions. Although Wilson had campaigned to expand antitrust laws, the Clayton and Federal Trade Commission Acts of 1914 contained significant compromises. Senator James Reed of Missouri mused, "When the Clayton Act was first written, it was a raging lion with a mouth full of teeth. It has degenerated into a tabby cat with soft gums, a plaintive mew, and an anemic appearance. It is a sort of legislative apology to the trusts, delivered hat in hand, and accompanied by assurances that no discourtesy is intended."[31]

Despite their intense lobbying, unions had to swallow a compromise that fell well short of giving them full immunity against antitrust laws. The original Clayton bill, introduced in 1913, *forbade outright* many business practices such as use of exclusive selling contracts, interlocking boards of directors, and interlocking stock. By the time the bill had become the Clayton Act such practices were forbidden only when they substantially lessened competition or created a monopoly. The final version of the Clayton Act was actually superior to the original bill on grounds of economic efficiency. Economists have shown that such business practices could promote cost reductions and greater efficiency for many types of smaller firms without conferring significant amounts of market power.[32]

Wilson had apparently focused his antitrust goals on the establishment of a strong Federal Trade Commission (FTC). The Federal Trade Commission Act outlawed unfair practices and gave the commission authority to oversee business activity and issue cease-and-desist orders when competition was illegally suppressed. The impact of the commission, however, would be determined by the attitudes of the commissioners appointed. The reformers who had hoped for a strong cop to monitor business practices were somewhat dismayed when Wilson stated that "it was no large part of his purpose that the Federal Trade Commission should be primarily a policeman to wield a club over the business community." Instead, he saw the restraining powers of the commission as a "necessary adjunct which he hoped and expected to be of minor rather than major use." Dismay turned to anger when the first chair of the FTC, Joseph Davies, who had headed the Bureau of Corporations, was ineffectual. His replacement, Edwin N. Hurley, believed that the commission should become "useful to businessmen" and preached "cooperation between business and government" (Link 1954, 74, 75).

The FTC's first real attempt to restrict industry by means of enforcement of antitrust laws after World War I was quickly slapped down. After significant investigations, the FTC charged that the leading meatpackers were "engaging in unlawful combinations and illegal restraint of trade." The commission's solution included major restructuring and even public ownership of a segment of the industry. In response, the meatpackers successfully lobbied to move oversight of their business from the FTC to the U.S. Department of Agriculture. The Supreme Court's decision in *Federal Trade Commission v. Gratz* (1920) sharply limited the FTC's regulatory authority by holding that the "unfair methods of competition" cited in the initial act were not defined well and thus required judicial interpretation. Until the ruling was overturned in the 1930s, the commission's duties were largely limited to fact-finding. The role played by the FTC as antitrust enforcer has waxed and waned with changes in administrations ever since.[33]

The Complex Impact of Workplace Safety Regulation

Numerous studies of modern federal safety regulations find that they have had limited impact in reducing workplace accidents. These findings are also present in studies of accident regulation conducted during the Progressive Era. Most regulations appear to have codified existing practices in the relevant industry. Only a handful of state coal safety regulations appear to have been associated with reductions in accident rates, and those were often laws that employers used to bind the behavior of independent miners. For example, restrictions on miners who blasted the coal face without making an undercut helped reduce the dangers of explosions in the mines. The restrictions were highly unpopular because they forced miners to spend significantly more time hacking away with a pick.[34]

In some settings the new technology created new safety hazards. Some equipment was heavy and made work more awkward, and the gas masks used in mining literally burnt the miners' lips while saving them from ingesting the dangerous gases. In other settings miners worried that employers might claim that use of the technology allowed them to eliminate other safety precautions.

Inadequate enforcement might also have contributed to the relative ineffectiveness of most safety regulations. Most state mining departments visited mines only once or twice, if at all, during the year. Inspections had some impact because states with more inspection resources were successful at lowering the number of fatal accidents. Spending on factory inspection may have been less effective than spending on mine inspection. The number of factories per inspector was huge, making it impossible for inspectors to visit all workplaces within a year. The deaths of a large number of women in the infamous Triangle Shirtwaist Factory fire in New York in 1911 could be attributed in part to violations of building and factory codes that had gone unpunished. Soon after New York State tightened the laws, however, New York newspapers were still describing the inadequacies of enforcement, and statistical studies show no effect of state factory inspection budgets on accident rates.[35]

Many contemporaries anticipated reductions in accident risk from the introduction of workers' compensation. In fact, the response of fatal accident rates to the introduction of workers' compensation and employer liability laws (which limited the assumption-of-risk, fellow-servant, or contributory negligence defenses) varied across industries. falling in railroading, possibly falling in manufacturing. and rising in coal mining. The differences may have been driven by the costs to employers of preventing the major types of accidents in which moral hazard problems might have arisen.[36]

Why do we see these differences in results across industries? Employer liability laws and workers' compensation generally increased the average post-accident compensation paid to workers; therefore, both types of laws gave employers incentives to increase their accident prevention efforts while potentially giving workers incentives to relax their efforts or increase the reporting of accidents, a problem known as moral hazard. Increased prevention efforts by employers appear to have dominated in manufacturing and the railroads, where the costs of preventing accidents via changes in machinery and supervision were relatively low. In contrast, in the coal industry, where workers had always played a much greater role in accident prevention deep within the mines, accident rates rose. The moral hazard problems led to the type of accidents whose prevention was very costly for the employer. Therefore, employers chose to pay the extra damages to workers. The rise in accident rates does not imply that workers' compensation lowered the welfare of coal workers. Given that most coal workers were paid piece rates, they relaxed safety precautions only because they were trading safety for higher earnings. The increased benefits offered by workers' compensation allowed workers to increase their current earnings by working faster, while compensating them better when they were injured.

The Legacy of the Progressive Era

Progressive-Era policies may have been more evolutionary than revolutionary, but they nonetheless have had long-term consequences for the American economy. Although the initial effects of many policies had been limited, the reformers could claim success in their long-range objective of changing the terms of the debate. Like the Bedouin camel, Progressive reformers pushed their nose inside the tent, and within the next few decades nearly the whole camel was inside.

The adoption of the income tax with the Sixteenth Amendment eliminated a significant constraint on the federal government's ability to collect revenue and thus on its ability to spend. When earlier relying on tariffs and excise taxes, the federal government always faced tight limits because taxes on specific goods could reach levels at which purchases declined enough that tax revenues fell. Tariffs that rose too high could eliminate all imports of a good and thus all tariff revenue. The institution of an income tax meant that incomes from all endeavors could be taxed. The initial effects were small; fewer than 7 percent of households paid taxes prior to 1941. Yet crises led to substantial changes. During World War I tax rates rose sharply for the relatively small number of households that paid taxes. During World War II the federal government not only raised rates but imposed income taxes on the vast majority of households. Since World War II federal spending and taxation have expanded such that the federal government collects approximately 20 percent of GDP in tax revenues.

Along with taxation and spending, monetary policy is a major part of macroeconomic policy. The Federal Reserve System, adopted in 1913, established the first true central bank in American history. As a result, federal monetary policy played an important role in the economic fluctuations of the twentieth century. The Federal Reserve has not always been a force that reduces fluctuations; many economists assign a significant portion of the blame for the Great Depression to the Fed's inaction. It has met with more success during the modern era. At any rate, the actions of the Fed are a part of daily discussion of the state of the economy today.

The modern social insurance system was first set in place during the Progressive Era. Workers' compensation has remained a state-level program, but most other programs have evolved into a mixture of state and federal action. The Social Security Act of 1935 replaced state-level mothers' pension laws, old-age pensions, and aid to the blind with federal-state versions, which evolved further into the modern Temporary Assistance to Needy Families and Supplemental Security Income programs. Expansions of eligibility in the federal pension programs for Civil War veterans circa 1900 meant that a significant number of the elderly in the North were receiving federal pensions. World War I pensions and bonuses for veterans continued this trend and laid additional groundwork for the eventual provision of old-age pensions for all citizens, adopted with the Social Security Act.

Modern federal regulation of hours and wages, enacted in 1938, had its precedents in state-level regulation of women's hours, child labor, and women's minimum wage. These precedents were reinforced by the restrictions on hours for railroad workers established by the Adamson Act and upheld by a 5–4 Supreme Court decision in *Wilson v. New* in 1917. Regulation of workplace safety, foods, drugs, and the environment has evolved in several stages to a mixed regime of national and state rules.[37]

Supporters of government intervention who believe that it is necessary to curb the excesses of market economies see the policies established during the early 1900s as progressive in that they are moves in the right directions. Those who are less sanguine about the success of regulatory efforts reject the Progressive label on the ground that the policies introduced during this era might have reduced the productivity of the nation's economy. All can agree, however, that these policies were progressive in the sense that they were forward-looking. The evolutionary steps taken during the Progressive Era anticipated and set precedents for the tremendous expansion of government witnessed in the twentieth century.

Notes

1. Higgs (1987) used the metaphor of the bridge to modern times to describe the Progressive Era.
2. Broesame (1990), Buenkner (1973), Ekrich (1974), Gould (1974), Hofstadter (1963), Rodgers (1998), and Higgs (1987) discuss the Progressive Era.
3. For discussions of the increase in the size of firms, see Lamoreaux 1985, Chandler 1977, and Bittlingmayer 1985. Conditions in the economy in the late 1890s and early 1900s are discussed in Engerman and Gallman 1996 and 2000.
4. See Wolman 1936, Commons 1966 (vol. 3), Foster and Dubofsky 1984, and Montgomery 1987.
5. The discussion of urban reforms in the next few paragraphs is based on Holli 1974.
6. For an example of changes in administration, see the changes in city police departments described in Monkkenon 1981. For a humorous view of Taylorism when applied to a family, see Gilbreth and Carey 1948 or the 1950 movie *Cheaper by the Dozen,* starring Clifton Webb and Myrna Loy. McCraw (1974, 184), Knier (1947), and Rice (1977) offer fuller discussions of the changes in city governments.
7. Troesken 1996 and chapter 9 of this book contain broader discussions of the development of utilities and public works.
8. On antitrust policy see Bittlingmayer 1996, Sklar 1988, Lamoreaux 1985 (159–86), and Link 1954. A. Johnson (1959) discusses Roosevelt and the Bureau of Corporations. The case is Minnesota v. Northern Securities Co., 194 U.S. 48 (1904).
9. Link (1954) and Wilson (1956) offer insights into Wilson's attacks on the tariff. Irwin (1993) provides the historical economists' views of the tariff.
10. On the cigarette bans, see Alston, Dupre, and Nonnenmacher 2002. On state and federal prohibition and their impact on health see Dills and Miron 2004.
11. Baack and Ray 1985.
12. For an examination of the impact of antitrust activity and presidential attacks on business on stock markets and recessions, see Bittlingmayer 1992. For more on the Federal Reserve and its role, see chapters 5, 14, and 17 of this book. See also Friedman and Schwartz 1963, Livingston, 1986, Meltzer 2003, and Timberlake 1993.
13. For estimates of these compensating wage differentials, see Fishback 1992, 1998; Fishback and Kantor 1992, 2000; and Kim and Fishback 1993. For discussions of the operation of employer liability laws, see Fishback and Kantor 2000.
14. On benefits for federal employees, see Johnson and Libecap 1994. Kim and Fishback (1993) discuss the railroad liability laws. The federal government

also established a Bureau of Mines, but it was an informational agency and had no regulatory authority (Fishback 1992).

15. Lochner v. New York, 198 U.S. 45 (1905) (http://straylight.law.cornell .edu/supct/cases/name.htm [accessed August 18, 2005]), which declared limits on bakers' hours in New York to be unconstitutional, chilled efforts to establish limits on wages and hours for male workers for some time. On the limits on liability contracts, see Fishback and Kantor (2000).

16. The quotation is from Muller v. Oregon, 208 U.S. 412 (1908). http:// straylight.law.cornell.edu/supct/cases/name.htm (accessed August 18, 2005), also found in Hofstadter 1963, 66–68. For comprehensive descriptions of state labor legislation, see Brandeis 1966 and Holmes 2003. Margo and Finegan (1996) and Goldin and Katz (2003) examine the impact of school attendance requirements.

17. Ziliak (1996), Hannon (1984), Ziliak and Hannon (2006), and Margo and Kiesling (1997) provide quantitative information on public assistance in the nineteenth century. Skocpol (1992) provides an extensive discussion of the development of mothers' pensions and retirement and disability benefits for veterans. Lubove (1968) and Berkowitz and McQuaid (1992) provide overviews of the moves toward social insurance and welfare. For a listing of states that adopted mothers' pensions, aid to the blind, and old-age relief see Fishback and Thomasson 2006.

18. See Hofstadter 1963 for samples of the writings of muckrakers and other Progressives. Moss (1996) and Rodgers (1998) provide extensive discussions of the roles played by academic economists.

19. Roosevelt and Wilson are quoted in Link 1954, 21. The main features of the 1912 Progressive platform are found in Hofstadter 1963, 128–34.

20. See Fishback and Kantor 2000; Kolko 1963; Lubove 1967, 1968; Moss 1996; Wiebe 1962; and Weinstein 1968 for the roles played by businessmen. Jacoby (1997), Brandes (1976), and Fishback (1992) discuss welfare capitalism. For an extensive discussion of violence in coal strikes, see Fishback 1995 and sources cited thereim.

21. The paragraph is based on Higgs 1987, 114–16. See also Rodgers 1998 and Moss 1996. Sylla (1992, 547–48) speculates that big government arose in response to the rise of big business. He argues that the Progressive Era was a shift of regulation toward the federal level. Businesses were hampered by state regulations that had been used by local businesses to maintain their local advantages. Businesses therefore tried to shift the regulation to the federal level. This is true with regard to regulation of railroads and food and drugs, but the vast majority of Progressive policies stayed centered in the states.

22. See Moss 1996, Sylla 1992, Fishback and Kantor 2000, Holmes 2003, and Brandeis 1966.

23. Wabash, St. L. & P. R. Co. v. Illinois, 118 U.S. 557 (1886).

24. The section about pure food regulations is based on Dupre 1999; Law 2003a, 2003b; Law and Libecap 2006; and Libecap 1992. For discussion of the development of drug regulation see Temin 1980. Near the end of the Progressive Era, the Department of Agriculture began a program to eradicate bovine

tuberculosis when state regulations concerning cattle were ineffective owing to evasion. In this case federal regulation of food was a response to a severe health crisis. See Olmstead and Rhode 2004.

25. See Law and Libecap 2006, 338–40.

26. The quotations are from Hofstadter 1963, 3.

27. The section is based on Fishback and Kantor 2000. See also Witt 2004.

28. This section is based on discussions of child labor trends and legislation in Sanderson 1974, Osterman 1979, Brown, Christiansen, and Phillips 1982, Carter and Sutch 1996, and Moehling 1999. The impact of compulsory schooling legislation on child labor appears to have been mixed. Margo and Finegan (1996) find a significant effect of compulsory schooling legislation on school attendance in 1900. Meanwhile, Goldin and Katz (2003) find that compulsory high school legislation accounts for only a small portion of changes in high school attendance.

29. See Goldin 1990, 192–98; Whaples 1990a, 290–94, 357–58; 1990b, 398–402.

30. Estimating the legislative burden of tariffs is complicated because the taxes on imports vary across a large number of goods. Discussion of the changes in tariff rates associated with the tariff acts is based on Doug Irwin's (1998) estimates of tariffs as percentages of import prices and the contributions of changes in tariff legislation and in import prices to changes in the tariff percentage of import prices. For further discussion, see Taussig 1964 and Link 1954.

31. Reed is quoted in Link 1954, 72–73. Bittlingmayer (1996), Sklar (1988), and McCraw (1974) provide extensive discussion of the political economy of antitrust activity in the Progressive Era.

32. For discussions of economic and legal theories of antitrust policy, see Bork 1978, Posner 1977, and Viscusi, Vernon, and Harrington 1998. The unions obtained some concessions, including jury trials for criminal contempt cases, limits on injunctions that might halt their organizing efforts, and the declaration that unions would not be considered "illegal combinations in restraint of trade when they lawfully sought legitimate objectives." Link (1954) suggests that the unions were unhappy with this compromise but in public loudly proclaimed a victory. The welfare of unions rose dramatically by government fiat during World War I but declined sharply in the 1920s, suggesting that the Clayton Act's protections were relatively weak.

33. The quotations are from Link 1954, 75–76. McCraw (1974, 197–98) describes the post–World War I FTC. The Supreme Court case was Federal Trade Commission v. Gratz, 253 U.S. 427 (1920).

34. For modern studies see Viscusi 1992 and Bartel and Thomas 1985. For a summary of statistical studies of the impact of Progressive Era safety legislation, see Fishback 1998, which summarizes work on mining, railroads, and manufacturing by Fishback 1986, 1992; Aldrich 1997; Graebner 1976; Buffum 1992; and Chelius 1976, 1977. See also Fishback 2006.

35. See Stein 1962, McEvoy 1995, and Fishback 2006 on the Triangle Shirtwaist Factory fire. For statistical studies, see Buffum 1992 and Chelius 1976, 1977.

36. To avoid problems with reporting of accidents, all of the studies of the impact of workers' compensation on accident risk have focused on fatal accidents (Fishback 1998).

37. Wilson v. New, 243 U.S. 332 (1917).

References

Aldrich, Mark. 1997. *Safety First: Technology, Labor, and Business in the Building of American Work Safety, 1870–1939.* Baltimore: Johns Hopkins University Press.

Alston, Lee, Ruth Dupre, and Tomas Nonnemacher. 2002. "Social Reformers and Regulation: The Prohibition of Cigarettes in the United States and Canada." *Explorations in Economic History* 39 (October): 425–45.

Baack, Benjamin, and Edward Ray. 1985. "Special Interests and the Adoption of the Income Tax in the United States." *Journal of Economic History* 45 (September): 607–25.

Bartel, Ann P., and Lacy Glenn Thomas. 1985. "Direct and Indirect Effects of Regulation: A New Look at OSHA's Impact." *Journal of Law and Economics* 28 (April): 1–25.

Berkowitz, Edward, and Kim McQuaid. 1992. *Creating the Welfare State: The Political Economy of Twentieth-Century Reform.* Lawrence: University of Kansas Press.

Bittlingmayer, George. 1985. "Did Antitrust Policy Cause the Great Merger Wave?" *Journal of Law and Economics* 28 (April): 77–118.

———. 1992. "Stock Returns, Real Activity, and the Trust Question." *Journal of Finance* 47 (December): 1701–30.

———. 1996. "Antitrust and Business Activity: The First Quarter Century." *Business History Review* 70 (Autumn): 363–401.

Bork, Robert. 1978. *The Antitrust Paradox: A Policy at War with Itself.* New York: Basic.

Brandeis, Elizabeth. 1966. "Labor Legislation." In *History of Labor in the United States,* ed. John R. Commons and Associates, 3:399–70. 1935; repr., New York: Augustus Kelley.

Brandes, Stuart. 1976. *American Welfare Capitalism, 1880–1940.* Chicago: University of Chicago Press.

Broesame, John J. 1990. *Reform and Reaction in Twentieth Century American Politics.* New York: Greenwood.

Brown, Martin, Jens Christiansen, and Peter Phillips. 1992. "The Decline of Child Labor in the U.S. Fruit and Vegetable Canning Industry: Law or Economics?" *Business History Review* 66 (Winter): 723–70.

Buenkner, John D. 1973. *Urban Liberalism and Progressive Reform.* New York: Charles Scribner and Sons.

Buffum, David. 1992. "Workmen's Compensation: Passage and Impact." PhD diss., University of Pennsylvania.

Carter, Susan, and Richard Sutch. 1996. "Fixing the Facts: Editing of the 1880 U.S. Census of Occupations with Implications for Long-Term Labor Force Trends and the Sociology of Official Statistics." *Historical Methods* 29 (Winter): 5–24.

Chandler, Alfred. 1977. *The Visible Hand: The Managerial Revolution in American Business.* Cambridge: Harvard University Press, Belknap Press, 1977.

Chelius, James R. 1976. "Liability for Industrial Accidents: A Comparison of Negligence and Strict Liability Systems." *Journal of Legal Studies* 5 (June): 293–309.

———. 1977. *Workplace Safety and Health: The Role of Workers' Compensation.* Washington, DC: American Enterprise Institute Press.

Commons, John R., and Associates. 1966. *History of Labor in the United States,* 4 vols. 1916–; repr., New York: Augustus Kelley.

Dills, Angela, and Jeff Miron. 2004. "Alcohol Prohibition and Cirrhosis." *American Law and Economics Review* 6 (Fall): 285–318.

Dupre, Ruth. 1999. "If It's Yellow, It Must Be Butter: Margarine Regulation in North America since 1886." *Journal of Economic History* 59 (June): 353–71.

Ekrich, Arthur. 1974. *Progressivism in America: A Study of the Era from Theodore Roosevelt to Woodrow Wilson.* New York: New Viewpoints.

Engerman, Stanley, and Robert Gallman. 1996–2000. *The Cambridge Economic History of the United States.* 3 vols. New York: Cambridge University Press.

Fishback, Price V. 1986. "Workplace Safety during the Progressive Era: Fatal Accidents in Bituminous Coal Mining, 1912–1923." *Explorations in Economic History* 23 (July): 269–98.

———. 1987. "Liability Rules and Accident Prevention in the Workplace: Empirical Evidence from the Early Twentieth Century." *Journal of Legal Studies* 16 (June): 305–28.

———. 1992. *Soft Coal, Hard Choices: The Economic Welfare of Bituminous Coal Miners, 1890 to 1930.* New York: Oxford University Press, 1992.

———. 1995. "An Alternative View of Violence in Strikes: The Bituminous Coal Industry, 1890–1930." *Labor History* 36 (Summer): 426–56.

———. 1998. "Operations of 'Unfettered' Labor Markets: Exit and Voice in American Labor Markets at the Turn of the Century." *Journal of Economic Literature* 36 (June 1998): 722–65.

———. 2006. "The Irony of Reform: Did Large Employers Subvert Workplace Safety Reform, 1869 to 1930?" In *Corruption and Reform,* ed. Edward Glaeser and Claudia Goldin, 285–318. Chicago: University of Chicago Press.

Fishback, Price V., and Kantor, Shawn Everett. 1992. "'Square Deal' or Raw Deal? Market Compensation for Workplace Disamenities, 1884–1903." *Journal of Economic History* 52 (December): 826–48.

———. 2000. *A Prelude to the Welfare State: The Origins of Workers' Compensation.* Chicago: University of Chicago Press.

Fishback, Price V., and Melissa Thomasson. 2006. "Social Welfare Spending: 1929 to the Present." In *Historical Statistics of the United States, Earliest Times to the Present, Millennial Edition,* ed. Susan B. Carter et al. vol. 2, pt. B, "Work and Welfare," 2-700–2-719. New York: Cambridge University Press.

Foster, Rhea Dulles, and Melvyn Dubofsky. 1984. *Labor in America: A History.* 4th ed. Arlington Heights, IL: Harlan Davidson.

Friedman, Milton, and Anna Schwartz. 1963. *A Monetary History of the United States, 1867–1960.* Princeton: Princeton University Press.

Gilbreth, Frank B., and Ernestine Gilbreth Carey. 1948. *Cheaper by the Dozen*. New York: Crowell.

Goldin, Claudia. 1990. *Understanding the Gender Gap: An Economic History of Women*. New York: Oxford University Press.

Goldin, Claudia, and Lawrence Katz. 2003. "Mass Secondary Schooling and the State: The Role of State Compulsion in the High School Movement." National Bureau of Economic Research Working Paper No. 10075, Cambridge, MA (November).

Gould, Lewis L., ed. 1974. *The Progressive Era*. Syracuse, NY: Syracuse University Press.

Graebner, William. 1976. *Coal-Mining Safety in the Progressive Era*. Lexington: University of Kentucky Press.

Hamilton, Alexander, James Madison, and John Jay. 1961. *The Federalist Papers*. New York: New American Library.

Hannon, Joan. 1984. "The Generosity of Antebellum Poor Relief." *Journal of Economic History* 44.3 (September): 810–21.

Higgs, Robert. 1987. *Crisis and Leviathan: Critical Episodes in the Growth of American Government*. New York: Oxford University Press.

Hofstadter, Richard. 1963. *The Progressive Movement, 1900–1915*. Englewood Cliffs: Prentice-Hall.

Holli, Melvin. 1974. "Urban Reform." In *The Progressive Era*, ed. Lewis L. Gould. Syracuse, NY: Syracuse University Press.

Holmes, Rebecca. 2003. "The Impact of State Labor Regulations on Manufacturing Input Demand during the Progressive Era." PhD diss., University of Arizona.

Irwin, Douglas. 1993. *Against the Tide: An Intellectual History of Free Trade*. Princeton: Princeton University Press.

———. 1998. "Changes in U.S. Tariffs: The Role of Import Prices and Commercial Policies." *American Economic Review* (September): 1015–26.

Jacoby, Sanford. 1997. *Modern Manors: Welfare Capitalism since the New Deal*. Princeton: Princeton University Press.

Johnson, Arthur. 1959. "Theodore Roosevelt and the Bureau of Corporations." *Mississippi Valley Historical Review* 45 (March): 571–90.

Johnson, Ronald N., and Gary D. Libecap. 1994. *The Federal Civil Service System and the Problem of Bureaucracy: The Economics and Politics of Institutional Change*. Chicago: University of Chicago Press.

Kaufman, Bruce. 1993. *The Origins and Evolution of the Labor Relations Field in the United States*. Cornell Studies in Industrial and Labor Relations, no. 25. Ithaca: ILR Press.

Kim, Seung-Wook, and Fishback, Price V. 1993. "Institutional Change, Compensating Differentials and Accident Risk in American Railroading, 1892–1945." *Journal of Economic History* 53 (December): 796–823.

Knier, Charles M. 1947. *City Government in the United States*. Rev. ed. New York: Harper & Brothers.

Kolko, Gabriel. 1963. *The Triumph of Conservatism: A Reinterpretation of American History, 1900–1916*. New York: Free Press of Glencoe.

Lamoreaux, Naomi R. 1985. *The Great Merger Movement in American Business, 1895–1904*. New York: Cambridge University Press.

Landes, William M., and Richard A. Posner. 1987. *The Economic Structure of Tort Law.* Cambridge: Harvard University Press.

Law, Marc. 2003a. "Specialization, Information, and Regulation in American Economic History." PhD diss., Washington University.

——. 2003b. "The Origins of State Pure Food Regulation." *Journal of Economic History* 63 (December 2003): 1103–30.

Law, Marc, and Gary Libecap. 2006. "The Determinants of Progressive Era Reform: The Pure Food and Drug Act of 1906." In *Corruption and Reform,* ed. Edward Glaeser and Claudia Goldin, 319–42. Chicago: University of Chicago Press.

Libecap, Gary. 1992. "The Rise of the Chicago Packers and the Origins of Meat Inspection and Antitrust." *Economic Inquiry* 30.2 (April 1992): 242–62.

Link, Arthur S. 1954. *Woodrow Wilson and the Progressive Era, 1910–1917.* New York: Harper & Brothers.

Livingston, James. 1986. *Origins of the Federal Reserve System: Money, Class, and Corporate Capitalism, 1890–1913.* Ithaca: Cornell University Press.

Lubove, Roy. 1967. "Workmen's Compensation and the Prerogatives of Voluntarism." *Labor History* 8 (Fall): 254–27.

——. 1968. *The Struggle for Social Security: 1900–1935.* Cambridge: Harvard University Press.

Margo, Robert, and Aldrich Finegan. 1996. "Compulsory Schooling Legislation and School Attendance in Turn of the Century America: A "Natural Experiment' Approach." *Economic Letters* 53 (October): 103–10.

Margo, Robert, and Lynn Kiesling. 1997. "Explaining the Rise in Antebellum Pauperism, 1850–1860: New Evidence." *Quarterly Review of Economics and Finance* 37 (Summer): 405–17.

McCraw, Thomas. 1974. "The Progressive Legacy." In *The Progressive Era,* ed. Lewis L. Gould, 181–201. Syracuse NY: Syracuse University Press.

McEvoy, Arthur. 1995. "The Triangle Shirtwaist Fire of 1911: Social Change, Industrial Accidents, and the Evolution of Common-Sense Causality." *Law and Social Inquiry* 20:621–51.

Meltzer, Allan. 2003. *A History of the Federal Reserve.* Vol. 1, *1913–1951.* Chicago: University of Chicago Press.

Moehling, Carolyn. 1999. "State Child Labor Laws and the Decline of Child Labor." *Explorations in Economic History* 36 (January): 72–106.

Monkkenon, Eric H. 1981. *Police in Urban America, 1860–1920.* New York: Cambridge University Press.

Montgomery, David. 1987. *The Fall of the House of Labor.* New York: Cambridge University Press.

Moss, David. 1996. *Socializing Security: Progressive-Era Economists and the Origins of American Social Policy.* Cambridge: Harvard University Press.

Olmstead, Alan, and Paul Rhode. 2004. "An Impossible Undertaking: The Eradication of Bovine Tuberculosis in the United States." *Journal of Economic History* 64 (September): 734–72.

Osterman, Paul. 1979. "Education and Labor Markets at the Turn of the Century." *Politics and Society* 9 (March): 103–22.

Posner, Richard A. 1977. *Antitrust Law: An Economic Perspective*. Chicago: University of Chicago Press.

Rice, Bradley Robert. 1977. *Progressive Cities: The Commission Government Movement in American, 1901–1920*. Austin: University of Texas Press.

Rodgers, Daniel. 1998. *Atlantic Crossings: Social Politics in a Progressive Age*. Cambridge: Harvard University Press, Belknap Press.

Sanderson, Allen. 1974. "Child-Labor Legislation and the Labor Force Participation of Children." *Journal of Economic History* 34 (March): 297–99.

Sklar, Martin. 1988. *The Corporate Reconstruction of American Capitalism, 1890–1916: The Market, the Law, and Politics*. New York: Cambridge University Press.

Skocpol, Theda. 1992. *Protecting Soldiers and Mothers: The Political Origins of Social Policy in the United States*. Cambridge: Harvard University Press.

Stein, Leon. 1962. *The Triangle Fire*. New York: Lippincott.

Sylla, Richard. 1992. "The Progressive Era and the Political Economy of Big Government." *Critical Review* 5:531–57.

Taussig, F. W. 1964. *The Tariff History of the United States*. 8th ed. New York: Capricorn.

Temin, Peter. 1980. *Taking Your Medicine: Drug Regulation in the United States*. Cambridge: Harvard University Press.

Timberlake, Richard. 1993. *Monetary Policy in the United States: An Intellectual and Institutional History*. Chicago: University of Chicago Press.

Troesken, Werner. 1996. *Why Regulate Utilities? The New Institutional Economics and the Chicago Gas Industry, 1849–1924*. Ann Arbor: Michigan University Press.

Viscusi, W. Kip. 1992. *Fatal Tradeoffs: Private and Public Responsibilities toward Risk*. New York: Oxford University Press.

Viscusi, W. Kip, John Vernon, and Joseph Harrington. 1998. *Economics of Regulation and Antitrust*. Cambridge: MIT Press.

Weinstein, James. 1968. *The Corporate Ideal in the Liberal State: 1900–1918*. Boston: Beacon.

Whaples, Robert. 1990a. "The Shortening of the American Work Week: An Economic and Historical Analysis of Its Context, Causes, and Consequences." PhD diss., University of Pennsylvania.

———. 1990b. "Winning the Eight-Hour Day, 1909–1919." *Journal of Economic History* 50 (June): 393–406.

Wiebe, Robert. 1962. *Businessmen and Reform: A Study of the Progressive Movement*. Cambridge: Harvard University Press.

Wilson, Woodrow. 1956. *A Crossroads of Freedom: The 1912 Campaign Speeches of Woodrow Wilson*. Ed. John Wells Davidson. New Haven: Yale University Press.

Witt, John Fabian. 2004. *The Accidental Republic: Crippled Workingmen, Destitute Widows, and the Remaking of American Law*. Cambridge: Harvard University Press.

Witte, Edwin. 1932. *The Government in Labor Disputes*. New York: McGraw-Hill.

Wolman, Leo. 1936. *The Ebb and Flow of Trade Unionism*. New York: National Bureau of Economic Research.

Ziliak, Stephen. 1996. "The End of Welfare and the Contradiction of Compassion." *Independent Review* 1 (Spring): 55–73.

Ziliak, Stephen, and Joan Underhill Hannon. 2006. "Public Assistance: Colonial Times to the 1920s." In *Historical Statistics of the United States: Earliest Times to the Present, Millennial Edition,* ed. Susan B. Carter et al., vol. 2, pt. B., "Work and Welfare," 2-693–2-700. New York: Cambridge University Press.

SUMNER J. LA CROIX

11

Government and the People:
Labor, Education, and Health

THE POPULATION of the United States is the beneficiary of the fruits of U.S. economic development, and the labor force, a subset of the population, has played a leading role in generating growth. In this chapter I consider the historical role of the U.S. government in determining the size of the population and the labor force, investments in human capital (that is, education and health), and the organization of labor markets. The national government played a very limited role in determining the size of the population and the labor force until after the Civil War. Restrictions on immigration, originally targeted at specific ethnic groups from the 1880s to the early 1970s, have shaped the growth of the population. Restrictive federal policies concerning birth control adopted in the late nineteenth century were replaced by more liberal policies after World War II, and they have contributed to reductions in the birthrate and participation of women in the labor force. The building of public works at the local level and expansions in government-sponsored medical research have contributed to longer lives. State and local governments, and more recently the federal government, have played major roles in the development of general human capital with the introduction of public schools in the 1800s and the establishment of compulsory minimum requirements for child education. The expansions in public health, water treatment, and sewage control facilities have contributed to better health in the workforce, as have social insurance and tax policies designed to subsidize health care. Ultimately, governments shaped the organization of labor markets through regulations and changes in the treatment of collective bargaining during the Great Depression and afterward.

The influence of government spending and regulation on population growth, labor force participation, education, job training, and the

N__
L__

operation of labor markets has increased dramatically since the 1930s. Some of these initiatives have been complementary to market institutions, that is, the spending and regulations have supported institutions that underpin markets and have increased economic growth, whereas other interventions have been designed to transfer income to specific interest groups with the transfer costs varying widely by intervention. The ratchet mechanism so clearly set forth by Robert Higgs in *Crisis and Leviathan,* in which individual liberties to participate in markets disappear in a two-steps-backward, one-step-forward process, should be discernable in many aspects of this chapter.

Despite this mixed legacy, in a few critical areas, some U.S. citizens have reaped large gains in freedom as a result of government interventions in labor markets over the course of the last two hundred years. Slavery has been abolished. Legal restrictions on the voting rights of African Americans have been abolished, albeit more than one hundred years after voting rights had been promised. Women have gained a constitutional right—discovered in the penumbra of the Constitution—to control their fertility and have gained more legal control over their lives while they are married. And although the employment of disabled Americans fell substantially after the passage of the Americans with Disabilities Act (ADA), the act has arguably brought millions of disabled Americans from the shadows to the mainstream of American life.

Government, Population, and Health

The population of the United States has, like all populations, found its proximate determinates in only three factors: birthrates, mortality rates, and immigration. Although I treat each factor separately in this section, it is important to point out that between 1800 and 1930, American birth and death rates evolved following a pattern that demographers have identified in virtually all countries and that they have labeled the "Demographic Transition." It is a singular historical period during which birth and death rates decline significantly from high to low levels in a particular country or region. Because the decline in U.S. death rates preceded the decline in birthrates with a long lag, the result was an increase in population growth rates that persisted through the 1920s.[1] With this connection clearly in mind, I present separate discussions of birth and death rates and immigration.

Birthrates

White birthrates per 1,000 women in North America were between 45 and 50 per year in the seventeenth and eighteenth centuries, considerably higher than the 30 per 1,000 women observed in Europe during the same period. In the United States, white birthrates peaked at 55 per 1,000 women in 1800 and underwent a long period of secular decline through 1936, when there were only 17.6 births per 1,000 women. Reliable black birthrates prior to 1850, a year in which 88 percent of U.S. blacks were enslaved, are unavailable. In subsequent years black birthrates closely followed trends in white birthrates but were at higher levels throughout. Black birthrates averaged 58.6 per 1000 women over the 1850–1859 period (see table 11.1). From this peak level, black birthrates underwent a long secular decline, falling to 34.4 births per 1,000 women in 1915.[2]

A number of forces combined, starting in the early nineteenth century, to lower American fertility rates and thereby contribute to the demographic transition in the United States. First, rising wage rates from 1815 onward increased the opportunity costs of children and lowered fertility rates.[3] Second, advances in knowledge about infectious diseases lowered infant mortality, thereby lowering the number of births required to reach a targeted level of children. Third, agricultural families often had high fertility rates due to the potential use of children for farm labor; as families moved to manufacturing and service jobs in urban areas, the demand for children fell, depressing birthrates. Although government policies had an indirect influence via their influence on these factors, government had almost no direct influence on birthrates through the end of the nineteenth century.

During the Great Depression, there was a sharp fall in fertility in the United States that continued though World War II. Government policies that helped deepen and prolong the depression and that drafted millions of young men into the military were indirect causes of the fertility decline. Accompanying the booming economy after World War II was a rise in U.S. birthrates from 1946 to 1960 to levels more than sufficient to replace lost wartime fertility. The resulting "baby boom" produced large swings in age structure among white and black populations. Rising wages drew women into the labor force during the 1950s and early 1960s, thereby increasing the "price" of raising a child and depressing U.S. fertility in the mid-1960s.[4] Birthrates continued to fall significantly in the 1970s and 1980s and then increased slightly after 1990. The post-1990 boom was the echo of the earlier boom and was triggered not by an increased number of children per family but by an increased number of women of child-bearing age.

How, if at all, did government affect the birthrate? Two regulations that the national and state governments enacted—and later repudiated— had major effects on fertility choices. In 1873 the national government

placed restrictions on the use of birth control devices with the enactment of the Comstock Law. A 1938 federal court decision ended the use of the Comstock Law to regulate birth control, but state laws quickly filled the gap. The state of Connecticut, for example, explicitly prohibited individuals from using drugs or instruments to prevent conception, and it also prohibited health care professionals from advising patients as to their use.[5]

In 1965 the U.S. Supreme Court, in a pathbreaking decision, *Griswold v. Connecticut,* overturned the state birth control bans, ruling that a "statute forbidding use of contraceptives violates the right of marital privacy which is within the penumbra of specific guarantees of the Bill of Rights." The legalization of contraceptives and the subsequent changes in state laws reducing the age of majority were enacted just as a new form of contraception—the birth control pill—was becoming widely available. The pill was to have major effects on women's careers and lives. As a direct effect, the pill virtually eliminated the chance of pregnancy, thereby reducing the cost to women of having sex. As an indirect effect, the pill delayed the age of first marriage. This reduced the costs to a career woman of engaging in extended professional education as it became more likely that a male with matching education and interests would still be available for marriage after graduation. The timing of the introduction of the pill thereby coincided with the substantial increase in the fraction of female U.S. college graduates entering professional programs around 1970 and the increase in the age at first marriage among all female U.S. college graduates just after 1972.[6]

In the 1820s the states began to enact laws criminalizing abortion after the first trimester, and by 1900 abortions had generally been banned by the states. Sixty-five years later, the abortion ban was still in place, with exceptions allowed only in limited instances such as rape, incest, and endangerment of the life or health of the mother. In 1969 the California Supreme Court ruled that California's law prohibiting abortion was unconstitutional, and by the end of 1970, four other states (Alaska, Hawaii, New York, and Washington) had repealed laws prohibiting abortion. In 1973 the landmark U.S. Supreme Court decision *Roe v. Wade* established the right of U.S. women to choose an abortion until the time when the fetus becomes viable. By providing a form of insurance against unexpected economic, social, and personal events during a pregnancy, legalized abortion should be expected to have increased pregnancies, decreased unwanted births, and had an indeterminate effect on the birthrate. Using data from the transition from illegal to legal abortion in the 1970s, it has been estimated that if abortion were to be criminalized by the federal government, then U.S. birthrates would increase by 10.8 percent, or 432,000 births annually. If, however, the U.S. Supreme Court were to overturn *Roe,* the Congress declined to criminalize abortion, and abortion remained legal in only the five states that allowed it in 1970, then estimates of the increase in birthrates decline to only 4.1 percent, or 123,000 births annually.[7]

Death Rates and Investments in Health

Mortality data are less well documented than fertility data because few states implemented death registries until the late nineteenth century. We know that mortality rates stabilized around 1800 before increasing in the 1840s and 1850s. After the Civil War, mortality rates began a long trend of slow decline, a pattern that has persisted into the twenty-first century.[8] The decline in death rates is generally due to improvements in the standard of living resulting from better nutrition and housing, better provision of public sanitation, improvements in personal hygiene, improvements in medical care and knowledge, and reduced deaths from infectious disease. By its provision of sanitation and water treatment, the government contributed significantly to reductions in death rates among urban workers (see chapter 9). In any case, the improvements in nutrition, personal hygiene, and medical care and knowledge have only indirect roots in government expenditures or government intervention in labor markets until after World War II.

The national government's declared and undeclared wars led to sporadic increases in U.S. death rates, with increases being particularly large during the Civil War (360,000 Union soldiers and 258,000 Confederate soldiers killed) and World War II (407,000 U.S. soldiers killed). Increases in mortality from the Revolutionary War, World War I, the Korean War, and the Vietnam War were also considerable. (See table 11.2; also see chapters 7 and 14 for additional discussion.) Recent research on the fate of soldiers who were injured, contracted infectious diseases, or were exposed to more combat while in service during the Civil War shows that these soldiers accumulated substantially less wealth ($868 per soldier) by 1870 than those who did not serve.

The experience of soldiers in the Civil War provides a clear illustration of a more general proposition: that health and income are interdependent. Increases in income allow individuals and their government to undertake a wide range of activities to improve their health. Autonomous increases in health also generate increases in incomes by allowing

Table 11.2 U.S. CASUALTIES OF WAR

Conflict	Population (millions)	Enrolled (thousands)	Dead (thousands)	Wounded (thousands)
Revolutionary War	3.5	200.0	4.4	6.2
War of 1812	7.6	286.0	2.3	4.5
Mexican War	21.1	78.7	13.3	4.2
Civil War: Union	26.2	2,803.3	359.5	275.2
Confederate	8.1	1,064.2	198.5	137.0
Combined	34.3	3,867.5	558.0	412.2
Spanish-American War	74.6	306.8	2.4	1.7
World War I	102.8	4,743.8	117.0	204.0
World War II	133.5	16,353.7	307.3	670.8
Korean War	151.7	5,764.1	33.7	103.3
Vietnam War	204.9	8,744.0	58.2	153.3
Gulf War	260.0	2,750.0	0.3	0.5

individuals to work harder and to be available for work on more days. Government policies have affected this dual feedback mechanism via several channels. First, policies affect income and economic growth, and higher levels of income tend to increase many (but not all) dimensions of health. Second, policies toward the pharmaceutical industry, the health insurance industry, and the health care industry generally have direct implications for the production of health care, which, in turn, typically improves health. (See chapter 17 for a discussion of the effects of the Food and Drug Administration's regulation of pharmaceutical products.) Third, government involvement in the rapid development, international diffusion, and implementation of public health knowledge, nutritional practices, vaccines, and birth control practices has been responsible in part for greater life expectancy and health status in the United States and throughout the world. (See chapter 9 for a more complete discussion of how urbanization and structural change affected the demand for public health measures.) Finally, federal spending on health care research, much of administered by the National Institutes of Health and conducted by private and public research units and universities throughout the United States, has increased substantially since 1960. The discussion below focuses on the ways federal tax incentives and federally provided health insurance programs have affected markets for health insurance, which now cover more than 70 percent of U.S. residents.[9]

The health insurance industry began to assume its modern form in the 1930s when the nonprofit Blue Cross and Blue Shield plans emerged to offer prepaid coverage for physician services and hospitalization.

States that passed an enabling law that provided a coherent legal framework for the operation of the Blues saw rapid expansion of the health care industry during the 1930s. The success of the Blues induced for-profit insurance companies to enter the market, thereby allowing for additional choice and product variety. Yet despite these pro-growth measures and a decade of industry expansion, only 12.3 million Americans (9 percent of the population) were covered by private health insurance in 1940. The plunge into World War II would, however, lead to dramatic increases in coverage in just five years: 32 million Americans (22.9 percent of the population) had private health insurance coverage in 1945. What led to the dramatic increases in coverage during a period of wartime scarcity? [10]

During World War II, large corporations that produced goods for the U.S. military struggled to attract and retain workers as government-imposed wage controls made it virtually impossible for firms to use the carrot of higher wages. The national government responded to this problem by allowing firms (under the auspices of the 1942 Stabilization Act) to offer health benefit packages to their current workers and prospective employees and thereby raise total compensation without raising wages and salaries. The pot was sweetened by a 1943 administrative tax court ruling that allowed employer payments to commercial health insurance companies on behalf of their employees to avoid taxation as employee income. The subsidization of health insurance benefits may have resulted in firms' being more likely to buy coverage for their employees and buying additional coverage on top of existing coverage. [11]

Despite the end of wage and price controls after World War II, the national and state governments continued to allow the wartime benefit package to be offered as untaxed worker compensation. There was, however, considerable confusion about the type and scope of benefits that could be subsidized, and this confusion restricted the expansion of health insurance coverage after World War II. It was not until the Internal Revenue Service codified these provisions in 1954 that a firm could be sure that its contributions to health insurance plans would not be taxed as employee income. By 1957 the IRS regulations had increased the mean value of coverage by 9.5 percent, reduced the net cost of coverage by 17.5 percent, and expanded access to group health coverage by employers.

The private health insurance market would be strongly influenced in the 1960s by the enactment of the Medicare and Medicaid programs, which replaced earlier federal grants to the states dedicated to providing medical care to welfare recipients and the aged. Medicare provides hospital insurance to the elderly (Part A) and provides a voluntary supplementary insurance program (Part B) covering outpatient physician services. Medicaid provides a variety of health care services to individuals meeting means tests. This provision of universal acute-care coverage for Americans over the age of sixty-five represented a dramatic turnaround for the federal government because earlier bills in Congress with this aim had failed to gather sufficient support. On the eve of the passage of Medicare and Medicaid in 1965, less than 2 percent of the annual federal budget was devoted to health care. Medicare and Medicaid changed that equation as expenditures on these programs jumped. Federal expenditures on the Medicaid program accounted for 3.3 percent and 7.3 percent of federal outlays in FY1990 and FY2002, respectively, while the Medicare program accounted for 8.5 percent and 12.6 percent of federal outlays in FY1990 and FY2002, respectively.[12] The aging of the baby boom generation, increases in the cost of health care, and the enactment in 2003 of a complex prescription drug benefit program for the Medicare-eligible population are expected to lead to significant increases in future Medicare expenditures.

Has the program improved the health of its elderly beneficiaries? An exhaustive study of the Medicare-eligible population in the 1990s has concluded that the program has been one of the most effective—if not necessarily the most efficient—social welfare programs in the nation's history. The study arrives at the surprising conclusion that in the Medicare-eligible population, socioeconomic status is connected neither to mortality rates nor to the incidence of most sudden-onset health conditions. These results stand in sharp contrast to those for the rest of the population, in which mortality rates rise as socioeconomic status falls.[13]

Coerced and Free Immigration

Between 1610 and 1807 there were three types of immigrant flows: free, indentured, and coerced. Africans were forcibly brought to the English North American colonies to be slaves, and between 1630 and 1780, roughly 219,000 African American net migrants came to the thirteen colonies. This compares with 475,000 white migrants to the colonies in the same period. The proportion of the total population that was enslaved increased from 4 percent in 1670 to 21 percent in 1780, a combination of higher immigration and birthrates. In 1807 the United States Congress passed legislation to end the coerced immigration of African slaves to the United States effective January 1, 1808.[14]

Many European immigrants financed their voyage to North America by becoming indentured servants. In return for their passage, indentured servants agreed to serve for a fixed term with an employer on terms set in the indenture contract. Although they freely entered into their contracts, they were not free during the term of their contracts. Colonial and state courts played a role in enforcing these contracts but generally did not dispute their terms. The flow of indentured servants declined as slaves became more readily available to the southern colonies after 1750. Remarkably, indentured servitude did not end with the dramatic action of the legislature and the pen of the executive but instead ended in 1835 with the development of superior methods of financing immigration. United States governments did not prohibit immigrant servitude until 1885.[15]

From the beginning of English settlement in the seventeenth century until 1882, free immigration proceeded without significant subsidies or restrictions from either the colonial governments or the national government. Immigration did not proceed evenly but came in waves, with large numbers arriving between 1845 and 1860, during the 1880s, and between 1897 and 1914 (see figure 11.1). Shifts after the Civil War in the composition of immigrant groups from northern Europe to southern Europe, eastern Europe, and China and increases in the overall flow of immigrants to the United States led to a backlash against immigrant workers in the late 1870s as increased competition from unskilled newcomers generated legislative measures to restrict their arrival. Growing political opposition to Chinese immigration in the West and the South led the U.S. Congress in 1879 to pass the "Fifteen Passenger Bill," a measure designed to limit this group that was vetoed by President Rutherford B. Hayes. The first major restrictions on immigration to the United States came with the Chinese Exclusion Act of 1882, which barred additional Chinese from coming to the United States and prevented those already here from becoming citizens. The act was the first major immigration measure to identify an ethnic group for exclusion and stands in stark contrast to the Burlingame Treaty, effected between China and the United States—signed only seventeen years earlier, in 1865—which encouraged Chinese laborers to come to the United States. Between 1891 and 1905, Chinese migrants frequently contested their exclusion in federal courts, and this prompted Congress to transfer responsibility for the enforcement of immigration law from federal courts to the national bureaucracy.[16]

The restrictions on Chinese immigration were extended to Japanese immigration by the 1907–1908 gentlemen's agreement between the United States and Japanese governments. The agreement effectively

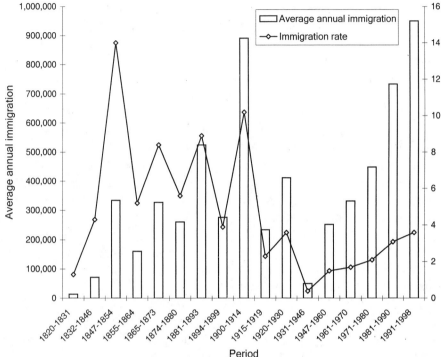

Figure 11.1. Immigration and immigration rate

ended the immigration of Japanese male laborers from Japan and from Hawaii (a U.S. possession after August 1898) to the West Coast of the United States. The 1917 Immigration Act denied entry to people from a "barred zone," a triangular region running from the Arabian peninsula to Indochina to Japan that included Polynesia, Indonesia, and Malaysia and excluded Iran, the Philippines, and Guam.[17]

Although Congress did not impose any restrictions on European immigration prior to 1917, strong political support had been building in Congress after 1897 for additional controls on immigration from southern Europe, with the preferred instrument of exclusion being a literacy test. Between 1897 and 1917, immigration bills containing a literacy test were approved by the House of Representatives on five separate occasions and by the Senate on four occasions. Presidential vetoes prevented early literacy tests from becoming law, but it is noteworthy that the House twice voted to override vetoes of the test, and the Senate voted to override once, when the literacy test was enacted in 1917. States with few foreign-born residents and lightly populated urban areas opposed increased immigration restrictions. The literacy test eventually passed because the South shifted sides in the debate between 1897 and 1917. Reasons for the shift are hard to disentangle, but it may have been due to the South's desire to prevent the North from acquiring a cheaper labor force or the South's recent passage of Jim Crow laws.[18]

The passage of the literacy test requirement was less limiting in 1917 than it would have been in 1897 because literacy was improving in the sending countries. Thus, Congress moved to enact highly restrictive quotas in 1921, 1924, and 1929. Between 1919 and 1965, immigration to the United States was highly limited and for all intents and purposes restricted to European countries, particularly northern and eastern European countries. Trade restrictions imposed in 1930 by the Smoot-Hawley Tariff—and not fully relaxed until the 1950s and 1960s—reinforced the immigration restrictions by shutting off another channel by which foreign unskilled labor could compete with unskilled labor in the United States.[19]

The passage of the 1965 reforms opened the door to larger immigrant flows from a broader mix of countries and placed an emphasis on family reunification. After 1965, the U.S. government began to allow immigration to relieve labor shortages in particular sectors such as agriculture in the 1960s and 1970s and software engineering in the 1990s. From the mid-1980s to the September 11, 2001, terrorist attack, U.S. immigration flows were about the same as in the early twentieth century. They have, however, had a smaller impact on the U.S. economy and on sending economies because the U.S. population has almost tripled, growing from 99 million in 1910 to 287 million in 2002, and the world population has more than tripled, increasing from 1.75 billion in 1910 to 6.14 billion in 2001. Some sending countries have experienced significant reductions in their skilled and overall workforces in recent years.[20] Since the 9/11 attack, legal immigration has declined dramatically while illegal immigration from Mexico and Central America had continued at a rapid pace.

Labor Force Participation

Numerous factors determine whether an individual decides to participate in the labor market and what types of jobs are ultimately found. Market forces and personal choices play major roles, with marital status, education, health, number and age of children, the length of the workday, family wealth, and wage rate all important factors. The national government has played a role in determining labor force participation and choice of jobs via social insurance program, gender bars, racial segregation requirements, federal income tax rates for married couples, and publicly subsidized secondary and higher education programs.

Five major trends in labor force participation can be identified beginning in the late eighteenth century. First, participation by women has exhibited a U-shaped pattern, with declines throughout the nineteenth century, reentry beginning in the 1920s, and sharp increases starting in the 1950s. The U.S. government played a role in cementing the low participation rates of the early twentieth century by enacting "marriage bars" that banned married women from employment in large private firms hiring clerical workers and in public schools. The marriage bars appeared in the late 1800s and reached their peak during World War II. The Great Depression prompted the formalization of these policies by both private firms and government agencies. Section 213 of the 1932 Federal Economy Act prohibited husbands and wives from working simultaneously in the federal civil service. Numerous state and local governments enacted similar restrictions during the 1930s. The marriage bars mirrored and reinforced female labor force participation patterns during this period. "In 1939, of all married women not currently working, but who had worked prior to marriage, more than 80% exited the workplace at the precise time of marriage."[21]

The second major trend is in the rate of nonparticipation in the labor force by men aged forty-five to fifty-four. The nonparticipation rate increased from 4.2 percent in 1948 to 8.4 percent in 1976 to 11.5 percent in 2002. Econometric research has attributed a large portion of this increase to the generous benefits available to totally and permanently disabled workers offered by the Social Security Disability Insurance Program, a program set up in 1956 by amendments to the Social Security Act.[22]

Third, labor force participation rates of young men and women declined over the course of the twentieth century. Although for some young people this may have been due to the effects of legislation restricting child labor, legislation mandating compulsory minimum years of education, or the post–World War II minimum wage, the decline is primarily due to their choice to invest in more years of education. This choice was facilitated (as I discuss below) by the rapid growth of publicly subsidized secondary education after 1890 and publicly subsidized higher education after 1944.

Fourth, there was a secular decline in the retirement age over the course of the twentieth century. Labor force participation rates of sixty-year-olds fell from 96 percent in 1880 to 81 percent in 1940 to 66 percent in 1990; the rates for sixty-five-year-olds fell from 90 percent in 1880 to 68 percent in 1940 to 39 percent in 1990. Rates fell even further for those at higher ages, with rates for seventy-year-olds falling from 81 percent in 1880 to 22 percent in 1990. Earlier retirement from the labor force has been partially induced by the presence of the federal government's Social Security program, as the wealth embodied in the promised annuity payments has raised the demand for leisure among older Americans.[23]

Fifth, since the establishment of the federal income tax in 1913, economists have regularly debated the effect of federal payroll and income tax rates on labor force participation. The issue is of particular importance because marginal federal and state income tax rates, Social Security payroll tax rates, and Medicare payroll taxes rates have changed substantially over the course of the past century.[24] The U.S. Congress has episodically increased the Medicare tax, the Social Security tax, and the labor income base against which both taxes are applied. In 1937, the Social Security payroll tax was rolled out at 3 percent of the wage (on wages up to $3,000), with employers withholding 1.5 percent of an employee's compensation and making a matching payment. By 1990, the sum of employer and employee Social Security taxes had increased to 12.4 percent on labor compensation up to a specified cap. By 2004, the cap had increased to $87,900. In 1966 the Medicare payroll tax was rolled out with a tax rate of 0.35 percent of labor compensation up to a cap of $6,600, with employers withholding 0.175 percent of an employee's compensation and making a matching payment. In 1994, the cap on labor compensation subject to the Medicare tax was repealed, thereby subjecting all labor earnings to the tax. Marginal rates for the federal income tax have varied considerably over time, but average marginal rates have tended to drift upward, a trend corresponding to the increase in the size of the national government. State income taxes were generally enacted after World War II, and state marginal tax rates drifted upward through the 1980s before stabilizing and declining in some states during the 1990s.[25]

Consider the following computations of an average marginal tax rate using the federal income tax, the Social Security payroll tax, and the Medicare payroll tax. From 1915 to 1939, the average marginal tax rate fluctuated between 0.3 and 2.8, rising during World War I, falling during the 1920s, and rising again in the 1930s owing to income tax increases engineered by Presidents Herbert Hoover and Franklin Roosevelt. The World War II period represents a discrete jump, with the average marginal tax rate increasing to 15.0 percent in 1945. The average marginal tax rate fell slightly in the late 1940s, increased again during the Korean War, and by 1963 exceeded its wartime peak with a value of 15.5 percent. The tax cuts sponsored by President John F. Kennedy—which reduced the statutory marginal federal income tax rate of the highest-income taxpayers from 90 to 70 percent—reduced the average marginal rate to 13.7 percent in 1965, but the decrease proved to be short-lived. The rate showed an upward trend starting in 1966, reaching a value of 20.2 percent in 1981. The 1981–1984 tax cuts proposed by President Ronald Reagan—which reduced the statutory marginal federal income tax rate of higher-income taxpayers from 70 to 50 percent—were partly offset by increases in the Social Security and Medicare payroll tax rates as the average marginal tax rate fluctuated between 17.1 and 18.9 percent from 1982 to 1994.[26]

The effects of changes in state and federal payroll and income taxes on labor force participation, hours, and effort have been hotly debated. In general, cross-sectional studies of men between the ages of twenty-five and fifty-five show that changes in after-tax wages produced only small responses in number of hours worked and in participation. Among married women—particularly those in upper-income families that previously faced high marginal rates during the 1970s and early 1980s—the response in terms of hours worked was, once again, small, but the response in labor force participation was considerably larger.[27]

Education and Job Training Programs

Studies of economic growth patterns have identified the education of the population as a key determinant of the economic success of nations. The U.S. practice of providing increasing amounts of education to the general public has been a key factor in maintaining America's position as the leading economy in the world. Although education was largely a private affair in the colonial period, local governments and later state governments became heavily involved in providing universal education to the populace. In the latter half of the twentieth century the national government increasingly expanded its role in funding and overseeing the educational process.

Primary Education

Households in the colonies invested substantially in primary education; literacy rates among free adult males were typically higher than those in England in the mid-seventeenth century. Colonial literacy rates appear to have declined somewhat at the end of the century owing to geographic dispersion of the growing population and the difficulty that new towns experienced in building schools. Literacy rates in English America rose throughout the eighteenth century and remained higher than those in England.[28]

From the seventeenth century to the early nineteenth century, young boys and girls in New England were often sent to a "dame school," where women taught basic subjects—reading, writing, spelling, arithmetic, and religion—in their homes for a fee. In some instances, towns paid the fee for poor students. After completing dame school, boys would then either train in a trade or go to a "Latin" school where they would learn mathematics, Latin, Greek, history, literature, and some natural science. In the middle colonies, religious orders ran most schools. Their support came from a variety of public and private sources, including appropriations, land grants, endowments, and tuition. In the South, the distances between large farms often meant that students were home-schooled, with children from wealthier families receiving training from tutors.

The United States has a long history of state government passage of compulsory education and attendance laws dating back to the Massachusetts Act of 1642, the first compulsory education law in the English colonies. Enacted in response to concerns of Puritan leaders that non-Puritan settlers were not educating their children sufficiently, the act required that parents ensure that their children learn to read and write or face loss of custody. In 1647 Massachusetts passed additional legislation (the "Old Deluder Satan" school law) requiring towns with more than fifty households to form a school and towns with more than one hundred households to form a secondary ("Latin grammar") school. Funding for these schools came from a variety of sources, including tuition, taxes, entrance fees, and charges for firewood.

A specific mechanism for providing some public support to schools offering primary education was embodied in the Land Ordinance, passed by the Continental Congress on May 20, 1785. The ordinance specified the way in which U.S. government lands would be surveyed and sold in the Northwest Territory. It required that one section of land (section 16) in new townships be set aside for the maintenance of a school. In 1853 Congress increased the number of sections of land to be set aside in California from one to two (sections 16 and 36), and later it would reserve four sections of each township in the southwestern territories. The changes were instituted because of the low value of land in these regions.

The Ordinance of the Northwest Territory—enacted by the Continental Congress on July 13, 1787, to form a territorial government, to secure settler rights, and to set conditions for admission as a state—sets forth a broad justification for the new territorial governments to encourage the founding of new schools to serve their new settlers. Article III of the ordinance states simply that "[r]eligion, morality, and knowledge, being necessary to good government and the happiness of mankind, schools and the means of education shall forever be encouraged." By stressing the link between schools and good governance (which is, in the economist's parlance, a "public good"), the ordinance opens the door for government to "encourage" schools, a broad declaration that might involve subsidies or merely careful attention by territorial and county governments to the legal and financial frameworks within which schools were founded and maintained.

In 1779 Thomas Jefferson suggested that all white children in Virginia receive three years of free primary education. Boys with strong records in primary school would continue their schooling at privately operated academies receiving some public funds. The cream of the crop would then attend the College of William and Mary, which would provide scholarships for smart students and indigent students. Jefferson's vision of universal, free primary education would, however, not begin to take form in U.S. schools until the 1820s.

Between 1780 and 1820, the colonial pattern of many distinct types of schools receiving funds from both private and public sources persisted, with enrollments expanding to cover an increasing percentage of school-age children. Local government revenues from property taxes were combined with state revenues from the sale of new surveyed lands (in states that still had new lands to survey) and revenues from "rate bills," which were tuition bills assessed to children's families based on attendance (for days exceeding a fixed number of free days) or the school term. For example, between 1828 and 1868, state and local tax revenues financed 50 percent of teacher salaries in New York school districts, and rate bills financed the other half. Wealthier families in rate bill states often chose to send their children to private schools because the funds used to pay the rate bill could otherwise be used to pay private tuition. Children of poor families who could not afford to pay the rate bill were relegated to "pauper" schools.[29]

From 1794 through the 1820s, states in the Northeast passed laws enabling towns to impose property taxes to finance private and public schools and allowing parents to be assessed with the rate bills that covered a portion of the costs associated with their children's enrollment in public schools. A backlash against the bills developed soon after their imposition as education reformers led movements in several Northeast

states to abolish rate bills and eliminate pauper schools. Two prominent educators, Horace Mann in Massachusetts and Henry Barnard in
Connecticut, argued that states should ensure free access to primary
schools, compel attendance by young students, and mandate that certain
topics be taught in all primary schools. They believed that "common
schools" would help assimilate the new waves of immigrants of different nationalities and religions into American life. They would provide
students with a mixture of academic and social skills that would later
enhance their productivity at jobs in the rising manufacturing sector.
Mann, Barnard, and other prominent educators pushed for more than
just the establishment of common schools: they also worked to establish
mechanisms to ensure their quality, to raise the standards required of
their teachers, and to lengthen the school year and school day.

Their arguments provided the rationale for state governments to become more extensively involved in regulating the provision of primary
education in the 1830s and 1840s, when some states repealed rate laws
and formed state boards of education that developed curriculum criteria
for use by all primary schools. The new "common schools" that emerged
from this process shared several important characteristics. They had
the goal of providing a common education to rich and poor children.
They were controlled and maintained by towns. They were nondenom-
inational, a critical feature in communities with both Protestant and
Catholic populations. They were open to free youth; those in the South
excluded African Americans. And, rather than being financed by user
fees, their revenues came primarily (but not exclusively) from property
taxes paid by an older property-owning generation, many of whom no
longer had children enrolled in school.

In 1827 Massachusetts became the first state to repeal its rate bill
law, imposing a requirement that towns with more than fifty families
provide free primary education. The repeal process took hold gradually
in other states, with large cities often repealing rate bills and establishing common schools before the state government repealed the enabling
legislation. Repeal was not achieved in some northeastern states until
after the Civil War. By 1871, all states in the North and the West had
followed suit. Repeal of rate bill laws was imposed on southern states
during the 1870s by various Reconstruction-Era measures.

Did the repeal of rate bills and the establishment of common schools
make a difference in enrollment and attendance rates? Sparse, low-
quality data for public school enrollment during this period limit our
ability to draw strong conclusions. Studies of this question have found

that the repeal of the rate bills was associated with only small changes in enrollment and attendance rates. One rationale for this result is that enrollment rates had already risen to high levels in rate bill states owing to the substantial number of free days provided before daily rates were charged.[30]

With free primary education available to all children nationwide by the end of the 1870s, states turned their attention to compulsory education laws, which required all children to complete a primary education. By 1918, all forty-eight states had passed such requirements. A study of the impact of compulsory education laws on primary enrollments concluded that they were largely ineffective.[31]

Secondary Education

The first publicly supported high school in the English colonies, the Boston Latin School, was established in 1635, but it did not set a trend. For the next 250 years, the overwhelming majority of students desiring a secondary education (grades 9–12) would attend a private school or receive instruction from private tutors. During the first half of the nineteenth century, privately provided and almost exclusively privately supported secondary schools, known as academies, proliferated throughout the United States. Some academies focused on preparing students for college, and others provided a mixture of academic and vocational training. One study estimated that by 1850 academies (outside the South) enrolled 13.5 percent of children eligible to enroll in secondary schools.[32]

Declining enrollment rates of secondary school-age children from 1850 and 1880 and the rise of the free public high school after the Civil War generated a downward spiral in the number of academies. The seeds of their demise were already being sown even as they spread rapidly between 1820 and 1850. In the 1820s several large cities opened free public high schools, and by the eve of the Civil War, there were more than 320 such schools. As free public high schools became more common in both urban and rural school districts, parents increasingly chose to send their children to the free public high school rather than to pay the substantial tuitions charged by private academies.

The stage for increased local government funding of high schools was set by the "Kalamazoo Case," the 1874 decision of the Michigan Supreme Court which established that Michigan school districts could use public funds to support secondary education.[33] States outside the South supported the growth of public secondary schools by passing "free tuition" laws from 1907 to 1925. These laws mandated that a child's home school district pay tuition to a nearby district if the home district did not provide a public secondary school for the student to attend. The free tuition laws were not enforced for African American children in the South. Such laws may have had an impact on secondary enrollment because as late as 1932 (the first year for which these data were collected), only one in five of the nation's 130,000 school districts had a public high school. (The number of school districts has since steadily declined, leaving only 15,000 districts in 2000.)

School enrollment rates of children eligible for secondary school declined between 1850 and 1880, but the demand for secondary education increased dramatically thereafter. In part this was because business and government needed workers with more specialized education. Advances in science required an increased specialization of academic disciplines, and the rise of big business and large-scale retailing fueled demands for workers who could use new office machineries, work with numbers, and read directions. Enrollment rates in public and private high schools increased to 18 percent in 1910 and then soared to 71 percent in 1940. High school graduation rates increased concomitantly from 9 percent in 1910 to 51 percent in 1940.[34]

Did laws requiring children to attend an additional year of secondary school—implemented by increasing the age for obtaining a work permit—increase educational attainment, or were these laws merely enacted in tandem with the increased demand for education? A recent study found that one additional year of required education increased overall attainment of individuals who reached age fourteen between 1915 and 1939 by roughly 5 percent. In addition, the study concluded that continuation laws—mandating that working youth attend school on a part-time basis—were ineffective at improving education for those in the upper half of the education distribution but were highly effective in increasing educational attainment among individuals in the lower 25 percent of the distribution. Another recent study reaffirmed the initial study, finding that only 5 percent of the increase in high school enrollment and educational attainment for individuals reaching age fourteen between 1910 and 1939 was due to the passage of state-level compulsory schooling and child labor laws.[35]

State governments provided an increasingly large share of the funding of primary and secondary education over the course of the twentieth century. In 1925, local governments financed 84 percent of such expenditures. By 1940, local governments financed 68 percent of such expenditures, the states 30 percent, and the federal government 2 percent.

In 1999, local governments financed only 44 percent of such expenditures, the states 49 percent, and the federal government 7 percent.[36] A portion of the increased financing by state governments was due to state legislation requiring some equalization of expenditure across school districts and to state court decisions mandating such equalization, usually under the guise of equal protection clauses in state constitutions.

The federal government's involvement in primary and secondary education was virtually nonexistent until 1898, when the U.S. Supreme Court issued its famous ruling in *Plessy v. Ferguson,* which allowed public school districts to run racially segregated but "equal" schools. This decision signaled to school districts that the federal courts would not intervene with respect to their treatment of African American and white children. The equally famous decision in *Brown v. Board of Education* (1954) would trigger massive federal involvement in education, with federal judges ordering elementary and secondary schools throughout the country to desegregate. To accomplish that objective, federal judges ordered school districts in the North and the South to bus black and white students to new schools and in some cases took over the administration of the school district when their orders were defied. Integration of public schools led some white families, particularly in the South, to change the enrollment of their children from public to private schools and to move from inner-city neighborhoods to suburban ones that were, at least initially, outside the scope of the court-ordered busing plans.

The *Brown* decision ushered in a new era in which minorities, women, and learning-disabled students had increasing access to primary and secondary education from public schools.[37] Title VII of the Civil Rights Act of 1964 had enormous implications for women because it forced public schools across the educational spectrum to provide programs for women that had previously been offered only for men. Highly visible effects are the expansion in sports programs for women and the increase in admissions to and graduations from professional schools (for example, law, medicine, and architecture) that graduated predominantly male classes as late as the mid-1960s. (See chapter 8 for a discussion of the impact of civil rights legislation on the education of African Americans.)

In the nineteenth century, federal involvement in secondary education was limited to its grants of public lands. Federal appropriations dedicated to secondary education had a relatively late start. They began with the Smith-Hughes Vocational Act of 1917, which subsidized high school courses focusing on agriculture, trades, and home economics.

The federal share of public elementary and secondary revenues had gradually increased to 4.4 percent in 1957, before it bounced up to roughly 8 percent in the mid-1960s with the passage of the National Defense Education Act of 1958 (providing aid for teaching science, mathematics, and foreign languages) and the Elementary and Secondary Education Act of 1965. The federal share of public education expenditures continued to increase through the 1970s, reaching 11.9 percent in 1980, the year in which the Department of Education was established as a U.S. cabinet agency. The federal share of education expenditures then abruptly reversed course, falling to just 8 percent in 1996.[38]

The fall in federal expenditures is somewhat surprising, because in 1983 a federal commission had issued a report titled *A Nation at Risk* that harshly criticized the state of public education in the United States. It found that test scores of U.S. students had declined since the 1960s while the performance of overseas students had increased dramatically. The commission's report set in motion a two-decade-long examination of the nation's public school systems and prompted Congress to pass several rounds of legislation in the 1990s that increased federal regulation of the K–12 education provided by public schools. This intrusion into education policy increased significantly in 2002 when President George W. Bush signed the No Child Left Behind Act. The act requires states to test students in grades 3–8 in reading and math in order to identify poorly performing schools. School districts are mandated to allow parents to transfer their children out of schools that fail to attain stipulated gains in math and reading achievement. Schools that fail to improve are required to offer their students additional services, such as private tutoring, to replace poorly performing teachers, and to change their curriculum to facilitate learning of basic math and reading skills. Failure to respond to the act's strict rules opens the door for the State Board of Education to assume control over the failing school.[39]

Higher Education

Until the late eighteenth century all colleges and universities in the United States were private institutions. Harvard College, the first such institution, was founded in 1636 to educate Puritan ministers. As other religious groups became more firmly established, new colleges were founded to educate ministers in their theologies and traditions. Consider the College of William and Mary (1693; Anglican), Yale University (1701; Congregationalist), Princeton University (1746; New Lights Presbyterian), Columbia University (1754; Anglican), Brown University

(1765; Baptist), and Rutgers University (1766; Dutch Reformed). The minority of students who attended and did not become ministers often studied law and became some of the most prominent lawyers and politicians of the late eighteenth and early nineteenth century—among them John Adams, Thomas Jefferson, James Madison, and Alexander Hamilton. Private colleges enrolling women came much later, with Mt. Holyoke Female Seminary (1837), Elmira College (1853), Vassar College (1861), Wellesley College (1871), Smith College (1871), and Bryn Mawr College (1881) among the first to be established.

Public provision of higher education began in the South. The University of Georgia was chartered in 1785 although no students matriculated until 1801; North Carolina chartered its state university in 1787 and started teaching in 1795. Publicly funded universities received a strong boost from the Morrill Act of 1862, which provided each state with thirty thousand acres of federal land per Congressman in the U.S. Senate and the House. The act directed the states to sell these lands and to invest the proceeds in an endowment fund to support "land grant" colleges specializing in agriculture and mechanical arts. The 1887 Hatch Act, providing funds to establish agriculture experimentation stations at the land grant colleges, the second Morrill Act of 1890, and the Bankhead-Jones Act of 1935 all provided additional federal funding or grants of federal lands to support the land-grant universities.

State support for public colleges and universities increased from 5.1 percent of state and local government expenditures in 1929 to 11.0 percent in 1940. Support varied greatly across states, with New England states spending only $458 per one thousand residents in 1929 and mountain states spending $2,057. States with higher expenditures tended to be newer states without established private colleges and universities, wealthier states, states with more homogeneous populations (reducing the potential for political clashes over the amount and composition of public expenditures), and states with higher shares of employment in mining, manufacturing, and agriculture. History matters with respect to public support for higher education. There is a strong positive correlation (.44) between state support for higher education in 1929 and state support in 1994, and there is a strong positive correlation (.61) between public college enrollments in 1929 and public college enrollments in 1994.

Several million members of the U.S. military who were demobilized after World War II received a big bonus: education benefits conferred by the Serviceman's Readjustment Act, known more popularly as the GI Bill. Educational benefits were awarded to individuals (rather than institutions), they depended on length of service and age, and they could be used at colleges and universities or for vocational, technical, and apprenticeship training. Turner and Bound (2003) have argued that the GI Bill had an enormous effect on educational aspirations of veterans. "One study, conducted by the Information and Education Division of the Army in 1944, just after the announcement of the GI Bill, showed the remarkable power of the benefits in changing educational aspirations. Prior to the announcement of benefits, only 7 percent of enlisted men indicated that they planned further training or education after the war. After the announcement, 29 percent of white enlisted men and 43 percent of black enlisted men expressed a definite interest in education and training after the war." [40]

The GI Bill was, however, not extended to broader federal funding of higher education owing to opposition in Congress to an increased federal presence in higher education. The shock (and awe) caused by the Soviet Union's launch of the *Sputnik I* satellite on October 4, 1957, led to widespread concern that the United States was falling behind the Soviet Union in mathematics and the sciences. Congress responded by passing the National Defense Education Act of 1958, which provided for low-interest student loans for private and public college students; cancellation of loans for students who became teachers; funds to promote the teaching of natural sciences in high schools; and graduate fellowships in the sciences, mathematics, and engineering.

Congress authorized a massive expansion of aid to college students with the 1965 passage of the Higher Education Act. Title IV authorized the College Work-Study Program and the Guaranteed Student Loan Program, both of which would expand massively during the following decade. In 1972 Congress modified the legislation to allow students enrolled in community colleges, vocational schools, and qualified training programs to receive federal grants and loans. Basic Grants (renamed Pell Grants) were established in the 1972 legislation to provide a minimum level of support for needy students. Since 1972 Congress has repeatedly tinkered with the details of these programs. The overall result has been a massive expansion of federal grants and guaranteed loans to students enrolled in postsecondary education programs. By 1993–94, the federal government was guaranteeing roughly $35 billion in student loans.

Job Training Programs

Federal job training programs got their start in 1958 and have taken many forms. Some of the programs have served clients who have voluntarily signed up, and others have been tied to public assistance benefits. Some programs help clients search for work, and others provide classroom training at vocational schools or community colleges, in-plant training, and comprehensive services. Federal job training programs have proceeded through three major programmatic phases.[41]

Phase one began with the passage of the Manpower Development and Training Act (MDTA) in 1962, which, after the passage of the Economic Opportunity Act in 1964, was directed toward serving welfare recipients and youths from low-income families. In 1968 "MDTA programs provided 140,000 persons classroom training at a cost of $6,500 (1994 dollars) per participant, and 125,000 persons on-the-job training at a cost of $3,000 per participant," according to Robert LaLonde. One MDTA program, the Job Corps, which provides comprehensive residential services such as counseling, education, training, work experience, and health care to disadvantaged youth, is still in place. The program has increased the number of clients served and been reduced in scope since its inception, serving 40,600 persons in FY1966 at an annual per-person cost of $37,000 (in 1994 dollars) and 104,000 persons in FY1994 at an annual per-person cost of $16,000.[42]

During the second phase, in the early 1970s, Congress replaced MDTA with the Comprehensive Employment and Training Act (CETA). The act transferred the operation and administration of training and employment programs to the states while providing them with block grants to aid low-income unemployed and economically disadvantaged people. The law also took over and received increased funding for a program providing temporary public service jobs to eligible unemployed persons. Total spending amounted to $8.4 billion dollars by FY1981.

In the 1980s, during the third phase, Congress replaced CETA with the Job Training Partnership Act (JTPA), ending the public service jobs component of CETA and reorienting its programs from training disadvantaged workers to providing services for unemployed dislocated (but not necessarily disadvantaged) workers. These new services complemented those provided under a program established in the early 1960s, the Trade Adjustment Assistance (TAA) program, which provided assistance to workers who lost their jobs owing to export competition. Another group of federal programs mandates that welfare recipients participate in these programs.

Have these job training programs been effective? A number of studies have concluded that adult women tend to attain modest earnings gains after participation in these training programs, men attain lower and more variable earnings gains, and, with the possible exception of the Job Corps, disadvantaged youth typically do not attain consistently positive earnings gains. Even for programs that initially generated positive benefits for participants, their earnings gains usually evaporated after several years. Mandatory programs are also notable for not consistently generating positive gains for their clients. Job search assistance programs directed toward displaced workers stand out from the pack, because they typically generate positive earnings benefits. A recent study aptly summarized the literature by concluding that the "aggregate effects of JTPA are minimal, both on the legally defined target population and on the labor force as a whole" and that the contributions of mandatory programs "to reducing poverty almost certainly have been slight."[43]

Regulation of Labor Markets after World War II

After World War II, the U.S. Congress enacted numerous regulations and programs that have collectively dropped onto labor markets like an avalanche. A national minimum wage was established in 1938; it was greatly increased and its scope expanded after World War II. Economists have hotly debated its impact ever since. Social insurance programs funded by payroll taxes have expanded, increasing payroll taxes and potentially affecting both the supply of and demand for labor. With the Taft-Hartley Act of 1947 and the Landrum-Griffin Act of 1959, Congress has twice passed legislation designed to restrict union behavior and influence and to structure union governance. The Occupational Safety and Health Administration has imposed numerous restrictions on the type of job environments within which employees can legally work (see chapter 15 for a discussion of the impact of OSHA on labor markets). And the 1964 Civil Rights Act and the 1991 Americans with Disabilities Act both imposed new requirements on the personnel practices of small, medium, and large firms.

Labor Unions after World War II

Chapter 13 chronicles how the passage of the National Industrial Recovery Act in 1933 and the introduction of the National Labor Relations Board dramatically changed the atmosphere for collective bargaining in the United States. The recognition of workers' rights to collectively bargain with employers and the development of a legal framework for collective bargaining led to a dramatic surge in union membership from less than 3.5 million workers in 1929 to 8.5 million workers in 1940. During World War II (see chapter 14), there were only a few strikes (which had little impact on production), union leaders served on federal regulatory commissions, the War Labor Board was instituted to settle labor disputes, and union recruitment of new workers accelerated. By 1946, union membership had soared to more than 14 million workers.

After World War II, unions and employers fought over the readjustment of compensation packages when the federal government ended its wartime wage and price controls in 1946. Work stoppages soared to record levels in the 1945–46 period, and public concern about the disruptions produced new legislation restricting union activity: the 1947 Taft-Hartley Act, passed over President Harry S. Truman's veto. Although the act mandated collective bargaining between an employer and a union and prohibited very narrowly defined "featherbedding" practices, its key provision was section 14B, which permitted states to pass right-to-work laws, which prohibited firms from requiring workers to become union members to keep their jobs. By 1966 nineteen states, most of them in the South, had passed right-to-work laws. Over the course of the next forty years, most states stuck with their original choices. During that time only five states would change their status. In 2006, twenty-two states had right-to-work laws after Indiana repealed its law and four states passed new right-to-work laws.[44]

A 1975 study of the initial impact found that states that had them in 1953 had unionization rates 4.6 percent lower than other states had in 1939, eight years prior to the enactment of Taft-Hartley, and unionization rates 4.5 percent lower than those of other states in 1953, six years after the law's passage. It concluded that Taft-Hartley's section 14B had little initial effect on unionization. A survey of more recent econometric studies of right-to-work laws found very different results: such laws generally have negative effects on unionization rates, positive effects on worker free-riding (defined as workers' receiving union benefits on the job without joining the union), and variable effects on wages.[45]

A series of congressional right-to-work hearings held in 1957–58 uncovered corrupt behavior by union leaders and instances in which dissenting union members were punished and their voices suppressed. The hearings made the chief counsel of the Senate Select Committee on Improper Activities in the Labor or Management Field, Robert Kennedy Jr., famous and also led to the passage of the Landrum-Griffin Act in 1959. The act required unions to issue periodic reports on their finances, allow free speech by members, and hold regular elections of officers.

Union membership peaked in 1953 at 26 percent of the civilian labor force and has been in continual decline since then, with just 11.6 percent of the civilian labor force counted as union members in 2000. There are four main reasons for the decline, the primary one being the decline of U.S. manufacturing industries. Since manufacturing workers are more likely to be unionized than other workers, the decline in the share of the manufacturing sector in national output and the even more rapid decline in the share of manufacturing workers in employment led to a decline in the overall rate of employee unionization. Similar reasoning applies to the rapid growth of female labor force participation starting in the 1950s, because females have historically been less likely to become union members than males. The steady postwar migration of the U.S. population from union states in the Northeast and the Midwest to right-to-work states in the South and West has also contributed to the decline in union membership. Finally, since the mid-1970s large firms in oligopolistic industries (where a few firms account for most of total production) have encountered more competition from foreign and domestic firms owing to globalization, trade liberalization, and domestic deregulation. Since increased competition in a firm's product market makes the quantity it can sell more responsive to price changes (creates an increase in the elasticity of demand, in the economists' parlance), firms find that paying wage premiums to unionized workers risks large reductions in sales and employment. Recognizing this, employees have become less interested in being represented by a labor union.

The decline in union membership among private-sector workers has been offset partially by a rapid increase in union membership among state, local, and federal government workers in the past forty-five years. The 1935 Wagner Act specifically excluded government employees from collective bargaining, and it was not until 1959 that Wisconsin became the first state to allow some employees of the state and local governments to form unions and to bargain collectively. By 2001, thirty-five states had changed their laws to allow public workers to unionize. In ten of these states, some public employees including teachers are allowed to strike, whereas the police and some others are not. Federal employees' unions had existed in various forms since 1912 (when workers in navy shipyards organized) but only became a major force after President John F. Kennedy issued Executive Order 10988 in 1962. It allowed for exclusive recognition of federal employees' unions and established the right of the unions to bargain with the federal government. In 2001, 37.4 percent of local, state, and federal workers were union members.

Has unionization of public workers led to higher compensation packages? One study examined the compensation of union and nonunion fire departments during the early 1980s and found that union wages were only slightly higher than nonunion wages whereas the fringe benefits (pension, health plans, sick days, and vacation) in the union contracts were much higher than those in the nonunion contracts. Another study examined a broader set of public workers' contracts negotiated in the early 1980s and found that unions representing police, fire, sanitation, and other municipal workers were able to negotiate only small wage premiums—an average of 3.6 percent—compared to nonunion wages but were much more effective in achieving increases in fringe benefits, with large increases in paid time off from work and pensions being the most notable. These differences may occur because elected officials serving for a limited number of terms are more likely to agree to future benefit increases, which accrue far beyond their terms in office, than to wage bills due during their terms in office.[46]

State and Federal Minimum Wage Laws

The establishment of a national minimum wage in 1938 (discussed in chapter 13) had a strong impact on hours and employment during its first decade in force. A vast number of studies of the impact of the minimum wage on employment after World War II consistently found a negative relation between the level of the inflation-adjusted minimum wage and hours worked. Most of the controversy concerned the size of the reduction in hours, and debate focused on whether the trade-off between a higher wage for low-skill workers who kept their jobs and higher unemployment rates among youth and workers with fewer than twelve years of schooling was beneficial to society.[47]

Over the course of the past fifty years, some states have passed minimum wage laws that impose in-state minimums that are above the national minimum. One highly publicized study exploited these cross-state differences to study the effect of a 1992 hike in New Jersey's minimum wage on hours worked in fast-food restaurants. The neighboring state of Pennsylvania, which did not increase its minimum wage, was used as a control. The study concluded that the hike in the minimum wage did not seem to reduce hours worked by fast-food workers. Other researchers have criticized this study, finding that it lacked data about the number of hours worked by full-time and part-time workers and therefore had to make assumptions about the number of hours worked by each group. Using actual payroll data from fast-food restaurants in New Jersey and Pennsylvania, they found that the hike in New Jersey's minimum wage decreased employment.[48]

Other critics have noted that fast-food hamburgers are typically a nontraded good—most of us do not usually travel across state lines or international borders to find a cheaper burger, particularly if we live in Hawaii or Alaska. Since most consumers make up somewhat of a captive audience for fast-food restaurants in their area, the additional costs of the minimum wage are more likely to be passed on to consumers in the form of higher burger prices rather than realized as fewer fast-food establishments, shorter hours of operation, and employment losses. Manufacturers of a good traded in competitive interstate markets would, however, find it more difficult to maintain employment when the state's minimum wage increased, because they would not be able to raise the good's price in response to the state's minimum wage hike.

Lost in this discussion are two major points. First, although Congress has periodically increased the nominal minimum wage, the inflation-adjusted minimum wage has declined by more than 30 percent from its peak in the early 1970s (see figure 11.2). This means that the minimum wage has become a less binding constraint for businesses than it was

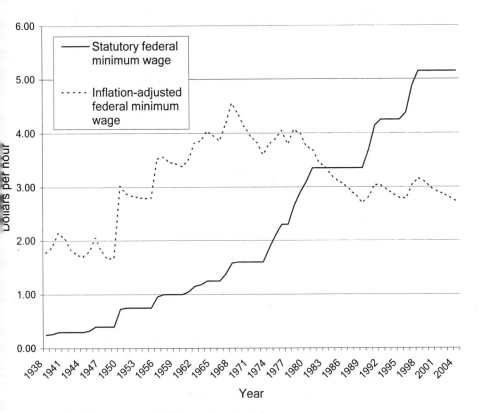

Figure 11.2. Statutory and inflation-adjusted minimum wage rates

Note: The statutory minimum wage was deflated by the Consumer Price Index—All Urban Consumers, with 1982–1984 as the base time period.

during the three decades following World War II. Second, although the inflation-adjusted federal minimum wage has shown a downward trend in the past three decades, as of 2005 seventeen states had state minimum wage rates that exceeded the federal minimum wage, sometimes by as much as 40 percent. The variation in rates across states is significant because it allows states to tie their minimum wage rates more closely to regional labor market conditions. This should serve to reduce the labor market distortions in lower-wage states that a higher federal minimum wage would have produced. Thus, the continuing controversy about the minimum wage seems to be somewhat of an academic discussion given the declining importance of this regulation in the national political economy.

Civil Rights Legislation

Three civil rights acts—the Equal Pay Act of 1963, the Civil Rights Act of 1964, and the Civil Rights Act of 1991—contain provisions focusing on discrimination in hiring, firing, and setting wages and salaries by race and gender. (See chapter 8 for a discussion of the ways national civil rights legislation has changed the treatment of African Americans in labor markets.) Between 1967 and 1988, Congress passed legislation banning certain types of age discrimination in employment and a number of bills regulating access of people with disabilities to public facilities and discrimination against people with disabilities in labor markets.

The Americans with Disabilities Act (ADA) was hailed as a landmark advance for people with disabilities when it was enacted in 1991. The ADA mandates that medium- and large-size firms offer "reasonable accommodation" to their disabled employees; it also prohibits firms from discrimination in hiring, firing, and setting wages on the basis of employee or applicant disabilities. Some have hailed the ADA as a mechanism for improving the productivity of disabled workers while others decry the expensive accommodations that it ostensibly requires and the litigation it generates. The ADA has reduced the employment of Americans with disabilities by middle-sized firms, with employment of men aged twenty-one to thirty-nine dropping sharply in 1991 and the employment of women in the same age group dropping sharply in 1992. Since the ADA provides protection against arbitrary firing of disabled workers, one might expect that the separation rate of disabled workers would fall after the ADA became law. Yet a 2001 study has found no evidence that the separation rate changed after the ADA's passage.[49]

Conclusion

The governments of the United States have played varying roles in determining the size of the population, its health and human capital, and the organization of labor markets. As in most areas, government's role, in particular that played by the federal government, has expanded over time. Immigration, which was virtually unrestricted prior to 1872, became highly regulated after World War I. In the post–9/11 environment, the ratchet effect appears to be operative once again, with new, discretionary standards emerging that leave substantial power over every entry in the hands of government officials. By contrast, birth control is less heavily regulated and more available in 2005 than it was in 1872, the eve of the passage of the restrictive Comstock Law. In most areas—health, education, and regulation of labor markets—an avalanche of new regulations and programs has left the United States with a crazy quilt of market-supporting interventions and income-transferring interventions. In a world of natural and artificial distortions, it is often difficult to sort out which regulations and programs fall into which boxes. And that, of course, is one role that historical economics can play, as the full range of the American experience forces us to realize that the effects of programs and regulations change over time, that programs and regulations evolve in both structure and efficacy as the environment changes, and that complex ones need intense study in their full historical range if we are ever to understand them.

Notes

1. Population growth had a fourth proximate determinate that was closely controlled by the U.S. government: territorial expansion. The purchase of the Louisiana Territory from France during the Napoleonic Wars, the conquest of the Southwest and California from Mexico, the settlement of claims in the Pacific Northwest, the purchase of Alaska from Russia, the annexation of Hawaii, and the annexation of some of Spain's former colonies (Puerto Rico and Guam) provided prime lands, ports, and natural resources to attract waves of new settlers.

2. All data on post-1850 birthrates are from Susan B. Carter, Scott Sigmund Gartner, Michael R. Haines, Alan L. Olmstead, Richard Sutch, and Gavin Wright, eds., *Historical Statistics of the United States: Earliest Times to the Present, Millennial Edition*, vol. 1, table Ab40-51, p. 1-399 (New York: Cambridge University Press, 2006). The percentage of blacks enslaved in 1850 is taken from ibid., table Aa145-184, p. 1-48.

3. See Margo 2000 for a full discussion of wage trends in nineteenth-century labor markets.

4. The baby boom in the West resulted from rising birth rates, whereas the baby boom in the developing world resulted from declining infant and child

mortality rates. See Feeney and Mason 2001. Economists disagree about why the U.S. baby boom occurred. Economists affiliated with the University of Chicago emphasized the competing effects of income on the ability to afford children and of the value of women's time on the affordability of children. See Becker 1960, Becker and Lewis 1974, and Willis 1974. By contrast, Butz and Ward (1979) argued that fertility increased after the war because rising income led to an increased demand for children. Although the wages of women and, hence, the opportunity costs of childbearing were also rising, the effects were muted because many women were not part of the labor force. See also Easterlin 1968 for a completely different perspective.

5. United States v. One Package Containing 120 More or Less, Rubber Pessaries to Prevent Conception, 86 F.2d 737 (2d Cir. 1936). The official title of the "Comstock Act" is the Postal Act of 1873. The law's nickname refers to Anthony Comstock, founder of the New York Society for the Suppression of Vice.

6. The discussion of the impact of the birth control pill relies on Goldin and Katz 2002. The full citation is Griswold v. Connecticut, 381 U.S. 489 (1965). In 1972 the Court extended the right to birth control to single people. Eisenstadt v. Baird, 405 U.S. 432 (1972).

7. The discussion in the text draws extensively from Levine 2004. The full citation of the decision is Roe v. Wade, 410 U.S. 113 (1973). Roe must be considered in light of a subsequent decision, Webster v. Reproductive Health Services, 492 U.S. 490 (1989), in which the Court provided states with substantial room to regulate and restrict abortions, while affirming the fundamental right to an abortion. By November 2005, thirty states had legislated a waiting period before a minor's abortion. Forty-four states require parental consent or notification prior to a minor's abortion. Thirty-six states prohibit later-term abortions, with most restrictions coming after twenty-four weeks' gestation, because viability is frequently estimated to begin at around twenty-two to twenty-four weeks. Thirty-one states ban partial-birth abortion, a rare procedure performed to protect the welfare of the mother should a late-term pregnancy experience severe problems. Seventeen states fund all or most medically necessary abortion (beyond federal minimum requirements) for Medicaid clients. Eight states allow some providers and insurers to refuse to prescribe contraceptive services, and eight states allow provision of emergency contraception without a prescription. More than half of state Medicaid programs cover emergency contraception. http://statehealthfacts.kff.org (accessed April 3, 2006).

8. The first half of the nineteenth century is an anomaly because death rates among white males were rising. Data about death rates in the United States are rough estimates until the 1930s owing to incomplete death registrations in many U.S. counties.

9. See Arora 2001 and Fogel 1992 for more complete discussions of the complex interrelationship between income and health.

10. This discussion is based on Thomasson 2003a, 2003b.

11. See Thomasson 2003b, 1374, and 1943 Fed. Tax Rep. (CCH) ¶6587 (1943).

12. Federal government expenditures on the Medicaid program as a percentage of GDP amounted to 0.7 percent in 1990 and 1.4 percent in 2002, and expenditures on the Medicare program amounted to 1.9 percent in 1990 and 2.4

percent in 2002. The Medicare program also covers some disabled individuals under the age of sixty-five as well as individuals with end-stage renal disease.

13. The study of the Medicare program referred to in the text is Adams, Hurd, McFadden, Merrill, and Ribiero 2003. They also find no evidence that therapies for acute diseases which are linked to socioeconomic status lead to mortality differentials. They find some association between socioeconomic status and the incidence of gradual-onset health conditions such as mental illness and some chronic conditions.

14. See Galenson 1996, 178–80 for a full discussion of coerced immigration.

15. The quotation is from Walton and Rockoff 1998, 35. See Grubb 1994 for a discussion of the end of indentured servitude.

16. See Hatton and Williamson 1998 for a far-reaching analysis of immigration to the Americas. The political coalition between the South and the West in 1882 to restrict immigration from China may have been due to the South's desire not to have a region with a cheaper labor force. The 1840s and 1850s saw an earlier burst of nativism that was a major factor behind the rise of the Republican Party. The Chinese Exclusion Extension Act of 1904 indefinitely extended the ban on Chinese immigration set forth in the earlier legislation.

17. Some relatives of earlier migrants from Japan and picture brides from Korea and Japan were allowed to migrate to Hawaii until 1924.

18. This discussion draws heavily on Goldin 1994.

19. The three acts are the Emergency Quota Act of 1921, the Immigration Act of 1924, and the National Origins Act of 1929. See Williamson 1998 for an analysis of the backlash to the liberal immigration policies in effect before World War I.

20. The discussion of immigration relies heavily on Martin and Widgren 2002.

21. See Goldin 1990, 1991 and Cohen 1985, 1988. The quotation is from Goldin 1990, 13.

22. See Parsons 1980 for the pioneering research on this topic. Haveman and Wolfe (1984) provide a critical perspective on Parsons's study.

23. This discussion in the text draws heavily on Costa 1998.

24. Most analysts recognize that individuals make labor-supply decisions on the basis of the marginal tax on labor.

25. Another important payroll tax is the federal unemployment tax. It takes 0.8 percent of the first $7,000 of labor income.

26. These calculations are taken from Stephenson 1998.

27. McCarty (1990) found that Social Security taxes reduced the labor force participation of older upper-income women. Gruber (2003) studied the effects of changing taxation rates on social security income when a taxpayer's total income exceeded certain thresholds. He found that the earnings test reduced the labor supply of older women but had no robust effect on the labor supply of older men. Eissa (1995) studied the effects of the 1986 tax reform, which substantially lowered the average marginal tax for married women in families at the 99th and 90th income percentiles. This study found that the tax reduction increased both labor force participation rates and hours worked.

28. See Galenson 1996 for a excellent discussion of literacy in England and the English colonies during the eighteenth century.

29. This section relies heavily on the discussion in Goldin and Katz 2003b of school finance in the nineteenth century.

30. Fishlow (1966) concluded that enrollment increases typically preceded state repeal of rate bills. Kaestle and Vinovskis (1980) provided additional evidence using data on school attendance. Goldin and Katz (2003b) provide a critical review of nineteenth-century enrollment statistics.

31. See Landes and Solomon (1972) for a classic early study of compulsory schooling.

32. Goldin and Katz 2003b, 44.

33. Stuart v. School District No. 1 of the Village of Kalamazoo, 30 Mich. 69 (1878). See Goldin (1998, 2001) and Goldin and Katz (1999a, 199b, 2003) for more complete discussion of the forces that led to an increase in the demand for a high school education and to the rapid supply response in most areas.

34. See Goldin 2001 for a more complete discussion of the forces behind the increase in demand for a high school education. Carter et al. 2006, vol. 2, table Bb9-56 is the source for enrollment figures.

35. The discussion in the text is based on the work of Lleras-Muney (2002a), who conducted an econometric analysis using state panel data of the effects of compulsory schooling laws in the 1920s and 1930s. Goldin and Katz (2003a) investigated the same research question for both secondary enrollment and educational attainment, while using an expanded time period (1910 to 1939) and a corrected data set for compulsory school laws. Margo and Finegan (1996) used 1900 census data to investigate the impact of compulsory schooling laws on schooling of individuals reaching fourteen years of age. They identify a small impact on educational attainment when compulsory schooling laws are combined with child labor laws in their econometric analysis.

36. Http://www.doe.gov reports statistics relating to school enrollment and finance for the past ten to thirty years, depending on the series.

37. The full citations are Plessy v. Ferguson, 163 U.S. 537 (1896), and Brown v. Board of Education, 347 U.S. 483 (1954).

38. Data are from http://nces.ed.gov/pubs/97384.pdf (accessed April 25, 2006).

39. Each teacher is required to become "highly qualified" in a particular subject area by the end of the 2005–6 school year.

40. The discussion is based on Turner and Bound 2003; the quotation is at 148–49.

41. The description of job training programs relies heavily on LaLonde 1995, 150–54.

42. The quotation is from ibid., 150.

43. The studies referred to in the text are LaLonde 1995, Friedlander, Greenberg, and Robins 1997 (the quotation is on 1847), and Ashenfelter 1978.

44. See chapter 9 and chapter 14 for a more complete discussion of the rise of unions through World War II. The term *featherbedding* refers to union work rules that require more workers than needed to complete a job.

45. Lumsden and Peterson 1975 studied the initial impact of right-to-work laws; Moore 1998 is an excellent survey of more recent econometric literature about right-to-work laws.

46. Ichniowski (1980) studied wages and benefits of union and nonunion firefighters, and Zax (1988) studied wages and benefits of a broader group of union and nonunion government workers.

47. See Brown, Gilroy, and Kohen 1982 for an excellent survey of earlier research on the impact of federal minimum wage increases on hours, employment, and unemployment.

48. Card and Krueger's 1994 study started the recent controversy over whether increases in the minimum wage lead to declines in hours worked. Their study has provoked numerous responses, including those by Hyclak, Johnes, and Thornton 2005 and Neumark and Wascher 2000 (the study discussed in this paragraph).

49. The federal laws referred to in this paragraph as precursors of the ADA are the Age Discrimination in Employment Act of 1967, the Architectural Barriers Act of 1968, the Rehabilitation Act of 1973, the Fair Housing Amendments of 1988, and the Air Carriers Access Act of 1989. DeLeire (2000) and Acemoglu and Angrist (2001) analyzed large data sets with information about disabled and nondisabled workers. The discussion in the text refers to results from Acemoglu and Angrist 2001.

References

Acemoglu, Daron, and Joshua D. Angrist. 2000. "How Large Are Human Capital Externalities? Evidence from Compulsory Schooling Laws," *NBER Macroeconomics Annual* 15:9–59.

———. 2001. "Consequences of Employment Protection: The Case of the Americans with Disabilities Act." *Journal of Political Economy* 109 (July): 730–70.

Adams, Peter, Michael D. Hurd, Daniel McFadden, Angela Merrill, and Tiago Ribeiro. 2003. "Healthy, Wealthy, and Wise? Tests for Direct Causal Paths between Health and Socioeconomic Status." *Journal of Econometrics* 112:3–56.

Arora, Suchit. 2001. "Health, Human Productivity, and Long-Term Economic Growth." *Journal of Economic History* 61 (September): 699–749.

Ashenfelter, Orly. 1978. "Estimating the Effect of Training Programs on Earnings." *Review of Economics and Statistics* 60 (February): 47–57.

Becker, Gary S. 1960. "An Economic Analysis of Fertility," in *Demographic and Economic Change in Developed Countries*. Universities–National Bureau Conference Series, no. 11. Princeton: Princeton University Press, 209–31.

Becker, Gary S., and H. Gregg Lewis. 1973. "Interaction between Quantity and Quality of Children." *Journal of Political Economy* 81 (March–April): S279–S288.

Carter, Susan B., et al. 2006. *Historical Statistics of the United States: Earliest Times to the Present, Millennial Edition*. New York: Cambridge University Press.

Bloom, David, and Jeffrey G. Williamson. 1998. "Demographic Transitions and Economic Miracles in Emerging Asia." *World Bank Economic Review* 12 (September): 419–55.

Brown, Charles, Curtis Gilroy, and Andrew Kohen. 1982. "The Effect of the Minimum Wage on Employment and Unemployment." *Journal of Economic Literature* 20 (June): 487–528.

Card, David, and Alan B. Krueger. 1994. "Minimum Wages and Employment: A Case Study of the Fast Food Industry in New Jersey and Pennsylvania." *American Economic Review* 84 (September): 772–93.

Chesnais, Jean-Claude. 1992. *The Demographic Transition: Stages, Patterns, and Economic Implications; A Longitudinal Study of Sixty-Seven Countries Covering the Period 1720–1984.* Trans. Elizabeth Kreager and Philip Kreager. New York: Oxford University Press.

Costa, Dora L. 1998. *The Evolution of Retirement: An American Economic History, 1880–1990.* Chicago: University of Chicago Press.

———. 2000. "Hours of Work and the Fair Labor Standards Act: A Study of Retail and Wholesale Trade, 1938–1950." *Industrial and Labor Relations Review* 53 (July): 648–64.

DeLeire, Thomas. 2000. "The Wage and Employment Effects of the Americans with Disabilities Act." *Journal of Human Resources* 35 (Fall): 693–715.

Easterlin, Richard A. 1968. *Population, Labor Force, and Long Swings in Economic Growth: The American Experience.* New York: Columbia University Press.

Easterlin, Richard A., Michael L. Wachter, and Susan M. Wachter. 1978. "The Changing Impact of Population Swings on the American Economy." *Proceedings of the American Philosophical Society* 122 (June): 119–30.

Eissa, Nada. 1995. "Taxation and Labor Supply of Married Women: The Tax Reform Act of 1986 as a Natural Experiment." National Bureau of Economic Research Working Paper no. 5023, Cambridge, MA, February.

Feeney, Griffith, and Andrew Mason. 2001. "Population in East Asia," in *Population Change and Economic Development in East Asia: Challenges Met, Opportunities Seized,* ed. Andrew Mason, Stanford: Stanford University Press.

Fishlow, Albert. 1966. "The American Common School Revival: Fact or Fancy?" In *Industrialization in Two Systems: Essays in Honor of Alexander Gerschenkron,* ed. Henry Rosovsky, 40–67. New York: Wiley.

Fogel, Robert W. 1994. "Economic Growth, Population Theory, and Physiology: The Bearing of Long-Term Processes on the Making of Economic Policy." *American Economic Review* 84 (June): 369–95.

Freeman, Richard. 1988. "Contraction and Expansion: The Divergence of Private Sector and Public Sector Unionism in the United States." *Journal of Economic Perspectives* 2 (Spring): 63–88.

Friedlander, Daniel, David H. Greenberg, and Philip K. Robins. 1997. "Evaluating Government Training Programs for the Economically Disadvantaged." *Journal of Economic Literature* 35 (December): 1809–55.

Galenson, David. 1996. "The Settlement and Growth of the Colonies: Population, Labor and Economic Development." In *The Cambridge Economic History of the United States,* vol. 1, *The Colonial Era,* ed. Stanley L. Engerman and Robert E. Gallman, 135–207. New York: Cambridge University Press.

Goldin, Claudia. 1990. *Understanding the Gender Gap: An Economic History of American Women.* New York: Oxford University Press.

———. 1991. "The Role of World War II in the Rise of Women's Employment." *American Economic Review* 81 (September): 741–56.

———. 1994. "The Political Economy of Immigration Restriction in the United States: 1890 to 1921." In *The Regulated Economy: A Historical Approach to Political Economy,* ed. Claudia Goldin and Gary Libecap, 223–57. Chicago: University of Chicago Press.

———. 1995. "The U-Shaped Female Labor Force Function in Economic Development and Economic History." In *Investment in Women's Human Capital and Economic Development,* ed. T. Paul Schultz, 61–90. Chicago: University of Chicago Press.

———. 1998. "America's Graduation from High School: The Evolution and Spread of Secondary Schooling in the Twentieth Century." *Journal of Economic History* 58 (June): 345–74.

———. 2001. "The Human Capital Century and American Leadership: Virtues of the Past." *Journal of Economic History* 61 (June): 263–91.

Goldin, Claudia, and Lawrence F. Katz. 1999a. "The Returns to Skill in the United States across the Twentieth Century." National Bureau of Economics Research Working Paper no. 7126, Cambridge, MA, May.

———. 1999b. "The Shaping of Higher Education: The Formative Years in the United States, 1890 to 1940." *Journal of Economic Perspectives* 13 (Winter): 37–62.

———. 2002. "The Power of the Pill." *Journal of Political Economy* 110 (August): 730–70.

———. 2003. "The 'Virtues' of the Past: Education in the First One Hundred Years of the New Republic." National Bureau of Economics Research Working Paper no. 9958, Cambridge, MA, September.

Grove, Wayne, and Craig Heinicke. 2003. "Better Opportunities or Worse? The Demise of Cotton Harvest Labor, 1949–64." *Journal of Economic History* 63 (September): 736–67.

Grubb, Farley. 1994. "The End of European Immigrant Servitude in the United States: An Economic Analysis of Market Collapse, 1772–1835." *Journal of Economic History* 54 (December): 794–824.

Gruber, Jonathan. 2003. "Does the Social Security Earnings Test Affect Labor Supply and Benefits Receipt?" *National Tax Journal* 56 (December): 755–73.

Haines, Michael R. 2000. "The Population of the United States, 1790–1920." In *The Cambridge Economic History of the United States,* ed. Stanley Engerman and Robert E. Gallman, 2:143–205. New York: Cambridge University Press.

Hatton, Timothy J., and Jeffrey G. Williamson. 1998. *The Age of Mass Migration: An Economic Analysis.* New York: Oxford University Press.

Haveman, Robert H., and Barbara L. Wolfe. 1984. "Decline in Male Labor Force Participation: Comment." *Journal of Political Economy* 92 (June): 532–41.

Higgs, Robert. 1987. *Crisis and Leviathan: Critical Episodes in the Growth of American Government.* New York: Oxford University Press.

Hyclak, Thomas, Geraint Johnes, and Robert Thornton. 2005. *Fundamentals of Labor Economics.* Boston: Houghton Mifflin.

Ichniowski, Casey. 1980. "Economic Effects of the Firefighters Union." *Industrial and Labor Relations Review* 33: 405–25.

Kaestle, Carl, and Maris Vinovskis. 1980. *Education and Social Change in Nineteenth Century Massachusetts.* Cambridge: Harvard University Press.

LaLonde, Robert J. 1995. "The Promise of Public Sector–Sponsored Training Programs." *Journal of Economic Perspectives* 9 (Spring): 149–68.

Landes, William M., and Lewis C. Solomon. 1972. "Compulsory Schooling Legislation: An Economic Analysis of Social Change in the Nineteenth Century." *Journal of Economic History* 32 (March): 54–91.

Lee, Chulhee. 2005. "Wealth Accumulation and the Health of Union Army Veterans, 1860–1870." *Journal of Economic History* 65 (June): 352–87.

Levine, Phillip B. 2004. *Sex and Consequences: Abortion, Public Policy, and the Economics of Fertility.* Princeton: Princeton University Press.

Lleras-Muney, Adrianna. 2002a. "Were Compulsory Attendance and Child Labor Laws Effective? An Analysis from 1915 to 1939." Pt. 1. *Journal of Law and Economics* 45 (October): 401–35.

———. 2002b. "The Relationship between Education and Adult Mortality in the United States." National Bureau of Economic Research Working Paper no. 8986, Cambridge, MA, June.

Lumsden, Keith, and Craig Petersen. 1975. "The Effect of Right-to-Work Laws on Unionization in the United States," *Journal of Political Economy* 83 (December): 1237–48.

Margo, Robert A. 2000. "The Labor Force in the Nineteenth Century." *The Cambridge Economic History of the United States,* ed. Stanley L. Engerman and Robert E. Gallman, 2:207–43. New York: Cambridge University Press.

Margo, Robert A., and T. Aldrich Finegan. 1996. "Compulsory Schooling Legislation and School Attendance in Turn-of the Century America: A 'Natural Experiments' Approach." *Economics Letters* 53:103–10.

Martin, Philip, and Jonas Widgren. 2002. "International Migration: Facing the Challenge." *Population Bulletin* 57 (March): 1–40.

McCarty, Theresa A. 1990. "The Effect of Social Security on Married Women's Labor Force Participation." *National Tax Journal* 43 (March): 95–110.

Moore, William J. 1998. "The Determinants and Effects of Right-to-Work Laws: A Review of the Recent Literature." *Journal of Labor Research* 19 (Summer): 445–69.

Neumark, David, and William Wascher. 2000. "Minimum Wages and Employment: A Case Study of the Fast-Food Industry in New Jersey and Pennsylvania: Comment." *American Economic Review* 90 (December): 1362–96.

O'Neill, June, and Solomon Polachek. 1993. "Why the Gender Gap in Wages Narrowed in the 1980s." *Journal of Labor Economics* 2 (January): 205–28.

Parsons, Donald O. 1980. "The Decline in Male Labor Force Participation." *Journal of Political Economy* 88 (February): 117–34.

Ransom, Roger, and Richard Sutch. 1986. "The Labor of Older Americans: Retirement of Men on and off the Job." *Journal of Economic History* 46 (March): 1–30.

Scofea, Laura A. 1994. "The Development and Growth of Employer-Provided Health Insurance." *Monthly Labor Review* 117 (March): 3–10.

Seltzer, Andrew J. 1995. "The Political Economy of the Fair Labor Standards Act of 1938." *Journal of Political Economy* 103 (June): 1302–44.

———. 1997. "The Effects of the Fair Labor Standards Act of 1938 on the Southern Seamless Hosiery and Lumber Industries." *Journal of Economic History* 57 (June): 396–415.

———. 2004. "Democratic Opposition to the Fair Labor Standards Act: A Comment on Fleck." *Journal of Economic History* 64 (March): 226–30.

Stephenson, E. Frank. 1998. "Average Marginal Tax Rates Revisited," *Journal of Monetary Economics* 41 (April): 389–409.

Thomasson, Melissa A. 2003a. "From Sickness to Health: The Twentieth Century Development of U.S. Health Insurance." *Explorations in Economic History* 39 (July): 233–53.

———. 2003b. "The Importance of Group Coverage: How Tax Policy Shaped U.S. Health Insurance." *American Economic Review* 93 (September): 1373–84.

Turner, Sarah, and John Bound. 2003. "Closing the Gap or Widening the Divide: The Effects of the G.I. Bill and World War II on the Educational Outcomes of Black Americans." *Journal of Economic History* 63 (March): 145–77.

Walton, Gary M., and Hugh Rockoff, 1998. *History of the American Economy*, 8th ed. Fort Worth: Dryden.

Williamson, Jeffrey G. 1998. "Globalization, Labor Markets, and Policy Backlash in the Past." *Journal of Economic Perspectives* 12 (Fall): 51–72.

Willis, Robert J. 1973. "A New Approach to the Economic Theory of Fertility Behavior." *Journal of Political Economy* 81 (March–April): S14–S64.

Zax, Jeffrey. 1988. "Wages, Compensation, and Municipal Unions." *Industrial Relations* 27:301–17.

GARY D. LIBECAP

12

The Federal Bureaucracy: *From Patronage to Civil Service*

SOME OF THE SHARPEST political debates in current American politics revolve around the size, role, and performance of government, specifically the federal government.[1] Since 1933 the expenditures of this level of government in the economy have far exceeded those of the state and local levels (Wallis 1984, 141). Via a myriad of social programs, regulations, taxes, and payments, the federal government permeates virtually every aspect of life in the United States. The size of government has grown in the twentieth and twenty-first centuries, often following a ratchet-like pattern, following major crises including World War I, the Great Depression, World War II, and the terrorist attacks of September 11, 2001.[2] Accordingly, the debate about the performance and accountability of government necessarily focuses on the federal government and, in turn, on the structure of its labor force, the federal bureaucracy.

The current federal bureaucracy is largely autonomous. It generally is insulated from political control by politicians by civil service rules, and there are few institutional provisions within the civil service system to encourage efficiency in delivery or responsiveness to citizens. This is not to say that the bureaucracy is uncaring or indifferent to the provision of goods and services, but rather that the motivation for effective service delivery largely is due to internal personal factors or agency agendas and cultures and not to bureaucratic rules regarding hiring, salary, and promotion or to direct political management of the government labor force by elected officials.

As such, the government bureaucracy in the twenty-first century is a far cry from that which existed in the nineteenth century, when the government was run by patronage. In the system of patronage there was no question of political control. Each government worker owed his or her job to an elected politician and the local political machine and was careful to follow the benefactor's wishes. Politicians, in turn, had to be responsive to key voting constituencies within the electorate and hence directed patronage workers to meet the needs of those constituencies as well.

Only when the federal labor force became too large to effectively manage in the latter part of the nineteenth century were federal politicians willing to give up some patronage positions. By that time, the patronage workforce had become too cumbersome for politicians to control and direct, and it began to inflict growing costs on politicians. Gradually, patronage was replaced by the civil service system.

The Federal Civil Service System

Structure

Table 12.1 shows federal civilian employment within the executive branch for 1949, 1969, 1989, and 2002. The General Schedule (GS 1–15) sector makes up the bulk of federal civilian employment in the executive branch, and it is the major component of the civil service system. Higher-level officials, those in grades GS 16–18 (both career and appointed), are in the Senior Executive Service, also part of the civil service system; in 2002 it numbered approximately 6,946 individuals. In addition, in 2002 there were 446 very senior officials in the Executive Schedule for the management of executive departments (U.S. Office of Personnel Management 2002, 12). The federal wage system covers blue-collar employees. The president has the authority to appoint only a small number of top-level officers in the civil service, approximately 5,800 individuals (Johnson and Libecap 1994a, 161). The remaining federal civilian employees are covered by one of the federal employment systems described in the table. Other than senior presidential appointees, there is no patronage left in the federal government in the twenty-first century.

Table 12.1 FEDERAL CIVILIAN EMPLOYEES, EXECUTIVE BRANCH, 1949–2002

Year	General schedule (thousands)	Federal wage system (thousands)	Postal (thousands)
1949	830	502	361
1969	1,274	592	654
1989	1,494	374	827
2002	1,238	193	812

Sources: Johnson and Libecap (1994a, 98) and U.S. Office of Personnel Management 2002, 12; 2003, 28.

An Autonomous, Professional Bureaucracy

Patronage has few adherents today, but it may have had some uses for aligning the interests of voters, politicians, and government workers. It is often argued instead that part of the infrastructure necessary for successful economic development is a politically neutral, professional bureaucracy. The notion is that a civil service protected from competing political pressures can administer programs for citizens more effectively than can one that, like patronage, is subject to direct political interference. Such intervention would corrupt the bureaucracy and channel government services and transfers toward favored constituencies, rather than to those who were the original intended targets. Despite the logic of these arguments, there is, however, a problem with a completely protected, ostensibly politically neutral bureaucracy.

An autonomous bureaucracy has the potential to operate in a self-directed manner with advancement as the objective. This objective is unlikely to coincide with effective delivery of government services. With limited political oversight and direction, an insulated bureaucracy has less incentive to be responsive to citizens' demands. There may be few options for citizens who complain about arbitrary bureaucratic decisions or the poor provision of government services. Policies may be implemented and administered in a manner that aids in building bureaucratic budgets, staffing, and political influence but meets few of the citizens' needs. With bureaucracies writing the rules for implementing the legislation passed by Congress, remedies for the problems of excessive autonomy may be very costly to enact for citizens and politicians alike.

This chapter is not an attack on the federal bureaucracy. Rather, it cautions against overly sanguine conclusions about the effectiveness and desirability of an autonomous, politically neutral bureaucracy. The chapter describes how the current civil service system, which covers career government employees, emerged from patronage in the late nineteenth century and how government employees' unions have played a direct role in molding the development of today's civil service, which today occupies a privileged position in the American labor force.

Controlling for individual characteristics and job attributes, career federal employees generally earn more than do their counterparts in the private sector (Venti 1987, 147–82). Advancement is more or less automatic, with pay increases based on the passage of time, rather than merit. Salary growth is not tied to the growth or decline of agency budgets, with individuals receiving salary adjustments as part of the civil service system and not as the direct result of the expansion or contraction of their agency. Further, there is comparatively little use of incentive or performance pay by government managers to reward productivity by their subordinates. Federal employees also have tenure in their positions. It is extremely costly for government employees to be fired or otherwise removed from their offices for poor performance.

Federal employees' unions are among the most influential lobbying groups in American politics and are among the largest political campaign contributors. Federal politicians who have many government employees in their districts pay particular attention to the concerns of these unions. Although Congress has enacted a variety of mechanisms to control bureaucratic drift, which is the manipulation of policy by administrative agencies, career officials still have considerable discretion in the actual implementation of government programs. And there is concern that they use this discretion to promote personal and agency agendas, rather than the desires of voters and their elected representatives.

Career government employees are not necessarily "politically neutral," that is, guided solely by scientific or technical management principles. Highly protected employees with strong ideological or professional attachments to political causes or policies are in a position to influence the administrative actions of their agencies. A number of scholars such as Gordon Tullock, William Niskanen, Frederick Mosher, Hugh Heclo, and James Wilson have voiced concern that bureaucrats are both opportunistic in pursuit of their own interests and influential in shaping policy away from what was desired by the president and the Congress.[3] Indeed, the president and agency heads, who are his political appointees, often have conflicts with the career agency officials who administer policy.

The incentives of bureaucrats to resist or promote policy change are increased because of the very nature of many government services. Federal agencies administer policies regarding the environment, welfare, health care, transportation, and defense, and people have strong preferences about what the government's role in these areas should be. Professionals seeking employment with the government often are attracted to a particular agency because of its stated mission or for the opportunity to help change the way in which it operates.

Although it is difficult empirically to determine how much bureaucratic manipulation of policy occurs, anecdotal evidence suggests the possibilities. For example, at the Federal Trade Commission and in the Department of Justice, lawyers and economists, who are not political appointees but career civil servants, decide whether a case is worth pursuing and whether a particular piece of evidence is relevant. Similarly, at the Environmental Protection Agency, field investigators have considerable leeway in the enforcement of the Clean Air Act and other environmental regulations authorized by Congress. These officials may use their discretion to direct policy in ways that they personally prefer and not strictly as desired by Congress.

Another example is provided by the U.S. Forest Service. Throughout much of its history, its mission centered largely on providing services and commodities to the timber and grazing industries. In the 1960s and 1970s, the professional staff of the agency was composed mainly of people trained in timber management and harvesting, foresters and engineers who supervised timber sales and construction of roads to access sites. The political success of the environmental movement, however, greatly changed the mission of the agency and pitted new interest groups against old ones. These conflicts resulted in a change in the types of professionals employed by the Forest Service. Individuals trained in wildlife management, biologists, and specialists in recreation became much more common. Since this change in professional orientation more employees have actively challenged past agency policy. These individuals want the Forest Service to move further toward environmental goals such as wilderness preservation and away from support of the timber industry.

Politicians bear the political costs of such policy adjustments and hence must act more judiciously and more slowly. Agency employees, on the other hand, with professional ties to new policies and strongly held beliefs about their implementation, have latitude within the civil service system to act as advocates. In the private sector, such advocacy actions would likely bring dismissal, but with the job protection rules available to career federal employees, dismissal is not an easy option. As a result, the system has evolved into an institution that provides neither strong incentives for performance nor a policy-neutral workforce.

Patronage

Until the early part of the twentieth century, most federal employees in the United States were hired on the basis of political patronage. Patronage was viewed as a necessary and useful method for staffing federal offices. Indeed, it was the currency of political exchange when political parties were loose national coalitions of local organizations or machines held together by national politicians such as the president. In his study of the Jacksonian era, Leonard White emphasized that the connection between national politicians and the local party was patronage: "The success of . . . local organizations seemed to depend much more on securing offices, contracts, and favors for their members than on campaigning over disputed issues of statesmanship" (White 1954, 84).

The right to place the local party faithful in relatively high-paying federal jobs (generally as postmasters, customhouse employees, land office clerks, and surveyors) was coveted by members of the House of Representatives, Senators, cabinet members, and local political bosses. The president, who had the constitutional power to staff executive branch positions, traded these positions to such lower-level politicians in exchange for their support for legislation and reelection.

The awarding of patronage positions was a means by which politicians could motivate and reward their supporters, and because the latter could be fired at will, patronage was a means by which politicians could insure that government employees did their bidding. As political currents shifted among the electorate, politicians could respond, knowing that their appointees would follow their directives. In no sense was there a politically independent bureaucracy. To obtain the party's nomination and support in the campaign, candidates for federal office were required to permit the local party machine to play a role in the dispensation of the jobs and favors they acquired on election and to be responsive to the demands of local party leaders.

Gaining the support of the local party machine depended on congressional candidates' ability to obtain patronage positions from the president. The president in turn used the distribution of patronage to build and enforce political coalitions. As Theodore Roosevelt noted with regard to his bargaining with members of Congress, "If they'll vote for my measures I'll appoint their nominees to Federal jobs. And I'm going to tell them so."[4] Although nominees for senior offices required Senate approval, appointments to the more numerous lower-level positions could be made without the consent of the Senate, and there were few restrictions on who could be hired. The positions could then be used to promote the president, members of Congress, and local politicians. So long as the interests of federal politicians and the local party machine coincided, the spoils system was mutually beneficial.

Although patronage positions were known to be temporary, they were highly sought after both as means of employment and as means of establishing political and social positions and contacts within the political party structure and the local community. Because government employment depended on the political fortunes of each worker's benefactor and party, appointees were motivated to deliver services and other government benefits as effectively as possible to key constituents. Patronage workers therefore were expected to be politically active on behalf of their mentors, to engage in campaign work, and to contribute part of their salaries in the form of political assessments.

These assessments were a legal means of transferring federal tax revenues to political parties. The payments ranged from 2 to 20 percent of an individual patronage worker's salary, depending on the position held. Solicitation letters were sent by the party to each worker, return envelopes were provided to ensure that payments were made, and compliance was carefully monitored. Those who did not contribute lost their jobs (Fowler 1943, 157–60). Federal patronage positions appear to have paid more than the market wage for comparable private jobs in order to compensate for the assessments.[5] Payments by federal workers were important sources of campaign financing, and their control rested with the local party apparatus.[6]

Those who held patronage positions were well aware that they did not have job tenure and would be removed routinely after elections in which their political benefactors were defeated. For example, after twenty-five years of Republican domination of the presidency, when Grover Cleveland first took office in 1885, 43,087 fourth-class postmasters were removed, suspended, or asked to resign to make room for Democratic Party stalwarts (Fowler 1943, 306). These were the rules of the game, and they provided for a partisan federal bureaucracy. When the government was small, patronage provided for close allegiance between appointees and politicians, and employee behavior could be monitored at relatively low cost.

The number of federal positions was relatively low at first, reflecting the limited role of the federal government in the economy and society. There were perhaps five thousand federal jobs in 1816, five hundred of them in Washington, DC. Throughout the nineteenth century most federal employees worked for the Post Office as postmasters, postal clerks, or mail carriers. In 1881, for example, 59 percent of all federal employees were in the Post Office.[7]

The allocation of these positions among the various competing claimants involved considerable negotiation among the relevant members of Congress, the president, and the Postmaster General. The Postmaster General was one of the president's chief strategists and advisors in allocating positions, and the decisions often were delicate ones. In 1890 there were, on average, 250 postal workers per congressional district and 1,700 applications for those positions (Fowler 1943, 140–45, 215).

Although there were early conflicts over patronage, neither politicians nor voters thought the system needed to change. Indeed, if anything, patronage was seen as promoting the ideals of equality and social mobility by allowing common people to fill public offices. Anyone with the right political connections could obtain a government job, at least for a short while. There was to be no long-term holding of federal offices, a practice that could lead to the development of an entrenched civil service elite counter to the democratic goals of the new government.

The push for a shift from patronage came with the growth of government after the Civil War. Table 12.2 outlines the size of the federal civilian labor force in the nineteenth century. As indicated, prior to the Civil War, the federal workforce was relatively small at approximately twenty-six thousand in 1851, but by 1871, the number of civilian employees had grown to fifty-one thousand and by 1881, to one hundred thousand. As the bureaucracy grew, its performance became more and more consequential for businesses' profitability, and politicians came under growing pressure from business groups to provide government services more effectively than was possible under patronage. At the same time, it was becoming increasingly costly for federal politicians to control and benefit from a larger number of patronage employees. Monitoring was the key problem. Business groups were especially critical of the system, and they were instrumental in the formation of groups such as the National Civil Service Reform League.

When the government labor force was small, federal politicians could oversee the actions of their appointees to guarantee their allegiance and to see that they responded to the demands of influential constituents. As the federal labor force grew, however, careful selection and supervision of patronage workers by the president or members of Congress became more difficult. Workers failed to attend to their jobs and corruption increased. By the late nineteenth century, patronage

Table 12.2 FEDERAL EMPLOYMENT OF CIVILIANS, 1816–1911

Year	Employment	Year	Employment
1816	4,837	1871	51,020
1821	6,914	1881	100,020
1831	11,491	1891	157,442
1841	18,038	1901	239,476
1851	26,274	1911	395,905
1861	36,672		

Source: U.S. Department of Commerce 1975, 1102–3.

came to be viewed by many as supplying a costly, inefficient, and corrupt labor force. This new condition strained the personal nature of the patronage staffing process and the political exchanges built around it. Members of Congress and the president often had to meet with job seekers to evaluate their political merits and fitness, placing a tremendous burden on their time. In 1870 James Garfield claimed that "one-third of the working hours of Senators and Representatives is hardly sufficient to meet the demands made upon them in reference to appointments of office."[8] Increasingly, the president in particular was becoming a position broker, dispensing hundreds of jobs under great pressure. These duties diverted attention from other responsibilities, and in the case of President Garfield, the costs of allocating patronage were especially high. On the morning of July 2, 1881, a disgruntled office seeker shot and killed him.

AS THE ECONOMY grew after the Civil War, businesses became more and more dependent on the smooth processing of international and interstate trade and information through the postal system and customhouses. Bills had to be sent and collected. Orders had to be received and merchandise shipped. Primary products and intermediate goods, such as fabric dyes and machine tools, often were imported from Europe or elsewhere. But under patronage these systems were not up to the task. Scandals and charges of fraud and inefficiency were directed at the largest post offices and customhouses.

The *New York Times* discussed efforts to improve the performance of the New York customhouse, reporting, "At no point had the defects of the previous method of appointment [patronage] seemed more obvious. . . . The customs service at the Port of New York had been properly considered as the climax of inefficiency and corruption"; the *Chicago Tribune* reported that "the appointees of congressmen and private individuals are expected to render a dual service, a service to the government and service to their patrons."[9]

The Jay Commission, appointed by the U.S. House of Representatives in 1877 to investigate the country's largest customhouses, found them to be much less efficient than were those in Great Britain, where staffing was done via a merit system. It found that a merit-based labor force "promised merchants and bankers an administrative system that would 'protect their interests and secure efficient services in the departments in which they were most directly affected.'"[10]

Dissatisfaction with the performance of the patronage system was particularly worrisome to the president, whose administration was charged with the adequate performance of government. The reputation of the president was on the line. By contrast, with their more narrow constituencies, members of Congress and local political bosses might still benefit from the distribution of patronage positions, even if the individuals involved were corrupt or inefficient. Increasingly, the president and members of Congress came into conflict over appointments to and management of the federal labor force.

One of the most notorious conflicts involved a battle beginning in 1871 for control of patronage appointments to the New York customhouse, the nation's largest and most important, handling three-fourths of all customs duties. Following embarrassing public exposure of corruption, Presidents Ulysses S. Grant and Rutherford B. Hayes attempted to obtain greater authority over hiring and management of customs officials, but New York state senator Roscoe Conkling and the local party machine aligned with him resisted their efforts.

Although support for patronage was particularly strong within the local political machine, in the latter half of the nineteenth century presidents and many members of Congress were finding that patronage was losing its appeal as a source of votes. Not only did patronage provide an inept and corrupt labor force and prove to be a source of increasing scandal and embarrassment, as congressional hearings held in the 1870s indicate, but assessments on the salaries of patronage workers were also becoming insufficient to fund the growing costs of national-, state-, and district-level political campaigns.[11] Politicians increasingly turned to wealthy individuals and interest groups for donations, but these groups demanded more efficient provision of government services, and more patronage was not the solution.

The rising costs of screening, monitoring, and negotiating with patronage workers were intensified by important changes in the structure of the political party system in the United States in the latter part of the nineteenth century. Prior to the Civil War, American political parties were loose confederations of local factions, not well-organized national groups. In this way the parties mirrored the national economy, which, because of high transportation costs, was more or less a collection of regional economies. Parties focused on parochial concerns to win elections for their candidates, and patronage was used to organize campaigns and to fill appointive offices. After the Civil War, however, the rural, relatively isolated nature of the economy began to change rapidly. The economy became increasingly urbanized, industrialized, and integrated owing to reductions in transportation and information costs. Market size grew and per capita income rose. Politics and political parties began to be more national in scope (Skowronek 1982, 39–40).

There was a corresponding rise in demands by private interest groups for new and more complex services from the federal government that went beyond their local areas. Interstate coalitions such as the Grangers, the National Association of Manufacturers, and the National Civil Service Reform League lobbied Congress for legislation that they desired. One such bill, the Pendleton Act of 1883, was designed to implement a limited merit system for federal hiring.

The Pendleton Act

Although there had been earlier attempts to enact merit-hiring legislation, the shift from patronage to merit began with the Pendleton Act of 1883. The law required that applicants for certain federal jobs be ranked on the basis of examination results or merit and not on their party membership or service. The Act created two groups within the federal labor force: classified (merit) employees and unclassified (patronage) employees. The classified service made up only 10 percent of the federal labor force in 1883. Not until twenty-one years later did more than 50 percent of the total federal civilian labor force work within the merit provisions.

Patronage was left for smaller, less critical facilities where monitoring was possible and where inefficiencies would be less politically costly. By partitioning the federal labor force in this way, the Pendleton Act could be responsive to the demands of business and reform groups with merit employment where it mattered while upholding patronage in less sensitive areas to meet the needs of the local party machines.

The positions targeted for the classified service were those in which performance was especially important: 2,573 positions in the customs service (in the largest customhouses), 5,699 in the postal service (in the largest post offices), and 5,652 in the departmental service in Washington, DC (headquarters of executive branch departments with more technical responsibilities) in a total of 131,860 federal positions.[12] As the government grew, the size of the merit labor force also grew as a proportion of overall federal civilian employment. Figure 12.1 details the rise the share of the merit labor force.

In part, this growth took place routinely as the postal and customs services grew in size and as executive department offices in Washington expanded (pursuant to section 6 of the Pendleton Act). The merit service also grew owing to explicit actions of the president, often the in face of opposition from members of Congress and local party officials who still benefited from patronage appointments. With the broadest

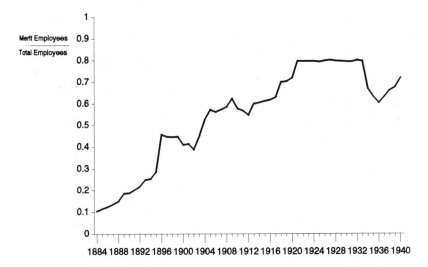

Figure 12.1. Proportion of merit to total federal civilian employees, 1884–1940
Source: Johnson and Libecap 1994a, 61.

national constituencies and the most remote ties to local political machines, the president was the most avid supporter of the merit system.

By means of executive orders and rules revisions drafted by executive department heads, the president could extend the merit system. Gradually after 1883, federal employees in the Railway Mail Service, the Indian Service, the Agriculture and Interior Departments, the Treasury, the IRS, and the War Department were added to the classified service.

Most of the positions that were left in the unclassified service were fourth-class postmasterships, which were part-time offices in virtually every town and village in the country. There were about seventy-six thousand of them in 1896, and they were coveted by members of Congress as means of rewarding political supporters. They were routinely dismissed whenever administrations and political parties changed, and every new president was under intense pressure to dismiss existing officeholders and make these offices available to the party loyal.

Beginning as early as the term of Grover Cleveland, these pressures were a burden and a diversion from public affairs that needed consideration. In addition, the National Civil Service Reform League demanded that these "plums of the spoils system" be placed in the classified service. Nevertheless, they remained patronage positions until early in the twentieth century, when Theodore Roosevelt moved most to the classified service (Johnson and Libecap 1994a, 53–63).

The demands on members of Congress also were severe as hordes of office seekers streamed to Washington to place their demands whenever there was a new Congress (Sageser 1935, 132–33). Lame-duck presidents were pressured to "blanket in" political appointees by placing them in the merit service, thereby giving them some possible protection from dismissal by the incoming administration. But because the Pendleton Act did not grant tenure to government employees, such actions may have provided little job security. Further, lame-duck appointments accounted for only about one-fifth of the growth of the classified labor force (Johnson and Libecap 1994a, 61–66). More and more, patronage was becoming too unpopular with critical constituent groups to be maintained, and presidents were more interested in using their classification ability to expand presidential authority and the efficiency of government than in satisfying the demands of local party bosses.

The Role of Federal Employees' Unions in the Growth of the Civil Service System

The Pendleton Act did not give government employees job tenure. Merit and patronage employees could be removed for lack of performance. The Pendleton Act also was unclear as to who controlled the new bureaucracy, and the president and the Congress subsequently competed for control. This competition provided an opportunity for government employees to play the two parties against one another and achieve additional protections. Limited tenure was first granted to government employees in 1897 by the president to limit the influence of Congress. Gradually, one side or the other granted more job security to federal employees until complete tenure was provided. The move from patronage was made complete with the Hatch Acts of 1939 and 1940, which prohibited the direct involvement of federal employees in political campaigns.

These actions appear to have had the unintended effect of creating a new and independent group of federal employees, who became a critical third party in the continued development of the bureaucracy in the twentieth century. Federal employees' unions became influential in the enactment of laws defining job descriptions, pay classifications, salaries, and job ladders. With job security and merit-based hiring and promotion, career government employees did not owe allegiance to the incumbent party or to a particular politician.

Although the Pendleton Act, in part, was designed to improve the efficiency of the delivery of federal services, the cumulative effect of the law and related legislation was to limit the leverage available to politicians over the federal bureaucracy. The old issue of whether the president or the Congress controlled the federal labor force was largely replaced by new questions about whether either had real control of the bureaucracy.

Prior to 1880, the federal labor movement was splintered and limited in size. With civilian employment based on patronage, federal workers owed allegiance to their mentors, not to their peers. Federal labor unions were virtually nonexistent (Nesbitt 1976, 3–80). But with the creation and growth of the classified service, conditions began to change. With the gradual demise of patronage, members of Congress began to take less interest in government employees while those employees began to view their positions as more permanent. They maneuvered to make them so and to increase their salaries and benefits (Spero 1927, 61).

The earliest federal employees' unions lobbied to expand the classified service, extend civil service reforms and protection from dismissal, and to institute more automatic pay increases. They were assisted by private-sector unions in pushing for greater job classification and security, higher salaries, limits on hours of work, workers' compensation, and retirement benefits. Gradually, federal employees' unions, especially postal unions, became a major lobbying force with headquarters in Washington, DC, where they drafted laws for the classified service, carefully followed legislation that affected them, appeared in committee hearings to support or oppose critical legislation, and organized campaigns for supportive politicians and agency administrators, especially the chairs of the House and Senate Civil Service Committees.

Federal employees' unions demonstrated that they could mobilize their membership to further their interests. As W. M. Collins, president of the Railway Mail Association, admonished its members, "[Y]ou should remember your friends on election day." [13] One natural area of attention was salaries. Data assembled by Paul Douglas in 1930 show that weekly salaries for federal employees exceeded that of their private-sector counterparts in 1900 but that their relative position declined through 1917.[14] With the slow decline of patronage, politicians were less concerned with maintaining the relatively high salaries that compensated for patronage assessments. In addition, federal agency heads had considerable discretion in placing individuals and determining their salaries.

Federal Salaries

After 1917, however, the relative salary position of federal workers improved. This improvement coincided with expansion of membership in federal unions and their associated lobbing for salary legislation. The unions, led by the National Federation of Federal Employees (NFFE), were particularly interested in legislation that authorized automatic salary increases with the passage of time and avoided efficiency ratings as a basis for pay adjustments.

The most important legislation was the Classification Act of 1923, which called for uniform position definitions and salaries throughout the classified service. With the uniform position structure defined by statute, federal unions could better lobby Congress for general salary increases that would apply broadly to federal employees without intervention by the agency heads involved. Over time, via the Civil Service Reform Act of 1978, the 1990 Federal Employees Pay Comparability Act, and related legislation, they achieved a pay structure that rigidly defined a pay system with automatic step increases and very limited reliance on merit provisions. There were also favorable mechanisms for increasing federal salaries in response to changes in private-sector compensation.

Federal employees' unions such as the NFFE and the American Federation of Government Employees (AFGE) have played a key role in molding their compensation system, and studies using standard human capital earnings regressions indicate that most federal workers earn more than their private-sector counterparts.[15] Further, their salaries are not linked to the fortunes of their agency but rise with the passage of time (Johnson and Libecap 1989a). Federal workers effectively have job tenure, so it is extremely difficult to remove them, and under civil service rules, federal government supervisors have little discretion in rewarding employees for exemplary performance or in punishing those who underperform (Johnson and Libecap 1989b).

Not only were federal employees able to raise their salaries by lobbying for pay legislation, but they were also able to obtain workplace benefits generally ahead of those in the private sector. Indeed, the federal government became a model for many of these benefits, which subsequently were granted elsewhere in the economy. One benefit was the eight-hour day, which was advocated by postal unions, and though collaboration with private-sector unions, was extended first throughout the Postal Service and other federal agencies and then to other parts of the labor force.

Other benefits garnered by federal employees by active lobbying of Congress included compulsory workers' compensation provisions for death and injuries due to accidents and expanded pension and retirement benefits. For example, the 1920 Federal Retirement Act was considerably more generous than either state government or private pension provisions at the time.[16]

Tenure

A final and critical benefit secured by federal employees was effective job tenure. Job security, which insulates career government workers from direct political manipulation or management, emerged from competition between the president and Congress over control of the federal labor force. Although the Pendleton Act created a bureaucratic structure that limited the authority of local politicians over federal employees, the legislation was not clear as to whether the president or Congress had authority over the new classified service. Each side had an incentive to use government employees in its own interest, but conflict over control could have led to a return of the some of the dangers inherent in the old patronage system.

This could have arisen, for example, if either the President or Congress threatened employees with dismissal for failure to support their political objectives or to campaign for them. Because the president had the most to lose under patronage-like conditions and their associated political costs, it is not surprising that the first move toward job tenure came through an executive order issued by President McKinley in 1897, requiring that dismissal from the classified service be made solely for cause with written notification. This order limited arbitrary dismissals by angry members of Congress.[17]

In 1912, however, Congress became concerned about growing presidential pressure on the classified service and enacted the Lloyd-LaFollette Act, which, among other things, prohibited dismissal of classified employees for any reason except inefficiency. More ironclad tenure provisions were added in the Civil Service Retirement Act of 1920 and subsequent legislation by implementation of elaborate grievance, notification, and arbitration procedures. These provisions naturally were strongly supported by federal employees' unions, and they profoundly changed the nature of the federal bureaucracy and its relation with the president and Congress.

The Emergence of an Autonomous Federal Bureaucracy

In the end, the efforts of the executive and legislative branches to reduce partisan influence on federal employees by the creation and gradual extension of the civil service system and the subsequent addition of tenure protection dramatically increased the autonomy of the bureaucracy. What previously had been an explicitly political arrangement between politicians and patronage workers was replaced by merit requirements, high salaries and other benefits, and substantial job security. The actions taken by the president and Congress not only set the stage for a relatively insulated, protected, and privileged bureaucracy but, through federal employees' unions, created an influential third party in the continued development of the civil service system.

Ironically, it appears that the very depoliticization of the federal labor force created a new set of problems. Although the Pendleton Act was designed to improve the efficiency of the delivery of federal services, the cumulative effect of this institutional change was to limit the leverage available to politicians over the federal bureaucracy in insuring adherence to policy and effective delivery of services.

The shift to a merit system facilitated the development of a new interest group, federal employees' unions, with an important stake in the nature of the civil service system. This interest group was able to secure additional favorable legislation covering salaries, benefits, and expanded job tenure. At the same time, the "problem of bureaucracy" and associated criticisms of government were largely issues of accountability, intrusiveness, cost, and productivity. None of these will be easily resolved within the confines of the existing civil service system with its insulated but politically powerful bureaucracy.

Conclusion

We have come a long way from the federal labor force that existed after the Civil War. The federal government is not only far, far larger and growing, but federal career employees are relatively insulated from direct political control with limited structural incentives for efficient performance. Further, federal employees' unions are politically powerful as major contributors to electoral campaigns and as mobilizers of their members in voting for supportive politicians and against those who oppose them.

In a time of large federal deficits and constraints on budgets, there are pressures for greater productivity from government employees. In countering civil service reform, however, federal unions have resorted to the use of popular myths about patronage and political manipulation (Johnson and Libecap 1995). Any effort to reduce the privileges held by government workers and to strengthen political control of the bureaucracy is cast as a return to patronage or, at minimum, increased political interference. In this way the bureaucracy attempts to control or to mold the flow of information in the debate about civil service reform. By raising fears of patronage and political manipulation of government workers, the bureaucracy diverts the discussion from an analysis of the private benefits received by career employees under the current system to a debate about the risks of dismantling civil service protections and reinstating patronage.

The fear of patronage and loss of political neutrality are convenient ploys for federal employees' unions to turn to in responding to criticisms about the performance of the bureaucracy. There is no returning to patronage as it existed in the nineteenth century. But a system whereby greater control over the bureaucracy is granted to politicians via greater use of merit pay and some increased authority in hiring and firing would provide a remedy to current problems with performance and accountability within the federal bureaucracy.

Given the growing size of the federal government in the economy, the costs and effectiveness of the delivery of government goods and services assume greater importance in determining the ability of the overall economy to meet the needs of citizens. Accordingly, the quest for neutral competence within the bureaucracy has been replaced with a quest for its greater accountability and motivation.[18] This objective certainly fits well with initial goal of the politicians who pushed for and enacted the Pendleton Act of 1883.

Notes

1. The material in this chapter is drawn from joint research and publication with Ron Johnson, especially Johnson and Libecap 1994a.

2. Higgs 1987. See also Goldin and Libecap 1994.

3. Weingast and Moran (1983), however, argue that by controlling the budget, Congress can exert influence over the administration of policy. For discussion of the concerns and issues, see Johnson and Libecap 1994a, 154–71.

4. Roosevelt is quoted in Van Riper 1958, 185.

5. See Johnson and Libecap 1994a, 42, endnote 4 for discussion of the evidence concerning this issue.

6. Overacker 1932, 103–9; Reeves 1969, 581.

7. U.S. Civil Service Commission, *Annual Report*, 1893, 9, 230.

8. Garfield is quoted in U.S. House of Representatives 1976, 156.

9. *New York Times*, March 24, 1873; *Chicago Tribune*, November 18, 1882.

10. *New York Times*, September 9, 1881, quoted in Skowronek, 1982, 52.

11. See Johnson and Libecap 1994a, 23.

12. U.S. Civil Service Commission, *Annual Report*, 1889, 15.

13. Collins is quoted in Spero 1927, 47–48.

14. Johnson and Libecap 1994a, 83–85. See also Conyngton 1920, 15–20.

15. Smith 1977; Gyourko and Tracy 1988; Venti 1987; and others noted by Johnson and Libecap 1994a, 110–11.

16. Johnson and Libecap 1994a, 88–91. See also Clark, Craig, and Wilson 2003.

17. U.S. Civil Service Commission, *Annual Report,* 1899, 19; Johnson and Libecap 1994b, 114.

18. Knott and Miller (1987, 231–51) describe the efforts of various presidential administrations in a chapter titled "The Quest for Neutral Competence."

References

Clark, Robert L., Lee A. Craig, and Jack W. Wilson. 2003. *A History of Public Sector Pensions in the United States.* Philadelphia: University of Pennsylvania Press.

Conyngton, Mary. 1920. "Separations from the Government Service." *Monthly Labor Review* 11 (December): 1131–44.

Fowler, Dorothy G. 1943. *The Cabinet Politician: The Postmaster General, 1829–1909.* New York: Columbia University Press.

Goldin, Claudia, and Gary D. Libecap, eds. 1994. *The Regulated Economy: A Historical Approach to Political Economy.* Chicago: University of Chicago Press.

Gyourko, Joseph, and Joseph Tracy. 1988. "An analysis of Public and Private-Sector Wages Allowing for Endogenous Choices of Both Government and Union Status." *Journal of Labor Economics* 6.2 (April): 229–53.

Higgs, Robert. 1987. *Crisis and Leviathan: Critical Episodes in the Growth of American Government.* New York: Oxford University Press.

Johnson, Ronald N., and Gary D. Libecap. 1989a. "Agency Growth, Salaries and the Protected Bureaucrat." *Economic Inquiry* 27 (July): 431–51.

———. 1989b. "Bureaucratic Rules, Supervisor Behavior, and the Effect on Salaries in the Federal Government." *Journal of Law, Economics, and Organization* 5.1 (Spring): 53–82.

———. 1994a. *The Federal Civil Service System and the Problem of Bureaucracy: The Economics and Politics of Institutional Change.* Chicago: University of Chicago Press.

———. 1994b. "Patronage to Merit and Control of the Federal Government Labor Force." *Explorations in Economic History* 31.1 (January): 91–119.

———. 1995. "Courts, a Protected Bureaucracy, and Reinventing Government." *Arizona Law Review* 37.3: 791–823.

Knott, Jack H., and Gary J. Miller. 1987. *Performing Bureaucracy: The Politics of Institutional Choice.* Englewood Cliffs, NJ: Prentice-Hall.

Nesbitt, Murray, B. 1976. *Labor Relations in the Federal Government Service.* Washington, DC: Bureau of National Affairs.

Overacker, Louise. 1932. *Money in Elections.* New York: Macmillan.

Reeves, Thomas C. 1969. "Chester A. Arthur and Campaign Assessments in the Election of 1880." *Historian* 31.4:573–82.

Sageser, A. Bower. 1935. *The First Decades of the Pendleton Act: A Study of Civil Service Reform.* University Studies, nos. 34–35. Lincoln: University of Nebraska Press.

Skowronek, Stephen. 1982. *Building a New American State: The Expansion of National Administrative Capacities, 1877–1920.* New York: Cambridge University Press.

Smith, Sharon. 1977. *Equal Pay in the Public Sector: Fact or Fantasy?* Princeton: Princeton University Press.

Spero, Sterling D. 1927. *The Labor Movement in a Government Industry: A Study of Employee Organization in the Postal Service.* New York: Macmillan.

U.S. Civil Service Commission. [Various years.] *Annual Report.* Washington, DC: Government Printing Office.

U.S. Department of Commerce. 1975. *Historical Statistics of the United States.* Washington, DC: Government Printing Office.

U.S. House of Representatives. 1976. *History of Civil Service Merit Systems of the United States and Selected Foreign Countries.* Committee on Post Office and Civil Service. 94th Cong., 2nd sess. Washington, DC: Government Printing Office.

U.S. Office of Personnel Management. 2002. *Federal Civilian Workforce Statistics: Pay Structure of the Federal Civil Service.* Washington, DC: Government Printing Office.

——. 2003. *Federal Civilian Workforce Statistics: Fact Book.* Washington, DC: Government Printing Office.

Van Riper, Paul P. 1958. *History of the United States Civil Service.* Evanston, IL: Row Peterson.

Venti, Stephen F. 1987. "Wages in the Federal and Private Sectors." In *Public Sector Payrolls*, ed. David A. Wise, 147–82. Chicago: University of Chicago Press.

Wallis, John, J. 1984. "The Birth of the Old Federalism: Financing the New Deal, 1932–1940." *Journal of Economic History* 44.1 (March): 139–59.

Weingast, Barry R., and Mark J. Moran. 1983. "Bureaucratic Discretion or Congressional Control? Regulatory Policymaking by the Federal Trade Commission." *Journal of Political Economy* 91.6 (December): 765–800.

White, Leonard D. 1954. *The Jacksonians: A Study in Administrative History.* New York: Macmillan.

13

The New Deal

AFTER THE largely evolutionary changes in the government's role during the Progressive Era and the emergency expansion of that role during World War I, government activity continued to grow along its long-term path. While many of the temporary wartime programs were being phased out, other programs continued to expand. Governments were building a rapidly expanding network of roads and highways that could accommodate the increasing use of the automobile, and districts and states continued to add high schools. Meanwhile, lobbyists from a variety of interest groups and reform movements were sowing the seeds for later expansions. In many ways, however, the decade of the 1920s was the calm before the storm, as the Great Depression soon encouraged drastic changes in the landscape of government and the economy.

Just prior to the stock market crash of 1929, the economy turned downward. Despite optimism after the crash that the economy would soon recover, it continued its downward slide into the worst depression in American history. By 1933 real output in the United States was 30 percent below its 1929 peak, and prices had fallen dramatically. Unemployment rates eventually peaked above 25 percent in 1933 but remained above 10 percent for the entire decade of the 1930s. Ironically, given the shift toward increased government involvement in the economy, federal macroeconomic policies likely contributed significantly to the depth of the Depression.

As the Depression deepened, President Herbert Hoover, a strong Progressive in his own right, experimented with a variety of new policies that called on the government to combat the growing problems. His most prominent effort was the establishment of the Reconstruction Finance Corporation (RFC). Modeled on the War Finance Corporation of World War I, the RFC sought to resurrect the economy by means of massive loans to banks, railroads, industry, and governments. Hoover's actions met with little success in counteracting the downward slide, and the 1932 elections swept Franklin Delano Roosevelt and a large Democratic congressional majority into office.

The U.S. economy had always rebounded from sharp downturns, but after four years of continued decline, this downturn seemed different, and notions that market economies could be self-correcting were dismissed with increasing frequency. Problems could be found in nearly every nook and cranny of the economy. State and local governments, which had long held responsibility for providing aid to those in trouble, were overwhelmed. Citing a peacetime emergency, the administration rolled up its sleeves and within the First Hundred Days in office established a "New Deal" for America. Identify a problem and the Roosevelt administration offered a program to solve it. The programs had laudable goals: raising farm incomes, raising wages, helping the unemployed, stimulating industrial output by raising prices, offering liquidity to housing markets, providing insurance for bank deposits, building social overhead capital—such as dams, roads, sewers, and pubic buildings—and still more. Yet the many programs at times worked at cross purposes. For example, programs designed to raise farm prices by limiting acreage contributed to greater unemployment in the farm sector and certainly made life more difficult for consumers of farm products.

The New Deal programs went through several transformations. In 1935 the Supreme Court declared the Agricultural Adjustment and the National Industrial Recovery Acts unconstitutional in the *Butler* and *Schechter Poultry* cases, eliminating major features of Roosevelt's farm programs and industrial policy. Further, the federal government's role in providing relief to the unemployed and indigent was revamped. The federal government continued to provide temporary work relief through the Works Progress Administration, while the Social Security Act of 1935 established long-term programs for old-age pensions and state-federal administration of unemployment insurance and welfare policy.[1]

During the 1930s the role of government, in particular the role of the federal government, in the economy ratcheted upward in ways unanticipated by the Progressives of the early 1900s. Several New Deal emergency programs were temporary and were phased out during or after World War II. Some were successful based on several standards of measurement. Others were failures best not repeated. In the end the New Deal established a legacy of social insurance programs, regulations, and procedures that are largely still in place today. Many have served as the bases on which new programs have been built.

Macroeconomic Policy during the 1930s

A leading aspect of economic thought developed during the twentieth century was an explicit role for federal government in macroeconomic policy. In the Employment Act of 1946 the U.S. Congress gave the federal government the explicit responsibility to use monetary and fiscal policy to help smooth the path of economic growth, maintain full employment, and avoid inflation. The nation's central bank, the Federal Reserve System (known as the Fed), handles the reins of monetary policy, and Congress, subject to the presidential veto, determines fiscal policy through its decisions about spending and taxation. The implicit use of fiscal and monetary policy stretches back to the early days of the century, and macroeconomic policy used during the 1930s has long dominated discussions of the Great Depression. The formation of the Federal Reserve System in 1913 established a full-blown central bank armed with policy tools that could influence the money supply.[2] Meanwhile, the Keynesian ideas of using government spending and taxation to stimulate the economy were being developed as the Depression progressed.

The Central Bank Policy as a Contributor to the Great Depression

The Holy Grail among American economists is an explanation of the cause of the Great Depression that is convincing to the profession at large. Numerous explanations have been proposed. Some argue that economies tend to be cyclical, with both short-term fluctuations and long Kondratieff cycles, and that at various times every thirty to ninety years, there is a downturn of biblical proportions. Others emphasize a sharp decline in investment and construction following the booms of the 1920s. Still others emphasize a decline in consumption, particularly of durable goods, that might have been fueled in part by the uncertainties in the stock market. Most scholars, however, agree that the monetary policies of the Federal Reserve to some degree contributed to the decline of the early 1930s, although there is still disagreement about the magnitude of the Fed's actions and the reasons why its policy was misguided.[3]

Milton Friedman and Anna Schwartz originated the argument that the Fed bears significant responsibility for the tremendous drop in output between 1929 and 1933. In the Federal Reserve Act of 1913, the Fed was given the responsibility of creating an "elastic" currency. Although the concept of an elastic currency was vague, most observers thought that the Fed was expected to help solve liquidity crises during bank runs. By the 1920s the Fed had two effective tools for influencing the money supply: the discount rate at which member banks borrowed from the Fed to meet their reserve requirements and open-market operations. The open-market operations involved the purchase or sale of existing bonds. Reductions in the discount rate and purchases of bonds contributed to increases in the money supply. Thus, if the Fed was focused on problems with bank failures and unemployment within the U.S. economy, its optimal strategy was to lower the discount rate and purchase bonds.[4]

Yet it also had to pay attention to the gold supply in the United States. The nation generally adhered to the international gold standard, which was essentially a promise that the Federal Reserve and U.S. banks would pay out an ounce of gold for every $20.67 in Federal Reserve notes received in international transactions. To remain on the gold standard, the Fed was required to provide adequate U.S. gold reserves to make this promise credible. If changes in the relative attractiveness of the dollar led the nation's supply of gold to fall below the appropriate level, the Fed was expected to take action to make the dollar more attractive. At the time the standard policies used in response to gold outflows included raising the discount rate and selling (or at least reducing purchases of) existing bonds.

The Federal Reserve's attempts to slow the speculative boom in stocks contributed to slowing the money supply between 1928 and 1929. Over the following four years there were a series of negative shocks to the money supply, including the stock market crash in 1929, banking crises in 1930–31, 1931, and 1932–33, and Britain's abandonment of the gold standard in November 1931. The Fed's response to these crises is best described as too little, too late. Had the Fed offset the early crises quickly with much larger open-market purchases of bonds and faster cuts in the discount rate, it could have limited the damage and prevented the rapid decline in the money supply. The economy would have been in a much better position when the next crises hit or some of the later crises would have been prevented or softened significantly. The Fed's boldest move, an open-market purchase of $1 billion in bonds in the spring of 1932, would have been extremely effective in 1930, but two years later it essentially served to close the drain after most of the water had already run out.[5]

Why was the Federal Reserve so recalcitrant? Friedman and Schwartz argued that it lacked strong leadership of the right kind. Benjamin Strong, a powerful advocate for a focus on protecting the domestic economy as the head of the New York Federal Reserve Bank, had died in 1928. Although his replacements at the New York Fed argued for expansive bond purchases in the early 1930s, they were overridden by the rest of the Fed's policymakers, who tended to hold the Austrian view that such interference would prolong the problems.

Not all agree that the Fed changed directions with the death of Strong. Statistical comparisons of Federal Reserve policy in the 1920s and 1930s suggest that the Fed seemed to be responding to domestic and international changes in largely the same way in both decades. The Fed likely failed to recognize that the problems of the Great Depression were so large that they required the Fed to take much greater action to save banks and stimulate the money supply. For example, the Fed allowed thousands of banks to fail during the 1920s because they believed them to be weaker banks that normally would not survive in a market economy. The banks that failed in the early 1930s, having survived through the 1920s, were generally stronger, and the Fed did not realize that many were failing owing to extraordinary circumstances.[6]

Some of the Fed's actions might best be understood by examining its international role in defending the gold standard. Until 1933 the Fed maintained a strong commitment to the international gold standard, a commitment that tied its hands. Although the money supply and the economy were continuing to decline, the outflows of gold that occurred when Britain left the gold standard in 1931 and during the banking crisis in March of 1933 led the Fed to raise the discount rate. Once the United States left the gold standard in 1933, it was freer to focus on domestic policy and the money supply, and the economy began to recover. This same pattern was repeated throughout the world. In country after country, central banks that sought to maintain the gold standard saw their domestic economies sink. As each left the gold standard, its economy rebounded. By leaving the gold standard, the United States received a substantial flow of gold into the American economy caused by the devaluation of the dollar to $35 per ounce of gold and by political developments in Europe that stimulated the money supply.[7]

In addition to leaving the gold standard, the Roosevelt administration sought to ease the pressure on banks in March 1933 by declaring a national "Bank Holiday." During a series of bank runs between October 1932 and March 1933, thirty states declared bank holidays, which took the pressure off the deposits in states where the banks were closed but increased runs by depositors in the states where banks remained open. During the national Bank Holiday all banks and thrift institutions were temporarily closed, and auditors examined the banks. Banks declared to be sound were reopened shortly afterward. Conservators were appointed to improve the positions of the insolvent banks, and the Reconstruction Finance Corporation was given the power to subscribe to stock issues from the reorganized banks. These seals of approval conferred on the reopened banks helped change expectations about the solvency of the bank system.[8]

With the benefit of hindsight, the appropriate choices for the central bank now seem more obvious, although there are still debates about the effectiveness of different policies. Recognize, however, that the Federal Reserve was less than twenty years old, and its administrators were relatively inexperienced as central bankers. Learning from the mistakes of countries with a longer history of central banking was of little use, because nearly every other central bank in the world was making the same mistakes.

And the Fed still had more lessons to learn. The Banking Act of 1935 reorganized the Federal Reserve System and also gave it direct administrative control over the reserve requirements for its member banks. Under the fractional reserve system member banks were required to hold a share of deposits with the Fed as backing for their deposits. By 1935 the economy had been moving through two years of recovery. The real GDP growth rate was very rapid, in large part because the economy was starting from a base that was 36 percent below the 1929 level. The number of unemployed persons had dropped significantly, although they still composed more than 15 percent of the labor force. Noting that banks were holding reserves above and beyond the reserve requirements, the Fed began to be concerned about the possibility of inflation. If the banks started lending out their excess reserves, the Fed worried, the increase in the money supply, which would be multiplied via successive loans, would lead to rapid inflation that would halt the recovery. Feeling that the recovery was far enough along, the Federal Reserve doubled reserve requirements in three steps between 1935 and 1937. It had not recognized that the banks were holding the excess reserves in order to protect themselves against bank runs. Recent experience had given them little confidence that the Fed would act as a lender of last resort. Therefore, the banks increased their reserves to make sure that they kept roughly the same cushion. The policy contributed to a reduction in the money supply, a spike in unemployment, and a decline in real GDP growth in 1937–38.[9]

Federal Fiscal Policy: Spending and Taxation at the National Level

During the Great Depression with its severe worldwide problems, John Maynard Keynes developed his seminal theories about the impact of government spending and taxation on income and wealth. Keynes actively discussed his ideas with his colleagues during the early 1930s, and they were published in *The General Theory of Employment, Interest, and Money* in 1936. The theories of the classical economists suggested that periods of high unemployment would lead to downward adjustments to wages in the labor markets and prices in product markets that would naturally cause the economy to return to an equilibrium at full employment. Keynes argued that wages were sometimes "sticky" in a generally downward direction and that long-term contracts between workers and employers, union strength, and a host of factors might prevent wages from falling. Similarly, product prices might not always adjust. As a result, the economy might settle into a new long-term equilibrium in which resources would not be fully employed. One solution to the problem was for governments to stimulate the economy by increasing government spending or reducing tax collections. These moves would lead to budget deficits that could move the economy back toward a new equilibrium in which all resources would be fully employed.

During the New Deal the Roosevelt administration embarked on an ambitious spending program, more than doubling the Hoover administration's federal spending in real terms (1958 dollars) from an average of $7.3 billion in the period 1930–32 to an average of $15.7 billion in the period 1934–39 (see figure 13.1). The increase was so large that it seems obvious that Roosevelt was following the Keynesian prescriptions for a depressed economy. But closer study casts significant doubt on that interpretation. Keynes published an open letter to Roosevelt in the *New York Times* in December 1933 suggesting that Roosevelt practice stimulative spending policies. They met in 1934, but most observers believed that Keynes had little impact on the president's thinking. Although Keynes's ideas were in circulation by 1933, the lag between academic advances and their use in policy tends to take decades. In fact, Keynes once claimed: "Madmen in authority, who hear voices in the air, are distilling their frenzy from some academic scribblers of a few years back." Several of Roosevelt's advisers also argued for using government programs as a stimulus, but they followed a different logical path for their arguments.[10]

Roosevelt was following a far more conservative path because he, like Hoover, sought to avoid leaving the federal budget too far out of balance. As a result, average federal tax collections also more than doubled between 1930 and 1939 from $4.7 billion to $11.8 billion. The Revenue Act of 1932, passed by the Hoover administration, had sharply raised rates for the less than 10 percent of the households that were paying federal taxes during the 1930s. Individuals earning between two and three thousand dollars saw their effective tax rates rise from 0.1 percent to 2 percent in 1932. Those earning more than $1 million experienced a rate increase from 23.1 to 57.1 percent. The Roosevelt administration could have opted to lower the rates but only made slight adjustments during the rest of the decade, lowering them a bit for those earning less than ten thousand dollars and raising them a bit for those earning more than one hundred thousand dollars.

As a result, the federal budget deficit was never very large relative to economic shortfalls during the 1930s. Writing in 1941, Alva Hansen, a major figure in aiding the diffusion of Keynesian thought in the economics profession, stated, "Despite the fairly good showing made in the recovery up to 1937, the fact is that neither before nor since has the administration pursued a really positive expansionist program. . . . For the most part the federal government engaged in a salvaging program and not in a program of positive expansion." Figure 13.1 bears this out. It shows the federal budget deficit in billions of 1958 dollars from 1929 through 1941. After running surpluses in 1929 and 1930, the Hoover

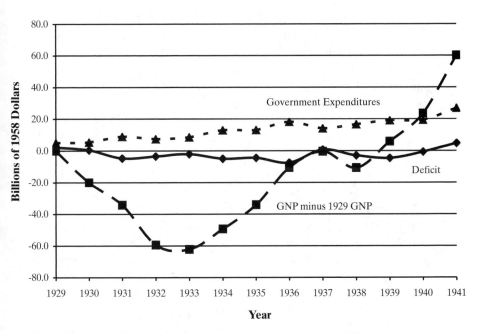

Figure 13.1. Federal budget deficit, government expenditures, and difference between GNP and 1929 GNP, all in 1958 dollars

government ran budget deficits of 4.7 billion and $3.5 billion in 1931 and 1932. The Roosevelt administration ran one surplus in 1937 and deficits in other years ranging from $2 billion in 1933 to $7.5 billion in 1936. The peaks in both administrations were probably not attempts to establish a Keynesian stimulus package. In 1931 and 1936 Congress passed large-scale payments to veterans over the vetoes of Hoover and Roosevelt, and these composed the bulk of the budget deficit.[11]

As a share of GNP, these budget deficits pale in comparison to some periods during the postwar era. Budget deficits during the 1930s never reached more than 3.9 percent of GNP in any one year. This was true even though the GNP had fallen drastically. Based on this metric, in the 1980s Ronald Reagan looked far more Keynesian than Roosevelt because budget deficits exceeded 5 percent in some years during the Reagan era.

The ultimate goal of any stimulus program is to reach full employment. Figure 13.1 also shows the difference between real GNP (in 1958 dollars) in each year and the 1929 full-employment peak of $203.6 billion. If these were attempts at Keynesian stimuli aimed at returning to full employment, the budget deficits were mere cupfuls of dollars that would have barely filled the target bucket. Real GNP in 1933 was $62.1 billion below its 1929 level, whereas the real budget deficit was only $2 billion. In 1934 a $5 billion dollar deficit was matched with a GNP shortfall of $49.3 billion; in 1935 the $4.5 billion deficit was offsetting a $34.1 billion shortfall. The figures look strongest in 1936, when a 7.5 billion deficit was matched with a $10.6 billion GNP shortfall. Keynesians argue that budget deficits have multiplier effects. For these deficits to be meaningful for returning to full employment, the multiplier effects would have had to be almost ten, yet the most ardent Keynesians find multipliers of only around two.

One of the Keynesian concepts was the balanced budget multiplier: a dollar increase in government spending matched by a dollar increase in taxation would lead incomes to rise by a dollar. Thus, we should look at government spending relative to the GNP shortfalls. Yet the real government spending estimates in the 1933 to 1936 period range from $8.7 billion in 1933 to $13.1 billion in 1934 and 1935. In 1936, the year of the veterans' bonus, real spending peaked at $18.1 billion. These figures pale in comparison to the shortfall in national income.[12]

Any impact that the federal deficits had in promoting recovery had to compete with the contractionary changes in state and local government budgets after 1933. Prior to 1933, state and local governments generally held nearly full responsibility for relief of the indigent and the unemployed. By 1933 they were overwhelmed by these and other responsibilities in the midst of a sharp decline in their revenues. A number were forced to run short-term deficits in the early 1930s. Yet state constitutions generally require balanced year-to-year budgets. To repay the budget shortfalls and also the debt issued during the early 1930s, state and local governments began raising taxes and establishing new taxes after 1933. The problem was further exacerbated when the federal government dumped responsibility for direct relief to "unemployables" back onto the state and local governments in 1935 after two years of extensive spending. Thus, in the latter half of the 1930s, they were often running small surpluses.

Not all taxes were designed to raise revenue. The Smoot-Hawley Tariff Act of 1930 raised taxes on imports substantially on top of a 1922 increase in an attempt to protect American manufacturers from competition from foreign imports. International trade was a small enough percentage of the American economy at the time that most economists ascribe to the tariff a secondary role as a contributor to the Depression in the United States, but it had far worse implications at the international level. The Smoot-Hawley tariff was matched by a series of protectionist measures enacted by countries throughout the world. As each nation tried to protect its home production interests by means of higher tariffs and restrictions on imports, world trade spiraled downward. By 1933 the total imports for seventy-five countries had fallen to roughly one-third of the level seen in 1929.

The Roosevelt administration contributed to a recovery in world trade by relaxing these tariff barriers. The Reciprocal Trade Agreement Act of 1934 freed the administration to sign a series of tariff reduction agreements with key trading partners. Agreements with Canada, several South American countries, Britain, and key European trading partners loosened the trade restrictions markedly. As a result, American imports rose from a twenty-year low in 1932–33 to an all-time high by 1940.[13]

The Reconstruction Finance Corporation: The Transition Agency

Because the Federal Reserve System did too little and too late in the early 1930s, the Hoover administration sought another way to inject liquidity into the economy by forming the Reconstruction Finance Corporation (RFC) in February 1932. The RFC was modeled after the War Finance Corporation of World War I. Its first moves included making loans to four thousand banks, railroads, credit unions, and mortgage

loan companies to provide assets that would jumpstart commercial lending. Among the most important programs was the provision of loans to
troubled banks in an attempt to provide them with enough liquidity to
survive bank runs. Recent studies suggest that these initial loans were
not successful because repayment of the RFC loans were given first
priority over depositors and other lenders when the borrowing banks
failed. As a result, banks had to hold the assets that they could sell most
easily to insure repayment of the RFC loans. These assets could not
then be used to repay depositors when the bank failed. When the RFC
began to accept more risk by purchasing preferred stock in the troubled
banks, it was more successful at staving off failures.[14]

The Roosevelt administration immediately saw uses for the RFC and
gave the off-budget corporation extraordinary leeway. The RFC retained
control of a large supply of funds that could be loaned out and had the
authority to borrow still more funds without having to constantly return
to Congress for new appropriations. As the loans were repaid, the RFC
continually had new funds to loan out again. The president and Congress
quickly came to love the RFC because it gave them so much flexibility.
James Olson describes the breadth of its activity: "By the mid-1930s, the
RFC was making loans to banks, savings banks, building and loan associations, credit unions, railroads, industrial banks, farmers, commercial
businesses, federal land banks, production credit associations, farm cooperative, mortgage loan companies, insurance companies, school districts, and livestock credit corporations" (Olson 1988, 43–44). Perhaps
more important, the RFC became the banker to many New Deal programs, providing loans or startup working capital to the Public Works
Administration (PWA), the Home Owners' Loan Corporation (HOLC),
the Farm Credit Administration (FCA), the Federal Housing Administration (FHA), the Rural Electrification Administration (REA), and
the Works Progress Administration (WPA).

It is clear that the RFC was central to the operation of Roosevelt's
New Deal. Its record at stimulating recovery is somewhat mixed.
Hoover's original goal for the RFC was to expand commercial credit
to 1929 levels, but this probably unobtainable short-term goal was not
met until the end of the 1930s. As one example, RFC loans to railroads and industries did contribute to delaying bankruptcies. Yet the
delay of bankruptcies may have been a mixed blessing. On the plus side,
the delays gave financial institutions more time to reduce their holdings of railroad bonds and avoid more banking crises. On the minus
side, the delays may have retarded needed maintenance and capital

expenditures. When railroads were in trouble they tended to cut back on maintenance of their rolling stock and rails and other capital equipment. One advantage of bankruptcies is that they forced railroads that could be viable again to make the proper investments in order to attract the necessary capital for reorganization. A recent study suggests that railroads that received RFC support continued to delay these types of expenditures when compared with the railroads that went through bankruptcy proceedings.[15]

The RFC was designed to be a temporary emergency agency, and by 1939 there were extensive discussions about winding it down. The Nazi invasion of France in 1940 led to a transformation of the RFC into a wartime agency that more closely resembled its ancestor the War Finance Corporation. The RFC established a series of companies to stockpile materials and products considered strategic for national defense, finance construction of new defense plants, and provide loans for housing construction for defense workers and made a wide variety of loans to businesses taking part in the war effort. At the end of the war the RFC finally was wound down.

Emergency Relief and Public Works Programs

Federal spending during the 1930s was less about macroeconomic stimulus in the modern sense of the word and more about solving the harsh problems that had arisen during the Depression. One of the central problems was determining how to aid the huge numbers of unemployed and discouraged workers. Prior to the Depression, the federal government had assumed virtually no responsibility for the provision of relief payments to low-income people and the unemployed. Unemployment and poverty were seen as local problems best dealt with by state and local governments and charities. As these relief structures became overwhelmed by unprecedented levels of unemployment in the early 1930s, views of the federal role shifted. The Hoover administration worked within the existing framework by authorizing the Reconstruction Finance Corporation in 1932 to lend up to $300 million to cities to provide relief. Originally, these loans were meant to be repaid at three percent interest via reductions in future highway apportionments, but the RFC was allowed to write them off in 1938.[16]

By the time Roosevelt took office in March 1933, unemployment rates had surged well past 20 percent. Arguing that the Great Depression was a national peacetime emergency, the federal government temporarily took over the lion's share of the responsibility for relief. During the First Hundred Days the Roosevelt administration established the Federal Emergency Relief Administration (FERA). The FERA distributed federal monies to the states, which, in turn, distributed the monies to local areas, which administered the payments to households. The FERA program offered either direct relief payments (with no work requirement) or work relief that required a family member to work for the funds. The amounts paid were determined by a "budget-deficit" principle. Local administrators compared the household's income to a hypothetical budget for a family that size and the maximum amount of relief would be determined by its deficit. The actual payments often fell short of the maximum when relief officials, faced with large caseloads and limited funds, cut payments to provide relief for more families.[17]

By November 1933 the administration was wary about the still-large number of unemployed people given the anticipation of a harsh winter. As a short-term fix, the Civil Works Administration (CWA) was established to immediately put people to work on public jobs, ranging from "make-work" activities to maintenance jobs such as raking leaves to the building of roads and schools. By December 1933 the CWA employed 3.6 million people. Eligibility for CWA employment was based on the budget-deficit principle, but the CWA wage payments were not specifically tied to the size of the household deficit. It was closed down in March 1934, and most of those employed were eventually transferred to FERA projects. Between July 1933 and July 1935, the FERA and the CWA distributed roughly $3.5 billion in relief to families throughout the United States.

In mid-1935 the Roosevelt administration redesigned the federal government's role in providing relief. It continued to provide work relief for unemployed persons who were employable in the Works Progress Administration but returned much of the responsibility for direct relief of "unemployables" to state and local governments. Applicants for aid were still certified by state and local officials, who continued to consider a family's budget deficit when assessing its need for relief employment. The WPA then hired certified people and paid them a wage for a restricted number of hours each month. Dissatisfied with its lack of control over work relief under the FERA, the federal government administered WPA more centrally. Yet the WPA, like FERA, faced a mixture of pressures as administrators decided how to distribute spending across the nation. State and local governments lobbied for funds, and federal administrators appear to have paid attention to local economic distress and political necessities. Roosevelt saw all of these emergency relief programs as temporary. Even though some officials wished to make them permanent features of the economy, the WPA was phased out by the end of 1942.[18]

The relief grants were composed of an unusual mixture of transfer payments, work, and the building of public projects. They were more closely associated with the workhouses of the past than to the modern welfare state, although they operated on a dramatically larger scale. In 1933 the administration could simply have relied on making direct relief payments without a work requirement. At that time, however, the vast majority of Americans considered collecting government payments to be a badge of shame. The pre-Depression attitudes that the poor (but not disabled) were responsible for their own fate still held sway even as it became obvious that many hardworking people had lost their jobs. One of the harshest outcomes of the Depression was the loss of confidence among the populace, which learned that it was not enough to work hard to maintain a comfortable life. Long after the Depression ended, this loss of confidence continued to influence the choices and attitudes toward risk of the generations who lived through the era. The trade of work for relief payments was considered less shameful, although even then a number of people were hesitant to accept the government's largesse. Harry Hopkins, the head of the FERA, the CWA, and later the WPA, preferred work relief, which "provided a man with something to do, put money in his pocket, and kept his self-respect."[19]

In the administration's view the work relief programs were not revolutionary. They were explicitly designed so as not to go beyond the public sector into the private sector. The projects were traditional government projects such as building and maintaining public buildings, schools, parks, roads, and sanitation facilities. Production of manufactured goods, creation of stores, and other private-sector activities were off-limits. Further, the work relief pay was designed to be below-market wage rates to encourage workers to seek private employment. To combat fears that private jobs would end quickly, the WPA assured people that they would be accepted back on work relief if they lost their private job. Even so, a significant percentage of workers stayed on work relief jobs for periods as long as a year and in some cases several years.[20]

As an alternative to work relief, the federal government (and state and local governments) might have funded public projects in the usual way, either directly hiring employees at market wages or contracting with construction firms that hired their workers in the private market. Hopkins and his aides appear to have rejected this alternative for several reasons. First, they wanted to provide relief as quickly as possible to a large number of struggling households. Had the work relief funds been used to fund public projects in the usual way, the same budget would have directly helped fewer people and built fewer projects. Second, Roosevelt saw the work relief as temporary emergency funding. All the bills authorizing the funds had the word *emergency* in their titles, and these programs all ended when the Depression was over. Further, the people on work relief were still considered unemployed in the official statistics until they obtained private jobs. Although Roosevelt occasionally delighted in tweaking conservative big businessmen, he was sensitive to the traditional boundaries between private and public employment. He resisted many efforts by more socialistic advisers to see work relief as a permanent institution designed to help the unemployed. Instead, he proffered the public assistance and social insurance mechanisms established under the Social Security Act as his long-term legacy.[21]

The public works grants included expenditures by the Public Works Administration, the Public Buildings Administration (PBA), the Public Roads Administration (PRA), and the Tennessee Valley Authority (TVA). The PWA was established under the National Industrial Recovery Act of 1933, and the PBA and PRA were rearrangements of existing federal agencies that had offered grants to states and cities to build roads and federal structures outside Washington, DC. These grants were also used largely to employ workers, but the focus was less on hiring the unemployed than on building such large-scale forms of civil infrastructure as dams, roads, schools, and sanitation facilities. Consequently, the planning stages of the projects were longer and the labor policies were more like non-Depression norms. Public works projects paid substantially better wages than the relief projects, were freer to hire a broader class of skilled workers, and were required to hire only a proportion of people from the relief rolls. By the end of the 1930s, the PWA, the WPA, the PRA, and the PBA had been rolled into the Federal Works Agency (FWA). In 1942, the PWA and WPA had been terminated and the PBA and PRA's duties were distributed to new agencies.[22]

How successful were the public works and relief programs at achieving their goals? On the surface they were wildly successful. The works programs marshaled resources that put millions of people to work during the worst and longest depression in American history. The WPA records at the National Archives are filled with box after box of personal letters to Roosevelt and Harry Hopkins thanking them for helping their families survive and get back on their feet. Many of the roads, buildings, post offices, and public works built by these agencies in every county in America are still in place or renovated versions of the original projects bear their stamp.

On a more cynical level, the programs succeeded by helping Roosevelt and Democratic congressmen remain in office. In 1938 WPA administrator Harry Hopkins allegedly declared to friends that "we shall tax and tax and spend and spend and elect and elect." Hopkins claimed that he had never made such a statement, but plenty of contemporaries considered it to be the underlying truth. Millions of Americans could claim that the Roosevelt administration had provided them with funds, a work relief job, or in-kind benefits during their time of need, a fact that was easily remembered on Election Day.[23]

There is another counterfactual standard against which these projects should be measured. How much better did the local economies perform in response to work relief and public works projects than they would have had the projects not been established? This is a more difficult question to answer because it involves trying to construct a hypothetical history of the era. It is a relevant question, however, when trying to assess the true impact of the projects and whether such projects might be effective in the future. The impact of public works and relief spending might have been mitigated by several factors. There was likely to be some "fiscal drag" to the extent that such spending led to higher incomes that generated more federal income taxes and greater consumption of goods on which excise taxes were charged. There is also the potential for "crowding out" of local activities. For example, local governments might have used federal funds to build projects that they had already planned to build in the near future. To obtain federal funds, state and local authorities often had to propose projects for federal funding. Thus, the New Deal funds might have moved the projects forward by one or two years as opposed to creating something that would never have been built. To some extent the public works and work relief opportunities might have forced private companies to pay higher wages to attract workers to new opportunities, which in turn would have retarded private employment. Certainly, there were complaints by private employers to the WPA that this was happening. Given the extremely high levels of unemployment, it might seem as if the federal projects would have simply soaked up the unemployed and thus such crowding out of private activity would not have been great. This is an empirical question that scholars are just now beginning to answer.[24]

In the past two decades, a number of economists have used the geographic variation in New Deal spending to measure the effect of the

New Deal programs. The results still tell a relatively optimistic story for public works and relief programs, although there may have been some crowding out of private activity. In the labor market the relief programs may have reduced employment in private industry. Studies of cross-sectional data that provide a snapshot of the country in a single year suggest that areas with greater relief employment did not see crowding out of private employment. But studies using panel data, which allow for variation both across geographic areas and over time, find some crowding out. At the state level, for every relief job created the private sector shed half of a private job; therefore, the net gain was half a job.

The relief jobs may have helped workers in ways that, oddly enough, caused the official measures of unemployment to rise. High unemployment rates often discourage workers from seeking work. These "discouraged" workers are not considered unemployed under standard definitions of unemployment, which require that someone be actively seeking work. Meanwhile, during the 1930s relief workers were treated as unemployed in the official statistics. As a result, when a relief job became available and was filled by a discouraged worker, the number of unemployed persons in the official statistics rose by one. Hence we see the odd result that the creation of an additional relief job could make the official unemployment statistics look worse during the 1930s.[25]

The impact of public works and relief programs extended well beyond the labor market. An added dollar of public works and relief spending in a U.S. county was associated with an increase in retail sales of roughly forty to fifty cents between 1933 and 1939. Given typical ratios of retail sales to income, this suggests that incomes in the county grew roughly eighty-five cents at the mean when a dollar was added to public works and relief spending. Counties with greater levels of such spending appeared to be more attractive to workers because these counties experienced more in-migration during the 1930s. Greater relief spending also reduced property crime rates in cities during the Depression.[26]

By putting resources into the hands of struggling families and by building public works that contributed to better public health, the relief and public works programs also may have staved off a potential rise in infant mortality rates during the 1930s. Improvements to public health in the early 1900s had led to sharp declines in infant mortality through the early 1930s, but in the heart of the Depression the decline stalled temporarily. Studies of the experience of black and white infants throughout the South and a panel of cities across the entire United States suggest that the relief and public works programs contributed to a decrease in infant mortality rates. In cities greater relief spending also reduced suicides, homicides, and deaths due to diarrhea, infections, and parasites. The relief expenditures associated with preventing a death from these causes ranged from $840,000 to roughly $9 million in year 2000 dollars. This is approximately the value of life found in labor market studies and is a substantially smaller cost than the cost of many modern safety programs. Increases in relief spending also helped offset the sharp decline in the birth rate that occurred during the heart of the Depression.[27]

The Farm Programs

The situation for farmers in some ways may have been more dire than in cities and industries. An expansion of farms during World War I had followed a golden era of farm prices in the early 1900s. As the Europeans recovered from the war in the early 1920s, demand for American farm products declined, and the farm sector went through a difficult shakeout in the early 1920s. After a decade of troubles farmers were hit still harder by the Great Depression.

Since the Gilded Age farmers had been protesting their plight and seeking ways to limit output and raise prices. The large number of American farmers and the competition from foreign producers had combined to prevent the farmers from successfully combining forces to limit output. By the 1920s they had begun pressing the federal government to limit production. In 1927 and 1928 Congress passed versions of the McNary-Haugen bill designed to raise farm prices without supply controls, but each was vetoed by the president. In 1929 the federal government began experimenting in a small way with a program in which the Federal Farm Board purchased output from producers who limited production. The Roosevelt administration responded to farmers' pleas during the First Hundred Days by establishing a series of measures that became the basis for the nation's modern farm programs.[28]

The goal was to limit supply and thus raise the ratio of farm prices to nonfarm prices to levels seen during the golden era just prior to World War I. The centerpiece of the New Deal program was the rental and benefit program administered by the Agricultural Adjustment Administration (AAA). For a wide variety of farm products the AAA offered agreements to farmers that paid them to take land out of production. The funds for the program came from a tax on farm output at the location where it was first processed, for example, at the cotton gin for cotton. Farmers were not required to accept the agreements, but the AAA set attractive terms and actively marketed the programs through county agents and local boards of farmers. In the tobacco and cotton programs federal decision makers added a degree of coercion to the system by levying heavy taxes on any production beyond designated limits. As a result, the sign-up rates ranged between 70 and 95 percent for most types of crops. In 1935 the program was nullified by the U.S. Supreme Court *United States v. Butler* on grounds that the processing tax used to finance the program was unconstitutional. Farm interests that had warmed to the AAA pressed the Roosevelt administration to enact a similar program that would overcome the constitutional objections. Soon thereafter, a new AAA was established that made payments to curtail land use, adjust production, and conserve the soil under the Soil Conservation and Domestic Allotment Act.[29]

Many farmers also benefited from a wide range of loan programs. The Commodity Credit Corporation (CCC) lent funds to farmers for crops in storage with terms that contributed to keeping prices high. When repayment time came, if crop prices exceeded the target level, the farmer would sell the crop on the market and repay the government loan. If crop prices were below the target, the farmer gave the crop to the government as payment of the loan. In the 1930s the CCC set the target prices above market prices, so the program operated as a price support program. The program has continued to the present day.

Farmers had long lobbied for federal intervention to provide cheaper and more adequate sources of credit. With the National Farm Loan Act of 1916 and the establishment of Federal Intermediate Credit Banks (FICBs) in 1923, the federal government had developed a farm credit system with two types of land banks: those that aided in mortgage lending and those that would purchase nine-month to three-year bank loans, which freed up more funds for the banks to expand lending for seed, provisions, and other short-term needs. By 1932 the land banks held about one-seventh of the total outstanding farm-mortgage debt, although the joint-stock land banks were liquidating because they had never generated sufficient capital to operate profitably. The intermediate credit banks had not succeeded in generating the amount of short-term credit desired by farmers. As the Hoover administration ended, the land bank system expanded its lending power. But the true boom in farm lending resulted when the Farm Credit Administration was created in 1933 to revamp and administer the entire farm credit system. Within two years the FCA programs had lent out more than had been lent in the prior sixteen years. Consequently, the federal government was involved in more than half of farm mortgages by the mid-1930s.[30]

The AAA and most loan programs were primarily oriented toward large farmers but also distributed smaller amounts of funds in programs designed to eliminate areas of persistent rural poverty. The original FERA legislation called for aid to low-income farmers in the form of relief, the Resettlement Administration moved some farmers to better land, and loans and grants from other programs were provided to aid small family farms. These farm programs were later transferred to the Farm Security Administration when it was formed in 1937.[31]

Chapter 15 deals with the long-term effects of the farm programs. Observers of the short-term impact in mid-1930s were unsure whether the AAA's practice of paying farmers to take land out of production was effective in raising prices. Several studies suggest that farmers took the lowest-quality land out of production first and then found ways to raise the productivity on other acreage by using more fertilizers and adopting new technologies (such as tractors) as labor-saving devices. Efforts to determine the AAA's impact have been confounded because a series of major climatic disasters, including droughts in some areas, floods in others, and the Dust Bowl, coincided with the program's introduction and also contributed to drops in production and higher prices.[32]

Given that the programs were voluntary, the AAA likely benefited the farmers who accepted the production agreements. But it might well have had an adverse effect on the incomes of farm laborers, tenants, and sharecroppers. The program was strongly oriented toward larger farms. Although sharecroppers and tenants were supposed to be eligible for AAA payments, in some areas they did not receive their full share and some were demoted to wage labor. Further, farmers receiving AAA payments were required to remove land from production, likely causing the demand for farm labor to fall and leading to lower incomes for farm workers. Recent studies of the impact of the AAA grants on retail sales growth and on net migration at the county level during the 1930s suggest that the gains to recipients of the grants were offset by losses to farm workers, croppers, and tenants. Greater payments did not lead to faster growth in general economic activity during the 1930s, and counties with more AAA spending tended to experience more net out-migration than other parts of the country. In the South, where, according to observers, the impact on low-income farmers was greatest, areas with higher AAA spending experienced higher infant mortality for both black and white families. The association was stronger for black families than for white ones.[33]

On the positive side, the AAA helped prevent recurrences of the Dust Bowl of the 1930s, in which high winds combined with drought and soil erosion to create enormous dust clouds that blew through areas of Kansas, Colorado, Oklahoma, and Texas. Inadequate efforts to prevent soil erosion by the large numbers of small farmers who had first settled the area in the homesteading period helped create the problem. Each of the small farmers had little incentive to use methods to prevent soil erosion. Such efforts cut the amount of their production below a level that would allow them to farm profitably, while the benefits of their efforts would have accrued to their neighbors and not to them. The AAA, in particular the retooled Soil Conservation version in operation after 1935, encouraged the development of large farms and required farmers receiving benefits to use techniques that cut soil erosion. One sign that these changes were effective was that the same climactic conditions of strong winds and terrible droughts hit the region again in the 1970s, but no Dust Bowl developed.[34]

The National Recovery Administration: A Misguided Experiment

Just as they offered programs to reorganize the farm sector, Roosevelt's advisers sought to develop new institutions that would revive the industrial sector. Some saw the problem as lack of supply caused by "destructive" competition that had sent prices lower, driving many firms out of business and reducing surviving firms' incentives to produce. Coal companies, farmers, and others in troubled sectors had lobbied Congress or protections from such competition during the 1920s. Meanwhile, the Roosevelt administration needed solutions for the demand-side problems that continued to haunt the economy. After all, higher prices meant that consumers would buy less. To counteract the price effect and stimulate purchasing, the Roosevelt administration followed in the footsteps of the Hoover administration and sought ways to keep wages high so that workers and consumers would have higher incomes. Realizing that high wages might contribute to unemployment, the administration sought to spread the work by reducing the number of hours worked per person. It was hoped that less exhausted workers would increase their hourly productivity, so that monthly earnings would not be reduced much.

This logic was the basis for the National Industrial Recovery Act (NIRA) of 1933. The act established the National Recovery Administration (NRA) to foster the development of "fair" codes of competition in the various industries. Industrialists, workers, and consumers in each industry met to establish rules for minimum prices, quality standards, and trade practices. The workers were to be protected by minimum wages, limits on hours, and rules related to working conditions. Section 7a of the NIRA established standard language for the codes that gave workers the right to bargain collectively through the agent of their choice. Once approved by the NRA the codes were to be binding to all firms in the industry, even those not involved in the code-writing process.

It is quite clear in hindsight that creating the NRA was a disastrous policy. United States law had always banned cartels and price-fixing agreements in restraint of trade. Suddenly, the federal government was giving industry leaders antitrust exemptions as well as carte blanche to establish the basis for competition. Effective cartels require an enforcer because in the long run cartel arrangements tend to fall apart; each firm has an incentive to raise output and find ways to break their agreements by lowering prices and improving quality. To put it bluntly, the federal government had become the enforcer of cartel agreements in the majority of industries in America. Adam Smith's observation that "people of the same trade seldom meet together, even for merriment and diversion, but the conversation ends in a conspiracy against the public, or in some contrivance raise prices" seems to have held true for many of the NRA code negotiations (Smith 1937, 128). The codes in quite a few sectors were largely written by the leaders of trade associations in each industry with some influence by consumers because relatively few industries had a strong union presence. Many small firms complained that the codes favored the large firms that had been so influential in writing them. Cartel agreements do raise prices, but they do so by limiting output. Wholesale prices jumped 23 percent in two years although consumer prices were much slower to rise, and industrial production was still slow to recover.

The Roosevelt administration did want workers in the industries to share in the economic profits generated by the codes. It is unclear, however, that their wages rose enough to overcome the higher industrial prices they would pay. With regard to job sharing engendered by limits on hours, the NRA was just as likely (if not more) to contribute to unemployment as to solve it. Given that the Roosevelt administration tried so many policies simultaneously, it is difficult to isolate the impact of the NRA. Yet recent studies that perform policy simulations with and without the NRA suggest that the NRA might well have substantially slowed the recovery from the depths of the Depression.[35]

Even the businessmen who anticipated benefiting the most from the NRA restrictions were not uniformly satisfied. In industries with greater diversity among the participants, the process of writing the codes was often fraught with controversy, and many firms considered the codes illegitimate and thus felt free to violate them. Firms signaled that they were following the codes by displaying the symbol of the NRA, a blue eagle, but town gossip suggested that a number of violators were displaying the symbol just as prominently. The Supreme Court struck down the NRA as unconstitutional in the *Schechter Poultry* case in 1935. Unlike the AAA, there was little support for reenacting the NRA, and the Roosevelt administration let it die.[36]

The Geographic Distribution of Federal Funds: Promoting Relief, Recovery, and Reform, or Politics as Usual?

From the beginning the New Deal was controversial. In a famous Fireside Chat, Roosevelt proclaimed that the New Deal would promote "relief, recovery, and reform." Conservatives, critics, and big businessmen charged the New Dealers with the more cynical purpose of using government programs to build patronage and to "buy" voters to ensure the continuation of the Democrats' hegemony over the federal government. Over the course of the past thirty-five years scholars have been examining these claims by closely examining the geographic distribution of New Deal funds. The variation in spending per person across the states is striking, ranging from highs for the decade of nearly $900 per person in the mountainous West to lows of roughly $100 per person in some southern regions. The United States is an economically diverse country and there was substantial regional variation in the extent of the downturn, so we might expect the spending figures to vary. Among the patterns that drew attention was the relatively small amount received by southern states, although southern per capita incomes were the lowest in the nation and some southern states experienced among the worst of the downturns.[37]

Many modern programs have explicit formulas that determine the distribution of spending via matching grants and specific counts. The inner workings of the emergency New Deal programs are more difficult to fathom. Explicit formulas for matching funds written into the FERA legislation were largely deemed unworkable after the first three months. Senate testimony from FERA administrators about the distribution of funds offers a long list of factors that were considered but little guidance as to the weights each factor was given. Similarly, the WPA matching requirements were routinely ignored, and the shares of funds provided by state and local governments varied widely.

Therefore, scholars of the New Deal have turned to statistical analysis of the geographic patterns. More than thirty years of study suggest that the funds were distributed in response to a complex mix of factors, although there is not full agreement about how much weight to give to each factor. The rhetoric of the Roosevelt administration suggested that they were seeking to promote recovery, relief, and reform. Many studies, but not all, find evidence that the administration promoted recovery and relief by spending more in areas with higher unemployment and in areas where the economic downturn from 1929 to 1933 was more pronounced. Relatively few find signs of reform or redistribution of income because areas with more long-term poverty tended not to receive extra funds. Most programs required that state and local governments develop and help fund projects in order to obtain federal grants. Some areas received substantially less funding if leaders were leery of possible strings attached to New Deal largesse or because they did not press as aggressively for funding. Areas with more federally owned land tended to receive more funds as the administration sought to enhance the value of the federal lands.

Nearly every study finds that political considerations were important to the Roosevelt administration. More funds per capita were distributed in areas that were more likely to swing toward voting for Roosevelt and areas where high voter turnout suggested strong political interest. The administration appeared to be innovative in its use of radio to reach the public, and there is evidence that more funds were spent in areas where more families had radios. Some studies find that the administration might also have been rewarding districts that had long voted for the Democratic presidential candidate. Since Congress holds the purse strings, the distribution of New Deal funds was likely influenced by the congressional power structure. There is some evidence that members of important committees and congressional leaders were effective at helping their constituents obtain more New Deal funds

The nation's political leaders rarely talk about the overall distribution of the federal budget when promoting their solutions to problems. They instead describe how they develop specific programs to deal with each issue. Recent studies of specific programs suggest that the determinants of the geographic patterns were quite different from program to program. The New Deal seemed to offer something for everybody. The relief programs spent more in areas where the downturn was more problematic and also appeared to spend more in areas with lower incomes. Meanwhile, the large-scale farm programs appear to have been targeted mainly at aiding large farms, with smaller amounts devoted to helping small farmers and tenants.

Federal loan and mortgage insurance programs operated by the RFC, the HOLC, and the FHA, tended to be targeted at areas with higher incomes. To obtain loans the recipients had to have money to help ensure repayment. The administration worried that a record of substantial loan defaults would lead the public to call a halt to existing loan programs and prevent the creation of future programs.

At the program level, there is evidence that political maneuvering played a role in determining the distribution of funds at the margin. But political success did not mean that the Roosevelt administration needed to focus strongly on cynically manipulating the elections by targeting spending on swing states. By operating the relief programs and spending money where the problems were greatest, the administration could do well in the upcoming elections by also doing good for those in trouble.

One of the central worries of handing out such large sums around the country was the potential for corruption. Many of these programs had to be set up from scratch in less than three months. The Civil Works Administration was set up in two weeks. The potential for skimming of funds was enormous, particularly given the past record of scandals at all level of governments. Roosevelt knew that for the New Deal to be a success, scandals had to be minimized, or else the result would be disaster for his administration. He would bear the blame while reaping little reward from petty corruption by others. Thus, mechanisms were established to try to limit corrupt activity. The relief programs, for example, included an investigations division charged with the task of examining the hundreds of boxes of complaints, investigating them more thoroughly, and then providing support to the Attorney General's office when prosecution was warranted. The investigations considered complaints ranging from charges that a local relief administrator had hired a relief worker for lawn work around her home to charging the governor of North Dakota with fraud. Cynics and critics of the New Deal might argue that the division was investigating everybody except Roosevelt's administrators. Yet the establishment of an investigative division as part of the basic structure of a program was certainly not common in state and local government structures at the time. Further, there is evidence that when the federal government exerted more control of programs, the programs were more likely to work toward the administration's stated goal. When the federal government exerted more control over how monies were distributed within states with the move from the FERA to the WPA, the distribution of funds within states became more carefully targeted at relief, recovery, and reform.[38]

Long-Term Legacies of the New Deal

By the end of World War II, many of the New Deal agencies—the emergency relief and public works programs, the RFC, and the NRA—

had been shut down. Yet the New Deal left a series of lasting legacies, in addition to the farm programs, that remain in place today. Under the Roosevelt administration's aegis, workers' collective bargaining rights were expanded, federal limits on wages and hours were instituted, financial markets were more strongly regulated, and the federal government became involved in an extensive public assistance and social insurance network.

Labor Policy

Although the NRA's cartel-like features were not reenacted after the agency was eliminated, the Roosevelt administration sought to maintain its high-wage policies via legislation that reestablished the rules for union recognition and the passage of a minimum wage law. The National Labor Relations (Wagner) Act of 1935 reconstituted from section 7a of the NIRA the right of workers to bargain collectively via their own representatives. Prior to the 1930s public policy concerning unionization had focused on the "at will" doctrine. Either the employer or the worker could terminate the employment relationship. Thus, employers had the right to refuse to negotiate with union representatives and the right to refuse to recognize a union even in cases where the vast majority of workers had unionized. Under New Deal legislation workers had the right to hold elections to seek unionization status. When a majority of workers voted to accept union representation, the employer was required to recognize the union and enter into a collective bargaining agreement. In addition, employers could no longer establish company unions as alternatives to independent organizations. The National Labor Relations Board (NLRB) was established to oversee union elections and the collective bargaining process.

The New Deal policies dramatically changed the landscape of the workplace, and union organization expanded rapidly during the 1930s using a mixture of recognition strikes and union elections. In some cases before and during the 1930s, when the press for union recognition met staunch resistance from employers, strikes could turn violent. One of the benefits of the NLRB policies was to regularize the union recognition process, and the incidence of violent strikes has diminished sharply since.[39]

The Fair Labor Standards Act (FSLA) of 1938 established a federal role in setting a national minimum wage, overtime requirements, and child labor restrictions. During the Progressive Era, proponents of wage and hour limits for male workers had long been frustrated by court decisions preventing limits on male labor contracts and by a federal structure in which states were considered responsible for labor issues. Under the New Deal federal responses became widespread. After the demise of the NRA, which had been struck down for delegating too much of Congress's authority to private groups in setting the codes of competition, proponents of limits on wages and hours turned their attention to Congress. Supreme Court cases decided after the famous attempt by Roosevelt to pack the court gave reformers more confidence that national labor market policies would survive Court scrutiny.

The passage of the FLSA is a classic example of an interest group struggle in which a significant subset of employers joined with union leaders and reformers to impose limits on other employers. The proposed minimum wage was expected to raise the wages of low-wage workers, who tended to be younger, less skilled, black, and located in the South. High-wage employers who supported the legislation anticipated gains from imposing higher wages on competitors who had relied on low wages. They readily joined reformers and unions in calling for the end of the payment of "substandard" and "oppressive" wages. After the bill was first reported out of committee in July 1937 it went through many revisions before passage in 1938. A series of compromises made the bill more palatable to interests that had been on the fence, including elimination of regional differences in the minimum wage and limits on the authority of the administrative body. The pattern of votes on the various versions of the bill show that Democrats and legislators from areas with high-wage industries, more unionization, and more advocates of teenage workers voted for the FLSA. Meanwhile, those from areas with more retail trade and low wages tended to vote against it. Congressmen from agricultural areas were more likely to oppose the bill in anticipation that the exemption for agriculture might eventually be lifted. Many southern legislators actively opposed the FLSA because the South, a low-wage region, would be most heavily affected by the legislation. Yet they were not unanimously opposed. Hugo Black of Alabama was the Senate sponsor of the bill, and Claude Peppers of Florida and Lister Hill of Alabama were ardent supporters who worked to move the bill out of committee.

The FLSA imposed a national minimum wage, although agricultural workers, domestic workers, and employers not involved in interstate commerce were exempted from the act. The introduction of the minimum wage had its largest effects in the South. Some observers suggest that it was a key factor in an increase in southern wages that helped close the gap in regional wages. An in-depth description of the law's impact on two key southern industries, lumber and seamless hosiery, illustrates its other immediate effects, which are best illustrated by comparing the choices of southern firms, for which the minimum wage was higher than the prevailing wage, with those of firms in the North, where it was not. The seamless hosiery firms followed the classic predictions of economists. When northern firms were expanding employment, southern firms reduced employment, particularly for knitters in low-wage plants, as they shifted toward new mechanized production processes that reduced the need for labor.

The story in the lumber industry is more complex but still supports the standard predictions of economists. War-related government purchases of lumber fueled a large boom in lumber output. As a result, southern lumber firms actually increased employment after the introduction of the minimum wage, but output from higher-wage northern areas rose substantially faster. Southern employment likely would have risen less or declined except for three factors. The boom in demand led southern firms to begin cutting in forests where labor-saving devices were less effective, the majority of southern lumber firms actively avoided the law by dropping out of interstate commerce to become exempt from the FLSA, and others illegally paid less than the minimum.

The FLSA is a major legacy of the New Deal. The provision of time-and-a-half pay for overtime hours worked by hourly workers has become a major feature of employment arrangements. The minimum wage provisions have long been a source of controversy both among economists and in the public policy arena. Chapter 11 discusses the debates about the minimum wage in the postwar era.[40]

Financial Regulations

Roosevelt's Bank Holiday and the RFC bank loans were temporary solutions to bank panics. The stock market crash and the vast array of problems in the banking and construction industries, however, led to pressures for more permanent solutions, including a wide variety of regulations and the development of new financial institutions that still exist today. The Securities and Exchange Commission (SEC) was established to monitor the stock markets, reporting requirements for firms issuing stock, and insider trading and to enforce rules governing market trades.

To preclude future bank runs on deposits, the Roosevelt administration established the Federal Deposit Insurance Corporation (FDIC) and the Federal Savings and Loan Insurance Corporation (FSLIC) to provide federal government insurance of deposits up to a set limit. Small banks that were not members of the Federal Reserve System played an important role in promoting the FDIC and heavily influenced its initial rate structure. Banks paid the FDIC insurance rate on all deposits, but protection was given only to the first $5,000 in each account. This structure meant that larger banks with larger deposits were providing subsidies to the smaller banks.

Until the late 1970s, FDIC and FSLIC insurance were considered key factors in the absence of bank runs. The demise of savings and loans in the 1980s led to reexamination of the history of government deposit insurance, and people are more wary of the institution today. Studies of the state governments' experiments with deposit insurance in the early 1900s suggest that the state programs often created more problems than they solved. The main problem was *moral hazard*. Knowing that their deposits were insured, bankers had incentives to make riskier loans, which in turn increased the likelihood of bank failures and government bailouts of the banks. For government deposit insurance to work well, the insurer had to monitor the quality of the banks' loans and investments and raise insurance rates for banks that took riskier actions. Alternatively, the government as insurer had to impose limits on the banks' actions before providing insurance. The FDIC and FSLIC appeared to be working well in preventing bank failures when financial institutions were tightly regulated through the late 1970s, but the savings and loan industry was experiencing declines in income and net worth that led to potential insolvencies that would have overwhelmed the FSLIC's reserves. The savings and loans' intense lobbying of the FSLIC and Congress postponed restructuring of the industry. In 1980 and 1982 banks, savings and loans, and other financial institutions successfully pressed for deregulation that would allow them more latitude in making loans and investments and in the interest payments they could offer depositors. Meanwhile, the account coverage limit was raised from $40,000 to $100,000. Ultimately, the combination of aggressive investment strategies by the savings and loans and insufficient discipline by the FSLIC led to a crisis that shook the industry.[41]

During the 1930s the problems faced by financial institutions were intimately linked with housing loans. In an attempt to provide liquidity to housing markets and enhance the quality of many banks' loan portfolio, the Home Owners' Loan Corporation was established. Between 1933 and 1936 HOLC funds were used to refinance more than $3 billion in mortgage loans already on the verge of foreclosure. In 1934 the

Federal Housing Administration was formed to offer federal insurance for mortgage loans both for new and existing homes and for repair and reconstruction. In 1938 the Federal National Mortgage Administration (Fannie Mae) began providing a secondary market for mortgage loans in which banks could sell the loans as assets and then use the funds to make new mortgages.

Both the HOLC and the FHA carefully vetted the loans that they refinanced and insured to avoid a large cascade of defaults. As a result, the programs were primarily targeted at people with higher income or who clearly were faced with only short-term difficulties. The long-term impact of the FHA and Fannie Mae was probably much greater than their short-term effects because they contributed to a permanent restructuring of mortgage lending. Prior to the 1930s most mortgage loans had been five-year loans on which the borrower paid interest during the life of the loan. At the end of the loan period the borrower repaid the entire principal or sought to roll the loan over for a new term. Borrowers typically could borrow only up to 50 percent of the value of their home. The New Deal housing programs chose loan structures that had been used for only a small share of loans in the 1920s. The length of the loans was extended to fifteen or twenty years (today they range up to thirty years) with lower down payment requirements and amortized repayment schedules in which the borrower made the same monthly payment over the term of the loan with no balloon at the end. It is possible that the changes in payment structures contributed to a reduction in defaults associated with the inability to pay balloon payments, and the programs may have increased liquidity in housing markets.

The Social Security Act of 1935:
Federal Social Insurance and Public Assistance

Roosevelt saw the FERA programs for direct relief and work relief as temporary emergency measures. When the New Deal emergency relief programs were revamped with new legislation in 1935, the federal government returned responsibility for unemployables to state and local governments and focused instead on using work relief in its emergency programs. Recognizing that the existing state and local relief meant that there was quite large variation in opportunities for direct relief and in the way it was organized, the administration sought to reorganize certain forms of state and local relief into a federal system that allowed states to operate their own programs within federal guidelines and with some funds from the federal government. The Aid to Dependent

Children (ADC), Aid to the Blind (AB), and Old-Age Assistance (OAA) programs essentially took over the roles played by the parallel state programs. Once all of the states had passed enabling legislation allowing them to join the system, the new federal-state combination insured that low-income persons in these categories had nationwide access to public assistance. The program, however, gave states latitude in setting benefit levels and some of the eligibility requirements for aid.

A similar state-level flexibility was established for unemployment insurance (UI) programs. Prior to the Depression, UI had met with the least success in state legislatures of any social insurance program proposed by the Progressives. Although they were liable for workplace accidents, employers under common law had never been liable for aiding their unemployed workers. Several studies have shown that, at the time, workers in industries that suffered from layoffs and unemployment generally received higher wages to compensate for this risk. Several states had rejected bills requiring compulsory unemployment insurance prior to the Depression, but the number of states considering unemployment compensation rose as unemployment soared. Roosevelt's campaign promises had included unemployment insurance provided under state laws. By 1934, when the Social Security Act was being developed by the Committee on Economic Security (CES), only Wisconsin had adopted an unemployment insurance system. Several other states passed similar bills in 1935. Although the CES strongly considered a national bill, the long-standing precedent of state control over labor issues and fears that a system run exclusively by the national government might not survive constitutional scrutiny led them to choose a joint federal-state arrangement. The final Social Security Act established a basic structure for all state unemployment insurance programs. Employers pay a tax that goes into an unemployment reserve fund for each state that is managed by the national government. In enabling legislation the states established the benefits to be paid, the maximum benefit payment, eligibility requirements, and the maximum duration of unemployment.

One of the major features of U.S. unemployment insurance is experience rating. The states adopted a wide variety of experience rating systems, but the basic principle is the same. Employers who lay off a higher share of their workers and impose more burdens on the UI system are expected to pay higher taxes. In comparison with other unemployment systems around the world, experience rating is unique, but it is designed to solve the same moral hazard problems that arise under workers' compensation, deposit insurance, and other forms of insurance. In a sense, the UI reserve fund is a common pool. In the absence of experience rating, employers faced with a downturn in their business face extra temptation to lay off workers rather than to continue paying wages to underutilized workers and losing profits. Although they may have to pay higher wage rates to compensate workers for the increased layoffs, by dumping a disproportionate share of their workers into the UI system, they force other employers to subsidize the higher wage rates. With experience rating the employer faces additional taxes when he lays off too many workers and thus has less incentive to dump workers onto UI. In fact, studies of UI that compare the experience rating systems in different states and that compare northern states with Canada, which has no experience rating, show that greater experience rating serves to reduce seasonal unemployment fluctuations.[42]

The basic UI system established under the Social Security Act has been largely unchanged since the New Deal. In comparison with the rest of the world, the U.S. system is unique in that the states offer a wide variety of benefit levels, the unemployment taxes are experience-rated, and there are limits on the duration of benefits. Had UI been adopted at a later date, some argue, the system might have been a national one, because a series of Supreme Court decisions and other national policies have moved away from the long legacy of emphasis on state hegemony over labor markets. But in some ways this idiosyncratic UI system may have been beneficial in dealing with the shocks to the global economy. A number of studies suggest that relatively low unemployment benefits, limited duration of benefits, and experience rating have made unemployment less attractive to workers in the United States than in Europe and have given U.S. labor markets much more flexibility in responding to downturns. The state systems may also have given the diverse regions of the nation more flexibility in designing systems that better fit their economies.

The centerpiece of the Social Security Act of 1935 was the establishment of a federal old-age retirement system. There was a loose precedent for the federal government's involvement in old-age pensions. The Civil War disability pension had expanded its eligibility requirements so broadly that the infirmities of old age were largely covered, so that a substantial share of the elderly in the North in the early 1900s were receiving federal military pensions. In 1925 a trust fund had been established to pay an average bonus of $1,000 to World War I veterans in 1945. As the Depression worsened, veterans began calling for early payment of the bonus. Events surrounding a march on Washington in 1932 had culminated in troops led by Douglas MacArthur destroying a tent encampment constructed by protesting veterans. Veterans continued to press for payment after Roosevelt was elected, and Congress finally voted a payment over his veto in 1936. In the meantime pundits such as Francis Townsend were calling for substantial old-age pensions that proved popular among the American public. The popularity was somewhat surprising because the details called for about 40 percent of GDP to be distributed to the elderly. Huey Long's press for "Share the Wealth" programs raised fears that he would siphon votes away from Roosevelt in the 1936 election. These were the proximate political causes, but there was a broad recognition that the share of elderly in the U.S. population was rising and was expected to continue to rise. Because the elderly were more likely to be infirm and less able to work, the pension program was seen as a means of keeping the elderly off of public assistance rolls.

In seeking to establish an old-age retirement program, the Roosevelt administration had two options: an insurance model or a social adequacy model. In the insurance model people would pay premiums into a retirement fund, which would be invested. When people retired they would receive benefits based on the accumulated monies in the retirement fund. The benefits from such a model would have tended to be relatively low given the proposed premiums to be paid. Some considered the benefits to be inadequate to offset poverty in old age and instead proposed that the government provide a subsidy to overcome what they considered society's failure to provide enough income to adequately provide for old age.

Roosevelt himself demanded the insurance principles when the program was being considered because he was uncertain of the need for old-age pensions and worried about saddling future generations with a large debt load. The initial plan tried to split the difference, providing a subsidy for the elderly as of 1940 who had not had time to accumulate much in the funds and then making the transition to the insurance plan. By 1939 it became clear that splitting the difference would not work. The Social Security Act was amended to become a pay-as-you-go plan funded by taxes on earnings for wage and salary workers and the self-employed.[43]

Under a pay-as-you-go system the government collects taxes from current workers and pays benefits to the retirees, but no explicit contract ties the taxes paid during the person's working life to the benefits received. When the taxes collected exceed the benefits paid, the government does "invest" the surplus in a trust fund. But the trust fund is composed of the government's promises to itself to collect enough taxes to pay benefits to retirees at some future date.

Neither the tax rates nor the benefit rates have been set in stone. In 1940 workers and employers were each paying 1 percent of earnings for the old-age program, and the retirees received benefits equal to roughly one-fourth of the average earnings of those paying taxes. Because the ratio of retirees to workers was less than one per hundred, the system started with a surplus and the early retirees received payments that far surpassed their contributions to the system. Over the course of the past six decades tax rates and benefits have been restructured several times. Retirement benefits are now about 40 percent of average earnings for workers. Continued declines in the number of workers relative to retirees have led Social Security taxes to rise so that workers and employers each now pay rates of more than 5 percent. Because the retiree's share of the population is expected to continue to rise, we can expect some mixture of Social Security tax increases, cuts in benefits, and restructuring of the program over the next few decades.

Conclusion

In 1933 the U.S. economy was in the heart of a horrendous depression. Hoover's attempts to offset the economic decline barely retarded the slide into oblivion. Banks had been failing everywhere, and a new round of panics was just around the corner. Claiming that "We have nothing to fear but fear itself," Roosevelt fearlessly plunged ahead. In his First Hundred Days Roosevelt, using both hands, threw just about every policy his advisers and Congress could think of at the emergency. You name it and the Roosevelt administration tried it: aid for the destitute and the unemployed, public works projects, bank holidays, loans, reorganizations of industry, farm programs (see table 13.1). Some programs ran at cross-purposes with others, worsening problems that the other programs were assigned to resolve.

There were so many changes and so many programs and so many problems that it is hard to sort out how successful the New Deal programs were at resolving these issues. It is quite clear that the U.S. government was a novice at macroeconomic policies because many fiscal and monetary policy moves appear inadequate in hindsight. Of course, even today there is substantial disagreement among leading economists about how effectively monetary and fiscal policy can influence real output. So we remain more advanced novices with some conflicting opinions about the experiences under our belt.

At the operational level many of the programs seem to have worked reasonably well. In a short time the Roosevelt administration established

Table 13.1 MAJOR NEW DEAL PROGRAMS

Agency or regulation	Enacted	Permanent or temporary	Description
Agricultural Adjustment Administration	1933	permanent	Promoted higher farm prices through restrictions on output
Civil Works Administration	1933	temporary	Made grants for work relief jobs for public works and provided maintenance for public buildings and parks
Commodity Credit Corporation	1933	permanent	Provided loans that guaranteed minimum farm prices
Fair Labor Standards Act	1938	permanent	Established federal minimum wage and work hour restrictions for workers involved in interstate commerce
Farm Credit Administration	1933	permanent	Reorganized and coordinated programs that provided loans to farmers for seed and crops and for farm mortgages
Farm Security Administration	1937	temporary	Provided loans and grants to farmers to provide relief and better farming opportunities
Federal Communications Commission	1934	permanent	Regulated interstate communications
Federal Deposit Insurance Corporation	1933	permanent	Insured bank deposits
Federal Emergency Relief Administration	1933	temporary	Provided grants for relief payments (direct and as work relief) to households with inadequate income
Federal Farm Mortgage Corporation	1933	permanent	Issued bonds to help finance farm mortgage and improvement loans
Federal Housing Administration	1934	permanent	Provided federal insurance for home mortgages
Federal National Mortgage Association	1938	permanent	Purchased FHA-insured mortgages to provide liquidity in banking markets
Federal Savings and Loan Insurance Corporation	1934	permanent	Provided federal insurance of savings and loan deposits
Home Owners Loan Corporation	1933	temporary	Provided loan funds to aid banks in refinancing troubled mortgage loans
National Labor Relations Board	1935	permanent	Monitored and adjudicated disputes over collective bargaining agreements
National Recovery Administration	1933	temporary	Oversaw development of industrial competition codes
Public Buildings Administration	1932	permanent	Provided grants for constructing federal government buildings
Public Roads Administration	1932	permanent	Provided grants for building public highways
Public Works Administration	1933	temporary	Provided grants and loans to build large-scale public works

Table 13.1 (CONTINUED)

Agency or regulation	Enacted	Permanent or temporary	Description
Public Works Administration, Housing Division	1933	temporary	Provided grants and loans for the building of public housing projects
Reconstruction Finance Corporation	1932	temporary	Provided loans for banks, rail roads, industry, local governments; served as backer for many New Deal programs
Resettlement Administration	1935	temporary	Provided loans and grants to farmers to provide relief and better farming opportunities
Rural Electrification Administration	1935	permanent	Provided loans to extend electricity service to rural areas and farmers
Securities and Exchange Commission	1933	permanent	Regulated financial markets
Social Security Administration, Aid to Dependent Children	1935	permanent	Gave federal and state funds to provide aid to children who lost parents
Social Security Administration, Aid to the Blind	1935	permanent	Provided federal and state aid to the blind
Social Security Administration, Old-Age Assistance	1935	permanent	Provided federal and state relief funds for indigent seniors
Social Security Administration, Old-Age Pensions	1935	permanent	Provided old-age pensions to retired workers
Tennessee Valley Authority	1933	permanent	Large-scale project building dams to create reservoirs and provide electric power
U.S. Housing Administration	1937	permanent	Established loans for public housing projects
Unemployment insurance	1935	permanent	Established state and federal insurance funds to provide benefits to unemployed workers
Works Progress Administration	1935	temporary	Provided grants for work relief jobs on smaller-scale public projects

Note: Temporary implies that program was ended after the Depression with no transfer of duties to other programs.

organizations designed to distribute funds to state and local governments and to millions of people. Given the difficulties of establishing any successful organization, some of the agencies were service operations miracles. A great many people directly benefited from work relief and the new federal-state public assistance programs. Huge numbers of roads, public buildings, and public works were constructed. Lives were saved by better public health programs. Banks stopped failing at such a high rate. The unemployment rate lurched downward and GNP eventually returned to the peak of 1929, getting set to take off once the economy had pushed past the harsh economic realities of World War II.

Yet a simple relation of better times with the presence of the programs is not enough to effectively measure the impact of the policies. When we ask the counterfactual question of how the economy would have fared without the New Deal policies, the answer is more complex. At no time in American economic history has the economy failed to rebound and soar to new heights within a few years, so there is a natural expectation that a rebound would have occurred. Of course, the administration followed these policies because after four years of sharp decline, no end to the decline appeared in sight. The situation was so complex with so many things happening at once, it is hard to sort out the successes and failures. Talented and very intelligent scholars of the New Deal find plenty of room for disagreement about its short-term effects. Some have argued that the sheer volume of policies and changes in direction, along with anticipation that new policies might be adopted, created so much uncertainty that it retarded economic growth. Nearly every economist considers the cartel-like features of the National Recovery Administration to have been a misguided experiment that retarded the benefits of competition in markets. In the farm sector the new policies led to gains for farm owners but may well have harmed farm workers, tenants, and croppers. Studies that try to control for the fact that policies were put in place to counteract economic problems in a number of cases find that some of the New Deal programs made positive contributions, but their impact was not nearly as large as the surface comparisons suggest.[44]

The New Deal had tremendous long-range consequences for government in the American economy. The degree to which the role of government was ratcheted up during the peacetime "crisis" of the 1930s, was a central event that led Robert Higgs (1987) to develop his theories of the government ratchet effect. Higgs's theory does not imply that there was no retrenchment of government activity. Work relief programs, the RFC, the HOLC, the NRA, and other temporary arrangements were phased out, but much of the New Deal legacy remains. The ratchet effect implies that after the crisis ends, the long-term expansion of the government's role begins again, but at a new and higher base. By its end the New Deal had established a federal network of social insurance and public assistance programs, federal oversight and insurance of large parts of the financial industry, substantial changes in the rules under which labor markets operated, a whole network of programs in the farm sector, and many more programs. Succeeding generations have tinkered with some of these roles. In response to the increasing sophistication of financial markets and institutions, financial regulation was scaled back during the late 1970s. Yet even in this area there have been few serious challenges to the idea that the government has some role in regulating these markets. The mere mention of elimination of social insurance and public assistance programs would be political suicide. The debates focus instead on better ways to make them work in a context where they have become a growing share of the national economy. The farm programs, which are the bane of market-oriented economists and a worldwide sticking point in trade negotiations, seem to have infinite lives. Despite an ever-shrinking farm sector and scandals about the wealth of those receiving farm subsidies, the politicians who come to office suggesting their demise often end up expanding the programs.

Only a very small percentage of the American public today participated in the pre–New Deal economy, and for this group the experience of the Depression forever influenced their views of the role of government. Given that nearly all Americans have spent a lifetime with the long-standing New Deal institutions, it is unlikely that they will be eliminated lightly. Even the many critics of specific policies recognize that the debate is hardly ever devoted to eliminating the New Deal programs. The discussion instead focuses on how to make these programs work better in a mixed economy.

Notes

1. United States v. Butler, 297 U.S. 1 (1936). In A. L. A. Schechter Poultry Corp. v. United States, 295 U.S. 495 (1935), the National Industrial Recovery Act was nullified because Congress had delegated too much power to the administrative branch.

2. See chapter 5.

3. For discussions of long cycles see Schumpeter 1939. Scholars who emphasize declines in investment and consumption include Field (1992) and Gordon (1974), while Romer (1990) and Temin (1976) emphasize the sharp declines in consumption. See Cole and Ohanian 1999, Bordo, Erceg, and Evans 2000, and Chari, Kehoe, and McGratton 2003 for assessments of the impact of monetary policy shocks, fiscal policy shocks, and technology shocks as determinants of the path of macroeconomic activity. Their models predict the drop in income from 1929 to 1933 well but predict a much more rapid recovery than actually occurred. For recent efforts to explain the slow recovery, see Cole and Ohanian 2004, Harrison and Weder 2003, and Romer 1992.

4. See Friedman and Schwartz 1963, 299–419.

5. There is a huge literature on the causes of the Depression, and not all scholars agree with Friedman and Schwartz's assessment of the Fed's role. See Friedman and Schwartz 1963, Wheelock 1991, Temin 1976, 1989, Gordon 1974, Romer 1992, Rothbard 2000, Eichengreen 1992, Cole and Ohanian 1999, and Bordo, Erceg, and Evans 2000. Atack and Passell 1994, 583–624, and Smiley 2002 offer highly readable summaries of the debates that strongly influenced the description given here.

6. For the Austrian view, see Rothbard 2000. The statistical study of Federal Reserve policy in the 1920s and 1930s was performed by Wheelock (1992).

7. Barry Eichengreen (1992) is a leading proponent of the view that remaining on the gold standard was a problem for the United States and a series of other countries. See also Temin and Wigmore 1990.

8. See Smiley 2002, 26–28, 74–75 and sources cited there.

9. This description is based on Friedman and Schwartz 1963. For a view that puts less emphasis on the Fed's role, see Romer 1992.

10. Barber (1996, 52, 83–84) discusses the relation between Keynes and Roosevelt. He also offers extensive discussions of the economic thinking of policymakers in the Roosevelt administration. The quotation is from Keynes 1964, 383.

11. Hansen is quoted in Brown 1956, 866.

12. Learning the extent to which fiscal policy is stimulative involves more complex calculations than the ones described here. See Brown (1956) and Peppers (1973), who find that the New Deal deficits were even less stimulative than the raw numbers shown here suggest. In fact, Peppers argues that Hoover was following more stimulative fiscal policies than was Roosevelt. The discussion of state and local government budgets in the chapter is based on their work as well.

13. For historical comparisons of the impact of tariff rates, see Irwin 1998. Kindleberger (1986, 170) and Atack and Passell (1994, 602) describe the international trade developments of the 1930s.

14. The descriptions in this section are based on Olson 1988 and Jones 1939, 1951. Jones was the director of the RFC.

15. The discussion of the RFC's impact on railroad investments is based on Mason and Schiffman 2004. The impact of the RFC on bank failures is discussed in Mason 2001.

16. The federal government had established programs for disability payments to military veterans, workers' compensation for federal employees, and retirement pensions for federal workers. See chapter 12 in this volume. For discussion of the RFC relief loans see Jones 1951, 178.

17. Another New Deal relief program was the popular Civilian Conservation Corps, which provided short-term jobs to youths who moved to camps where they worked to conserve natural resources and returned a portion of earnings to their families.

18. The best description of the operation of the WPA is found in Howard 1943. A large number of statistical studies describe the distribution of the New Deal relief funds, including most recently Fleck 1999a, 1999b, and 2001a, Stromberg 2004, and Fishback, Kantor, and Wallis 2003, which summarizes the results of many studies of all New Deal programs. After 1935 the federal

government did not completely stop providing direct relief to "unemployables" because the Social Security Act of 1935 introduced joint state-federal versions of some earlier state programs such as old-age assistance, aid to dependent children (replacing mothers' pensions), and aid to the blind.

19. Hopkins is quoted in Adams 1977, 53.

20. Margo (1993, 1991) describes the characteristics of workers on relief in the late 1930s.

21. In fact, Hopkins succeeded in obtaining a substantially larger share of the total public works and relief budgets in part because he pleased Roosevelt by helping so many people much more quickly than Harold Ickes had with the PWA monies. In part Hopkins did this by breaking large projects that might have been built by the PWA into subprojects (Schlesinger 1958, 283–96).

22. See Clarke 1996, 62–68 and Schlesinger 1958, 263–96.

23. The Hopkins quotation is from McJimsey 1987, 124.

24. The cross-sectional studies of the relation between relief and employment were performed by Wallis and Benjamin (1981) and Fleck (1999b), and the panel study of employment across states across time was done by Wallis and Benjamin (1989).

25. Darby (1976) showed that the definition of relief workers as unemployed had significant implications for measures of unemployment in the 1930s, while Fleck (1999b) established the one-to-one relation between relief jobs and measured unemployment.

26. The retail sales and migration studies were performed by Fishback, Horrace, and Kantor (2005, 2006). The crime study is by Johnson, Kantor, and Fishback (2003).

27. The results for the mortality and birth measures can be found in Fishback, Haines, and Kantor (2001, forthcoming).

28. Libecap (1998, 188–99) describes the development of farm programs from 1870 to the present. For a long-term view of the farm programs see chapter 15.

29. United States v. Butler, 297 U.S. 1 (1936). For a detailed description of the first three years of the AAA, see Nourse et al. 1937. The AAA's efforts to curtail hog and cotton production generated enormous controversy in 1933. The program required farmers to destroy six million pigs and plow under roughly ten million acres of cotton. An enormous outcry arose although most of the pigs were purchased by the Federal Surplus Relief Corporation and distributed to households on relief (Chandler 1970, pp. 218).

30. The paragraph is based on Halcrow 1953, 342–43.

31. For more discussion of this program, see Alston and Ferrie 1999.

32. For discussions of the impact of the AAA on crop output, see Libecap 1998, 193nn. Its effects on reducing problems with the Dust Bowl are discussed in Hansen and Libecap 2004.

33. Discussions of the AAA, the switch to wage labor, and denial of payments to sharecroppers and share tenants are found in Whatley 1983, Biles 1994, 39–43, and Saloutos 1982. Alston (1981) describes a reduction in the demand for farm labor. The impact of the AAA on retail sales and migration is examined in Fishback, Horrace, and Kantor 2005, 2006. The effects of the AAA on infant mortality are found in Fishback, Haines, and Kantor 2001.

34. The effects of the AAA on reducing problems with the Dust Bowl are discussed in Hansen and Libecap 2004.

35. Bellush (1975) offers a good administrative history of the NRA. Cole and Ohanian (2004) find that the high-wage policies and retrenchment in antitrust action associated with the NRA and the Roosevelt administration's post-NRA policies significantly slowed the recovery.

36. Alexander (1997) and Alexander and Libecap (2000) discuss the problems the industries had in establishing the codes of "fair" competition and the reasons why businesses did not press for a new NRA when it was declared unconstitutional. In A. L. A. Shechter Poultry Corp. v. United States, 295 U.S. 495 (1935), the Supreme Court struck down the National Industrial Recovery Act because Congress had delegated too much authority to the executive branch.

37. For descriptions of the program, see Howard 1943 and Williams 1968. Among many statistical analyses of the distribution of funds in the discussion below, Fishback, Kantor, and Wallis (2003) summarize a series of studies including Couch and Shughart 1998; Wallis 1984, 1987, 1998, 2001; Wright 1974; Reading 1973; Anderson and Tollison 1991; Fleck 1999a, 1999b, 1999c, 2001; Stromberg 2004; Arrington 1970; and Mason 2003.

38. For discussions of corruption, see Fishback, Kantor, and Wallis 2006.

39. See Freeman 1998. The Norris-LaGuardia Act of 1932 had also smoothed the path for union recognition. During the Progressive Era a number of states had limited the use of antitrust laws to treat unions as illegal combinations in restraint of trade, prevented contracts in which workers pledged not to join unions (yellow-dog contracts), and limited the use of injunctions in labor disputes.

40. The political economy of the Fair Labor Standards Act is discussed in Seltzer 1995, 1997. See also Fleck 2002 for a discussion of political issues. Wright (1986) suggests that the minimum wage helped raise southern wages to levels closer to wages in the rest of the country.

41. White (1998) provides an excellent summary of the New Deal banking policies. The studies of state deposit insurance and problems in the banking industry were performed by Alston, Grove, and Wheelock (1994), Wheelock (1992), White (1983), Calomiris and White (2000), and Richardson and Chung (2003). White (1998) and Kane (1991) offer good descriptions of the problems with savings and loans. Another problem, known as adverse selection, also arises in the deposit insurance markets. When insurers cannot tell the difference between risky and safe bankers easily, setting of insurance rates can be difficult. Say a state offered deposit insurance at a rate based on the average probability of failure. If bankers were not required to purchase deposit insurance, the state insurance fund was likely to attract primarily bankers facing higher-than-average risk. Consequently, this adverse selection of bankers would lead to problems with the solvency of the fund. When states began offering deposit insurance, there was a potential problem in that riskier bankers might have been more likely to move into the state.

42. This discussion is based on work by Baicker, Goldin, and Katz (1998). For modern comparisons of labor markets and unemployment institutions across countries see Blau and Kahn 2002.

43. For a lucid description of the development of social security, changes in policies over time, and the future problems associated with it, see Scheiber and Shoven 1999. See also Berkowitz and McQuaid 1992, 123–25, 130–36, Quadagno 1988, 119–21, Lubove 1968, and Costa 1998.

44. Higgs (1997) and Smiley (2002) have recently laid out the uncertainty argument.

References

Adams, Henry H. 1977. *Harry Hopkins: A Biography.* New York: G. P. Putnam's Sons.

Alexander, Barbara. 1997. "Failed Cooperation in Heterogeneous Industries under the National Recovery Administration." *Journal of Economic History* 57 (June): 322–44.

Alexander, Barbara, and Gary Libecap. 2000. "The Effect of Cost Heterogeneity in the Success and Failure of the New Deal's Agricultural and Industrial Programs." *Explorations in Economic History* 37 (October): 370–400.

Alston, Lee. 1981. "Tenure Choice in Southern Agriculture, 1930-1960." *Explorations in Economic History* 18 (July): 211–32.

Alston, Lee, and Joseph Ferrie. 1999. *Southern Paternalism and the American Welfare State.* New York: Cambridge University Press.

Alston, Lee, Wayne Grove, and David Wheelock. 1994. "Why Do Banks Fail? Evidence from the 1920s." *Explorations in Economic History* 31 (October): 409–31.

Alston, Lee, and Randal Rucker. 1987 "Farm Failures and Government Intervention: A Case Study from the 1930s." *American Economic Review* 77 (September): 724–30.

Anderson, Gary M., and Robert D. Tollison. 1991. "Congressional Influence and Patterns of New Deal Spending, 1933–1939." *Journal of Law and Economics.* 34 (April): 161–75.

Arrington, Leonard J. 1970. "Western Agriculture and the New Deal." *Agricultural History* 49 (October): 337–16.

Atack, Jeremy, and Peter Passell. 1994. *A New Economic View of American History from Colonial Times to 1940.* 2nd ed. New York: Norton.

Baicker, Katherine, Claudia Goldin, and Lawrence Katz. 1998. "A Distinctive System: Origins and Impact of U.S. Unemployment Compensation." In *The Defining Moment: The Great Depression and the American Economy in the Twentieth Century,* ed. Michael Bordo, Claudia Goldin, and Eugene N. White, 227–64. Chicago: University of Chicago Press.

Barber, William J. 1996. *Designs within Disorder: Franklin D. Roosevelt, the Economists, and the Shaping of American Economic Policy, 1933–1945.* New York: Cambridge University Press.

Bellush, Bernard. 1975. *The Failure of the NRA.* New York: Norton.

Berkowitz, Edward, and Kim McQuaid. 1992. *Creating the Welfare States: The Political Economy of Twentieth Century Reform.* Rev. ed. Lawrence: University of Kansas Press.

Biles, Roger. 1994. *The South and the New Deal.* Lexington: University of Kentucky Press.

Blau, Francine, and Lawrence Kahn 2002. *At Home and Abroad: U.S. Labor Market Performance in International Perspective*. New York: Russell Sage Foundation.

Bordo, Michael, Christopher Erceg, and Charles L. Evans. 2000. "Money, Sticky Wages, and the Great Depression." *American Economic Review* 90 (December), 1447–63.

Brown, E. Cary. 1956. "Fiscal Policy in the 'Thirties: A Reappraisal." *American Economic Review* 46 (December): 857–79.

Calomiris, Charles, and Eugene N. White. 2000. "The Origins of Federal Deposit Insurance." In *U.S. Bank Deregulation in Historical Perspective*. New York: Cambridge University Press.

Chandler, Lester. 1970. *America's Greatest Depression, 1929–1941*. New York: Harper & Row.

Chari, V. V., Patrick Kehoe, and Ellen McGrattan. 2003. "Accounting for the Great Depression." *Federal Reserve Bank of Minneapolis Quarterly Review* 27 (Spring 2003): 2–8.

Clarke, Jeanne Nienaber. 1996. *Roosevelt's Warrior: Harold L. Ickes and the New Deal*. Baltimore: Johns Hopkins University Press.

Cole, Harold, and Lee Ohanian. 1999. "The Great Depression in the United States from a Neoclassical Perspective." *Federal Reserve Bank of Minneapolis Quarterly Review* 23 (Winter): 2–24.

———. 2004. "New Deal Policies and the Persistence of the Great Depression: A General Equilibrium Analysis." *Journal of Political Economy* 112 (August): 779–816.

Costa, Dora. 1998. *The Evolution of Retirement: An American Economic History, 1880–1990*. Chicago: University of Chicago Press.

Couch, Jim, and William Shughart II. 1998. *The Political Economy of the New Deal*. New York: Elgar.

Darby, Michael R. 1976. "Three and a Half Million U.S. Employees Have Been Mislaid: Or, an Explanation of Unemployment, 1934–1941." *Journal of Political Economy* 84 (February): 1–16.

Eichengreen, Barry. 1992. *Golden Fetters: The Gold Standard and the Depression, 1919–1939*. New York: Oxford University Press, 1992.

Field, Alexander. 1992. "Uncontrolled Land Development and the Duration of the Depression in the United States." *Journal of Economic History* 52 (December): 785–805.

Fishback, Price, Michael R. Haines, and Shawn Kantor. 2001. "The Impact of the New Deal on Black and White Infant Mortality in the South." *Explorations in Economic History* 38 (January): 93–122.

———. Forthcoming. "Births, Deaths, and New Deal Relief during the Great Depression." *Review of Economics and Statistics*.

Fishback, Price, William Horrace, and Shawn Kantor. 2005. "The Impact of New Deal Expenditures on Local Economic Activity: An Examination of Retail Sales, 1929–1939." *Journal of Economic History* 65 (March): 36–71.

———. 2006. "Do Federal Programs Affect Internal Migration? The Impact of New Deal Expenditures on Mobility during the Great Depression." *Explorations in Economic History* 43 (April): 179–222.

Fishback, Price, Shawn Kantor, and John Wallis. 2003. "Can the New Deal's Three R's Be Rehabilitated? A Program-by-Program, County-by-County Analysis." *Explorations in Economic History* (October): 278–307.

———. 2006. "Institutional Designs and the Problem of Corruption during the New Deal." In *Corruption and Reform,* ed. Claudia Goldin and Edward Glaeser, 343–72. Chicago: University of Chicago Press.

Fleck, Robert. 1999a. "Electoral Incentives, Public Policy, and the New Deal Realignment." *Southern Economic Journal* 63 (January): 377–404.

———. 1999b. "The Marginal Effect of New Deal Relief Work on County-Level Unemployment Statistics." *Journal of Economic History* 59 (September): 659–87.

———. 1999c. "The Value of the Vote: A Model and Test of the Effects of Turnout on Distributive Policy." *Economic Inquiry* 37 (October): 609–23.

———. 2001a. "Inter-Party Competition, Intra-Party Competition, and Distributive Policy: A Model and Test Using New Deal Data." *Public Choice* 108 (July): 77–100.

———. 2001b. "Population, Land, Economic Conditions, and the Allocation of New Deal Spending." *Explorations in Economic History* 38 (April): 296–304.

———. 2002. "Democratic Opposition to the Fair Labor Standards Act of 1938." *Journal of Economic History* 62 (March): 25–54.

Freeman, Richard. 1998. "Spurts in Union Growth: Defining Moments and Social Processes." In *The Defining Moment: The Great Depression and the American Economy in the Twentieth Century,* ed. Michael Bordo, Claudia Goldin, and Eugene N. White, 265–96. Chicago: University of Chicago Press.

Friedman, Milton, and Anna Schwartz. 1963. *A Monetary History of the United States, 1867–1960.* Princeton: Princeton University Press.

Gordon, Robert Aaron. 1974. *Economic Instability and Growth: The American Record.* New York: Harper & Row.

Halcrow, Harold G. 1953. *Agricultural Policy of the United States.* New York: Prentice-Hall.

Hansen, Zeynep, and Gary Libecap. 2004. "Small Farms, Externalities, and the Dust Bowl of the 1930s." *Journal of Political Economy* 112 (June): 665–94.

Harrison, Sharon, and Mark Weder. 2003. "Did Sunspot Forces Cause the Great Depression?" Paper presented at the Cliometrics Conference in Raleigh, NC, May.

Higgs, Robert. 1987. *Crisis and Leviathan: Critical Episodes in the Growth of American Government.* New York: Oxford University Press.

———. 1997. "Regime Uncertainty: Why the Great Depression Lasted So Long and Why Prosperity Resumed after the War." *Independent Review* 1 (Spring): 561–90.

Howard, Donald S. 1943. *The WPA and Federal Relief Policy.* New York: Russell Sage Foundation.

Irwin, Douglas. 1998. "Changes in U.S. Tariffs: The Role of Import Prices and Commercial Policies." *American Economic Review* 88 (September): 1015–26.

Johnson, Ryan, Shawn Kantor, and Price Fishback. 2003. "The Effects of Relief Spending on Criminal Behavior during the Great Depression." Working paper presented at the ASSA meetings in Washington, DC, January.

Jones, Jesse H. 1939. *Reconstruction Finance Corporation Seven-Year Report to the President and the Congress of the United States, February 2, 1932 to February 2, 1939.* Washington, DC: Reconstruction Finance Corporation.

Jones, Jesse H.. with Edward Angly. 1951. *Fifty Billion Dollars: My Thirteen Years with the RFC, 1932–1945.* New York: Macmillan.

Kane, Edward. 1991. *The S&L Insurance Mess.* Washington, DC: Urban Institute.

Keynes, John Maynard. 1964. *The General Theory of Employment, Interest, and Money.* New York: Harcourt, Brace and World.

Kindleberger, Charles. 1986. *The World in Depression, 1929–1939.* Rev. ed. Berkeley: University of California Press.

Libecap, Gary. 1998. "The Great Depression and the Regulating State: Federal Government Regulation of Agriculture, 1884–1970." In *The Defining Moment: The Great Depression and the American Economy in the Twentieth Century,* ed. Michael Bordo, Claudia Goldin, and Eugene N. White, 181–226. Chicago: Chicago University Press.

Lubove, Roy. 1968. *The Struggle for Social Security, 1900–1935.* Cambridge: Harvard University Press.

Margo, Robert. 1991. "The Microeconomics of Depression Unemployment." *Journal of Economic History* 51 (June): 333–41.

———. 1993. "Employment and Unemployment in the 1930s." *Journal of Economic Perspectives* 7 (Spring): 41–59.

Mason, Joseph. 2001. "Do Lenders of Last Resort Policies Matter? The Effects of the Reconstruction Finance Corporation Assistance to Banks during the Great Depression." *Journal of Financial Services Research* 20 (September): 77–95.

Mason, Joseph. 2003. "The Political Economy of Reconstruction Finance Corporation Assistance during the Great Depression." *Explorations in Economic History* 40 (April): 101–21.

Mason, Joseph, and Daniel Schiffman. 2004. "Too-Big-to-Fail, Government Bailouts, and Managerial Incentives: The Case of Reconstruction Finance Corporation Assistance to the Railroad Industry during the Great Depression." Working paper presented at the meeting of the American Social Science Association in San Diego, January.

McJimsey, George. 1987. *Harry Hopkins: Ally of the Poor and Defender of Democracy.* Cambridge: Harvard University Press.

Nourse, Edwin G., Joseph S. Davis, and John D. Black. 1937. *Three Years of the Agricultural Adjustment Administration.* Washington, DC: Brookings Institution.

Olson, James S. 1998. *Saving Capitalism: The Reconstruction Finance Corporation and the New Deal.* Princeton: Princeton University Press.

Peppers, Larry. 1973. "Full Employment Surplus Analysis and Structural Change: The 1930s:" *Explorations in Economic History* 10 (Winter): 197–210.

Quadagno, Jill. 1988. *The Transformation of Old Age Security: Class and Politics in the American Welfare State.* Chicago: University of Chicago Press.

Reading, Don C. 1973. "New Deal Activity and the States, 1933 to 1939." *Journal of Economic History* 33 (December): 792–810.

Richardson, Gary, and Ching-Yi Chung. 2003. "Deposit Insurance in Developing Economies: Lessons from the Archives of the Board of Governors and the 1920s State Deposit-Insurance Experiments." Paper presented at the Cliometrics Conference in Raleigh, NC, May.

Romer, Christina D. 1990. "The Great Crash and the Onset of the Great Depression." *Quarterly Journal of Economics* 105 (August): 597–624.

———. 1992. "What Ended the Great Depression?" *Journal of Economic History* 52 (December): 757–84.

———. 1999. "Why Did Prices Rise in the 1930s?" *Journal of Economic History* 59 (March): 167–99.

Rothbard, Murray. 2000. *America's Greatest Depression.* 5th ed. Auburn, AL: Ludwig von Mises Institute.

Saloutos, Theodore. 1982. *The American Farmer and the New Deal.* Ames: Iowa State University Press.

Schieber, Sylvester J., and John B. Shoven. 1999. *The Real Deal: The History and Future of Social Security.* New Haven: Yale University Press.

Schlesinger, Arthur, Jr. 1958. *The Age of Roosevelt: The Coming of the New Deal.* Boston: Houghton Mifflin.

Schumpeter, Joseph. 1939. *Business Cycles: A Theoretical, Historical, and Statistical Analysis of the Capitalist Process.* New York: McGraw Hill.'

Seltzer, Andrew J. 1995. "The Political Economy of the Fair Labor Standards Act." *Journal of Political Economy* 103 (December): 1302–42.

———. 1997. "The Effects of the Fair Labor Standards Act of 1938 on the Southern Seamless Hosiery and Lumber Industries." *Journal of Economic History* 57 (June): 396–415.

Smiley, Gene. 2002. *Rethinking the Great Depression: A New View of Its Causes and Consequences.* Chicago: Ivan R. Dee.

Smith, Adam. 1937. *An Inquiry into the Wealth and Causes of the Wealth of Nations.* New York: Modern Library.

Stromberg, David. 2004. "Radio's Impact on Public Spending." *Quarterly Journal of Economics* 119 (February): 189–221.

Temin, Peter. 1976. *Did Monetary Forces Cause the Great Depression?* New York: Norton.

———. 1989. *Lessons from the Great Depression.* Cambridge: MIT Press.

Temin, Peter, and Barry Wigmore. 1990. "The End of One Big Deflation." *Explorations in Economic History* 27 (October): 483–502.

Wallis, John Joseph. 1984. "The Birth of the Old Federalism: Financing the New Deal, 1932–1940." *Journal of Economic History* 44 (March): 139–59.

———. 1985. "Why 1933? The Origins and Timing of National Government Growth, 1933–1940." *Research in Economic History* 4:1–51.

———. 1987. "Employment, Politics, and Economic Recovery during the Great Depression." *Review of Economics and Statistics* 69 (August): 516–20.

———. 1991. "The Political Economy of New Deal Fiscal Federalism." *Economic Inquiry* 39 (July): 510–24.

———. 1998. "The Political Economy of New Deal Spending Revisited, Again: With and without Nevada." *Explorations in Economic History* 35 (April), 140–70.

———. 2001. "The Political Economy of New Deal Spending, Yet Again: A Reply to Fleck." *Explorations in Economic History* 38 (April): 305–14.

Wallis, John Joseph, and Daniel K. Benjamin. 1981. "Public Relief and Private Employment in the Great Depression." *Journal of Economic History* 41 (March): 97–102.

———. 1989. "Private Employment and Public Relief during the Great Depression." Working paper, Department of Economics, University of Maryland.

Whatley, Warren C. 1983. "Labor for the Picking: The New Deal in the South." *Journal of Economic History* 43 (December): 905–29.

Wheelock, David. 1991. *The Strategy and Consistency of Federal Reserve Monetary Policy, 1924–1933.* New York: Cambridge University Press.

———. 1992. "Deposit Insurance and Bank Failures: New Evidence from the 1920s." *Economic Inquiry* 30 (July): 530–43.

White, Eugene Nelson. 1983. *The Regulation and Reform of the American Banking System: 1900–1929.* Princeton: Princeton University Press.

———. 1998. "The Legacy of Deposit Insurance: The Growth, Spread, and Cost of Insuring Financial Intermediaries." In *The Defining Moment: The Great Depression and the American Economy in the Twentieth Century,* ed. Michael D. Bordo, Claudia Goldin, and Eugene N. White, 87–121. Chicago: University of Chicago Press..

Williams, Edward Ainsworth. 1968. *Federal Aid for Relief.* New York: AMS Press.

Wright, Gavin. 1974. "The Political Economy of New Deal Spending: An Econometric Analysis." *Review of Economics and Statistics* 56 (February): 30–38.

———. 1986. *Old South, New South: Revolutions in the Southern Economy since the Civil War.* New York: Basic.

ROBERT HIGGS

14

The World Wars

THE UNITED States' participation in the world wars gave rise to massive increases in the extent of government involvement in economic life and brought about many important, enduring changes in the government's relations with private economic actors. In both wars, the federal government expanded enormously the amount of its expenditure, taxation, and regulation as well as its direct participation in productive activities, creating what contemporaries described during World War I as "war socialism." Each of these great experiences left a multitude of legacies—fiscal, institutional, and ideological—many of which continue to shape the country's political economy. As William Graham Sumner wisely observed, "[I]t is not possible to experiment with a society and just drop the experiment whenever we choose. The experiment enters into the life of the society and never can be got out again." The world wars are among the greatest "experiments" that American society ever endured.[1]

World War I

The outbreak of war in Europe in the fall of 1914 surprised nearly everybody in the United States, a country with little desire and no significant preparation to enter such a war. President Woodrow Wilson declared the nation's neutrality and urged all Americans to "be neutral in fact, as well as in name, during these days that are to try men's souls"—a position from which he himself began to retreat before long, especially after a German U-boat sank the (munitions-laden) British liner *Lusitania* on May 7, 1915, causing the deaths of 128 Americans.

Notwithstanding the official neutrality, some Americans, in particular some of the well-heeled financial and business elites of the Northeast, had no doubt whose side they favored. As Morgan partner Thomas W. Lamont said, "we wanted the Allies to win, from the outset of the war. We were pro-Ally by inheritance, by instinct, by opinion." Soon

J. P. Morgan and Company became the sole purchasing agent for the French and British governments in the United States and also helped steer about $1.5 billion in private credits to the Allies (Chernow 1990, 200). With the bellicose National Security League and former president Theodore Roosevelt beating the war drums on Wilson's right flank, the president moved steadily closer to his ultimate decision to seek a U.S. declaration of war.[2]

Meanwhile, various advocates of "preparedness" undertook to survey the nation's resources and to empower the government to mobilize those resources for war. The National Defense Act of 1916 authorized the president to place obligatory orders for munitions at prices set by the government. The Army Appropriations Act of 1916 authorized the president to take control of transportation systems during wartime and to create a high-level Council of National Defense charged with determining how the economy might best be mobilized for war.

As the war proceeded, the belligerent European nations diverted many of their ships from commercial service to military purposes. In addition, some ships were sunk by enemy action, interned in foreign ports, or confined to home ports. As the supply of shipping services constricted, shipping rates skyrocketed. In response, the Shipping Act of 1916 was enacted, creating the U.S. Shipping Board and authorizing it to regulate the rates and practices of waterborne common carriers in foreign and interstate commerce and, through a subsidiary, to acquire, construct, and operate merchant vessels. In 1917 the subsidiary, known as the Emergency Fleet Corporation, began operation, and between 1917 and 1922 it built more than 2,350 ships (hundreds of them nearly worthless wooden vessels) at a cost of more than $3 billion—approximately one-tenth of the entire financial cost of the war. Meanwhile, the Shipping Board commandeered 431 steel ships of more than 2,500 deadweight tons under construction in U.S. yards, and it took control of all existing U.S. steel cargo vessels of more than 2,500 deadweight tons and all existing U.S. passenger vessels of more than 2,500 deadweight tons suitable for ocean service.[3]

Even before the U.S. declaration of war on April 6, 1917, military leaders and the president had decided to rely on conscription to fill the ranks of the wartime army. In Congress, great opposition arose to a military draft. Missouri senator James A. Reed warned that "the streets of our American cities [will be] running red with blood on Registration day." Despite such grave apprehensions, a draft law ultimately was enacted on May 18, 1917. The government mounted a massive propaganda campaign to whip up support for the draft, and the registration of about ten million men aged twenty-one to thirty took place on June 5 without major incident. Not content to rely on moral suasion and hoopla, the government also provided penalties of a year in prison for failure to register and a fine of as much as $10,000 and imprisonment for as long as twenty years for obstruction of the draft—draconian punishments that were imposed later on hundreds of people who had the temerity to speak out against conscription.[4]

By employing thousands of local civilian boards rather than the military to administer the draft, the government operated the system with considerable success. As Provost Marshall General Enoch H. Crowder, who headed the system, observed with rare frankness, the local draft boards served as "buffers between the individual citizen and the Federal Government, and thus they attracted and diverted, like local grounding wires in an electric coil, such resentment or discontent as might have proved a serious obstacle to war measures, had it been focussed on the central authorities." All told, the draft snared 2,820,000 men, or roughly 72 percent of all those who served in the army in 1917 and 1918, and no doubt many of those who volunteered for military or naval service did so only because of the looming threat of the draft (the rate of evasion, however, was 11 percent, which showed that not everybody was intimidated).[5]

Although the government could draft men for war, it could not simply conscript the vast resources needed to feed, clothe, shelter, train, and transport these men and to equip them with modern arms and ammunition, and therefore it had to find ways to obtain sufficient cash to purchase the requisite goods and services. Federal outlays, which had been considerably less than a billion dollars per year in the period just before the war, jumped to $12.7 billion in fiscal year 1918 and $18.5 billion in fiscal year 1919 (see table 14.1); hence the government needed to acquire an unprecedented amount of revenue.

To do so, it imposed a variety of new taxes, including many excise taxes and steep taxes on "excess" corporate profits, and it raised both individual and corporate income tax rates enormously. Before the war, the highest individual income tax rate had been 7 percent on taxable income in excess of $500,000. In 1918, in stark contrast, the highest rate stood at 77 percent on income in excess of $1,000,000. More important, before the war the lowest rate had been 1 percent on income in excess of $20,000, but in 1918, it was 6 percent on income in excess of $4,000. Thus, a substantial portion of the middle class found itself liable for

Table 14.1 FEDERAL RECEIPTS, OUTLAYS, AND SURPLUS (FY), FEDERAL DEBT AND MONEY STOCK (MID-YEAR), AND GDP DEFLATOR, 1913–1926

Year	(1) Federal receipts	(2) Federal outlays	(3) Surplus or deficit	(4) Federal debt	(5) Money stock	(6) GDP deflator (1996 = 100)
1913	0.714	0.715	—	1.2	15.4	7.2
1914	0.725	0.726	—	1.2	16.1	7.3
1915	0.683	0.746	−0.063	1.2	17.1	7.5
1916	0.761	0.713	0.048	1.2	20.4	8.1
1917	1.101	1.954	−0.853	3.0	23.9	9.7
1918	3.645	12.677	−9.032	12.5	25.8	11.4
1919	5.130	18.493	−13.363	25.5	30.3	13.0
1920	6.649	6.358	0.291	24.3	34.7	15.0
1921	5.571	5.062	0.509	24.0	32.2	13.1
1922	4.026	3.289	0.736	23.0	33.6	12.1
1923	3.853	3.140	0.713	22.3	36.4	12.5
1924	3.871	2.908	0.963	21.3	38.0	12.5
1925	3.641	2.924	0.717	20.5	41.7	12.7
1926	3.795	2.930	0.865	19.6	43.5	12.8

Sources: Columns 1–3, U.S. Office of Management and Budget 2002, 21; column 4, U.S. Bureau of the Census 1975, 1104; column 5, Friedman and Schwartz 1963, 707–11 (currency held by the public plus all commercial bank deposits); column 6, Johnson and Williamson 2002.

Note: Figures are given in billions of current dollars except for deflator.

payment of a tax that had been touted originally as aimed exclusively at extracting money from the very rich. Owing to the new taxes and the increased rates of existing taxes, federal revenues rose from well under a billion dollars in fiscal year 1916 to $6.6 billion in fiscal year 1920 (see table 14.1).[6]

Still, the tax revenue the government obtained fell far short of its expenditure, and the rest had to be borrowed. The Treasury mounted a series of Liberty Bond drives, accompanied by considerable propaganda and hoopla, to stir the public's desire to lend at what would turn out to be (owing to unanticipated inflation) substantially negative real rates of interest. As the government's borrowing proceeded apace, the national debt climbed steeply, from a little more than $1 billion before the war to more than $25 billion at the end (see table 14.1). Thus, the public came to be saddled with the burden of servicing a government debt destined never again to be paid off, although some debt reduction did take place as the Treasury ran budget surpluses during the 1920s (see table 14.1).

To ease the Treasury's task of selling its huge bond issues, the newly created Federal Reserve System ("the Fed") swung into action, adopting low lending rates and setting other conditions that encouraged commercial banks to borrow reserves from the Fed. Flush with reserves, the commercial banking system then flooded the economy with an outpouring of new credit and money (Friedman and Schwartz 1963, 213–20). As table 14.1 shows, the money stock (narrowly defined as currency held by the public plus all deposits in commercial banks) doubled between 1915 and 1920. The upshot of this doubling illustrated perfectly the quantity theory of money: the purchasing power of money fell precisely by half, as shown in the table by the doubling of the GDP deflator.

Because of the rapid inflation that the Treasury and Fed policies caused, the economy had a spuriously prosperous appearance during the war: money incomes were soaring, but the real value of civilian output was falling. Between 1916 and 1920, nominal GNP increased by 79 percent, but real GNP increased by only 6 percent. More important, real *private* GNP (that is, real GNP minus real government purchases of final goods and services) increased by only 5 percent—less than the rate of population growth—and nearly all of that small increase was wiped out in the postwar depression of 1921. In 1917 and 1918 real private GNP actually fell substantially, by 6 percent in each year (see table 14.2)—a classic illustration of guns displacing butter.[7]

Just as the government declined to pay free-market prices to lure men into military service, so it displaced free markets elsewhere as it sought to hasten the rapid reallocation of many other resources deemed

Table 14.2 GNP, GOVERNMENT PURCHASES, AND GROSS PRIVATE PRODUCT, 1913–1926

Year	(1) GNP (current $)	(2) GNP (1929 $)	(3) Government purchases (current $)	(4) Government purchases (1929 $)	(5) GPP (current $)	(6) GPP (1929 $)
1913	39.1	63.5	2.5	4.5	36.6	59.0
1914	36.4	58.6	2.7	4.8	33.7	53.8
1915	38.7	60.4	2.8	5.0	35.9	55.4
1916	49.8	68.9	2.9	4.7	45.9	64.2
1917	59.9	67.3	5.4	7.0	54.5	60.3
1918	76.2	73.4	16.2	16.5	60.0	56.9
1919	78.9	74.2	9.5	9.7	69.4	64.5
1920	88.9	73.3	5.9	5.6	83.0	67.7
1921	73.9	71.6	6.3	6.5	67.6	65.1
1922	74.0	75.8	6.0	6.4	68.0	69.4
1923	86.1	85.8	6.2	6.4	79.9	79.4
1924	87.6	88.4	6.7	6.9	80.9	81.5
1925	91.3	90.5	7.3	7.4	84.0	83.1
1926	97.7	96.4	7.3	7.4	90.4	89.0

Sources: Columns 1–4, Kendrick 1961, 294, 297; columns 5–6 are computed from columns 1–4.

Note: Figures are in billions of dollars.

essential to its prosecution of the war. Although public opinion obstructed outright conscription of food, fuel, and many other goods and services, the government promoted its war program by means of various interventions in the markets. These controls quickly proliferated and penetrated deeply into the operation of the market economy, which soon became more rigged than free in countless ways.

A major step in this direction was the enactment of the Food and Fuel Control Act (usually called the Lever Act) on August 10, 1917, giving sweeping statutory authority to the U.S. Fuel Administration and the U.S. Food Administration, the latter of which the president had created by executive order in May, appointing Herbert Hoover as its head. The law empowered the government to exert a panoply of controls over the production, distribution, consumption, and pricing of food, feed, fuel, fertilizer, and the equipment used to produce these goods. The agencies proceeded to wield their vast powers on a wide scale, dictating the prices of wheat, sugar, and coal and imposing a variety of "conservation" orders to stimulate greater production of basic commodities and to steer them toward war uses, including the subsistence of European allies (a contemporary slogan stated, "Wheat Will Win the War"). The Lever Act also forbade the production of "distilled spirits for beverage purposes," a wartime concession to the prohibitionists that presaged the ratification of the Eighteenth ("Prohibition") Amendment to the U.S. Constitution just two months after the Armistice ended the war.

To control industrial raw materials, components, and finished products, President Wilson created the War Industries Board (WIB) by executive order in July 1917, then strengthened it substantially in March 1918, appointing Wall Street speculator Bernard M. Baruch as its chairman. The WIB sought to steer goods to uses the government favored for its war-production program, primarily by issuing priority ratings that established the sequence in which sellers were to fill various customer orders. As the WIB exerted, in Baruch's words, "the power to determine who gets what and when" (Baruch 1960, 55), the price system lost its essential rationale as a signaling and allocation system. Thinly veiled threats that other government agencies might withhold fuel or transportation services or even confiscate production facilities outright served to enforce the WIB's ostensibly voluntary agreements with industrialists.

A WIB price-fixing committee, which reported directly to the president, undertook to fix at low levels the prices of scores of goods in especially keen demand for the government's war-production program (such as metals, chemicals, construction materials, textiles, and leather goods), thus keeping the financial costs of that program artificially low and concealing its true economic cost. These price controls were not intended to contain overall price inflation, nor did they do so inadvertently to any appreciable degree.[8]

Many other wartime government agencies also sought to shape the allocation of goods and services in support of the government's war-production program: the War Trade Board, the War Finance Corporation, the War Labor Administration, and thousands of others, including a multitude that operated at the state and local levels of government. To call the whole apparatus "central planning" would be to suggest a greater degree of coherence than it actually possessed. (Of course, central planning as practiced later in places such as the USSR and China never had the coherence it purported to have, either.) Nevertheless, war socialism as practiced in the United States during World War I constituted a massive departure from the market-oriented system in operation prior to the war, and sloughing off every vestige of this emergency contrivance after the war had ended would prove to be impossible.[9]

The railroad industry, perhaps as much as any, emerged from the war permanently altered. Of course, the government had already become deeply engaged in regulating the interstate railroads decades before the war, and legislation passed in the early twentieth century had strengthened the Interstate Commerce Commission's powers substantially. Indeed, the faulty exercise of those powers had put the industry into a tight price-cost squeeze, and as a result it had entered the war period poorly equipped to provide the services it was then called on to provide in connection with the government's wartime economic and military mobilizations.[10]

Actions taken by the railroad labor unions made matters even worse. Just prior to U.S. entry into the war, in 1916, a nationwide strike of the operating brotherhoods had been averted only after President Wilson intervened and gained congressional approval of the Adamson Act, which effectively raised wage rates by 25 percent by reducing the standard workday from ten to eight hours with no change in daily pay. Toward the end of 1917, the unions again threatened a nationwide strike unless their further demands were met, this time jeopardizing the entire war-production program, which the government had rendered especially vulnerable by concentrating its munitions orders and its use of ports of embarkation in the northeastern part of the country.[11]

When severe winter weather brought an already shaky railroad system to a near standstill in December 1917, the Wilson administration chose to resolve the matter by nationalizing the interstate railroad companies and placing them under the control of the U.S. Railroad Administration, headed by the Treasury secretary (who was also Wilson's son-in-law), William Gibbs McAdoo. The Railroad Administration proceeded in effect to cartelize the railroad industry, operating the various companies as a single economic unit. To assuage the restive unions, McAdoo soon approved a substantial wage increase, retroactive to January 1, 1918, shifting the cost of this increase onto shippers and taxpayers. Although the government promised to pay the owners of the commandeered railroads an annual rent equal to each company's average net operating income during the three years ending June 30, 1917, the real value of this payment declined steadily as the purchasing power of the dollar fell continually during the time of the government's possession—the GDP deflator rose 55 percent between 1917 and 1920 (see table 14.1). When the government finally returned the railroad properties to their private owners under the terms of the Transportation Act of 1920, it did so only with many strings attached, shifting vital aspects of managerial discretion from the owners to the ICC. As a legal historian observed, the 1920 law "stopped only short of nationalization."[12]

Wartime labor disputes also prompted the government to nationalize other industries, including the telephone, the domestic telegraph, and the international telegraphic cable industries. In addition, for various reasons, it took over eleven specific industrial plants and in effect nationalized the ocean-shipping industry. Exercising its wartime censorship powers, the government shut down more than a hundred publications, taking an especially heavy toll on the foreign-language press (Linfield 1990, 34, 46–47).

Although U.S. participation in World War I lasted only nineteen months, the experience affected the society, the polity, and the economy deeply and permanently. Fiscal, institutional, and ideological effects loomed large.

The war effected a permanent shift in the federal government's sources of revenue away from consumption taxes such as the tariff and domestic excise taxes and toward individual and corporate income taxes. Never again, however, would the federal income tax be a forthright "class tax" laid only on the well-to-do. Instead, henceforth, it would bring substantial portions of the middle class within its reach (in this respect, World War II proved to be even more significant). Never again would individual income tax rates range from 1 to 7 percent. In 1929, after a series of tax cuts passed during the Harding and Coolidge administrations, the top rate stood at 24 percent on income in excess of $100,000—more than three times the top prewar rate (U.S. Bureau of the Census 1975, 1095). Armed with a strengthened capacity to collect taxes, the federal government kept its spending at a substantially higher level after the war bulge itself had come and gone. In the seven prewar fiscal years 1910–16, federal outlays averaged $707 million per year; in the seven postwar fiscal years 1923–29, they averaged $2,978 million per year, or 321 percent greater (an increase of 73 percent would have been sufficient to compensate for the reduced purchasing power of the dollar). In this respect, among many others, the war produced a "ratchet effect" on the growth of government.[13]

The institutional legacies of World War I loomed still larger than the fiscal legacies. "The Administrative Revolution in Government," observed Sir John Hicks, "can (almost) be precisely dated. . . . [I]t was during [World War I] that governments discovered—to their astonishment and sometimes to their dismay—what power, what economic power, what power over their own peoples had come into their hands. Some, when the war was over, endeavoured to forget it; only to be driven to resurrecting it, bit by bit, as the easiest way of coping with one after another of the emergencies, political and economic, which they encountered." In the United States, scarcely more than a decade had elapsed before this resurrection took place with a vengeance:[14]

In the depths of the Great Depression, the federal government employed the wartime measures as models for dealing with what Franklin Roosevelt called "a crisis in our national life comparable to war." Hence the War Finance Corporation came back to life as the Reconstruction Finance Corporation, the War Industries Board as the National Recovery Administration, the Food Administration as the Agricultural Adjustment Administration, the Capital Issues Committee as the Securities and Exchange Commission, the Fuel Administration as the Connolly Act apparatus for cartelizing the oil industry and the Guffey Act apparatus for cartelizing the bituminous coal industry. The military mobilization of young men came back as the quasi-military Civilian Conservation Corps. The Muscle Shoals hydroelectric munitions facility became the germ of the Tennessee Valley Authority. The wartime U.S. Housing Corporation reappeared first as part of the Public Works Administration in 1933 and then as the U.S. Housing Authority in 1937. The New Deal's federal social security program harked back to the wartime servicemen's life insurance and the payments made to the soldiers' dependents. The temporary wartime abandonment of the gold

standard became permanent in 1933–34, when the government nationalized
the monetary gold stock and abrogated all contractual obligations, both
public and private, to pay gold. Along with the revived agencies came many
of the wartime planners, including Baruch, Felix Frankfurter, George Peek,
Hugh Johnson, John Hancock, Leon Henderson, and John Dickerson, not
to mention FDR himself, as advisers or administrators. Obviously the wartime precedents were crucial in guiding the New Dealers and helping them
to justify and gain acceptance of their policies. (Higgs 1997, 314)

Less visibly, though ultimately perhaps most significantly, the war's
ideological legacies continued to shape the thinking of policymakers
and the public for decades. "It was from this type of experience," George
Soule observed of World War I, "that the possibilities of governmental
planning were first learned in the United States." Soule made reference
especially to the engineers and economists who had participated in the
wartime government planning operations; other observers noted the
same effect on businessmen and government officials. "We helped inter
the extreme dogmas of laissez faire," concluded Bernard Baruch, the
wartime industrial czar. "Our experience taught that government direction of the economy need not be inefficient or undemocratic, and suggested that in time of danger it was imperative." Baruch was scarcely a
disinterested historian of the wartime planning (and the "lessons" that
he and others drew from the experience were erroneous), yet no one
can deny that the wartime collectivism had a profound effect in "soft-
ening up" the middle classes for eventual acceptance of a big, active,
interventionist central government. Collectivists of various stripes, unable to maintain the full panoply of wartime programs after peace returned, bided their time, awaiting the next national emergency, when
they would be poised to propose—and much of the public would be
predisposed to accept—programs similar to those employed in managing the war economy.[15]

World War II

Soon after World War I ended, a revulsion against the war and its
seemingly pointless sacrifices set in, and during the 1920s and 1930s,
the public for the most part supported measures to preserve U.S. neutrality and to keep the armed forces on a near-starvation diet. In the
Senate the Nye Committee hearings of 1934–36 cast an accusing light
on the "merchants of death," the financiers and industrialists whom
many people blamed in those days for the ill-fated U.S. engagement in

the Great War. To preclude foreign entanglements that might drag the country into a future war, Congress passed strict neutrality laws in 1935, 1936, and 1937 and a less strict law in 1939. Therefore, despite some interwar planning by the War Department, the Navy Department, and a handful of big businessmen, the nation had made scant preparation for engagement in a great war when the conflagration broke out in Europe in 1939. The U.S. Army had only 190,000 officers and men, making it the world's sixteenth largest. Nor did the United States possess anything that deserved to be called a substantial munitions industry (U.S. Bureau of the Census 1975, 1141).

Whereas Woodrow Wilson in 1914 had urged his fellow citizens to remain neutral in thought as well as deed, Franklin D. Roosevelt in 1939 declared: "This nation will remain a neutral nation, but I cannot ask that every American remain neutral in thought as well." Roosevelt himself, however, had no intention of remaining neutral in either thought or deed, and he worked relentlessly, often behind the scenes, to move the country toward full engagement in the war against Germany and its allies. After France and the Low Countries fell to Hitler's forces in the spring of 1940, the government began to mobilize and organize resources for war much more seriously. A series of makeshift planning agencies guided these preparations: the National Defense Advisory Commission, the Office of Production Management, the Office of Price Administration and Civilian Supply, and the Supply Priorities and Allocations Board all drew their authority from presidential directives and operated under FDR's tight control within the Executive Office of the President. Only after the attack on Pearl Harbor did Congress enact war powers laws that created a firm statutory foundation for the War Production Board and the other agencies that would direct the wartime command economy during the following four years.[16]

Of all the measures taken during the eighteen-month "defense period" that preceded the formal U.S. declaration of war, none loomed larger than the reestablishment of military conscription. A proposal to reinstitute the draft ignited a fierce national debate in 1940. In the Senate, Arthur Vandenberg described a peacetime draft as "repugnant to the spirit of democracy and the soul of Republican institutions," Henry F. Ashurst opposed "riveting shackles of militarism upon the American people," and Walter F. George worried that Congress could not grant the president such power "and convince the American people that we are not ready and resigned and reconciled to the final, inevitable, short step of actually entering the war." Ultimately, however, the nation's first peacetime national conscription law was enacted on September 16, 1940. Still, the draft remained a contentious measure, and when the law came up for extension in the summer of 1941, with a provision to retain the existing draftees in service beyond the twelve months originally stipulated, the House passed it by the narrowest possible margin, 203 to 202.[17]

After the United States formally entered the war, the draft laws received periodic amendment. The ages of men subject to induction were extended at both ends to include all between the ages of eighteen and forty-five, and the period of service became the duration of the war plus six months. Deferments remained controversial, especially the general exemption of agricultural workers. Naturally, many men joined the navy or the army air forces to escape the draft and the consequent likelihood of assignment to the dreaded infantry. Once again, local civilian boards rather than the military administered the draft system, which contributed greatly to its acceptance by the draftees and their families. Secretary of War Henry L. Stimson praised the system as "a triumph of decentralization."[18]

Of the sixteen million who served in the armed forces at some time during the war, more than ten million, or about 63 percent, were drafted outright. The buildup of this enormous conscription-fed armed force has a crucial bearing on the claims made during and since the war that U.S. participation in World War II "got the economy out of the Great Depression." The explanation that has usually accompanied this claim is a species of vulgar Keynesianism: the "wartime prosperity" is said to have resulted from massive government spending financed for the most part by borrowing and creating money. Although the fiscal policies of the government during the war had major importance in many respects, the core of the claim about elimination of the Depression relates to the reduction of unemployment, not to the increase of national output (an increase that consisted entirely of military outputs, not of civilian goods and services). The truth, however, is simple: overwhelmingly, the reduction of unemployment occurred because of the buildup of the armed forces.[19]

As table 14.3 shows, the uniformed, active-duty ranks of the armed forces increased by 11.6 million persons between mid-1940 and mid-1945. That increase alone was more than sufficient to account for the simultaneous reduction of unemployment by 7.9 million persons. During those five years, however, the armed forces also increased their civilian employment by 2.3 million persons, and "private" employment in military supply industries increased by 10.7 million (the increase had been even

Table 14.3 EMPLOYMENT, UNEMPLOYMENT, AND LABOR FORCE, 1940–1948

Year	Uniformed military on active duty	Civilian military employees	Military supply industry employees	Total nonmilitary employees	Unemployed	Total labor force
1940	0.5	0.3	0.3	46.1	8.8	55.9
1941	1.8	0.6	2.5	45.2	6.8	56.9
1942	3.9	1.3	10.0	39.6	4.1	58.9
1943	9.0	2.2	13.4	36.0	1.9	62.5
1944	11.5	2.2	12.6	38.1	0.9	65.3
1945	12.1	2.6	11.0	39.1	0.9	65.7
1946	3.0	1.4	1.2	55.9	1.7	63.1
1947	1.6	0.9	0.8	55.4	2.3	61.0
1948	1.4	0.9	1.0	56.4	2.4	62.1

Source: U.S. Department of Defense, Office of the Assistant Secretary of Defense (Controller) 1987, 126.

Note: Figures represent millions of persons at mid-year.

greater during the peak war-production years 1943 and 1944). While this gigantic diversion of labor to military purposes was proceeding, however, total *nonmilitary* employment actually fell by 7 million persons (again, the drop had been even greater in 1943 and 1944).

Nobody needs a macroeconomic model to understand these events—not Keynesianism, not monetarism, not any modern refinements of those theories. The government forced millions of men into the armed forces, paid millions of others to equip those men with guns and ammunition, and hence unemployment disappeared—that's the end of the story, so far as the elimination of unemployment is concerned. None of this, however, had anything to do with the creation of genuine prosperity, and in no way does it support the oft-repeated claims that the war brought about a "carnival of consumption" and that "economically speaking, Americans had never had it so good." It would have been more than miraculous had the U.S. economy managed to improve the well-being of consumers (either currently or, via investment, subsequently) while reducing civilian employment by more than 10 million persons, or about 15 percent (22 percent between 1940 and 1943), and no such miracle occurred.[20]

The government did spend gargantuan amounts of money to prosecute the war; never before or since did the government's fiscal activities so dominate the nominal economy. As table 14.4 shows, federal outlays increased from $9.5 billion in fiscal year 1940 to $92.7 billion in fiscal year 1945, at which time those outlays amounted to almost 44 percent of officially measured GNP (U.S. Bureau of the Census 1975, 224).

Table 14.4 FEDERAL RECEIPTS, OUTLAYS, AND SURPLUS (FY), DEBT AND MONEY STOCK (MID-YEAR), AND GDP DEFLATOR, 1940–1948

Year	Federal receipts	Federal outlays	Surplus or deficit (−)	Federal debt	Money stock	GDP deflator (1996 = 100)
1940	6.548	9.468	−2.920	50.7	54.3	10.3
1941	8.712	13.653	−4.941	57.5	61.3	11.0
1942	14.634	35.137	−20.503	79.2	69.0	−
1943	24.001	78.555	−54.554	142.6	90.4	−
1944	43.747	91.304	−47.557	204.1	104.6	−
1945	45.159	92.712	−47.553	260.1	124.7	−
1946	39.296	55.232	−15.936	271.0	139.3	−
1947	38.514	34.496	4.018	257.1	146.0	−
1948	41.560	29.764	11.796	252.0	146.9	17.3

Sources: Columns 1–3, U.S. Office of Management and Budget 2002, 21; column 4, U.S. Bureau of the Census 1975, 1105; column 5, Friedman and Schwartz 1963, 716–18; column 6, Johnson and Williamson 2002.

Note: Figures are given in billions of current dollars except deflator.

To get the wherewithal to pay for this huge gush of spending, the government proceeded, as it had in 1917 and 1918, to impose new taxes, to increase the rates of existing taxes, and to lower the boundaries above which people became liable for the payment of taxes. Annual excise tax revenue more than trebled between 1940 and 1945. Employment tax revenue more than doubled. The major sources of increased revenue, however, were individual and corporate income taxes. The latter zoomed from $1.0 billion in 1940 to $16.4 billion in 1945 (the greater part representing an "excess profits" tax), while individual income taxes jumped from $1.1 billion to more than $18.4 billion. Before the war, fewer than fifteen million individuals filed an income tax return; in 1945, approximately fifty million did so (U.S. Bureau of the Census 1975, 1110). And not only did most income earners have to pay, but they also had to pay at much higher rates: the bottom bracket rose from 4.4 percent on income in excess of $4,000 in 1940 to 23 percent on income in excess of $2,000 in 1945. The top rate reached a virtually confiscatory rate of 94 percent on income in excess of $200,000 (ibid., 1095). In one mighty push, the government had completed the transformation of the income tax from a "class tax" to a "mass tax," which it would remain ever afterward. Moreover, the payroll withholding of income taxes, which the government imposed midway through the war, also remained an essential component of the great federal revenue-reaping machine.[21]

Notwithstanding the stupendous increase in taxation, the government's revenues amounted to less than half of its outlays (see table 14.4), and it had to obtain the rest by borrowing. Therefore, the national debt swelled from $51 billion in 1940 to $260 billion in 1945. The Federal Reserve System bought about $20 billion of government bonds itself, thereby acting as a de facto printing press for the Treasury, and it aided the government's bond sales indirectly by adopting policies that dramatically expanded the volume of commercial bank reserves and thereby contributed to the rapid increase of credit and money, which pumped up the demand for government bonds. As table 14.4 shows, the money stock increased by 171 percent between 1940 and 1948 (the latter being the first year that was almost completely free of the effects of wartime price controls), while the GDP deflator rose 68 percent—this time the simple quantity theory of money was an imperfect predictor, although its core relationship (more money → higher price level) still applied.

The reader will note that table 14.4 lists no figures for the GDP deflator from 1942 through 1947. Such figures have been computed, to be sure, and all too many economists and historians have taken them seriously. In truth, however, the operation of a massive military procurement system combined with a shrunken civilian economy subject to comprehensive price controls renders all such price-index calculations so problematic that for most purposes it is best not to use them at all. The government began to dictate selected prices in 1941; it expanded and tightened the controls considerably in 1942 after the enactment of the Emergency Price Control Act in January and the Economic Stabilization Act in October. Not until late 1946 did the government abandon the price controls, and not until 1948 had the economy shaken off the direct effects of those controls nearly completely.[22]

A massive bureaucracy, the Office of Price Administration, managed the maze of controls and—because the price controls gave rise to pervasive shortages—the related rationing of a number of important consumer goods, including gasoline, tires, canned foods, meats, fats, sugar, clothing, and shoes. Although many people evaded the price controls and rationing restrictions and a black market flourished for many items, the OPA's control of basic consumer markets proved a major nuisance to civilians from 1942 through 1946 (Rockoff 1984, 85–176).

Consumers might well have been thankful that the rationed goods were available at all, because many other goods were not. Early in 1942 the War Production Board forced the cessation of civilian automobile production, compelling this great industry to turn its factories and managerial talents to the production of war goods such as army tanks and bomber planes. Many other consumer durable goods, including most household appliances, were either unavailable or available only in tightly limited quantities during the war. New construction of private residential housing came to a halt as the government diverted construction materials to the building of military bases and other war-related facilities and to the construction of housing for munitions workers at places where existing living accommodations could not shelter the influx of Rosies seeking to rivet.

Closure of the civilian automobile industry was only one of thousands of measures taken by the War Production Board, the central agency of the government's wartime command economy. In 1940 and 1941 the WPB's predecessor agencies had begun to issue priority ratings similar to those the WIB used during World War I to give precedence to orders placed by critical munitions producers. Although the WPB inherited this system, expanded and refined it, and to some extent continued to use it throughout the war, the system proved highly unsatisfactory in practice. Excessive issuance of high priority ratings gave rise to "priorities inflation" and thus rendered the system incapable of serving its intended purpose. In 1943 the WPB implemented its Controlled Materials Plan for allocating three critical metals—steel, copper, and aluminum—to the major procurement agencies (Army, Navy, Army Air Forces, Maritime Commission, and Lend-Lease), which in turn allocated their quotas down the chain of their contractors and subcontractors. The idea was that the tail composed of these three materials would wag the dog of the entire war-production program. Although the authorities claimed success for this plan, they continued to supplement it with an array of other controls besides priorities, including spot allocations and production scheduling. Like any system of central planning, the entire apparatus was pervaded by conflicts, inconsistencies, and misdirections. The authors of one of the most careful studies of the system made liberal use of terms such as "administrative chaos," "administrative anarchy," "chasm between plan and operation," and "trial-and-error fumbling," and they concluded that the successes of the wartime planned economy were "less a testimony to the effectiveness with which we mobilized our resources than they are to the tremendous economic wealth which this nation possessed." [23]

Amid the sound and fury of the wartime command economy, no area proved more troublesome than labor. Owing to the massive withdrawal of prime workers from the civilian labor force by the draft and by voluntary enlistments, labor grew ever scarcer, and the civilian labor force consisted increasingly of youths, elderly people, and inexperienced women who were drawn to seek employment, especially in relatively high-paying

THE WORLD WARS 447

munitions industries such as aircraft manufacturing and shipbuilding. The War Manpower Commission attempted to steer labor to the occupations and locations where it would make the greatest contribution to the war-production program, but labor proved difficult to steer. Toward the end of the war the president proposed that a national service law be enacted that in effect would make all workers subject to an industrial draft, but powerful opponents of this idea, including the labor unions and the major business associations, blocked its congressional approval.

Labor unions, which had prospered after passage of the National Labor Relations Act in 1935 and had become leading players in the New Deal coalition, continued to flex their muscles during the war. They finagled constantly to push wages and other compensation above the limits the government had set in an effort to restrain the wage-price spiral that its inflationary monetary policy was causing. In general, the government enforced a "maintenance of membership" rule, which helped the unions add about four million new members to their ranks—an increase of approximately 40 percent—during the war years. Some powerful unions, most prominently the railroad operating brotherhoods (as usual) and the United Mine Workers (UMW), took advantage of their choke hold on the production of critical war services and materials to demand large wage increases, striking when their demands were not met. Twice in 1943 the government seized the bituminous coal mines and threatened to draft the striking miners, but the miners eventually achieved their objectives for the most part. (Roosevelt, who despised the UMW's charismatic leader, John L. Lewis, promised that he would resign from the presidency if Lewis would just commit suicide, but the president got no satisfaction in that regard, either.) Altogether, the government took over more than forty production facilities—in some cases entire industries—during the war, and half that many during the immediate postwar years, to settle union-management disputes and thus to avoid protracted work stoppages.[24]

Not content with the regimentation of workers and capitalists in the private sector, the government undertook to build enormous industrial facilities on its own account, thus embracing war socialism in its pure form. Of the $25.8 billion invested in new manufacturing plants and equipment between mid-1940 and mid-1945, $17.2 billion, or precisely two-thirds, was federally financed, much of it directly by the armed forces and the rest for the most part by the Defense Plant Corporation, a wartime subsidiary of the Reconstruction Finance Corporation. As the head of the latter, Jesse Jones, observed, "At the close of World War II, Defense Plant Corporation's investment alone embraced 96 per cent of the nation's synthetic rubber capacity, 90 per cent in magnesium metal, 71 per cent in the manufacture of aircraft and their engines, 58 per cent in aluminum metal, and nearly 50 per cent of the facilities for fabricating aluminum" (Jones 1951, 316). The Navy and the Maritime Commission plowed $2.2 billion into the construction of shipyards and of plants for the production of ship components. Much of the government's wartime capital formation had little or no value for civilian production, and the government received only pennies on the dollar for the plants and equipment it sold to private purchasers in the latter 1940s (Higgs 2004).[25]

Like the previous world war, World War II left a multitude of fiscal, institutional, and ideological legacies. After this unprecedented experiment in government control of economic life, Americans would never be the same and, in ways both direct and indirect, the government's role in the economy would be permanently enlarged.

The fiscal effects of World War II loomed large. In fiscal year 1940, when the depression still lingered and the government was spending heavily for a number of relief programs, federal outlays amounted to $9.5 billion, but in fiscal year 1948, after the wartime command system had come and gone and the economy was once again enjoying genuine prosperity, outlays amounted to $29.8 billion, or 212 percent more (see table 14.4), even though a 68 percent increase would have been sufficient to compensate for the fallen purchasing power of the dollar. Relative to GNP, federal outlays amounted to 10 percent in fiscal year 1940 and 12.2 percent in fiscal year 1948.[26] Federal receipts had grown much more, however, rising by 535 percent between fiscal years 1940 and 1948. (In the former year the budget had a large deficit, in the latter year a much larger surplus [see table 14.4].)

The huge increase in federal revenues testified to the power of the wartime tax system, which the government retained when the war ended. Although some taxes were terminated, and some reductions were made in tax rates, many of the wartime changes remained, including the capture of the masses in the income tax net and the payroll withholding of taxes to prevent employees from avoiding payment. In 1940 the lowest individual tax rate was 4.4 percent on income in excess of $4,000; in 1948 it was 16.6 percent on income in excess of $2,000 (equivalent to little more than half that amount in 1940 dollars). In 1948, 11.5 million of the persons who paid individual federal income tax, or about 55 percent, had the tax withheld by employers (U.S. Bureau of the Census 1975, 1091). With this war-spawned tax system, the federal government possessed the fiscal engine it would use to propel the postwar warfare-welfare state.[27]

Despite the enormous increase in taxation during the war, the government had borrowed more than half of the funds it expended; hence, the national debt had ballooned from $51 billion in mid-1940 to $271 billion in mid-1946. Although a small amount was paid down in the late 1940s, the giant debt was destined to remain forever, and later to be bulked up even more, especially during the administrations of Ronald Reagan, George H. W. Bush, and George W. Bush. Thus, debt management became an important aspect of federal fiscal affairs in a way that it never had been before World War II except during wartime.

The misleadingly named Lend-Lease program, whereby the government had transferred $50 billion worth of goods and services to allied nations during the war, clearly prefigured the adoption of the postwar Marshall Plan, whereby $12.5 billion was transferred to European governments from 1948 to 1951 to aid their recovery from the war's devastation. The way was then clear for the U.S. government to undertake a permanent foreign aid program, which has continued to the present, to the benefit of favored foreign governments and well-connected U.S. exporters.

The postwar foreign aid program was but one aspect of the nation's new commitment to "internationalism." As the war ended, the United States and the USSR transformed their wartime alliance seamlessly into outright enmity, and forty-five years of global cold war ensued, a conflict with far-reaching political, social, cultural, and economic consequences, including the outbreak of devastating regional wars in Korea and Vietnam. World War II had shattered the nation's traditional commitment to noninterventionism—a policy smeared as isolationism and appeasement by the proponents of war during 1940 and subsequently— and the U.S. triumph in 1945 suggested to many Americans the desirability of their nation-state's acting as a global policeman thereafter. Among the many costs of this commitment was the devotion of 7.5 percent of annual GNP, on average, to purchases of military goods and services between 1948 and 1989.[28]

On the receiving end of much of this spending was the conglomeration of military contracting companies, universities, consultants, labor unions, and other recipients who formed one vertex of the iron triangle known as the military-industrial-congressional complex. The contractual arrangements that tied the parties of this arrangement together had been forged into their modern form first during the "defense period" prior to World War II, and the dimensions of the system had swelled hugely during the war. When the government's spending for military purposes plunged after 1945, the system endured a few lean years, but the outbreak of fighting in Korea in 1950 served as a catalyst for a big rebound, and the major participants have continued to prosper despite alternating ups and downs of the defense budget ever since. The military-industrial-congressional complex constitutes perhaps the most consequential of all the institutional legacies of World War II.[29]

Perhaps even more auspicious, however, was the war's ideological legacy. On one hand, the war shattered the remnants of serious opposition to government interventionism among businesspeople. The war, observed Calvin Hoover, "conditioned them to accept a degree of governmental intervention and control after the war which they had deeply resented prior to it."[30] Hence, even during the pro-business Eisenhower administration, no attempt was made to get rid of the pervasive interventionist programs that the government had created during Franklin D. Roosevelt's presidency. On the other hand, the general public's prevailing interpretation of the wartime experience gave unprecedented ideological support to a big federal government actively engaged in a wide range of domestic and international tasks:

> After all, the wartime central planners had just carried out successfully a complex undertaking of enormous dimensions. They had waged a global war, marshaling, organizing, and allocating the requisite resources to defeat two mighty adversaries while leaving American civilian consumers relatively well off, at least by comparison with the suffering populations of the Soviet Union, Japan, Germany, or Great Britain. Surely this great accomplishment testified to the planners' knowledge, abilities, and devotion to the public interest. Surely a central government capable of winning the greatest war in human history could carry out such relatively mundane tasks as stabilizing the business cycle, guaranteeing all citizens a good job and a high standard of living, and regulating the industrial life of the nation to achieve greater fairness than the unfettered market. Surely. (Higgs 1997, 318)

Passage of the Employment Act of 1946 formally committed the federal government to ongoing responsibility for the successful operation of the economy. While the government undertook to perform its newly authorized role as economic savior, the Veterans Administration carried out the wide-ranging responsibilities stipulated in the GI Bill of 1944, overseeing the operation of a vast welfare state within the welfare state.

In the six decades that followed the end of the war, the welfare state grew stupendously and assumed a multitude of specific forms. Although the public did not always approve of this sprawling system's operation, and sometimes its miscarriages were too obvious to deny, no amount of contradictory evidence seems to have dented the public's post–World War II faith in the government's ability somehow—usually by spending vast sums of money—to create personal and social security and to remedy the full range of human problems and pathologies.

Postscript

Students of the growth of government have sometimes treated the world wars as nearly irrelevant to the explanation they seek, viewing them as aberrations or even as "random" deviations from a long-term trajectory determined by more persistent structural changes. This way of viewing them is profoundly mistaken. In truth, nothing had greater importance than the world wars in determining the long-term growth of government in the United States in the twentieth century. Although direct belligerent participation in the first war lasted less than two years and in the second war less than four years, each of those brief periods brought about more extreme, pervasive, and consequential changes than several decades of normal peacetime development would have brought about. Not only did the wars provide auspicious occasions for a variety of ideological, political, and economic special-interest groups to achieve their long-cherished ends, but they brought about additional changes that no group could have effected in their absence, such as the validation of government-business planning "taught" by World War I and the "internationalist" transformation of U.S. foreign and defense policy occasioned by World War II, among many others. History follows a path-dependent course: what is likely to happen on any given day depends heavily on what has happened previously; hence, even seemingly abnormal events have the potential to alter the subsequent course of events substantially. The long run is indeed a series of short runs in which the potentialities of each short run are contingent on its inheritance from the past. "Experiments" so vast and traumatic as U.S. participation in the world wars entered deeply into the life of the society, with manifold consequences, and they continued to affect the economic, political, and social life of the nation at the dawn of the twenty-first century.

Notes

1. The quotation is from Sumner 1934, 2:473.
2. The quotation and the material about Morgan are from Chernow 1990, 186, 200.

3. See Day 1920, 592–93, and Sicotte 1999, 861, citing U.S. Shipping Board reports of the number of ships built. Hurley (1927, 32, 42) describes the commandeering of ships.

4. Reed is quoted in Higgs 1987, 132; Linfield (1990, 43–45) describes draft penalties.

5. Crowder is quoted by Kennedy (1980, 152), and the draft details are from U.S. Bureau of the Census 1975, 1140, and Farrell 1985, 18–19, 206.

6. U.S. Bureau of the Census (1975, 1095) reports the tax rates.

7. A similar conclusion is reached by Romer (1988, 107–8).

8. See Taussig 1919, 210. Haney 1919, 105–6, contains a list of products that were affected.

9. Paxson 1920, 76 refers to a War Department General Staff guide to "nearly three thousand separate agencies."

10. See Martin 1971.

11. See Higgs 1987, 116–21.

12. The quotation is from Murphy 1972, 6.

13. Outlay data are from U.S. Office of Management and Budget 2002, 21; the GDP deflator is from Johnson and Williamson 2002.

14. The quotation is from Hicks 1969, 162.

15. The quotations and related material are from Soule 1947, 32, 62–63, and Baruch 1960, 74.

16. See Kennedy 1999, 426–515 (the quotation is on 427) and Garrett 2003.

17. The legislators are quoted in Higgs 1987, 200.

18. See Stimson and Bundy 1947, 162.

19. The draft statistics are from Chambers 1987, 254–55, and Higgs 1987, 200–202. For a more in-depth discussion of the impact of the war on prosperity, see Higgs 1992, 44–49.

20. The quoted phrases are from Blum (1976, 90) and Melman (1985, 15), respectively.

21. U.S. Bureau of the Census 1975, 1105. The tax rates are at 1095.

22. For a fuller discussion of price controls and their impact on deflators, see Higgs 1992, 49–52.

23. For many details of the federal controls on industries, see U.S. Civilian Production Administration 1947). The quoted phrases are from Novick, Anshen, and Truppner 1949, 9, 110, 140, 219, 291, 394, 395, 400, 403.

24. See the detailed information about wartime seizures in Justice Frankfurter's concurring opinion in *Youngstown Sheet & Tube Co. et al. v. Sawyer*, 343 U.S. 679 (1952), 621–27.

25. Higgs (1993, 180, citing WPB data) describes the investment program. Lane (1951, 397) discusses the government's investment in shipbuilding. Higgs (2004) discusses the lack of value of war capital and the postwar fire sale.

26. These figures are computed from data from table 14.4 and U.S. Bureau of the Census 1975, 224.

27. The tax rates and withholding percentages are from U.S. Bureau of the Census 1975, 1095, 1091.

28. Higgs (1994) and Leebaert (2002) discuss the developments leading to the cold war. Military purchase share is calculated in Higgs 1994, 292.

29. Higgs (1993) describes the defense contracting process. Trevino and Higgs (1992) and Higgs (2001) discuss the military-industrial-congressional complex.
30. The quotation is from Hoover 1959, 212.

References

Baruch, Bernard M. 1960. *Baruch: The Public Years.* New York: Holt, Rinehart and Winston.

Blum, John Morton. 1976. *V Was for Victory: Politics and American Culture during World War II.* New York: Harcourt Brace Jovanovich.

Chambers, John Whiteclay III. 1987. *To Raise an Army: The Draft Comes to Modern America.* New York: Free Press.

Chernow, Ron. 1990. *The House of Morgan: An American Banking Dynasty and the Rise of Modern Finance.* New York: Simon & Schuster.

Day, Edmund E. 1920. "The American Merchant Fleet: A War Achievement, a Peace Problem." *Quarterly Journal of Economics* 34 (August): 567–606.

Farrell, Robert H. 1985. *Woodrow Wilson and World War I, 1917–1921.* New York: Harper & Row.

Friedman, Milton, and Anna Jacobson Schwartz. 1963. *A Monetary History of the United States, 1867–1960.* Princeton: Princeton University Press.

Garrett, Garet. 2003. *Defend America First: The Antiwar Editorials of the* Saturday Evening Post, *1939–1942.* Caldwell, ID: Caxton.

Haney, Lewis H. 1919. "Price Fixing in the United States during the War." *Political Science Quarterly* 34 (March): 104–26.

Hicks, John. 1969. *A Theory of Economic History.* Oxford: Oxford University Press.

Higgs, Robert. 1987. *Crisis and Leviathan: Critical Episodes in the Growth of American Government.* New York: Oxford University Press.

——. 1992. "Wartime Prosperity? A Reassessment of the U.S. Economy in the 1940s." *Journal of Economic History* 52 (March): 41–60.

——. 1993. "Private Profit, Public Risk: Institutional Antecedents of the Modern Military Procurement System in the Rearmament Program of 1940–1941." In *The Sinews of War: Essays on the Economic History of World War II,* ed. Geofrey T. Mills and Hugh Rockoff, 166–98. Ames: Iowa State University Press.

——. 1994. "The Cold War Economy: Opportunity Costs, Ideology, and the Politics of Crisis." *Explorations in Economic History* 31 (July): 283–312.

——. 1997. "War and Leviathan in Twentieth-Century America: Conscription as the Keystone." In *The Costs of War: America's Pyrrhic Victories,* ed. John V. Denson, 309–22. New Brunswick, NJ: Transaction.

——. 2001. "The Cold War Is Over, but U.S. Preparation for It Continues." *Independent Review* 6 (Fall): 287–305.

——. 2004. "Wartime Socialization of Investment: A Reassessment of U.S. Capital Formation in the 1940s." *Journal of Economic History* 64 (June): 500–20.

Hoover, Calvin B. 1959. *The Economy, Liberty, and the State.* New York: Twentieth Century Fund.

Hurley, Edward N. 1927. *The Bridge to France*. Philadelphia: Lippincott.

Johnson, Louis, and Samuel H. Williamson. 2002. "The Annual Real and Nominal GDP for the United States, 1789–Present." Economic History Services, April. http://www.eh.net/hmit/gdp.

Kendrick, John W. 1961. *Productivity Trends in the United States*. Princeton: Princeton University Press.

Kennedy, David M. 1980. *Over Here: The First World War and American Society*. New York: Oxford University Press.

———. 1999. *Freedom from Fear: The American People in Depression and War, 1929–1945*. New York: Oxford University Press.

Lane, Frederic C. 1951. *Ships for Victory: A History of Shipbuilding under the U.S. Maritime Commission in World War II*. Baltimore: Johns Hopkins University Press.

Leebaert, Derek. 2002. *The Fifty-Year Wound: The True Price of America's Cold War Victory*. Boston: Little, Brown.

Linfield, Michael. 1990. *Freedom under Fire: U.S. Civil Liberties in Times of War*. Boston: South End.

Martin, Albro. 1971. *Enterprise Denied: Origins of the Decline of American Railroads, 1897–1917*. New York: Columbia University Press.

Melman, Seymour. 1985. *The Permanent War Economy: American Capitalism in Decline*, rev. ed. New York: Simon & Schuster.

Murphy, Paul L. 1972. *The Constitution in Crisis Times, 1918–1969*. New York: Harper & Row.

Novick, David, Melvin Anshen, and W. C. Truppner. 1949. *Wartime Production Controls*. New York: Columbia University Press.

Paxson, Frederic L. 1920. "The American War Government, 1917–1918." *American Historical Review* 26 (October): 54–76.

Romer, Christina D. 1988. "World War I and the Postwar Depression: A Reinterpretation Based on Alternative Estimates of GNP." *Journal of Monetary Economics* 22:91–115.

Sicotte, Richard. 1999. "Economic Crisis and Political Response: The Political Economy of the Shipping Act of 1916." *Journal of Economic History* 59 (December): 861–84.

Soule, George. 1947. *Prosperity Decade: From War to Depression: 1917–1929*. New York: Holt, Rinehart and Winston.

Stimson, Henry L., and McGeorge Bundy. 1947. *On Active Service in Peace and War*. London: Hutchinson.

Sumner, William Graham. 1934. *Essays of William Graham Sumner*, ed. Albert G. Keller and Maurice R. Davie. New Haven: Yale University Press.

Taussig, F. W. 1919. "Price-Fixing as Seen by a Price-Fixer." *Quarterly Journal of Economics* 33 (February): 205–41.

Trevino, Ruben, and Robert Higgs. 1992. "Profits of U.S. Defense Contractors." *Defence Economics* 3:211–18.

U.S. Bureau of the Census. 1975. *Historical Statistics of the United States, Colonial Times to 1975*. Washington, DC: Government Printing Office.

U.S. Civilian Production Administration. 1947. *Industrial Mobilization for War: History of the War Production Board and Predecessor Agencies, 1940–1945*. Washington, DC: Government Printing Office.

U.S. Department of Defense, Office of the Assistant Secretary of Defense (Controller). 1987. *National Defense Budget Estimates for FY1988/1989.* Washington, DC: Department of Defense.

U.S. Office of Management and Budget. 2002. *Budget of the United States Government, Fiscal Year 2003: Historical Tables.* Washington, DC: Office of Management and Budget.

RANDAL R. RUCKER AND
E. C. PASOUR JR.

15

The Growth of U.S. Farm Programs

THE DEVELOPMENT of federal farm programs in the twentieth century coincides with the overall expansion of the role of the federal government in the United States. The growth of farm programs is unusual, however, because the government's role in agriculture has expanded during a period when the share of American workers in the sector has become smaller and smaller. In the early days of the Republic, state and federal governments left the farm sector largely unregulated even though more than 70 percent of the American workforce labored in the agricultural sector and 40 percent of output originated in primary agriculture. Since then, both the share of the American workforce working directly in agriculture and the share of output from primary agriculture have fallen to less than 2 percent. During the same period, government involvement in the agricultural sector has expanded from being relatively minimal in the early 1800s to the present broad range of programs and policies that directly and indirectly affect production and prices through a multitude of channels.

Federal and state programs in the late nineteenth and early twentieth centuries were primarily designed to promote research into new methods of farming and to disseminate that information to enhance the productivity of American farmers. During the agricultural downturn that followed the boom of World War I, farmers increasingly pressured the federal government for more direct intervention in markets. After four years of a devastating depression, the Roosevelt administration responded to the continuing pressure from agricultural interests by establishing a wide range of programs that involved direct intervention in agricultural markets, as well as price and income subsidies for farmers. Although these programs have been modified over time, they remain the basis of our farm policy today. Their survival in the face of extensive criticism and declining numbers of farmers illustrates many of the key insights into interest group politics that have been developed by economists in the public choice literature.

Agricultural Policy Prior to 1933

Government policies have affected U.S. agriculture since colonial times.[1] Two examples of early policies include tobacco regulations and tariffs on sugar. In the colonies, tobacco production and marketing were marked by attempts to maintain prices above competitive levels. In 1621, for example, Governor Francis Wyatt of Virginia, acting on instructions from England, ordered production controls to limit the number of tobacco plants per head of family.[2] Such provisions were at times associated with "inspection laws" that restricted sales of poorer quality tobacco to ensure that market prices were maintained by sufficiently small crops. Although efforts to increase tobacco prices by restricting production can be traced to the 1600s, an effective producer cartel for tobacco was not achieved until the New Deal in 1933.

Sugar tariffs were first imposed in 1789 as a means of raising revenues for the government, and a total of thirty acts were passed dealing with sugar between 1789 and 1930. In the 1840s, the purpose of sugar tariffs was expanded to include the encouragement of domestic production and processing.[3] Prior to the 1890s, however, the sugar tariff remained primarily a revenue duty, and sugar was the most important single item in the revenue from customs.[4]

Before World War I, the federal government's role in regulating agricultural markets was limited. Its policy agenda during the late nineteenth and early twentieth centuries focused mainly on agricultural research and extension programs designed to increase productivity, address public goods problems, and maintain competitive markets. Although a few states instituted agricultural experiment stations in the early nineteenth century, the scope of their influence was relatively minor. The foundation for more extensive publicly financed agricultural research and extension programs was established in the second half of the nineteenth century. In 1862 the U.S. Department of Agriculture (USDA) was created as an information agency for farmers.[5] Also in 1862, Congress passed the Morrill Act to encourage the establishment of an agricultural and mechanical college in each state. The act provided for a grant of thirty thousand acres of land to each state for each representative and senator in Congress. The proceeds from sale of the land were to be used for the endowment and support of at least one land-grant college in each state. A second Morrill Act, enacted in 1890, provided annual federal appropriations to the states (with a maximum of $25,000 per state) to support instruction in the land-grant colleges. The act also contained provisions forbidding racial discrimination among prospective students by colleges receiving the funds.[6]

A second step in the creation of the nationwide system of agricultural education and research agencies was the Hatch Act, passed by Congress in 1887. This act established the system of state agricultural experiment stations that is associated with the land-grant colleges and universities. The Smith-Lever Act of 1914 offered aid to the states in developing a nationwide system of publicly supported agricultural extension activities to disseminate the research results from the experiment stations to farmers and their families. Finally, the Smith-Hughes Act of 1917 provided federal support for the teaching of vocational agriculture in high schools.

From 1862 to 1932, the USDA was mainly a scientific and statistical agency. Agricultural research was conducted on crops, soils, and animals with the primary objective of discovering cost-reducing methods of producing and marketing farm products. The extension and educational activities were designed to disseminate the latest research findings from the experiment stations to farmers. From the beginning, publicly funded agricultural research received support from three types of political supporters: public interest advocates who wished to improve agriculture through science, agricultural scientists, and farmers.[7] The first two groups were instrumental in founding the agricultural research institutions described above.

Prior to World War I, rather than implementing policies that directly affected commodity prices, Congress dealt largely with standard public goods problems by providing new mandates and appropriations to the USDA. Problems addressed included livestock and plant diseases and related issues associated with meat and drug inspection. In response to agrarian unrest in the late nineteenth century, Congress enacted legislation that provided indirect support in the form of, for example, lower tariffs on manufactured products, regulation of railroad rates, antitrust laws, food inspection to promote demand, and promotion of cooperatives.

The advent of World War I brought increased federal intervention into commodity markets, including the granting of broad powers to the president to regulate particular commodity prices. Although these powers expired with the end of the war, the experience demonstrated the ability of the government to influence prices. When agricultural prices dropped in the 1920s, farmers turned to the government for relief. Its initial response to these requests and to the growth in associated farm lobbying efforts was to sanction and encourage the development of cooperative marketing associations as a means of controlling supplies and increasing prices.[8] The Capper-Volstead Act of 1922 was an important early piece of legislation in the cooperative movement. The act gives producers the legal right to work together in jointly marketing their products. Thus, members of agricultural coops enjoy a favored status when contrasted with other business firms, which are legally prohibited from such collusive activity by antitrust laws. Without the act, many of the marketing activities currently engaged in by agricultural coops would be violations of one or both of the two primary statutes that govern antitrust policy in the United States—the Sherman Antitrust Act and the Clayton Act.

Cooperative arrangements have worked well for some agricultural products. The large number of farmers and associated cooperatives involved in the production of wheat and other major commodities, however, suggests that such arrangements are not likely to be successful for those products. As the difficulties associated with monitoring farmers' compliance with cooperative marketing controls for major commodities became apparent in the 1920s, efforts were made to obtain relief through measures that more directly increased prices. An important result of these efforts was the development of the McNary-Haugen bills, which were considered by Congress during the mid-1920s. These bills proposed a two-price plan that had the goal of raising farm product prices in the domestic market above those of the world market by the use of export subsidies. The subsidies were to be financed by assessment of a tax on processors or handlers of particular farm commodities. Under the McNary-Haugen plan, a government export corporation would buy wheat and other products as a way of increasing domestic farm prices. These surplus farm products were then to be "dumped" in international markets, and reimports were to be restricted by tariffs. Five McNary-Haugen bills were introduced from 1924 to 1928, but none of them was enacted into law. The principal features of these bills were adopted, however, in the New Deal legislation of the following decade, which provided for the financing of export subsidies from tariff receipts.

The Federal Farm Board was the most immediate forerunner of New Deal action programs in agriculture. The board was created in 1929 by President Herbert Hoover, who perceived the farm problem as one of temporary overproduction and low prices. The basic idea was to raise prices of wheat, cotton, and other "surplus" products via government purchase and storage of the products until some future period of production shortfalls. The board first attempted to support farm prices through a government-sponsored grain storage program. No shortfalls occurred, however, and the board's budget was soon exhausted. President Franklin Roosevelt abolished the Federal Farm Board in 1933.

The Agricultural Adjustment Act of 1933 and the Great Depression

Governmental activism in U.S. agriculture, as in the case of the Federal Farm Board, was the exception rather than the rule prior to 1933. Historically, the agricultural policy agenda focused mainly on agricultural research and extension programs to increase productivity and to maintain competitive markets. Federal intervention on a massive scale was initiated during the New Deal, and there was a pronounced change in program goals as the USDA, under Secretary of Agriculture Henry Wallace, developed a host of new action programs. Instead of increased production and competitive markets, the Agricultural Adjustment Act (AAA) of 1933 established the goals of "parity" prices and incomes in agriculture to raise farm product prices (and farm incomes) above free-market levels. The specific goal of the parity price approach was to raise product prices so that a physical unit of a particular product (pound, bushel, and so on) had the same buying power that prevailed during the base period of 1910 to 1914.

The 1933 AAA, which was enacted during the depths of the Great Depression, signaled a huge increase in government involvement in agriculture in the United States.[9] To understand this fundamental shift in policy, it is useful to put the events of the Great Depression in perspective by considering conditions in the agricultural sector for the two previous decades. The decade from 1910 to 1920 was a period of relative prosperity for U.S. agriculture. An important source of this prosperity was the war in Europe during the second half of the decade, which drastically reduced the productive capacity of Europe, thereby increasing the demand for U.S. products. Prices and farm incomes rose accordingly. After the war ended late in 1918, European productive capacity recovered slowly, and prosperity in U.S. agriculture continued for a period as commodity prices and net incomes remained at high levels. The fact that land prices and farm mortgage debt continued to increase immediately after the end of the war suggests that U.S. farmers expected prosperity to continue.

During 1920 and 1921, U.S. farm prices plummeted as European production recovered faster than expected. Declining production costs during this period only partly offset the effects of falling output prices.

Aggregate net farm income fell by 50 percent and land values fell by almost 20 percent during these two years. Between June 1920 and December 1921, corn prices fell from $1.85 to $0.41 per bushel, wheat prices fell from $2.58 to $0.92 per bushel, hog prices fell from $0.19 to $0.065 per pound, and the index of prices received by farmers fell by 41 percent.[10]

From 1923 to 1929, U.S. agricultural prices and net farm incomes were relatively stable, and although land prices continued to decline, the rate of decline was relatively low. Then came the Great Depression, which held the U.S. economy in its grip throughout the decade from 1929 to 1939. It was a period of economic chaos and massive economic contraction. During the three-year period from 1929 to 1932, stock (equity) prices lost nine-tenths of their value, real GNP decreased by one-third, industrial production was reduced by one-half, and unemployment reached 25 percent of the labor force. The overall level of prices fell by 9 percent in 1931 and by 11 percent in 1932.

Like other sectors of the economy, conditions in the U.S. farm sector were severe during the Great Depression. The index of prices received by farmers fell by 55 percent between 1929 and 1933. Grain, cotton, and livestock producers were particularly hard hit during this period, while changes in dairy, fruit, and poultry prices were somewhat less dramatic. Net farm revenues fell by 69 percent between 1929 and 1933, and an index of land values fell by 37 percent.

A useful indicator of the extent of the distress in the agricultural sector is the rate of farm failures. Failure rates were less than five per thousand per year until the early 1920s, when they increased to about fifteen per thousand. In 1932, farm failure rates skyrocketed to about thirty-eight per thousand! In other words, almost 4 percent of all farms in the United States failed in 1932. Failure rates gradually declined—thanks in part to several government relief programs implemented in the 1930s—and by the early 1940s had fallen back to less than five per thousand.[11] From that time until the mid-1980s, when collection of data for this particular data series was discontinued, the rate of farm failures never again approached five per thousand. Below we briefly discuss the causes of the Great Depression and then focus on the programs implemented in the 1930s to deal with problems in the agricultural sector.

The Great Depression and New Deal Measures in Agriculture

It has long been commonly held that the market economy is inherently unstable and that the Great Depression was merely a severe manifestation of this instability. Thus, it has been argued, the government must intervene in agriculture and other areas to regulate and stabilize the economy. There are, however, strong reasons for doubting this conventional explanation of the beneficial effects of government intervention during the Depression.[12] Contrary to what has been taught to generations of students and future policy makers, there is a great deal of evidence that government intervention in the form of high tariffs, high taxes, restrictive monetary policies, and programs to maintain wages and prices either caused or greatly exacerbated the economic chaos prevailing at that time.[13] The Smoot-Hawley Tariff Act, enacted in 1930, for example, raised import tariffs to the highest levels in the twentieth century—52.8 percent on an ad valorem basis. These actions by the United States led to retaliatory measures by foreign trading partners, and protectionism ran wild as countries worldwide raised tariffs and erected other trade barriers, including quotas. Prices of export commodities, notably U.S. farm products, dropped dramatically following the passage of the tariff bill, and exports of U.S. farm products were reduced by two-thirds from 1929 to 1933.[14] Agriculture was hit especially hard by the protectionist trade policies because of its heavy dependence on exports—farm prices plunged, many farm loans turned bad, and farm foreclosures skyrocketed.

In general, the programs instituted to restrict competition in agricultural markets were consistent with the collectivist thrust of various New Deal initiatives instituted to remedy alleged market failures. Included among the broad range of programs instituted to deal with problems in the agricultural sector were programs providing for production controls and price supports, subsidized food distribution, export subsidies, subsidized farm credit, conservation of land and water resources, crop insurance and disaster payments, and expanded agricultural research and extension services.

Programs in all of these areas are still in effect although many changes have been made since the programs began. The remainder of this chapter is devoted to an analysis of U.S. farm programs and policies, including a description of major changes in the programs over time. A notable aspect of the programs listed above is the inconsistencies among them, both in their objectives and in their effects. Agricultural research, for example, is designed to improve technology, which tends to increase supply and decrease product prices. Price support programs, on the other hand, are designed to increase product prices. The more effective the research and extension programs, the more costly it is for taxpayers to support product prices at any given level.

The Growth of Government in U.S. Agriculture

As can be seen in figure 15.1 (below) and table 15.1, the role of government in U.S. agriculture has grown dramatically since 1933. The first major increase occurred during the New Deal era. Expenditures by the USDA increased from less than $200 million in 1929 to $1.2 billion in fiscal 1935 (table 15.1). The USDA's outlays as a percentage of the total federal budget increased markedly in the 1930s, declined during World War II, rose again following the end of the war, slowly declined until 1970, increased again in the 1980s, and decreased in the 1990s. The USDA budget as a percent of the total federal budget increased from 4.3 percent in 1970 to about 6 percent in the early to mid-1980s, even as the total U.S. budget was rising at an unprecedented peacetime rate. Increases in food and nutrition programs were responsible for much of the USDA budget growth from 1970 to 1980. Price support program payments accounted for most of the large increase in USDA outlays during the 1980s, but food and nutrition programs again were responsible for most of the increase in government support to agriculture in the 1990s.

The growth in USDA expenditures since World War II has been dramatic, measured on either a per-farm or a per-farm-worker basis. As indicated in table 15.1, on a per-farm basis, expenditures increased from $549 in 1950 to almost $25,000 in fiscal 1998—which is equivalent to $3,700 in 1950 prices. A large proportion of this increase was not, of course, paid directly to farmers because there was a pronounced increase in the food stamp and other food assistance programs during this period. These programs, though not directly benefiting farmers, benefit them indirectly by providing politically acceptable means for disposing of surplus commodities.

Employment at the USDA increased continually from 1929 to 1980, although the number of farms and farmers decreased. Employment at the department rose most rapidly during the New Deal era, more than tripling from 1929 to 1935. Employment increased continuously following World War II until 1980 and has since shown a downward trend.

Outlays by the USDA for stabilization of farm prices and incomes increased dramatically in the early 1980s, peaking in 1986. Since then, outlays have varied widely, depending on product prices, price support levels, weather, export sales of farm products, and so on. Although payments to farmers were significantly lower in the early and mid-1990s than in the 1980s, additional disaster or emergency assistance dramatically increased stabilization outlays in 1998, 1999, 2000, and 2001 to levels considerably above those authorized under the 1996 farm bill.

Table 15.1 USDA EXPENDITURES AND EMPLOYMENT, 1929–1998

Year	USDA expenditures					USDA employment		
	Total outlays ($ billions)	Share of total budget (%)	Share of net farm income (%)	Per farm ($)	Per farm worker ($)	Total (thousands)	Per thousand farm workers	Per thousand farms
1929	0.2[a]	5.2	2.5	27	13	24.4	2	4
1935	1.2	16.2	21.4	175	94	85.1	7	12
1940	1.6	22.3	29.7	259	144	81.9	7	13
1945	2.3	2.3	16.9	386	226	82.0	8	14
1950	3.0	7.4	18.8	549	298	84.1	8	16
1955	4.6	7.2	34.3	996	553	85.5	10	18
1960	5.4	7.1	47.0	1,368	768	98.7	14	25
1965	6.9	5.9	54.0	2,068	1,237	113.0	20	34
1970	8.4	4.3	61.0	2,847	1,860	116.0	26	39
1975	15.6	4.7	61.0	6,170	3,583	121.0	28	48
1980	34.8	5.9	214.7	14,259	9,388	129.1	35	53
1985	55.5	5.9	192.8	24,219	17,819	117.8	38	51
1990	46.0	3.7	102.7	21,443	15,916	122.6	42	57
1995	56.7	3.7	157.4	25,799[b]	16,473	103.8	30	47
1998	53.9	3.2[b]	122.3	24,628[b]	15,970[b]	107.1	32	49[b]

Sources: USDA expenditures and total budget outlays for 1929–60 are from U.S. Department of Commerce, *Statistical Abstract of the United States* (Washington, DC: GPO), various issues. Those for 1961–98 are from U.S. Office of Management and Budget, *Historical Tables. Budget of the U.S. Government* (Washington, DC: GPO), various issues. Agricultural employment and net farm income are from *Economic Report of the President* (Washington, DC: GPO), various issues.
Number of farms is from U.S. Department of Agriculture, *Agricultural Statistics* (Washington, DC: GPO), various issues. USDA employment data are from U.S. Department of Commerce, *Statistical Abstract of the United States* and USDA, Office of Budget and Program Analysis, *Budgetary Tables* (Washington. DC: GPO), various issues.
[a]More than 50 percent of the expenditure was for road construction, an item not reported in later USDA budgets.
[b]Figure is preliminary.

Outlays for stabilization of farm prices and incomes continue to be augmented by increased outlays for other farm-related programs, most notably food and nutrition programs. Spending on the latter more than doubled from the mid-1980s to the mid-1990s and now constitutes two-thirds of the total USDA budget. This pattern of USDA activities is consistent with public-choice theory. In the classic expansion pattern of a bureaucracy, the USDA, having outgrown the area it was originally designed to aid, has maintained and increased its constituency by moving into tangential areas such as food and nutrition programs, as well as rural recreation, community facilities, urban nutrition, and so on.

Total USDA outlays decreased substantially for several years after 1986, but by the mid-1990s nominal outlays had again increased to mid-1980s levels. The 1995 USDA budget adjusted for inflation, however, was about 40 percent lower than that of a decade earlier. The reduction in real outlays can be attributed in part to increased pressure on farm programs because of heightened congressional concerns and actions taken to reduce federal budget deficits.

So long as government expenditures on agricultural programs were viewed as being in the public interest, these programs were subject to relatively little criticism. More and more, however, consumer groups have challenged marketing orders for milk, oranges, and other products, the sugar program, the tobacco and peanut programs, and other farm programs that benefit a relatively small number of (relatively large) agricultural producers at the expense of the general public. Agricultural programs are increasingly being viewed as income redistribution programs rather than as public interest activities. Despite this, a strong residue of public support remains for preserving the family farm. Although the family farm plays a key role in maintaining public support for farm programs, the distribution of government payments is highly skewed toward large farmers—almost half of all government agricultural payments go to fewer than 10 percent of farms.[15]

Agricultural Policy Tools

Three main types of government policy tools have been used to support (raise) agricultural product prices since the New Deal action programs were instituted in the 1930s: (1) price supports, which raise selected commodity prices directly; (2) restrictions on output or input (typically land) use, which raise prices indirectly; and (3) compensatory payments. Many past U.S. commodity price support programs, as well as those currently in effect, use one or more of these policy tools. Before recounting the overall historical development of U.S. commodity programs, it is useful to describe these primary policy tools and discuss their economic effects.

Price Supports Alone

The simplest type of price support program is one in which the government merely sets a price (on the basis of parity, cost of production, or some other criterion) above the market-clearing level.[16] If the price support is set above the normal market-clearing price, there will be a surplus, with the amount produced exceeding the amount purchased by consumers. In a pure price support program of this type, the government buys the surplus quantity at the support price. The net cost to taxpayers is these acquisition costs plus the costs of storing the surplus minus the revenue the government receives from selling the surplus.

Although government price support programs typically are much more complex than the simple description above implies, it can provide useful insights into the impacts of commodity programs. For example, surpluses are inevitable and fully predictable when government uses price supports to raise farm product prices above competitive levels. In fact, the U.S. government has purchased large amounts of dairy products, wheat, feed grains, cotton, and other commodities at various times during the past sixty years in the operation of price support programs.

Price Supports with Restrictions on Output Levels or Input Use

Price supports inevitably lead to increased production, which, as indicated above, leads to surpluses and treasury costs, thereby creating an incentive for further government involvement through programs to control production. A price support program that involves government acquisition of surpluses will be costly to taxpayers, with the magnitude of the treasury cost determined largely by how high the price support is set relative to the market-clearing price. Agricultural production in the United States has been restricted either indirectly, by limiting the use of one or more inputs, or directly, by restricting output levels.

Although it would be possible to reduce output via restrictions on the use of labor or capital, land is the input whose usage is most commonly restricted in production control programs. At various times since the 1930s, restrictions on acreage—which have taken various forms, including both mandatory allotments and voluntary set-asides—have been used in price support programs for cotton, corn, wheat, tobacco, peanuts, and other products.

A major purpose of the acreage restrictions has been to alleviate the surplus-related problems that arise under the price support programs.

Remember that a price support set at a level above the market-clearing price leads to a surplus that the government must purchase. The amount of surplus production and the associated costs can be reduced by establishing acreage restrictions. Their effectiveness in decreasing surpluses is limited by the fact that farmers have incentives to find ways to take advantage of the high price support levels. One way farmers can accomplish this is by using more fertilizer and pesticides and planting more intensively than they would have in the absence of the acreage restrictions. These alternative practices increase costs (relative to costs when there are no restrictions on acreage). Moreover, although acreage restrictions reduce the surplus, the reduction is not as large as the policy maker might have originally intended. The more difficult it is to effectively substitute labor and fertilizer for land in producing the output, the more costs will increase and the more effective will be the acreage restrictions at eliminating the surplus.

The effectiveness of acreage allotments in restricting production is also undermined by advances in production technology. In the tobacco program, for example, as technology advanced and other inputs were substituted for land, tobacco yields with allotments in force increased from 1,083 pounds per acre in 1944 to 2,208 pounds in 1964. Thus, acreage allotments had to be reduced repeatedly during this period to limit production to the desired level.[17]

Whereas some U.S. commodity programs have mandated participation by all producers, in other programs participation has been voluntary. The voluntary programs that have included provisions designed to reduce acreage have had to offer financial incentives to induce farmers to participate. In the Soil Bank program, which was instituted in the Agricultural Act of 1956, for example, farmers were paid to take land out of production.

The overall objective of farm programs involving the voluntary diversion of land is the same as for mandatory acreage allotment programs: to reduce production and increase product prices. The basic difference is that in voluntary diversion programs the individual producer's choice of whether to participate is based on economic incentives rather than legal coercion. Prior to the 1996 farm bill, farmers who voluntarily chose to obtain price supports under the cotton, wheat, and feed grain programs were, as a condition of participation, required to set aside specified amounts of land for conservation uses.

For some commodities, problems associated with mandatory acreage allotments have resulted in legal restrictions on the amount of output each producer can legally produce and sell. For example, in 1965 the tobacco price support program was changed so that production was restricted by a marketing poundage quota, which specified the number of pounds that a producer could sell in a given year. From 1978 until the passage of the 2002 farm bill, the peanut price support program also involved the use of marketing quotas.[18] Marketing quotas typically are—in some respects—more effective means of restricting production (or sales into particular markets) than restrictions on input use. This is because (as discussed above) when operating under acreage restrictions, farmers can continue to increase output, at least to some extent, by substituting other inputs for land. In contrast, farmers cannot legally circumvent mandated restrictions on the number of units of output that they may produce and sell.

Compensatory Payments

An early proposal to adopt price supports that involved the use of compensatory payments was contained in the "Brannan Plan" of the late 1940s, which was named after Charles Brannan, the Secretary of Agriculture in the Truman administration. Like the simple price support programs discussed above, a compensatory payment program involves a specified price level that is greater than the market-clearing price. In the compensatory payment approach, however, the government does not purchase the amount that consumers do not buy at the supported price. Instead, the farmers base their production decisions on the supported price and then sell the amount produced at whatever price will clear the market.[19] The government then makes per-unit payments to farmers equal to the difference between the support price and the market-clearing price for each unit. Producers know in advance what price they will get, but they do not know how much of this price they will receive from market transactions and how much they will receive in the form of government payments.[20]

Prior to the passage of the 1996 farm bill, the compensatory payment approach was a major component of the cotton, rice, wheat, and feed grain programs, where a "target price" was guaranteed by paying producers the difference between the target price and the market price (or a government-established loan rate). These government outlays were referred to as "deficiency payments." Although target prices were reintroduced in the 2002 farm bill, deficiency payments per se no longer exist, having been replaced by direct payments with different names.

History and Operation of Production-Control Programs

The Agricultural Adjustment Administration, which was created in the Agricultural Adjustment Act (AAA) of 1933, quickly initiated price supports and production controls for the "basic crops" listed in the act, including wheat, cotton, corn, tobacco, milk, and dairy products.[21] As indicated previously, the AAA was one of many New Deal measures that restricted production, set prices, restricted imports, and so on. The implementation of these programs marked the turning point from a largely free to a highly controlled U.S. farm economy. Below we discuss the evolution of U.S. farm programs since the 1930s. We divide this evolution into three phases: supply management, surplus problems and export subsidies, and direct payments. We also discuss whether recent changes in farm programs constitute a distinct fourth phase in U.S. farm programs. For each phase, we discuss the primary policy tools employed, as well as the problems encountered—notably, mounting surpluses and increasing treasury costs—that led to further program changes.

The First Phase: Supply Management

The primary policy tools used in the first phase of the evolution of U.S. farm programs were price supports and acreage restrictions. In this phase, which lasted from 1933 to the mid-1950s, the emphasis was placed on supply management to reduce output as a means of preventing unacceptably large treasury costs. Under the AAA of 1933, acreage allotments restricted farmers to planting only specified numbers of acres of particular crops such as rice, wheat, cotton, peanuts, and tobacco. A national acreage allotment for a crop was set at a level that would meet anticipated domestic and export consumption at the support price. The national allotment was then apportioned among individual farms based on historical plantings of the crop. Alternative production control measures received a great deal of criticism. For example, farmers were paid to plow under their cotton, and the government, in a widely publicized and much-criticized program, bought up pigs and killed them to reduce the supply of pork.

Prices paid to farmers for the basic crops were guaranteed by the U.S. government by granting producers "nonrecourse loans" on commodities stored by the Commodity Credit Corporation (CCC). The CCC, a government agency, was created in 1933 to provide for loans to farmers and storage when production was "too large." A wheat farmer, for example, could store wheat and obtain a loan from the CCC using the wheat as collateral. The loan rate per bushel was the support price of wheat. If the price of wheat fell below the predetermined support price, wheat farmers could satisfy their loan obligations by forfeiting their rights to the commodities held by the CCC. In such a situation the corporation had no recourse other than to assume ownership of the commodity. Through the years these stocks have provided a good measure of surplus production attributable to farm programs.

The initial production controls in the form of acreage allotments, combined with unusually severe droughts in the mid-1930s, resulted in lower output of most of the controlled crops during this period. Total acreage of crops grown, however, changed little as farmers substituted noncontrolled for controlled crops. Sharp increases occurred, for example, in acreage of soybeans, rice, and grain sorghum. Moreover, surpluses of corn and other controlled crops soon mounted because of sharp increases in yields as farmers intensified their farming practices on the restricted acreage. And to the extent that noncontrolled crops such as grain sorghum were good substitutes for corn as feed for livestock, increases in noncontrolled crops further exacerbated surplus problems in the corn market.[22]

The surplus stock problem resulted from the government's setting prices above the market level. As a result, in part, of severe droughts, problems of overproduction and surplus stocks remained manageable from the initiation of the AAA farm programs in 1933 until World War II. Production controls were removed during the war as commodity prices increased and stocks were liquidated because of increased demand. The economic recovery of war-ravaged Europe and Asia and then the Korean War kept demand strong so that surpluses of U.S. farm products were not a major problem as late as the early 1950s. In the mid-1950s, however, high price supports led to mounting surplus problems. The pace of advancements in agricultural technology quickened following the Korean War, and accumulating surpluses led the Eisenhower administration to launch several new initiatives to cope with the overproduction.

Supply management failed for two reasons. First, farmers minimized the effect of planting restrictions by taking less productive land out of production and by increasing the use of nonland inputs such as chemical fertilizers, lime, and improved seed. Second, other programs worked against the stated policy goal of decreasing farm output. For example, expanded subsidies for federal research and farmer education, along with the institution of new programs to subsidize farm credit, led to increases in farm output.

The Second Phase: Surplus Problems and Export Subsidies

As the surpluses of farm products mounted in the 1950s following the end of the Korean conflict, a political consensus emerged that farm programs should be modified. Although measures were instituted at this time to alleviate surpluses, including flexible and lower price supports, land retirement, and programs to increase the demand for farm products, ongoing dramatic advances in agricultural technology, along with government subsidies for nonland inputs, continued to lower the market-clearing price for farm products throughout the 1950s.

Continuing surplus problems in this era led to the enactment of the 1956 Soil Bank program, in which farmers were paid to take cropland out of production. The program represented an alternative to acreage allotments and marketing quotas. Sections of farms and entire farms were removed from production for periods ranging from three to fifteen years. This program was designed to reduce the output of crops then in greatest surplus and to shift land out of cultivation and into forage, trees, and so on. During the period from 1961 to 1972 an average of 12 percent of U.S. farmland was enrolled in the Soil Bank program.[23] The annual cost of the program reached a peak of almost $1 billion in 1971. In addition to cost, other objections to the program were based on its negative impacts on rural businesses and institutions in communities where farmers placed whole farms in the Soil Bank.

In addition to these measures to reduce farm output, beginning in the mid-1950s, government initiatives were launched to increase the consumption of farm products. A massive government-subsidized export plan, known initially as Public Law 480 and later as Food for Peace, was implemented to encourage the export of price-supported commodities to countries that were unable to make commercial purchases and to assist agricultural development in less developed countries. Although this program did provide an additional outlet for U.S. farm products, it is not consistent with open markets and it has had harmful effects on producers in the recipient countries.[24] This subsidized effort to increase foreign demand for farm products was augmented by an expansion of domestic food subsidies including the school lunch and food stamp programs. These measures to dispose of overproduction in a politically acceptable manner, which are discussed in more detail later in this chapter, contributed substantially to the dramatic increase in the costs of government farm programs from the early 1950s to the early 1960s.

The Third Phase: Direct Payments

Despite the increasing costs of farm programs, it became apparent that existing price support and acreage control programs were not solving the income problem in agriculture—net farm income, for example, was lower in the early 1960s than it had been a decade earlier. Direct payments to farmers jumped with the Soil Bank program in 1956 and remained important under succeeding farm bills in 1961, 1965, and 1970. Direct payments from the government assumed even greater importance with the 1973 farm bill, which implemented for the first time an entirely new system of direct payments—target prices.[25] The target price method of supporting prices for wheat, cotton, and feed grains remained in effect for more than twenty years, was discontinued under the 1996 farm bill, and has been revived in a modified form in the 2002 farm bill. Under the target price system, participating farmers received a government-determined target price for their crops. Farmers either sold the product at the market price (the price at which the quantity supplied by farmers at the target price equals the quantity demanded) or placed it in CCC storage at a specified loan rate. The government then paid the farmers an amount—known as a deficiency payment—to ensure that they received the target price. Direct payments to U.S. farmers reached unprecedented levels in the severe recession of the mid-1980s (figure 15.1). When the 1981 farm bill was enacted, the anticipated annual budgetary costs were $1–2 billion.[26] Program costs increased sharply, however, with direct payments reaching nearly $19 billion in 1983 as commodity markets weakened in the early 1980s and price supports remained high. Although many believed as the 1985 farm bill was being debated that major changes would be made in farm policy, their expectations were not realized and the changes actually implemented in the bill were relatively minor. Although a few bells and whistles were added to hold down treasury costs, the basic structure of farm programs remained intact. Similarly, the 1990 farm bill saw only minor changes.

Direct payments to farmers remained important in the 1996 farm bill, in which farmers who participated in the target price programs were guaranteed "transition payments" for seven years. Direct payments continued to play a major role in the 2002 farm bill.

The 1996 and 2002 Farm Bills: Decoupled Payments—A Fourth Phase?

For some time after its passage, it was thought the Federal Agricultural Improvement and Reform (FAIR) Act of 1996, commonly referred to as either the 1996 farm bill or the Freedom to Farm Act, represented a sweeping change in direction for U.S. farm commodity programs. Starting with the Agricultural Adjustment Act in 1933, price and income support payments for wheat, feed grains, and cotton had been linked to a farm's current production. Under the 1996 farm bill, annual lump-sum payments (known as *production flexibility contract payments*) were made to producers of these commodities. These contract payments were linked to past production but were independent of a producer's production of these commodities in any given year. This *decoupling* of the link between government payments and production was viewed as a landmark change in commodity policy because of the reduced impact of government commodity payments on farmers' production decisions.

The FAIR Act also included loan rates for many commodities, including those designated to receive the lump-sum contract payments. Although the legislated rates were considerably below market prices for a period after the bill was enacted, when market prices fell in the

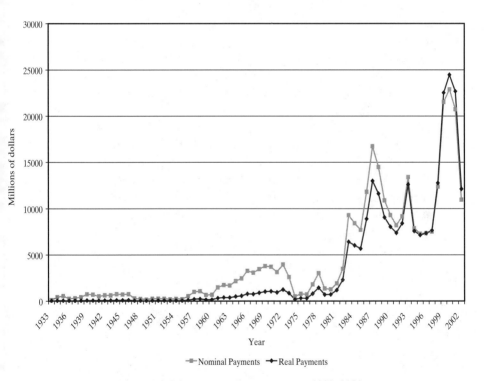

Figure 15.1. Direct government payments, 1933–2002

Sources: U.S. and State Farm Income Data, Government Payments, United States by Program 1933–2002 at http://www.ers.usda.gov/data/farmincome/finfidmu.htm (accessed April 5, 2006). Amounts include only cash payments made directly to farmers, not including farmer-owned reserve payments.

Note: Payments are deflated using the implicit price deflator (1996 = 100) at http://www.econstats .com/deflator.xls (accessed April 5, 2006).

late 1990s, the loan rates became effective. Because federal payments related to the loan rate program are based on current production, this component of government payments still influences farmers' planting decisions.[27]

At the time the 1996 farm bill was passed, its provisions for de-coupled payments, increased planting flexibility to encourage more re-sponsiveness to market conditions, and declining schedule of contract payments between 1996 and 2002 (see figure 15.2) were interpreted by some industry participants and observers as an indication that govern-ment's involvement in U.S. agriculture would be ending soon. In reality, total payments to farmers under the 1996 legislation—including con-tract, conservation, loan deficiency, and disaster aid payments—were dramatically higher than specified in the act, largely as a consequence of emergency annual ad hoc assistance legislation enacted in 1998, 1999, 2000, and 2001 (see figure 15.3).

The 2002 farm bill generally increased the level of government ex-penditures on a wide variety of farm programs.[28] Loan rates for most commodities were increased, and marketing loans and loan deficiency payments were continued for wheat, feed grains, and cotton (as well as for a number of other commodities), with all production eligible for these payments. Annual direct (lump sum) payments were continued for these commodities, with the level of payment based on past produc-tion levels. The fact that farmers have been allowed to update their base acreage and program yields using 1998–2001 acreage and yields, how-ever, suggests that current production may influence future government payment levels. Further, target prices were reinstituted in the 2002 farm bill, and producers receive decoupled *countercyclical payments,* the magnitude of which varies inversely with market prices.

THE PRECEDING DISCUSSION describes the evolution of U.S. farm pro-grams for major agricultural commodities (wheat, corn, cotton, and so forth). There are also federal farm programs for a number of other com-modities, including dairy, sugar, tobacco, peanuts, honey, and wool and mohair.[29] A common characteristic of these programs is that (with the possible exception of the dairy program) the constituencies supporting them are small enough or geographically focused enough that they can-not marshall enough political support to survive without substantial cost to the Treasury. Moreover, these programs illustrate the public-choice argument that small constituencies with large potential benefits will pre-vail in political markets over larger constituencies with small potential costs. Thus, peanut, sugar, honey, and tobacco producers have received thousands of dollars in benefits annually from their programs while consumers of these products incur a few dollars each in costs annually.

Demand-Enhancing Programs

A major purpose of the crop programs was to increase farm incomes and prices. A simple price support program will result in a surplus and corresponding treasury costs. One of the most dramatic features of agricultural production in the United States in the past century has been the remarkable rate at which production technology has advanced. Such advances result in increases in supply and concomitant increases in costs to the Treasury. There are three apparent ways to decrease the politically problematic treasury costs: reductions in the level of the price support,

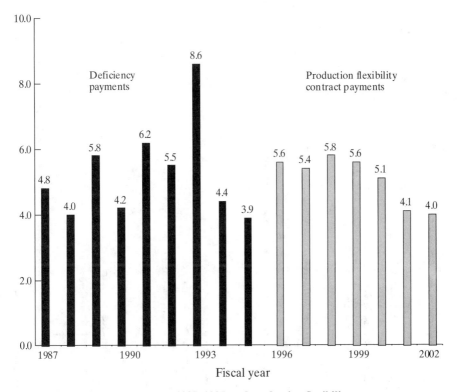

Figure 15.2. Deficiency payments, 1987–1995, and production flexibility contract payments under FAIR, 1996–2002

Source: Frederick J. Nelson and Lyle P. Schertz, Provisions of the Federal Agriculture Improvement and Reform Act of 1996, AIB no. 729, p. 6. http://www.ers.usda.gov/Publications/aib729/ (accessed April 5, 2006).

reductions in supply, and increases in demand. Reductions in the level of prices supports have occasionally been implemented, but substantial reductions in nominal support levels have been uncommon.[30] Supply reductions have been accomplished by restricting supply both directly, with production or marketing quotas, and indirectly, through restrictions on the use of inputs (typically land). These approaches were discussed in detail above. Several different programs have been implemented for the purpose of increasing demand. Food stamps, export subsidies, foreign aid, and school lunch programs were mentioned briefly above. These and another notable demand-enhancing program (the ethanol program) are discussed in more detail below.[31]

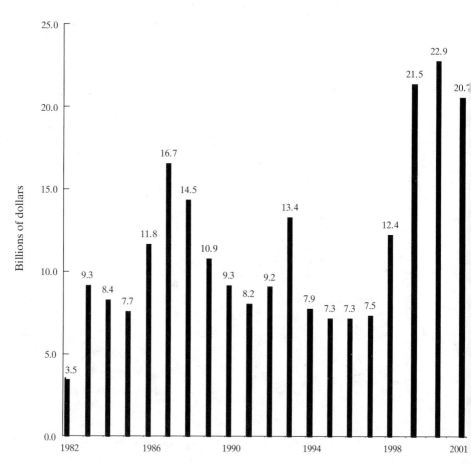

Figure 15.3. Direct government payments to agricultural producers and farm owners, 1982–2001 (calendar years)

Sources: U.S. and State Farm Income Data, Government Payments, Unites States, by Program, 1933–2004. http://www.ers.usda.gov/data/farmincome/finfidmu.htm (accessed April 5, 2006).

Subsidized Food Programs

Government-operated food assistance programs provide food at no cost or below-market prices to targeted groups of consumers. These programs originated in the 1930s, and their scope has increased dramatically since 1970. Although the food stamp and school lunch programs are the best known, there are a number of others. Below we present a brief history of these programs, describe their major features, and discuss a few issues and problems associated with the programs.

The original purpose of food stamp, school lunch, and other subsidized food programs was to facilitate the operation of price support programs for farm products. One view of these programs is that they increased the demand for farm products. Another view is that they provided politically acceptable means of disposing of surpluses acquired in conjunction with product price supports. The first of these programs involved the purchase in the 1930s by the Federal Surplus Commodities Corporation (FSCC), in cooperation with the Agricultural Adjustment Administration, of surplus agricultural commodities for direct distribution to the unemployed and their families.

Surplus commodities have been used in various ways over the years, with three major pieces of legislation making up the cornerstone for the funding of food assistance programs. Section 32, an amendment to the Agricultural Adjustment Act of 1933, provides for the appropriation of 30 percent of the import duties imposed on all commodities for use by the secretary of agriculture to encourage exports and the domestic consumption of "surplus" agricultural commodities. Under this program, meats, fruits, and vegetables have been purchased with section 32 funds and donated to school lunch and breakfast programs. Dairy products, rice, peanuts, wheat, and other price-supported products have also been purchased and donated to schools and other nonprofit agencies under section 416 of the 1949 Agricultural Act. Finally, section 6 of the National School Lunch Act of 1946 provides additional authorization for the purchase of agricultural commodities to be donated to schools and service institutions.[32]

Programs involving cash subsidies present an alternative to direct donation programs as a means of subsidizing food consumption. The importance of government-donated commodities relative to cash subsidies has decreased over time, largely as a result of dramatic increases in cash subsidy programs since the mid-1960s. The food stamp program is the largest of the cash subsidy programs. There is now an array of frequently overlapping federal food assistance programs, but the following discussion mainly focuses on the food stamp and school lunch programs.

Food Stamps. The food stamp program of the 1930s grew out of dissatisfaction with earlier direct food distribution programs, which reduced regular market food purchases and afforded no choice to recipients of the commodities received. In the initial program, low-income families received stamps that allowed them to buy food at reduced prices. The initial program ended during World War II but was resumed after the war. Permanent food stamp legislation was enacted in 1964.

The food stamp program is the major food assistance program in the United States, accounting for about two-thirds of all food assistance spending. Outlays for the program continue to increase. Estimates for 2005 suggested that almost twenty-six million people received food stamps at a cost of roughly $31.1 billion.[33] Before 1979, recipients were required to pay a portion of the value of food stamps. In 1979 the purchase requirement was eliminated and food stamps now are provided free to qualified recipients.

Various issues and problems are associated with the program. One issue relates to the magnitude of the impact of the program on food expenditures. Research suggests that for each dollar spent on food stamps, food expenditures increase by twenty to forty-five cents. This is because recipients, to some extent, substitute food stamps for food purchases they would have made without the food stamps. The numbers given above suggest that the billions of dollars spent on food stamp programs have a relatively small effect on the demand for food—they probably increase total food expenditures by less than 2 percent.[34]

An important problem that has plagued the food stamp program from the beginning is abuse of the system. The USDA has estimated that 25 percent of the $260 million in food stamp coupons distributed during the period from 1939 to 1943 were misused.[35] Misuse continues to be a major problem; the Government Accounting Office found that as recently as 1993, overpayments of food stamp benefits totaled almost $2 billion.[36] To a considerable extent, these problems are due to inaccurate information provided by recipients (particularly regarding their incomes) to those administering the program. Methods that have been discussed for dealing with these problems include the implementation of electronic benefit transfer systems and replacing food stamps (and other special assistance programs) with a single cash payment for individual participants.

School Lunch Program. The school lunch program was also begun in connection with surplus disposal activities of the FSCC in the 1930s.

Food donations to schools dropped off during World War II, but a permanent program was established under the National School Lunch Act of 1946. Both the scope and cost of the school lunch and other nutrition programs for children have increased dramatically since that time. Annual federal expenditures on the school lunch program were less than $100 million in 1947. By 2002, federal outlays for school lunch, school breakfast, and other child nutrition programs had increased to more than $10 billion.[37]

In the school lunch program, both a cash subsidy and a donated food subsidy are provided for *all* lunches. More than half of the students receive meals free or at greatly reduced prices. Indeed, of the estimated twenty-eight million participants in 2002, 13.6 million received free school lunches.[38] The per-meal subsidy, including commodities, was recently estimated to be $.36 for "paid" school lunches, $2.46 for free lunches, and $2.05 for reduced-price lunches.[39]

The operation of the national school lunch program poses a number of problems and issues. First, successful application of producer pressure to use the program as a means to dispose of surplus influences what schools serve in their lunches. Surplus products such as cheese, butter, and honey are not likely to be the foods that schools would prefer to have.

Second, there are problems related to USDA dietary guidelines and minimum nutrient requirements for school lunches. When a Clinton administration study found that school lunches substantially exceeded the government's guidelines for saturated fat and sodium, regulations were changed, and now school meals must comply with the dietary guidelines.[40] The USDA mandates for more fruits and vegetables on school menus are controversial and politically sensitive because any increase in those products at the expense of beef and other meats is harmful to the meat industry.

Third, the federal subsidy in school lunch programs is an important public policy issue that has received little public attention. As indicated above, all school lunches are subsidized to some extent. The subsidization of school lunches, particularly for children from upper- and middle-income families, remains an important public policy issue. Why should the public at large, including low-income taxpayers, be taxed to provide school lunches at subsidized prices for those who can afford to pay?

Other Food Assistance Programs. The 1964 permanent food stamp legislation led to a tremendous expansion of subsidized food programs, not only in food stamp and school lunch programs, but also in other

programs targeted toward nutrition for children and the elderly. Total
food assistance increased from $1 billion in 1969 to about $39 billion in
2002.[41] According to the USDA Food and Consumer Service's 1997 Mission Statement, one in six people in the United States receives domestic
food assistance.[42] As with the programs discussed above, an important
public policy issue related to many of these programs is the provision
of food assistance to individuals in middle- and upper-income families.

Export Subsidies and Foreign Aid. The price support and production
control programs instituted during the 1930s, in which domestic prices
were held above world price levels, resulted in the chronic accumulation
of surplus stocks. Over the years there has been pressure to subsidize exports to reduce the surpluses. Such subsidies effectively increase the demand faced by producers in the export market. Export subsidies began
with an amendment to the 1933 AAA—section 32—which, as discussed
above, authorized the use of import tariff revenues to subsidize agricultural exports and domestic consumption of "surplus" commodities.[43]
Subsidized exports using section 32 funds have been relatively limited
except for a period during and immediately after World War II. Between
1936 and 1976, less than 10 percent of section 32 money was allocated to
subsidizing agricultural exports (most section 32 funds have been spent
on subsidized food programs, mainly the school lunch program).[44]

Domestic and Foreign Credit Programs That Affect U.S. Agriculture

Federal intervention in agricultural credit markets dates back to the
Federal Farm Loan Act in 1916.[45] This act established credit institutions,
which later were folded into the Farm Credit System (FCS), whose
purpose was to make long-term loans on farm real estate. The FCS,
although privately owned, is a government-sponsored enterprise. As
such, it is able to borrow and lend at preferential rates. The FCS now
makes short- and long-term loans to farmers and in 2000 held about
25 percent of farm business debt.

The USDA also has a number of credit programs for agriculture
and related purposes. The CCC makes commodity loans, and the Farm
Service Agency provides a range of credit services in housing, utility
services, and business assistance programs in rural areas. Although the
USDA once was an important source of credit in agriculture, over time it
has shifted its focus from direct lending to acting as a guarantor of loans.

The federal government is also involved in providing foreign credit
that has important impacts on U.S. agricultural markets. Public Law 480,

which was a component of the Agricultural Trade Development and Assistance Act of 1954 (the 1954 farm bill), is commonly called the Food for Peace program. It was designed to reduce the CCC stocks acquired through price support programs. Under Title I of this legislation, long-term sales to foreign buyers are made with repayment periods of up to forty years at low interest rates. Under Title II, food is donated by the U.S. government to people in foreign countries in response to malnutrition, famine, and so on. The food is mainly distributed by private voluntary organizations, cooperatives, or international organizations.

Export subsidies have become strongly embedded in U.S. farm policy as a result of this program. During the 1950s and 1960s concessionary sales under government programs, including Food for Peace, often accounted for as much as one-third of export sales.[46] The gross cost to taxpayers of financing such exports from 1955 to 1979 was about $40 billion.[47] Food for Peace expenditures during the 1980s and 1990s typically have been somewhat less in real terms—running from $1 billion to $2 billion per year. In recent years, the United States has used targeted export subsidies as opposed to the general subsidies used in the 1950s and 1960s.[48]

Another program that has had substantial impacts on U.S. exports of farm products has been the Export Credit Guarantee Program. This legislation guarantees payment to U.S. lenders should a foreign buyer fail to repay any loan used to purchase U.S. agricultural commodities. From 1982 to 1986, the USDA provided about $22 billion in export credit guarantees.[49] These programs increase exports to buyers where credit is necessary to make sales but where financing may not be available without CCC guarantees that payments will be made. Currently, the USDA provides about $4 billion annually in export credit guarantees. Under the 1996 and 2002 farm bills, at least $1 billion in direct credit and credit guarantees must be targeted annually to "emerging markets" that are taking steps toward market-oriented economies.

Although U.S. foreign food aid programs in the past provided a means of disposing of surplus crops, their nature has changed in recent years. With the advent of the 1996 farm bill, the federal government's role in storing farm commodities for the purpose of supporting farm incomes and prices has been greatly reduced. Currently, the government purchases crops directly from farmers, even though there are no longer any program-induced surpluses. The USDA estimated the total value of U.S. food aid to be about $2.3 billion in 2005 and the value of all direct export subsidies (which includes such subsidies as export credit guarantees and market development programs in addition to food aid) to be almost $5.4 billion.[50]

There has been a great deal of controversy about the impact in the recipient countries of Food for Peace and other programs that encourage U.S. exports. The increase in supply available to recipient countries reduces prices received by local farmers, which leads to decreases in output and makes local farmers worse off. Thus, in the long run, U.S. export subsidies may reduce availability of domestically grown food in the recipient countries and aggravate rather than alleviate hunger problems.[51]

The Ethanol Program

Following the Arab oil embargo of 1973 and the resulting increases in oil and gasoline prices, politicians looked for methods of encouraging the development of renewable domestic sources of energy.[52] One approach was legislation that provided subsidies for biomass-derived fuels. The primary fuel of this type was gasohol, a mixture of 90 percent gasoline and 10 percent ethanol.[53] The ethanol subsidy was in the form of exemptions from federal excise taxes, which have been in the range of $.50 to $.60 per gallon of ethanol ($.05 to $.06 per gallon of gasohol). The aggregate value of the ethanol subsidy amounted to more than $7.1 billion between 1979 and 1995 and was projected by the General Accounting Office to equal another $3.3 billion between 1996 and 2000.[54]

The impact of the subsidy can be understood by thinking in terms of the compensatory payments described above. Until 1996, the corn market was regulated with a target price program. Recall that the price received by farmers was an above-market price that was composed of two parts: the market price the farmer received for the corn and a government subsidy that made up the difference between the target price and the market price. The impact of the ethanol program was to provide a new use for corn, thereby increasing the demand for corn. Evidence suggests that in many (if not most) years, the increase in demand was not sufficiently large to cause the supply and demand curves to intersect at a price above the target price. The effect of the ethanol program was thus to increase the market price of corn and to decrease deficiency payments and treasury costs. The program, however, had little or no effect on the incomes of corn farmers.[55]

Why then, did corn producers lobby in support of the ethanol program? Johnson and Libecap (2001) argue that producers benefited from ethanol subsidies because they made a portion of the transfer from taxpayers less visible. Deficiency payments are highly visible—the government writes checks to eligible producers. This visibility creates political problems for farm programs, especially when large checks are written to large farmers and to high-profile individuals and corporations. Replacing these payments with the benefits arising from ethanol subsidies had (and continues to have) political benefits for corn producers.

Water Subsidies in the West

Although not funded through the USDA, water subsidies in the West—especially California—are critical in maintaining the current importance of agriculture in that region.[56] Irrigation subsidies are provided via water projects of the Department of the Interior.[57] Irrigation districts use artificially low-priced electricity produced by federally funded dams to pump water. The subsidies are quite substantial. It has been estimated, for example, that the capitalized value of water subsidies for a 160-acre California farm may exceed $100,000. Without subsidized water—worth billions of dollars over time—California would play a greatly reduced role in U.S. agriculture. Water and power subsidies distort the geographical pattern of agricultural production in the United States and also reduce the water available for recreational and urban uses in the West.

Conclusions and Political Economy Issues

Since the 1930s, farm programs have been used to support the incomes of U.S. farmers. Advocates of these programs have walked a fine line in transferring income to farmers without unacceptably high treasury costs. Technological advances in agriculture have increased commodity supply, thereby increasing surpluses and treasury costs. Similarly, producers have been ingenious in finding ways to increase their production in response to the incentives presented to them by farm programs, further increasing surpluses and treasury costs.

The history of U.S. farm programs illustrates several concepts and models that have been developed in the public-choice literature, four of which we summarize here. First, insights into the political economy of farm programs can be gleaned from the argument that small constituencies with large potential per-person benefits from a program will tend to prevail in political markets over larger constituencies with small potential per-person costs. Over the years, peanut, sugar, honey, and tobacco producers on average have received thousands of dollars in benefits annually from their programs, while consumers of these products incur a few dollars each in annual costs.

Second, economic models of regulation suggest that for a given industry, a political equilibrium will be established that balances at the margin the competing interests of consumers, producers, and taxpayers.[58] Shocks to the industry result in adjustment to a new political equilibrium. The history of U.S. farm programs, from an overall perspective and at the level of individual programs, can be interpreted as the outcome of such an equilibrating process, wherein the driving forces behind program changes have been rightward shifts in supply that increase costs to taxpayers.[59]

Third, the historical pattern of USDA activities is consistent with public-choice theory. In recent years the USDA has outgrown the constituency it was originally designed to aid: production agriculture. In response, in the classic expansion pattern of a bureaucracy, the USDA has maintained and increased its base by expanding into such tangential areas as urban nutrition, rural recreation, and community facilities.

Fourth, U.S. agricultural programs provide an excellent example of the *transitional gains trap* and associated problems. The value of government price support programs, for instance, gets incorporated into such asset prices as land and marketing quotas. Producers operating when a program is implemented (or when a price support is unexpectedly increased) receive windfall gains. Producers who enter the industry later receive no windfall gains from the program because the prices they pay for assets (and associated production costs) reflect the value of the government program. Thus, the gains from government programs are transitional. Moreover, once a price support program is begun, there is no way to abolish it without imposing windfall losses on asset owners—many of whom are not the ones who received the original windfall gain. The transitional gains trap is inherent in price support programs of all types.

Limited government intervention in U.S. agriculture began in the colonial era and continued on a relatively small scale into the twentieth century. Current U.S. farm programs form a costly and anachronistic legacy of the New Deal era. Although often rationalized as necessary to cope with changing economic conditions, government farm programs have not succeeded in increasing the long-term profitability of American agriculture. Short-term gains, obtained at the expense of U.S. consumers and taxpayers, go mainly to individuals whose incomes are above those of the nonfarm population. Moreover, price support programs are inherently protectionist and are inconsistent with the World Trade Organization's objective of reducing trade barriers and fostering trade between countries.

Notes

1. Pasour and Rucker 2005, the primary source of information and material for this chapter, contains more detailed discussions of many of the issues addressed in the chapter. Another important source of information for this chapter is Libecap 1998.

2. See Gray 1933, 261.

3. See Alvarez and Polopolus 2002 for a discussion of the history of U.S. sugar programs.

4. See Taussig 1967, 276.

5. See Hadwiger 1982, 15.

6. See Huffman and Evenson 1993.

7. Ibid, 15–16.

8. See Libecap 1998 for more detail.

9. See chapter 13 for a more exhaustive discussion of numerous aspects of the Great Depression and the government programs that were implemented during the 1930s.

10. See Alston 1983, 885–903.

11. See Rucker and Alston 1987 for an analysis of the impacts of state and federal relief programs in the 1930s.

12. For more extensive discussions of the following, see Gwartney and Stroup, 2000, 383–84, and Saint-Etienne 1984.

13. Saint-Etienne 1984, 38.

14. See Anderson 1979, 229.

15. See Pasour and Rucker 2005, 81.

16. The market-clearing price is the price at which the quantity demanded by buyers equals the quantity supplied by sellers. The government's basis for determining the level of support prices has varied over time. The parity concept and costs of production have both been used extensively as bases. See Pasour and Rucker 2005, chap. 8, for a more detailed discussion and critiques of these approaches.

17. For a detailed discussion of these events, see Rucker 1995.

18. Marketing quotas also are used to restrict agricultural output in other countries. Examples of such programs in recent years include marketing quotas for dairy, eggs, and poultry in Canada, dairy production quotas in the EU, and (recently eliminated) quotas for tobacco, eggs, and milk in Australia.

19. The target price programs implemented in the 1970s serve as an example of the compensatory payment approach.

20. An increase in demand will decrease the proportion of farmers' income that is received from the government without altering their total income (this insight is relevant to the discussion of the ethanol program later in the chapter). Note that, unlike the simple price support program discussed above, a compensatory payment program may result in no surplus to be purchased by the government. See Pasour and Rucker 2005, chap. 10, for a detailed discussion and analysis of the impacts of compensatory payment programs.

21. This section draws heavily on Luttrell 1989.

22. Ibid., 32.

23. See Knutson, Penn, and Flinchbaugh 1998, 261.

24. Public Law 480 (P.L. 83-480 [July 10, 1954]) remains in effect. See Pasour and Rucker 2005, chap. 14, for further discussion of the features and effects of this program.

25. Target prices are an example of the "compensatory payments" discussed above.

26. This discussion draws heavily from Gardner 1995, chap. 1.

27. A substantial proportion of the costs of government programs in recent years has been accounted for by *marketing loans* and *loan deficiency payments.* Marketing loans, which were instituted in the 1985 farm bill, allow producers to repay their nonrecourse loans at rates less than the specified nonrecourse loan rate. Loan deficiency payments (LDPs) are similar to marketing loans, the primary difference being that producers can collect the difference between the loan rate and the lower repayment rate without putting their commodity under loan. After the 1996 farm bill was passed, during the "farm crisis" of the late 1990s, LDPs totaled $1.8 billion in 1998, $5.9 billion in 1999, $6.4 billion in 2000, and $5.5 billion in 2001. USDA/ERS, U.S. and State Farm Income from government payments data, http://www.ers.usda.gov/data/farmincome/finfidmu.htm (accessed April 2, 2006).

28. See the appendix to Pasour and Rucker 2005 for details of the provisions of the 2002 farm bill.

29. See Pasour and Rucker 2005, as well as other materials cited there, for discussions and analyses of each of these programs.

30. Possibly the most common method for decreasing price support levels is to freeze them in nominal terms and let the real value of the supported price decrease with inflation.

31. There is an extended history—not discussed in this chapter owing to space limitations—of programs working at cross purposes. Subsidized crop insurance and credit programs are two examples of programs that reduce the cost of agricultural production, thereby increasing the supply of agricultural products and ameliorating or reversing the impacts of policies designed to reduce surpluses and treasury costs. See Pasour and Rucker 2005, chaps. 15 and 16, for extended discussions of these programs.

32. See Longen 1990.

33. Based on information from USDA, *Food Stamp Program Annual Summary.* www.fns.usda.gov/pd/fssummar.htm (accessed April 2, 2006).

34. See Pasour and Rucker 2005, chap. 13, for details on the relevant calculations.

35. See Bovard 1983, and U.S. Department of Agriculture 1945, 577.

36. U.S. General Accounting Office 1995.

37. Source: http://www.usda.gov/agency/obpa (accessed April 4, 2006). This is the home page for the Office of Budget and Program Analysis of the U.S. Department of Agriculture. Program outlays for the food stamp, child nutrition, and other programs of the Food and Nutrition Service of the USDA may be found in the "Budget Summary" for recent years.

38. U.S. Department of Agriculture, Office of Budget and Program Analysis 2003, 53.

39. Ibid.

40. Ibid., 457.

41. Ibid., 49.

42. See Pasour and Rucker 2005, chap. 13, for more detail about other food programs.

43. See Knutson, Penn, and Flinchbaugh 1998, 451.

44. See Longen 1990, 24.

45. See Pasour and Rucker 2005, chap. 16.

46. See Knutson, Penn, and Flinchbaugh 1998, 176.

47. See Luttrell 1983, 6.

48. See Knutson, Penn, and Flinchbaugh 1998, 155.

49. See Wilson 1987.

50. See U.S. Office of Budget and Program Analysis [2006], 9.

51. See Pasour and Rucker 2005, chap. 14, for discussion of other agricultural export subsidy programs.

52. A primary source of information for the discussion in this section is Johnson and Libecap 2001.

53. Ethanol is a fuel produced from crops such as corn that is made by fermenting and distilling simple sugars.

54. See U.S. General Accounting Office 1997.

55. See Johnson and Libecap 2001 for further discussions of issues related to this discussion.

56. See Pasour and Rucker 2005, 307–8. Also see Gardner 1995, chap. 12.

57. See Rucker and Fishback 1983 for a historical examination of the nature, magnitude, and distribution of irrigation subsidies.

58. For seminal articles in this literature, see Stigler 1971, Peltzman 1976, and Becker 1983.

59. For interpretations of the history of specific programs in the context of these models of regulation, see Rucker and Thurman 1990 and Muth, Rucker, Thurman, and Chuang 2003.

References

Alston, Lee J. 1983. "Farm Foreclosures in the United States during the Interwar Period." *Journal of Economic History* 43 (December): 885–903.

Alvarez, Jose, and Leo C. Polopolus. 2002. "The History of U.S. Sugar Protection." Electronic Data Information Source (EDIS) document SC 019, Department of Food and Resource Economics, Florida Cooperative Extension Service, Institute of Food and Agricultural Sciences, University of Florida, Gainesville (June). http://edis.ifas.ufl.edu/BODY_SC019 (accessed April 4, 2006).

Anderson, Benjamin M. 1979. *Economics and the Public Welfare.* Indianapolis: Liberty.

Becker, Gary S. 1983. "A Theory of Competition among Pressure Groups for Political Influence." *Quarterly Journal of Economics* 98:371–401.

Bovard, James. 1983. "Feeding Everybody: How Federal Food Programs Grew and Grew." *Policy Review* 26 (Fall): 42.

Gardner, B. Delworth. 1995. *Plowing Ground in Washington: The Political Economy of U.S. Agriculture.* San Francisco: Pacific Research Institute for Public Policy.

Gray, Lewis Cecil. 1933. *History of Agriculture in the Southern United States to 1860,* vol. 1. Washington, DC: Carnegie Institution.

Gwartney, James D., and Richard L. Stroup. 2000. *Economics: Private and Public Choice,* 9th ed. Fort Worth: Harcourt Brace, Dryden Press.

Hadwiger, Don F. 1982. *The Politics of Agricultural Research.* Lincoln: University of Nebraska Press.

Huffman, Wallace E., and Robert E. Evenson. 1993. *Science for Agriculture: A Long-Term Perspective.* Ames: Iowa State University Press.

Johnson, Ronald N., and Gary D. Libecap. 2001. "Information Distortion and Competitive Remedies in Government Transfer Programs: The Case of Ethanol." *Economics of Governance* 2.2 (July): 101–34.

Knutson, Ronald D., J. B. Penn, and B. L. Flinchbaugh. 1998. *Agricultural and Food Policy,* 4th ed. Englewood Cliffs: Prentice-Hall.

Libecap, Gary D. 1998. "The Great Depression and the Regulating State: Federal Government Regulation of Agriculture, 1884–1970." In *The Defining Moment: The Great Depression and the American Economy in the Twentieth Century,* ed. Michael D. Bordo, Claudia Goldin, and Eugene N. White, 181–226. Chicago: University of Chicago Press.

Longen, Kathryn. 1980. *Domestic Food Programs: An Overview.* Washington, DC: U.S. Department of Agriculture, ESCS 81.

Luttrell, Clifton B. 1983. *Down on the Farm with Uncle Sam.* Los Angeles: International Institute for Economic Research.

———. 1989. *The High Cost of Farm Welfare.* Washington, DC: Cato Institute.

Muth, Mary K., Randal R. Rucker, Walter N. Thurman, and Ching-Ta Chuang. 2003. "The Fable of the Bees Revisited: Causes and Consequences of the U.S. Honey Program." *Journal of Law and Economics* 46.2 (October): 479–516.

Pasour, E. C., Jr., and Randal R. Rucker. 2005. *Plowshares and Pork Barrels: The Political Economy of Agriculture.* Oakland, CA: Independent Institute.

Peltzman, Sam. 1976. "Toward a More General Theory of Regulation." *Journal of Law and Economics* 19:211–40.

Rucker, Randal R. 1995. "Endogenous Policy Dynamics, the Visibility of Rents, and Changes in the Transferability of Production Rights: The Case of Flue-Cured Tobacco." Montana State University, Bozeman.

Rucker, Randal R., and Lee J. Alston. 1987. "The Effects of State Farm Relief Legislation on Private Lenders: The Experience of the 1930s." *American Economic Review* (December): 724–30.

Rucker, Randal R., and Price V. Fishback. 1983. "The Federal Reclamation Program: An Analysis of Rent-Seeking Behavior." In *Water Rights: Scarce Resource Allocation, Bureaucracy, and the Environment,* ed. Terry L. Anderson. San Francisco: Pacific Institute for Public Policy Research; Cambridge, MA: Ballinger.

Rucker, Randal R., and Walter N. Thurman. 1990. "The Economic Effects of Supply Controls: The Simple Analytics of the U.S. Peanut Program." *Journal of Law and Economics* 33:483–515.

Saint-Etienne, Christian. 1984. *The Great Depression, 1929–1938*. Stanford, CA: Hoover Institution Press.

Stigler, George J. 1971. "The Theory of Economic Regulation." *Bell Journal of Economics and Management Science* 2:3–21.

Taussig, F. W. 1931. *The Tariff History of the United States*. 8th ed. Repr., New York: Augustus M. Kelley, 1967.

U.S. Department of Agriculture. 1945. *Agricultural Statistics, 1945*. Washington, DC: Government Printing Office.

U.S. Department of Agriculture, Office of Budget and Program Analysis. 2003. "2003 Budget Summary." http://www.usda.gov/agency/obpa/Budget-Summary/2003/2003budsum.htm (accessed April 4, 2006).

U.S. General Accounting Office. 1995. "Food Assistance: Reducing Food Stamp Benefit Overpayments and Trafficking: Report to the Committee on Agriculture, House of Representatives," GAO/RCED-95-198. http://www.gao.gov/archive/1995/rc95198.pdf (accessed April 4, 2006).

———. 1997. *Tax Policy: Effects of the Alcohol Fuels Tax Incentives*. General Government Division Report no. 97–41. Washington, DC: Government Printing Office. http://www.unclefed.com/GAOReports/ggd97-41.pdf (accessed April 4, 2006).

U.S. Office of Budget and Program Analysis. [2006]. *FY 2007 Budget Summary and Annual Performance Plan*. http://www.usda/gov/agency/obpa/Budget-Summary/2007/FY07budsum.pdf (accessed April 5, 2006).

Wilson, W. Gene. 1987. "Government Policies: Will They Increase Farm Exports?" *Federal Reserve Bank of Atlanta Economic Review* 72 (January–February): 22.

LEE J. ALSTON AND
JOSEPH P. FERRIE

16

Shaping Welfare Policy: *The Role of the South*

THE U.S. welfare system developed later and was always more decentralized than its European counterparts. The federal political system in the United States, which grants much more policy discretion to states, explains some of this difference. But the difference also results from the role of economic interests in the southern United States and their disproportionate political power. Until the mechanization of cotton cultivation in the South, large-scale agricultural interests in that region had the economic incentive and the political ability to prevent the expansion of the welfare state in ways that would interfere with prevailing race or labor relations. With the mechanization of cotton picking and accompanying technological advances in seeds, defoliants, and gins, we begin to see profound changes in the South's political landscape that also manifested themselves at the national level such that currently the South's attitudes toward welfare differ far less from the attitudes of rest of the nation.

The Contractual Mix in Southern Agriculture and the Rationale for Paternalism

Under slavery, cotton was produced by slaves working in gangs. Owners of plantations or their overseers closely monitored the slaves' efforts, and shirking, if detected, frequently resulted in whipping. On emancipation, slaveowners attempted to work the freedmen in gangs, but those who chose this mode of production discovered that they had difficulty retaining labor: the greatest asset of freedmen was their ability to move.[1] The ex-slaves also had labor scarcity on their side. With emancipation, freed women and children opted to work fewer hours in the field than under slavery. The withdrawal of their labor raised the bargaining power of men.

Over time, the use of gangs gave way to experimentation. Some planters tried share contracts with their entire labor force. For example, a former slaveowner would offer to supply the land, the seeds, the work stock, and the marketing of cotton and in return receive 50 percent of the output. In return for their labor, workers collectively would receive the remaining 50 percent, to be divided among the workers. This system of group contracting succumbed to what economists term the "free-rider" problem, in which some get the benefits without bearing the costs. A free-rider problem emerges whenever the individual reward to a worker is only partly tied to individual effort. In the context of cotton a rational worker would ask: Why should I work so hard when a large part of my effort results in rewarding another?[2] Differences in the abilities of workers, their attitudes toward labor and leisure, and the size of the group exacerbate the free-rider problem. As a result plantation owners increasingly relied on contracts with individuals and households.[3]

The transition took time, but eventually a mix of wage, sharecropper, and tenant contracts emerged.[4] A wage contract pays the worker a fixed amount per unit of time, for example, per month or per day. As such, labor effort is divorced from the reward to labor. Without monitoring, shirking would abound. In a sharecropper contract, workers supply effort and in return receive a percentage of the output, most frequently, but not always, 50 percent. A tenant contract leaves the worker as the residual claimant; that is, he owes the landlord a rent in cash, in kind, or as a percentage of the output, and the remaining profits, if any, are his.

The individual contract negotiated between workers and landlords depended on their respective endowments. The underlying motivation for the contract was the cost of supervising labor. Prior to the mechanization of cotton, the production of cotton was very labor-intensive. With direct supervision and direct physical punishment (or at least the credible threat of punishment), the gang system used under slavery had reduced monitoring costs directly. With the gang system no longer an option after emancipation, plantation owners still had an incentive to reduce monitoring costs, which vary depending on what factors the workers bring to the production process. To simplify, suppose only four factors are used to produce cotton: land, work stock (a mule), know-how, and labor effort. Landlords always supply land and workers always supply labor effort. If farmers have considerable experience (human capital) and own their own mule, they supply all but the land to the production process. This means that the only reason for the landowner to be on the farm is to monitor the worker's effort. Compare this to the situation of workers who just started farming and do not own a mule. In this case the landowner needs to be on the farm to monitor the treatment of his work stock. Given that the landowner is there for these reasons, the additional costs of monitoring the work effort of inexperienced farmers are low compared to the costs of monitoring the effort of experienced farmers. As such, tenancy emerged in part to lower the cost of monitoring the work of experienced farmers.[5]

To say that contracts adapted to monitoring costs does not mean that monitoring costs disappeared. Over time landlords found an additional mechanism to reduce them further; it was known as *paternalism*.[6] Paternalism in southern agricultural contracts was an implicit contract between landlords and certain agricultural workers whereby the workers exchanged "good and faithful" labor for a variety of in-kind goods and services. For black workers, the most important of these benefits was protection from civil rights abuses. Plantation owners reduced labor turnover and induced greater work effort by offering workers a variety of goods and services that were difficult, if not impossible, to procure in the market. The variety of goods ranged from garden plots to old-age assistance to de facto crop insurance. The essence of the contract was that it raised the opportunity cost of leaving the current employer for an alternative employer because the benefits were individual; they depended on the good and faithful effort of employees to specific employers and the willingness of employers to deliver the goods and services.[7]

The Politics of Paternalism—Reconstruction to the New Deal

The benefits to workers of entering into a paternalistic labor contract increased during the postbellum period as political competition waned. During the Reconstruction period (1865–76) Republicans and Democrats competed for votes. Republicans represented the poor white and ex-slave vote, and Democrats catered to the upper-class plantation elite.[8] Though political divisions over class lines occur frequently, other types of divisions occur. In the South racism did not disappear with emancipation. Indeed, some analysts argue that emancipation fostered racism. The Freedmen's Bureau prevented the ugliest forms of racism from persisting, but its stay in the South came to an end following the presidential election of 1876 between Rutherford B. Hayes and Samuel J. Tilden. The electoral returns were close, and in a questionable recount, South Carolina and Louisiana tipped the balance in favor of Hayes. Scholars have argued that a quid quo pro was at work; in exchange for electing

Hayes, the North agreed to leave the South and not interfere in the region's labor or race relations.

Without federal interference, southern Democrats exploited the race issue and eventually passed poll taxes and literacy tests, which had the effect of disenfranchising most blacks and many poor whites. Once blacks were effectively prevented from voting, politicians did not need to promote the economic and political progress of blacks. In the words of W. E. B. Du Bois, "the South became an armed camp for intimidating black folk" (Du Bois 1965,). The number of lynchings soared. In the 1890s, the number of lynchings averaged 111 per year. A black man was hung every third day. For blacks other governmental goods and services declined. The gap between expenditures for white and black schools widened significantly. For example, in 1910 Louisiana spent only seventeen cents on black schools for every dollar that it allocated for white schools (Margo 1990). Though Louisiana had the lowest ratio of black to white school expenditures, the rest of the Deep South did not lavish money on black schools. The Jim Crow laws provided separate but vastly unequal public accommodations for blacks and whites. Many unions further promoted racism by relegating blacks to particular jobs (Higgs 1974). In the face of such a hostile atmosphere, a black in the South had an incentive to "stay in his or her place" and seek the refuge of a white protector.

Because of their wealth and social position, white plantation owners could offer certain paternalistic benefits at relatively low cost. Interventions ranged from bailing a good tenant's son out of jail to the particularly striking example of William Alexander Percy, who stood on the steps of the courthouse in Washington County, Mississippi, and warned the Ku Klux Klan not to set foot in his county. Other anecdotal evidence abounds about the actions of plantation owners and, more important, the beliefs of workers concerning the willingness of plantation owners to take care of their workers. Many of these benefits could be considered as substitutes for welfare or insurance schemes, such as workmen's compensation (Fishback and Kantor 2000). There was an important difference; not all workers received paternalism. It was earned over time by loyalty. On the part of plantation owners the system became known as *noblesse oblige*. The elite could, on one hand, foster or condone general racist attitudes and policies (for example, relatively low schooling and welfare expenditures), and on the other hand offer protection or old-age assistance for individual workers. Lower government expenditures on welfare and a more hostile social environment increased the value to workers of accepting the paternalistic packages offered by the landed elite.

An expansion of the welfare state would have diminished the value of paternalism to workers and reduced the incentive effects reaped by plantation owners. But the plantation elite had little to fear in the period from Reconstruction until the Great Depression. Within the South, rural Democrats controlled the political landscape, while outside the South, nascent attempts at welfare policy occurred only at the state and local levels. Any threat to paternalism from the beginnings of the federal welfare system awaited the New Deal.

New Deal Welfare Policies and the Role of the South

Until the Great Depression the northern policy of not interfering in labor or race issues in the South created a political equilibrium. As a result, U.S. welfare policy was truly federalist in the sense that states varied dramatically in the welfare benefits that they offered to residents. Some, such as Wisconsin, were pioneers in offering early social security systems, whereas the southern states stood out as offering little in the way of governmental programs. By the time the nation was in the depths of the Depression in 1934, thirty-one states had established old-age pension programs, but none of the thirty-one was in the South. The region was not distinctive because industrial states provided more generous welfare benefits than agricultural states: most Midwestern agricultural states provided generous benefits, as did California. The early precursors to general welfare legislation were programs of Mothers' Aid. Though southern states did have programs for Mothers' Aid, their benefit levels were on average 25 percent below those of the rest of the nation. Moreover, the programs tended to come with strings attached. For example, in Louisiana, to receive aid mothers has to be available to work in the fields.

The United States might have left policies concerning welfare to the states had it not been for the Great Depression. In the depths of the Depression, state budgets for relief and welfare pensions were overwhelmed by the large number of unemployed workers and their families. As a result, many states turned to the federal government for help. Little was forthcoming during the Hoover administration, but FDR welcomed the opportunity to do something. His first response was the Federal Emergency Relief Administration (FERA). At first FERA issued two types of grants: matching grants (three federal dollars for every state dollar) and discretionary grants. By the end of 1933

FERA moved solely to discretionary grants on a "take it or leave it" basis. The program required states that wanted benefits to conform to its standards. For example, it stipulated that recipients of work relief be paid a minimum wage of thirty cents per hour. The concern in the South was that this would drive up wages in agriculture or make it more difficult to attract workers as sharecroppers. Initially more irksome to the southern way of life was FERA's dictate that eligibility for work relief could not be based on race. Southerners quickly learned, however, that eligibility decisions remained in local hands. The end result was that the South welcomed the money, without which expenditures on relief in the region would have been extremely meager. From 1933 to 1935, the federal government provided more than 90 percent of the South's total expenditures for relief as compared to 60 percent for the Northeast.

At times FERA sanctioned states that did not comply with its dictates. In 1934 and 1935 the program brought relief administration under direct federal control in six states: Georgia, Louisiana, Massachusetts, North Dakota, Ohio, and Oklahoma. In four other states, Alabama, Colorado, Illinois, and Missouri, FERA withheld funds until states complied with their dictates. As with many welfare programs, it was not only the southern states that complained of interference from Washington. The voices of states' rights advocates echoed across the country, but the political power of southerners seemed to amplify southern voices in Washington. In the early years of the New Deal, Roosevelt viewed the southern Democrats as among his most loyal supporters. For example, Rexford Tugwell, one of Roosevelt's most radical advisors, described this branch of the party as "the only dependable body of men who can be counted on to stick by their bargains and pass legislation" (Schlesinger 1965, 415). Roosevelt was explicit about his fear of retaliation if he crossed them: "The Southerners by reason of seniority in Congress are chairmen or occupy strategic places on most of the Senate and House Committees. If I come out for the anti-lynching bill now (1935), they will block every bill I ask Congress to pass to keep America from collapsing. I just can't take that risk" (ibid., 438).

Over time, opposition to FERA mounted, and the government wanted to move to a more permanent solution to welfare. This was the impetus for the Social Security Act of 1935. The starting point for a policy of social insurance was Roosevelt's Committee on Economic Security (CES), established in 1934. The CES produced numerous studies about all aspects of the social security question and endorsed including agricultural workers in a governmental unemployment and old-age pension system. For the most part, Roosevelt used the reports of the CES as the basis for the social security bill he presented to Congress in 1935. The bill included agricultural workers in both the unemployment and old-age provisions of social security. In our view, the inclusion of agricultural workers threatened the viability of paternalism in southern agriculture.

Roosevelt's bill came under the auspices of the House Ways and Means Committee and the Senate Finance Committee, both dominated by southerners: Robert Doughton (D-NC) chaired the Ways and Means Committee and Pat Harrison (D-MS) chaired the Senate Finance Committee. In addition, southerners held many of the more senior seats. Southern opposition to including agriculture under social security emerged quickly in the deliberations. Both committees moved quickly to exclude all agricultural workers from the provisions of the unemployment benefits associated with the social security bill. In the words of Edwin Witte, the chair of the CES and architect of the pioneering social security system in Wisconsin, the exclusion was "a matter of course" (Witte 1962, 132). Debate about whether to exclude agricultural workers from the old-age provisions was prolonged, but at the end of the day the bills that emerged from both committees excluded agricultural workers from all provisions of social security. Again, we stress that many Congressmen from outside the South also opposed many of the initial provisions proposed by Roosevelt, so the South did not fight a solo battle against the administration, but no other region collectively was as politically powerful, a fact reflected in southerners' seniority on committees.

After the passage of the Social Security Act, lobbyists began to press for the inclusion of more of the population under its umbrella. In the late 1930s and throughout the 1940s prominent advocates for covering agricultural workers under social security include organized labor, the National Association for the Advancement of Colored People (NAACP), the National Urban League, and the Social Security Board. Their efforts came to naught. It was not until 1954 that Congress included agricultural workers under Social Security, and this was done over the protests of many southern Congressmen who had temporarily lost some of their agenda control because the GOP had a majority in the House and Senate following the 1952 general election. This meant that the senior southern Democrats lost their control over the Senate Finance Committee and the House Ways and Means Committee. As testimony to their opposition, Walter George (Georgia) and Harry Byrd (Virginia), who served on the conference committee to reconcile the differences between the House and Senate versions of the amended Social Security bill, refused to sign the conference report. Without the Democrats' loss of power during the legislative session from 1953 to 1954, the inclusion of agricultural workers likely would have been postponed until southerners had less need for their exclusion.

The South needed relief, so southern politicians shaped federal programs as best they could. For some in Washington and elsewhere, though, relief for the South was the starting point and reform was the ultimate goal. This was the case with the Farm Security Administration (FSA). The FSA was created in 1937, though it was essentially a consolidation and expansion of programs formerly operating under the auspices of the Resettlement Administration, FERA, and the Division of Subsistence Homesteads in the U.S. Department of the Interior. The former programs included meager efforts at rehabilitation and resettlement and posed little threat to southern elites, who were able to coopt most of the programs to suit their local needs. The FSA was bigger in scope and scale. At the heart of paternalism was dependency based on a personal relationship. The goal of many FSA programs was for tenants to become independent farm operators. The program that provided credit and technical assistance to tenants posed the greatest threat to paternalism because it sought to make the landlord-tenant relationship more impersonal, for example, by promoting the use of written leases. The FSA began to be seen in the South and elsewhere as a radical organization aimed at reform. Adding to this perception was the FSA's sponsorship of a project that produced a powerful set of photographs depicting the plight of tenant farmers.

The opposition by the South to the FSA was part of a more general conservative reaction in the late 1930s to the New Deal, as recovery seemed more imminent. Early opposition took the form of cooptation. Increasingly, decision making devolved to local county boards controlled (naturally) by the established local agricultural elites. Still, the FSA was seen as a threat. By 1940 the opponents of the FSA turned to cutting off funding for the agency rather than simply tinkering with the administration of programs. Again, the South was not alone in its opposition. The FSA operated outside the established agricultural organizations such as the USDA Extension Service, so opposition was also significant within government bureaucracies trying to protect their own turf. The FSA's opponents charged it not only with waste and inefficiency but also with harming the free enterprise system, an accusation that increasingly resonated in Congress. The testimony of Oscar

Johnston, the president of the National Cotton Council, at hearings on an agriculture appropriations bill characterizes much of the discussion:

> The FSA is so functioning and conditioning its activities as to promote gross inefficiency in the matter of culture and production of cotton and cottonseed; to seriously impede the cost of production of cotton and cottonseed; to lower the morale of farm workers engaged in the production of the commodities under consideration; to threaten to disturb and disrupt economic and social conditions and relationships throughout the cotton belt; to threaten those who produce cotton and cottonseed on a commercial basis; to depress the morale of the cotton farmers throughout the belt; and ultimately to destroy the business of farming as a free enterprise and a respectable means of earning social and economic security by American farmers. (House Committee on Agriculture 1944, 1619)

By 1943 the supporters of the FSA either gave in or lost: the House Appropriations Committee voted to abolish the FSA. The Senate did not want to abolish it completely, but in the compromise bill rural rehabilitation funding was slashed 43 percent and promotion of cooperatives and land leasing was outlawed. The FSA limped along until, 1946 when Truman signed legislation creating the Farmers Home Administration, thereby abolishing the FSA. The reflections of Sidney Baldwin, a leading FSA official, capture the sentiment of the southern elite: "Those Southerners who were bitterly opposed to us were opposed to us for understandable reasons. We were in many ways subversive of the status quo. . . . The programs of the FSA represented a serious threat to the dependence of the farm tenant and sharecropper on his landlord, the store-keeper, and the court-house gang. . . . It didn't take many FSA clients in a Southern county to prove the fact that the FSA was real, that it was there, that the poor farmer need not be so entirely dependent on the rules of this community" (Baldwin 1968, 282).

World War II and the Threat of Labor Shortages

While the skirmishes over funding of the FSA occurred, agricultural interests in the United States faced a much more serious issue beginning in the 1940s: a switch from surplus labor to shortages because of the manpower demands of World War II. This change threatened to undermine the region's system of paternalistic labor relations by providing an opportunity for southern workers to obtain alternative employment in labor-deficit regions. This would have substantially reduced the value of paternalism and undermined the discipline among workers that it promoted. Southerners responded in three ways: (1) by directly preventing workers from leaving the South via legislation barring labor agents who could have recruited workers for northern factories; (2) by providing draft deferments to workers who remained in the South; and (3) by indirectly making out-migration a less attractive option by increasing the migration of temporary farm workers, mainly from Mexico, to areas outside the region that otherwise would have represented attractive destinations for southern workers.

The emigrant agent legislation passed in a number of southern states was a quick and easy solution to the threat that workers would decamp for industrial employment in the North. These laws were enacted at the state level, where the plantation elites exercised considerable influence, and prompted little resistance from other economic interests. By 1942, twelve states across the country had placed restrictions on the recruitment of labor by agents from outside the state. Eleven of the twelve states were in the South.

A more potent source of competition for workers was the federal government. The war effort required both the mobilization of troops and the relocation of workers to sites of wartime production. Either would have undermined paternalism, but both were fought successfully in Congress by the region's political agents. Generous criteria for deferment were inserted into the rules of the Selective Service System to allow even relatively unproductive southern farm workers to avoid conscription if their county's farm establishment (dominated by large planters) attested that they were necessary for maintaining farm production levels. The federal government was also barred from expending funds to reallocate workers across regions in 1943, an outcome that was recognized at the time as beneficial mainly to southern planters.

Only one avenue remained for workers who hoped to escape from the system of paternalistic labor relations: self-financed and self-directed migration to labor deficit regions. Southerners could do little to dampen the demand for workers in war industries. But they could reduce the demand for farm workers outside the South. By encouraging the importation of Mexican farm workers under the Bracero Program (Public Law 78), plantation interests succeeded in making migration out of the South by farm workers considerably less attractive.

Temporary Mexican farm workers were brought into the United States pursuant to a variety of agreements beginning in 1942. These initiatives enjoyed the strong support of representatives in Congress from across the South, leading to the institutionalization of labor importation in the *Bracero* Program in 1951. Two southern Congressmen played key roles: Representative William R. Poage (D-TX) and Senator Allen J. Ellender (D-LA), both chairmen of their respective Agriculture Committees, negotiated the initial wartime labor agreement with the Mexican government. Though only Texas and Arkansas ever employed significant numbers of these workers in the South, the region's representatives provided strong support for the program throughout its existence. This is consistent with their interest in reducing migration to regions such as the Southwest, where many more *braceros* were employed. The program continued long after the war with strong southern support and ended only in 1963, when the mechanization of the cotton harvest was a viable substitute for labor across the entire South.

Welfare Expansion in the 1960s

Though southerners were successful from the New Deal through the early 1950s in preventing the expansion of federal programs that would have made paternalism less attractive, the American welfare state nonetheless expanded. As we noted above, the Social Security system was broadened to include farmers and farm workers in the 1950s, during a period when southern Democrats lacked the veto power they had exercised over welfare legislation up to that point. Even more dramatic changes to the national welfare system occurred in the 1960s and early 1970s as new programs were introduced.

What led to this dramatic reversal? Whenever Democrats had held the upper hand in Congress, southerners had been positioned to block the expansion of the welfare system. Democrats retained control in Congress throughout the 1960s, yet legislation previously blocked by southerners was enacted. Did their preferences change, or did changes in their place within the congressional power structure diminish their ability to resist new initiatives?

The second argument is the easier to address directly. For much of the twentieth century and particularly after World War II, committees crafted most of the legislation in Congress. Without the approval of the relevant committee, a bill could not be easily advanced to the floor for a vote by the full body. Within committees, chairmen exercised almost absolute authority to direct the committee's work. Because of the dominance of Democrats in the South, the region's representatives in Congress tended to enjoy much greater seniority than other legislators, and that longevity gave them a disproportionate share of committee chairmanships. This gave southerners veto power over legislation they found objectionable, veto power that they successfully exercised throughout the 1930s and 1940s. If their power in the congressional committee structure is measured by the number of chairmanships they held and the number of the most senior committee positions they occupied, it is clear that southern veto power did not wane in the 1960s. Table 16.1 shows the seniority of southern Congressmen on certain committees in the House of Representatives. The information in the table starts in 1947 because this was the year that Congress reorganized committees in ways that gave more power to committees and to committee chairs in particular. We chose 1960 as our first break point because there is a consensus that at least until 1960 southern Democrats controlled the legislative agenda. Another break point was established in 1964 with the election of Lyndon Johnson. Information is provided for the Rules, Appropriations, and Ways and Means committees because they are the most powerful committees in the House. The Rules committee is the gatekeeper: all legislation must pass through it before proceeding to the floor for a vote. If a bill does not meet the preferences of the senior members of this committee, the bill is simply left to die. The Rules Committee also determines whether legislation is deemed to be constitutional. Appropriations controls spending, and Ways and Means controls taxation. The remaining committees were selected because of their importance in determining legislation affecting race or labor relations in the South.

It is apparent that southerners dominated in terms of seniority. Moreover, their seniority increased in the 1960s. They chaired the Rules, Ways and Means, and Agriculture Committees throughout the 1960s, and in many years they commanded a majority of the senior seats.[9] Note that a veto over the legislative agenda can be sustained by simply controlling seniority in either the House or the Senate.

Table 16.1 SENIORITY OF SOUTHERN DEMOCRATS IN THE HOUSE OF REPRESENTATIVES, 1947–1970

Committee	Years chaired			Average of 5 senior seats		
	1947–60	1961–64	1965–70	1947–60	1961–64	1965–70
Rules	6	4	6	3.0	3.0	1.7
Appropriations	0	0	6	2.3	2.0	3.3
Ways and Means	10	4	6	3.4	2.0	2.7
Agriculture	10	4	6	4.7	5.0	5.0
Education and Labor	8	0	4	2.0	2.0	1.0
Judiciary	0	0	0	1.3	1.5	1.0

By constitutional design the Senate is more conservative than the House. By *conservative* we simply mean that the Senate is more likely to uphold the status quo. Because they serve six-year terms, senators have less fear of voting their preferences than do members of the House, and thus Senators are better insulated from public opinion. In addition, terms in the Senate are staggered so that during any electoral cycle only one-third of the seats turn over. This further insulated the South from popular opinion. The power of the Senate is a negative power in that it could block legislation. One instrument in the arsenal of power is the filibuster, a practice strengthened over time by precedent according to which a senator cannot be called to order because of the irrelevance of his discourse during a debate. This means that a bloc of senators can simply wear out other members by a continual discussion, preventing a measure from coming to a vote. Robert Caro has described the veto power of the Senate as "an impenetrable wall against the democratic impulses it had originally been supposed only to 'refine' and 'filter,' . . . a dam against which waves of social reform, attempts to ameliorate the human condition, dashed themselves in vain" (Caro 2002, 105).

Table 16.2 shows the seniority of southern Congressmen in the Senate. Like their House counterparts, they dominated many committees. Moreover, in the Senate their dominance clearly increased in the 1960s. With regard to welfare and civil rights the conservatism of the Senate showed up in chairmanships of the Labor and Judiciary Committees, chaired by southerners throughout the decade. The only powerful committee on which the South did not dominate the chairmanship was the Appropriations Committee, but it did occupy the majority of the top seats during the 1960s.

Though Southerners' power was undiminished, there is a good deal of evidence that their willingness to use that power to block welfare legislation was reduced by several developments in the 1960s. The mecha-

Table 16.2 SENIORITY OF SOUTHERN DEMOCRATS IN THE SENATE, 1947–1970

Committee	Years chaired			Average of 5 senior seats		
	1947–60	1961–64	1965–70	1947–60	1961–64	1965–70
Rules	0	2	6	1.0	1.0	1.3
Appropriations	4	0	2	2.7	3.5	4.0
Finance	10	4	6	3.5	3.5	3.3
Agriculture	10	4	6	4.0	5.0	5.0
Labor	6	4	6	1.4	2.0	1.7
Judiciary	4	4	6	2.3	4.7	3.2

nization of cotton harvesting probably had the most direct impact on that willingness: though less than half of the cotton in the South was harvested mechanically at the end of the 1950s, more than eighty percent was picked by machines by 1965. This had the direct effect of reducing the need for paternalism as new machine technology standardized production and reduced the scope for shirking. It also reduced the value of paternalism indirectly by increasing unemployment in southern agriculture. The threat of unemployment now served to motivate workers, as had the promise of benefits contingent on their perceived effort.

The value of paternalism had rested on a lack of civil rights, particularly for blacks, in the South. The nation's changing attitudes toward civil rights in the late 1950s and early 1960s also made the long-term viability of paternalism less likely. Part of the increased demand for civil rights and more equality in welfare came from blacks who had migrated north and become an important core constituency for the Democratic Party, particularly in certain states (Young and Burstein 1995). As workers and employers foresaw the day when the government would protect workers from violence, both groups had less reason to enter into long-term relationships in which current efforts were rewarded with future benefits. The logic of paternalism began to unravel.

Southerners were not powerless in the face of these developments, however. As we have seen, they maintained their hold over the congressional committee structure until well into the 1970s, when it was significantly reduced by a series of reforms. Though they no longer blocked as much welfare legislation in the 1960s as they had previously, they continued to play a large role in welfare policy. The difference in the 1960s was that rather than blocking legislation that threatened their interests, as they had since the New Deal, they now sought to alter legislation in ways that encouraged migration out of the South by farm workers rendered superfluous by mechanization. The Great Society programs of the Johnson administration were crafted by southerners, who still occupied crucial nodes of power in Congress, in order to reduce the burden on local elites that unemployed farm workers would have imposed. Together with northern urban legislators for whom migrants from southern farms represented a powerful new constituency, southern farm interests now supported programs directed at poverty in the nation's cities. Southern representatives were decisive in passage of both the Economic Opportunity Act of 1964 and the Food Stamp program's genesis in 1963.

The decline in the influence of rural agricultural interests at the state and federal levels had effects at both levels. At the federal level welfare expenditures became more homogeneous. In the short period between 1960 and 1970 total benefit levels divided by population in the North and the South started to converge. In 1960, when cotton production was 50 percent mechanized, the ratio of southern benefit levels (AFDC, Food Stamps and Medicaid) per capita to benefits per capita in the rest of the country was .80. By 1970, when cotton was nearly fully mechanized, the ratio climbed to .87.[10] If we restrict the comparison to the South and the Midwest, the convergence is more striking, increasing from .74 in 1960 to nearly .90 in 1970. In short, over time we saw much more convergence between the South and the rest of the country with regard to welfare systems.

Concluding Remarks

The South witnessed changes that went beyond the institution of welfare. The Economic Opportunity Act initially encouraged the out-migration of labor from the South, but equally important, the region began to recruit capital actively.[11] The recruiting involved not so much lowering corporate taxes across the board as offering tax breaks to selected large firms. These moves attracted a number of major automobile manufacturers to the South in the 1980s and 1990s.

In addition to changes within the South. the Voting Rights Act had a profound impact on the region. Not only did it enable millions of African Americans to vote, but it set in motion a transition away from a solid one-party Democratic South to a mixed and eventually dominant though not solid Republican South. Considerable migration from the rest of the nation into the South also contributed to more convergence of regional attitudes. Perhaps the most dramatic change was the southward migration of the elderly, who, in some states, most notably Florida, have accumulated considerable economic and political clout. Ironically, though the South is now less distinct than the rest of the nation in its attitudes toward welfare policies, it has retained its disproportionate force in shaping policies overall.

Notes

1. Of course, a former slave's ability to switch employers required some knowledge of alternative employment opportunities. Over time competition among landowners for scarce labor generated this information (Higgs 1974). For an analysis of the transition to free labor contracting, see Shlomowitz 1978.

2. The free-rider problem is familiar to anybody who has been involved in a group project.

3. Households face less of a free-rider problem because of ties of affection and fear. Nevertheless, most households with teenagers find that they confront a variety of free-rider problems, e.g., the length of a shower, which affects the amount of hot water for other members of the family.

4. Alston and Higgs (1982) provide an analysis of the evolution of contracts as well as tests of the determinants of contract mixes across plantations in Georgia in the early part of the twentieth century.

5. The use of tenant contracts to reduce monitoring costs dates back to Roman antiquity. See Alston 2003.

6. The following discussion draws heavily on Alston and Ferrie 1999.

7. Numerous employers use perquisites to reduce turnover and increase effort. Wherever monitoring costs loom large, management has an incentive to try to raise the opportunity costs of quitting or being fired. For example, it is not surprising that software producers were among the first to eliminate dress codes and punch clocks in order to motivate and retain creative engineers, whose work effort was difficult to monitor.

8. These distinctions are painted sharply; as always, reality is more nuanced. See Kousser 1974 for an analysis of the political forces at work in this period.

9. Note that the power of the South on the House Education and Labor Committee was weakest in the early 1960s and it was not coincidental that the Economic Opportunity Act was written by this committee.

10. These calculations are based on data contained in Robert Moffitt's website: http://www.econ.jhu.edu/People/Moffitt/DataSets.html.

11. Recruitment of northern capital was made all the easier given the open-shop right-to-work laws in place in many southern states.

References

Alston, Lee J. 2003. "Tenant Farming." In *The Oxford Encyclopedia of Economic History,* ed. Joel Mokyr, 5:97–101. New York: Oxford University Press.

Alston, Lee J., and Joseph P. Ferrie. 1999. *Paternalism and the American Welfare State: Economics, Politics, and Institutions in the U.S. South, 1865–1965.* Cambridge: Cambridge University Press.

Alston, Lee J., and Robert Higgs. 1982. "Contractual Mix in Southern Agriculture since the Civil War: Facts, Hypotheses and Tests." *Journal of Economic History* 42:327–53.

Baldwin, Sidney. 1968. *Poverty and Politics: The Rise and Decline of the Farm Security Administration.* Chapel Hill: University of North Carolina Press.

Caro, Robert A. 2002. *Master of the Senate: The Years of Lyndon Johnson.* New York: Knopf.

Du Bois, W. E. B. 1965. *The Souls of Black Folk.* 1903; repr., New York: Avon.

Fishback, Price, and Shawn Kantor. 2000. *A Prelude to the Welfare State: The Origin of Workers' Compensation.* Chicago: University of Chicago Press.

Higgs, Robert. 1974. *Competition and Coercion.* Cambridge: Cambridge University Press.

House Committee on Agriculture. 1944. Hearings on the Department of Agriculture Appropriations Bill. 78th Cong., 1st sess.

Kousser, J. Morgan. 1974. *The Shaping of Southern Politics: Suffrage Restriction and the Establishment of the One-Party South, 1880–1910.* New Haven: Yale University Press.

Margo, Robert. 1990. *Race and Schooling in the South, 1880–1950.* Chicago: University of Chicago Press.

Shlomowitz, Ralph. 1978. "The Freedmen's Bureau." PhD diss., University of Chicago.

Witte, Edwin E. 1962. *The Development of the Social Security Act.* Madison: University of Wisconsin Press.

Young, Richard P., and Jerome S. Bernstein. 1995. "Federalism and the Demise of Prescriptive Racism in the United States." *Studies in American Political Development* 9 (Spring): 1–5.

PRICE FISHBACK

17

Seeking Security in the Postwar Era

WHEN WORLD War II ended in the late summer of 1945, the United States entered a new era in its economic and political history. During the preceding sixteen years, the American people had endured twelve years of economic depression, then four years of wartime economic privation and regimentation. Those sixteen years had composed a seemingly endless period of national emergency, to which governments at all levels, but most strikingly the federal government, had responded in unprecedented ways. Consequently, as the postwar era began, the size, scope, and power of governments in the United States greatly exceeded their magnitudes in the "good old days" before the onset on the depression. Although some of the emergency measures had already been terminated or soon would be, many persisted, sometimes under a new name or lodged in a different agency. In countless ways, an era of permanent big government had arrived.[1]

Amid the storms of two world wars and a deep, lengthy depression, long-standing beliefs in individual responsibility and free markets had lost much ground. In their stead, people had embraced a faith in the government's capacity to provide security, not only against foreign threats but also against many sorts of workaday economic hazards such as unemployment or low earnings during the working-age years and insufficient income during old age. In the mid-1940s, Bertrand de Jouvenel wrote, "The essential psychological characteristic of our age is the predominance of fear over self-confidence. . . . Everyone of every class tries to rest his individual existence on the bosom of the state and tends to regard the state as the universal provider." With the passage of time, Americans would look to government for more and more sorts of security—protection from the risk of workplace accidents, from race or sex discrimination, from the adverse side effects of drugs, from environmental pollution, and so on and on. This protection, however, cost the public far more than the high taxes required to fund its provision; de Jouvenel observed: "[I]f the state is to guarantee to a man what the consequences of his actions shall be, it must take control of his activities . . . to keep him out of the way of risks." Just as de Jouvenel foresaw, after World War II the demand for government protection in the United States rose to new heights, and the corresponding loss of individual economic liberties proceeded apace.[2]

Erosion of Constitutional Checks
and the Expansion of Rent-Seeking

In the postwar era the Constitution no longer served as it once had to constrain the public's hunger for the redistribution of income and wealth or the politicians' ambitions for power. As the constitutional scholar Edward S. Corwin wrote after the war, for the first time in U.S. history, the country did not return to a "peacetime Constitution." Supreme Court cases decided during the war had embedded more deeply in the U.S. system of government the revolutionary changes first validated during the late 1930s. The Court's wartime pronouncements brought into greater prominence all of the following:

> (1) the attribution to Congress of a legislative power of indefinite scope; (2) the attribution to the President of the power and duty to stimulate constantly the positive exercise of this indefinite power for enlarged social objectives; (3) the right of Congress to delegate its powers *ad libitum* to the President for the achievement of such enlarged social objectives . . . ; (4) the attribution to the President of a broad prerogative in the meeting of "emergencies" defined by himself and in the creation of executive agencies to assist him; (5) a progressively expanding replacement of the judicial process by the administrative process in the enforcement of the law—sometimes even of constitutional law.[3]

This expansion in legislative and executive power over the economy has occurred at all levels of government. This development is best illustrated by the expansions in local governments' power of eminent domain, its ability to take private property with just compensation for public use under the Fifth Amendment to the Constitution. The key phrase is "public use." In the nineteenth century *public use* typically was defined narrowly as use by the general public. United States Supreme Court decisions in 1896 and 1906 broadened the definition of public use to include promoting development in the West by taking property for irrigation (1896) and for mining projects (1906). In the postwar era, the definition of public use continued to broaden. In *Berman v. Parker* (1954) the Supreme Court held that a reasonably successful department store in a blighted slum area could by taken for use in a redevelopment plan that would build streets, schools, and public facilities but also sell land to private developers to build housing. In *Hawaii Housing Authority v. Midkiff* (1984), the Court allowed the transfer of property from landlords to renters to eliminate the "social and economic evils of a land oligopoly."[4]

Most recently, in June 2005, the 6–3 decision in *Kelo et al. v. City of New London* allowed several private homes to be taken to allow the Connecticut city to execute a "carefully formulated" economic development plan "that it believes will provide appreciable benefits to the community, including but by no means limited to new jobs and increased tax revenue." Justice Sandra Day O'Connor dissented, arguing that the precedent set by this decision implies that nothing prevents "the State from replacing any Motel 6 with a Ritz-Carlton, any home with a shopping mall, or any farm with a factory." While many groups started to lobby state legislatures for narrower definitions of public use, one outraged citizen illustrated O'Connor's warning by proposing a local economic development plan to take Justice David Souter's home for the public purpose of building the "Lost Liberty Hotel," which would provide more jobs and tax revenue to the local government.[5]

As the public clamored for government guarantees of security of all sorts and as constitutional checks and balances became less effective at constraining the growth of government, the political system opened the door wide to "rent seeking" by special interests. More and more often previously unorganized groups formed political organizations, movements, and coalitions to seek to use the government for their own benefit. Eventually nearly everybody except taxpayers and consumers in general had a voice in the state capitals and in Washington, DC, demanding largesse, subsidies, privileges, protections from competition, and other favors. Legislators were happy to trade such favors for votes—politicians who declined to do so lost out in the political competition to those who would. This expansion of interest group activity naturally fostered a continuous growth of government in many different areas.

The Warfare State

Nowhere was the role of government magnified more than in international affairs. Traditionally, the United States had pursued a relatively modest foreign policy, complying for the most part with Washington

and Jefferson's advice to steer clear of entangling alliances and, especially, of the endless quarrels among the great European powers.
Although the United States had gained overseas colonies from the
Spanish-American War and although Woodrow Wilson's intervention
in World War I had constituted a highly significant deviation from the
country's traditional foreign policy, still, on the eve of World War II
the great majority of Americans favored a policy of neutrality, peaceful commerce with the people of all nations, and avoidance of military
interventions abroad. The war, however, shattered the old convictions
and arrangements irreparably.[6]

  The United States emerged from World War II as the world's richest
and most militarily powerful country, and its leaders soon determined
to follow a long-term policy of global military engagement in pursuit of
national security. In 1947 President Harry S. Truman proclaimed the
"Truman Doctrine," an open-ended pledge to assist virtually any government threatened by communists, whether from within or without.
To secure the U.S. position in Europe, the U.S. government devised
the Marshall Plan and entered into the North Atlantic Treaty, the first
formal U.S. alliance since the one with France during the American
Revolution. The Berlin crisis in 1948, the Communist victory in China,
the Soviet nuclear test, the establishment of the North Atlantic Treaty
Organization (NATO) in 1949, and the outbreak of the Korean War
in 1950 tipped the balance permanently in favor of a policy of active
global containment and deterrence of the USSR. For the next four decades there would be no distinct peacetime and wartime but instead a
continuing cold war punctuated by episodes of all-too-hot conflict in
Korea, Vietnam and, on a smaller scale, many other places. Maintenance of the postwar warfare state had tremendous repercussions for
all aspects of American life—economic, political, social, and cultural.[7]

  From 1950 to the late 1960s, the dominant cold war ideology and a
bipartisan consensus on defense and foreign policy, focused on global
containment of communism and deterrence of a Soviet attack on the
United States or its allies, gave nearly unchallenged support to the
unprecedented allocation of resources to the peacetime military establishment. Though weakened under the strains of the Vietnam War controversy and its political aftermath, both the ideology and the consensus persisted, now subject to considerable fraternal squabbling, notably
in Congress. President Ronald Reagan's rhetorical hostility toward the
Soviet Union's "evil empire" and the hawkish posture of his administrat
ion,especially during the first term, gave renewed luster to the tarnished

cold war ideology and preserved its vitality until the USSR had left the scene.[8]

The ideological climate was important—indeed, essential—in maintaining high levels of resource allocation to defense, but it was not sufficient. Ordinary citizens, almost none of whom had any direct contact with communists menacing the United States, easily came to suspect that maintaining the nation's security did not require such vast expenditures and that military interests, especially the uniformed services and the big weapons contractors, were spending far more than was necessary to deal with external threats. Frequent newspaper and television reports of waste, fraud, mismanagement, and bribery fostered the public's tendency, absent a crisis, to doubt what the defense authorities said. The underlying cold war ideology, however, created the potential for political leaders periodically to arouse the public's slumbering apprehensions.

Episodic crises offset the tendency of the background threat to lose its effectiveness in sustaining public support for high levels of military spending. Some crises presented themselves—for example, when the North Koreans crossed the 38th parallel in 1950 and when the Soviets invaded Afghanistan at the end of 1979—but ordinarily world events did not present such clear-cut cases. To maintain public interest in defense spending, the authorities alerted the public to a series of ominous "gaps." Just after World War II, U.S. leaders exaggerated Soviet force levels and offensive capabilities. A bomber gap in the mid-1950s became a missile gap between 1958 and 1961, followed within a few years by an antimissile gap and a first-strike missile gap. All were revealed in due course to have been false alarms. Meanwhile the American people received an almost wholly fictitious account of an incident in the Gulf of Tonkin in 1964, after which Congress gave its blessing to what soon became a major war. Subsequent gaps were alleged with regard to bombers (again), thermonuclear megatonnage, antisubmarine capabilities, and missile throw weights. An influential group of Republican hawks, calling themselves the Committee on the Present Danger, declared the 1970s to have been a "decade of neglect" that opened a dangerous "window of vulnerability." According to Secretary of Defense Caspar Weinberger, an "enormous gap" had "emerged since 1970 between the level of Soviet defense activities and our own," though fortunately the Reagan administration had "managed to close much of this gap." Subsequent events suggest that the alleged defense spending gap of the 1970s was largely illusory, the product of faulty methods of estimation. Still, as the cold war passed through its twilight years, government officials were warning that the country faced a space-based missile defense ("Star Wars") gap that could be closed only by spending vast amounts of money.[9]

Although not every gap scare led directly to a corresponding U.S. response, the succession of such episodes helped sustain an atmosphere of tension and insecurity that fostered the maintenance of an enormous ongoing arms program. Claims about gaps placed the burden of argument on relatively ill-informed opponents of military spending who were already vulnerable to charges of insufficiently robust patriotism or worse transgressions. During the cold war, the government adopted a rigorous cult of secrecy. Although some secrecy served a legitimate military purpose, some also merely protected U.S. policymakers from the public whose interest they ostensibly served. As one analyst observed, "what no one knows, no one can criticize." When the government released information, it did so in a way that served its own interests and embarrassed its critics.[10]

When the national security elite lacked persuasive strategic rationales to present to the public, they could only draw on the pool of patriotism, but that was not a bottomless reservoir, and without replenishment in a form that the public could understand and support, it tended to run dry. As the balance of public opinion became strongly negative, it worked its way through political processes, reaching both Congress and the administration, to affect the allocation of resources to the military establishment. Such negative feedback occurred strongly during the latter stages of the Korean and theVietnam Wars.[11]

The biggest problem for the defense authorities arose from that proverbially inevitable duo, death and taxes—the most evident manifestations of the costs of extensive commitments of resources to military purposes. Of the two, death was the more important. Statistical models fitted to public opinion data gathered during the Korean War and the Vietnam War show that in both cases "every time American casualties increased by a factor of 10, support for the war dropped by about 15 percentage points." Smith reported public opinion data showing that "complaints about taxes were high during the two limited wars and increased as the wars progressed." Discontent with U.S. engagement in the Asian wars fostered Dwight D. Eisenhower's electoral victory over incumbent Harry S Truman in 1952 and led to Lyndon B. Johnson's decision not to seek reelection in 1968.[12] The situation has repeated itself since September 11, 2001, when al Qaeda terrorists flew commercial airplanes into the World Trade Center towers and the Pentagon. A surge in American fears of further attacks led to a rapid rise in patriotic fervor and a willingness by many to support invasions in Afghanistan and Iraq as part of the War on Terror. Prior supporters lost faith when Iraqi weapons of mass destruction, the focus of the cries for war, were not found. Support diminished still further as the daily reports of deaths and injuries accumulated into the thousands after the war was "won."

Immediately after the end of World War II, military spending fell sharply: in inflation-adjusted dollars, it dropped by nearly 90 percent between fiscal years 1945 and 1948, after which it rebounded substantially, rising by almost 50 percent during the next two years, as the Truman administration sought to rebuild the military establishment to back up its foreign policy of resisting and containing the USSR and its satellites on a global scale (see table 17.1). A far greater change occurred, however, after the outbreak of the Korean War: real defense outlays jumped by 126 percent between fiscal years 1950 and 1953. The bulk of that increase, though, went not to fight the war in Korea but to strengthen overall U.S. forces and to deploy many of them around the world, especially in western Europe and Japan. Although military spending shrank somewhat after the 1953 armistice in Korea, it remained thereafter much greater than during the late 1940s—about 200 percent greater.

Atop the permanent cold war plateau of military spending, three distinct upsurges came and went. During the early years of the twenty-first century, a fourth upsurge began whose peak, at the time of this writing, remains impossible to forecast. The upsurge of the early 1950s was the biggest whether measured in percentage terms, relative to the size of the

Table 17.1 NATIONAL DEFENSE OUTLAYS, FISCAL YEARS 1945–2003

Fiscal year	National defense outlays (bil. 1996$)	Percent of federal budget	Percent of all net gov't. budgets	Percent of GDP
1945	717	89.5	82.1	37.5
1946	366	77.3	65.2	19.2
1947	99	37.1	27.3	5.5
1948	77	30.6	19.9	3.6
1949	109	33.9	23.0	4.8
1950	114	32.2	21.8	5.0
1951	186	51.8	34.8	7.3
1952	352	68.1	50.5	13.2
1953	372	69.4	52.2	14.1
1954	341	69.5	50.0	13.0
1955	285	62.4	43.2	10.8
1956	265	60.2	41.0	9.9
1957	270	59.3	40.2	10.1
1958	267	56.8	38.3	10.2
1959	268	53.2	36.4	10.0

(*continued*)

Table 17.1 (Continued)

Fiscal year	National defense outlays (bil. 1996$)	Percent of federal budget	Percent of all net gov't. budgets	Percent of GDP
1960	273	52.2	35.1	9.3
1961	274	50.8	33.8	9.3
1962	287	49.0	32.9	9.2
1963	282	48.0	32.0	8.9
1964	287	46.2	30.8	8.5
1965	265	42.8	27.8	7.4
1966	292	43.2	28.4	7.7
1967	347	45.4	30.3	8.8
1968	378	46.0	31.3	9.5
1969	361	44.9	29.4	8.7
1970	339	41.8	27.0	8.1
1971	309	37.5	23.7	7.3
1972	283	34.3	21.7	6.7
1973	255	31.2	19.9	5.9
1974	245	29.5	18.7	5.5
1975	241	26.0	16.9	5.5
1976	232	24.1	15.7	5.2
1977	230	23.8	15.8	4.9
1978	231	22.8	15.4	4.7
1979	237	23.1	15.5	4.6
1980	245	22.7	15.4	4.9
1981	259	23.2	15.9	5.1
1982	282	24.8	16.9	5.7
1983	305	26.0	17.8	6.1
1984	309	26.7	18.1	5.9
1985	331	26.7	18.1	6.1
1986	354	27.6	18.4	6.2
1987	361	28.1	18.2	6.1
1988	365	27.3	17.6	5.8
1989	370	26.5	17.0	5.6
1990	355	23.9	15.3	5.2
1991	310	20.6	13.2	4.6
1992	327	21.6	13.7	4.8
1993	314	20.7	13.0	4.4
1994	298	19.3	12.1	4.1
1995	282	17.9	11.1	3.7
1996	266	17.0	10.5	3.5
1997	265	16.9	10.3	3.3
1998	260	16.2	9.9	3.1
1999	261	16.2	9.7	3.0
2000	271	16.5	9.8	3.0
2001	276	16.4	9.6	3.0
2002	308	17.3	10.3	3.4
2003	327	17.6	10.6	3.5

Source: U.S. Department of Defense 2003, 206–7, 216–17.

federal budget, or relative to the overall economy (see table 17.1). The Vietnam War brought about an upsurge of roughly 43 percent between fiscal years 1965 and 1968. The Reagan buildup of the 1980s, which actually began during the latter part of the Carter administration, pushed real military outlays up about 56 percent between fiscal years 1979 and 1989. After each upsurge, spending fell back toward or even slightly below the level of the cold war plateau. In fiscal year 2001, a decade after the breakup of the USSR, however, real military outlays were as great as they had been during the height of the cold war in the late 1950s and early 1960s, although the United States no longer had any current or potential military rival in sight. Its invasions of Afghanistan in 2001 and Iraq in 2003, followed by military occupation and ongoing combat operations against resistance forces in those countries, fostered greatly increased arms spending. Legislation enacted late in 2003 ensured that U.S. military spending in fiscal year 2004 would be greater than at any time since World War II.[13]

The immense military spending during the sixty years after World War II fostered the operation of a new politico-economic arrangement that had assumed its modern form during the early 1940s: the military-industrial-congressional complex (MICC). Before leaving the presidency in 1961, Dwight D. Eisenhower warned in his farewell speech to the American people against "the military-industrial complex," which he characterized as the "conjunction of an immense military establishment and a large arms industry" and whose influence, he feared, posed dangers to "our liberties or democratic processes." Beginning in the 1960s and gaining impetus during the 1970s and 1980s, congressional involvement grew ever greater as members of Congress sought to turn military-industrial funding and operations to their own political advantage—hence the congressional component of the MICC. Each incumbent senator and representative works to "bring home the bacon" to the home district and keep it there. A failure to do so spurs fears of defeat in the next election. As an example, the Department of Defense had been seeking to close a series of military bases for a decade starting in the 1970s, but pork-barrel negotiations in Congress prevented individual closures, as did requirements that an environmental impact statement be filed for each closure. Only after Congressman Richard Armey and one hundred others co-sponsored a bill with an all-or-nothing list of bases to be closed could the Defense Department succeed in closing down bases it no longer wanted. Even then the political negotiations were complicated as congressman from districts facing base closures sought other forms of redress. Observers experienced déjà vu in 2005, when a new all-or-nothing base closing bill was introduced. Only the locations and the names of (some of) the Congressmen had changed.[14]

Of all the government's military measures, none loomed larger for the personal liberties of the American people than the military draft, a system of compulsory service employed during both world wars and extended repeatedly during the cold war until the Nixon administration sponsored its ultimate abandonment in 1973. Over the years, millions of young men suffered involuntary induction into the military services, usually the army, and millions of other lived in fear that they might be snared, often taking otherwise undesirable actions, such as relocation to foreign countries or extended enrollment in college or seminary, merely to reduce their risk of conscription. Not only were these inductees paid, in cash and in kind, well below the wages they would have earned in civilian jobs, but hundreds of thousands of draftees lost their lives in the U.S. wars of the twentieth century. Although in most respects the government has grown more powerful and intrusive during the postwar era, the abolition of the draft and the development of an all-volunteer military constitutes a tremendous advance of personal liberty.

The Warfare State and Research and Development

Besides funding gigantic military-industrial operations, the government also funded for military purposes a huge part of the most advanced scientific and technological research and development in the late 1940s and 1950s. Such developments led Eisenhower to warn also against the "danger that public policy could itself become the captive of a scientific-technological elite." To some extent Eisenhower's fears proved justified, although historians and other observers continue to debate the extent to which, and the precise manner in which, the nation's permanent military mobilization shaped its social, political, technological, and economic institutions and conduct.[15]

No one can deny the vast repercussions of militarily motivated activities. During World War II, the military dominated research and development even more than it had the economy as a whole. Under the time pressure of the need to "develop it or lose the war," the Manhattan Project developed nuclear weaponry, which contributed the technologies that led to later development of nuclear power plants. Crash wartime programs sped the development of penicillin, the microelectronics associated with radar, synthetic rubber, and the early vacuum-tube computers. After the war the Defense Department, the National Bureau of

Standards, and the Census Bureau were among the few organizations with sufficient needs for making calculations to provide the demand for the cumbersome room-size computers of the late 1940s and 1950s. Meanwhile, the military continued its demand for improved nuclear technology, missile guidance systems, and communications. Such militarily motivated enactments as the Interstate Highway Act of 1956 provided the basic plan for building the national system of interstate and defense highways The National Defense Education Act of 1958 gave the federal government another big foot in the door of higher education, following hard on the heel of the first big foot, the GI Bill of 1944.[16]

These interactions led to a quite different structure of research and development (R&D) institutions than had been in place prior to World War II. Contemporaries in the early 1900s saw the rise of the corporate research laboratory, in which large companies often borrowed foreign technologies and developed them for commercial uses inside the United States. Aside from federal funding of agricultural research, university research received relatively little government support. During and after World War II, a symbiotic relationship developed among the federal government, universities, and businesses. The federal government, particularly the military, was the leading financier of U.S. research during the Korean War and the early phases of the cold war. Between 1953 and 1964 the federal share of R&D spending rose from 54 to 67 percent, and the military share accounted for 48 percent of total R&D in 1953, peaking at 54 percent in the late 1950s. Since then, business R&D spending has risen rapidly, causing the federal government's share to fall below 30 percent by 2000. Meanwhile, the military share declined to 24 percent by 1980, peaked again during the Reagan buildup, and declined below 15 percent on the eve of September 11, 2001. Unlike many other countries, the United States allows government- and military-funded research to be performed largely by universities and private firms. Research performed and financed by federal agencies fell from only 20 percent in 1953 to 7 percent circa 2000, replaced by a rise from 8 to 15 percent in federally funded university research.[17]

The level of U.S. research and development spending in the postwar era has been the highest in the world, and the United States currently ranks in the top five countries in R&D spending as a share of GNP. Various studies attribute a substantial portion of U.S. economic growth in the twentieth century to technological changes and improvements in workforce productivity. No one questions the importance of military R&D in maintaining the nation's standing as a world power.

The potential free-rider problems associated with the public good features of national defense suggest that the national government is probably the appropriate funding source. Government also has a role in funding basic civilian research with external benefits to society in the accumulation of knowledge that we cannot immediately anticipate. The economic questions raised about federal military and basic research dollars are centered more on determining the optimal amount and assessing the extent to which military R&D leads to spillover benefits in the private economy. Many military innovations have limited spillover benefits to the rest of society, either because they are focused on death and destruction or because the "do or die" atmosphere of technological development raises costs of development and production in ways that make it difficult to transfer them to consumer products. Military spillovers are most commonly seen where the military seeks to resolve problems that are similar in nature to what would arise in the commercial sector. Yet this raises an important question. Would the same or fewer resources spent in the commercial sector have led to similar or more feasible innovations that fit the needs of consumers better.[18]

The Military and the Development of the Internet

The development of the modern Internet and World Wide Web offers a good case study of these issues. The military played a central role in financing the early development of cross-computer networks and communications that eventually formed the backbone of the Web. Ironically, the development of the Internet and personal computers has probably done more for personal liberty worldwide than most innovations of the twentieth century. Like most innovations, the Internet and the Web have come about through the interaction of literally hundreds if not thousands of innovations. The interactions between the military and the National Science Foundation with universities and private companies sped the development of the Web in some ways but slowed it in other ways.[19]

The original military funding in the 1960s for cross-computer communication was meant to set up durable communications systems that would allow the U.S. to retaliate in response to a first-strike missile attack by the Soviets. Military funding for Paul Baran at the Rand Corporation allowed him to develop the theories of packet-switching (breaking messages into multiple same-size units), networks with multiple nodes, and random resending of packets and other error correction methods that became the basis for the operation of the Net. Computer science funding from the Department of Defense's Advanced Research Projects Agency (ARPA) in the 1960s and 1970s gave university and business researchers the resources to build on these theories to develop hardware and software protocols such as FTP (file transfer protocol) and TCP/IP (transmission control protocol/Internet protocol) that are found on modern PCs. Students who trained at these institutions expanded on the research, and some became the leading entrepreneurs of the commercial Internet boom.

The military funding contributed spillover benefits to the development of the commercial Internet for several reasons. First, the military only loosely controlled the projects. No one anticipated that the true "killer app" of the ARPANET would be email, developed in 1972. Most of those messages, already with the funky @ in the address, involved discussions of sci-fi, sex, drugs, and rock and roll, moves in long-distance chess matches, and the occasional remote printing of a dissertation or paper. Bob Kahn, a leading developer of the ARPANET and the Internet, observed that ARPA "would never have funded a computer network in order to facilitate email" because the telephone already served person-to-person communications well. Second, the military encouraged the researchers to widely disseminate their work, figuring in game-theoretic fashion that if both sides knew that the other had durable communications that would survive a first strike, they would be less likely to choose mutually assured destruction. Third, the military was willing to fund small firms, contributing to a significant wave of start-ups.[20]

Throwing large amounts of resources at smart people sped the early development of the ARPANET, but military security limited access to a relatively small number of universities and consultants until the early 1980s, when a separate military Net was spun off and the ARPANET was opened to more researchers. The National Science Foundation funded an NSFNET backbone in the early 1980s that eventually replaced the ARPANET but legally NSF funding could not be used for commercial purposes. Such restrictions were particularly problematic because the value of a network is raised substantially when more people have access. Ultimately, in the mid-1990s, the NSFNET was shut down, and the Internet has been run by a wide range of competing service providers since.[21]

The Internet was clearly a case in which military research eventually spilled over into the private sector. Would we have seen a version of the modern Internet in a counterfactual world with no military funding? You bet. The alternative version likely would have been different because innovation is a path-dependent process, in which each new development relies on prior findings. Even with more limited non-military funding, most of the key participants, the brightest computer minds at the leading schools, likely would have received some funding either from the NSF or the private sector. In the 1960s the NSF funded computer science research at schools with no ARPANET dollars, so there is little doubt that the NSF would have shifted funding to the AR-PANET schools in the absence of military financing. Other researchers without military funding, such as Donald Daviess, developed packet-switching theories for use in British telecommunications independent of Paul Baran, although a few years later. Researchers funded by the NSF at the University of Delaware established regional computer net-works with alternative protocols for addressing packets.[22]

In the absence of government funding we likely would have had email systems and a substantial World Wide Web, although it might have arrived more slowly. By the late 1970s there were all sorts of alternative ways of operating email, electronic "bulletin boards," chat rooms, news-groups, and electronic newsletters that were developed using Unix on AT&T's time-sharing systems, IBM protocols, and personal computers with modems.[23] Xerox, seeking to develop the paperless office, funded the extraordinarily innovative Palo Alto Research Center (PARC), where researchers, many with ARPANET experience, developed an in-credible array of innovations: ethernet local area networks, laser print-ers, BITMAPS for color monitors, word-processing programs, and the graphical user interface (GUI) used by Apple and Windows. When Xe-rox failed to exploit most of the innovations, the researchers themselves commercialized them through companies such as 3COM, Microsoft, Apple, and Adobe. Meanwhile, the use of GUI by Internet service pro-viders such as CompuServe, America Online, and Prodigy gave large number of personal computer users easy access to other computers.[24]

Ultimately, researchers at the CERN particle physics research lab in Europe developed the first World Wide Web based on ideas first written up in 1974 in Ted Nelson's *Computer Lib,* a counterculture manifesto calling for "the people" to gain control of computers. The CERN team developed and distributed HTML (hypertext mark-up language) to for-mat Web pages, HTTP (hypertext transfer protocol) to help browsers and servers exchange information, and the URL (uniform resource locator) to establish the computer address and application protocol of the page. Marc Andreessen and a team of researchers at the University of Illinois NSF supercomputer site soon developed the MOSAIC Web browser and then left to commercialize a "MOSAIC killer" by developing the Netscape browser. Netscape's success, in turn, led Bill Gates and Microsoft to bundle a Web browser with its operating system. The browser "war" led both companies to distribute their browsers for free, and the rapid expansion and investment in Internet businesses in the late 1990s was off and running.[25]

The case study illustrates that military financing played a central early role in the actual development of the Internet and the World Wide Web. The military's role was clearly sufficient to develop the early technologies, but arguably it was not necessary. The credit for these technologies should go to the actual people performing the research. Most were likely to have been involved in a less defense-focused institutional structure. The role of the National Science Foundation in funding basic research in computer science might have been more difficult to replace, but there was enough private activity that this was possible as well.

Other Government Policies Toward Innovation

The federal government's policies regarding innovation were not confined to financing or procurement. A key to commercial use of the Internet, for example, was the moratorium on taxes on the Internet passed by Congress in 1998. The moratorium was recently extended in 2004 but not without considerable debate because opponents of the moratorium abhorred the "lost" tax revenue. Tax subsidies for investment and environmental and safety regulations have influenced the path of innovations in many industries.[26]

Property rights in ideas and innovation have always had conflicting impacts on technology by creating incentives to invent via the award of short-term monopoly rights to the inventor but slowing diffusion as the monopolist seeks profits by charging licensing fees that are above competitive levels. Supreme Court decisions handed down in 1898 and 1908 that tightened patent protections and the streamlining of application processes by the Patent Office enhanced the development activities of corporate labs in the prewar era. Meanwhile, the relatively weak legal protections of intellectual property in the computer and microelectronics industry contributed to rapid innovations in software through the mid-1990s. Specific software code could by copyrighted, but any change in the code that still accomplished the same objective did not infringe the copyright. In 1996 the U.S. Patent Office began to allow for software patents. Since then, a number of large firms have begun to develop portfolios of patents, and some policymakers fear that innovation in software might be slowed because the creation of software relies heavily on the cumulative body of software written earlier.[27]

Antitrust policies, particularly threats of costly antitrust suits, have strongly influenced the development of technology. Corporate research labs arose in the early 1900s in part due to Justice Department antitrust policies that threatened action against dominance in a single industry but allowed for efforts to develop new technologies and diversify into new industries. Ironically, this likely led to a more oligopolistic structure in the pre–World War II economy as firms that conducted more R&D were more likely to stay among the top two hundred firms throughout that era. From 1938 through the 1970s a series of consent decrees made it tougher for large firms to acquire firms in "related" technologies or industries. This worked either to increase the size of firms or to lead to new start-ups, depending on the setting. Large firms performed more internal research, which led to further expansions, whereas other firms followed conglomeration strategies that combined products into one firm with few technological links. In contrast, in microelectronics and computing liberal licensing and cross-licensing policies were driven in part by 1956 consent decrees that settled antitrust suits against IBM and AT&T. The break-up of AT&T in 1984 led to more competition in telecommunications, in large part due to built-in pricing advantages given to MCI, Sprint, and other AT&T competitors. High-tech industries held their breath while awaiting the outcome of an antitrust suit against Microsoft for its bundling of the Internet Explorer browser with the operating system and other strategies. After the U.S. District Court ruled against it, the Appeals Court in 2001 gave more leeway to Microsoft, and the settlement with the Department of Justice that followed allowed Microsoft to retain the right to bundle new software into its operating system while limiting its control of the desktop screen on personal computers and preventing other practices.[28]

The Welfare State

Parallel to its vastly enlarged tasks as an international military power, the postwar U.S. government inherited from the New Deal and the wartime command economy a panoply of greatly expanded activities at home, especially in managing the domestic economy. After experimenting with temporary emergency relief and public works programs designed to right the listing economic ship of the 1930s, the federal government formalized its role as macroeconomic overseer by enacting the Employment Act of 1946. The act declared that "it is the continuing policy and responsibility of the Federal Government to use all practicable means . . . to promote maximum employment, production, and purchasing power." Thus it became the federal government's permanent policy to prevent macroeconomic malfunctions such as the Great Depression. Henceforth, "doing something" would be official policy, although the precise nature of the "something" would vary with political circumstances and calculations.[29]

As Keynesian economics became generally accepted in the 1960s, the government tinkered with government spending and taxation, occasionally raising spending and cutting taxes to "lean against the wind" during recessions. Monetarism, rational expectations, and adaptive expectations theories came to the fore in the 1970s as the economy experienced the despair of "stagflation," combining the twin evils of high inflation and high unemployment at the same time. After inflation in consumer prices reached a peacetime high above 11 percent in 1979 and 1980, Federal Reserve chairman Paul Volcker followed a monetarist prescription of tightening monetary policy. After the resulting anticipated recession in 1982 and 1983, inflationary expectations appear to have been wrung out of the economy, and the nation has experienced relatively low inflation rates since.[30]

Ronald Reagan had run for president in 1980 on a platform of rolling back the government's role in the economy. In 1986 he succeeded in cutting personal income tax rates (the top rate fell from 50 to 28 percent) to promote the supply-side agenda of eliminating disincentives to work. The cut was designed to be revenue-neutral, however, and therefore it called for a substantial increase in taxes on businesses. As a result, federal tax receipts relative to gross domestic product remained above 17 percent, the same level as during the recession in 1983. In fact, Reagan and George H. W. B ush looked far more like Keynesians than any of the peacetime presidents. Federal outlays exceeded an unprecedented 22 percent of the GDP level in most years of the Reagan and George H. W. Bush presidencies, and the budget deficit exceeded 4 percent relative to GDP in more than half the years in their terms. Only the Truman and Ford administrations in 1946 and 1976, respectively, had reached such budget deficit levels after World War II. Bill Clinton and a Republican Congress handed off the only budget surpluses that the United States has seen since the mid-1950s to George W. Bush, who then proceeded to cut personal income tax rates from the levels reached after his father's failure to keep his pledge—"Read my lips. No new taxes"—and the Clinton tax rate increases. This move and the recession at the end of the Internet boom contributed to a decline in receipts to

15.7 percent of the GDP level and an increase in the budget deficit above 4 percent of GDP by 2004. In the past twenty-five years, the economy has managed to experience recessions only once every decade, a highly unusual run for a U.S. economy that typically saw recessions once every three to seven years prior to 1980. Some observers attributed this to luck given the muddled statements made about budget policies by the politicians making the decisions. Many suggest that the key to this success has been the wizardry practiced by Federal Reserve head Alan Greenspan, who held a highly pragmatic view of the Fed's role in influencing interest rates and the money supply.

Although the federal government's acceptance of responsibility to reduce unemployment is a post–New Deal phenomenon, it is a myth that prior to the New Deal the United States had a brutal laissez-faire economy. The roots of the modern welfare state wind deeply through American history. Local governments always provided a modicum of relief to the destitute who had no one to help them. After the Civil War the federal government extended its veterans' pension system to cover hundreds of thousands of northern veterans and their dependents. Soon after 1910 the states adopted workmen's compensation systems to insure workers against injuries on the job. By the early 1930s, almost all states paid "mother's pensions" to impoverished widows with young children, thirty states had adopted old-age relief payment legislation, and twenty-eight states offered aid to the blind.[31]

The Social Security Act of 1935 created joint state-federal versions of the public assistance programs for mothers (Aid to Dependent Children, or simply "welfare"), the aged, and the blind. That landmark federal statute also offered state-administered unemployment insurance (subject to federal requirements) and old-age pensions. So, by the beginning of the postwar era, the United States already had a fairly well developed welfare state, although at that time it served relatively few beneficiaries and cost relatively little—not until 1960 did annual Social Security payments exceed $10 billion (see table 17.2). During the 1950s, 1960s, and 1970s, members of Congress repeatedly raised the amounts of existing benefits, expanding the types of benefits (for example, adding disability insurance in 1956), and easing the eligibility requirements for receiving benefits. In addition, minimum wages and prescribed working conditions, first provided by permanent federal law in 1938, fleshed out the postwar welfare state. Much more important, the GI Bill of 1944 provided a variety of benefits—including educational stipends and loan guarantees for the purchase of homes, farms, and businesses—to millions of veterans of the Big One and set an irresistible precedent for Congress.

Table 17.2 GOVERNMENT EXPENDITURES, TOTAL AND SELECTED COMPONENTS, FISCAL
YEARS 1948–2002

| Fiscal year | Total government spending | Defense and international spending | Federal payments to individuals | | State and local spending from own sources |
			Social Security and Medicare	Other	
1948	42.3	13.7	0.5	8.5	12.3
1949	52.6	19.2	0.6	9.5	13.6
1950	57.9	18.4	0.7	12.9	15.2
1951	61.8	27.2	1.5	8.8	16.1
1952	85.0	48.8	2.0	8.9	17.1
1953	94.4	54.9	2.6	8.3	18.1
1954	90.3	50.9	3.3	9.3	19.2
1955	90.0	45.0	4.3	10.0	21.1
1957	101.9	48.6	6.5	10.5	24.8
1958	110.6	50.2	8.0	12.9	27.6
1959	122.5	52.2	9.5	13.2	29.7
1960	124.7	51.1	11.4	12.8	31.7
1961	133.3	52.8	12.2	15.3	34.7
1962	145.2	58.0	14.0	14.9	37.3
1963	151.9	58.7	15.5	15.5	39.5
1964	162.3	59.7	16.2	16.0	42.5
1965	165.5	55.9	17.1	16.0	46.2
1966	186.0	63.7	20.3	16.8	50.4
1967	214.3	77.0	24.5	18.7	56.0
1968	242.4	87.2	28.4	21.4	63.2
1969	257.6	87.1	33.0	24.2	73.1
1970	278.3	86.0	36.4	28.4	81.9
1971	304.4	83.0	42.6	38.0	93.0
1972	333.5	84.0	47.7	45.3	100.7
1973	354.9	80.8	57.2	47.5	107.2
1974	393.3	85.1	65.7	54.7	123.3
1975	475.4	93.6	77.7	76.2	142.6
1976	531.9	96.1	89.6	91.0	157.8
1977	585.5	103.6	104.5	92.5	173.1
1978	646.0	112.0	116.7	95.0	185.8
1979	709.5	123.8	130.8	103.1	206.9
1980	820.3	146.7	151.0	127.5	234.0
1981	934.9	170.6	179.1	146.1	263.8
1982	1032.8	197.6	203.1	155.3	294.7
1983	1118.7	221.8	224.0	172.9	315.8
1984	1182.3	243.3	237.0	164.9	336.6
1985	1303.9	268.9	256.1	172.0	365.4
1986	1379.5	287.5	270.7	181.3	395.3
1987	1435.6	293.6	285.0	187.1	434.9
1988	1524.6	300.8	302.5	199.1	463.5
1989	1634.6	313.1	324.4	212.9	497.0
1990	1789.5	313.1	353.8	231.9	543.0
1991	1906.2	289.1	380.7	271.3	585.2
1992	2002.8	314.5	414.3	315.5	619.4

(*continued*)

Table 17.2 (Continued)

Fiscal year	Total government spending	Defense and international spending	Federal payments to individuals		State and local spending from own sources
			Social Security and Medicare	Other	
1993	2062.6	308.3	444.8	340.3	647.9
1994	2142.9	298.7	476.2	348.6	675.9
1995	2229.3	288.5	510.1	367.4	712.2
1996	2299.4	279.2	538.1	374.7	738.2
1997	2376.4	285.7	569.4	384.4	775.5
1998	2465.4	281.6	586.2	395.5	812.9
1999	2561.3	290.1	595.2	406.4	859.6
2000	2718.9	311.7	621.0	433.3	932.6
2001	2863.5	322.0	666.1	462.2	1002.0
2002	3050.7	370.9	704.6	539.8	1041.6

Source: U.S. Office of Management and Budget 2003, 296.

Note: Figures are in billions of current dollars.

The first fifteen years of the postwar era brought relatively few new welfare-state measures. The country seemed content for the most part to digest the many legacies of the New Deal and the war. When ambitious New Dealer Lyndon B. Johnson became president late in 1963, the drive to expand the welfare state became ascendant again. Johnson's landslide victory over conservative Barry Goldwater in 1964 was accompanied by the election of large Democratic majorities in both houses of Congress. The landslide was seen as a public mandate to expand the government's role in the economy. Keynesian economists were assuring the public that they could fine-tune the economy, taking for granted a high rate of economic growth from which the government could reap a perpetual "fiscal dividend" to fund new programs. John Kenneth Galbraith, Michael Harrington, and other popular social critics condemned the failures of the market system and ridiculed its defenders. The public seemed prepared to support new measures to fight a "War on Poverty," establish "social justice," and end racial discrimination—hence the Great Society.[32]

Congress proceeded to pass a variety of statutes injecting the federal government more deeply into education, job training, housing, and urban redevelopment. The Food Stamp Act of 1964 gave rise to one of the government's most rapidly growing benefit programs: in 1969, fewer than three million persons received the stamps, and federal outlays for the program totaled $250 million; in 1981, twenty-two million persons received the stamps, and federal outlays for the program totaled $11 billion.

The Community Action Program aimed to mobilize the poor and to raise their incomes. When Congress appropriated $300 million to create community action agencies, a wild scramble to get the money ensued, led by local politicians and, in some cities, criminal gangs—as vividly portrayed in Tom Wolfe's tragicomic tale *Radical Chic and Mau-Mauing the Flak Catchers* (1970). In 1965 Congress effected a huge and enduring federal intrusion into basic public education—traditionally a local government matter—by enacting the Elementary and Secondary Education Act. Aid to Dependent Children expanded resources to provide for more benefits in the form of Aid to Families with Dependent Children.[33]

Although the growth in scope of the welfare state slowed after the mid-1970s, it did not stop—and the Reagan administration certainly did not reverse the growth, as conservative Republican legend maintains. Democratic president Bill Clinton, in negotiations with Republicans who had gained control of Congress promising a new "Contract with America," tightened the standards for remaining on assistance with the passage of the Temporary Assistance to Needy Families (TANF) Act in 1996. A reduction in the number of recipients and the average length of time on welfare rolls followed, although some of the reductions are attributable to a booming economy at the time.

The largest expansion in social insurance and public assistance came in the form of programs for the elderly. In 1965, Congress added Medicare to the Social Security system, ensuring medical care for everyone over sixty-five years of age. Simultaneously, Medicaid, a cooperatively administered and financed (state and federal) program, assured medical care for welfare recipients and the medically indigent. In the early days the federal payments crowded out the charitable treatment of the indigent. "Most of the government's medical payments on behalf of the poor compensated doctors and hospitals for services once rendered free of charge or at reduced prices," historian Allen Matusow has observed. "Medicare-Medicaid, then, primarily transferred income from middle-class taxpayers to middle-class health-care professions."[34]

The federal government's health programs became fiscal time bombs, as Medicare outlays (excluding premiums paid by beneficiaries) rose to $256.8 billion and federal Medicaid outlays rose to $147.5 billion by 2002. Like Social Security's old-age pensions, the federal health programs grew at a rate that could not be sustained indefinitely. All federal health programs together consumed 7.1 percent of total federal outlays (equivalent to 1.4 percent of GDP) in 1970 and 23.5 percent of total federal outlays (equivalent to 4.6 percent of GDP) in 2002.[35]

In the past fifteen years, as the elderly have become a major political force in America, serious reform of Medicare and Social Security has been considered the "third rail" of American politics. Touch the rail and watch your political ambitions sizzle into smoke. After winning reelection President George W. Bush grabbed the rail and proposed fixes to the system, including allowing a limited amount of money to be put into private accounts. The private accounts have some appeal because they give individuals ownership and control of the investments in their accounts. Social Security benefits for the recently retired yield a very low rate of return on all of the taxes the retirees had earlier paid into the system. There are fears that the private accounts will lead to people choosing investments that are too risky, thus leading to a bailout for those individuals when their chosen investments fail. But there are risks that benefits will have to be cut in the regular Social Security system as well.

The "iron rules of the pay-go" system for Social Security old-age pensions require that the current tax revenues at least equal the current payments to retirees for the system to work. As the ratio of retirees to workers continues to rise, either higher taxes will have to be borne by society's working generations or benefits will have to be cut, either by lowering the ratio of benefits to earnings from roughly 40 percent or raising the retirement age. In the past sixty years the nation has seen several Social Security tax increases, and the retirement age at which full benefits are paid has increased by two years. One 2005 proposal called for future benefits to rise at the same rate as the cost of living—setting benefits based on the standard of living at the time of retirement—rather than the current practice of having them rise at the same rate as wages, which allows retirees to share in advances in the average standard of living. It remains to be seen whether Congress and the president succeed in a reform that fixes social security. The "fix for all time" of the 1980s, regrettably, did not work for long.[36]

The debates about Social Security have masked the potentially more serious problems that analysts believe will arise in funding Medicare. The rapid growth in medical expenses, particularly in the last year of life, seems as if it will continue for some time. Yet in the face of that rapid growth, Congress and George W. Bush added an enormously expensive prescription drug benefit to the Medicare system late in 2003, a benefit whose cost is certain to exceed even the huge projected amounts before long.

Public assistance and protection against income risk extend well beyond the low-income segments of society. In fact, the payments to the poor fall well short of the benefits provided to companies and those with higher levels of incomes. In countless ways, postwar governments actively engaged in doling out subsidies, some of them direct (for example, cash and in-kind services), others indirect (for example, tariffs on competing imported products). Agricultural interests, which began to reap such subsidies early in the twentieth century, acquired them whole hog during the latter half of the century, as seen in chapter 15. Defense contractors also gained huge subsidies, often disguised as reimbursed costs in their supply contracts for military goods and services.

Once the federal government got into the business of extending college loans, millions of college students every year became the beneficiaries of credit extended at below-market rates of interest. Government loan guarantees likewise effectively subsidized a multitude of business and household borrowers. The entire real-estate sector became pervaded by various forms of subsidized lending. Joseph P. Stiglitz observed in 1989, "In the US today, approximately a quarter of all lending (to the private sector) is either through a government agency or with government guarantees. . . . The magnitudes of the implicit subsidies and costs—both the total value, and who receives how much—are hidden."[37] Inspection of the government's organization chart reveals many federal agencies that supply subsidized credit (for example, the Maritime Administration, the Small Business Administration, the Export-Import Bank, the Farm Credit System, and the Rural Utilities Service). Besides doling out subsidized credit and loan guarantees to privileged recipients, the postwar U.S. government has stood ready to bail out firms deemed "too big to fail," whether they be defense contractors (for example, Lockheed in 1974), industrial firms (for example, Chrysler in 1979), banks (for example, Continental Illinois Bank in 1984), or other financial institutions (for example, Long-Term Capital Management in 1998), regardless of whether bad luck or bad management brought them to the brink of bankruptcy. Because loan guarantees do not automatically entail a government outlay, their extension ordinarily does not leave any trace in conventional measures of the size and growth of government.

Regulation

Ever since the establishment of the British colonies in North America, governments have engaged in regulating certain economic and social activities, the details differing from place to place and over time. In the nineteenth century, nearly all such regulation and subsidization took place at the state and local levels, and governments at those levels have continued to involve themselves actively right up to the present day. Only in the late nineteenth century did the federal government begin to engage in important, enduring forms of such intervention (aside from the de facto subsidies associated with tariff protection). Thereafter, during "normal" times the federal government gradually added to the scope of its interventions. Moreover, each of the great crises of the first half of the twentieth century—the two world wars and the Great Depression—became the occasion for government officials to expand their interventions abruptly.

As a result, by the beginning of the postwar era, federal regulators had entrenched themselves in agriculture and food processing, banking and finance, corporate and industrial organization and trade practices, airline, railroad, and highway transportation, telecommunications and radio broadcasting, oil and gas production and distribution, electricity transmission, coal mining, maritime shipping, labor-management relations, pharmaceutical innovation and marketing, international trade and finance, nearly every labor market, and many other areas of economic life. One might have thought that the scope of regulation in the late 1940s was more than sufficient in what was still described as a market economy, but evidently the politically potent actors thought otherwise, because despite a few significant reversals (most of them in the late 1970s and early 1980s), the scope of regulation and subsidization continued to grow during the following half-century. Anyone who believes that the current U.S. economic system is accurately described by the term *capitalism* or *market system* needs to take a closer look at the current *Code of Federal Regulations.*[38]

During the Korean War, the federal government reinstituted many of the World War II–era controls over industrial production, wages, prices, credit, shipping, and the allocation of raw materials. This time the controls did not bind as tightly or as comprehensively as before, nor did they last as long. Most were permitted to lapse by the war's end in 1953, although some, such as the Defense Production Act of 1950, remained on the statute books as a framework for future mobilizations (and to facilitate continued subsidies to selected defense contractors).[39]

The Great Society Regulations

During the presidential terms of Dwight D. Eisenhower and John F. Kennedy, the United States took a respite from the imposition of significant new federal regulation of economic activities. The period from 1964 through 1975, however, during the Lyndon B. Johnson and Richard M.

Nixon presidencies, brought forth a deluge of new regulations comparable only to the torrent unleashed during the heyday of Franklin D. Roosevelt's New Deal.

Congress loosed a legislative flood of new regulations aimed at preventing discrimination based on race, sex, age, or handicap: the Civil Rights Act of 1964, the Equal Pay Act of 1963, the Age Discrimination in Employment Act of 1967, and later the Americans with Disabilities Act of 1990 and the Civil Rights Act of 1991. The acts were passed with the laudable goals of trying to ensure equality of treatment in politics, the economy, and society in general. The original ideal of the civil rights movement and the 1964 act was a color-blind society. Within a few years, however, there was a shift toward "affirmative action." Affirmative action originally was meant as a means of giving a helping hand to people who suffered disadvantages based on prior discrimination. Over time affirmative action has become the centerpiece of efforts to promote diversity throughout society. It has aided many members of the designated groups. See, for example, the impact of the laws relating to African Americans in chapter 8. At the societal level many forms of segregation, intimidation, and limits on opportunity that were obvious and commonplace in the 1950s are rare and considered unthinkable by the generations born since. As is the case for many laws, there were unintended consequences. Increases in the likelihood of antidiscrimination litigation over employment separations has raised the anticipated costs of hiring minorities at companies where the first few months traditionally are periods of assessing job candidates, leading in some cases to an economic chill on minority hiring. The legislative and judicial push and pull over affirmative action policies reveals an undercurrent of antagonism between groups that may have been worsened by the preference policies themselves. Finally, a highly litigious environment combined with an emphasis on political correctness has imposed increasing limits on the freedoms of speech, the press, association, and the practice of religion long guaranteed by the First Amendment.[40]

Many Great Society regulations were meant to protect people, including the Cigarette Labeling and Advertising Act of 1965, the Fair Packaging and Labeling Act of 1966, the Child Protection Act of 1966, the National Traffic and Motor Vehicle Safety Act of 1966, the Flammable Fabrics Act of 1967, and the Consumer Credit Protection (Truth-in-Lending) Act of 1968. The regulations tend to be most successful when they control practices that have long-range impact that consumers find difficult to gather information about. But the passage of regulation is a political process wherein lobbying by powerful interests and compromise are common. The high-minded titles of the complex acts in some cases were misleading descriptions of the actual regulations, and specific segments of the regulations matched already prevailing practices by most firms or the rules benefited some firms by reducing competition from other firms that faced high costs of meeting the regulatory standard.

The regulatory change in the 1960s that likely had the biggest impact on modern society was the expansion of the authority of the Food and Drug Administration (FDA) in 1962. Since that date, the FDA has become steadily more powerful, exercising regulatory control over goods that account for roughly 25 percent of all consumer spending—processed foods, pharmaceuticals, medical devices, and cosmetics, among others. The FDA's regulation of pharmaceuticals and medical devices offers a number of insights into the development of protective regulations. It illustrates the expansion of public demands for regulation in times of crisis, the steady expansion of regulatory authority via administrative decisions between major legislative changes, and the complicated evaluation of costs and benefits of various regulatory regimes.

The FDA was created in its modern form by the Food, Drug, and Cosmetic Act of 1938, a response to the tragedy that arose when the Massengill Company tried developing a liquid form of the medicine Elixir Sulfanilamide by dissolving it in the chemical equivalent of antifreeze. The act provided that firms demonstrate their product's safety to the FDA before marketing the product. After the rapid expansion in wonder drugs during the 1940s, concerns about the marketing of drugs led to the Humphrey-Durham amendment of 1951, which codified the difference between prescription and nonprescription drugs. In the late 1950s antitrust hearings into the pharmaceutical industry coincided with another tragic after-effect, the flipperlike hands and feet of infants born to women who were given thalidomide as a cure for morning sickness. The Kefauver-Harris amendments to the Food, Drug, and Cosmetic Act in 1962 gave the agency much greater control over drug-testing procedures, and more important, expanded the FDA's mandate to insure not only the safety of a new drug but also the effectiveness of the drug in dealing with the condition it was purported to treat. Ironically, thalidomide is now approved as a treatment for multiple-myeloma cancer patients. Later amendments and administrative decisions about adequate testing continued to increase the cost and time lag in the development of pharmaceuticals. Meanwhile, the FDA, via the Medical Device Amendments of 1976, the Safe Medical Devices Act of 1990, and a series of administrative rulings, was expanding its role as gate-keeper

for the development of medical devices and it oversight of existing production of medical devices.[41]

Most of the expansion in FDA regulatory authority, whether legislated or achieved by incremental changes in interpretation and administration of existing law, has served to delay and raise the costs of introduction of new drugs and medical devices. Estimates suggest that the shift
from focusing only on safety to also requiring effectiveness raised the
costs of getting a drug approved between threefold and tenfold in the
1960s and 1970s relative to the pre-1962 era, and costs appear to be doubling every ten years or so since. The delay between first application and
approval rose from six years in the 1970s to eight years in the 1980s. The
FDA is two years slower than British agencies in approving drugs, and
the result has been a shift by many companies toward production and
testing of drugs and medical devices in other countries. At the same time
the FDA has sought increased authority over cigarettes and the herbal
and organic remedies that have become popular alternative therapies.[42]

The FDA's incentives are all weighted toward taking great care and
time to prevent an unsafe or ineffective drug from appearing on the
market because the administration has faced very high costs in the form
of bad publicity and loss of jobs when approved drugs are found to be
dangerous. This focus has a grisly cost because delays in approval of
successful drugs also mean lives lost or diminished by pain and suffering. One illustration is the FDA commissioner's March 1988 ban (now
rescinded) on advertising the fifty-percent reduction in first heart attacks for middle-aged males associated with taking an aspirin a day.
The reason? Aspirin had not gone through the approval process for
preventing heart attacks. Although the Federal Trade Commission, not
the FDA, oversaw advertising of aspirin, an over-the-counter medicine,
the companies acceded to the ban to avoid angering the FDA regulators who decide about approval of their other products. The companies
avoided the large costs of the approval process because the information
was widely known among doctors, who could prescribe medicines for
conditions not covered by FDA testing. The ban meant that after the
initial burst of media reports of the studies, consumers reaching ages at
which heart health becomes an issue have since learned about the heart
benefits haphazardly through word of mouth and occasional newspaper
articles. Many first found out about the benefits from their doctor after
experiencing their first heart-related event, too late for those struck by
a heart attack with no warning. It has been estimated that tens of thousands of lives per year may have been lost during the advertising ban.[43]

Over the past twenty years the FDA has responded to increased criticisms of the delays and costs of approving drugs by trying to streamline procedures. In the late 1980s legislation was passed to allow it to give "priority review" to drugs treating life-threatening or severely disabling conditions, including AZT for AIDS sufferers and L-Dopa for Parkinson's disease. Yet in 2005 recent discoveries of heightened risks of heart failure with pain relievers such as Vioxx and problems with pacemakers led FDA officials to respond to public criticism by talking of exercising further caution in approving drugs and even tighter regulation of medical device production.[44]

During this period both market institutions and the courts also have served to "regulate" the drug industry. Consumers have found decent information about the effectiveness of drugs and medical devices in medical journals, consumer reports, consultations with doctors, National Institute of Health studies, and advertising of brands by companies with the intention of remaining in business for the long run. Access to information has been eased by the recent expansion of the Internet. Court regulation came in the form of product liability claims. Successful claims forced negligent firms to pay large penalties in the form of replacement of the successful plaintiffs' lost earnings, medical bills, funds for pain and suffering, and punitive damages, which ultimately served as deterrents to firms marketing unsafe drugs. Yet the liability system has its own imperfections. Large payments were made to many people allegedly injured by silicone breast implants even though the science suggested no connection between implants and injury. Meanwhile, some companies established subsidiaries with few assets to shield the main company's assets from liability claims. Further, litigation often lasted several years and resulted in costs paid to lawyers, expert witness, and the courts that led to large gaps between the amounts paid by the negligent company and those received by the injured party. Little wonder that most claims are settled out of court. Theoretical and empirical work on the optimal mix of reliance on markets, regulation, and liability rules depends on complicated interactions between administrative costs, negotiations costs, information costs, and the operations of product and insurance markets. The interactions are complex enough that there is no single answer that can be applied to all settings.[45]

Nixon's Regulatory Expansion

After Richard Nixon became president, regulations continued to pour forth from the federal government, including wage and price controls and long-term regulatory regimes established by the Occupational Safety and Health Act of 1970, the Consumer Product Safety Act of 1972, the Equal Employment Opportunity Act of 1972, and the Employee Retirement Income Security Act of 1974, and a series of environmental regulations. The wage and price controls had tremendous short-term effects, whereas the environmental regulations continue to influence nearly all aspects of modern American life.

By his willingness to sign so many significant regulatory acts, the supposedly conservative Nixon displayed his political hallmark: he was, above all, an opportunist. Nothing illustrates that opportunism better than his imposition of mandatory wage and price controls, anathema to conservatives, in August 1971. Twenty-five years later, Herbert Stein, a member and later chairman of Nixon's Council of Economic Advisers, characterized the adoption of the controls as utterly heedless of the longer term. Recalling the meetings at which the plan was laid, Stein wrote: "Even after 25 years I am amazed by how little we looked ahead during that exciting weekend at Camp David, when we (the president, really) made those big decisions." Everybody seemed to have assumed without discussion that after a ninety-day wage-and-price freeze, the government would somehow ease back to a regime of flexible prices. "As it turned out, we were in the price and wage control business not for 90 days but for nearly 1,000. [Moreover, w]e were in the business of controlling energy prices for much longer." [46]

If Nixon could not be bothered to look ahead, he surely had a keen view of—some might say, an obsession with—the past. He believed that he had lost the presidential election in 1960 because of the Eisenhower administration's failure to generate favorable macroeconomic conditions on the eve of the election, and he was determined not to repeat that mistake in 1972. His calculations and machinations proved astute, no matter how wrongheaded they were with regard to serving the general interest. The public, as always, reacted with great approval to the imposition of wage and price controls, as indicated by favorable opinion polls, a soaring stock market, and, most of all, Nixon's landslide reelection. Although Nixon ultimately suffered ignominy when he was driven from office by hostile reaction to his Watergate gambit, his far more damaging economic mismanagement, in contrast, never caused him any personal or political harm whatsoever.

The wage and price controls passed through several phases of greater or lesser stringency until finally, with relief all around, they were allowed to lapse in the spring of 1974. While they remained in force, they gave rise to significant distortions in the allocation of resources and hence to economic inefficiency, and they created congenial conditions for the adoption of unusually bad monetary policies by the Federal Reserve System. Fed policy led to rates of inflation not seen since the 1940s and not squeezed back to tolerable levels until the early 1980s, after the failure of Gerald Ford's Whip Inflation Now (WIN) buttons and the Carter administration's sham anti-inflation program, the so-called wage and price guidelines. Of course, the Nixon wage and price controls did not actually prevent inflation—only changes in the underlying supply of or demand for money can affect its true exchange value—but they did suppress the manifestation of the actual inflation and produce the politically profitable appearance of having been successful temporarily.[47]

The most important legacies of Nixon's wage and price controls were the energy-price controls and allocations that persisted long after the comprehensive price controls had expired. When the first energy crisis struck, the administration was looking forward to disengagement from its no-longer-useful price controls, but given the lingering presence of those controls, the Arab oil embargo and the OPEC price hikes of late 1973 and early 1974 quickly led in many areas to shortages that were rationed for the most part by the customers' waiting in the infamous gas lines. The inconvenience and uncertainty proved to be more than the public could bear and, in William E. Simon's words, "collective hysteria" arose. "The political heat was on both Congress and the executive to solve the problem overnight."[48]

To deal with the crisis, the president created by executive order the Federal Energy Office (which by statute later became the Federal Energy Administration and later still the Department of Energy) and named Simon to head it. Overnight, Simon became the "energy czar," authorized by Nixon "to decide everything and to decide it rapidly." The president equated the energy crisis with a wartime situation. Finding the government's energy allocation procedures tangled and ineffective, Simon and his assistants worked frantically for months to channel existing supplies to the areas with the most desperate shortages. Although eventually some improvements were made and the gas lines shortened and began to disappear by the spring of 1974, the whole arrangement remained fundamentally defective. Simon concluded: "There is nothing like becoming an economic planner oneself to learn what is desperately, stupidly wrong with such a system."[49]

The energy situation got no better as Congress passed ever more complicated energy legislation in the mid-1970s. Inevitably another crisis struck, and early in 1979 the gas lines reappeared. The Energy Department's erratic efforts to fix the problem only made it worse. Only after Ronald Reagan assumed the presidency and scrapped all oil-price controls was the mess permitted to clean itself up via market processes. Even then, however, a complex system of price controls for natural gas lingered for more than a decade until complete decontrol of wellhead gas prices took effect at the beginning of 1993, terminating a forty-year experiment in the federal regulation of natural gas prices that had produced nothing but market distortions and wholly avoidable energy crises.[50]

Environmental Regulation

The Nixon-era regulations with the broadest implications for society today relate to the environment. The new era of environmental regulation began with passage of the National Environmental Policy Act in 1969—the authority for requiring the preparation and approval of a detailed "environmental impact statement" (EIS) for federal construction projects or private projects subject to any form of federal permission. The EIS process immediately became a substantial source of delay, cost escalation, and exasperation for developers. In 1970 Nixon created the Environmental Protection Agency (EPA) to set and enforce environmental standards, consolidating into a single agency about fifteen different federal programs then dealing with air and water pollution, waste disposal, and radiation. The EPA acquired sharper teeth from enactment of the Clean Air Act of 1970 (and later amendments), the Water Pollution Control Act of 1972 (and later amendments), the Toxic Substances Control Act of 1976, and the Comprehensive Environmental Response, Compensation, and Liability Act (often called the Superfund law) of 1980, among other statutes. The EPA quickly became one of the most intrusive and controversial of all federal regulatory agencies, and it has remained so to the present day.

If big corporations have the Commerce Department and labor unions have the Labor Department, then environmental organizations have the EPA—none of this, of course, without great ongoing ideological, political, and legal struggle. Yet the environmental organizations have not had free reign because they have had to counteract lobbying activities by a broad range of labor, business, and state and local government interests. Trade associations in some highly profitable industries succeeded in lobbying for water discharge standards for total suspended solids and biochemical oxygen demand that imposed much higher costs on other industries than on theirs. Business and interest-group lobbies strongly influenced the regulation of chemical ingredients under the pesticide rules. The choice of Superfund clean-up sites was influenced by pressures from legislators in particularly powerful positions. Meanwhile, congressmen from the Northeast imposed nationwide standards that raised costs in other regions in ways that kept northeastern industries from losing jobs and factories to the rapidly growing West and South. These interest-group pressures did not keep the regulations from actually focusing on health and environmental hazards. In fact, environmental policy in the United States has tended to be more proactive than in many countries. In general, countries similar to the United States in protecting both economic freedoms and civil liberties tend to spend more on eliminating pollution and have lower emission levels than the rest of the world.[51]

One important issue for environment policy is the appropriate location for government responsibility in the federal system. Economic theories of federalism suggest that the optimal assignment of responsibility should be imposed at the lowest level of government that fully encompasses the costs and benefits of the program. Thus, environmental problems with lead in the local water supply would best be handled by city or county governments, while higher levels of government might be required to act when pollution of rivers by plants in one city caused problems for other cities downstream. The main fear expressed about focusing environmental policy below the federal level is that state or local governments might "race to the bottom" in setting standards as they try to attract jobs and businesses to their communities. Several but not all studies of moves toward state and local standard-setting do not find evidence of a race to the bottom. In some cases communities have moved toward setting more exacting standards than had previously been set by the federal government.[52]

How successful have the environmental regulations been? It depends on careful measurement of the benefits and costs of the regulations. The majority of EPA regulations listed in table 17.3 focused on promoting health by limiting pollution. Pollution problems arise when property rights are poorly specified. The classic example is air pollution. No one owns the atmosphere, so people damaged by air pollution from a factory cannot obtain appropriate compensation for their losses. This is a failure of the American property rights system as much as or more than of markets because polluters do not bear the full costs of their pollution and thus the full costs of the hazards are not incorporated into market prices for the goods. Regulation is one of several alternatives that might be effective at reducing pollution.

Table 17.3 Cost-benefit assessments of key environmental acts

Program	Date passed	Goal	Overall net benefits	Discussion of net benefits
Clean Air Act	1970	Protect human health by limiting pollution from sulfur dioxide, nitrogen oxides, particulate matter, carbon monoxide, ozone, and lead;	Positive	Benefits from reducing mortality and chronic bronchitis substantially outweighed the costs of pollution controls (Freeman 1982, 2002).
		reduce particulates and emissions from factories and other stationary sources;	Positive	See above
		cut tailpipe emissions for new cars by up to 90 percent by mid-1970s with further cuts afterward;	Negative	Costs of pollution controls far exceeded small improvements in health and death rates (Freeman 1982, 2002).
		gasoline lead controls after 1985	Positive	Health benefit improvements significantly outweighed the costs (Freeman 2002).
Clean Water Act	1972	Fishable and swimmable bodies of water	Negative	Measured costs much larger than the benefits from modest improvements in nationwide water quality. However, certain very bad bodies of water were cleaned up "dramatically." In study of eight rules established between 1981 and 1996, costs were 20 times larger than benefits, but one rule between 1990 and 1995 had positive net benefits (Hahn 1996, 2000).
Safe Drinking Water Act	1974	Improved safety of drinking water	Positive	Cost per cancer death avoided of $4.7 million similar to values of life for relatively cost-effective programs. Costs of eliminating 10 most cost-effective compounds even lower at $2.9 million. Eliminating some other compounds cost about $127 million per death avoided (Raucher et al. 1993). Eliminating lead highly beneficial (Troesken 2005; Hahn 2000).

(continued)

Table 17.3 (CONTINUED)

Program	Date passed	Goal	Overall net benefits	Discussion of net benefits
Toxic Substances Control Act	1976	Improving health by limiting toxic substances	Negative	Asbestos bans led to cost per cancer case avoided of over $70 million (Van Houven and Cropper 1996).
Superfund	1980	Cleanups of sites with hazardous materials	Mixed	Cleanup at small number of sites cost less than $3.5 million per cancer death avoided. Cleanup at roughly 70 percent of sites cost more than $112 million per cancer death avoided (Hamilton and Viscusi 1999).
Federal Insecticide, Fungicide, and Rodenticide Act	1972	Reduction of health dangers from use of pesticides	Negative	Six major rules had established costs that far exceeded benefits quantified or identified by the EPA (Hahn 2000). Study of re-registration of pesticides in 245 cases found cost of $70 million per cancer case avoided (Van Houven and Cropper 1996).
Endangered Species Act	1973	Protection of species in danger of extinction	Negative	A few species removed from list are no longer in danger. More species removed from endangered status when further investigation showed they should not have been on list in the first place. In some cases very high costs to property owners and workers (Mann and Plummer 1995, 239–50; Simmons 2005b).

Sources: Cost-benefit analysis results for all but the Endangered Species Act are summarized in Freeman 2002 from various analyses of EPA studies performed by various environmental economists. The Endangered Species Act studies were performed in Mann and Plummer 1995 and also summarized in Simmons 2005b.

It is generally agreed that the EPA has been successful at dramatically cutting air pollution, improving the quality of drinking water, modestly improving the ability to fish and swim in many bodies of water, pressing for the cleanup of hazardous wastes, and reducing exposure to toxic substances. Yet these improvements came at a substantial cost. In nearly all cases, the American economy saw reductions in productivity to achieve these goals. One estimate suggests that GNP in 1990 might have been as much as 20 percent lower than it would have been without the acts overseen by the EPA. Although the original Clean Air and Clean Water Acts explicitly ignored the costs of the cleanups, several presidential executive orders have required the EPA to report estimates of costs and benefits from a variety of their programs. The benefits of the programs have been measured as reductions in the loss of life and acute chronic illnesses associated with exposure to the pollutants. These improvements are then converted into monetary values by estimates of the value of lives lost, medical costs, and lost income associated with illness. The monetary values are then compared to the EPA's costs of monitoring the environment and the costs to businesses of reducing the pollutants.[53]

Some see these as grisly and irrelevant calculations on the grounds that a human life cannot be measured in monetary terms. Yet societal institutions commonly make such calculations to reward injured parties. Workers' compensation laws list values for loss of life or body parts, and liability suits place values on lives all the time. When people choose to take a higher-paying but more dangerous job or to pay less for cars without airbags, they are implicitly weighing monetary values of potential injury or loss of life against monetary costs. Most estimates of how much people demand in terms of wages to accept greater risk or are willing to pay for less safe autos suggest that people's market decisions imply a statistical value of a life of between $1 million and $11 million dollars.[54]

Table 17.3 shows the results of a series of economic studies comparing the economic benefits and costs of the programs. The data in many cases were collected by the EPA and then reanalyzed by government or academic economists. Some EPA regulations have led to benefits that substantially outweigh the costs, including the portions of the Clean Air Act that called for factories and other stationary polluters to cut particulate emissions and the elimination of lead from gasoline in 1985. On the other hand, the EPA reductions in automobile tailpipe emissions in 1975 saved few lives and imposed quite large costs, and regulations for some pesticides and asbestos have cost more than $70 million for every cancer death prevented. Under the Superfund law s and the Clean Water Act, some cleanups of bodies of water and hazardous waste sites have been highly beneficial. In the majority of cases, however, water quality improvements were small, and the Superfund cleanups cost well over $112 million per cancer death prevented at some sites.

Such calculations of costs and benefits can be highly subjective. The studies summarized in table 17.3 focused on the health benefits mentioned prominently in the acts and the costs associated with the cleanups. The benefits may be understated to the extent that the flora, fauna, and other features of the environment are better protected by the regulations. Some may decide that values of human life should be much higher than the roughly $5 million typically incorporated in many studies. Others claim that the costs inadequately consider new technologies for cleanups, but the win-win situations in which the company simultaneously becomes "more green" and more productive have been overwhelmed by the settings where the costs of production have risen sharply in broad-based studies of the economy.

The cost side might also be understated. Many environmental economists suggest that the EPA cost-benefit calculations are too optimistic. The more subtle and not easily measured aspect of the regulations is the lost opportunity for development caused by the intrusiveness of regulations and the limitations on property rights that result. A recent study of housing prices across urban America suggests that increasingly tight regulation of land use has restricted the housing stock enough to raise housing prices significantly since 1970. One source of regulation has been the Endangered Species Act (ESA), which seeks to preserve habitats for species in danger of extinction, although with very little success at actually restoring species to the point where they could be removed from the list (see table 17.3). The ESA has been more successfully used by coalitions of environmental groups and existing homeowners to limit development and protect local amenities that include the natural environment. In African countries the use of positive economic incentives, such as purchasing land to protect elephant habitats, for example, proved far more effective than prior rules that simply made it illegal to harm elephants. The Nature Conservancy has been following a similar successful strategy of purchasing land to preserve natural environments. Over the past fifteen years environmental policy has recognized some of the problems associated with command-and-control types of regulation and have allowed polluters who find it costly to reduce emissions to purchase permits from other polluters who face much lower costs of complying with EPA standards. The early results of these market-based programs suggest that they have succeeded at reducing the costs of reducing pollution.[55]

Deregulation in Some Industries

Nearly all regulatory agencies and programs face periods of severe criticism. From time to time the critics succeed in slaying a regulatory dragon. The most notable episode of such counterattack occurred in the late 1970s and early 1980s when a slew of deregulatory statutes gained enactment. The upshot was the reduction or elimination of several forms of economic regulation that had been in place since the 1930s or earlier. In 1978 Congress passed the Airline Deregulation Act, providing for the gradual deregulation of commercial airlines. In accordance with this statute, the Civil Aeronautics Board ceased allocating domestic routes in 1981, stopped regulating fares in 1983, and closed up shop entirely in 1985—an exceedingly rare occurrence in the world of regulation. Airline passengers gained major benefits from the CAB's disappearance, which opened up competition A cluster of statutes implemented between 1976 and 1984 reduced the extent of the government's regulation of transportation by railroads, trucks, and buses, again with major benefits to consumers. At the end of 1995 the Interstate Commerce Commission, the oldest independent federal regulatory agency, dating to 1887, was abolished and its remaining functions transferred to the Surface Transportation Board in the Department of Transportation. Financial institutions were partially deregulated in 1980 and 1982, and telecommunications underwent revolutionary changes when a federal court ruling broke up the Bell Telephone System in 1984. After the mid-1980s, the deregulatory movement lost its momentum, and not much significant deregulation occurred during the following two decades.[56]

The deregulatory episode was an aberration. Much more notable was the relentless, ongoing flood of regulations, many of which purport to protect health, enhance safety, or prevent discrimination, that poured forth every year on the strength of the multitude of existing statutes authorizing agencies to impose such rules at all levels of government. As late as the 1950s the *Federal Register*—the official announcement of each year's new final and proposed rules—contained only 107,000 pages for the entire decade; the ten-year total jumped to more than 450,000 pages in the 1970s. It continued to rise in each decade thereafter, and in the early years of the twenty-first century it was running at a rate of more than 731,000 pages per decade. Federal regulatory agencies alone now issue more than four thousand new rules each year, and state and local regulators add countless others. Hardly ever is an old rule removed from the books, and so the aggregate mass of regulations in effect grows ever more immense, as even a casual inspection of the fifty volumes of the *Code of Federal Regulations* attests.[57]

Fiscal Dimensions of the Growth of Government

A great deal of the growth of government has taken forms that do not leave heavy footprints in government budgets. The bulk of the cost of regulations, for example, takes the form of higher private costs, higher prices, and sacrificed individual liberties. Yet a great deal of the expanded activity has required spending increasingly large sums of money, obtained by continuing to withhold and collect income taxes from the vast majority of the public. Table 17.2 provides data about certain dimensions of the fiscal growth of government in the postwar era.[58]

By the measures presented in the table, government grew enormously during those fifty-five years. Before considering just how much it grew, however, one might consider one or two adjustments. First, one might wish to adjust the data for changes in the purchasing power of the dollar. Because the government allowed the money supply to grow throughout the entire postwar period, the dollar's purchasing power has fallen 85 percent (alternatively, one can say that the overall price level rose by a factor of more than 6.5, according to the official chained price index for GDP). Thus, merely to maintain the same level of real expenditure, governments would have needed to spend more than 6.5 times more in 2002 than in 1948. Second, one might wish also to adjust for changes in the population, which increased by 91 percent during this period. Multiplying the dollar-depreciation factor (6.55) and the population-growth factor (1.91), one finds that government would have needed to increase its spending by a factor of approximately 12.5 in order to maintain the 1948 level of real expenditure per capita. One should recognize that the United States in 1948 was an economically advanced and relatively civilized country with actively engaged governments at all levels.[59]

Looking first at the growth of the total expenditures of all governments—federal, state, and local—between 1948 and 2002, one sees that they grew by a factor of 72, or almost six times the amount necessary to maintain the 1948 level of real expenditure per capita. The spending component associated with the nation's expansive global military activities (shown under the rubric "Defense and international spending" in table 17.2), grew by a factor of more than twenty-seven, or by more than twice what was needed to maintain the 1948 level of government. The greatest growth of all, however, occurred in the welfare-state elements of the budget, the transfer payments shown under the rubric "Federal payments to individuals" in the table (as well as those, not shown separately, that compose a substantial part of the state and local spending shown in the rightmost-right column). Federal Social Security and Medicare expenditures expanded by a mind-boggling factor of 1,409, while "other" federal transfer payments expanded by a factor of almost 64. Although the federal government's growth was in many respects the most remarkable, the state and local governments plunged into the tax-and-spend fray with full force as well. Spending at those levels of government (from their own revenue sources) increased nearly 85-fold, or by nearly seven times more than the amount needed to maintain the 1948 standard of real spending per capita. The growth was even greater if the amounts financed by federal revenue-sharing are included.

Perhaps the most notable aspect of the postwar growth of government was its relentlessness. In fifty-five years, only twice (in 1954 and 1955) did total government spending decline, and then only because of a $10 billion cutback in defense spending after the fighting ended in Korea (see table 17.2). From time to time over the years, defense spending fell slightly for a while, but not once did Social Security and Medicare spending fall, and not once did state and local spending (from state and local revenue sources) fall. Thus, besides relying on the certainty of death and taxes, Americans also could expect with complete confidence that every year the postwar welfare state would spend more dollars. The entitlements system, whereby governments fix an eligibility formula and then make transfer payments to everyone who fits that formula, has effectively placed the growth of the welfare state on autopilot for a guaranteed steep ascent.

Conclusion

"The natural tendency," said Thomas Jefferson, "is for government to gain ground and liberty to yield." Yet until the early twentieth century, the growth of government in the economy, especially the federal government, remained slow by comparison with its growth afterward. The difference between the two eras reflects in various degrees the political consequences of accumulating long-term structural changes (urbanization, industrialization, improvements in transportation and communication, and so forth), the enduring effects of great national emergencies (especially the world wars and the Great Depression), and the political consequences of ideological changes that favored the growth of government and were themselves fostered in part by the structural changes and the national crises. These fundamental changes promoted the formation of political interest groups in great and growing abundance, each seeking in some way to use the power of government to promote its members' ends at the expense of the general community, and the combination of ideological change and political maneuvering brought about the abandonment of constitutional doctrines that had long helped restrain the growth of government. The upshot was that by the beginning of the postwar era nothing fundamental remained to restrain the rapid growth of government except workaday political wrangling, and the politicians proved resourceful in working around their differences in order to provide something for everybody (everybody, that is, who possessed political resources and was organized for effective political action). Thus, nature has taken the course that Jefferson long ago perceived as its tendency. To be sure, the growth of government cannot continue forever, if only because an increasingly voracious predator ultimately must destroy its prey and therefore its means of sustenance. At present, however, there is no end in sight.[60]

For some, the foregoing account of the postwar growth of government and the consequent shrinkage of private property rights and economic liberties may seem unbalanced. Where else, they might ask, can we find so much security of private property rights and such expansive economic liberties as in the United States? Sure enough, in systematic studies of economic freedom, the United States in recent times always stands near the top of the ranking of the world's nation-states. Even today, people throughout much of the world look to the United States as a safe haven for their investments and bank deposits and as a relatively free labor market in which workers can find ample opportunities for well-compensated employment. Still, there is no contradiction between these undeniable facts and the vast growth of government in the United States since World War II. Government has grown enormously in *all* the economically advanced countries during this era. Despite that growth, the U.S. economy remains, overall, relatively free of government burdens and restraints. Nonetheless, the search for security by its nature has increasingly limited individual freedoms over time. As a British admirer of the United States remarked recently, "If the Americans today remain the freest people in the world, that is only because they started with so much more to lose."[61]

Notes

1. This chapter could not have been written without the support of Robert Higgs, who provided much of the organization, many of the insights, and his flair for writing.

2. Jouvenel 1993 [1945], 388–89. For many details of the dominant security-obsessed ideology of the postwar era, see Twight 2002, McClosky and Zaller 1984, and Page and Shapiro 1992.

3. The quotations are from Corwin 1947, 179.

4. Fallbrook Irrigation District v. Bradley, 164 U.S. 112 (1896); Strickley v. Highland Boy Gold Mining Co., 200 U.S. 527 (1906); Berman v. Parker, 348 U.S. 26 (1954); Hawaii Housing Authority v. Midkiff, 467 U.S. 299 (1984).

5. The path of U.S. Supreme Court decisions concerning "public use" in takings is provided in Kelo et al. v. City of New London et al., No. 04-108 (June 25). The quotations are from pp. 15, 36 and 37. The calls for lobbying are found in Mary Deibel, "Property Rights Issue Causing Legislative Woes across Nation," *Las Vegas Sun,* July 31, 2005, D1, D6; the story about the "taking" of Souter's home is in "They Paved Paradise: Joni Mitchell and Property Rights," *Wall Street Journal,* June 30, 2005, A12. The Supreme Court has made a series of decisions that have protected social rights, including reading of an arrestee's rights (the *Miranda* warning) and several aspects of the right to privacy. Privacy rights are a source of ongoing controversy, in part because their protection is central to the *Roe v. Wade* decision regulating abortion.

6. This section draws heavily on Higgs 1994a.

7. See Sherry 1995 and Leebaert 2002.

8. See Neu 1987, 91–92, 100–01; Rockman 1987, 18, 28–29; and Ambrose 1985, 221–22.

9. See Weiner 1990, 19–45, on the series of gaps, Kolodziej 1966, 77, on the immediate post-war period, Page and Shapiro 1992, 227–28, on the Gulf of Tonkin, and Weinberger 1987, 17, for the quotations about the 1970s and 1980s. The economist Franklyn D. Holzman (1992, 34) charges that the CIA's choice of methods was a "deliberate attempt [by the CIA, the DIA, and possibly the administration] to mislead our policy makers and the public."

10. The analyst is quoted in Sapolsky 1987, 122. On government information releases, see Page and Shapiro 1992, 172–284, 367–72.

11. Higgs and Kilduff 1993.

12. Statistical relationships between public opinion and war deaths were developed by John Mueller (1973, 60–61). The quotations are from Smith 1971, 250.

13. Higgs 2001.

14. The quotation is from Eisenhower 1961, 653. For discussions of the MICC, see Higgs 1989, 31; 1993. The base closings process is described by Stamato 1993.

15. The quotation is from Eisenhower 1961, 654. For the debates see Sherry 1995, Friedberg 2000, and Leebaert 2002.

16. See Mowery and Rosenberg 2000 on technologies arising from war programs; Fisher, McKie, and Mancke 1983 for discussions of early computers; Patterson 1996, 274, on highways; and Twight 2002, 143–54, on education.

17. See Mowery and Rosenberg 2000. The calculations are based on National Science Foundation 2003.

18. The standing of the United States is based on information in National Science Foundation 2003. The role of technology in promoting growth is discussed in Mowery and Rosenberg 2000 and Barro and Sala-i-Martin 2004.

19. The facts about the rise of the Internet in this section are from Abbate 1999, Cringely 1996, Segaller 1998, and Naughton 2000. The researchers who developed the innovations are a fascinating group of iconoclasts who are described in depth in these books. None of the authors address the counterfactual question of what would have happened in the absence of military funding. In fact, Abbate states that her purpose is to show the importance of defense financing to its development. My interpretation does not contradict her findings. She shows that the military financing played an important role. Her chapter 6, however, shows the incredible array of activity going on in other sectors, which buttresses the point made here that military funding was likely not necessary to have a functioning Internet today.

20. Kahn is quoted in Segaller 1998, 105.

21. See Abbate 1999, chap. 6. There was no guarantee that commercial access would have led to more rapid advancement of commercial uses. In fact, AT&T passed on an opportunity to purchase the ARPANET in 1972 on grounds that it was incompatible with their switching networks and that it was a competing technology to their primary business. However, AT&T and eventually the companies formed in the break-up of AT&T did develop commercial networks (Abate 1999, 195; Segaller 1998, 108–9).

22. On path dependence and technology, see David 1985 and Liebowitz and Margolis 2001.

23. Abbate 1999, chap. 6 included a Unix computer language feature called UUCP (Unix-to-Unix Copy) that was soon used to send email, distribute electronic newsletters, set up newsgroups, and ultimately form USENET. Email, chat rooms, and ultimately BITNET were built on IBM's RJE (remote job entry) protocol. Personal computer (PC) users with phone modems began posting messages on "bulletin boards" on host PCs, leading to message exchanges such as FidoNet. Despite skirting bankruptcy in the late 1970s, Telenet became a major force in interconnecting personal computers in the 1980s.

24. Segaller 1998, 159–74; Cringely 1996, 80–92, 106–111; and Abbate 1999, chap. 6.

25. Abbate 1999, chap. 6, Segaller 1998, 296–318, and Liebowitz and Margolis 2001, 219–23. The term "MOSAIC killer" is from Segaller 1998, 300.

26. Gross (2004) reports on the extension of the Internet moratorium. R. Nelson (1982) edited a superb and thoughtful volume by several scholars on government policy and technical progress in semiconductors, commercial aircraft, computers, agriculture, pharmaceuticals, autos, and residential construction.

27. Mowery and Rosenberg 2000; Thakur 2003. Some scholars ascribe a large role in technological advancement to the Bayh-Dole Act of 1980, which gave universities and small businesses the right to patent innovations that resulted from government research, but David Mowery (2005) suggests that Bayh-Dole was largely a continuation of a long-term trend in that direction.

28. The case is United States of America v. Microsoft Corporation, 253 F.2d 34 (2001). See Mowery and Rosenberg 2000, 826–29, Liebowitz and Margolis 2001, and James et al. (2002).

29. This section draws heavily on Higgs 1987, 246–56, and Higgs 1996. The quotation is from "Employment Act of 1946," 514–15.

30. Monetarism emphasizes the role of changes in the money supply in influencing economic activity and inflation. Rational expectations and adaptive expectations models emphasize the importance of the public's knowledge of federal macroeconomic policy. To the extent that people can rationally anticipate the government's plans, macroeconomic policy will have little influence over real GDP or unemployment and will likely manifest itself in the form of changes in the price level. Adaptive expectations models allow for people to have less information about the path of government policy and thus we would see short-term adjustments in GDP and unemployment in response to policy changes until people recognize the changes. For a discussion of the Volcker disinflation, see Goodfriend and King 2005. See also the discussions in the volume edited by Feldstein (1994).

31. See Fishback and Thomasson 2006; Ziliak and Hannon 2006.

32. Higgs 1987, 246–51.

33. The information about food stamps comes from Browning and Browning 1983, 128. Johnson and the congressmen who sought the 1965 education bill emphasized the War on Poverty; however, the actual structure of the bill left many loopholes through which aid leaked away from the poor. The act established a formula that multiplied a child poverty measure by a share of the typical amount of spending in the district. Richer school districts received more per poor child because of their higher average spending levels, and there were no guarantees that the money would be spent on the poor children or on the schools in the poor districts. See Twight 2002, 154–64.

34. Matusow 1984, 231–32.

35. The figures from U.S. Office of Management and Budget 2003, 299.

36. For the "iron rules of pay-go" and a lucid discussion of the economics of Social Security past, present, and future, see Scheiber and Shoven 1999.

37. Stiglitz 1989, 63.

38. The code can be found on line at http://www.gpoaccess.gov/cfr/index .html.

39. Williams 1954, 64–66; Higgs 1987, 244–46.

40. See Bernstein 2003, Glazer 1975, and Sowell 1984, 38–42.

41. Hansen 1995, Regan 2003, and Temin 1980.

42. See Hansen 1995, DiMasi 2001, and Regan 2003. Comanor (1986, 1199–1209) offers a careful overview of the studies of the impact of the 1962 regulatory change on the development of new drugs.

43. Rubin 1995; Mann and Plummer 1991.

44. Hansen 1995.

45. See Glaeser and Shleifer 2003 and Polinsky and Shavell 2000 for discussions of the economics of enforcement.

46. The quotations are from Herbert Stein, "Wage and Price Controls: 25 Years Later," *Wall Street Journal*, August 15. For a full account of this episode, see Stein 1984, 133–207.

47. See Higgs 1979a, 1979b, 1980, 1981.

48. Simon 1979, p. 54.

49. Ibid., 50, 55.

50. See Chapman 1980 and Glasner 1985, 130–37 for the gas lines and Bradley 1995 for many historical details about and insightful analysis of the energy industries and their regulation.

51. The discussion of the political economy of environmental regulations is based on the survey by Oates and Portney (2001).

52. See ibid.

53. The cost-benefit discussion is based on Freeman's (2002) survey and the studies cited there. See Viscusi 1992 for discussions of how to measure the value of life in markets.

54. See Hamilton and Viscusi 1999 and Viscusi 1992.

55. For evaluations of the success of the Endangered Species Act, see Mann and Plummer 1995 and Simmons 2005b. For a discussion of alternative methods of protection, see Simmons 2005a.

56. On the deregulatory episode, see Weidenbaum 1986, 178–202.

57. See Crews 2003, 11–12.

58. Higgs 1987, 229–31, and Twight 2002, 87–131.

59. Higgs (1991) argues against the common practice of adjusting government spending also for the growth of the national product. The figures in table 17.1, column 4, show military spending adjusted for inflation in terms of 1996 dollars and as a percentage of GDP.

60. Thomas Jefferson to Edward Carrington, May 27, 1788, in Jefferson 1950, 13:208. For more extended discussion of crises and expanding government, see Higgs 1987, 2005.

61. See, e.g., Gwartney, Lawson, and Block 1996. For international comparisons, see Higgs 2005. The quotation is from Gabb 2003.

References

Abbate, Janet. 1999. *Inventing the Internet.* Cambridge: MIT Press.

Ambrose, Stephen E. 1985. *Rise to Globalism: American Foreign Policy since 1938,* 4th ed. New York: Penguin.

Barro, Robert, and Xavier Sala-i-Martin. 2004. *Economic Growth.* 2d ed. Cambridge: MIT Press.

Bernstein, David E. 2003. *You Can't Say That! The Growing Threat to Civil Liberties from Antidiscrimination Laws.* Washington, DC: Cato Institute.

Bradley, Robert L. 1995. *Oil, Gas, and Government: The U.S. Experience.* Lanham, MD: Rowman & Littlefield and the Cato Institute.

Browning, Edgar K., and Jacquelene M. Browning. 1983. *Public Finance and the Price System,* 2nd ed. New York: Macmillan.

Chapman, Stephen. 1980. "The Gas Lines of '79." *Public Interest* (Summer): 40–49.

Comanor, William S. 1986. "The Political Economy of the Pharmaceutical Industry." *Journal of Economic Literature* 24 (September): 1178–1217.

Corwin, Edward S. 1947. *Total War and the Constitution.* New York: Knopf.

Crews, Clyde Wayne, Jr. 2003. *Ten Thousand Commandments: An Annual Snapshot of the Federal Regulatory State,* 2003 ed. Washington, DC: Cato Institute.

Cringely, Robert X. 1996. *Accidental Empires: How the Boys of Silicon Valley Make Their Millions, Battle Foreign Competition, and Still Can't Get a Date*. New York: HarperBusiness.

David, Paul A. 1985. "Clio and the Economics of QWERTY." *American Economic Review* 75:332–37.

DiMasi, Joseph A. 2001. "New Drug Development in the United States from 1963 to 1999." *Clinical Pharmacology and Therapeutics* 69:286–96.

Eisenhower, Dwight D. 1961. "Eisenhower's Farewell Address, January 17, 1961." In *Documents of American History*, vol. 2, *Since 1898*, 9th ed., ed. Henry Steele Commager, 652–54. Englewood Cliffs: Prentice-Hall.

"Employment Act of 1946, February 20, 1946." In *Documents of American History*, vol. 2, *Since 1898*, 9th ed., ed. Henry Steele Commager, 514–16. Englewood Cliffs: Prentice-Hall.

Feldstein, Martin, ed. 1994. *American Economic Policy in the 1980s*. Chicago: University of Chicago Press.

Fishback, Price, and Melissa Thomasson. 2006. "Social Welfare: 1929 to the Present." In *Historical Statistics of the United States: Earliest Times to the Present, Millennial Edition*, ed. Susan B. Carter et al., vol. 2, pt. B, "Work and Welfare," 2-700–2-719. New York: Cambridge University Press.

Fisher, Franklin, James McKie, and Richard Mancke. 1983. *IBM and the U.S. Data Processing Industry: An Economic History*. New York: Praeger.

Freeman, A. Myrick. 1982. *Air and Water Pollution Control: A Benefit-Cost Assessment*. New York: John Wiley.

———. 2002. "Environmental Policy since Earth Day I: What Have We Gained?" *Journal of Economic Perspectives* 16 (Winter): 125–46.

Friedberg, Aaron L. 2000. *In the Shadow of the Garrison State: America's Anti-Statism and Its Cold War Grand Strategy*. Princeton: Princeton University Press.

Gabb, Sean. 2003. "Why Criticising American Foreign Policy Is Not Anti-Americanism." *Free Life Commentary* no. 102 (April 29). http://www.seangabb.co.uk/flcomm/flc.htm (accessed August 2005).

Gieringer, Dale H. 1985. "The Safety and Efficacy of New Drug Approval." *Cato Journal* 5 (Spring–Summer): 177–201.

Glaeser, Edward L., Joseph Gyourko, and Raven Saks. 2005. "Why Have Housing Prices Gone Up?" National Bureau of Economic Research Working Paper No. 11129, Cambridge, MA.

Glaeser, Edward L., and Andrei Shleifer. 2003. "The Rise of the Regulatory State." *Journal of Economic Literature* 41 (June): 401–25.

Glasner, David. 1985. *Politics, Prices, and Petroleum*. Cambridge, MA: Ballinger.

Glazer, Nathan. 1975. *Affirmative Discrimination*. New York: Basic.

Goodfriend, Marvin, and Robert King. 2005. "The Incredible Volcker Disinflation." National Bureau of Economic Research Working Paper 11562, Cambridge, MA.

Gross, Grant. 2004. "Bush Signs Internet Tax Moratorium." *Infoworld* (December). http://www.infoworld.com/article/04/12/03/HNbushinternettax_1.html (accessed August 10, 2005).

Gwartney, James D., Robert Lawson, and Walter Block. 1996. *Economic Freedom of the World, 1975–1995.* Vancouver, BC: Fraser Institute.

Hahn, Robert W. 1996. "Regulatory Reform: What Do the Government's Numbers Tell Us?" In *Risks, Costs, and Lives Saved: Getting Better Results from Regulation,* ed. Robert Hahn, 208–53. New York: Oxford University Press.

———. 2000. *Reviving Regulatory Reform: A Global Perspective.* Washington, DC: AEI-Brookings Joint Center for Regulatory Studies.

Hamilton, James T. and W. Kip Viscusi. 1999. *Calculating Risks: The Spatial and Political Dimensions of Hazardous Waste Policy.* Cambridge: MIT Press.

Hansen, Ronald W. 1995. "FDA Regulation of the Pharmaceutical Industry." In *Hazardous to Our Health? FDA Regulation of Health Care Products,* ed. Robert Higgs, 13–28. Oakland, CA: Independent Institute.

Higgs, Robert. 1979a. "Inflation and the Destruction of the Free Market." *Intercollegiate Review* 14 (Spring): 67–76.

———. 1979b. "Blaming the Victim: The Government's Theory of Inflation." *Freeman* 29 (July): 397–404.

———. 1980. "Carter's Wage-Price Guidelines: A Review of the First Year." *Policy Review* 11 (Winter): 97–113.

———. 1981. "Wage-Price Guidelines: Retreat and Defeat." *Freeman* 31 (November): 643–52.

———. 1987. *Crisis and Leviathan: Critical Episodes in the Growth of American Government.* New York: Oxford University Press.

———. 1989. "Beware the Pork-Hawk: In Pursuit of Reelection, Congress Sells out the Nation's Defense." *Reason* 21 (June): 28–34.

———. 1991. "Eighteen Problematic Propositions in the Analysis of the Growth of Government." *Review of Austrian Economics* 5:3–40.

———. 1993. "Private Profit, Public Risk: Institutional Antecedents of the Modern Military Procurement System in the Rearmament Program of 1940–1941." In *The Sinews of War: Essays on the Economic History of World War II,* ed. Geofrey T. Mills and Hugh Rockoff, 166–98. Ames: Iowa State University Press.

———. 1994a. "The Cold War Economy: Opportunity Costs, Ideology, and the Politics of Crisis." *Explorations in Economic History* 31 (July): 283–312.

———. 1994b. "Banning a Risky Product Cannot Improve Any Consumer's Welfare (Properly Understood), with Applications to FDA Testing Requirements." *Review of Austrian Economics* 7:3–20.

———, ed. 1995. *Hazardous to Our Health? FDA Regulation of Health Care Products.* Oakland, CA: Independent Institute.

———. 1996. "The Welfare State: Promising Protection in an Age of Anxiety." *Freeman* 46 (May): 260–66.

———. 2001. "The Cold War Is Over, but U.S. Preparation for It Continues." *Independent Review* 6 (Fall): 287–305.

———. 2004. "The U.S. Food and Drug Administration: A Billy Club Is Not a Substitute for Eyeglasses." in *Against Leviathan: Government Power and a Free Society,* 59–73. Oakland, CA: Independent Institute.

———. 2005. "The Ongoing Growth of Government in the Economically Advanced Countries." *Advances in Austrian Economics* 8:279–300.

Higgs, Robert, and Anthony Kilduff. 1993. "Public Opinion: A Powerful Predictor of U.S. Defense Spending." *Defence Economics* 4:227–38.

Holzman, F. D. 1992. "The CIA's Military Spending Estimates: Deceit and Its Costs." *Challenge* 35:28–39.

James, Charles A., et al. 2002. "Memorandum of the United States in Support of Entry of the Proposed Final Judgement in *United States of America v. Microsoft Corporation.*" Civil Action No. 98-1232 (CKK). U.S. Dist. Ct. for the District of Columbia. February.

Jefferson, Thomas. 1950. *Papers of Thomas Jefferson.* Ed. Julian P. Boyd. Princeton: Princeton University Press.

Jouvenel, Bertrand de. 1993 [1945]. *On Power: The Natural History of Its Growth.* Indianapolis: Liberty Fund.

Kolodziej, E. A. 1966. *The Uncommon Defense and Congress, 1945–1963.* Columbus: Ohio State University Press.

Leebaert, Derek. 2002. *The Fifty-Year Wound: The True Price of America's Cold War Victory.* Boston: Little, Brown.

Leibowitz, Stan J., and Stephen E. Margolis. 2001. *Winners, Losers and Microsoft: Competition and Antitrust in High Technology.* Rev. ed. Oakland, CA: Independent Institute.

Mann, Charles, and Mark Plummer. 1991. *The Aspirin Wars.* Boston: Harvard Business School Press.

———. 1995. *Noah's Choice: The Future of the Endangered Species Act.* New York: Knopf.

Matusow, Allen J. 1984. *The Unraveling of America: A History of Liberalism in the 1960s.* New York: Harper & Row.

McClosky, Herbert, and John Zaller. 1984. *The American Ethos: Public Attitudes toward Capitalism and Democracy.* Cambridge: Harvard University Press.

Mowery, David. 2005. "The Bayh-Dole Act and High Technology Entrepreneurship in U.S. Universities: Chicken, Egg, or Something Else?" In *University Entrepreneurship and Technology Transfer: Process, Design, and Intellectual Property,* ed. Gary Libecap, 39–68. New York: Elsevier.

Mowery, David, and Nathan Rosenberg. 2000. "Twentieth Century Technological Change." In *The Cambridge Economic History of the United States,* vol. 3, ed. Stanley Engerman and Robert E. Gallman, 803–926. New York: Cambridge University Press.

Mueller, John E. 1973. *War, Presidents, and Public Opinion.* New York: Wiley.

National Science Foundation, Division of Science Resources Statistics. 2003. *National Patterns of R&D Resources: 2002 Data Update (current to October 2002).* Arlington, VA (NSF 03-313) [March]. http://www.nsf.gov/statistics/nsf03313 (accessed August 2, 2005).

Naughton, John. 2000. *A Brief History of the Future: From Radio Days to Internet Years in a Lifetime.* New York: Overlook.

Nelson, Richard, ed. 1982. *Government and Technical Progress: A Cross-Industry Analysis.* New York: Pergamon.

Nelson, Theodore. 1974. *Computer Lib: You Can and Must Understand Computers Now; Dream Machines.* Chicago: Hugo's Book Service.

Neu, C. E. 1987. "The Rise of the National Security Bureaucracy." In *The New American State: Bureaucracies and Politics since World War II*, ed. Louis Galambos, 85–108. Baltimore: Johns Hopkins University Press.

Oates, Wallace, and Paul Portney. 2001. "The Political Economy of Environmental Policy." Discussion Paper 01-55. Washington, DC: Resources for the Future.

Page, Benjamin I., and Robert Y. Shapiro. 1992. *The Rational Public: Fifty Years of Trends in Americans' Policy Preferences*. Chicago: University of Chicago Press.

Patterson, James T. 1996. *Grand Expectations: The United States, 1945–1974*. New York: Oxford University Press.

Polinsky, A. Mitchell, and Steven Shavell. 2000. "The Economic Theory of Public Enforcement of Law." *Journal of Economic Literature* 38 (March): 45–76.

Portney, Paul, and Wallace Oates. 1995. "Tightening Environmental Standards: The Benefit-Cost or No-Cost Paradigm." *Journal of Economic Perspectives* (Autumn): 119–32.

Raucher, Robert S., et al. 1993. *An Evaluation of the Federal Drinking Water Program under the Save Drinking Water Act as Amended in 1986*. Prepared for the American Waterworks Association by RCG/Hagler, Bailly, Inc. Boulder, CO.

Regan, Tracy. 2003. "Microeconomic Essays on Market Entry, Optimal Education, and Measured Experience." PhD diss., University of Arizona.

Rockman, B. A. 1987. "Mobilizing Political Support for U.S. National Security" *Armed Forces and Society* 14:17–41.

Rubin, Paul. 1995. "FTC Advertising Restrictions: Ignorance Is Death" In *Hazardous to Our Health? FDA Regulation of Health Care Products*, ed. Robert Higgs, 29–54. Oakland, CA: Independent Institute.

Sapolsky, H. M. 1987. "Equipping the Armed Forces." *Armed Forces and Society* 14:113–28.

Schieber, Sylvester J., and John B. Shoven. 1999. *The Real Deal: The History and Future of Social Security*. New Haven: Yale University Press.

Segaller, Stephen. 1998. *Nerds 2.0.1: A Brief History of the Internet*. New York: TV Books.

Sherry, Michael S. 1995. *In the Shadow of War: The United States since the 1930s*. New Haven: Yale University Press.

Simmons, Randy T. 2005a. "Fixing the Endangered Species Act." In *Re-Thinking Green: Alternatives to Environmental Bureaucracy*, ed. Robert Higgs and Carl P. Close, 129–56. Oakland, CA: Independent Institute.

———. 2005b. "The Endangered Species Act: Who's Saving What?" In *Re-Thinking Green: Alternatives to Environmental Bureaucracy*, ed. Robert Higgs and Carl P. Close, 109–28. Oakland, CA: Independent Institute.

Simon, William E. 1979. *A Time for Truth*. New York: Berkley Books.

Smith, R. B. 1971. "Disaffection, Delegitimation, and Consequences." In *Public Opinion and the Military Establishment*, ed. C. C. Moskos Jr., 221–51. Beverly Hills: Sage.

Sowell, Thomas. 1984. *Civil Rights: Rhetoric or Reality?* New York: William Morrow.

Stamato, Linda. 1993. "Planning and Politics: A Winning Strategy (Not Only) for Closing Military Bases." *Consortium on Negotiation and Conflict Resolution Newsletter* (Fall–Winter), 1–3. http://policy.rutgers.edu/CNCR/publications.html (accessed August 9, 2005).

Stein, Herbert. 1984. *Presidential Economics: The Making of Economic Policy from Roosevelt to Reagan and Beyond.* New York: Simon & Schuster.

Stiglitz, Joseph E. 1989. "On the Economic Role of the State." In *The Economic Role of the State,* ed. Arnold Heertje, 9–85. Oxford: Basil Blackwell.

Temin, Peter. 1980. *Taking Your Medicine: Drug Regulation in the United States.* Cambridge: Harvard University Press.

Thakur, Nidhi. 2003. "Essays in the Production of Patents, Engineers and Occupational Mobility." PhD diss., University of Arizona.

Troesken, Werner. *The Great Leadwater Pipe Disaster.* Forthcoming. Cambridge: MIT Press.

Twight, Charlotte A. 2002. *Dependent on D.C.: The Rise of Federal Control over the Lives of Ordinary Americans.* New York: Palgrave.

U.S. Department of Defense, Office of the Under Secretary of Defense (Controller). 2003. *National Defense Budget Estimates FY2004* (March). Washington, DC: U.S. Department of Defense.

U.S. Office of Management and Budget. 2003. *Budget of the United States Government, Fiscal Year 2004, Historical Tables.* Washington, DC: U.S. Office of Management and Budget.

Van Houtven, George, and Maureen Cropper. 1996. "When Is a Life Too Costly to Save? The Evidence from U.S. Environmental Regulations." *Journal of Environmental Economics and Management* 30:344–68.

Viscusi, W. Kip. 1992. *Fatal Tradeoffs: Public and Private Responsibilities for Risk.* New York: Oxford University Press.

Weidenbaum, Murray L. 1986. *Business, Government, and the Public.* 3rd ed. Englewood Cliffs: Prentice-Hall.

Weinberger, Caspar W. 1987. *Annual Report of the Secretary of Defense to the Congress, Fiscal Year 1988.* Washington, DC: Government Printing Office.

Weiner, Tim. 1990. *Blank Check: The Pentagon's Black Budget.* New York: Warner Books.

Williams, Benjamin H. 1954. *Emergency Management of the National Economy.* Vol. 21, *Reconversion and Partial Mobilization.* Washington, DC: Industrial College of the Armed Forces.

Wolfe, Tom. 1970. *Radical Chic and Mau-Mauing the Flak Catchers.* New York: Farrar, Straus and Giroux.

Ziliak, Stephen, and Joan Underhill Hannon. 2006. "Public Assistance: Colonial Times to the 1920s." In *Historical Statistics of the United States: Earliest Times to the Present, Millennial Edition,* ed. Susan B. Carter et al., vol. 2, pt. B, "Work and Welfare," 2-693–2-700. New York: Cambridge University Press.

JOHN JOSEPH WALLIS AND PRICE FISHBACK

KEY INDICATORS OF ECONOMIC
AND GOVERNMENT ACTIVITY

THE UNITED STATES currently has a federal system of governments with one national government, fifty state governments, more than ten thousand city governments, a handful of territorial governments, thousands of school districts, thousands of township and town governments, and thousands special districts for sewer, water, irrigation, and other purposes. To give a sense of the changes in government at all levels, this appendix provides estimates of expenditures, revenues, debt, and employment for the national, state, and local levels of government. We also provide information about gross domestic product (GDP)—the value of all goods and services produced within the economy annually, in both nominal dollars and in year 2000 dollars—population, and per capita nominal and real GDP (see table A.7). Good sources for extended series of data about government and the economy in general can be found at the EH.NET Web site, www.eh.net, which gives information about GDP, costs of living, wages, foreign exchanges rates, and a variety of other factors over a long period of time and in the new revision of the *Historical Statistics of the United States* (Carter et al. 2006).

Annual information is typically offered for the period from 1929 to the present because for the most part this information has been collected by the government in a consistent fashion over that time period. For earlier periods, we typically list the data only for census years ending in zero or government census years. There was no attempt to conduct a complete census of governments until 1902, so we have limited information about governments prior to that time. The estimates we do have required extensive digging by Richard Sylla, John Wallis, and John Legler (1995a, 1995b, 1995c, 1995d), who have made the data available for individual states and cities via the Inter-University Consortium for Political and Social Research. Readers interested in general histories of government finance in the United States prior to the 1960s can consult Dewey 1934 or Studenski and Kroos 1963.

Several clear patterns appear in these tables. First, the tables show the dramatic increase in government expenditures (including transfer payments to the elderly and welfare recipients) from roughly 4 percent of GDP in the 1840s to 8 percent in 1900 to 38 percent in 2000 (see tables A.1 and A.2). Meanwhile, government employment rose by a factor of 6.4 between 1929 and 2000, whereas the U.S. population grew by only a factor of 2.4 (see tables A.6 and A.7). The data about dollars and people show the easily measured footprints of government in terms of expenditures, revenues collected, debts, and people employed. They do not show the impact of government as seen in laws and court decisions. If the impact of these aspects of government were factored in, we would see that government likely grew in the twentieth century by amounts larger than those shown here. Those interested in the evolution of the state constitutions can find the original constitutions, revised constitutions, and amendments at John Joseph Wallis's NBER/Maryland Constitution Project, http://www.stateconstitutions.umd.edu.

War dominates the debt experience of the central government. Until World War II, the federal government accumulated substantial debts that were then paid down over the course of the following years. During World War II the United States again ran up a large debt, but since that time it has not been paid down. Nominal debt has risen by a factor of more than eighteen, and the debt measured in year 2000 dollars has risen by a factor of 2.4; however, the federal debt as a ratio to one year's GDP has fallen from roughly .83 to .43 (see tables A.5 and A.7).[1]

Over the course of the nation's history, government finance has gone through three distinct phases in terms of the relative importance of state, national, and federal activity. Each era was characterized by one level of government taking the lead in promoting economic development and by a dominant source of government revenue. Between 1790 and 1842 state governments took an active lead in promoting economic development through investments in transportation and legal innovation to promote development of corporations and banks. Infrastructure investment and land sales offered governments the opportunity to collect income from their assets. The prominent role played by state governments is best shown by the extent of government debt. By 1841, state government borrowing for banks, canals, and railroads had increased state debt to the point that it was roughly eight times the debts of the national and local governments combined (see table A.4). But the high level of debt created serious problems for state governments in the economic depression that began in 1839. By 1842 eight states and the territory of Florida were in default on their debts. In the 1840s and 1850s, constitutional changes in many states made it more difficult for states to borrow money and make investments in social infrastructure.

The second era began in the 1840s as local governments grew in size and importance and took over most of the important infrastructure investment in education, roads, water systems, sewer systems, and public utilities. By 1902 the debt situation had been reversed such that local debt was roughly eight times the amount of total state debt (table A.4). The ratio of expenditures by local government to those by state governments rose from about 1.4 in 1840 to 3.6 in 1900 (table A.2). As the Progressive Era dawned, local government was clearly the most active level of government in the United States. Not surprisingly, property taxes, the mainstay of local taxation, became the most prominent form of tax revenue by 1900.

On the eve of the Great Depression, local governments collected more than half of the tax revenues collected by all governments, they had incurred a debt for their investments equal to the national debt that remained from World War I, and property taxes made up more than 40 percent of all government revenues. The Great Depression and New Deal ushered in the national phase of government revenue and expenditures as the federal government offered more and more grants to state and local governments and spent large amounts on national defense during the cold war and became the primary source of funds for old-age security (see chapter 17). Federal debt became the dominant form of government debt, accounting for roughly 82 percent of total government debt by 1995 (see table A.5). Income and sales taxes became the most important sources of government revenue at the national and state levels. Although this system has not been static, the basic relations among national, state, and local governments remained in place for the rest of the twentieth century.

Table A.1 NATIONAL, STATE, AND LOCAL GOVERNMENT SPENDING PER PERSON, 1800–1900

Current dollars per capita

Year	National	State	Local	Total	Total as % of GNP
1800	1.96	0.42			
1810	1.80	0.36			
1820	2.52	0.56			
1830	2.07	0.54			
1840	1.50	0.88	1.23	3.60	4.0
1850	1.93	0.99	1.23	4.14	4.2
1860	3.32	1.72	2.17	7.20	5.4
1870	9.82	2.34	5.48	17.64	8.4
1880	6.39	1.70	4.98	13.07	5.7
1890	5.74	1.84	5.96	13.55	6.4
1900	6.42	2.43	8.83	17.68	7.2

Sources: Wallis 2000, p. 65. State revenues from 1800 to 1900 are from data collected by Sylla, Legler, and Wallis available from the Inter-University Consortium for Political and Social Research. Local revenues from 1840 to 1900 are from Legler, Sylla, and Wallis (1988). Data for GNP up to 1860 are from Gallman 1966; remaining years up to 1900 are from Balke and Gordon 1989.

Note: The figures for state and local government are listed in dollars per person because for the period prior to 1840, they are estimates for the entire country based on a subset of states and cities.

Table A.2 GOVERNMENT REVENUE AND EXPENDITURES: TOTAL, PER CAPITA, AND AS A PERCENTAGE OF GDP, 1902–1995

Fiscal year	Revenue Total in millions of dollars	Dollars per capita	Percentage of GDP	Expenditure Total in millions of dollars	Dollars per capita	Percentage of GDP
1902	1,694	21	7.8	1,660	21	7.6
1913	2,980	31	8.1	3,215	33	8.8
1922	9,322	85	12.9	9,297	84	12.8
1927	12,191	102	12.8	11,220	94	11.7
1932	10,289	82	17.5	12,437	100	21.2
1934	11,300	89	17.1	12,807	101	19.4
1936	13,588	106	16.2	16,758	131	20.0
1938	17,484	135	20.3	17,675	136	20.5
1940	17,804	135	17.6	20,417	155	20.1
1942	28,352	210	17.5	45,576	338	28.2
1944	64,778	468	29.5	109,947	794	50.0
1946	61,532	435	27.7	79,707	564	35.9
1948	67,005	457	24.9	55,081	376	20.5
1950	66,680	438	22.7	70,334	462	23.9
1952	100,245	636	28.0	99,847	634	27.9
1953	104,781	654	27.6	110,054	687	29.0
1954	108,255	664	28.5	111,332	683	29.3
1955	106,404	641	25.7	110,717	667	26.7

	Revenue			Expenditure		
iscal ear	Total in millions of dollars	Dollars per capita	Percentage of GDP	Total in millions of dollars	Dollars per capita	Percentage of GDP
956	119,651	708	27.3	115,796	686	26.5
957	129,151	751	28.0	125,463	730	27.2
958	130,403	746	27.9	134,931	772	28.9
959	133,085	748	26.3	145,748	820	28.8
960	153,135	848	29.1	151,288	837	28.7
961	158,774	864	29.1	164,875	898	30.3
962	168,100	901	28.7	176,240	945	30.1
963	181,192	957	29.3	186,058	983	30.1
964	192,451	1,003	29.0	196,431	1,024	29.6
965	202,585	1,043	28.2	205,682	1,059	28.6
966	225,547	1,147	28.6	224,813	1,144	28.5
967	252,562	1,271	30.3	257,799	1,297	31.0
968	265,639	1,324	29.2	282,645	1,408	31.1
969	312,638	1,543	31.8	308,344	1,521	31.3
970	333,810	1,628	32.1	332,985	1,624	32.1
971	342,482	1,649	30.4	369,423	1,779	32.8
972	382,935	1,824	30.9	399,099	1,901	32.2
973	432,164	2,039	31.3	436,967	2,062	31.6
974	484,659	2,266	32.3	478,340	2,237	31.9
975	519,599	2,406	31.7	560,131	2,594	34.2
976	570,997	2,619	31.3	625,076	2,867	34.2
977	657,206	2,984	32.4	682,492	3,099	33.6
978	731,737	3,287	31.9	747,172	3,357	32.6
979	829,328	3,685	32.4	832,514	3,699	32.5
980	932,198	4,094	33.4	958,656	4,210	34.4
981	1,075,387	4,676	34.4	1,109,814	4,826	35.5
982	1,146,271	4,937	35.2	1,233,263	5,311	37.9
983	1,181,182	5,041	33.4	1,346,476	5,747	38.1
984	1,307,483	5,532	33.2	1,427,673	6,041	36.3
985	1,418,781	5,950	33.6	1,580,814	6,629	37.5
986	1,515,657	6,298	34.0	1,696,121	7,048	38.0
987	1,679,165	6,916	35.4	1,811,733	7,462	38.2
988	1,775,999	7,248	34.8	1,920,097	7,836	37.6
989	1,917,736	7,753	35.0	2,030,753	8,210	37.0
990	2,046,998	8,184	35.3	2,218,826	8,871	38.2
991	2,124,211	8,380	35.4	2,379,169	9,386	39.7
992	2,266,765	8,824	35.8	2,494,424	9,710	39.4
993	2,377,235	9,134	35.7	2,575,970	9,898	38.7
994	2,511,556	9,534	35.5	2,673,006	10,147	37.8
995	2,680,424	10,056	36.2	2,818,796	10,575	38.1

Source: Totals are from U.S. Department of Commerce, Bureau of the Census 1985.

Note: The totals presented here equal the sum of the components and differ from the totals presented in the source. For more detail see the chapter on government in Carter et al. forthcoming. Population and real GDP sources are described in table A.7.

Table A.3 FEDERAL, STATE, AND LOCAL GOVERNMENT SHARES OF TOTAL GOVERNMENT EXPENDITURES
AND REVENUES

Fiscal Year (%)	Revenues			Expenditures		
	Federal (%)	State (%)	Local (%)	Federal (%)	State (%)	Local (%)
1902	38.6	10.8	50.7	34.0	8.2	57.8
1913	32.3	12.1	55.6	29.8	9.2	61.0
1922	45.7	13.2	41.1	39.2	11.7	49.1
1927	36.7	16.4	47.0	30.4	12.9	56.7
1932	25.6	22.1	52.3	32.4	16.3	51.3
1934	34.4	21.7	43.9	38.8	16.7	44.5
1936	38.1	24.0	37.9	49.3	14.6	36.1
1938	41.3	26.4	32.3	43.5	17.4	39.1
1940	39.3	28.2	32.5	45.0	17.4	37.6
1942	56.7	21.2	22.1	76.1	7.8	16.1
1944	79.4	10.4	10.3	90.5	3.0	6.5
1946	75.4	12.5	12.1	82.4	6.2	11.4
1948	70.5	15.1	14.4	61.4	14.3	24.3
1950	65.3	17.2	17.5	60.3	15.5	24.2
1952	71.6	14.3	14.1	69.1	10.8	20.1
1953	70.9	14.5	14.6	70.1	10.4	19.5
1954	70.1	14.7	15.2	67.1	11.7	21.2
1955	67.6	15.7	16.7	63.5	13.0	23.5
1956	67.9	15.8	16.3	62.7	13.1	24.2
1957	67.4	16.1	16.5	62.1	13.4	24.5
1958	66.0	16.4	17.6	60.2	14.8	25.0
1959	64.2	17.2	18.6	59.8	15.4	24.8
1960	65.2	17.0	17.8	59.7	14.6	25.7
1961	63.8	17.5	18.7	59.4	14.9	25.7
1962	63.3	17.9	18.8	60.0	14.5	25.6
1963	63.2	18.1	18.7	59.3	14.9	25.8
1964	62.9	18.6	18.6	59.0	15.1	25.9
1965	62.1	19.0	18.9	57.9	15.3	26.9
1966	62.6	19.1	18.4	57.8	15.2	27.0
1967	63.9	18.5	17.6	58.9	15.4	25.7
1968	62.2	19.8	18.0	58.9	15.7	25.5
1969	63.9	19.1	17.0	57.3	16.0	26.6
1970	61.6	20.6	17.8	55.5	16.9	27.6
1971	59.1	21.4	19.4	53.8	17.9	28.3
1972	58.3	22.0	19.6	52.3	18.2	29.6
1973	58.7	22.5	18.8	53.0	17.9	29.2
1974	59.5	22.2	18.3	52.8	18.0	29.2
1975	58.2	22.9	18.8	52.1	19.1	28.8
1976	56.6	24.4	19.0	51.5	19.7	28.8
1977	58.1	23.7	18.2	52.7	18.9	28.5
1978	58.7	23.4	17.8	53.8	18.3	27.9
1979	60.2	22.9	16.9	54.3	17.9	27.8
1980	60.5	22.8	16.7	54.9	18.1	27.0
1981	61.3	22.3	16.4	56.3	17.9	25.8
1982	59.8	22.8	17.3	57.6	17.1	25.3
1983	57.4	24.1	18.5	58.1	17.3	24.7
1984	57.6	24.1	18.3	58.1	17.0	24.9
1985	56.7	24.6	18.6	58.5	17.0	24.5
1986	55.8	25.3	19.0	57.8	17.2	24.9
1987	56.6	24.7	18.7	57.3	17.4	25.4

Fiscal Year (%)	Revenues			Expenditures		
	Federal (%)	State (%)	Local (%)	Federal (%)	State (%)	Local (%)
1988	56.8	24.5	18.7	57.1	17.3	25.6
1989	56.8	24.6	18.6	56.3	17.7	26.0
1990	56.3	24.7	19.0	56.2	17.9	25.9
1991	56.4	24.3	19.3	55.5	18.6	26.0
1992	55.4	25.3	19.3	53.8	20.0	26.2
1993	54.9	26.0	19.2	53.0	20.5	26.4
1994	55.6	25.4	19.1	52.8	20.6	26.6
1995	55.6	25.8	18.6	52.2	21.2	26.7

Source: Figures are from data files provided by the US. Census Bureau from the Census of Governments. See U.S. Bureau of the Census 1985, pp. 225–64 for published material through 1982.

Note: Duplicative transactions between governments are excluded. Also, revenues and expenditures are "direct" or "own-source." In other words, the figures do not include revenues from or expenditures for intergovernmental grants.

Table A.4 DEBT FOR STATE, LOCAL, AND NATIONAL GOVERNMENTS, 1838–1902

Year	Debt			Percentage of total		
	State	Local	National	State	Local	National
1838	172	25	3	86.0	12.5	1.5
1841	190	25	5	86.4	11.4	2.3
1870	352	516	2,436	10.7	15.6	73.7
1880	297	826	2,090	9.2	25.7	65.0
1890	228	905	1,122	10.1	40.1	49.8
1902	230	1,877	1,178	7.0	57.1	35.9

Sources: Wallis 2000, 66. National debt through 1932 is from U.S. Bureau of the Census 1975.

Note: Figures are given in Millions of dollars not adjusted for inflation

Table A.5 FEDERAL, STATE, AND LOCAL DEBT OUTSTANDING AND YEAR-TO-YEAR CHANGES IN DEBT, 1902–1995

Fiscal year	Outstanding at end of fiscal year				Change during year		
	Total	Federal	State	Local	Federal	State	Local
1902	3,285	1,178	230	1,877	−44	11	—
1913	5,607	1,193	379	4,035	−1	47	—
1922	33,072	22,963	1,131	8,978	−1,014	230	1,216
1927	33,393	18,512	1,971	12,910	−1,131	145	929
1932	38,692	19,487	2,832	16,373	2,686	223	9
1934	45,982	27,053	3,248	15,681	4,514	167	−826
1936	53,253	33,779	3,413	16,061	5,008	−9	306
1938	56,601	37,165	3,343	16,093	740	−32	6
1940	63,251	42,968	3,590	16,693	2,528	58	162

(continued)

Table A.5 (CONTINUED)

Fiscal year	Outstanding at end of fiscal year				Change during year		
	Total	Federal	State	Local	Federal	State	Local
1942	91,759	72,422	3,257	16,080	23,461	−233	−337
1944	218,482	201,003	2,776	14,703	64,307	−214	−1,080
1946	285,339	269,422	2,353	13,564	10,740	−154	−600
1948	270,948	252,292	3,676	14,980	−5,994	708	1,133
1950	281,472	257,357	5,285	18,830	4,587	1,137	1,979
1952	289,205	259,105	6,874	23,226	3,883	652	1,332
1953	299,852	266,071	7,824	25,957	6,966	950	2,731
1954	310,190	271,260	9,600	29,331	5,189	1,776	3,374
1955	318,641	274,374	11,198	33,069	3,114	1,598	3,738
1956	321,619	272,751	12,890	35,978	−1,623	1,692	2,909
1957	323,566	270,527	13,738	39,301	−2,224	848	3,323
1958	334,530	276,343	15,394	42,793	5,816	1,656	3,492
1959	348,816	284,706	16,930	47,180	8,363	1,536	4,387
1960	356,286	286,331	18,543	51,412	1,625	1,613	4,232
1961	363,994	288,971	19,993	55,030	2,640	1,450	3,618
1962	379,479	298,201	22,023	59,255	9,230	2,030	4,225
1963	393,312	305,860	23,176	64,276	7,659	1,153	5,021
1964	403,935	311,713	25,041	67,181	5,853	1,865	2,905
1965	416,786	317,274	27,034	72,478	5,561	1,993	5,297
1966	426,958	319,907	29,564	77,487	2,633	2,530	5,009
1967	439,880	326,221	32,472	81,187	6,314	2,908	3,700
1968	468,736	347,578	35,666	85,492	21,357	3,194	4,305
1969	487,268	353,720	39,555	93,995	6,142	3,889	8,503
1970	514,489	370,919	42,008	101,563	17,199	2,453	7,568
1971	568,286	409,459	47,793	111,034	38,540	5,785	9,471
1972	612,479	437,321	54,453	120,705	27,862	6,660	9,671
1973	656,903	468,418	59,375	129,110	31,097	4,922	8,405
1974	692,851	486,235	65,296	141,320	17,817	5,921	12,210
1975	764,054	544,129	72,127	147,798	57,894	6,831	6,478
1976	871,815	631,283	84,825	155,707	87,154	12,698	7,909
1977	968,794	709,136	90,200	169,458	77,853	5,375	13,751
1978	1,060,856	780,423	102,569	177,864	71,287	12,369	8,406
1979	1,137,853	833,750	111,740	192,363	53,327	9,171	14,499
1980	1,249,919	914,316	121,958	213,645	80,566	10,218	21,282
1981	1,367,831	1,003,939	134,847	229,045	89,623	12,889	15,400
1982	1,551,565	1,146,986	147,470	257,109	143,047	12,624	28,064
1983	1,836,387	1,381,886	167,290	287,211	234,900	19,820	30,102
1984	2,083,064	1,576,734	186,377	319,953	194,848	19,087	32,742
1985	2,396,084	1,827,451	211,917	356,716	250,717	25,540	36,763
1986	2,788,381	2,129,506	247,715	411,160	302,055	35,798	54,443
1987	3,081,205	2,354,073	265,551	461,580	224,567	17,836	50,420
1988	3,369,615	2,614,581	276,786	478,247	260,508	11,235	16,667
1989	3,680,189	2,881,112	295,500	503,577	266,531	18,714	25,330
1990	4,124,079	3,266,073	318,254	539,752	384,961	22,754	36,175
1991	4,598,765	3,683,054	345,554	570,157	416,981	27,300	30,405
1992	5,058,481	4,082,871	372,319	603,290	399,817	26,765	33,133
1993	5,453,857	4,436,171	389,721	627,965	353,300	17,402	24,675
1994	5,795,952	4,721,292	410,998	663,662	285,121	21,277	35,697
1995	6,116,315	5,000,945	427,239	688,131	279,653	16,241	24,469

Sources: Figures are from data files provided by the Section of the Bureau of Census from the Census of Governments. For published versions through 1982, see U.S. Bureau of the Census 1985.

Note: Figures are given in thousands of dollars unadjusted for inflation.

Table A.6 GOVERNMENT EMPLOYMENT BY LEVEL AND MAJOR FUNCTION, 1929–2000

		Federal			State and local		
Year	Total	Total	Military	Other	Total	Education	Other
1929	3,611	981	267	714	2,630	1,067	1,563
1930	3,779	1,034	310	724	2,745	1,095	1,650
1931	4,133	1,019	296	723	3,114	1,105	2,009
1932	4,373	1,006	290	716	3,367	1,093	2,274
1933	5,901	1,470	294	1,176	4,431	1,069	3,362
1934	6,820	2,227	357	1,870	4,593	1,069	3,524
1935	7,150	2,209	449	1,760	4,941	1,097	3,844
1936	8,050	4,993	521	4,472	3,057	1,118	1,939
1937	7,192	4,085	517	3,568	3,107	1,149	1,958
1938	8,197	4,987	507	4,480	3,210	1,180	2,030
1939	8,020	4,754	560	4,194	3,266	1,207	2,059
1940	7,917	4,652	642	4,010	3,265	1,194	2,071
1941	8,572	5,281	944	4,337	3,291	1,256	2,035
1942	10,486	7,252	1,702	5,550	3,234	1,264	1,970
1943	15,293	12,155	2,497	9,658	3,138	1,256	1,882
1944	17,527	14,405	2,520	11,885	3,122	1,256	1,866
1945	17,431	14,258	2,420	11,838	3,173	1,273	1,900
1946	9,311	5,902	1,822	4,080	3,409	1,347	2,062
1947	7,483	3,808	1,436	2,372	3,675	1,445	2,230
1948	7,894	4,007	1,428	2,579	3,887	1,504	2,383
1949	8,516	4,462	1,448	3,014	4,054	1,581	2,473
1950	8,802	4,603	1,468	3,135	4,199	1,636	2,563
1951	10,358	6,131	1,817	4,314	4,227	1,684	2,543
1952	11,102	6,737	1,910	4,827	4,365	1,762	2,603
1953	11,123	6,611	1,823	4,788	4,512	1,851	2,661
1954	11,114	6,394	1,702	4,692	4,720	1,946	2,774
1955	11,182	6,234	1,711	4,523	4,948	2,076	2,872
1956	11,414	6,202	1,738	4,464	5,212	2,199	3,013
1957	11,709	6,277	1,734	4,543	5,432	2,310	3,122
1958	11,756	6,044	1,691	4,353	5,712	2,430	3,282
1959	11,940	6,030	1,721	4,309	5,910	2,559	3,351
1960	12,275	6,090	1,770	4,320	6,185	2,732	3,453
1961	12,632	6,200	1,772	4,428	6,432	2,863	3,569
1962	12,992	6,349	1,833	4,516	6,643	3,012	3,631
1963	13,247	6,302	1,852	4,450	6,945	3,214	3,731
1964	13,683	6,382	1,838	4,544	7,301	3,431	3,870
1965	14,115	6,387	1,856	4,531	7,728	3,705	4,023
1966	15,322	7,057	1,978	5,079	8,265	4,049	4,216
1967	16,169	7,497	2,100	5,397	8,672	4,321	4,351
1968	16,670	7,551	2,112	5,439	9,119	4,582	4,537
1969	16,995	7,492	2,083	5,409	9,503	4,828	4,675
1970	17,068	7,129	2,042	5,087	9,939	5,060	4,879
1971	17,044	6,717	2,002	4,715	10,327	5,298	5,029
1972	17,036	6,308	2,017	4,291	10,728	5,467	5,261
1973	17,287	6,174	2,001	4,173	11,113	5,641	5,472
1974	17,647	6,146	2,049	4,097	11,501	5,858	5,643
1975	18,000	6,060	2,075	3,985	11,940	6,052	5,888
1976	17,997	5,934	2,085	3,849	12,063	6,124	5,939

(continued)

Table A.6 (CONTINUED)

		Federal			State and local		
Year	Total	Total	Military	Other	Total	Education	Other
1977	18,169	5,871	2,090	3,781	12,298	6,251	6,047
1978	18,492	5,881	2,117	3,764	12,611	6,292	6,319
1979	18,902	5,881	2,126	3,755	13,021	6,361	6,660
1980	19,273	6,010	2,221	3,789	13,263	6,481	6,782
1981	19,148	6,006	2,131	3,875	13,142	6,466	6,676
1982	19,149	6,084	2,113	3,971	13,065	6,421	6,644
1983	19,172	6,095	2,117	3,978	13,077	6,478	6,599
1984	19,428	6,196	2,143	4,053	13,232	6,581	6,651
1985	19,795	6,311	2,180	4,131	13,484	6,759	6,725
1986	20,170	6,384	2,164	4,220	13,786	6,940	6,846
1987	20,550	6,475	2,190	4,285	14,075	6,992	7,083
1988	20,906	6,470	2,192	4,278	14,436	7,257	7,179
1989	21,284	6,483	2,207	4,276	14,801	7,458	7,343
1990	21,779	6,532	2,315	4,217	15,247	7,668	7,579
1991	21,802	6,349	2,211	4,138	15,453	7,785	7,668
1992	21,839	6,177	2,231	3,946	15,662	7,885	7,777
1993	21,853	5,931	2,177	3,754	15,922	8,067	7,855
1994	21,911	5,720	2,100	3,620	16,191	8,223	7,968
1995	21,965	5,560	2,026	3,534	16,405	8,388	8,017
1996	21,935	5,387	1,951	3,436	16,548	8,522	8,026
1997	22,053	5,265	1,899	3,366	16,788	8,736	8,052
1998	22,262	5,194	1,878	3,316	17,068	8,928	8,140
1999	22,539	5,139	1,856	3,283	17,400	9,148	8,252
2000	22,996	5,235	1,976	3,259	17,761	9,382	8,379

Sources: U.S. Department of Commerce, Bureau of Economic Analysis, National Income and Product Accounts, "Full-Time and Part-Time Employees, by Industry," tables 6.4A, 6.4B, and 6.4C. http://www.bea.gov.

Note: Figures are in thousands of persons. Employment estimates are annual averages of monthly data. The category "federal military" includes the Coast Guard. Other federal workers include civilian workers and work relief workers under general government and workers in government enterprises. State and local other workers include general government workers, work relief workers, and workers in government enterprises.

Table A.7 GDP in current and year 2000 dollars, GDP deflator, and per capita GDP estimates in current and year 2000 dollars, 1790–2004

Year	GDP in billions of current dollars	GDP in billions of chained 2000 dollars	GDP Deflator (100 in year 2000)	Population in millions	GDP per capita	GDP per capita in year 2000 dollars
1790	0.24	4.793	4.99	3.930	61	1,220
1800	0.52	7.569	6.87	5.310	98	1,425
1810	0.81	10.867	7.50	7.220	113	1,505
1820	0.86	14.857	5.77	9.600	89	1,548
1830	1.09	21.415	5.07	12.900	84	1,660

Year	GDP in billions of current dollars	GDP in billions of chained 2000 dollars	GDP Deflator (100 in year 2000)	Population in millions	GDP per capita	GDP per capita in year 2000 dollars
840	1.73	31.847	5.43	17.120	101	1,860
850	2.54	47.329	5.36	23.260	109	2,035
860	4.49	77.721	5.77	31.510	142	2,467
870	8.49	104.473	8.13	39.910	213	2,618
880	11.14	170.329	6.54	50.260	222	3,389
890	13.56	228.133	5.94	63.000	215	3,621
900	18.68	327.954	5.70	76.090	245	4,310
902	21.73	373.801	5.81	79.160	275	4,722
910	31.30	472.706	6.62	92.410	339	5,115
913	36.63	536.236	6.83	97.230	377	5,515
920	86.76	606.692	14.30	106.460	815	5,699
922	72.43	625.911	11.57	110.050	658	5,688
927	95.60	798.408	11.97	119.000	803	6,709
929	103.60	865.200	12.00	121.770	851	7,105
930	91.20	790.700	11.50	123.080	741	6,424
931	76.50	739.900	10.30	124.040	617	5,965
932	58.70	643.700	9.10	124.840	470	5,156
933	56.40	635.500	8.90	125.580	449	5,061
934	66.00	704.200	9.40	126.370	522	5,573
935	73.30	766.900	9.60	127.250	576	6,027
936	83.80	866.600	9.70	128.050	654	6,768
937	91.90	911.100	10.10	128.820	713	7,073
938	86.10	879.700	9.80	129.820	663	6,776
939	92.20	950.700	9.70	130.880	704	7,264
940	101.40	1,034.100	9.80	132.122	767	7,827
941	126.70	1,211.100	10.50	133.402	950	9,079
942	161.90	1,435.400	11.30	134.860	1,201	10,644
943	198.60	1,670.900	11.90	136.739	1,452	12,220
944	219.80	1,806.500	12.20	138.397	1,588	13,053
945	223.10	1,786.300	12.50	139.928	1,594	12,766
946	222.30	1,589.400	14.00	141.389	1,572	11,241
947	244.20	1,574.500	15.50	144.126	1,694	10,924
948	269.20	1,643.200	16.40	146.631	1,836	11,206
949	267.30	1,634.600	16.40	149.188	1,792	10,957
950	293.80	1,777.300	16.50	152.271	1,929	11,672
951	339.30	1,915.000	17.70	154.878	2,191	12,365
952	358.30	1,988.300	18.00	157.553	2,274	12,620
953	379.40	2,079.500	18.20	160.184	2,369	12,982
954	380.40	2,065.400	18.40	163.026	2,333	12,669
955	414.80	2,212.800	18.70	165.931	2,500	13,336
956	437.50	2,255.800	19.40	168.903	2,590	13,356
957	461.10	2,301.100	20.00	171.984	2,681	13,380
958	467.20	2,279.200	20.50	174.882	2,672	13,033
959	506.60	2,441.300	20.80	177.830	2,849	13,728
960	526.40	2,501.800	21.00	180.671	2,914	13,847
961	544.70	2,560.000	21.30	183.691	2,965	13,936
962	585.60	2,715.200	21.60	186.538	3,139	14,556
963	617.70	2,834.000	21.80	189.242	3,264	14,976
964	663.60	2,998.600	22.10	191.889	3,458	15,627

(continued)

Table A.7 (Continued)

Year	GDP in billions of current dollars	GDP in billions of chained 2000 dollars	GDP Deflator (100 in year 2000)	Population in millions	GDP per capita	GDP per capita in year 2000 dollars
1965	719.10	3,191.100	22.50	194.303	3,701	16,423
1966	787.80	3,399.100	23.20	196.560	4,008	17,293
1967	832.60	3,484.600	23.90	198.712	4,190	17,536
1968	910.00	3,652.700	24.90	200.706	4,534	18,199
1969	984.60	3,765.400	26.10	202.677	4,858	18,578
1970	1,038.50	3,771.900	27.50	205.052	5,065	18,395
1971	1,127.10	3,898.600	28.90	207.661	5,428	18,774
1972	1,238.30	4,105.000	30.20	209.896	5,900	19,557
1973	1,382.70	4,341.500	31.80	211.909	6,525	20,488
1974	1,500.00	4,319.600	34.70	213.854	7,014	20,199
1975	1,638.30	4,311.200	38.00	215.973	7,586	19,962
1976	1,825.30	4,540.900	40.20	218.035	8,372	20,826
1977	2,030.90	4,750.500	42.80	220.239	9,221	21,570
1978	2,294.70	5,015.000	45.80	222.585	10,309	22,531
1979	2,563.30	5,173.400	49.50	225.055	11,390	22,987
1980	2,789.50	5,161.700	54.00	227.726	12,249	22,666
1981	3,128.40	5,291.700	59.10	229.966	13,604	23,011
1982	3,255.00	5,189.300	62.70	232.188	14,019	22,350
1983	3,536.70	5,423.800	65.20	234.307	15,094	23,148
1984	3,933.20	5,813.600	67.70	236.348	16,642	24,598
1985	4,220.30	6,053.700	69.70	238.466	17,698	25,386
1986	4,462.80	6,263.600	71.20	240.651	18,545	26,028
1987	4,739.50	6,475.100	73.20	242.804	19,520	26,668
1988	5,103.80	6,742.700	75.70	245.021	20,830	27,519
1989	5,484.40	6,981.400	78.60	247.342	22,173	28,226
1990	5,803.10	7,112.500	81.60	250.132	23,200	28,435
1991	5,995.90	7,100.500	84.40	253.493	23,653	28,011
1992	6,337.70	7,336.600	86.40	256.894	24,670	28,559
1993	6,657.40	7,532.700	88.40	260.255	25,580	28,944
1994	7,072.20	7,835.500	90.30	263.436	26,846	29,743
1995	7,397.70	8,031.700	92.10	266.557	27,753	30,131
1996	7,816.90	8,328.900	93.90	269.667	28,987	30,886
1997	8,304.30	8,703.500	95.40	272.912	30,428	31,891
1998	8,747.00	9,066.900	96.50	276.115	31,679	32,837
1999	9,268.40	9,470.300	97.90	279.295	33,185	33,908
2000	9,817.00	9,817.000	100.00	282.434	34,759	34,759
2001	10,128.00	9,890.700	102.40	285.545	35,469	34,638
2002	10,469.60	10,048.800	104.20	287.941	36,360	34,899
2003	10,971.20	10,320.600	106.30	290.789	37,729	35,492
2004	11,734.30	10,755.700	109.10	293.655	39,959	36,627

Sources: For real and nominal GDP and GDP price deflator for 1929–2004, see U.S. Bureau of Economic Analysis 2005. For population in all years and for the GDP figures prior to 1929, see Johnston and Williamson 2005. Annual estimates prior to 1929 can be found at www.eh.net/hmit.

Notes

1. To calculate federal debt in year 2000 dollars, divide the federal debt in a specific year by the GDP deflator (table A.7) and then divide by 100. The GDP deflator can also be used to calculate inflation rates from one year to the next by measuring the percentage change. Inflation in year 2004 relative to 2003 is (deflator in 2004 minus the deflator in 2003) divided by the deflator in 2003 and then multiplied by 100 to put it into percentage terms.

References

Balke, Nathan S., and Robert J. Gordon. 1989. "The Estimation of Gross National Product: Methodology and New Evidence." *Journal of Political Economy* 97 (February): 38–92.

Carter, Susan, et al., eds. 2006. *The Historical Statistics of the United States, Millennial Edition.* 5 vols. New York: Cambridge University Press.

Davis, Lance E., and John B. Legler. 1966. "Interrelations between Government Activities and Economic Growth: The Government in the American Economy, 1815–1902; A Quantitative Study." *Journal of Economic History* 26 (December 1966): 514–52.

Dewey, Davis R. 1934. *Financial History of the United States.* 12th ed. Repr. 1986, New York: Augustus Kelley.

Gallman, Robert. 1966. "Gross National Product in the United States, 1834–1909." In *Output, Employment, and Productivity in the United States after 1800.* Studies in Income and Wealth, vol. 30. Ed. Dorothy Brady. New York: Columbia University Press.

Johnson, Ronald N., and Gary D. Libecap. 1994. *The Federal Civil Service System and the Problem of Bureaucracy.* Chicago: University of Chicago Press.

Johnston, Louis D., and Samuel H. Williamson. 2005. "The Annual Real and Nominal GDP for the United States, 1790–Present." Economic History Services (October). http://www.eh.net/hmit/gdp/ (accessed November 15, 2005).

Legler, John B., Richard E. Sylla, and John Joseph Wallis. 1988. "U.S. City Finances and the Growth of Government, 1850–1902." *Journal of Economic History* 48 (June): 347–56.

Studenski, Paul, and Herman E. Kroos. 1963. *Financial History of the United States.* New York: McGraw-Hill.

Sylla, Richard E., Legler, John B., and Wallis, John. 1995a. *State and Local Government [United States]: Source and Uses of Funds, Census Statistics, Twentieth Century [Through 1982].* Inter-University Consortium for Political and Social Research Data Set 6304. http://www.icpsr.umich.edu.

———. 1995b. *State and Local Government [United States]: Source and Uses of Funds, City and County Data, Nineteenth Century.* Inter-University Consortium for Political and Social Research Data Set 6305. http://www.icpsr.umich.edu.

———. 1995c. *State and Local Government [United States]: Source and Uses of Funds, State Financial Statistics, 1933–1937.* Inter-University Consortium for Political and Social Research Data Set 6306. http://www.icpsr.umich.edu.

———. 1995d. *Sources and Uses of Funds in State and Local Governments, 1790–1915: [United States]*. Inter-University Consortium for Political and Social Research Data Set 9728. http://www.icpsr.umich.edu.

U.S. Bureau of Economic Analysis. 2005. "Current-Dollar and 'Real' Gross Domestic Product." http://www.bea.gov/bea/dn/gdplev.xls. Updated to October 28, 2005 (accessed November 18, 2005).

U.S. Bureau of the Census. 1907. *Wealth, Debt, and Taxation: 1902.* Washington, DC: Government Printing Office.

U.S. Bureau of the Census. 1915. *Wealth, Debt, and Taxation: 1913*, vols. 1–2. Washington, DC: Government Printing Office.

U.S. Bureau of the Census. 1975. *Historical Statistics of the United States, 1790–1970.* Washington, DC: Government Printing Office.

U.S. Bureau of the Census. 1985. "Historical Statistics on Government Finance and Employment." In *1982 Census of Governments*, vol. 6, no. 4, *Historical Statistics of Government Finance and Employment.* Washington, DC: Government Printing Office.

U.S. Department of the Interior. 1866. *Statistics of the United States in 1860.* Washington, DC: Government Printing Office.

U.S. Department of the Interior. 1872. *The Statistics of the Wealth and Industry of the United States.* Washington, DC: Government Printing Office.

U.S. Department of the Interior, Census Office. 1884. *Valuation, Taxation, and Public Indebtedness in the United States: 1880.* Washington, DC: Government Printing Office.

U.S. Department of the Interior, Census Office. 1895. *Report on Wealth Debt and Taxation*, pt. 2, *Valuation and Taxation.* Washington, DC: Government Printing Office.

U.S. Department of the Treasury. 1946. *Annual Report of the Secretary of the Treasury, 1946.* Washington, DC: Government Printing Office.

Wallis, John Joseph. 2000. "American Government Finance in the Long Run: 1790 to 1990." *Journal of Economic Perspectives* 2000 (Winter): 61–82.

———. 2001. "A History of the Property Tax in America." In *Property Taxation and Local Government Finance*, ed. Wallace E. Oates. Lincoln, NE: Lincoln Institute of Land Policy.

———. 2006. "Government Finance." In *Historical Statistics of the United States, Millennial Edition*, ed. Susan Carter et al., vol. 5, *Governance and International Relations*, 5-3–5-9. New York: Cambridge University Press.

APPENDIX B

THE ARTICLES OF CONFEDERATION

To all to whom these presents shall come, we the undersigned Delegates of the States affixed to our Names send greeting. Whereas the Delegates of the United States of America in Congress assembled did on the fifteenth day of November in the Year of our Lord One Thousand Seven Hundred and Seventy seven, and in the Second Year of the Independence of America agree to certain articles of Confederation and perpetual Union between the States of New Hampshire, Massachusetts Bay, Rhode Island and Providence Plantations, Connecticut, New York, New Jersey, Pennsylvania, Delaware, Maryland, Virginia, North Carolina, South Carolina and Georgia in the Words following, viz. "Articles of Confederation and perpetual Union between the states of New Hampshire, Massachusetts Bay, Rhode Island and Providence Plantations, Connecticut, New York, New Jersey, Pennsylvania, Delaware, Maryland, Virginia, North Carolina, South Carolina, and Georgia."

Art. i. The Stile of this confederacy shall be "The United States of America."

Art. ii. Each state retains its sovereignty, freedom and independence, and every power, jurisdiction and right, which is not by this confederation expressly delegated to the United States, in Congress assembled.

Art. iii. The said states hereby severally enter into a firm league of friendship with each other, for their common defence, the security of their liberties, and their mutual and general welfare, binding themselves to assist each other, against all force offered to, or attacks made upon them, or any of them, on account of religion, sovereignty, trade, or any other pretence whatever.

Art. iv. The better to secure and perpetuate mutual friendship and intercourse among the people of the different states in this union,

571

the free inhabitants of each of these states, paupers, vagabonds, and fugitives from justice excepted, shall be entitled to all privileges and immunities of free citizens in the several states; and the people of each state shall have free ingress and regress to and from any other state, and shall enjoy therein all the privileges of trade and commerce, subject to the same duties, impositions and restrictions, as the inhabitants thereof respectively, provided that such restriction shall not extend so far as to prevent the removal of property imported into any state, to any other state of which the owner is an inhabitant; provided also that no imposition, duties or restriction shall be laid by any state on the property of the United States, or either of them.

If any person guilty of or charged with treason, felony, or other high misdemeanor in any state, shall flee from Justice, and be found in any of the United States, he shall upon demand of the governor or executive power of the state from which he fled, be delivered up and removed to the state having jurisdiction of his offence.

Full faith and credit shall be given in each of these states to the records, acts and judicial proceedings of the courts and magistrates of every other state.

ART. V. For the more convenient management of the general interests of the United States, delegates shall be annually appointed in such manner as the legislature of each state shall direct, to meet in Congress on the first Monday in November, in every year, with a power reserved to each state, to recall its delegates, or any of them, at any time within the year, and to send others in their stead, for the remainder of the year.

No state shall be represented in Congress by less than two, nor by more than seven members; and no person shall be capable of being a delegate for more than three years in any term of six years; nor shall any person, being a delegate, be capable of holding any office under the United States for which he, or another for his benefit, receives any salary, fees or emolument of any kind.

Each state shall maintain its own delegates in a meeting of the states, and while they act as members of the committee of the states.

In determining questions in the United States, in Congress assembled, each state shall have one vote.

Freedom of speech and debate in Congress shall not be impeached or questioned in any court, or place out of Congress, and the members of Congress shall be protected in their persons from arrests and imprisonments, during the time of their going to and from, and attendance on Congress, except for treason, felony, or breach of the peace.

Art. vi. No state without the consent of the United States in Congress assembled, shall send any embassy to, or receive any embassy from, or enter into any conference, agreement, or alliance or treaty with any king, prince or state; nor shall any person holding any office of profit or trust under the United States, or any of them, accept of any present, emolument, office or title of any kind whatever from any king, prince or foreign state; nor shall the United States in Congress assembled, or any of them, grant any title of nobility.

No two or more states shall enter into any treaty, confederation or alliance whatever between them, without the consent of the United States in Congress assembled, specifying accurately the purposes for which the same is to be entered into, and how long it shall continue.

No state shall lay any imposts or duties, which may interfere with any stipulations in treaties entered into by the United States in Congress assembled, with any king, prince or state, in pursuance of any treaties already proposed by Congress, to the courts of France and Spain.

No vessels of war shall be kept up in time of peace by any state, except such number only as shall be deemed necessary by the United States in Congress assembled, for the defence of such state, or its trade; nor shall any body of forces be kept up any state, in time of peace, except such number only as in the judgment of the United States, in Congress assembled, shall be deemed requisite to garrison the forts necessary for the defence of such state; but every state shall always keep up a well regulated and disciplined militia, sufficiently armed and accoutred, and shall provide and constantly have ready for use, in public stores, a due number of field pieces and tents, and a proper quantity of arms, ammunition and camp equipage.

No state shall engage in any war without the consent of the United States in Congress assembled, unless such state be actually invaded by enemies, or shall have received certain advice of a resolution being formed by some nation of Indians to invade such state, and the danger is so imminent as not to admit of a delay, till the United States in Congress assembled can be consulted, nor shall any state grant commissions to any ships or vessels of war, nor letters of marque or reprisal, except it be after a declaration of war by the United States in Congress assembled, and then only against the kingdom or state and the subjects thereof against which war has been so declared, and under such regulations as shall be established by the United States in Congress assembled, unless such state be infested by pirates, in which case vessels of war may be fitted out for that occasion, and kept so long as the danger shall continue, or until the United States in Congress assembled shall determine otherwise.

ART. VII. When land forces are raised by any state for the common defence, all officers of or under the rank of colonel shall be appointed by the legislature of each state respectively by whom such forces shall be raised, or in such manner as such state shall direct, and all vacancies shall be filled up by the state which first made the appointment.

ART. VIII. All charges of war, and all other expences that shall be incurred for the common defence or general welfare, and allowed by the United States in Congress assembled, shall be defrayed out of a common treasury, which shall be supplied by the several states, in proportion to the value of all land within each state, granted to or surveyed for any person, as such land and the buildings and improvements thereon shall be estimated according to such mode as the United States, in Congress assembled, shall from time to time direct and appoint. The taxes for paying that proportion shall be laid and levied by the authority and direction of the legislatures of the several states within the time agreed upon by the United States in Congress assembled.

ART. IX. The United States in Congress assembled shall have the sole and exclusive right and power of determining on peace and war, except in the cases mentioned in the sixth article—of sending and receiving ambassadors—entering into treaties and alliances, provided that no treaty of commerce shall be made whereby the legislative power of the respective states shall be restrained from imposing such imposts and duties on foreigners as their own people are subjected to, or from prohibiting the exportation or importation of any species of goods or commodities whatsoever—of establishing rules for deciding in all cases what captures on land or water shall be legal, and in what manner prizes taken by land or naval forces in the service of the United States shall be divided or appropriated—of granting letters of marque and reprisal in times of peace—appointing courts for the trial of piracies and felonies committed on the high seas and establishing courts for receiving and determining finally appeals in all cases of captures, provided that no member of Congress shall be appointed a judge of any of the said courts.

The United States in Congress assembled shall also be the last resort on appeal in all disputes and differences now subsisting or that hereafter may arise between two or more states concerning boundary, jurisdiction or any other cause whatever, which authority shall always be exercised in the manner following. Whenever the legislative or executive authority or lawful agent of any state in controversy with another shall present a petition to Congress (stating the matter in question and praying for a

hearing), notice thereof shall be given by order of Congress to the legislative or executive authority of state in controversy, and a day assigned
for the appearance of the parties by their lawful agents, who shall then
be directed to appoint, by joint consent, commissioners or judges to
constitute a court for hearing and determining the matter in question;
but if they cannot agree, Congress shall name three persons out of each
of the United States, and from the list of such persons each party shall
alternately strike out one, the petitioners beginning, until the number
shall be reduced to thirteen; and from that number not less then seven,
nor more than nine names, as Congress shall direct, shall in the presence of Congress be drawn out by lot, and the persons whose names
shall be so drawn, or any five of them, shall be commissioners or judges,
to hear and finally determine the controversy, so always as a major part
of the judges who shall hear the cause shall agree in the determination.
And if either party shall neglect to attend at the day appointed, without
shewing reasons which Congress shall judge sufficient, or being present shall refuse to strike, the Congress shall proceed to nominate three
persons out of each state, and the secretary of Congress shall strike in
behalf of such party absent or refusing; and the judgment and sentence
of the court to be appointed, in the manner before prescribed, shall be
final and conclusive. And if any of the parties shall refuse to submit to
the authority of such court, or to appear to defend their claim or cause,
the court shall nevertheless proceed to pronounce sentence, or judgment, which shall in like manner be final and decisive, the judgment
or sentence and other proceedings being in either case transmitted to
Congress, and lodged among the acts of Congress for the security of the
parties concerned, provided that every commissioner, before he sits in
judgment, shall take an oath to be administered by one of the judges
of the supreme or superior court of the state where the cause shall be
tried, "well and truly to hear and determine the matter in question, according to the best of his judgment, without favour, affection or hope
of reward." Provided also that no state shall be deprived of territory for
the benefit of the United States.

All controversies concerning the private right of soil claimed under different grants of two or more states, whose jurisdictions, as they
may respect such lands, and the states which passed such grants, are adjusted, the said grants, or either of them, being at the same time claimed
to have originated antecedent to such settlement of jurisdiction, shall,
on the petition of either party to the Congress of the United States, be
finally determined as near as may be in the same manner as is before

prescribed for deciding disputes respecting territorial jurisdiction between different states.

The United States in Congress assembled shall also have the sole and exclusive right and power of regulating the alloy and value of coin struck by their own authority, or by that of the respective states—fixing the standard of weights and measures throughout the United States—regulating the trade and managing all affairs with the Indians, not members of any of the states, provided that the legislative right of any state within its own limits be not infringed or violated—establishing and regulating post-offices from one state to another, throughout all the United States, and exacting such postage on the papers passing thro' the same as may be requisite to defray the expences of the said office—appointing all officers of the land forces, in the service of the United States, excepting regimental officers—appointing all the officers of the naval forces, and commissioning all officers whatever in the service of the United States—making rules for the government and regulation of the said land and naval forces, and directing their operations.

The United States in Congress assembled shall have authority to appoint a committee, to sit in the recess of congress, to be denominated "A Committee of the States," and to consist of one delegate from each state; and to appoint such other committees and civil officers as may be necessary for managing the general affairs of the United States under their direction—to appoint one of their number to preside, provided that no person be allowed to serve in the office of president more than one year in any term of three years; to ascertain the necessary sums of money to be raised for the service of the United States, and to appropriate and apply the same for defraying the public expences—to borrow money, or emit bills on the credit of the United States, transmitting every half year to the respective states an account of the sums of money so borrowed or emitted—to build and equip a navy—to agree upon the number of land forces, and to make requisitions from each state for its quota, in proportion to the number of white inhabitants in such state; which requisition shall be binding, and thereupon the legislature of each state shall appoint the regimental officers, raise the men and cloath, arm and equip them in a soldier-like manner, at the expence of the United States, and the officers and men so cloathed, armed and equipped shall march to the place appointed, and within the time agreed on by the United States in Congress assembled. But if the United States in Congress assembled shall, on consideration of circumstances, judge proper that any state should not raise men, or should raise a smaller number than its quota, and that any other state should raise a greater number of men than the quota thereof, such extra number shall be raised, officered, cloathed, armed and equipped in the same manner as the quota of such state, unless the legislature of such state shall judge that such extra number cannot be safely spared out of the same, in which case they shall raise, officer, cloath, arm and equip as many of such extra number as they judge can be safely spared. And the officers and men so cloathed, armed and equipped, shall march to the place appointed, and within the time agreed on by the United States in Congress assembled.

The United States in Congress assembled shall never engage in a war, not grant letters of marque and reprisal in time of peace, nor enter into any treaties or alliances, nor coin money, nor regulate the value thereof, nor ascertain the sums and expences necessary for the defence and welfare of the United States, or any of them, nor emit bills, nor borrow money on the credit of the United States, nor appropriate money, nor agree upon the number of vessels of war to be built or purchased, or the number of land or sea forces to be raised, nor appoint a commander in chief of the army or navy, unless nine states assent to the same: nor shall a question on any other point, except for adjourning from day to day, be determined, unless by the votes of a majority of the United States in Congress assembled.

The Congress of the United States shall have power to adjourn to any time within the year, and to any place within the United States, so that no period of adjournment be for a longer duration than the space of six months, and shall publish the journal of their proceedings monthly, except such parts thereof relating to treaties, alliances or military operations as in their judgment require secresy; and the yeas and nays of the delegates of each state on any question shall be entered on the journal, when it is desired by any delegate; and the delegates of a state, or any of them, at his or their request shall be furnished with a transcript of the said journal, except such parts as are above excepted, to lay before the legislatures of the several states.

ART. X. The committee of the states, or any nine of them, shall be authorised to execute, in the recess of Congress, such of the powers of Congress as the United States in Congress assembled, by the consent of nine states, shall from time to time think expedient to vest them with; provided that no power be delegated to the said committee, for the exercise of which, by the articles of confederation, the voice of nine states in the Congress of the United States assembled is requisite.

ART. XI. Canada acceding to this confederation, and joining in the measures of the United States, shall be admitted into, and entitled to all the advantages of this union: but no other colony shall be admitted into the same unless such admission be agreed to by nine states.

ART. XII. All bills of credit emitted, monies borrowed and debts contracted by, or under the authority of Congress, before the assembling of the United States, in pursuance of the present confederation, shall be deemed and considered as a charge against the United States, for payment and satisfaction whereof the said United States, and the public faith are hereby solemnly pledged.

ART. XIII. Every state shall abide by the determinations of the United States in Congress assembled, on all questions which by this confederation are submitted to them. And the Articles of this Confederation shall be inviolably observed by every state, and the union shall be perpetual; nor shall any alteration at any time hereafter be made in any of them; unless such alteration be agreed to in a Congress of the United States, and be afterwards confirmed by the legislatures of every state.

And Whereas it hath pleased the Great Governor of the World to incline the hearts of the legislatures we respectively represent in Congress, to approve of, and to authorize us to ratify the said articles of confederation and perpetual union. Know Ye that we the undersigned delegates, by virtue of the power and authority to us given for that purpose, do by these presents, in the name and in behalf of our respective constituents, fully and entirely ratify and confirm each and every of the said articles of confederation and perpetual union, and all and singular the matters and things therein contained: And we do further solemnly plight and engage the faith of our respective constituents, that they shall abide by the determinations of the United States in Congress assembled, on all questions, which by the said confederation are submitted to them. And that the articles thereof shall be inviolably observed by the states we respectively represent, and that the union shall be perpetual. In Witness thereof we have hereunto set our hands in Congress. Done at Philadelphia in the state of Pennsylvania the ninth day of July in the Year of our Lord one Thousand Seven Hundred and Seventy-Eight, and in the third year of the independence of America.

JOSIAH BARTLETT
JOHN WENTWORTH JUN^R   } On the part and behalf of the State of
AUGUST 8TH 1778   New Hampshire

JOHN HANCOCK
SAMUEL ADAMS
ELBRIDGE GERRY
FRANCIS DANA
JAMES LOVELL
SAMUEL HOLTEN

On the part and behalf of The State of Massachusetts Bay

WILLIAM ELLERY
HENRY MARCHANT
JOHN COLLINS

On the part and behalf of the State of Rhode Island and Providence Plantations

ROGER SHERMAN
SAMUEL HUNTINGTON
OLIVER WOLCOTT
TITUS HOSMER
ANDREW ADAMS

On the part and behalf of the State of Connecticut

JS^S DUANE
FRA^S LEWIS
W^M DUER
GOUV MORRIS

On the part and behalf of the State of New York

JNO WITHERSPOON
NATH^L SCUDDER

On the part and behalf of the State of New Jersey NOV^R 26, 1778.–

ROB^T MORRIS
DANIEL ROBERDEAU
JON^A BAYARD SMITH
WILLIAM CLINGAN
JOSEPH REED
   22^D JULY 1778

On the part and behalf of the State of Pennsylvania

THO M:KEAN
   FEBY 12 1779
JOHN DICKINSON
   MAY 5TH 1779
NICHOLAS VAN DYKE

On the part and behalf of the State of Delaware

JOHN HANSON
   MARCH 1 1781
DANIEL CARROLL D^O

On the part and behalf of the State of Maryland

RICHARD HENRY LEE
JOHN BANISTER
THOMAS ADAMS
JN^O HARVIE
FRANCIS LIGHTFOOT LEE

On the part and behalf of the State of Virginia

JOHN PENN
    JULY 21ST 1778
CORNS HARNETT
JNO WILLIAMS
} On the part and behalf of State of NO Carolina

HENRY LAURENS
WILLIAM HENRY
DRAYTON
JNO MATHEWS
RICHD HUSTON
THOS HEYWARD JUNR
} On the part and behalf of the State of South Carolina

JNO WALTON
    24TH JULY 1778
EDWD TELFAIR
EDWD LANGWORTHY
} On the part and behalf of the State of Georgia

THE CONSTITUTION OF THE UNITED STATES

WE THE PEOPLE of the United States, in order to form a more perfect Union, establish Justice, insure domestic Tranquility, provide for the common defence, promote the general Welfare, and secure the Blessings of Liberty to ourselves and our Posterity, do ordain and establish this CONSTITUTION for the United States of America.

ARTICLE I

Section 1. All legislative Powers herein granted shall be vested in a Congress of the United States, which shall consist of a Senate and House of Representatives.

SECTION 2. The House of Representatives shall be composed of Members chosen every second Year by the People of the several States, and the Electors in each State shall have the Qualifications requisite for Electors of the most numerous Branch of the State Legislature.

No Person shall be a Representative who shall not have attained to the Age of twenty five Years, and been seven Years a Citizen of the United States, and who shall not, when elected, be an Inhabitant of that State in which he shall be chosen.

Representatives and direct Taxes shall be apportioned among the several States which may be included within this Union, according to their respective Numbers, which shall be determined by adding to the whole Number of free Persons, including those bound to Service for a Term of Years, and excluding Indians not taxed, three-fifths of all other Persons. The actual Enumeration shall be made within three Years after the first Meeting of the Congress of the United States, and within every subsequent Term of ten Years, in such Manner as they shall by Law direct. The Number of Representatives shall not exceed one for every thirty Thousand, but each State shall have at Least one Representative; and until such enumeration shall be made, the State of New Hampshire shall be entitled to chuse three, Massachusetts eight, Rhode

Island and Providence Plantations one, Connecticut five, New York six, New Jersey four, Pennsylvania eight, Delaware one, Maryland six, Virginia ten, North Carolina five, South Carolina five, and Georgia three.

When vacancies happen in the Representation from any State, the Executive Authority thereof shall issue Writs of Election to fill such Vacancies.

The House of Representatives shall chuse their Speaker and other Officers, and shall have the sole Power of Impeachment.

SECTION 3. The Senate of the United States shall be composed of two Senators from each State, chosen by the Legislature thereof, for six years; and each Senator shall have one vote.

Immediately after they shall be assembled in consequence of the first election, they shall be divided as equally as may be into three classes. The seats of the Senators of the first class shall be vacated at the expiration of the second year, of the second class at the expiration of the fourth year, and of the third class at the expiration of the sixth year, so that one third may be chosen every second year; and if vacancies happen by resignation, or otherwise, during the recess of the Legislature of any State, the Executive thereof may make temporary appointments until the next meeting of the Legislature, which shall then fill such vacancies.

No person shall be a Senator who shall not have attained to the age of thirty years, and been nine years a citizen of the United States, and who shall not, when elected, be an inhabitant of that State for which he shall be chosen.

The Vice President of the United States shall be President of the Senate, but shall have no vote, unless they be equally divided.

The Senate shall chuse their other Officers, and also a President pro tempore, in the absence of the Vice President, or when he shall exercise the Office of President of the United States.

The Senate shall have the sole power to try all impeachments. When sitting for that purpose, they shall be on oath or affirmation. When the President of the United States is tried, the Chief Justice shall preside; and no person shall be convicted without the concurrence of two thirds of the members present.

Judgment in cases of impeachment shall not extend further than to removal from office, and disqualification to hold and enjoy any office of honor, trust or profit under the United States; but the party convicted shall nevertheless be liable and subject to indictment, trial, judgment and punishment, according to law.

SECTION 4. The times, places and manner of holding elections for Senators and Representatives, shall be prescribed in each State by the Legislature thereof; but the Congress may, at any time, by Law, make or alter such regulations, except as to the places of chusing Senators.

The Congress shall assemble at least once in every year, and such meeting shall be on the first Monday in December, unless they shall by law appoint a different day.

SECTION 5. Each House shall be the judge of the elections, returns and qualifications of its own members, and a majority of each shall constitute a quorum to do business; but a smaller number may adjourn from day to day, and may be authorized to compel the attendance of absent members, in such manner, and under such penalties, as each House may provide.

Each House may determine the rules of its proceedings, punish its members for disorderly Behaviour, and, with the concurrence of two-thirds, expel a member.

Each House shall keep a journal of its proceedings, and from time to time publish the same, excepting such parts as may in their judgment require secrecy; and the yeas and nays of the Members of either House on any question shall, at the desire of one-fifth of those present, be entered on the journal.

Neither House, during the session of Congress, shall, without the consent of the other, adjourn for more than three days, nor to any other place than that in which the two Houses shall be sitting.

SECTION 6. The Senators and Representatives shall receive a compensation for their services, to be ascertained by law, and paid out of the Treasury of the United States. They shall in all cases, except treason, felony and breach of the peace, be privileged from arrest during their attendance at the session of their respective Houses, and in going to and returning from the same; and for any speech or debate in either House, they shall not be questioned in any other place.

No Senator or Representative shall, during the time for which he was elected, be appointed to any civil office under the authority of the United States, which shall have been created, or the emoluments whereof shall have been encreased during such time; and no person holding any office under the United States, shall be a member of either House during his continuance in office.

SECTION 7. All bills for raising revenue shall originate in the House of Representatives; but the Senate may propose or concur with amendments as on other bills.

Every bill which shall have passed the House of Representatives and the Senate, shall, before it become a law, be presented to the President of the United States; if he approve he shall sign it, but if not he shall return it, with his objections, to that House in which it shall have originated, who shall enter the objections at large on their journal, and proceed to reconsider it. If after such reconsideration two-thirds of that House shall agree to pass the bill, it shall be sent, together with the objections, to the other House, by which it shall likewise be reconsidered, and if approved by two-thirds of that House, it shall become a law. But in all such cases the votes of both Houses shall be determined by yeas and nays, and the names of the persons voting for and against the bill shall be entered on the journal of each House respectively. If any bill shall not be returned by the President within ten days (Sundays excepted) after it shall have been presented to him, the same shall be a law, in like manner as if he had signed it, unless the Congress by their adjournment prevent its return, in which case it shall not be a law.

Every order, resolution, or vote to which the concurrence of the Senate and House of Representatives may be necessary (except on a question of adjournment) shall be presented to the President of the United States; and before the same shall take effect, shall be approved by him, or, being disapproved by him, shall be repassed by two-thirds of the Senate and House of Representatives, according to the rules and limitations prescribed in the case of a bill.

SECTION 8. The Congress shall have power to lay and collect taxes, duties, imposts and excises, to pay the debts and provide for the common defence and general welfare of the United States; but all duties, imposts and excises shall be uniform throughout the United States;

To borrow money on the credit of the United States;

To regulate commerce with foreign nations, and among the several States, and with the Indian tribes;

To establish an uniform rule of naturalization, and uniform laws on the subject of bankruptcies throughout the United States;

To coin money, regulate the value thereof, and of foreign coin, and fix the standard of weights and measures;

To provide for the punishment of counterfeiting the securities and current coin of the United States;

To establish post offices and post roads;

To promote the progress of science and useful arts, by securing for limited times to authors and inventors the exclusive right to their respective writings and discoveries;

To constitute tribunals inferior to the supreme Court;

To define and punish piracies and felonies committed on the high seas, and offences against the law of nations;

To declare war, grant letters of marque and reprisal, and make rules concerning captures on land and water;

To raise and support armies, but no appropriation of money to that use shall be for a longer term than two years;

To provide and maintain a navy;

To make rules for the government and regulation of the land and naval forces;

To provide for calling forth the militia to execute the laws of the Union, suppress insurrections and repel invasions;

To provide for organizing, arming, and disciplining the militia, and for governing such part of them as may be employed in the service of the United States, reserving to the States respectively the appointment of the officers, and the authority of training the militia according to the discipline prescribed by Congress;

To exercise exclusive legislation in all cases whatsoever, over such district (not exceeding ten miles square) as may, by cession of particular States, and the acceptance of Congress, become the seat of the Government of the United States, and to exercise like authority over all places purchased by the consent of the legislature of the State in which the same shall be, for the erection of forts, magazines, arsenals, dock-yards, and other needful buildings; and

To make all laws which shall be necessary and proper for carrying into execution the foregoing powers, and all other powers vested by this Constitution in the Government of the United States, or in any department or officer thereof.

SECTION 9. The migration or importation of such persons as any of the States now existing shall think proper to admit, shall not be prohibited by the Congress prior to the year one thousand eight hundred and eight, but a tax or duty may be imposed on such importation, not exceeding ten dollars for each person.

The privilege of the writ of habeas corpus shall not be suspended, unless when in cases of rebellion or invasion the public safety may require it.

No bill of attainder, or ex post facto law, shall be passed.

No capitation or other direct tax shall be laid, unless in proportion to the census or enumeration herein before directed to be taken.

No tax or duty shall be laid on articles exported from any State.

No preference shall be given by any regulation of commerce or revenue to the ports of one State over those of another; nor shall vessels bound to, or from, one state be obliged to enter, clear, or pay duties in another.

No money shall be drawn from the treasury, but in consequence of appropriations made by law; and a regular statement and account of the receipts and expenditures of all public money shall be published from time to time.

No title of nobility shall be granted by the United States, and no person holding any office or profit or trust under them shall, without the consent of the Congress, accept of any present, emolument, office, or title, of any kind whatever, from any King, Prince, or foreign State.

SECTION 10. No State shall enter into any treaty, alliance, or confederation; grant letters of marque and reprisal; coin money; emit bills of credit; make any thing but gold and silver coin a tender in payment of debts; pass any bill of attainder, ex post facto law, or law impairing the obligation of contracts, or grant any title of nobility.

No State shall, without the consent of the Congress, lay any imposts or duties on imports or exports, except what may be absolutely necessary for executing its inspection laws; and the net produce of all duties and imposts laid by any State on imports or exports, shall be for the use of the Treasury of the United States; and all such laws shall be subject to the revision and controul of the Congress.

No State shall, without the consent of Congress, lay any duty of tonnage, keep troops, or ships of war in time of peace, enter into any agreement or compact with another State, or with a foreign Power, or engage in war, unless actually invaded, or in such imminent danger as will not admit of delay.

ARTICLE II

Section 1. The executive power shall be vested in a President of the United States of America. He shall hold his office during the term of four years, and, together with the Vice President, chosen for the same term, be elected as follows:

Each State shall appoint, in such manner as the legislature thereof may direct, a number of electors, equal to the whole number of Senators and Representatives to which the State may be entitled in the Congress;

but no Senator or Representative, or person holding an office of trust or profit under the United States, shall be appointed an elector.

The electors shall meet in their respective States, and vote by ballot for two persons, of whom one at least shall not be an inhabitant of the same State with themselves. And they shall make a list of all the persons voted for, and of the number of votes for each; which list they shall sign and certify, and transmit sealed to the Seat of the Government of the United States, directed to the President of the Senate. The President of the Senate shall, in the presence of the Senate and House of Representatives, open all the certificates, and the votes shall then be counted. The person having the greatest number of votes shall be the President, if such number be a majority of the whole number of electors appointed; and if there be more than one who have such majority, and have an equal number of votes, then the House of Representatives shall immediately chuse by ballot one of them for President; and if no person have a majority, then from the five highest on the list the said House shall in like manner chuse the President. But in chusing the President, the votes shall be taken by States, the Representation from each State having one vote; a quorum for this purpose shall consist of a member or members from two-thirds of the States, and a majority of all the States shall be necessary to a choice. In every case, after the choice of the President, the person having the greatest number of votes of the electors shall be the Vice President. But if there should remain two or more who have equal votes, the Senate shall chuse from them by ballot the Vice President.

The Congress may determine the time of chusing the electors, and the day on which they shall give their votes; which day shall be the same throughout the United States.

No person except a natural born citizen, or a citizen of the States, at the time of the adoption of this Constitution, shall be eligible to the office of President; neither shall any person be eligible to that office who shall not have attained to the age of thirty-five years, and been fourteen years a resident within the United States.

In case of the removal of the President from office, or of his death, resignation, or inability to discharge the powers and duties of the said office, the same shall devolve on the Vice President, and the Congress may by law provide for the case of removal, death, resignation or inability both of the President and Vice President, declaring what officer shall then act as President, and such officer shall act accordingly, until the disability be removed, or a President shall be elected.

The President shall, at stated times, receive for his services, a compensation, which shall neither be encreased nor diminished during the period for which he shall have been elected, and he shall not receive within that period any other emolument from the United States, or any of them.

Before he enter on the execution of his office, he shall take the following oath or affirmation:—"I do solemnly swear (or affirm) that I will faithfully execute the office of President of the United States, and will, to the best of my ability, preserve, protect and defend the Constitution of the United States."

SECTION 2. The President shall be commander-in-chief of the army and navy of the United States, and of the militia of the several States, when called into the actual service of the United States; he may require the opinion, in writing, of the principal officer in each of the executive departments, upon any subject relating to the duties of their respective offices; and he shall have power to grant reprieves and pardons for offences against the United States, except in cases of impeachment.

He shall have power, by and with the advice and consent of the Senate, to make treaties, provided two-thirds of the Senators present concur; and he shall nominate, and, by and with the advice and consent of the Senate, shall appoint ambassadors, other public ministers and consuls, judges of the supreme Court, and all other officers of the United States whose appointments are not herein otherwise provided for, and which shall be established by law. But the Congress may by law vest the appointment of such inferior officers as they think proper in the President alone, in the courts of law, or in the heads of departments.

The President shall have power to fill up all vacancies that may happen during the recess of the Senate, by granting commissions which shall expire at the end of their next session.

SECTION 3. He shall from time to time give to the Congress information of the state of the Union, and recommend to their consideration such measures as he shall judge necessary and expedient; he may, on extraordinary occasions, convene both Houses, or either of them, and in case of disagreement between them with respect to the time of adjournment, he may adjourn them to such time as he shall think proper; he shall receive ambassadors and other public ministers; he shall take care that the laws be faithfully executed, and shall commission all the officers of the United States.

SECTION 4. The President, Vice President and all civil officers of the United States shall be removed from office on impeachment for, and conviction of, treason, bribery, or other high crimes and misdemeanors.

ARTICLE III

Section 1. The judicial power of the United States shall be vested in one Supreme Court, and in such inferior courts as the Congress may from time to time ordain and establish. The judges, both of the supreme and inferior courts, shall hold their offices during good behaviour, and shall, at stated times, receive for their services a compensation which shall not be diminished during their continuance in office.

Section 2. The judicial power shall extend to all cases, in law and equity, arising under this Constitution, the laws of the United States, and treaties made, or which shall be made, under their authority;—to all cases affecting ambassadors, other public ministers and consuls;—to all cases of admiralty and maritime jurisdiction;—to controversies to which the United States shall be a party;—to controversies between two or more States;—between a State and citizens of another State;—between citizens of different States,—between citizens of the same State claiming lands under grants of different States, and between a State, or the citizens thereof, and foreign States, citizens or subjects.

In all cases affecting ambassadors, other public ministers and consuls, and those in which a State shall be party, the Supreme Court shall have original jurisdiction. In all the other cases before mentioned, the Supreme Court shall have appellate jurisdiction, both as to law and fact, with such exceptions, and under such regulations, as the Congress shall make.

The trial of all crimes, except in cases of impeachment, shall be by jury; and such trial shall be held in the State where the said crimes shall have been committed; but when not committed within any State, the trial shall be at such place or places as the Congress may by law have directed.

Section 3. Treason against the United States shall consist only in levying war against them, or in adhering to their enemies, giving them aid and comfort. No person shall be convicted of treason unless on the testimony of two witnesses to the same overt act, or on confession in open court.

The Congress shall have power to declare the punishment of treason; but no attainder of treason shall work corruption of blood, or forfeiture, except during the life of the person attainted.

ARTICLE IV

Section 1. Full faith and credit shall be given in each State to the public acts, records, and judicial proceedings of every other State. And the Congress may by general laws prescribe the manner in which such acts, records and proceedings shall be proved, and the effect thereof.

SECTION 2. The citizens of each State shall be entitled to all privileges and immunities of citizens in the several States.

A person charged in any State with treason, felony, or other crime, who shall flee from justice, and be found in another State, shall, on demand of the executive authority of the State from which he fled, be delivered up, to be removed to the State having jurisdiction of the crime.

No person held to service or labour in one State, under the laws thereof, escaping into another, shall, in consequence of any law or regulation therein, be discharged from such service or labour, but shall be delivered up on claim of the party to whom such service or labour may be due.

SECTION 3. New States may be admitted by the Congress into this Union; but no new State shall be formed or erected within the jurisdiction of any other State; nor any State be formed by the junction of two or more States, or parts of States, without the consent of the legislatures of the States concerned as well as of the Congress.

The Congress shall have power to dispose of and make all needful rules and regulations respecting the territory or other property belonging to the United States; and nothing in this Constitution shall be so construed as to prejudice any claims of the United States, or of any particular State.

SECTION 4. The United States shall guarantee to every State in this Union a republican form of Government, and shall protect each of them against invasion; and on application of the Legislature, or of the Executive (when the Legislature cannot be convened), against domestic violence.

ARTICLE V

The Congress, whenever two-thirds of both Houses shall deem it necessary, shall propose amendments to this Constitution, or, on the application of the Legislatures of two-thirds of the several States, shall call a convention for proposing amendments, which, in either case, shall be valid, to all intents and purposes, as part of this Constitution, when ratified by the Legislatures of three-fourths of the several States, or by conventions in three-fourths thereof, as the one or the other mode of ratification may be proposed by the Congress; provided that no amendment which may be made prior to the year one thousand eight hundred and eight shall in any manner affect the first and fourth clauses in the ninth section of the first article; and that no State, without its consent, shall be deprived of its equal suffrage in the Senate.

ARTICLE VI

All debts contracted and engagements entered into, before the adoption of this Constitution, shall be valid against the United States under this Constitution, as under the Confederation.

This constitution, and the laws of the United States which shall be made in pursuance thereof, and all treaties made, or which shall be made, under the authority of the United States, shall be the supreme law of the land; and the judges in every state shall be bound thereby, any thing in the constitution or laws of any State to the contrary notwithstanding.

The Senators and Representatives before mentioned, and the members of the several State Legislatures, and all executive and judicial officers, both of the United States and of the several States, shall be bound by oath or affirmation to support this Constitution; but no religious test shall ever be required as a qualification to any office or public trust under the United States.

ARTICLE VII

The ratification of the conventions of nine States shall be sufficient for the establishment of this Constitution between the States so ratifying the same.

Done in Convention by the unanimous consent of the States present the seventeenth day of September in the year of our Lord one thousand seven hundred and eighty seven and of the independence of the United States of America the twelfth. In witness whereof we have hereunto subscribed our names,

George Washington, President and deputy from Virginia

Attest William Jackson, Secretary

New Hampshire	JOHN LANGDON
	NICHOLAS GILMAN
Massachusetts	NATHANIEL GORHAM
	RUFUS KING
Connecticut	WM: SAML. JOHNSON
	ROGER SHERMAN

New York	{	ALEXANDER HAMILTON
New Jersey	{	WIL: LIVINGSTON
		DAVID BREARLEY
		WM. PATTERSON
		JONA: DAYTON
Pennsylvania	{	B. FRANKLIN
		THOMAS MIFFLIN
		ROBT. MORRIS
		GEO. CLYMER
		THOS. FITZSIMONS
		JARED INGERSOLL
		JAMES WILSON
		GOUV MORRIS
Delaware	{	GEO. READ
		GUNNING BEDFORD jun
		JOHN DICKINSON
		RICHARD BASSETT
		JACO: BROOM
Maryland	{	JAMES MCHENRY
		DANIEL OF ST. THOS. JENIFER
		DANIEL CARROLL
Virginia	{	JOHN BLAIR
		JAMES MADISON JR.
North Carolina	{	WM: BLOUNT
		RICHD. DOBBS SPAIGHT
		HU WILLIAMSON
South Carolina	{	J. RUTLEDGE
		CHARLES COTESWORTH PINCKNEY
		CHARLES PINCKNEY
		PIERCE BUTLER
Georgia	{	WILLIAM FEW
		ABR. BALDWIN

THE BILL OF RIGHTS
[DECEMBER 15, 1791]

ARTICLE I

Congress shall make no law respecting an establishment of religion, or prohibiting the free exercise thereof; or abridging the freedom of speech, or of the press; or the right of the people peaceably to assemble, and to petition the Government for a redress of grievances.

ARTICLE II

A well regulated Militia, being necessary to the security of a free State, the right of the people to keep and bear Arms, shall not be infringed.

ARTICLE III

No Soldier shall, in time of peace be quartered in any house, without the consent of the Owner, nor in time of war, but in a manner to be prescribed by law.

ARTICLE IV

The right of the people to be secure in their persons, houses, papers, and effects, against unreasonable searches and seizures, shall not be violated, and no Warrants shall issue, but upon probable cause, supported by Oath or affirmation, and particularly describing the place to be searched, and the persons or things to be seized.

ARTICLE V

No person shall be held to answer for a capital, or otherwise infamous crime, unless on a presentment or indictment of a Grand Jury, except in cases arising in the land or naval forces, or in the Militia, when in actual service in time of War or public danger; nor shall any person be subject for the same offence to be twice put in jeopardy of life or limb; nor shall be compelled in any Criminal Case to be a witness against himself, nor be deprived of life, liberty, or property, without due process of law; nor shall private property be taken for public use, without just compensation.

ARTICLE VI

In all criminal prosecutions, the accused shall enjoy the right to a speedy and public trial, by an impartial jury of the State and district wherein the crime shall have been committed, which district shall have been previously ascertained by law, and to be informed of the nature and cause of the accusation; to be confronted with the witnesses against him; to have compulsory process for obtaining witnesses in his favor, and to have the Assistance of Counsel for his defence.

ARTICLE VII

In Suits at common law, where the value in controversy shall exceed twenty dollars, the right of trial by jury shall be preserved, and no fact tried by a jury shall be otherwise re-examined in any Court of the United States, than according to the rules of the common law.

ARTICLE VIII

Excessive bail shall not be required, nor excessive fines imposed, nor cruel and unusual punishments inflicted.

ARTICLE IX

The enumeration in the Constitution, of certain rights, shall not be construed to deny or disparage others retained by the people.

ARTICLE X

The powers not delegated to the United States by the Constitution, nor prohibited by it to the States, are reserved to the States respectively, or to the people.

INDEX

abortion laws, 328–29, 356n7
Adams, John, 148, 346
Adams, Sam, 80
adaptive expectations theory, 523, 549n30
Addams, Jane, 299
adverse selection, 424n41
affirmative action, 531
African Americans, 213, 237, 240, 244–46, 276–77, 279, 325. *See also* racial discrimination; racial segregation; racism
age discrimination, 354, 531
agrarian protest, 256–61, 458
Agricultural Adjustment Administration (AAA), 401–4, 468–69
agricultural policy, 457–62, 465–68. *See also* farm programs
agricultural production restrictions, 466–68
agricultural research, 458, 462
agricultural workers, 496, 499–500
agriculture, 157–61, 265–66, 401–4, 456–57; plantation, 44–45, 192, 237, 490–94; small-farm model, 90, 95–96, 98, 103–7, 110, 465; southern, 490–98. *See also* farm programs
Aid to Dependent Children (ADC), 413–14, 527
Aid to Families with Dependent Children, 527
Aid to the Blind (AB), 414
airlines, and deregulation, 543
air pollution, 538
Akron, Ohio, 278
Alabama, 176, 202, 212, 495
Alaska, 94
Alston, Lee J., 30
American Federation of Government Employees (AFGE), 378

American Federation of Labor, 301
American Tobacco Company, 271, 294, 300
Andreessen, Marc, 520
Andrews, John C., 299
Annapolis Convention (1786), 64–65
antebellum era, 190–94
Anti-Federalists, 71–72, 79–81
antislavery sentiment, 193
antitrust laws, 267–73, 294–96, 300, 308–10, 522
appeasement, 449
Argentina, 1
Arkansas, 156, 167, 500
Armey, Richard, 515
Army, U.S., 211, 214, 441
ARPANET, 519, 548n21
Articles of Confederation, 25, 59, 62–67, 70–71, 120, 148–49, 180
Ashurst, Henry F., 441
Asian immigration, 333–34
AT&T, breakup of, 522, 548n21
"at will" doctrine, 409
authority, governmental, expansion of, 18–20
automobile industry, 445–46
autonomy, of federal bureaucracy, 366–68, 379–80

baby boom, post–World War II, 325, 355n4
bail-outs, corporate, 529
balanced budget multiplier, 392
balance rule, 167
Baldwin, Sidney, 498
bank, national. *See* Bank of the United States (BUS)
bank clearinghouses, 136
banking, international, 140